Studies in Celtic History IX

THE LITURGY AND RITUAL OF THE CELTIC CHURCH

STUDIES IN CELTIC HISTORY
General Editor   David Dumville

THE
LITURGY AND RITUAL
OF THE
CELTIC CHURCH

F. E. WARREN

SECOND EDITION
BY

JANE STEVENSON

with a foreword
by

The Very Revd Professor Henry Chadwick, F.B.A., M.R.I.A.

THE BOYDELL PRESS

Introduction and bibliography ©Jane Stevenson 1987

First published 1881

Second edition published 1987 by
The Boydell Press
an imprint of Boydell and Brewer Ltd
PO Box 9, Woodbridge, Suffolk IP12 3DF
and Wolfeboro, New Hampshire 03894-2069, USA

ISBN 0 85115 473 5

ISSN 0261-9865

British Library Cataloguing in Publication Data

Warren, F.E.
  The liturgy and ritual of the Celtic
  church.—— 2nd ed.——(Studies in Celtic
  history, ISSN 0261-9865; 9).
  1. Celtic Church—— Liturgy and ritual
  2. Celtic Church—— History
  I. Title II. Stevenson, Jane III. Series
  264'.00941   BR748

    ISBN 0-85115-473-5

Library of Congress Cataloging-in-Publication Data

  Warren, F. E. (Frederick Edward), 1842-1930.
    The liturgy and ritual of the Celtic Church.

    (Studies in Celtic history, ISSN 0261-9865 ; 9)
    Bibliography: p.
    Includes indexes.
    1. Celtic Church--Liturgy. I. Stevenson, Jane.
  II. Title. III. Series.
  BX1995.C4W37 1987   264'.0089916   87-6365
  ISBN 0-85115-473-5

Printed in Great Britain by
St Edmundsbury Press, Bury St Edmunds, Suffolk

CONTENTS

Foreword

Students of early Irish Church-history who ask themselves what actually happened during church-services quickly find that, among the various helps to the study of the subject, one rather old book written more than a hundred years ago by an Anglican clergyman remains remarkably useful and informative.

Frederick Edward Warren, F.S.A. (10 November 1842 – 20 December 1930) was an energetic and conscientious editor and gatherer of liturgical texts. His edition of the Leofric Missal (Oxford, Bodleian Library, MS. Bodley 579 [*S.C.* 2675]), his book on the Irish missal at Corpus Christi College, Oxford (M.S. 282), and in particular his work on the liturgy and ritual of the Celtic Church were all published when he was a young fellow of St John's College, Oxford. Educated at Bradfield and Reading, he had come to St John's as an undergraduate scholar to read Literae Humaniores, and in 1866 a year after taking his degree was admitted to holy orders. After a period working away from Oxford, he returned to St John's as a bachelor don in 1873, holding a series of college offices — Dean of Arts, Dean of Divinity, finally in 1877 Vice-President. In 1880 he was Junior Proctor, and so might have seemed set for an academic career in the University. However, in 1882 he married and moved away into the pastoral ministry in successive benefices of which his College is patron — first at Frenchay near Bristol until 1890, then at Bardwell in Suffolk where he was Rector for thirty-two years until his retirement as an octogenarian widower in 1922. During his time at Bardwell he published the Antiphonary of Bangor with the Henry Bradshaw Society (1893/5), and in 1913 a translation of the Sarum Missal. He contributed to *The Cambridge Medieval History*. The University of St Andrews recognised the distinction of his work by conferring an honorary doctorate in 1913. He was an honorary canon of Bury St Edmund's. His principal hobby, aside from his academic interests, was archery.

Warren had a special interest in the early Irish and Anglo-Saxon Churches. That interest reflected a frequent concern of one important stream in the tradition of Anglican divinity, current since Archbishop Matthew Parker and his manuscript-collections, namely a desire to find a catholic Church-life and order which were nevertheless independent of Roman control and centralising. Occasionally a polemical sentence or two in his book must be understood against the background of this concern. Whatever view one takes on such a matter, however, because of the high importance of the texts and documents which he made easily accessible in his book he provided material of lasting value both to Celtic scholars and to liturgists.

To the present reissue of his book Dr Jane Stevenson has prefixed her important monograph. This work of excellent learning and judgment not only provides a corrective of Warren's history, but also brings to the intricate subject a clarity of exposition for which many readers will be grateful. Not all Celtic scholars today can be simply assumed to be at home with the forms and patterns of christian rites — not at least in the way which Warren could take for granted in 1881. Liturgists on their part are glad to have a reliable guide through a field where they do not always sufficiently control the languages. Dr Stevenson moves easily in both fields of study, understanding both the manifold problems besetting our available sources for early Irish Church-history and also the function of the rites for the Celtic communities which produced them. Her work will surely provide a strong stimulus to the subject.

HENRY CHADWICK

Preface

The reissue of Warren's *The Liturgy and Ritual of the Celtic Church* is timely, since nothing has been written in the last hundred years which adequately replaces it. At the same time, both the Celtic Churches and Western liturgies have been the subject of so much concentrated and productive scholarly activity in this century that it has been necessary to provide a rather lengthy new Introduction and Bibliography.

The purpose of the Introduction is twofold. It is intended to provide a basic introductory survey of liturgy for celticists unacquainted with this field, and to offer an equally basic guide to current thought on Celtic history for anyone interested in comparative liturgy. It is inevitable that some readers will find some sections of the Introduction unwarrantably simplistic and obvious: it is hoped that they will nonetheless find other parts of it profitable.

There is a fundamental way, also, in which this Introduction opens the book to new readers. Warren wrote as a clergyman of the Church of England; and he could rely on the structures and to some extent the history of the Western Church as background knowledge common to anyone literate and interested enough to read his book. This is very far from being the case now, and I have attempted in this Introduction not to take for granted that the reader is familiar with christian ritual. It must also be said that Warren's writing from within a particular christian community had its disadvantages as well as its advantages; this may be seen most clearly when his somewhat unhistorical and controversialist treatment of the relationship between Rome and the early Irish Church is contrasted with my own.[1] It should be emphasised, incidentally, that the capitalisation of the words 'Celtic Church' and 'Irish Church' here and throughout the text is a matter of editorial policy for the series as a whole, and does not imply a belief on my part that there were organised national Churches in early mediaeval Britain and Ireland.

The footnotes to the Introduction also serve a dual purpose. In the main, of course, they give the sources for a particular fact or position. But in

---

[1]   Warren, *The Liturgy*; cf. pp. 29-46 below. In addition, Warren's terminology, and occasionally his facts, stand in need of revision. Professor Chadwick has asked that I clarify some minor points; most importantly, that Warren's contrast of 'Ephesine' (by which he means 'Eastern and/or Gallican') and 'Petrine' ('Roman') aspects of liturgy, for example on pp. 164 and 167 below, is misleading. He is also mistaken in thinking that British bishops attended either the council of Nicaea in 325, or Sardica (which was in 342 or 343, not 347); and the author of the tract *De Sacramentis* referred to below, p. 110*n*, is Ambrose, the fourth-century bishop of Milan.

the case of some controversial or complex points, they serve also as a guide to the Bibliography. Thus, a footnote citing various books or articles may offer several which argue differently or contradict the position which I have chosen to maintain: they are there to allow the interested reader to pursue the matter further with the minimum of effort. The Introduction, even if it were purely a summary of other peoples' views, would have had to be many times longer if minor issues were not curtailed in this way. I also hope to have given a full and accurate guide to new editions, the whereabouts of relevant manuscripts, and to the various relevant bibliographical guides, dictionaries and other aids to scholarship.

I should like to end this preface by thanking Henry Chadwick, David Dumville, Isabel Henderson, Michael Lapidge, and Richard Sharpe, all of whom have given generously of their time and advice. I am also particularly grateful to John Dawson and Rosemary Rodd, of Cambridge University's Literary and Linguistic Computing Centre, and to the staff and fellow-users of the central computing service, who have answered many questions and helped me to solve the problems that have arisen in preparing this monograph as camera-ready copy.

Jane Stevenson,
Pembroke College,
Cambridge

January 1987

INTRODUCTION

The Liturgy and Ritual of the Celtic Churches

F.E. Warren was one of the earliest writers seriously to engage the question of the Celtic Churches and their organisation. *The Liturgy and Ritual of the Celtic Church* was a remarkable achievement in its day, and most of it has stood the test of time extremely well. Pfaff described it as 'still astonishingly useful, despite its age',[2] and Gougaud similarly acknowledged that it 'marked a stage in this department of liturgical study'.[3] Although the last hundred years have seen great strides made in the analysis and understanding of early liturgy and the beginnings of monasticism, and of the specific problems raised by Celtic christianity, Warren's work continues to be useful, although many individual details must be reassessed in the light of our new information.

The title of Warren's book is faintly misleading, both in itself and as a description of the contents. The concept of a 'Celtic Church' is a curious one: it is not directly comparable with divisions like the 'Roman Church' or the 'Gallican Church', but implies that the ethnic and linguistic grouping of the Celtic peoples is paralleled by their ecclesiastical homogeneity.[4] In fact, once the book is opened, it becomes clear that Warren is talking almost exclusively about the Irish Church, not from myopia but because the pre-English christianity of Britain and the christian practices of the Welsh, Breton, Cornish, Pictish, and 'Scottish' Churches are alike shrouded in obscurity. Only the most meagre fragments of evidence remain, most of them discussed by Warren. Modern scholarship is increasingly inclined to emphasise the local, territorial, or tribal quality of Celtic society;[5] to doubt the existence of a sense of ethnic identity as Celts;[6] and to show the divergences of practice and activity not only between Celtic countries, but within them. Far from speaking

---

[2] Pfaff, *Medieval Latin Liturgy*, p. 69.

[3] Gougaud, 'The Celtic liturgies', p. 175.

[4] This point was made by Hennig in 'Old Ireland and her liturgy', p. 62, and seconded by Ní Chatháin in 'The liturgical background', p. 128.

[5] Byrne, 'Tribes and tribalism',

[6] The Anglo-Saxons had a well developed sense of ethnic identity, and were very much aware of their Germanic roots. This provided at least some part of the impulse towards evangelising the pagans of Germany. See Bede, *Historia Ecclesiastica*, V.9 (edd. & transl. Colgrave & Mynors, p. 476). Irish sources do not appear to express an equivalent sense of celticity. See for instance Byrne, '"Senchas"', p. 144: 'the Irish preserved no tradition of being Celts, and neither did the Welsh. The mediaeval pseudo-historical theories about their origin did not connect them either with one another or with the ancient Gauls.'

of a 'Celtic Church', we are now hardly in a position to use the term 'Irish Church' without qualification.[7] Without any strong centralised authority equivalent to that of Rome (for all Armagh's best efforts),[8] without the Roman tradition of rule from the centre and a bureaucracy to expedite it, and without any means of enforcing a national position, the churches and monasteries of Ireland were, like its secular rulers, relatively autonomous. In this balkanised society, one is sceptical of the assumption that there was a national liturgy.[9] The difficulty here is the meagre survival of direct evidence. This book contains almost all the texts directly relevant to Irish liturgy, for very little more has been unearthed since it was first published.[10] Of the little which we do have, some few manuscripts, most importantly the Antiphonary of Bangor,[11] the Stowe Missal, probably written at Tallaght in 792,[12] and the Book of Dimma, written at Roscrea (Co. Tipperary),[13] can be localised. However, no one has ever seriously attempted to take the evidence of manuscript-origins into account when discussing Irish liturgy. The temptation to generalise from our texts and draw conclusions about Irish liturgy (rather than the use of the specific, but often unknown, centre in which each one was written) is enormous, and we have very little way of telling how far it is

---

7   See Hughes, 'The Celtic Church'.

8   On Armagh and its attempts to exert primacy over Ireland, see Sharpe, 'St Patrick' and 'Armagh and Rome'.

9   However, Hennig's warning, that 'it is even more difficult to establish a multiplicity of liturgies in Ireland than it is to establish one "type" of ancient Irish liturgy' ('Sacramentaries', pp. 26-7), should be borne in mind.

10   Some fragments discovered by Bannister, a certain amount of palimpsest-material which we owe to the patience and industry of Dold, and the Turin fragment (ed. W. Meyer), a 'sister'-manuscript to the Antiphonary of Bangor, are the main additions. They are discussed below, pp. lxvii, xlviii.

11   Milano, Biblioteca Ambrosiana, MS. C.5.inf.: ed. Warren, *The Antiphonary*; Gamber, *Codices*, I.146-7 (no. 150); Lowe, *Codices*, III.311, 'Irish minuscule, *saec.* vii *ex* (A.D. 680/91)'; Lapidge & Sharpe, *A Bibliography*, pp. 138-9 (no. 532). See also Bishop, 'A service-book', and Curran, *The Antiphonary*.

12   This manuscript, incidentally, is so named because it was part of the Duke of Buckingham's library at Stowe House before its eventual deposition in the Royal Irish Academy, and not for any more significant reason. For bibliography, see below, p. lviii. Byrne, 'The Stowe Missal', pp. 48-50, warns that the attribution of this manuscript to Tallaght is probable but not absolutely certain.

13   Dublin, Trinity College, MS. 59 (A.4.23) (unprinted): Gamber, *Codices*, I.143-4 (no. 145); Lowe, *Codices*, II.275: 'Irish cursive, *saec.* viii 2'; Lapidge & Sharpe, *A Bibliography*, p. 134 (no. 517); and Best, 'On the *subscriptiones*'. Its liturgical *subscriptiones* (also written at Roscrea) are separately listed by Lapidge & Sharpe, *A Bibliography*, p. 142 (no. 541), and Kenney, *The Sources*, pp. 703-4 (no. 563).

justifiable.

Liturgy and ritual are intricate and difficult subjects, but of particular importance for the history of Insular christianity. Their interest is not purely religious and spiritual: for the Celtic Churches, the surviving liturgical material provides valuable insights into the historical context of Celtic christianity, its sources, its contacts, and its outlook. The liturgists — in particular Edmund Bishop, in a seminal paper[14] — were the first to provide hard evidence for the influence of Spanish christianity on Irish, not only in Irish reliance on the works of Isidore of Seville, but also in their use of Spanish ritual and formulae.[15]

---

[14] 'Liturgical note', followed by his *Liturgica Historica*, pp. 163 and 165-202. It should be noted, however, that Bishop's methods and his conclusions have been recently criticised by Sims-Williams, 'Thoughts on Ephrem the Syrian', pp. 213-17.

[15] The contacts between Isidore's Spain and early Ireland have been examined by Hillgarth in a series of articles: 'The East', 'Visigothic Spain', and 'Ireland and Spain' (reprinted together in his *Visigothic Spain, Byzantium*).

1. Western Liturgies

The study of the early liturgy has received a good deal of specialist attention since Warren's day. Many more liturgical texts have been edited, and a whole series, the Henry Bradshaw Society's publications, is devoted to this area. All early liturgical manuscripts have been described by Gamber in his *Codices Liturgici*, with bibliography on each. There are also two separate bibliographies of mediaeval liturgy[16] and the documents for the Celtic liturgies in particular are listed by Lapidge & Sharpe,[17] and by Kenney, *The Sources*.[18] There are several guides to the early liturgy, such as Jungmann's *The Early Liturgy* and Duchesne's *Christian Worship*.[19] Vogel's *Introduction aux sources* is also very useful. An entire dictionary (albeit of uneven quality) was devoted to the subject, Cabrol & Leclercq's *Dictionnaire d'archéologie chrétienne et de liturgie*, as are two periodicals, *Archiv für Liturgiewissenschaft* and *Ephemerides Liturgicae*. There are also, of course, many important articles in other periodicals. This section is intended merely as the briefest of introductions to a vast and complex subject, providing a context and background for the liturgical developments of the Celtic Churches.

All liturgies are interrelated, and all alike are based on the moment of the Last Supper when Christ bade his followers to 'do this in remembrance of me' (Matthew XXVI.26-28, Mark XIV.22-24). In the earliest Church, the celebration of the eucharist seems to have been closely based on the

---

16   Pfaff, *Medieval Latin Liturgy*, and Vismans & Brinkhoff, *Critical Bibliography*.

17   *A Bibliography*, pp. 39-42 (nos 118-26); pp. 130-50 (nos 505-91); pp. 210-15 (nos 785-800); pp. 264-70 (nos 960-84); pp. 287-9 (nos 1031-7).

18   Kenney, *The Sources*, pp. 683-718 (nos 548-74).

19   See Vismans & Brinkhoff, *Critical Bibliography*, pp. 22-7. It is perhaps worth pointing out that complete novices in this area will also find *The Oxford Dictionary of the Christian Church*, edd. Cross & Livingstone, extremely useful since it provides concise and lucid definitions of all the specialist liturgical vocabulary. Useful basic introductory guides are Jones *et al.*, *The Study of Liturgy*, Martimort (ed.), *The Church at Prayer*, and Hughes, *Medieval Manuscripts*. Pfaff, *Medieval Latin Liturgy*, may also be used as an introduction.

20   Duchesne, *Christian Worship*, p. 49: 'The only permanent element, on the whole, which Christianity added to the liturgy of the synagogue was thus the sacred meal instituted by Jesus Christ as a perpetual commemoration of Himself'.

biblical form[20] combined with the structure of Jewish synagogue-worship,[21] and to have been celebrated as a joint evening meal in private houses.[22] With the passage of time, christian worship became formalised into the beginnings of mass and the divine office as we know them, and lost all connexion with the idea of the *Agape*, the christian communal meal.[23] Over the centuries, the liturgy has been subject to slow, organic change, new additions, and radical shifts of emphasis from time to time and place to place, while retaining the same basic form. There are three basic subdivisions of liturgical material which I intend to consider in this section: mass, divine office, and initiation.

i. *The Mass*[24]

The mass is bipartite in structure.[25] This structure goes back to the 'mystery-religion' aspect of the early Church,[26] where it was normal not to receive baptism and become a full communicating member of the Church until a long period of instruction and probation, the catechumenate, had been undergone.[27] The first half of the service therefore consisted of lections, prayers, and edification, followed by a break in the service while the catechumens left the church, leaving the communicants to celebrate the mystery of the mass proper in private. This second half, the *missa fidelium*, is, theologically speaking, organised around two main concepts: offering and intercession. The former focusses on the presence of Christ's body and blood and the unity of the

---

21   Baumstark & Botte, *Comparative Liturgy*, pp. 10-12 and 43-7. The subject is discussed more fully by Bradshaw, *Daily Prayer*, pp. 1-46; and see also Dugmore, *The Influence of the Synagogue*.

22   Jungmann, *The Early Liturgy*, pp. 13-14.

23   Duchesne, *Christian Worship*, p. 49, n. 1: 'The liturgical Agape disappeared, or nearly so, within less than a hundred years after the first preaching of the Gospel'. Cf. Jungmann, *The Early Liturgy*, pp. 29-38.

24   Jungmann's *Missarum Sollemnia* is the single most comprehensive study of the Western mass, translated as *The Mass of the Roman Rite*. See further Fortescue, *The Mass*, Cabrol, *The Mass*, and Pfaff, *Medieval Latin Liturgy*, p. 18.

25   Jungmann, *Missarum Sollemnia*, I.328.

26   See the Epistle of James of Edessa, as given by Brightman, *Liturgies*, I.490-1; Klauser, *A Short History*, pp. 24-30; Jungmann, *The Early Liturgy*, pp. 158-65, and *The Mass*, p. 51; and Baumstark & Botte, *Comparative Liturgy*, pp. 138-9.

27   Tertullian, *De Praescriptione*, XLI.4 (ed. R.F. Refoulé, *apud* Dekkers *et al.*, *Tertulliani Opera*, I.185-224, at p. 221), said that only heretics fail to distinguish between catechumens and the baptised. See also Augustine, *Sermones*, XLIX.8 (ed. Lambot, p. 620): 'ecce post sermonem fit missa [viz, "dismissal"] catechumenis. Manebunt fideles'; Ratcliff (ed.), *Expositio*, p. 9 ('de caticumino', § 15); Jungmann, *The Early Liturgy*, pp. 77-80.

faithful, evoked in the one commemorative sacrificial and sacramental act. The latter focusses on Christ's redemptive action as the grounds for pleading for human salvation. The prayers, psalms and collects of the mass interweave the two themes. Structurally, the *missa fidelium* may be divided into three parts:[28] oblation (the offering of bread and wine to be consecrated), consecration, and the actual communion itself.

From at least the fourth century, regional variation can be seen in the celebration of the mass.[29] This is to be expected since, in the earliest stages of christian worship, the celebrant was relatively free to choose, or even to compose, his own prayers. This freedom was curtailed towards the end of the fourth century, although the popes retained some individual latitude down to the eighth.[30] By the time of Gregory the Great, several definite groupings had appeared, the Roman rite, practised in Italy and North Africa, and the Gallican rites, which may be subdivided into the Gallican rite proper, the Milanese (or 'Ambrosian'), the early mediaeval Spanish rite (often called 'Mozarabic'), and the British/Irish rite.

Edmund Bishop made a masterly summary of the features which distinguish the Roman rite (which is the rite underlying modern Catholic worship).[31] He emphasised its solemnity, gravity, conciseness and dignity —in short, its display of the old Classical virtues within the new christian context. This is contrasted with the relative diffuseness, prolixity, and emotionalism of what might loosely be called the 'barbarian' (as opposed to 'Classical') rites.[32] It must be remembered that liturgical celebration has always to be spiritually and aesthetically satisfying to the participants. Consequently, a different aesthetic basis will tend to produce a different liturgy, which is not necessarily better or worse.[33] Who is to say that the very long and repetitive prayers of the Mozarabic rite did not, in the cumulative effect of their marathon petitioning, produce as fervent and genuine a devotional effect as the far briefer and more intense prayers of the Roman Church?

Duchesne suggested that the Gallican liturgy was originally developed

---

28   Young, *The Drama*, I.19.

29   Duchesne, *Christian Worship*, p. 55, defines the main divisions as Syrian and Alexandrian (the Eastern tradition: Hebraic and Greek respectively), and Roman and Gallican (the Western tradition: in Latin). Cabrol formulates the divisions slightly differently: *The Mass*, pp. 24-30.

30   Moreton, *The Eighth-Century Gelasian*, p. 20. See also Vogel, *Introduction*, pp. 20-2.

31   Bishop, *Liturgica Historica*, pp. 1-20.

32   *Ibid.*, pp. 4-5.

33   Baumstark & Botte, *Comparative Liturgy*, pp. 3-4.

at Milan in the fourth century,[34] a view which has not been universally accepted.[35] The interrelations between the various Western traditions are not easy to determine: the Milanese ('Ambrosian') rite was the most Greek-influenced of Western rites, reflecting the cosmopolitan status of Milan as a cultural and political centre.[36] In any case, the Gallican rite, whatever its origins, was gradually superseded by the Roman from the eighth century onwards. A major impetus towards liturgical uniformity was provided by Charlemagne (768-814) who instituted a programme to introduce the 'Gregorian sacramentary', a Roman mass-book, across his empire, although the Roman book had necessarily to be modified by the addition of some Gallican prayers, formulae, and festivals. Some Gallican elements have remained in the Catholic liturgy to this day.[37]

The most important witnesses to the early Gallican rite are the collection of masses first discovered in the nineteenth century by Franz Josef Mone (and thus often referred to as 'Mone-Messe', more recently edited by Mohlberg),[38] Dold's 'älteste Liturgiebuch',[39] the Bobbio Missal,[40] the *Missale Gothicum*,[41] and the *Missale Francorum*.[42] The characteristic elements of the

---

[34] *Christian Worship*, pp. 91-5.

[35] He has been followed by Jungmann, *The Early Liturgy*, p. 233, but contradicted by Griffe, 'Aux origines'.

[36] Bäumer, *Histoire*, I.189-90. For the Milanese rite, see Ratti & Magistretti (edd.), *Missale Ambrosianum*, and discussion by Cabrol, *The Mass*, pp. 90-102.

[37] The purely Roman elements of the Catholic mass were outlined by Bishop, *Liturgica Historica*, p. 7.

[38] Karlsruhe, Badische Landesbibliothek, MS. Aug. perg. 253: Lowe, *Codices*, VIII.1102; ed. Mohlberg, *Missale Gallicanum Vetus*; Gamber, *Codices*, I.158-9 (no. 203), Dekkers, *Clavis*, p. 434 (no. 1917). See also Wilmart, 'L'âge'. There is a detailed bibliographical guide to individual mediaeval mass-books by Gamber, *Codices*, and a briefer one by Dekkers, *Clavis*, pp. 423-39. Liturgical manuscripts earlier than the ninth century appear in Lowe, *Codices*.

[39] Wolfenbüttel, Herzog-August Bibliothek, MS. Weissenb. 76: Lowe, *Codices*, IX.1392; ed. Dold, *Das älteste Liturgiebuch*; Gamber, *Codices*, I.174-6 (no. 250).

[40] Paris, Bibliothèque nationale, MS. latin 13246: Lowe, *Codices*, V.653; ed. Lowe, *The Bobbio Missal*; Gamber, *Codices*, I.167-8 (no. 220); Dekkers, *Clavis*, p. 437 (no. 1924). It is also briefly discussed by Warren, *The Liturgy*, pp. 272-3, under the name *Missale Vesontionense*.

[41] Roma, Biblioteca Apostolica Vaticana, MS. Reginensis lat. 317: Lowe, *Codices*, I.106; ed. Mohlberg, *Missale Gothicum*; Gamber, *Codices*, I.161-2 (no. 210); Dekkers, *Clavis*, pp. 456-7 (no. 1919).

[42] Roma, Biblioteca Apostolica Vaticana, MS. Reginensis lat. 257: Lowe, *Codices*, I.103; ed. Mohlberg, *Missale Francorum*; Gamber, *Codices*, I.231-2 (no. 410), Dekkers, *Clavis*, p. 437 (no. 1923).

Gallican liturgy were described by Duchesne.[43] The sacramentary and *liber ordinum* used in early mediaeval Spain, and inaccurately called Mozarabic, are related to the Gallican rite, and were edited by Férotin.[44]

For the Roman rite, there are three significant traditions:[45] the first is the Sacramentary of Verona (once arbitrarily known as the Leonine Sacramentary),[46] which is not a true sacramentary at all but a single seventh-century manuscript found at Verona and possibly originating there, containing many allusions to liturgical practice in Rome. It is a private collection of many alternative masses,[47] but it is a priceless witness to worship in the city of Rome in the seventh century. The second is the Gelasian tradition of sacramentaries,[48] Roman massbooks somewhat contaminated with Gallican elements. There are two traditions of Gelasian sacramentary, the Old Gelasian, whose main witness is the earliest (seventh-century) Gelasian manuscript,[49] and the eighth-century Gelasians, described by Coebergh as 'une fusion entre deux livres authentiquement romains, le *Gélasien ancien* du type Vat. Regin. 316 et du *Grégorien* du type Paduensis D 47', with additional *ordines* from both Roman and Gallican sources.[50] The most important eighth-century Gelasian books are the Sacramentary of Rheinau[51] and the Sacramentary of

---

[43] *Christian Worship*, pp. 190-225. There is also a summary of its peculiar characteristics in Deanesly, *The Pre-Conquest Church*, p. 188; and see also Pfaff, *Medieval Latin Liturgy*, pp. 69-71.

[44] *Le Liber Mozarabicus*, and *Le Liber Ordinum*; discussed by Bishop, *The Mozarabic and Ambrosian Rites*, and see Pfaff, *Medieval Latin Liturgy*, pp. 65-8.

[45] These witnesses to the Roman liturgy are listed by Dekkers, *Clavis*, pp. 422-32 (nos 1897-1905), and discussed by Fortescue, *The Mass*, pp. 117-24, and by Martimort, *The Church at Prayer*, pp. 25-8.

[46] Verona, Biblioteca Capitolare, MS. 85 (80): Lowe, *Codices*, IV.514; ed. Mohlberg, *Sacramentarium Veronense*; Gamber, *Codices*, I.294-6 (no. 60), Dekkers, *Clavis*, p. 423 (no. 1897).

[47] Hope, *The Leonine*, pp. 23-37 and 138-9. See also Pfaff, *Medieval Latin Liturgy*, pp. 73-4.

[48] Coebergh, 'Le sacramentaire', Moreton, *The Eighth-Century Gelasian*, especially pp. 175-205, and Vogel, *Introduction*, pp. 50-7.

[49] Roma, Biblioteca Apostolica Vaticana, MS. Reginensis lat. 316: Lowe, *Codices*, I.105; ed. Mohlberg, *Liber Sacramentorum*; Gamber, *Codices*, I.301-3 (no. 610), Dekkers, *Clavis*, p. 424 (no. 1899). See also Pfaff, *Medieval Latin Liturgy*, pp. 74-5.

[50] Vogel, 'La réforme', p. 219. See also Pfaff, *Medieval Latin Liturgy*, pp. 75-6.

[51] Zürich, Zentralbibliothek Rheinau 30, Lowe, *Codices*, VII.109; edd. Hänggi & Schönherr, *Sacramentarium Rhenaugiense*; Gamber, *Codices*, II.371-2 (no. 802); Dekkers, *Clavis*, p. 431 (no. 1905).

Gellone.[52] The third Roman massbook is the Gregorian Sacramentary, allegedly the sacramentary of Gregory the Great, but in fact reflecting Roman practice in the late eighth century.[53] This was the sacramentary sent, on his request, to Charlemagne by Pope Hadrian. Although the king had hoped for a definitive massbook as an instrument of liturgical reform throughout his empire, the book as sent turned out to have many omissions. Alcuin therefore remedied its defects, heading his additions with a preface (known from its *incipit* as *Hucusque*) explaining his procedure, which was to supplement the book with additional masses and prayers for various purposes of both Gallican and Roman origins.[54] The important Gregorian manuscripts include the Sacramentary of Padua[55] and the Sacramentary of Hildoard.[56]

There were Greek and Eastern influences on the Gallican liturgy,[57] and also on the Roman liturgy.[58] Even Syriac and Coptic texts, ideas, and practices could and did cross linguistic and cultural frontiers into the West.[59] The human channels for this interchange are shown by the *Epistola* of Cummian: when the Irish deputation arrived at a hostel in Rome in the mid-seventh century, they found a Greek, an Egyptian, a Scythian, and a Jew already resident.[60] Particularly notable among the Eastern elements which transferred to the West are the Syriac practice of hymns and psalmody, and the transmission of apocrypha. The diversity of liturgy in the sixth century is witnessed by a letter from Pope John III to Edaldus, bishop of Vienne. The letter also demonstrates the increasing papal desire to get the situation under control:[61]

De officiis missarum, de quibus in literis uestris requisistis, sciat caritas uestra quia uarie apud diuersas ecclesias fiant; aliter enim Alexandrina ecclesia, aliter Hierosolymitana, aliter Ephesina,

---

52 Paris, Bibliothèque nationale MS. latin 12048: Lowe, *Codices*, V.618; ed. A. Dumas, *Liber sacramentorum*; Gamber, *Codices*, II.392 (no. 855); Dekkers, *Clavis*, p. 429 (no. 1905).

53 Ed. Deshusses, *Le sacramentaire grégorien*; Gamber, *Codices*, II.325-67 (nos 701-96). See also Pfaff, *Medieval Latin Liturgy*, pp. 76-8.

54 Ellard, *Master Alcuin*, pp. 109-43. See also Gamber, *Codices*, II.347-59 (nos 740-78).

55 Padova, Biblioteca Capitolare, MS. D.47: ed. Mohlberg, *Die älteste erreichbare Gestalt*; Gamber, *Codices*, II.398-9 (no. 880), Dekkers, *Clavis*, p. 429 (no. 1902).

56 Cambrai, Bibliothèque municipale, MS. 164 (159): Gamber, *Codices*, II.339-40 (no. 720); Dekkers, *Clavis*, p. 428 (no. 1904).

57 Quasten, 'Oriental influences'; Baumstark & Botte, *Comparative Liturgy*, p. 137.

58 *Ibid.*, pp. 98-102, and Harris, *The Codex Bezae*, p. 179.

59 Jungmann, *The Early Liturgy*, pp. 204-5.

60 Cummian, *Epistola* (ed. Migne, *Patrologia Latina*, LXXXVII.969-78, at cols 977-8).

61 Mansi, *Concilia*, IX.760-1.

aliter Romana facit; cuius morem et instituta debet seruare ecclesia tua, quae fundamentum sancti habitus ab illa sumpsit.

Although, as this letter shows, the instinct to centralise and standardise the liturgy on Roman lines existed from the sixth century, it was not really feasible to achieve this (except in some special cases, of which the nascent English Church is the clearest example)[62] until, with Charlemagne, secular and ecclesiastical politics were perceived as mutually reinforcing.[63] It should also perhaps be noticed that the chief executive of the Carolingian liturgical reform would appear to have been the Englishman Alcuin, the product of a Church which, as Bede, Stephanus, and others witness, held Rome in general and Gregory the Great in particular in peculiar reverence.[64] By the tenth century, the structure of the mass had more or less assumed the shape which it retains to this day.[65]

ii. The Divine Office[66]

The mass was not the only important element in christian religious life; equally significant, though in a different way, was the daily office. Celtic sources have relatively little to say about this, but it must still be briefly summarised here. In the early centuries of the faith, the committed christian was not only expected to attend mass, but to devote part of his or her day to prayer, not only in a private and unstructured way, but by taking part in corporate worship, consisting mainly of prayers for divine help and support, and the singing of psalms. These were the prayers of the entire christian community, not just of the clerics. Tertullian, advising against mixed

---

[62] But it should be noted that, even with the English Church, Gregory gave Augustine *carte blanche* to develop his own liturgy by supplementing his Roman books according to his own judgment: Bede, *Historia Ecclesiastica*, I.27 (edd. & transl. Colgrave & Mynors, p. 80-1). See also Warren, *The Liturgy*, p. 62.

[63] This development is described by Ellard, *Master Alcuin*; and see further Vogel, 'La réforme'.

[64] See Deanesly, 'The Anglo-Saxon Church', pp. 44-53, and also Brooks, *The Early History*, pp. 91-3. The Council of Clofeshoh (A.D. 747) decreed in its Canon XIII that mass should be celebrated throughout England according to Roman custom (edd. Haddan & Stubbs, *Councils*, III.367).

[65] This shape is usefully outlined by Young, *The Drama*, I.21-43.

[66] Some basic guides to the divine office and its history include Bäumer, *Histoire*, Hanssens, *Aux Origines*, Batiffol, *History*, and Bradshaw, *Daily Prayer*. See further Pfaff, *Medieval Latin Liturgy*, pp. 26-8.

marriage, gives as an example of the problems involved the marital friction which would be caused when a christian wife nightly disturbed her pagan husband's slumbers by getting up to pray.[67] Furthermore, the nights of Wednesday and Friday each week were given over to special vigils and prayers.[68] The liturgy of the hours developed a more concise form in the West than it had in the East,[69] but the structure of the daily hours of prayer was common to both, and goes back to the second century at least. The hours of prayer were well established by the fourth century. Augustine's pious mother Monica is an example of the devout lay person of the Patristic age: he mentioned in his *Confessiones* that she sedulously attended church twice a day, for services at daybreak and dusk.[70] The other hours of prayer were the third, sixth, and ninth hours of the day, the middle of the night, and cockcrow.[71] These offices consisted mainly of psalms and prayers, together with lections, collects, and hymns, the number of psalms and the composition of the office varying considerably from time to time and place to place. Men of affairs, such as lawyers, were not excused from this régime, although John Chrysostom allowed that a person on business need only say a prayer in his heart at the appropriate times.[72]

The Patristic age (fourth to sixth centuries) saw considerable development in the content and arrangement of these communal prayers for various reasons, one of which is the rise of monasticism. Although, as I have stressed, the liturgy of the hours was enjoined on *all* christians, the many distinguished monk-bishops of this period inevitably induced fruitful interaction between monastic and cathedral liturgy. The very existence of a group, within the christian community, which focussed its entire existence on the praise of God, unencumbered by the ties of family-life, administration, and the cares of the world, was bound to have an effect. The eventual result of the

---

[67] Tertullian, *Ad Uxorem*, II.4,2 and II.5,2 (edd. Dekkers *et al.*, *Tertulliani Opera*, I.371-94, at pp. 388-9).

[68] Bäumer, *Histoire*, I.72-3, and Bradshaw, *Daily Prayer*, pp. 40-2.

[69] Bäumer, *Histoire*, I.102.

[70] Augustine, *Confessiones*, V.9,17 (ed. Verheijen, pp. 66-7). On the morning's hour of prayer, see Hanssens, *Aux Origines*, and Jungmann, *Pastoral Liturgy*.

[71] Tertullian, *De Oratione*, §§ 24-5 (edd. Dekkers *et al.*, *Tertulliani Opera*, I.255-74, at pp. 272-3).

[72] John Chrysostom, *De Anna Sermo*, IV.5 (ed. & transl. Migne, *Patrologia Graeca*, LIV.631-76, at col. 666).

influence of monasticism was twofold, although both aspects are due to their status as specialists. Cathedral office was assimilated to the form of monastic office, which gradually supplanted it completely in the Western Church; and the laity were gradually squeezed out of involvement in the service, becoming spectators rather than active participants.[73]

The office, like the mass, was liable to variation and to attempts at control. Provincial councils from the sixth century onwards legislated for uniformity in the practice of psalmody and the performance of the office, although the repetition of the legislation suggests that it was ineffective.[74] The Council of Gerona (A.D. 517) is particularly noteworthy in that it insists that the ritual of the mass itself, as well as the custom of psalmody and ministering observed in the metropolitan church, should be followed in the whole province of Tarragona.[75] Another Iberian council, that of Braga, laid down that the same order of psalmody was to be observed in the morning- and evening-offices, and that monastic rules were not to be interpolated into the ecclesiastical rule.[76] This last council bears witness that the gradual supersession of cathedral office by monastic was not completely smooth and unopposed. Relations between monks and clerics in the early middle ages were not invariably conducted in a spirit of fraternal charity: issues of demarcation and status were apt to come up from time to time, with the daily office as the most obvious field of controversy.

iii. *Rites of Initiation*[77]

The early history of the rites of christian initiation should also be considered

---

[73] Bradshaw, *Daily Prayer*, p. 123.

[74] *ibid.*, p. 115. See, for example, *Concilium Epaonense* (Epaon; A.D. 517), § 27 (ed. de Clercq, *Concilia*, pp. 20-37, at 30); *Concilium Veneticum* (Vannes; A.D. 461-91), § 15 (ed. Munier, *Concilia Galliae*, pp. 150-7, at 155).

[75] *Concilium Gerundense*, § 1 (ed. Mansi, *Concilia*, VIII.547-54, at col. 549).

[76] *Concilium Bracarense Primum* (Braga; A.D. 599), § 1: 'neque monasteriorum consuetudines cum ecclesiastica regula sint permixtae' (ed. Barlow, *Martini Episcopi Bracarensis Opera*, pp. 104-15, at 111).

[77] The documents for the history of the baptismal liturgy are collected in translation by Whitaker, *Documents*. See also Fisher, *Christian Initiation*, Stenzel, *Die Taufe*, and Pfaff, *Medieval Latin Liturgy*, pp. 38-41. Duchesne outlined early Roman and Gallican baptismal rites in *Christian Worship*, pp. 294-327.

briefly here: that is, baptism and confirmation, and the ordination of deacons, priests, and bishops. Both sets of ceremonial created rifts between the Celtic Churches and their neighbours at one time or another and so will be discussed from this angle later on, in 'The Celtic Mass'; but it may be helpful to outline the background here. Baptism, like the other rituals of the Church, only gradually assumed a fixed form. The irreducible core of the ceremony is baptism with water (whether by immersing the candidate, or by pouring it over him),[78] meanwhile saying 'Baptizo te, N., in nomine Patris et Filii et Spiritus Sancti'. This is normally followed by the clothing of the neophyte in a ceremonial white garment, symbolising his new state. The words of baptism are crucial. Anyone baptised without invocation of the Trinity in this form does not receive the sacrament of regeneration. The words matter infinitely more than the character of the person performing the baptism.[79] Baptism may be performed by a priest or, at a pinch, by anyone, even a woman (thus, moribund infants could be baptised immediately on their arrival in the world, by any devout bystander, and the act was binding). The importance of baptism was such that even when it was performed in unorthodox circumstances — by heretics, by women, or with a garbled form of words[80] — its efficacy was usually deemed to be unimpaired.[81] The basic validity of baptism in any form lends a particular tone to Alcuin's vigorous attempts to standardise the baptismal service to what he saw as the most correct form.[82] He was particularly concerned that the Spanish Church followed the custom of single immersion, whereas he believed that a triple immersion, symbolising the three persons of the Trinity, was required.[83]

Confirmation was not always, as it is now, a ritual usually separated

---

[78] Thomas, *Christianity*, pp. 204-6.

[79] This is spelled out in a letter of Pope Zacharias to Boniface, dated May 1, 748: *Epistola LXXX* (ed. Tangl, *Die Briefe*, pp. 172-80, at 174).

[80] Zacharias to Boniface, July 1, 746: *Epistola LXVIII* (*ibid.*, pp. 141-2, at 141). Gregory III to Boniface, October 29, 739: *Epistola XLV* (*ibid.*, pp. 71-4, at 73).

[81] Gregory II to Boniface, November 22, 726: *Epistola XXVI* (*ibid.*, pp. 44-7, at 46). See Thompson, *The Offices*, pp. 194-5.

[82] Alcuin outlined the correct ceremony in *Epistola CXXXVII* (ed. Dümmler, *Epistolae*, II.210-16, at 214-15), on which see Ellard, *Master Alcuin*, pp. 68-85.

[83] Alcuin, *Epistola CXXXVII* (ed. Dümmler, *Epistolae*, II.212). The Spanish-Gallican baptismal rite has been set out by Bishop, *The Mozarabic*, pp. 11-14.

from baptism.[84] It originated in the laying on of hands described in Acts VIII.17, administered to newly baptised converts. The basic characteristics of confirmation are that it consists of anointing and the laying on of hands, and that it is performed by a bishop. It is the sacrament of the descent of the Holy Spirit to the newly baptised christian. The two sacraments were naturally performed together when most candidates were adult catechumens: in the early middle ages they continued to be performed together even on infants.[85] As baptism by heretics was not invalid, another important function of confirmation was as a rite of reconciliation between penitent heretics and the Church.[86] It was also used for people who had been baptised privately (that is, not by a priest) for some reason of urgency.[87] By the seventh century at the latest, both Roman and Gallican forms of baptism treat confirmation as the final stage of the baptismal service, in which the head is anointed with chrism, the first communion is made, and there is a laying on of hands by the officiating bishop.[88] The important thing to notice is that, although baptism can very well be performed by a priest, confirmation, at least in the West, must be performed by a bishop.[89] For example, the seventh-century Ildefonsus of Toledo, though unconcerned about single versus triple immersion, is quite emphatic about the episcopal role in anointing:[90]

nam presbyteris, seu extra episcoporum, siue praesente episcopo, cum baptizant, chrismate baptizatos unguere licet, sed quod ab episcopo fuerit consecratum; non tamen frontam ex eodem oleo signare, quod solis debetur episcopis, cum tradunt spiritum paracletum.

Bede spoke of Bishop Cuthbert journeying about Northumbria to confirm the

---

[84] On confirmation, see Thompson, *The Offices*; Fisher, *Christian Initiation*, pp. 141-8; and Angenendt, 'Bonifatius'.

[85] Thompson, *The Offices*, pp. 180-5.

[86] *Concilium Laodicenum* (Laodicea; A.D. 320), § 7 (ed. Mansi, *Concilia*, II.563-600, at col. 565). Zacharias to Boniface, July 1, 746: *Epistola* LXVIII (ed. Tangl, pp. 141-2, at 141).

[87] *Concilium Eliberitanum* (Elvira; A.D. 305), § 38 (ed. Mansi, *Concilia*, II.2-55, at col. 12).

[88] Pepperdene, 'Baptism', pp. 118-19, gives the Roman form of confirmation as found in the Gelasian Sacramentary, and the Gallican form found in *De Sacramentis*, on which see Duchesne, *Christian Worship*, p. 325 and n. 4.

[89] Innocent, *Epistola XXV, ad Decentium* (A.D. 416), § 6: 'de consignandis uero infantibus manifestum est non ab alio quam ab episcopo fieri licet' (ed. Migne, *Patrologia Latina*, XX.457-612, at cols 554-5).

[90] Ildefonsus, *Annotationum de cognitione baptismi liber* (ed. Migne, *Patrologia Latina*, XCVI.111-72, at cols 165-6).

baptised.[91]

Ordination of bishops similarly appears to be a ceremonial which appears in the West initially in a starkly simple form, and acquires various accretions over the centuries.[92] The form used in the West in the third century was very basic. It required first of all that the candidate be elected to a vacant see, that his ordination should take place in his own church, and that priests should assist at the ordination, but without taking part. The actual ceremony consisted of the bishops present laying their hands on the bishop-elect, and one of their number pronouncing the prayer of consecration. This was all that was necessary.[93] In order to prevent unsuitable candidates being ordained, rules of clerical celibacy were stringent: a future bishop might not have been married more than once,[94] his wife had to have been a virgin, not a widow, when he married her,[95] and their marital life had to cease with his ordination.[96] Another safeguard was the requirement that at least three bishops had to join together in ordaining each candidate[97] and that the clerics and people of the region should assent to his ordination.[98]

There are many other aspects of liturgical ceremony, such as pontifical ceremonies for the consecration of churches, which need not be considered here as there is no early Celtic evidence. The only pontifical ceremony for

---

[91] Bede, *Uita*, § 32 (ed. & transl. Colgrave, *Two Lives*, p. 252-3).

[92] See Ellard, *Ordination Anointings*, Porter, *The Ordination Prayers*, and Michels, *Beiträge*.

[93] Batiffol, 'La liturgie du sacre', p. 735.

[94] *Concilium Epaonense* (Epaon; A.D. 517), § 2 (ed. de Clercq, *Concilia*, pp. 20-37, at 24).

[95] Innocent, *Epistola XXXVII*, II.4: 'nam ea, quae habuerit ante uirum, licet defunctus sit, tamen si clerico postea fuerit copulata, clericus, qui eam acceperit, esse non poterit' (*Epistola et Decreta*, ed. Migne, *Patrologia Latina*, XX.457-612, at col. 604).

[96] *Concilium Turonense* (Tours; A.D. 567), § 13: 'episcopus coniugem ut sororem habeat' (ed. de Clercq, *Concilia*, pp. 175-99, at 180).

[97] *Concilium Arelantense* (Arles; A.D. 314), § 20 (ed. Munier, *Concilia Galliae*, pp. 3-25, at 13); *Concilium Carthaginense* (Carthage; A.D. 390), § 12 (ed. Munier, *Concilia Africae*, pp. 11-19, at 18); *Concilium Regense* (Riez; A.D. 439), § 1 (ed. Munier, *Concilia Galliae*, pp. 61-75, at 65). See also Gaudemet, *L'Église*, p. 339.

[98] *Concilium Aurelianense* (Orléans; A.D. 549), § 10 (ed. de Clercq, *Concilia*, pp. 147-61, at 151-2).

which we do have Celtic evidence is the consecration of virgins.[99] I have only the briefest addition to make to Warren's account of the Zürich fragment, which is mentioned here for the sake of completeness. The fullest exposition of the history of the consecration of virgins in the West is that of Metz who does not discuss the Irish fragment.[100] But Mohlberg, as Sims-Williams has noted, was able to find Continental parallels for three of its four prayers.[101] The third prayer, the one not found elsewhere, contains the phrase 'in factis, in dictis, in cogitationibus', which is particularly associated with Ireland, as Sims-Williams has demonstrated in the same article.

---

[99] Warren, *The Liturgy*, pp. 23-4. On the manuscript (Zürich, Staatsarchiv, MS. A.G. 19, no. xxxvi), see Lowe, *Codices*, VII.1012, Kenney, *The Sources*, p. 565 (no. 565), and Lapidge & Sharpe, *A Bibliography*, p. 213 (no. 793).

[100] Metz, *La consécration*.

[101] Sims-Williams, 'Thought', p. 93.

2. The British Isles and the Christian World

The liturgy and ritual of the British and Irish Churches were naturally based on imported models, however much they diverged from them. We have very little information about the British Church, except that in the period when Britain was a Roman province it was in communication with the rest of christendom and sent small numbers of bishops to the major fourth-century synods.[102] Monasticism formed a part of British christian life from an early stage, as is shown by the remarkable British heresiarch, Pelagius,[103] who was a monk,[104] by some ascetic writings connected with the early British Church,[105] and by one or two of the early British inscriptions.[106] But monasticism does not seem to have been a major or influential part of the life of the British Church until after Gildas wrote his *De Excidio Britanniae*.[107] It is usual to assume that, when Britain was ruled from Rome, its religious life was also based on Roman models. However, once the legions had left, Britain became increasingly detached from the Roman world. The fifth and sixth centuries in Britain are the darkest part of the Dark Ages. The only writers whose works have come down to us are the fifth-century Patrick (the apostle of Ireland)[108] and the sixth-century Gildas,[109] neither of whom wrote directly about ecclesiastical organisation. Gildas does provide the interesting hints that in his day the Church was wealthy and prestigious enough for a bishopric to be a valuable prize[110] and that men went overseas to seek ordination.[111] He also speaks of relying on *transmarina relatio*, showing that expatriate Britons

---

[102] See Warren, *The Liturgy*, p. 29; and Haddan & Stubbs, *Councils*, I.7-8.

[103] Lapidge & Sharpe, *A Bibliography*, pp. 3-7 (nos 2-20).

[104] However, he became a monk in Rome, and thus is not a witness to early British monasticism.

[105] See Frend, 'The christianization', pp. 45-6, and Lapidge & Sharpe, *A Bibliography*, pp. 7-9 (nos 4 and 21-24).

[106] Nash-Williams, *The Early Christian Monuments of Wales*, especially no. 78 (p. 84), and no. 223 (p. 144).

[107] A work which cannot, unfortunately, be precisely dated: see Dumville, 'Gildas and Maelgwn', and 'The chronology of *De Excidio*'. Gildas said that a group of holy Britons (probably monks) was so small in number that Mother Church could scarcely feel them as they rested in her bosom (I.26,3: ed. Winterbottom, p. 99).

[108] Lapidge & Sharpe, *A Bibliography*, pp. 9-11 (nos 25-6).

[109] *Ibid.*, pp. 12-13 (nos 27-28).

[110] III.67,1-2 (ed. Winterbottom, p. 119).

[111] III.67,5 (*ibid.*, p. 120).

remained in touch with their homeland.[112] Very few Continental writers appear to have had any knowledge of British affairs,[113] and British attendance at Church-councils ceased. One may draw from this the hypothesis that British liturgy, no longer in contact with Roman traditions, was not brought up to date with new developments[114] and is likely to have developed some local peculiarities, thus becoming increasingly eccentric.[115] The well known paschal controversy which bedevilled the relationship of the Irish Church with its neighbours for centuries is an analogous phenomenon: the reckoning used by the Irish was neither unique nor invented by them; it was merely archaic, and long since superseded in the Western Church at large.[116] The continued use of archaic *Uetus Latina* versions of parts of the Old Testament in the British Isles, at least down to the sixth century, is another fact pointing in the same direction.[117]

There are faint indications that some parts at least of the British christian community were rather unorthodox even in the fourth century.[118] The Water Newton hoard of fourth-century Romano-British christian silverware[119] suggests some degree of syncretism or accommodation with pagan religious practice on the part of its users.[120] It contains a number of triangular silver plaques marked with the chi-rho monogram, but otherwise modelled on pagan

---

[112] I.4,4 (*ibid.*, p. 90). See also Thomas, *Christianity*, pp. 51 and 271-4, on sub-Roman contacts between Britain and Gaul.

[113] Two exceptions are Sidonius Apollinaris (*ca* 430-*ca* 479), who wrote of a priest and monk called Riochatus who acted as a messenger between Gaul and Britain (in *Epistola*, IX.9,6, ed. & transl. Anderson, *Sidonius*, II.534-7), and Victricius of Rouen (*floruit saec.* iv *ex.*), who actually visited Britain, having been called over to help resolve ecclesiastical controversies (ed. & transl. Herval, *Origines chrétiennes*, pp. 110-13).

[114] See Markus, 'Pelagianism', pp. 199-201.

[115] Hughes, *The Church*, p. 31, doubted, on the basis of epigraphic evidence, that the Northern and Western branches of the British Church really lost touch with Gaul in the fifth and sixth centuries. But some contact could continue without affecting the general thesis that Britain was becoming more isolated, perhaps especially in the levels of society which produced bishops, administrators, and teachers.

[116] This is why Columbanus insisted on its orthodoxy in his *Epistola* I, §§ 3-5 (edd. & transl. Walker [& Bieler], pp. 2-9).

[117] Williams (ed. & transl.), *Gildas*, I.90-7, and see below, p. lxxiii-lxxviii.

[118] Warren, *The Liturgy*, pp. 26-9, denied this; but it should be said that most of the evidence brought forward here is archaeological and was discovered after his time.

[119] On the date, see Painter, *The Water Newton Early Christian Silver*, pp. 20-1.

[120] Painter, *ibid.*; Thomas, *Christianity*, pp. 113-21.

ex uoto plaques. No other christian *ex uoto* objects have ever been found.[121] Still more surprising is the Hinton St Mary mosaic pavement, with its head of Christ which would offend iconoclasts and iconodules alike: the first group because it was an image of Christ, and the second because it would necessarily be trampled on.[122] These two survivals suggest the possibility that christianity was adopted by the wealthiest sections of the Romano-British community in a relatively lukewarm or even frivolous manner,[123] although this of course tells us nothing about the enthusiasm or orthodoxy of the community's spiritual leaders, or of the christian rank and file either.

Other indications which are more general in their implications are the apparent lack of continuity between pagan and christian burial sites in the fourth and fifth centuries.[124] Provided that no 'mixed' sites are found to explode the theory, this could show that there was a major shift in British religious attitudes, towards a wider adoption of christianity, at just about the time when the island slipped away from the Roman Empire.

The Irish Church is more visible to us, although much of its early history remains obscure. It is clear that from the outset there were several different traditions feeding into it. St Patrick was a Briton, engaged for most of his life in evangelisation in Ireland, but in the teeth of opposition from some of his *seniores* at home.[125] This opposition may have been general, or it may have been personal: that is, the British bishops might have had a general disapproval of christianising the Irish pirates who were harrying their people, or they may have had serious doubts about Patrick's fitness for the job. E.A. Thompson has noted that[126]

The Catholic Church did not send out missionaries beyond the imperial frontier in order to convert the heathen at this date.

---

121 Painter, *The Water Newton Early Christian Silver*, pp. 16-19 (nos 10, 12-27) and 22. See also Frend, 'Romano-British christianity', p. 8.

122 Thomas, *Christianity*, pp. 106, 121. Toynbee points out in 'Pagan motifs and practices', pp. 181-4, that the other motifs on this site were all drawn from Classical, and consequently pagan, iconography, although they may perhaps be regarded as symbolic or allegorical representations of christian truths.

123 An idea which may be supported by Gildas's opinion (*De Excidio*, I.9,1) that the British accepted the Word without enthusiasm: 'licet ab incolis tepide suscepta sunt' (ed. Winterbottom, p. 91). See also Thompson, *Saint Germanus*, pp. 26-32

124 Thomas, *Christianity*, pp. 238-9.

125 Patrick, *Confessio*, § 26 (ed. Hood, p. 28). There are also editions by Hanson & Blanc, *Saint Patrick*, and Bieler, *Libri Epistolarum*.

126 'St. Patrick and Coroticus', p. 18. See also his 'Christianity and the Northern barbarians', p. 9.

He goes on to suggest that the first British christian presence in Ireland was almost entirely involuntary, consisting mainly of captives with perhaps a handful of traders, and that consequently the first Church in Ireland was not a Church of the Irish. He also raises the possibility that Palladius was sent to minister to this community of British christians in Ireland, and not to the Irish at all.[127] In any case, even if it is legitimate to deduce an originally negative attitude towards the Irish from Patrick's problems with his *seniores*, the British Church did not remain hostile. In the sixth century, the age of the great monastic founders, the Irish received much assistance and support from the Britons.[128] 'St Finnian', who is named as the master of most of the major Irish saints,[129] was himself a Briton resident in Ireland[130] and is also recorded by Columbanus, as having appealed to Gildas for advice.[131] Various Irish ecclesiastical sites and saints' Lives record their debt to the Britons.[132] The inference from this is that the early Irish Church was indebted, both for inspiration and some part of its day-to-day guidance, to British models. Richard Sharpe has noted that that 'the mainspring of developments in the Celtic Churches during the sixth century was a movement from western Britain'.[133]

For all that, the Irish Church was not an exclusively British product.[134] Prosper of Aquitaine tells us that the pope sent Palladius as first bishop to

---

[127] 'St. Patrick and Coroticus'.

[128] This is confirmed by the testimony of language, on which see Greene, 'Some linguistic evidence', Jackson, *Language and History*, and MacNeill, 'The beginnings'.

[129] Pádraig Ó Riain ('St. Finnbarr') has put forward a strong argument that Finnian of Clonard and Finnian of Moville were in fact the same man. Finnian's status as a monastic educator is attested as early as Adomnán's *Uita S. Columbae*, I.1 (edd. & transl. Anderson & Anderson, pp. 196-7); cf. II.1 (pp. 324-5).

[130] The name is British, and should be spelt Uinniau. See Dumville, 'Gildas and Uinniau'.

[131] *Epistola* I, § 7 (edd. & transl. Walker [& Bieler], pp. 8-9). See also Sharpe, 'Gildas'.

[132] Dumville, 'Some British aspects', pp. 19-20; Plummer, *Vitae*, I.ç and cxxiv-cxxv; Slover, 'Early literary channels', especially pt. 2, pp. 6-38; Smyth, *Celtic Leinster*, p. 9; Loth, 'Bretons insulaires'.

[133] Share, 'Gildas', pp. 200.

[134] Dumville 'Some British aspects', p. 24, concluded: 'it remains possible at the moment to speak only of British aspects of the earliest Irish Christianity, not of a clear British background to (and much less a British model for) the developing Irish Church'.

'the Irish believing in Christ'.[135] Palladius has been all but edited out of the Irish Church's own version of its history in order to leave Patrick in solitary apostolic glory, but it is not necessarily the case that Palladius made as little impact on the country as Patrician apologists have claimed. Ireland was, from a Continental viewpoint, on the edge of the known world,[136] but it was not completely isolated.[137] A very early stratum of loanwords indicates trading contacts with the Roman world,[138] and Ionas's *Uita S. Columbani* mentioned quite casually that one could expect to find an Irish trading vessel in the harbour at Nantes,[139] which would at least permit, even if it did not specifically encourage, contacts between Ireland and the Gallican Church.[140] Columba (*ob.* 597) on distant Iona received some Italian news — not fast, to be sure, but it did reach him eventually.[141] These links with the Continent provide a possible context in which Gaulish and Roman christianity could make some impact on the Irish, ratified by Celestine's appointment of

---

[135] See Warren, *The Liturgy*, pp. 30-1, and Corish, 'The early Irish Church'. Note the argument of Thompson ('St. Patrick and Coroticus') on the identity of these *Scotti*. The evidence for the activities of Palladius has been discussed by Bieler, 'The mission of Palladius'.

[136] Both Patrick and Columbanus saw it in this way. Patrick spoke of the Irish as living 'in ultimis terrae' (*Confessio*, § 58: ed. Hood, p. 34; see also his §§ 38-40, pp. 30-31). Columbanus (*Epistola* V, § 3: edd. Walker [& Bieler], p. 38, line 23), wrote that his people were 'ultimi habitatores mundi'.

[137] The archaeological evidence was put together by Ó Ríordáin, in 'Roman material in Ireland', and more recently by Bateson, 'Roman material from Ireland', and 'Further finds'.

[138] See Carney, 'Three Old Irish accentual poems', pp. 69-70, where he demonstrates that there is a stratum of non-christian Latin loanwords, including *legión* (*legio*) and *trebun* (*tribunus*) in the very early Irish poetry associated with Leinster and datable to the sixth century; and also Jackson, *Language and History*, pp. 122-48, Mc Manus, 'A chronology', pp. 42-4, and Ó Cróinín, 'The oldest Irish names', p. 112.

[139] *Uita*, I.23 (ed. Krusch, pp. 205-6). On this whole topic, see James, 'Ireland and western Gaul'; Zimmer, 'Über direkte Handelsverbindungen'; Doherty, 'Exchange and trade', pp. 76-85; and Thomas, 'Imported Late-Roman Mediterranean pottery', p. 254, where he discusses the use of *bordgal* (presumably from *Burdigala*: 'Bordeaux') as an Irish word meaning 'market' or 'meeting place'.

[140] Some of the differences and similarities between Irish and Gallic christianity were noted by Gaudemet, *L'Église*; but the mixed ancestry postulated for Irish christianity would account for these divergencies. Gaudemet assumed (probably mistakenly) that St Patrick was trained in Gaul (p. 96).

[141] Adomnán, *Uita S. Columbae*, I.28 (edd. & transl. Anderson & Anderson, pp. 262-5).

Palladius as the first bishop in Ireland.[142]

It is perhaps strange that this papal appointment, for which we have very little context, was not followed up: the papacy made few attempts to guide Irish ecclesiastical affairs for several hundred years. But it is interesting in this connexion that Columbanus spoke of Rome, rather than Britain or Gaul, as the *fons et origo* of Irish christianity,[143] although his contemporary Gregory the Great, who vigorously oversaw all the Churches of the Western Empire, sometimes to the point of interfering in minute matters of local government[144] (and who, of course, was the driving force behind the Roman mission to the English), was apparently almost completely ignorant about the British and Irish Churches and made no identifiable attempt to remedy this ignorance.[145] A little later, in the 630s, Cummian wrote of an Irish deputation, sent to Rome to try to solve the paschal controversy, as going 'uelut natos ad matrem'.[146]

The impression given by the various strata of evidence is that the Irish Churches were inspired from British, Gaulish, and Roman sources.[147] Thus, one religious centre might diverge considerably in practice from another, each following the traditions laid down by its founder or founders. No other conclusion is possible, since a unifying and controlling centre of evangelisation, deferred to by all parties, is an anachronistic concept.[148] In the seventh century, when most of our evidence for Ireland begins, we see markedly variant practice on the central issues of the tonsure and the date of Easter, and an enormous amount of emotion generated, in which some groups of churches (for which Cummian became spokesman) allowed overriding

---

[142] There are some further remarks, on Roman contacts with seventh-century Ireland, by Ó Cróinín, 'Pride', p. 354, and Warren, *The Liturgy*, pp. 58-62.

[143] *Epistola* V, § 3 (edd. & transl. Walker [& Bieler], pp. 38-9, lines 21-7). Adomnán also spoke of Rome as 'caput omnium ciuitatum': *Uita S. Columbae*, III.23 (edd. & transl. Anderson & Anderson, pp. 542-3).

[144] Wallace-Hadrill, *The Frankish Church*, pp. 115-18.

[145] Dudden, *Gregory the Great*, II.118-19.

[146] *Epistola* (ed. Migne, *Patrologia Latina*, LXXXVII.969-78, at col. 977B). Note, however, the practical point that it was only in the third year that the deputation returned. On Cummian, see Lapidge & Sharpe, *A Bibliography*, p. 78 (no. 289).

[147] Thomas, *Christianity*, pp. 271-4.

[148] Thompson, 'The origins', pp. 17-19.

power to the Roman position in the name of christian unity while others adhered obstinately to the methods of their own particular founders and *seniores*. Apart from making a contribution to the christianisation of Ireland, the Romano-British Church itself continued to survive in several different branches: the Church of Brittany, the Welsh and Cornish Churches, the Church of Pictland (whose supposed founder, Nynia, had a recognizably British name),[149] and apparently an outlying remnant in Bretoña in Galicia, about which very little is known.[150]

The export of the British Church to Brittany can be deduced from Gildas, who describes christian refugees fleeing the country:[151]

alii transmarinas regiones cum ululatu magno ceu celeumatis uice hoc modo sub uelorum sinibus cantantes, 'Dedisti nos tamquam oues escarum' (Ps. XLIII.12).

The Breton peninsula remained very British in its outlook for centuries. There is an interesting note in the Book of Llandaf, about a Welsh prince who did public penance in Brittany in the second half of the ninth century, of whom it was noted that he, the Bretons, and the archbishop of that country 'were of the same language and the same nation'.[152] Gerald of Wales claimed that the two languages were all but mutually intelligible even in the late twelfth century.[153] The Bretons also had much contact with the Irish from the sixth century to the ninth.[154] Columbanus had some contact with Brittany, and three and four centuries later the Breton monasteries were to be a major link in the transmission of many Hiberno-Latin texts. The country was of course subject to religious influence from the Gauls and later the Franks, but it continued to look northward and westward until the coming of the Northmen in the ninth century, and to some extent even beyond this time.

---

[149] See Thomas, *Christianity*, pp. 274-94, on Nynia; and also Thompson, 'The origins', and MacQueen, *St. Nynia*.

[150] Thompson, 'Britonia', and De Jubainville, 'Périodiques', p. 256, n. 3.

[151] *De Excidio*, I.25,1 (ed. Winterbottom, p. 98). See also Chadwick, 'The colonization', and Fleuriot, *Les origines*. Thompson, on the other hand, thinks that these emigrants are going to Ireland, not Brittany. But since British settlement in both countries demonstrably occurred, Gildas's statement does not favour one destination over the other.

[152] *Ibid.*, pp. 272-3.

[153] *Descriptio Kambriae*, I.4 (edd. Brewer *et al.*, *Giraldi Cambrensis Opera*, VI.155-227, at p. 177).

[154] Dumville, 'Some British aspects', pp. 20-3.

In Wales the Church remained even more intransigent about its regional peculiarities than did the Church of Iona, and showed no sign of conforming to general custom on the Easter-question and other matters of Church-discipline until 768.[155] The reasons may lie partly in the obstinate conservatism which seems to have been common to all the Celtic Churches, and partly in the fact that the message of the Church Universal came chiefly through the medium of the Church among the English, against which Welsh christians continued to nurture a profound animosity for centuries after the *aduentus Saxonum*.[156] Both Bede and Aldhelm noted that British (and Irish) clergy treated English clergy as excommunicates and consequently would not eat with them.[157] The slow process of the assimilation of the various Celtic Churches into the community of Catholic christendom and the gradual abandonment of their characteristic peculiarities has been summarised by Gougaud.[158]

The Welsh Church remained to some extent provincial until the Norman conquest. The most sophisticated Welsh writer of the ninth century, Bishop Asser, continued to use a *Uetus Latina* Bible when this had long since been superseded both on the Continent and in Ireland.[159] In the later eleventh and twelfth centuries, the careers of Bishop Sulien and his sons at Llanbadarn Fawr also illuminate a somewhat backward-looking Church in which even the

---

[155] *Annales Cambriae, s.a.* 768: 'Pasca commutatur apud Brittones, emendante Elbodugo homine Dei' (ed. Phillimore, p. 162). The *Annales* were discussed by Hughes, who suggested that 'The contemporary chronicle began soon after Wales accepted the Roman Easter' (*Celtic Britain*, p. 100). Their testimony for this date may therefore be accepted, although the entry is rather unspecific, and it may not be appropriate to conclude that all of Wales conformed at the same time. On Iona, see Hughes, *The Church*, pp. 106-7.

[156] Hughes, 'The Celtic Church and the papacy', pp. 12-13.

[157] Bede, *Historia Ecclesiastica*, II.4 (edd. & transl. Colgrave & Mynors, p. 146-7), and Aldhelm, *Epistola ad Geruntium* (ed. Ehwald, p. 484; transl. [Lapidge &] Herren, p. 158). See also Gougaud, *Christianity*, pp. 200-7, and Warren, *The Liturgy*, pp. 40-1. Proper behaviour towards excommunicates was laid down in *Synodus Diocesana Autissiodorensis* (Auxerre: A.D. 561×605), § 38 (ed. de Clercq, *Concilia*, pp. 264-72, at 269).

[158] *Christianity*, ch. xi: 'The Gradual Decline of Celtic Particularism' (pp. 386-426).

[159] Keynes & Lapidge, *Alfred the Great*, pp. 53-4. See further Lapidge, 'Latin learning', pp. 91-4.

principle of episcopal celibacy had apparently failed to take root.[160]

---

[160] Lapidge, 'The Welsh-Latin poetry', pp. 69-76, and Warren, *The Liturgy*, pp. 13-14. On the Welsh Church, see further Davies, *Wales in the Early Middle Ages*, and Davies, 'The Church in Wales'.

3. Monasticism in Celtic Lands

The ascetic impulse, the longing for a life devoted entirely to God, was naturally present in the christian Church from the beginning.[161] The developments which transformed the Church from its beginnings as a community of social outcasts into a state-supported and increasingly wealthy institution caused an inevitable backlash from more fervent souls, leading them to seek more austere and spiritual forms of life outside the ordinary boundaries of the christian community. Monasticism was a gradual and *ad hoc* development of the third and fourth centuries, when more and more people began to want to devote their entire lives to prayer and the contemplation of God, unencumbered by worldly cares.[162] The first major turning point was the third-century movement into the Egyptian desert, of which St Anthony was the guiding inspiration and classic example. The ascetics and hermits of Egypt worked out a variety of ways of life, ranging from the original solitary hermitages implied by the word *monachus* (from Greek μόνος, 'one') to cenobitic communities, such as those of Pachomius and Shenute, which introduced the concept of obedience to a superior alongside the virtues of poverty, chastity, and humility. The transformation of the yearning for a truly spiritual life into a coherent and practical scheme for achieving this end took hundreds of years.[163] Finally, St Benedict, an older contemporary of Gregory the Great and Columbanus, produced a guide to the monastic life so lucid and sensible that it came to overshadow or completely to supersede all other rules from about the year 800 onwards, and formed the basis for almost all subsequent developments of Western monasticism.[164] Its great strength is not originality, for it draws on many pre-existing traditions,[165] but its comprehensiveness, common sense, and organisation.

---

161 See Constable, *Medieval Monasticism*, for bibliography.

162 See Hughes, *The Church*, pp. 12-20, and Knowles, *Christian Monasticism*, pp. 9-24.

163 The development of monastic practice from the fourth century to the sixth has been discussed by Heiming, 'Zum monastischen Offizium'.

164 Benedict, *Regula Monasteriorum* (ed. de Vogüé).

165 Especially the so-called *Regula Magistri*: see Knowles, *Great Historical Enterprises*, pp. 139-95, de Vogüé (ed.), *La Règle du Maître*, I.19-24, and De Vogüé & Neufville (edd.), *La Règle de Saint Benoît*, I.33-79.

Irish monasticism was established in the pre-Benedictine period, before any consensus on the conduct of the monastic life had been achieved, and at a time when there were practically as many *regulae* as there were abbots.[166] The main impetus (if there *was* a main impetus) could have come either from Gaul or from Britain. We are a great deal better informed about Gaulish than about British monastic developments, since we have only Gildas as a contemporary witness to the British scene,[167] and there are several substantial near-contemporary accounts of monasticism in Gaul.[168] St Patrick stressed that some of his Irish converts had become monks and virgins of Christ, not merely christians,[169] which suggests that by his time monks were already a highly regarded sector of the christian community. The earliest phase of the Irish Church to have left any contemporary records was not organised on a monastic basis, as St Patrick's writings show us. He spoke of himself as a bishop.[170] Palladius, also, was despatched to be a *bishop* in Ireland, not a monastic leader. Although Patrick venerated monasticism, the main principle of ecclesiastical organisation was clerical — bishops, not abbots, were the central authorities. How quickly this was influenced by the monasticism which looms so large in our surviving sources from the late sixth century onwards is a matter for debate.[171] Columbanus, our next reference-point, regarded *clerici* and *monachi* as essentially different. He wrote as an abbot to bishops in

---

[166] Ryan, 'The Church at the end of the sixth century', p. 26: 'The main cause of difference was the *consuetudinarium* or customary. The Rule proper dealt with the substance of religious life, and, as this was the same for all, there was not room for much originality. But between custom and custom there could be the widest divergence.' See for example 'Mac Eclaise','The Rule of St Carthage', O Neill,'The Rule', Gwynn, 'The Rule', and also O'Carroll, 'Monastic rules'.

[167] Bowen, *Saints*, pp. 209-10, notes the close resemblance of the early Breton monastery of the Île de Lavret to the Syrian *lauras*, suggesting that this may be the remains of one of the earliest Western monasteries. It may also be a witness to the style of monasticism in the early *British* Church. The excavations there have been reported by Giot, 'Saint Budoc'.

[168] For example, the *uitae* of Martin and Honoratus. See the convenient collection of translations by Hoare, *The Western Fathers*, and discussion by Wallace-Hadrill, *The Frankish Church*, pp. 5-9.

[169] Patrick, *Confessio*, §§ 41-42 (ed. Hood, p. 31). It is clear that these people have to go on living in their respective communities, with all the difficulties which this entailed, especially for slave-women.

[170] *Confessio*, § 32 (ed. Hood, p. 29); *Epistola*, § 1 (*ibid.*, p. 35).

[171] See Firey, 'Cross-examining', pp. 37-40, on the lack of real evidence for the traditional picture of the development of monastic *paruchiae*, and on the continuing episcopal basis for power at Kildare down to the eighth century.

Epistola, II, with a due sense of the dignities of both.[172] His Penitential is divided into three sections, dealing with monks, clerics, and the laity.[173] By the seventh century, when most of our written sources begin, the balance of power has been understood as having shifted, so that the Irish Church was developing towards a system in which the main temporal power and authority was wielded by abbots, who had bishops as honoured subordinates.[174] This has recently been disputed by Richard Sharpe, who has suggested that the perceived change is chimerical, deriving from the ascetic and monastic bias of much of the early evidence. He argues that the powers of jurisdiction of a bishop and his rights within a given territory were in no sense set aside, although control of the *temporalities* of the Church did indeed come to be administered mainly by abbots.[175] Kathleen Hughes also emphasised the continued dignity and independence of some bishops into the seventh century:[176]

We are forced to the conclusion that an episcopacy controlling ecclesiastical administration survived into the seventh century, where it co-existed with the monastic *paruchiae* under presbyter-abbots which had been founded in the sixth.

However we may argue over the monastic or episcopal structure of the Irish Church, it is fairly clear that the Welsh Church remained essentially episcopal. Hughes associated this with the greater powers enjoyed by Welsh kings than by their Irish counterparts.[177]

Bede's understanding of life at contemporary Lindisfarne was that the bishop chose the abbot, with the advice of the brethren, but then lived under his rule.[178]

Unde ab illo omnes loci ipsius antistes usque hodie sic episcopate exercent officium, ut regente

---

[172] *Epistola* II, § 8 (edd. & transl. Walker [& Bieler], p. 20): 'alia enim sunt et alia clericorum et monachorum documenta, ea et longe ab inuicem separata' (although he went on to commend the heroism of those who attempted both).

[173] *Poenitentiale*, edd. & transl. Walker [& Bieler], pp. 168-81.

[174] For example Hughes, *The Church*, pp. 39-90.

[175] Sharpe, 'Some problems', pp. 263-5. See also Firey, 'Cross-examining', as above, n. 171

[176] *The Church*, p. 81. The honourable status of bishops in early mediaeval Ireland is also emphasised by the eighth-century vernacular law-tract *Críth Gablach*, § 48 (ed. Binchy, p. 24).

[177] Hughes, 'The Celtic Church'.

[178] Bede is here describing the position of Aidán at Lindisfarne (*Two* Lives, ed. & transl. Colgrave, pp. 206-9).

monasterium abbate, quem ipsi cum consilio fratrum elegerint, omnes presbiteri, diacones, cantores, lectores, caeterique gradus aecclesiastici, monachicam per omnia cum ipso episcopo regulam seruit.

His view that the bishop chose the abbot might be challenged, and might not be applicable to all Irish monasteries: if, as was the case at Lindisfarne's mother-house, Iona, the abbot was almost invariably a member of the founder's family, the bishop's choice must have been extremely restricted. Bede also noted that the combination of monastic and clerical ways of life was approved by Gregory the Great (who was himself monk and pope at the same time). It was not peculiar to Ireland.[179]

In this section, I shall be discussing monastic life almost exclusively, but it must be remembered that this does not necessarily represent the whole picture.[180] The text usually known as the 'First Synod of St Patrick' (*Synodus Episcoporum*) may shed some light on the early Irish bishops.[181] It has been variously dated from the fifth to the seventh century.[182] The text concerns itself mainly with episcopal authority, particularly with regard to *clerici* and *presbyteri*, although it also lays down some rulings on the behaviour of monks and nuns.[183] These could, of course, be interpolations, added to a basically early text in order to accomodate it to the developed monastic structure of the seventh and eighth centuries. The synod also legislated against one bishop 'poaching' on another's territory by ordaining anyone outside his own diocese. The last canon is interesting in that it prohibits a *diaconus* from

---

[179] See Sheehy's summary of the situation ('Concerning the origin', p. 139): 'On the Continent, the episcopal and clerical structure which had been temporarily confused with monasticism during the fourth and fifth centuries, asserted itself in the sixth century and re-established its rightful place in ecclesiastical organisation. In Ireland, on the other hand, the same evolved into a perverted monastic organisation.' See also Rousseau, 'The spiritual authority', pp. 406-16.

[180] Sharpe has commented on the 'distortion' imposed on our picture of the early Irish Church by Ryan's influential study *Irish Monasticism* ('Some problems', pp. 232-6).

[181] See *The Bishops' Synod*, ed. Faris; see also *The Irish Penitentials*, edd. & transl. Bieler [& Binchy], pp. 54-9.

[182] Bieler thought it to be contemporary with St Patrick. See his 'Patrick's Synod: a revision'. Binchy, 'Patrick and his biographers', pp. 45-9, and 'St Patrick's "First Synod"', held it to be a product of the 'romanising' party of the sixth or seventh century. Hughes, *The Church*, pp. 44-52, argued for a mid-sixth-century date.

[183] For example, *Synodus Episcoporum*, § 9 (*apud* Faris, *The Bishops' Synod*, pp. 1-2), § 17 (pp. 3-4).

wandering about *inconsulto suo abbate*.[184] It implies that deacons (a clerical grade) could find themselves under the jurisdiction of an abbot.[185] This synod is not incompatible with a generally monastic Church, even although it is preoccupied with the rights of bishops with respect to minor clergy and other bishops. These rights would hold good even if the bishops were themselves living under abbots.[186]

The conferring of holy orders, in Ireland as elsewhere, carried with it some specific privileges and responsibilities. It was priests and bishops, not monks, who confirmed the faithful and who celebrated the mass. This purely spiritual authority, regarding the bishop as the 'Vicar of Christ', was unaffected by lack of temporal authority. We know very little about cathedral offices in Ireland, although the cathedral office of morning- and evening-prayer, with vigils on Saturday-nights and the eves of feasts, performed by clerics and devout lay people, preceded and existed alongside the more elaborate offices performed by monks.[187] There is one reference in the 'First Synod of St Patrick' to what appears to be cathedral office:[188]

Quicumque clericus ussus neglegentiae causa ad collectas mane uel uespere non occurrerit alienus habeatur nisi forte iugo seruituti sit detentus.

Compare the ruling of the Council of Agde (A.D. 506): '[ab episcopis uel presbyteris] hymni matutini uel uespertini diebus omnibus decantentur'.[189]

On the Gaulish side, two major figures require specific mention. One is Cassian of Marseille (*ca* 360-435).[190] It was Cassian's special contribution that, after spending many years in the East, first at Bethlehem and then in Egypt, and sitting eagerly at the feet of the great Egyptian founders of monasticism, he settled in Gaul *ca* 415 and, in lucid Latin, wrote up monastic spirituality and thought and the nature of the monastic life. He also succeeded

---

184 *Synodus Episcoporum*, § 34 (*ibid.*, pp. 7-8).

185 If it can be taken at face-value, and not as a slip of the pen. The phrase *inconsulto suo abbate* may have drifted up from the next sentence, where it appears again.

186 See Ryan, *Irish Monasticism*, pp. 167-90, on episcopal jurisdiction.

187 Baumstark & Botte, *Comparative Liturgy*, pp. 111-16.

188 *Synodus Episcoporum*, § 7 (*apud* Faris, *The Bishops' Synod*, pp. 1-2).

189 *Concilium Agathense*, § 30 (ed. Munier, *Concilia Galliae*, pp. 189-219, at 206).

190 Cassian, *Conlationes*, ed. Petschenig; Cassian, *De Institutis*, ed. Petschenig. See also Chadwick, *John Cassian*.

in translating the austere principles of the Egyptian desert into Gaul, sensibly making allowance in matters of diet and clothing for the harsher climate.[191] His work and his writings were enormously influential — the other great names of early Gaulish monasticism, Honoratus of Lérins, Caesarius of Arles, and so on, owed a great deal to him. His work was used by Columbanus.[192] The other major figure is St Martin, bishop of Tours.[193] He was very highly regarded in early mediaeval Ireland; for example, Sulpicius Seuerus's *Uita S. Martini* and *Dialogi* appear alongside the Patrician *dossier* in the Book of Armagh. Henry Mayr-Harting has commented that 'the bishops of the Irish tradition looked to Martin's life for inspiration in many ways'.[194] He was celebrated by Columba, according to Adomnán who seems to imply that this was a general practice.[195] Columbanus also had a special devotion to him, witnessed in Ionas's *Uita*.[196] There is a (so-called) *Deprecatio S. Martini pro populo* in the Stowe Missal.[197] Perhaps one of the reasons for the veneration of Martin in Ireland is that he was an ascetic and monk who was also a bishop, and thus provided a model for the Irish combination of the clerical and monastic traditions. This idea was first argued by Heinrich Zimmer, and

---

[191] Cassian, *De Institutis, Praefatio*, §§ 8-9 (ed. Petschenig, p. 7). Sulpicius Seuerus also sheds light on the less heroic Gaulish attitude to self-denial —see, for example, *Dialogi*, I.5 (ed. Halm, p. 157): 'Enimuero, Postumianus [ait], cauebo posthac cuiusquam abstinentiam praedicare, ne Gallos nostros arduum penitus offendat exemplum'.

[192] The extent of Cassian's direct influence on the development of early Irish monastic culture deserves further scrutiny, since Chadwick asserted in *John Cassian*, pp. 148-9, that his works were not known in Ireland. But, in addition to the use of Cassian by Columbanus, particularly in his penitential, Cassianic practice is also found at Iona, for example the custom of an extra meal on Sundays and festivals: compare *Uita S. Columbae*, III.12 (edd. & transl. Anderson & Anderson, pp. 488-9), 'aliquam quasi in dominico prandioli adjectionem fieri', and Cassian, *De Institutis*, III.2 (ed. Petschenig, p. 45), 'in ipsis diebus, id est sabbato uel dominica seu ferialis temporibus, quibus prandium pariter et cena solet fratribus exhiberi'. The term *prandium* is used in both, although Adomnán, as is his wont, has used a diminutive form.

[193] The main sources for the life of St Martin are the works of Sulpicius Seuerus (ed. Halm).

[194] *The Coming*, p. 97.

[195] Adomnán, *Uita S. Columbae*, III.12 (edd. & transl. Anderson & Anderson, pp. 490-1): 'illa consueta decantaretur deprecatio in qua sancti Martini commemoratur nomen'.

[196] Ionas, *Uita S. Columbani*, I.22 (ed. Krusch, pp. 200-2). There is a good deal of other evidence for the Irish devotion to Martin: see Grosjean, 'Gloria postuma', and Gwynn, 'The cult'.

[197] Warner, *The Stowe Missal*, II.6.

has recently been revived by Edward James.[198]

One point which it is important to clarify is that monasticism in Ireland in the fifth, sixth, and seventh centuries did not have a single source. It was part of a vast, widespread enthusiasm for cenobitic and eremitic ways of life which can be found all over the christian world at this time. The possibility of direct contact with Egypt — suggested by romantically minded scholars in the past — can reasonably be discounted,[199] although Irish ecclesiastics would be aware, via Cassian, of the supreme reputation for holy living enjoyed by the Desert Fathers.[200] There were strong-minded, charismatic, and evangelical leaders nearer at hand, who adopted the monastic life and found flocks of eager postulants surrounding them. Martin of Tours, Cassian of Marseille, Honoratus of Lérins, are all examples.[201] Any or all of these, and others like them, could have given impetus to the monastic movement in Ireland, if only through their writings or their reputation.

The *Uitae Sanctorum Hiberniae*, many of which are Lives of the founders of important Irish monasteries, often suggest a specific source of inspiration for a saint's vocation to the monastic life.[202] These are *not*

---

[198] See Sulpicius Seuerus, *Uita S. Martini*, § 10 (ed. Halm, pp. 119-20); James, 'Ireland and western Gaul', pp. 366-7. Also see Kenney, *The Sources*, pp. 158-9 and 324.

[199] See Raftery, 'Ex oriente...', for a sceptical view —but note that this is challenged by Crehan, 'The liturgical trade route', pp. 88-90. There is some evidence of the remains of North African and Eastern pottery on British and Irish sites, notably Tintagel, although of course their route to the British Isles need not have been direct (Thomas, 'East and West', pp. 21-7).

[200] Chadwick (*John Cassian*, pp. 148-9), followed by Mayr-Harting (*The Coming*, p. 84), asserted that Cassian was little read in Ireland. This is incorrect. Apart from the use made of Cassian by Columbanus, he is an important source for the hymns and collects in the Antiphonary of Bangor (including the sixth-century hymn 'Precamur patrem'), and for the seventh-century poem 'Altus Prosator'.

[201] Luff, 'A survey'.

[202] For instance, Comgall spends time with both Fintan and Ciarán before founding Bangor (*Uita S. Comgalli*, § 11: Plummer, *Vitae*, II.6), and Ciarán himself goes to learn with Finnian (*Uita S. Ciarani*, § 15: *ibid.*, I.205). For what it is worth, these *uitae* name Irish and British masters: aside from Finnian (on whose British name see Dumville, 'Gildas and Uinniau'), Énda of Aran (*Uita S. Endei*, §§ 6-7: Plummer, *Vitae*, II.62-3) was associated with 'Rosnat' (identified by Ryan, *Irish Monasticism*, p. 106, with Candida Casa in Galloway, and by Thomas, 'Rosnat', with Tintagel —a view he has recently withdrawn, in 'East and West', p. 17 —, and Maedóc of Ferns is said to have been educated at David's *Meneuia* (*Uita S. Aedi*, § 12: Plummer, *Vitae*, I.44).

contemporary lives, and many are more or less fantastic; so their evidence cannot be trusted. Legend is different from history, and these Lives evidently contain a great deal of folklore, wild surmise, bad guessing, and ammunition for inter-church squabbling. In any case, one cannot imagine much uniformity between churches. Each abbot worked out for himself the most spiritual way of life which he could devise — to the limits of what flesh and blood could be expected to stand, in many cases[203] — based, presumably, on the direct method of 'apprenticing' himself in his youth to a senior, or the less personal approach of reading the works of his predecessors, and/or seeking personal advice.[204] This, as far as I can see, was the situation in Gaul and Britain as well. Compare the words which Bede gave to Benedict Biscop in *Historia Abbatum*:[205]

Ex decem quippe et septem monasteriis quae inter longes meae crebre peregrinationis discursus optima conperi, haec uniuersos didici, et uobis salubriter obseruando contradidi.

That is, before the widespread adoption of *Regula S. Benedicti*, there was no central authority to legislate on the monastic life.

As far as the monasticism of the fifth and early sixth centuries goes, we have only later evidence, chiefly in the form of the *uitae* of the founding saints. The picture begins to clarify a little in the late sixth century, mainly on account of the *Regula Monachorum* and *Regula Coenobialis* of Columbanus.[206] Columbanus said that he was basing his rules on the wisdom of his *seniores*; therefore they may give us a glimpse of life at Bangor under the régime of Comgall himself,[207] although Riché has noted that[208]

the chapters of the Rule tell us nothing about the relation between abbot and *prepositus*, the

---

203 For example, *Uita S. Comgalli*, § 56 (ed. Plummer, *Vitae*, II.21): 'alii enim dicebant, quod tanti dolores super eum a Deo dati sunt propter duriciam et asperitatem regule eius in monachis suis'.

204 See n. 202 for examples of the first approach. Columbanus's knowledge of Cassian suggests that he also used the second, and there is an example of the third in Uinniau's appeal to Gildas, recorded by Columbanus in his *Epistola* I, § 7 (edd. & transl. Walker [& Bieler], pp. 8-9).

205 § 11 (ed. Plummer, *Venerabilis Baedae Opera*, I.374-5).

206 Edd. & transl. Walker [& Bieler], pp. 122-43, 142-69. See also Laporte, 'Étude d'authenticité', and discussion by Bradshaw, *Daily Prayer*, pp. 133-4.

207 *Regula Monachorum*, § 7: 'de synaxi... quaedam sunt distinguenda, quia uarie a diuersis memoriae de eo traditum est', and a little later, 'inde et cum senioribus nostris...' (edd. & transl. Walker [& Bieler], p. 128).

208 Riché, 'Columbanus', p. 67.

liturgical *horarium*, the times of meals and so on. What matters is obedience, silence, fasting, chastity, mortification and penance.

The evidence of Columbanus's *Regulae* is strengthened by two Continental *Regulae* based on his practice, that of Donatus,[209] and another known as *Regula cuiusdam patris*.[210] There is also some information in the seventh-century *Uita S. Columbani* by Ionas of Bobbio. Another seventh-century view of sixth-century monasticism can be found in Adomnán's *Uita S. Columbae*.

The rule of life specified by Columbanus is extremely harsh in all aspects — food, clothing, sleep, and comfort of any kind are all ruthlessly restricted. His office is in line with this austerity. There are eight services (one every three hours of the twenty-four). They are as follows.[211]

ad secundam (Prime, in modern terminology): 6 a.m.

ad tertiam (Terce): 9 a.m.

ad sextam (Sext): 12 noon

ad nonam (None): 3 p.m.

ad uespertinam (Vespers): 6 p.m.

ad initium noctis (1 Nocturn): 9 p.m.

ad medium noctis (2 Nocturn): 12 midnight

ad matutinam (Lauds/Matins): 3 a.m.

Columbanus arranged the psalms into groups of three, called *chori*. Within each group, the first two were sung straight through, the third antiphonally (with the congregation divided into two, singing verses alternately). He makes a distinction between the holy nights of Saturday and Sunday and the rest of the week. In every case, *ad matutinam* is the longest and most important service of the day. In the four day-hours from *ad secundam* to *ad nonam*, only three psalms were sung, so as not to interfere with the day's labours, together with a series of short intercessory prayers for various categories of

---

209 The relevant section was given by Warren, *The Antiphonary*, II.xiv-xv. Donatus studied monasticism under Columbanus. He is mentioned in Ionas's *Uita S. Columbani*, I.14 (ed. Krusch, pp. 175-6). His rule is a fusion of Columbanian, Benedictine, and Caesarian traditions — see Luff, 'A survey', p. 193, and Wallace-Hadrill, *The Frankish Church*, p. 59.

210 ed. Migne, *Patrologia Latina*, LXVI.937-94. See § 20 (at col. 994).

211 Warren, *The Antiphonary*, II.xvi; Warren, *The Liturgy*, p. 17.

people.[212] In the three Night-hours, *ad uespertinam* to *ad medium noctis*, twelve psalms were sung. *Ad matutinam*, the number varies with the seasons. On ordinary nights, twenty-four psalms were sung in summer, rising to thirty-six in winter. On Saturdays and Sundays, the minimum was thirty-six and the maximum seventy-five. He also mentioned in the *Regula Coenobialis* that hymns were sung when the eucharist was celebrated[213] and on Sundays.

The prospect of singing psalms continuously for (at a guess) about two and a half hours in the small hours of a winter's night, with barely time to rest one's voice before starting all over again, is a régime which only the most fervent religious devotee could bear to contemplate. While on the subject of Columbanus, I should like to put forward the suggestion that the *cursus psalmorum* outlined above represented the whole of his office. It is generally assumed that he used canticles, antiphons, collects, hymns, prayers, and other addenda as well, since these are mentioned in the Antiphonary of Bangor, to which I shall turn later.[214] This does not strike me as a safe assumption.

In his *De Institutis*, which I mentioned earlier, Cassian explained the practice of the Egyptian desert-saints.[215] The Egyptians sang twelve psalms at a service, this number having been decreed by an angel. Columbanus similarly refers to 'canonicus duodenarius psalmorum numerus'.[216] The Egyptians also used to have two readings (*lectiones*), from the Old and New Testaments respectively, but these were regarded as edifying rather than essential.[217] The use of only three psalms at each day-hour is also a practice recorded by Cassian as occurring in Palestinian, Mesopotamian, and other Eastern monasteries.[218] He gave the same practical reason as Columbanus. The Rule of Caesarius of Arles, influenced by Cassian, has an office composed of psalms

---

[212] *Regula Monachorum*, § 7 (edd. & transl. Walker [& Bieler], p. 130). The monasticism of Columbanus is discussed by Bäumer, *Histoire*, I.236-9, who noted an 'Egyptian' tendency in early Irish monasticism, and by Hanssens, *Aux Origines*, pp. 88-90.

[213] Probably at dawn —see § 5, p. lviii, and also Warren, *The Liturgy*, p. 142.

[214] See Curran, *The Antiphonary*, p. 166.

[215] *De Institutis*, II.4 (ed. Petschenig, p. 20). See also Heiming, 'Zum monastischen Offizium', p. 106.

[216] *Regula Monachorum*, § 7 (edd. & transl. Walker [& Bieler], p. 132).

[217] *De Institutis*, II.6 (ed. Petschenig, pp. 22-3).

[218] *Ibid.*, III.3 (ed. Petschenig, p. 34).

xlv

and lections.[219] The Columbanian *Regula cuiusdam patris* similarly specifies psalms and lections.[220] I therefore suggest that practice at Bangor and at Columbanus's foundations in the later sixth century was of this austere and unelaborated kind, and that the more complex office of the Antiphonary was a seventh-century development.

Even with the relatively small amount of data available, it is clear that (as one might expect) there was no one sixth-century Irish monastic rule. Columbanus himself mentions a somewhat different *cursus psalmorum* known to him: there is no particular reason to assume that it was not also Irish.[221] There are also several hints in Adomnán's *Uita S. Columbae* to suggest that the office at Iona in Columba's time differed from that of Bangor, although it may also have had a long *ad matutinam*.[222]

In the seventh century, our primary witness is the Antiphonary of Bangor, supported by the Turin fragment, with some help from later texts.[223] The Antiphonary shows that at Bangor *ad matutinam* was still the most important hour. The manuscript contains many collects, two sets of eight (one for each Hour), but seven different sets *ad matutinam*. The *Canticum Moysi* ('Cantemus Domino'), which it contains, was sung at this hour, and also has collects after it. The three last psalms (148-50 — often known as the 'Laudate' psalms) are always associated with the morning-service,[224] so the Antiphonary's seven collects *post tres psalmos* also belong to this hour.[225] Another practice which is suggested, though not explicitly confirmed, by the

---

[219]   *Regula Caesarii Arelatensis*, § 25 (ed. Migne, *Patrologia Latina*, LXVII.1099-1104, at col. 1103).

[220]   *Regula cuiusdam patris*, § 20 (ed. Migne, *Patrologia Latina*, LXVI.987-94, at col. 994).

[221]   *Regula Monachorum*, § 7 (edd. & transl. Walker [& Bieler], pp. 132-3).

[222]   Adomnán, *Uita S. Columbae*, III.23. This chapter mentions three night-hours, vespers (edd. & transl. Anderson & Anderson, pp. 526-7), midnight (pp. 528-9), and *ymni matutinales* (pp. 536-7).

[223]   See Curran, *The Antiphonary* — a book which requires cautious handling. The author was better informed about liturgy than about Hiberno-Latin literature.

[224]   Although this has been challenged by Bradshaw, *Daily Prayer*, pp. 109-10, who suggested that the initial association of these psalms was with the end of the monastic vigil, and that, as this flowed together with the beginning of the morning-office, they became linked with this instead.

[225]   Warren, *The Antiphonary*, II.xxi.

Antiphonary is that specific psalms were tied to specific hours because their contents were especially appropriate.[226] Columbanus made no mention of this, and so there is no way of telling whether he practised *psalterium currens* (running straight through in order) or had even a few fixed psalms at some or all of his services.[227] Jungmann noted that praying through the psalms in their biblical sequence rather than with regard to theme is 'a basic feature of the monastic Office'.[228] Jenner advanced the suggestion that the sets of collects in the Antiphonary's *ad matutinam* may embody a skeleton of the Bangor office for this hour.[229] The order within each set is *post canticum* ('Cantemus Domino'), *post benedictionem trium puerorum*, *post tres psalmos* (148-50), *post euangelium* (which might mean the New Testament canticle, 'Benedictus Deus Israel'), *super hymnum*, and *de martyribus*. This suggests that these canticles and psalms may indeed have been sung in the order implied.

The Antiphonary's *cursus*, as far as it can be established, is in agreement with one found in a later text — the eighth-century(?) *Nauigatio S. Brendani*.[230] It might not occur to one to look for information about the Irish office in this egregious fantasy, but in fact the diurnal round of psalms is noted in two places, the chapters on the Island of Birds and the Island of the Three Choirs. In the latter episode, all the hours are mentioned but Sext. Each is given three specific psalms with, additionally, the Gradual Psalms (Pss. 119-133) at Vespers, and another twelve psalms in the order of the psalter at Matins. Thus, the two night-hours are considerably longer than the day-hours, though not nearly as long as those of Columbanus. This *cursus* is unlike any found in Continental offices, for example, in *Regula S. Benedicti*.[231] Curran has seized on the agreement between the Antiphonary and the *Nauigatio*, two texts quite widely separated in place, function, and possibly time, and argues that they can be put together with the *Regulae* of Columbanus to show that

---

[226] *Ibid.*, II.xi.

[227] For example, practically every system of worship in Western christendom had Psalms 148-150 at Lauds, or whatever the first service of the day may have been. It would be quite surprising if Columbanus did not have them thus. See Jungmann, *Pastoral Liturgy*, pp. 134-5 and 144.

[228] *ibid.*, p. 151. See also Baumstark, *Nocturna Laus*, pp. 156-66.

[229] 'Celtic rite', p. 498.

[230] *Nauigatio S. Brendani*, § 11 (ed. Selmer, pp. 22-8), and § 17 (pp. 49-58).

[231] See Curran, *The Antiphonary*, pp. 169-73, and the Marquess of Bute, 'Brendan's fabulous voyage', pp. 386-7.

there was a single Irish office. Another reference which might lend support to Curran's thesis is a story about St Columba in the fifteenth-century Great Book of Lecan, in which the celebration of the household of heaven is begun with Psalms 64, 102, and 112, in that order.[232] The same combination of psalms is given for Vespers in the *Nauigatio*.[233]

However, in the eighth and ninth centuries the texts associated with the *céli Dé* movement suggest that there is a multiplicity of customs once more.[234] The Rule of Tallaght records many variations of monastic practice,[235] although it is true to say that it devotes much more space to individual asceticism and devotion than to the structure of corporate worship. Monastic practice may have become a little more uniform as time went on, since the heads of houses were in communication with each other;[236] but, since there was no one monastery which had the power to legislate for Ireland as a whole, it is probably wisest to accept that unlocalised evidence is of relatively little use. The Turin fragment[237] has only two small pieces in it which are *not* in the Antiphonary. It does not contain any item of peculiarly Bangor interest. Was it, for example, written at Bobbio (the script is clearly Irish), in which case is it simply a sister-manuscript of the Antiphonary?[238] Alternatively, it might be

---

[232] Dublin, Royal Irish Academy, MS. 23.P.2 (535), fo 183r. Translated by Reeves, *The Life of St. Columba*, p. 205, n. a.

[233] *Nauigatio*, § 17 (ed. Selmer, p. 51).

[234] See Gougaud, *Christianity*, pp. 76-81, who referred (p. 78) to 'the singularity of some of [the culdees'] liturgical practices'; and also Reeves, *The Culdees*.

[235] Gwynn & Purton, 'The Monastery of Tallaght'. See for example §§ 33-34, pp. 140-1, and § 68, pp. 155-6.

[236] See the many notes in Adomnán's *Uita S. Columbae* of Columba's contacts with Comgall, Brendan, Cainnech, and others; and see also the often quoted interchange between the eighth-century Dublitir of Finglas and Mael Ruain of Tallaght on the subject of beer-drinking (edd. & transl. Gwynn & Purton, 'The Monastery of Tallaght', pp. 129-30 [§ 6]).

[237] Torino, Biblioteca Nazionale, MS. F.iv.1, fasc. 9, ed. Meyer, 'Das turiner Bruchstück', and described in Lowe, *Codices*, IV.454, as 'Insular majuscule, *saec.* viii *in.*, written doubtless in Ireland'. See also Gamber, *Codices*, I.147 (no. 151), Lapidge & Sharpe, *A Bibliography*, p. 211 (no. 786), and Warren, 'An early Irish liturgical fragment'. This is the remnant of a 'sister'-manuscript to the Antiphonary, containing canticles, two hymns, and some collects, only a tiny proportion of which is not also found in the Antiphonary.

[238] The surviving manuscripts of Bobbio provenance are mainly divided between the Ambrosian Library at Milan, home of the Antiphonary, and the Biblioteca Nazionale at Turin, home of the Turin fragment. See Ferrari, 'Spigolature Bobbiesi', pp. 1-14.

an independent witness to the Irish office, showing that there was widespread agreement on the form which this took by the late seventh century. In fact, it really cannot be used to prove either case, unless more clues to its origins can be found.[239]

The text known as *Catalogus Sanctorum Hiberniae* which was, before Grosjean's reassessment, usually attributed to the eighth century,[240] sheds light on how one Irish churchman viewed the past history of his own national Church. It claims that the first order, which was of bishops (A.D. 440-534), observed one mass and one celebration. The second order, mainly of presbyters (A.D. 534-572), celebrated different masses and had different rules,[241] and the third, again of presbyters, differed from one another in almost all possible respects (A.D. 572-660).[242] The first order is almost entirely legendary. As far as the second and third orders go, the *Catalogus* does not contradict the contemporary evidence, such as it is. Irish monastic practice not only differed from the Benedictine tradition, but it also differed from place to place in the way of life practised and the treatment of the office.

One variant on the usual round of the monastic hours should perhaps be mentioned, the *laus perennis*,[243] a form of devotion in which at least a part of the monastic community was singing psalms all the time, day and night, in response to the Pauline injunction, 'sine intermissione orate' (1 Thess. V.17). This was in origin a Greek practice, but was followed at the important Burgundian monastery of Agaune in the early sixth century.[244] This suggests that Merovingian monasticism, before Columbanus, was not universally as

---

[239] Hughes emphasised the diversity and lack of centralised authority or common standards: *The Church*, p. 183.

[240] Warren, *The Liturgy*, pp. 80-1. Warren even attributed the text to Tírechán, the seventh-century biographer of St Patrick. Grosjean ('Édition', pp. 212-13) dated it to the ninth or tenth century, casting even further doubts on its reliability. But even an eighth-century document is unlikely to be a reliable witness for the fifth, sixth, or seventh century.

[241] Grosjean, 'Édition', p. 206: 'diuersos celebrandi ritus habebant et diuersas regulas uiuendi'.

[242] These dates are based on the regnal dates given in three of the four redactions, for example, 'a tempore Leodegarii filii Neyl... ad tempora extrema Tuahal Meylgarb durauit' ('Édition', p. 206, discussed on pp. 301-6).

[243] See Luff, 'British monasticism'.

[244] Wood, 'A prelude', pp. 16-17.

decadent and spiritually torpid as has sometimes been said.[245] The *laus perennis* was only claimed for the early mediaeval Irish Church by writers working at a distance from it; St Bernard in his *Uita S. Malachiae* claimed it for pre-viking Bangor,[246] and Jocelin of Furness said that it was followed in a foundation of the British saint, Kentigern.[247] The *Teagasg Maoil Ruain* ('Teaching of Mael Ruain') specified a perpetual night-office in which the Psalter is recited twice through by two teams each of two monks,[248] and also specified that each monk must recite the entire Psalter through in the course of each day, in addition to his other work.[249]

Our evidence from specific localities shows some un-Continental features of Irish custom, which may have been more or less widespread. The psalms were particularly assiduously sung both in Columbanus's monasteries and later at Tallaght. The *cursus psalmorum* apparently shared by the Antiphonary and *Nauigatio S. Brendani* is quite different from Continental arrangements. The intercessory prayers used by Columbanus and in the Antiphonary also seem anomalous: they resemble Continental litanies, to which they may be related, but not very closely.[250]

The whole basis of Irish ecclesiastical and monastic as well as secular life was deeply shaken by the advent of the vikings.[251] Monasteries were, of course, an obvious source of plunder, whether slaves and livestock or chalices and precious metalwork, because they were large centres of population in a townless land, and possibly (though not necessarily) because they were less

---

[245] Wallace-Hadrill, *The Frankish Church*, pp. 56-9, and Prinz, *Frühes Mönchtum*, pp. 19-112.

[246] Bernard, *Uita S. Malachiae*, VI.12 (ed. A. Gwynn, *apud* Leclercq & Rochais [edd.], *Sancti Bernardi Opera*, III.295-378, at 322). See Gougaud, *Christianity*, pp. 330-1.

[247] *Uita S. Kentigerni*, § 25 (ed. Forbes, *Lives*, p. 205). It should be remembered that Jocelin certainly knew his Bernard, and was desperate to flesh out some very scanty relics of his subject. Additional references to the practice may be found in Luff, 'British monasticism', pp. 149-51, but none is either very early or very convincing.

[248] *Teagasg*, § 79 (ed. & transl. Gwynn, 'The Rule', pp. 46-7). See also *Riagail na Céle nDé*, § 30 (*ibid.*, pp. 72-3).

[249] *Teagasg*, § 65 (*ibid.*, pp. 38-9).

[250] Curran, *The Antiphonary*, pp. 106-13. See my discussion below, p. lxxxi.

[251] Binchy, 'The passing', and Hughes, *The Church*, pp. 197-214; although, as Ó Fiaich has said, 'all the troubles of ninth and tenth century Ireland are [not] to be laid at the door of the foreigner' ('The Church of Armagh', p. 79).

well defended than royal or other secular strongholds.[252] One complication was that the great monasteries were frequently sited coastally or on major arteries, whether rivers or roads, and this immediately turned from a strength to a weakness. Even a monastery as great as Bangor (situated on the shore of Belfast Lough) was so vulnerable that it was apparently completely destroyed.[253] Others showed greater powers of recuperation (or bargaining). The centre of the Columban group moved from the now-dangerous site of Iona to Kells, with a Scottish sub-group centred at Dunkeld.[254] Various kinds of accommodation were made with the new power in Ireland but, as Binchy emphasised,[255] things could never be the same again.

The demoralisation and economic difficulties caused by vikings must have contributed to the ecclesiastical developments of the tenth century onwards, of which an important feature was that the eventual recovery of monasticism was not a renaissance of native Irish traditions but an introduction of Continental forms which had previously made little headway. The eleventh century found the outside world — most specifically the pope and the archbishop of Canterbury — focussing attention on Irish christian and monastic practices, and not liking what it saw. For example, the succession of lay abbots of Armagh from the tenth to early twelfth century was highly irregular by normal ecclesiastical standards, and attracted the criticism of St Bernard.[256] Irish monasteries were perceived as lax, eccentric, and worldly, and Gaelic Church-leaders tolerated practices (especially a casual attitude to marriage)[257] which the rest of christendom regarded with horror. Part of the solution was the introduction of Continental monastic rules. The Cistercians,

---

[252] Henry, *Irish Art during the Viking Invasions*, pp. 17-25.

[253] Annals of Ulster, *s.a.* 823.8, 'Gentiles inuaserunt Bennchur Mor', and 824.2, 'Orggain Benncair' (edd. & transl. Mac Airt & Mac Niocaill, pp. 280-1). The Annals of Ulster continue to record 'abbots of Bangor' for centuries, but according to St Bernard (*Uita S. Malachiae*, VI.13, ed. A. Gwynn, *apud* Leclercq & Rochais [edd.], *Sancti Bernadi Opera*, III.295-378, at 322-3) the title was honorary only.

[254] There is an eloquent pair of entries in the Annals of Ulster (edd. & transl. Mac Airt and Mac Niocaill): *s.aa.* 802.9 'I Columbę Cille a gentibus combusta est' (p. 258); and 807.4, 'Constructio nouę ciuitatis Columbę Cille hi Ceninnus' (p. 262).

[255] 'The passing'.

[256] *Uita S. Malachiae*, X.19 (ed. A. Gwynn, *apud* Leclercq & Rochais [edd.], *Sancti Bernardi Opera*, III.295-378, at 328-30. See also Ó Fiaich, 'The Church of Armagh'.

[257] Gwynn, *The Twelfth-century Reform*, pp. 16-19.

following the lead of the formidable St Malachy, built many houses in Ireland,[258] although they were rapidly accused of backsliding into comfortable old Irish ways.[259] The Augustinian canons were another extremely successful introduction.[260] Some, perhaps many, of Ireland's ancient monasteries adopted the Augustinian rule, whereas the Cistercian and Benedictine monasteries were new foundations on new sites.[261] Other religious orders were also well represented.[262] The native Celtic monasticism was gradually superseded by the international monastic tradition of Western Europe.[263]

---

[258] Gwynn & Hadcock, *Medieval Religious Houses: Ireland*, pp. 114-44; Watt, *The Church in Medieval Ireland*, pp. 15-21;

[259] *Ibid.*, pp. 52-9.

[260] *Ibid.*, pp. 44-9; Gwynn & Hadcock, *Medieval Religious Houses: Ireland*, pp. 146-216 (including minor orders associated with the Augustinian rule).

[261] Both old and new monasteries occupied by Augustinians and Cistercians have been discussed by Carville, *The Occupation*.

[262] Gwynn & Hadcock, *Medieval Religious Houses: Ireland*.

[263] But it should be noted that native Irish habits and outlook continued to affect or modify the new ecclesiastical structures right through the middle ages. See Mooney, *The Church in Gaelic Ireland*.

4. Celtic Baptism and Ordination

Practically nothing specific can be said about the Romano-British liturgy. Charles Thomas was perhaps right to guess that it was both somewhat archaic and divergent from Continental practice,[264] but the guess cannot be substantiated. The *Collectio canonum Hibernensis* contains the note, 'Gildas ait: Brittones toto mundo contrarii, moribus Romanis inimici non solum in missa sed etiam in tonsura...',[265] but, although the genuine Gildas was used in the *Hibernensis*,[266] this particular remark reeks of seventh-century controversy and is not to be trusted.[267] In sixth-century Brittany, which took its traditions from the British Church, we find a case where the service of women (*conhospitae*) was permitted in the liturgy, against all orthodox custom.[268] If the two Breton priests censured by the bishop of Tours and his episcopal colleagues for this outlandish custom were following British practice, then this would certainly confirm Thomas's suggestion that the British liturgy was peculiar. There does appear to have been something strange about British *baptism*: it was one of the subjects on which Augustine of Canterbury took issue with the British bishops, according to Bede.[269] He did not say what was wrong with their practice, although Thomas has offered some suggestions.[270] The best solution is probably that offered by Margaret Pepperdene who pointed out that Bede's precise form of words is 'ut ministerium baptizandi que Deo renascimur iuxta morem sanctae romanae et apostolicae ecclesiae conpleatis', suggesting that the problem is not one of baptism, but of confirmation, at this time normally performed at the end of the baptismal service, but by a bishop rather than a priest. The Celtic Churches could have

---

264 Thomas, *Christianity*, p. 83.

265 ed. Wasserschleben, *Die irische Kanonensammlung*, p. 212 (LII.6).

266 Sharpe, 'Gildas', pp. 194-8.

267 Hughes, *The Church*, pp. 125-6, linked this passage with the seventh-century Irish romanising party.

268 De Labriolle, *Les sources*, pp. 226-7, discussed by Chadwick, *Early Brittany*, pp. 271-2, Jackson, *Language and History*, p. 14, Reynolds, '*Virgines subintroductae*', p. 556. Lapidge & Sharpe, *A Bibliography*, p. 225 (no. 823).

269 *Historia Ecclesiastica*, II.2 (edd. & transl. Colgrave & Mynors, pp. 138-9). See also Warren, *The Liturgy*, pp. 64-7.

270 Thomas, *Christianity*, pp. 209 and 212-13. British baptism has also been discussed by McKillop, 'A Romano-British baptismal liturgy?'.

been anomalous either in omitting the rite altogether, or in permitting it to be performed by a priest.[271] There is a baptismal service in the Stowe Missal, basically Roman though with some Gallican elements,[272] in which the infant or catechumen is anointed (twice) with oil and chrism[273] and sprinkled thrice with water (in the Roman fashion),[274] but where the rites of confirmation are not specifically assigned to a bishop. The baptism ends with a rite of footwashing, which is Gallican, not Roman.[275] Curiously, the Stowe baptism fails to specify the all-important words 'Baptizo te…'.[276] The Stowe prayer, 'Deus omnipotens pater', said immediately after baptism, is common to both Roman and Gallican traditions.[277] Doubts have been cast on whether Celtic priests were properly anointed at their ordination,[278] but this problem cannot be shown to extend to baptism. St Patrick himself referred to 'crismati neophyti in ueste candidi'.[279] The apparently casual attitude to the role of the bishop in Stowe is not found in all Celtic christian sources. The Breton *Uita I S. Samsonis*, which may be as early as the seventh century but whose date is hotly disputed, goes out of its way to stress the role of the bishop in baptism on two occasions.[280]

---

[271] Pepperdene, 'Baptism', p. 119.

[272] *The Stowe Missal*, ed. Warner, II.26-36.

[273] *Ibid.*, II.28 and 31.

[274] *Ibid.*, II.31.

[275] Duchesne, *Christian Worship*, p. 326.

[276] It is not the only sacramentary to omit this: the Old Gelasian Sacramentary in Roma, Biblioteca Apostolica Vaticana, MS. Reginensis lat. 316 (ed. Mohlberg, *Liber Sacramentorum*, p. 96) similarly takes it for granted. This has been discussed by Ellard, *Master Alcuin*, pp. 12-15.

[277] It appears in the same position in both Gelasian traditions; it is found in the Old Gelasian, ed. Mohlberg (*Liber Sacramentorum*, p. 96), and in Dumas's edition of the eighth-century Gelasian Sacramentary of Gellone (*Liber Sacramentorum*, I.336). Orthodox Roman practice contemporary with the Stowe Missal is discussed by Ellard, *Master Alcuin*, pp. 68-85, especially 75-9. By contrast, the Gallican rite as used in Spain (Mozarabic rite) differed in many important respects, which suggests that Tallaght at least followed Roman rather than Gallican baptismal practice (see Bishop, *The Mozarabic and Ambrosian Rites*, pp. 10-14).

[278] See below, pp. liv-lviii, and Warren, *The Liturgy*, pp. 65-6.

[279] Patrick, *Epistola*, § 3 (ed. Hood, p. 35).

[280] *Uita I S. Samsonis*, I.50 and II.7 (ed. Fawtier, pp. 145 and 163). See Lapidge & Sharpe, *A Bibliography*, p. 261 (no. 950), and Duine, *Inventaire Liturgique*.

Another christian initiation-ritual should perhaps be discussed at this point, as, once again, Celtic practice has been regarded as heterodox. This is the ordination of bishops. There are two aspects which caused trouble with other Churches: the first was that bishops were sometimes created by one rather than three other bishops, contrary to canon law, and the second was the form of episcopal anointing. The actual form of ordination practised in the Irish Church is not recoverable, but Hugh Williams pointed out that Gildas gives us a skeleton of the British rite in De Excidio Britanniae.[281] Gildas did not mention the imposition of hands, but only that two lessons were said, one involving 1 Peter I-II and Acts I.15-21, and the other 1 Timothy III and Matthew XXI.13-19. Gildas also said that the hands of an ordinand were blessed (in some unspecified way),[282] and that he stood by the altar for the ceremony.[283] Ordination by a single bishop worried early mediaeval Continental and English churchmen.[284] It did not worry a scholiast on Félire Oengusso, who gives us a picture of Columba presenting himself for ordination before a single bishop who proceeds to confer the wrong orders on him.[285] A unique practice is referred to in Uita II S. Samsonis, which is perhaps of the ninth or tenth century; the author claims that the custom was that when three bishops met to ordain, they should have three candidates for ordination.[286] Another problem is mentioned in later sources, in which doubts are expressed as to the British and Irish ordination of priests, on account of the skimping of the rite of anointing, oiling the head only and not the hands.[287] One obvious reason for this is a practical one. Alcuin said in a letter to the Irishman Colcu in 790: 'Misi caritate tua aliquid de oleo, quod uix

---

281   Williams (ed.), Gildas, II.230-45. See De Excidio, III.106-7 (ed. Winterbottom, pp. 138-40).

282   De Excidio, III.106 (ed. Winterbottom, p. 138).

283   Ibid., II.108,3 (ed. Winterbottom, p. 140).

284   For example Bede, Historia Ecclesiastica, I.27 (edd. & transl. Colgrave & Mynors, pp. 86-7), and see also Warren, The Liturgy, pp. 68-75. However, episcopal consecration in fifth-century Gaul seems to have been effected by only two bishops without causing concern — see Hanson, 'The Church', p. 3.

285   Félire Oengusso, note on February 11 (ed. & transl. Stokes, pp. 72-3).

286   Uita II S. Samsonis, § 14: 'ut mos ibi est a tribus episcopis tres ordinari' (ed. Plaine, 'Vita Antiqua', p. 105). Lapidge & Sharpe, A Bibliography, pp. 261-2 (no. 951).

287   This is claimed by Jocelin of Furness in his Uita S. Kentigerni, § 11 (ed. Forbes, Lives, p. 182) 'mos inoleuit in Britannia, in consecratione pontificum, tantummodo capita eorum sacri crismati infusione perungere'. What justification he has for this one cannot say.

modo in Britannia inuenitur, ut dispensares per loca necessaria episcoporum ad utilitatem uel honoris Dei'.[288]

A further complication here is that the anointing of bishops and priests was not in fact part of Roman ordination-practice until the late ninth century.[289] The custom, however, was vigorously promoted in the influential forgeries known as the Pseudo-Isidorean Decretals which successfully gave the impression that it was ancient practice. The hands and head of the priest were anointed in some parts of the Gallican Church from the eighth century, as witnessed by the Sacramentary of Gellone[290] and confirmed by Alcuin's letter quoted above, which may imply that unction was common to the Gallican and Insular Churches by this time.[291] The anointing of priests therefore offers a peculiar although hardly unparalleled case of the Celtic Churches acting in a way which was perfectly orthodox by contemporary Continental standards, but subsequently being castigated once Roman custom had changed — the change in this case being far more recent than the Roman Church itself was aware.

It has even been suggested that the practice of anointing the hands began in the British Church,[292] but this is based on a passage of Gildas, discussed above, which could equally well be interpreted as a quotation from Leviticus XVI.32.[293] However, there is a far more significant passage in Cogitosus's seventh-century *Uita S. Brigidae*, where he refers to a bishop as *unctum caput*. This seems to imply that he regards unction as the distinguishing feature of episcopacy, and this a century before there is a trace

---

[288] ed. Dümmler, *Epistolae*, II.32-3. See also Pepperdene, 'Baptism', p. 117.

[289] Ellard, *Ordination Anointings*, pp. 51-61. The earliest example in the Roman tradition of the anointing of the head of a bishop is in the ninth-century Milanese rite, on which see Batiffol, 'La liturgie du sacre', pp. 745-50.

[290] Paris, Bibliothèque Nationale, MS. latin 12048 (*saec.* viii *ex.*): Lowe, *Codices*, V.618; ed. Dumas, *Liber Sacramentorum*, I.394-5; Gamber, *Codices*, II.392 (no. 855). There is no direct rubrical statement of the anointing, but its implied presence is demonstrated by Ellard, *Ordination Anointings*, p. 31, who also (pp. 30-3) mentions Gallican mass-books (such as the *Missale Francorum*) which refer to the anointing of hands of priests and bishops, although only Gellone implies unction of the head.

[291] An alternative possibility is that Alcuin envisaged the oil being used for confirmations, which could be administered by bishops only.

[292] *Ibid.*, pp. 9-13, and Warren, *The Liturgy*, pp. 70-2.

[293] *De Excidio*, III.106, ed. Winterbottom, p. 138.

of it on the Continent.[294] Here again, we should probably look to Leviticus, but in a slightly different spirit. Leviticus XXI.10 says:

Pontifex, id est sacerdos maximus inter fratres suos, super cuius caput fusum est unctionis oleum, et cuius manus in sacerdoti consecratae sunt...

The high priest is distinguished by the unction of the head and consecration of the hands, the two features of episcopal consecration highlighted by, respectively, Cogitosus and Gildas. It would be in keeping with early Irish ecclesiastics' use of Old-Testament practice if they had adopted this rite for the consecration of a bishop. As Donnchadh Ó Corráin has pointed out:[295]

there was, it seems, a 'tribe of the Church', with differing orders, grades and functions; it was consciously modelled on the tribe of Levi, many of whose institutions it made its own.

He has also observed that[296]

careful comparison of Irish law with scripture shows that where the Pentateuch provided detailed rules of the law, these were very often adopted to the letter... in laying down the rules governing the priesthood, the Irish canonists follow the rules of the Pentateuch very closely.

The peculiar characteristics of early Irish christianity thus provide a context for the adoption of this Semitic practice into Western liturgy.

---

[294] *Uita*, ed. Bollandists, p. 135D. See also Kottje, *Studien*, pp. 94-105.

[295] Ó Corráin *et al.*, 'The laws', p. 405.

[296] *Ibid.*, p. 396.

5. The Celtic Mass

Information about the liturgy of the mass in Ireland is relatively scanty, and based mainly on the Stowe Missal, probably written at Tallaght in 792.[297] One important consideration is whether the Irish mass was based on Gallican or Roman models. It must be remembered that before the efforts which were made in Charlemagne's time to standardise the mass, there was a great deal of variety from one Continental Church to another.[298] The early missals can be sorted into families but, as the term 'family' suggests, they are similar rather than identical. Hennig has remarked:[299]

There is no evidence whatsoever of a Celtic liturgy originally pure and gradually more and more contaminated. On the contrary, it seems that, as far as we can trace it, the Irish liturgy was distinguished from the Gallican liturgy by a more generous acceptance of Roman, Spanish and above all, Oriental influences.

Edmund Bishop spoke of 'the Irish eclectic, or tinkering, method in liturgy' in his discussion of the Stowe Missal.[300] So it is reasonable to envisage the early Irish Churches taking whatever Continental models they could get hold of, and recombining elements to make the most suitable and beautiful celebration which they could devise.

Columbanus wrote of the Irish Church as deriving from Rome:[301]

Sed fides catholica, sicut a uobis primum, sanctorum uidelicet apostolorum successoribus, tradita est, inconcussa tenentur.

---

[297] Dublin, Royal Irish Academy, MS. Stowe D.ii.3 (1238): Lowe, *Codices*, II.268, Irish Half-uncial, *saec.* viii/ix, 'written in Ireland, probably at Tallaght'; ed. Warner, *The Stowe Missal*; see also bibliography in Kenney, *The Sources*, pp. 692-9 (no. 555), Lapidge & Sharpe, *A Bibliography*, pp. 140-1 (no. 537), and Gamber, *Codices*, I.132-3 (no. 101). For other remains of the Irish liturgy, see Lapidge & Sharpe, *A Bibliography*, pp. 130-50 (nos 505-91), and Gamber, *Codices*, I.133-52 (nos 102-77).

[298] Vogel, *Introduction*, pp. 43-203. Bishop, *Liturgica Historica*, pp. 14-15, wrote: 'The state of things in France, so far as mass and missal are concerned, at the accession of Charles the Great in 769 [*recte* 768], may be summed up in two words: liturgical anarchy'. See also Wallace-Hadrill, *The Frankish Church*, pp. 118-21.

[299] Hennig, 'Studies', p. 321.

[300] Bishop, *Liturgica Historica*, p. 166. Gougaud, 'The Celtic liturgies', p. 180, noted that the Celtic liturgies were eclectic, but not innovative. He suggested that the only original contribution which they made to the development of liturgy was to institute a blessing of the new fire at Easter.

[301] *Epistola* V, § 3 (edd. & transl. Walker [& Bieler], pp. 38-9).

We cannot tell whether he was talking about matters of practice as well as of the faith.[302] But there are indeed signs of Roman influence on Irish practice. In the *Catalogus Sanctorum Hiberniae*, the 'mass of the Second Order' is said to have been British in origin:[303]

Hii ritum celebrandum missam acceperunt a sanctis uiris de Britannia, scilicet a sancto Dauid et a sancto Gilda et a sancto Doco.

There is no evidence against the idea that the Irish liturgy was indebted to British models, but there is no evidence for it either: the early British liturgy is completely obscure. Grosjean is sceptical that the *Catalogus* can be taken on trust.[304]

It may be noted that one of the charges brought by the Gaulish clergy against the Columban churches was to do with Irish liturgical customs. At the Council of Mâcon in 623, charges were preferred against the Irish by one Agrestius. These included the following:[305]

In summa quod a caeterorum ritu ac norma desciscerent et sacra mysteria sollemnia orationum et collectarum multiplici uarietate celebrarent.

This might mean the use of many collects rather than one before the Epistle,[306] or collects which varied from Roman practice throughout the mass as a whole. Another attack on superfluous collects is to be found in the seventh-century *Expositio antiquae liturgiae gallicanae*: 'Inter benedictionem et euangelium collectio non intercedat nisi tantummodo responsurium quod a paruolis canitur'.[307] The Antiphonary of Bangor and the Turin fragment have a multiplicity of collects (including six for after the *Benedicite*),[308] many of them rhymed quatrains, unique to the Irish liturgical tradition. Only prose prayers were used on the Continent; so these quatrains would have sounded very

---

[302] Gamber argued that he was (*Missa Romensis*, pp. 87-8).

[303] Grosjean, 'Édition', p. 206.

[304] His discussion is *ibid.*, pp. 293-6.

[305] Mabillon, *Annales*, I.320-1. See also Jenner, 'Celtic rite', p. 495; and Warren, *The Liturgy*, pp. 96-7.

[306] Note that the Stowe Missal has *hic augmentum* (an extra collect or collects?) before the Epistle (ed. Warner, II.5).

[307] *Expositio*, § 9 (ed. Ratcliff, pp. 6-7).

[308] *The Antiphonary*, ed. Warren, II.24-7 (nos 63, 69, 72, 77, 82, 92); also no. 99 (II.29-30), a set of 'Antiphonae super cantemus et benedicite'.

strange to Continental ears.[309] Eustasius, speaking for Columbanus's order, did not deny Agrestius's charges, but pleaded for toleration of their divergent practice (as Columbanus himself did in *Epistola* II), since they were in no way contrary to christian doctrine. Liturgy before the Carolingian reforms was subject to local modifications, but there were evidently limits set by some sense of liturgical propriety which the Irish *peregrini* had overstepped.[310]

Mass was normally celebrated at dawn in Ireland. There is plenty of evidence for this in Adomnán's *Uita S. Columbae*.[311] Adomnán mentions two exceptions, but both appear to be *ad hoc*: in one case, Columba became aware, just as everyone was preparing to start an ordinary day, that Colmán had just died in Ireland, and ordered a mass.[312] In the other, Adomnán himself was delayed in getting back to Iona for Columba's festival on June 9, and mass was not begun till sext, after his arrival. Since he was the head of the house, they were probably waiting for him.[313] Gall celebrated at daybreak, after *ad matutinam*, in the space of time after this office when the monks would otherwise go back to bed and snatch another hour or so of sleep.[314] On this point there is no specific evidence in the life or writings of Columbanus. The dawn-celebration of the Irish Church has recently been challenged, on inadequate grounds. Pádraig Ó Néill has referred to the seventh-century Mo Chuaróc moccu Neth Semon as '[abolishing] the venerable Celtic tradition of celebrating mass in the evening at Nones in favour of morning'.[315] But Ó Néill (who was developing a suggestion of Grosjean's) has here misinterpreted

---

[309] Baumstark & Botte, *Comparative Liturgy*, pp. 61-2, noted that some Roman collects do take on a highly oratorical form, but they do not fall into verse. There is also a completely anomalous Gallican mass (one of the so-called 'Mone-Messen') entirely in hexameters, printed by Mohlberg, *Missale Gallicanum Vetus*, pp. 74-6.

[310] It was suggested by Dumville in 'Liturgical drama', pp. 381 and 384-5, that the origins of liturgical drama might lie in Ireland. If this were so, it would be another instance of the originality and unorthodoxy of the Irish response to the inherited liturgical tradition.

[311] For example III.11 (edd. & transl. Anderson & Anderson, pp. 486-7). See also Warren, *The Liturgy*, pp. 142-3.

[312] *Uita S. Columbae*, III.12, pp. 488-9.

[313] *Ibid.*, II.45, pp. 458-9.

[314] Walahfrid Strabo, *Uita S. Galli*, § 26 (ed. Migne, *Patrologia Latina*, CXIV.975-1030, at col. 999): 'Quadam itaque die, dum post laborem matutinalis officii quiescendi gratia lectos suos reuiserent, primo diluculo, uir Dei uocauit Magnoaldum diaconem suum, dicens illi, "instrue sacrae oblationis ministerium"', etc.

[315] 'Romani influences', p. 280.

the title 'Mo Chuaróc of the None' given to this worthy, which in fact probably relates to his introduction into Ireland of the computistical poem beginning 'Nonae Aprilis norunt quinis'.[316] There is no other evidence for an evening-celebration in Ireland, and it should be remembered that mass had already moved to the early morning by the time of Tertullian (*ob. ca* 240).[317] It would have been a strange anachronism in seventh-century Ireland.

Mass was celebrated on Sundays and on feast-days, which included saints' days. Adomnán notes a Sunday-celebration as *die dominica ex more*.[318] He also refers to a celebration on saints' days.[319] Kathleen Hughes drew attention to the early occurrence of mass on saints' days in Ireland.[320] She commented that this is at odds with Hennig's assertion that early Ireland had no *sanctorale*.[321] The Irish Church seems also to have followed the practice of celebrating private masses: that is, masses in which the priest celebrated alone, with no congregation, either for his own or for others' intentions.[322] Godel has even suggested that the Stowe Missal (as also the Bobbio Missal) was designed primarily for this kind of private celebration.[323]

---

[316] Ó Cróinín, 'Mo-Sinnu', p. 286.

[317] Jungmann, *Pastoral Liturgy*, p. 107; Tertullian, *De Corona*, III.3 (edd. Dekkers *et al.*, *Tertulliani Opera*, II.1039-65, at p. 1043).

[318] *Uita S. Columbae*, III.17 (edd. & transl. Anderson & Anderson, pp. 500-1). The *Synodus Episcoporum*, § 30 (edd. Bieler [& Binchy], *The Irish Penitentials*, pp. 58-9) also stated that mass was said on Sundays —by implication, therefore, not on other days. See Warren, *The Liturgy*, pp. 140-2.

[319] In II.45 (edd. & transl. Anderson & Anderson, pp. 456-7) and III.12 (pp. 488-91).

[320] *Early Christian Ireland*, pp. 206-7.

[321] Hennig, 'Old Ireland and her liturgy', pp. 68, 80-4, and 'The function', pp. 318, 327. It may be relevant to note that Irish ecclesiastics were certainly very interested in both native and foreign saints, as is witnessed by their martyrologies. The most important of these are *Félire Oengusso* (ed. & transl. Stokes; and see Kenney, *The Sources*, pp. 479-81, no. 272); *The Martyrology of Tallaght* (edd. Best & Lawlor; and see Lapidge & Sharpe, *A Bibliography*, pp. 141-2, no. 540, and Kenney, *The Sources*, pp. 481-2, no. 273); and *Félire Húi Gormain* (ed. & transl. Stokes; see also Kenney, *The Sources*, pp. 482-4, no. 275). For martyrologies in general, see Hennig, 'Kalendar und Martyrologium', and Pfaff, *Medieval Latin Liturgy*, pp. 55-6.

[322] Crehan, 'The liturgical trade route', pp. 96-7; see also Jungmann, *Missarum Sollemnia*, II.248, and the recent study by Angenendt, 'Missa Specialis'.

[323] Godel, 'Irisches Beten' (translated as 'Irish prayer'), p. 266. Note also the strange mass for protection against sickness found in the Book of Mulling, printed in *The Irish Liber Hymnorum* (edd. Bernard & Atkinson, I.xxiii). See Lawlor, *Chapters*, pp. 145-66.

The Antiphonary of Bangor contains material for both the mass and the office. It is not always clear which is which. For example, it contains many collects and a hymn devoted to the martyrs, heavily dependent on Spanish sources.[324] Do these relate to a mass for commemoration of the martyrs, on the lines, perhaps, of the tiny fragment of a mass for the martyrs found in the Irish liturgical palimpsest in Karlsruhe, Badische Landesbibliothek, MS. Aug. perg. 195,[325] or were they fitted into the *ad matutinam* service? The canticles 'Cantemus Domino' and 'Benedicite' are also liable to be dual-purpose. The hymns are rather a problem. It would be most unusual in terms of the development of Western liturgy if they formed part of the mass rather than of the office at this early time. Yet one of them, 'Sancti, uenite', is specifically eucharistic. It is headed, in the Antiphonary, *Ymnum quando commonicarent sacerdotes*.[326] There are also seven communion-antiphons.[327]

The seven communion-antiphons of the Antiphonary are particularly interesting. The antiphon 'Corpus Domini accepimus et sanguine eius potati sumus; ab omni malo non timebimus, quia Dominus nobiscum est' found in the Antiphonary[328] appears to be a direct translation of a *Greek* antiphon originating in sixth-century Palestine,[329] which was used in an independent Latin version in the Ambrosian mass of Milan.[330] Daniel[331] printed what is apparently a much longer Gallican communion-antiphon whose first clause is related to Warren's no. 112:

Uenite populi ad sacrum et immortale mysterium et libamen agendum. Cum timore et fide accedamus manibus mundis poenitentiae munus communicemus, quoniam propter nos agnus Dei patri sacrificium propositum est. Ipsum solum adoremus, ipsum glorificemus cum angelis clamantes. Alleluia.

---

[324] *Ibid.*, pp. 118-24.

[325] Dold, 'Liturgie-Fragmente', p. 275 (on Karlsruhe, Badische Landesbibliothek, MS. Aug. perg. 195, fo 33r). The fragment is described by Lowe, *Codices*, VIII.1091, as eighth-century Irish Half-uncial.

[326] Warren, *The Antiphonary*, I.10v-11r, and II.10-11.

[327] *Ibid.*, II.30-1.

[328] Warren, *The Antiphonary*, II.30 (no. 109).

[329] Baumstark & Botte, *Comparative Liturgy*, p. 97.

[330] Ratti & Magistretti (edd.), *Missale Ambrosianum*, p. 357. This version reads 'Corpus Christi accepimus et sanguinem eius potauimus: ab omni malo non timebimus; quia Dominus nobiscum est'.

[331] *Thesaurus Hymnologicus*, IV.109.

Daniel claimed to have found this in the *De Miraculis S. Martini* of Gregory of Tours, II.13, which would make it a relic of sixth-century Gallican practice (as its style suggests), but it is not to be found there; nor have I managed to locate it in any other text. These Irish antiphons therefore appear to suggest connexions with both the Milanese and, less certainly, the Gallican Churches.[332]

The Antiphonary's no. 122 deserves further mention, aside from its putative Gallican connexions.[333] It runs:

Hoc sacrum corpus Domini et Saluatoris sanguinem sumite uobis in uitam perennem.

It evidently bears some relationship to the hymn 'Sancti, uenite': either it is a paraphrase of the hymn's first stanza, or that first stanza is based on it.[334] It is also one of the few Irish liturgical fragments to appear in several different contexts. Ionas of Bobbio said that it was sung at the eucharist by St Burgundofara, who followed the Columban rule.[335] He gives *exactly* the same wording. St Burgundofara was within the Bangor axis, though twice removed, as it were; it is still more interesting that the identical formula appears in the Stowe Missal,[336] in the Irish sacramentary-fragment in Sankt Gallen, Stiftsbibliothek, MS. 1394,[337] and in *Nauigatio S. Brendani*.[338] This suggests the possibility that the core at least of the Irish mass was both relatively standardised across the country and quite different from the eucharistic formulae of any other rite. The Stowe Missal was probably written at

---

[332] Jenner, 'Celtic rite', p. 501, thought the communion-antiphons and responsory particularly characteristic of the Irish Church. But Duchesne, *Christian Worship*, pp. 186-8, noted that it was normal to sing an antiphon during communion in the Roman mass. In the Gallican mass, three verses of a psalm (the *Trecanus*) were sung, followed by 'Te laudamus' (pp. 224-5; see also Anglès, 'Latin chant', p. 29, and *Expositio*, § 28a, ed. Ratcliff, p. 16).

[333] Warren, *The Antiphonary*, II.31.

[334] Sancti, uenite
Christi corpus sumite
Sanctum bibentes
Quo redempti, sanguinem.

[335] *Uita S. Columbani*, II.16 (ed. Krusch, p. 267). Its presence here makes it likely that this antiphon dates from the sixth century, since presumably it formed part of the Bangor office as Columbanus learned it before he left for the Continent.

[336] Warner, *The Stowe Missal*, II.18.

[337] Warren, *The Liturgy*, p. 178.

[338] *Nauigatio*, § 17 (ed. Selmer, p. 52).

Tallaght; at any rate, it is in no way associated with Bangor, and neither is the *Nauigatio*. There is also a fractionally different version of the formula in the *Uita S. Brendani* printed by Plummer:[339]

Omnes communicabant, dicentes 'hoc sacrum corpus Domini et Saluatoris nostri sanguinemque sumite uobis in uitam eternam'.

The ultimate inspiration for this Irish antiphon may be the communion-prayer which the priest said to himself in the Mozarabic rite while placing a particle of the host in the chalice:[340]

Sancta sanctis et coniunctio corporis et sanguinis Domini nostri Iesu Christi sit sumentibus et potantibus nobis ad ueniam, et defunctis fidelibus praestetur ad requiem.

The Mozarabic formula itself appears to have Eastern antecedents going back at least to the time of Cyril of Jerusalem.[341] The tentative conclusion to be drawn from the wide distribution of 'Hoc sacrum corpus' within Ireland is that there may have been some degree of uniformity in the central core of the mass used in Ireland. It is, however, tenuous evidence with which to support such a conclusion.

Another apparently unique feature of the Irish eucharist had to do with the Fraction. It shows that, for all the importance of abbots in the early Irish Church, the unique spiritual authority of the bishop was venerated. In Adomnán's *Uita S. Columbae*, Columba broke the bread *jointly* with a visitor whom he believed to be a presbyter, but commented that, had he realised that the stranger was a bishop, he would have handed over the celebration to him.[342] Issues of courtesy, authority, and precedence were apparently involved — on another occasion, Columba was invited as a mark of respect to

---

[339] *Uita S. Brendani*, § 49 (ed. Plummer, *Vitae*, I.125). Plummer explained ('Some new light', pp. 124-33), that this *uita* is a conflation of the *Nauigatio* and a lost *uita*, and thus not independent evidence for the antiphon. Since its two manuscripts (described by Plummer, 'On two collections', p. 429), are thirteenth- or fourteenth-century in date, the variant wording carries little authority.

[340] This is found only in Cardinal Ximines's late fifteenth-century record of the then fast-disappearing Mozarabic rite, the *Missale Mixtum* (ed. Lesley, p. 6).

[341] *Missale Mixtum*, ed. Migne, *Patrologia Latina*, LXXXV.561, n. A. See also Cabrol, *The Mass*, pp. 132-3.

[342] *Uita S. Columbae*, I.44 (edd. & transl. Anderson & Anderson, pp. 304-5); Warren, *The Liturgy*, pp. 128-30. See also Gougaud, 'Les rites'.

celebrate alone, despite the presence of three fellow presbyter-abbots.[343] But that there is here an underlying principle of respect for bishops is confirmed by the eighth-century *Uita S. Albei*: 'sacerdos coram episcopo non debet nisi illo iubente celebrare'.[344] Interestingly, this detail in the version in *Codex Salmanticensis* has been cut out of the later redaction printed by Plummer. The principle of the precedence of bishops has also been emphasised by Richard Sharpe: 'Bishops sign before priests, who precede ecclesiastics in minor orders, even when the latter hold important positions... sacerdotal standing takes precedence over the headship of important monastic foundations such as Iona'.[345]

The eclecticism of Irish liturgical practice is witnessed by our one surviving early mass-book, the Stowe Missal.[346] It shares collects and prayers with Gallican mass-books like the Bobbio Missal,[347] and also with Roman sacramentaries, Gelasian, Gregorian, and that of Verona. These common elements have been completely rearranged. The main non-Roman elements in the Stowe Missal include the Gradual placed between Epistle and Gospel (in the Gallican mass, it came after the Gospel), the post-*Sanctus* prayer, the responsory at the Fraction, the elaboration of the Fraction (the bread was broken into many pieces, and arranged in a cross-shape),[348] and its position before rather than after the *Pater Noster*.[349] The prayer 'pro pissimis [*sic*] imperatoribus et omni romano exercitu' in the Stowe Missal's *deprecatio S. Martini*[350] is a translated fossil remaining from the Greek liturgy of John

---

[343] *Uita S. Columbae*, III.17 (edd. & transl. Anderson & Anderson, pp. 500-1). Another odd feature in the same chapter is that the mass is started outside the church, moving into it only after the reading of the lection from the Pauline Epistles.

[344] *Uita S. Albei*, § 21 (ed. Heist, *Vitae*, p. 123).

[345] Sharpe, 'Armagh and Rome', p. 66.

[346] A second book resembling Stowe survived to the sixteenth century in the library of Fulda where it was seen and described by Georg Witzel. See Bishop, 'Liturgical note', pp. 235-6, Kenney, *The Sources*, pp. 699-700 (no. 556), and Gamber, *Codices*, I.133-4 (no. 102).

[347] The Bobbio Missal is not now thought to be Irish. Its resemblances to Stowe are due to their common but independent derivation of material from the *Missa Romensis* of Pope Vigilius. See Hennig, 'Sacramentaries', p. 25.

[348] This practice was also followed, although less elaborately, in the Gallican rites of Spain and Gaul: see *Missale Mixtum*, ed. Lesley, p. 5, and *Concilium Turonensis* (Tours; A.D. 567), § 3 (ed. de Clercq, *Concilia*, pp. 175-99, at 178).

[349] Jenner, 'Celtic rite', pp. 501-2.

[350] Warner, *The Stowe Missal*, II.6.

Chrysostom.[351]

Another interesting feature of the mass in the Stowe Missal is its 'Hanc igitur'.[352] This prayer of intercession directly before communion is common to the Western tradition, though not absolutely fixed in form. The Stowe version is closest to that of the (Gallican) Bobbio Missal.[353] However, the Irish version is unique in ending with a petition that the founder of the church in which the prayer is being said, and also the people in general, may be converted from idol-worship.[354]

The Stowe Missal does not stand entirely alone. Some further fragments of sacramentary in Irish hands, found and described by Bannister, should also be mentioned.[355] As Bannister pointed out, the 'B'-fragment of an Irish sacramentary from Reichenau (possibly written at Clondalkin, Co. Leinster) is 'moulded after the type of the Stowe missal'.[356] He notes further that 'just as the Stowe missal has three masses only, viz. for the common of saints, for penitents, and for the dead, fragments A and B reveal three masses

351 Brightman, *Liturgies*, I.333. See also King, *Liturgies of the Past*, p. 254: he notes that the lost Fulda book gave the reading *piissimo imperatore*, and that the twelfth-century Irish Corpus Missal substituted *rex* and *exercitu Hibernensium*, adaptations of this now meaningless formula. Incidentally, Deshusses, *Le sacramentaire grégorien*, I.59, mentions that the seventh-century Gregorian palimpsest sacramentary-fragment in Monte Cassino, Archivio della Badia, MS. 271 (on which see Gamber, *Codices*, II.330 [no. 701]) has Good-Friday prayers 'pro christianissimis imperatoribus nostris'. There is further discussion of the *deprecatio* below, p. lxxxi.

352 *The Stowe Missal*, ed. Warner, II.12.

353 Bobbio Missal, § 12 (ed. Lowe, II.11). The Gregorian Sacramentary (ed. Deshusses, *Le sacramentaire grégorien*, I.88) and the Gelasian Sacramentary (ed. Mohlberg, *Liber Sacramentorum*, p. 185) have identical versions. Bannister also notes ('Some recently discovered fragments', pp. 53-4) that his fragment C contains material related to the Bobbio Missal, and that it may have a Bobbio provenance. It forms another link between Irish and Gallican liturgies.

354 There is some evidence that pagan worship continued in Ireland long after the introduction of christianity: Sharpe, 'Hiberno-Latin *laicus*'.

355 'Some recently discovered fragments'; Piacenza, Archivio della Basilica di S. Antonio, MS. C.48: Gamber, *Codices*, I.139 (no. 125); Lowe, *Codices*, IV.409, Half-uncial, *saec.* vii. Karlsruhe, Badische Landesbibliothek, MS. fragm. Aug. 17 and 18 (from the binding of MS. Aug. perg. 167): Gamber, *Codices*, I.138-9 (nos 120-1); Lowe, *Codices*, VIII.1085, Irish Half-uncial, *saec.* viii, written probably in Ireland. The complete corpus, of Irish sacramentary-fragments is listed by Gamber, *Codices* I.134-40 (nos 103-29).

356 'Some recently discovered fragments', pp. 61-6, 70.

which, although they have no title, correspond exactly with these three'.[357] This could be purely coincidental, but perhaps it is not. The Sankt Gallen fragments (printed by Warren)[358] also contain material paralleled in the Stowe Missal. The connexions, between the Stowe Missal and these Continental fragments which cannot be linked with any specific centres, may serve to support the apparent implication of the 'hoc sacrum corpus' antiphon discussed above, that the Stowe Missal can reasonably be taken as evidence for Irish liturgical practice beyond Tallaght itself.

On the other hand, this anomalous Irish mass did not go unchallenged even in Ireland. The palimpsest-sacramentary, München, Bayerische Staatsbibliothek, Clm 14429, written in Ireland in the seventh century, is completely un-Irish in its contents.[359] Hennig offered the theory that 'this sacramentary would appear to have been an abortive attempt to introduce — along with the Roman point-of-view in the Paschal controversy — Continental conceptions into the liturgy of the Irish Church'.[360] Dold claimed that both this Munich sacramentary and Karlsruhe, Badische Landesbibliothek, MS. Aug. perg. 195 are Irish, and that they are closely related to one another.[361] Gamber described Clm 14429 as Old-Gallican, although it is contaminated with foreign elements.[362] Therefore these fragments can be seen as representing a purer Gallican liturgy in use in some unidentifiable part of seventh-century Ireland.

There are also some important references to a 'Roman' mass in Irish hagiography. The *Salmanticensis*-redaction of *Uita S. Albei*, already referred to, says:[363]

[357] *Ibid.*, pp. 71-2.

[358] Sankt Gallen, Stiftsbibliothek, MS. 1394; Lowe, *Codices*, VII.979; Sankt Gallen, Stiftsbibliothek, MS. 1395; Lowe, *Codices*, VII.988 & 989. *The Liturgy*, pp. 174-83.

[359] It was edited by Dold & Eizenhöfer, *Das irische Palimpsestsakramentar*. A preliminary and far less complete attempt was printed by Dold, 'Liturgie-Fragmente'.

[360] Hennig, 'Old Ireland', p. 89.

[361] Dold, 'Liturgie-Fragmente' pp. 273-7, and Hennig, 'Sacramentaries', p. 25. See also Gamber, *Sakramentartypen*, p. 31, and Lowe, *Codices*, VIII.1091 and IX.1298.

[362] Gamber, *Sakramentartypen*, p. 23, and *Codices*, I.162-4 (no. 211). These foreign elements, incidentally, include Eastern and even Gnostic influences, on which see Dold & Eizenhöfer, *Das irische Palimpsestsakramentar*, pp. 127*-128*.

[363] *Uita S. Albei*, § 45 (ed. Heist, *Vitae*, p. 128).

Quodam tempore, misit Albeus duos uiros, scilicet Lugith et Keilchenne, qui sunt hi Formuig, ut nouum ordinem celebrandi *a Roma* deducerunt.

Again, this statement has been deleted from the text as presented by the later version. In the *Uita S. Brigidae* which is attributed to Ultán,[364] Brigit is also said to have arranged for the importation of the Roman mass:[365]

'...nimis desidero, ut ad me istius ordo et uniuersa regula feratur a Roma.' Tunc misit Brigida uiros sapientes et detulerunt inde missas, et regulam. Item dixit post aliquantum tempus Brigida ad illos uiros, 'ego sentio quod quidam commutauerunt in Roma missas postquam uenistis ab ea, Exite iterum.' Et illi exierunt et detulerunt ut inuenerunt.

Van Dijk pointed out that this story shows that the seventh-century Irish Church was sufficiently in contact with Rome to be aware of liturgical *changes* there, even if these are anachronistically ascribed to the fifth century.[366] The Roman features even in the basically Gallican Stowe Missal suggested to Gamber that there was a Roman element in Irish practice from a very early date, going back to the mission of Palladius from Rome,[367] and that the early Irish mass-books are in part precious witnesses to the earliest developments of the Roman mass.[368] Thus the 'Romanising' efforts of the seventh and eighth century do not necessarily reflect an extraneous element, but one which had been present in some ecclesiastical centres (such as, perhaps, Kildare) from their foundation. Note also that the singing of 'Kyrie eleison' at every hour was allegedly recommended by Patrick because it was a

---

364 Written in the seventh century, according to Sharpe, '*Vitae S Brigidae*', pp. 89-96. McCone, 'Brigit', pp. 131-2, assigns far less significance to this *uita*, describing it as the work of a mere '"scissors and paper" conflater of a few written works', and dating it to the eighth century.

365 *Uita III S. Brigidae*, § 91, ed. Colgan, pp. 527a-545b, at 527a. Incidentally, even the vestments of Kildare's first bishop, Conlaed, are said by Cogitosus to come from overseas: they are described as 'uestimenta transmarina et peregrina Episcopi Conlaei decorati culminis' at *Uita*, VII.31 (ed. Bollandus, *Acta Sanctorum*, February, I.129-41, at 139E).

366 Van Dijk, 'The urban and papal rites', pp. 469-70. Fantastic stories, of Brigit trying but *failing* to get a rule from Rome, occur in later texts: see *The Irish Liber Hymnorum*, edd. Bernard & Atkinson, II.191, and the references given there.

367 Gamber, 'Die irischen Messlibelli', and *Missa Romensis*, pp. 87-8.

368 Cabrol, *The Mass*, p. 161. Other evidence for early Irish contact with Rome is mentioned by Ó Cróinín, 'Pride', p. 354.

Roman custom,[369] although it was also practised in the Gallican Church from the sixth century.[370]

The preceding discussion will have given the impression that there was substantial diversity in the form of mass celebrated in early Ireland. Próinséas Ní Chatháin has also gained this impression:[371]

There is room in early Ireland for the celebration of mass on the model of Gallican and Roman prototypes. It would also go a long way towards explaining the anomalies and eclecticism and tinkering and waywardness which have on occasions been laid at the door of Irish liturgical scribes if what they were doing can be interpreted in some ways as attempting to reconcile differing practices of respectable antiquity.

The Irish were aware of the peculiarity of their own mass. There is an essay by, probably, a ninth-century Irishman working on the Continent, in which he discussed the ancestry of the various liturgies known to him.[372] He gave an elaborate ancestry for the Irish liturgy, which was basically Gallican/Eastern. He claimed that it originated with St Mark the Evangelist, passed through Basil and Gregory Nazianzen to the Egyptian Desert Fathers, thence to Cassian.[373] Cassian passed it on to Honoratus of Lérins, Caesarius of Arles, and others. Patrick learned it from these Gaulish saints, and passed it on to Comgall and one Wandilochus. Columbanus and his Continental foundations had it from Comgall. This is an extraordinary story which arouses immediate scepticism. However, deleting Mark the Evangelist and the Greek Fathers as evidence only of the Irish mania for genealogy, we are left with a line of descent running from Egypt via Cassian to Gaul, and from Gaul to Ireland. This is very much the outline of the influences on Irish *monasticism* sketched in the previous section. This suggests that the author is not inventing out of whole cloth, but has some actual knowledge of Irish Church-history — although whether this is relevant, as he claimed, to the development of the

---

[369] *Dicta Patricii*, in *The Patrician Texts*, edd. & transl. Bieler & Kelly, pp. 124-5 (and see the note on p. 214). The Greek custom of singing the 'Kyrie' was probably introduced into Rome at the end of the fifth century, as part of the litanic *deprecatio S. Gelasii*. See Capelle, 'Le *Kyrie*', pp. 142-3. Its later developments have been discussed by Callewaert, 'Les étapes'.

[370] *Concilium Vasense III* (Vaison; A.D. 529), § 3 (ed. de Clercq, *Concilia*, pp. 77-81, at 79). See also Bishop, *Liturgica Historica*, pp. 116-36.

[371] 'The liturgical background', p. 128.

[372] 'Ratio de cursus', ed. Hallinger. See also Warren, *The Liturgy*, pp. 77-80.

[373] Interestingly, Cassian himself claimed that the Egyptian monks were instructed by St Mark, *De Institutis*, II.5 (ed. Petschenig, pp. 20-1).

mass in Ireland is another matter.

Some later Irish missals should also be mentioned, although they date from the twelfth century and later, when the Irish Church was increasingly assimilated to Continental (which by this time means Roman) norms. St Bernard claimed that Malachy was the first to introduce Roman liturgy into Ireland.[374] Gilbert of Limerick also insisted on the Roman rite in his letter *Ad episcopos Hiberniae de usu ecclesiastico*.[375] Both these writers bear witness to the eleventh- and twelfth-century drive towards ecclesiastical conformity with international norms. A little later in the twelfth century, the Irish mass is specifically aligned with that of the English Church. The Drummond,[376] Corpus[377] and Rosslyn[378] missals, a trio of twelfth-century Irish mass-books, have distinct affinities with early missals of the Sarum rite.[379]

The surviving early Irish liturgical texts pertaining to the mass suggest two things; first, that the main traceable influence on Irish liturgical developments was Gallican; secondly, that Irish churchmen did not regard liturgy as 'holy writ' — fixed, immutable and not to be tampered with. They seem to have collected books from all parts of the Western world.[380] Hymns for the hours from Arles are used as the basis for the verse collects in the Antiphonary;[381] and a variety of Spanish collects forms the basis for the Irish

---

[374] *Uita*, III.7 (ed. A. Gwynn, *apud* Leclercq & Rochais [edd.], *Sancti Bernardi Opera*, III.295-378, at pp. 315-16).

[375] 'sed uestrae cupiens parere piisimae iussioni, ut diuersi et schismatici ordines, quibus Hibernia pene tota delusa est, uni catholico et romano cedant officio' (ed. Migne, *Patrologia Latina*, CLIX.995-6).

[376] *Missale Drummondiense*, ed. Forbes, and described by Kenney, *The Sources*, pp. 705-6 (no. 566), and by Lapidge & Sharpe, *A Bibliography*, p. 288 (no. 1034).

[377] *The Manuscript Irish Missal*, ed. Warren, and described by Kenney, *The Sources*, p. 706 (no. 567), and by Lapidge & Sharpe, *A Bibliography*, p. 144 (no. 566). See also Gwynn, 'The Irish missal', Quigley, 'The Clones Missal' (another name for the Corpus Missal), and Henry, *Irish Art in the Romanesque Period*.

[378] *The Rosslyn Missal*, ed. Lawlor, pp. xix-xxv.

[379] Gwynn, 'The Irish missal', p. 53.

[380] Of course, it was only gradually that *any* liturgy assumed a fixed form. The only thing which distinguished the Irish in this matter was the extent and degree of their eclecticism, together with their maintenance of a flexible attitude after the rest of Western christendom had become relatively centralised and fixed in its liturgical usages.

[381] Curran, *The Antiphonary*, pp. 93-6.

collects on the martyrs in the same codex.[382] The fragmentary surviving sacramentaries in Irish script are all basically Gallican in type, in their various ways; yet there is some Roman influence on the mass in the Stowe Missal. One should not get unduly carried away by this. Hennig warned that 'it is even more difficult to establish a multiplicity of liturgies in Ireland than it is to establish one "type" of ancient Irish liturgy'.[383] Nonetheless, despite the miserable lack of evidence, which leaves us in complete ignorance of, for instance, the public cathedral liturgy of a major episcopal centre like Armagh or Kildare, the surviving fragments seem to point in so many different directions that probably Ní Cháthain, quoted above, is near to the truth.

Another point which has emerged from this study is the crucial importance of two monastic centres. For the sixth and seventh centuries, we depend for our knowledge of mass and office almost entirely on the traditions of Bangor as mediated through Columbanus's foundation of Bobbio. The works of Columbanus, the Antiphonary of Bangor, and probably the Turin fragment have this provenance. The reason for this might lie simply in the improved survival-rate of books written on, or taken to, the Continent as against those remaining in Ireland, or it might be something more complex, now irrecoverable. For the eighth and ninth centuries, we are equally dependent on the monastery of Tallaght.[384] Our only Irish massbook, the Stowe Missal, was probably written at Tallaght. The main sources for later Irish monastic practice, *Teagasg Maoil Ruain* and the Rule of Tallaght, come from the same source. So do the two most important Irish martyrologies, *Félire Oengusso* and the Martyrology of Tallaght. There is one further witness to the Latin culture of this monastery, the hymn 'Archangelum mirum

---

[382] *Ibid.*, pp. 118-24.

[383] Hennig, 'Sacramentaries', pp. 26-7.

[384] Tallaght was founded in 767: see Gwynn & Hadcock, *Medieval Religious Houses: Ireland*, p. 45.

magnum', attributed to Mael Ruain himself.[385] We know a great deal, in consequence, of the customs and preoccupations of eighth-century Tallaght, even although there is no surviving *uita* of Mael Ruain. We can do little more than guess at how representative its liturgical customs are of Ireland as a whole — the mere fact of this extraordinary florescence of religious writing in both Irish and Latin, together with its own proud claims to distinction as a centre of the *céli Dé* movement, shows that it was hardly average.[386] Byrne pointed out that the Stowe Missal, which contains Roman elements, including the Gelasian canon of the mass, is contemporary with Carolingian reform of the liturgy on Romanising lines, so it might, if we only had more context for it, be innovative and radical rather than an average missal illustrating the norm of Irish liturgical practice.[387] We are forced, in evaluating the Stowe Missal, to take a product of a particularly lively and innovative monastery, and treat it as our guide to both monastic and ecclesiastical practice in Ireland as a whole. There is no alternative source of information, so this cannot be helped, but the unsatisfactory nature of the evidence should not be glossed over.

---

[385] The sole manuscript of this hymn is Karlsruhe, Badische Landesbibliothek, MS. Aug. perg. 221, fo 192 (Lowe, *Codices*, VIII.1095, described it as Reichenau minuscule, *saec.* ix *in.*: see also Brambach *et al.*, *Die Handschriften*, V.503-5). The writer added a macaronic Latin-Irish collect to it which runs 'Benedicat Dé te et Michael for Moilrum, amen'. 'Archangelum mirum magnum' is a fine example of eighth-century Hiberno-Latin hymnody, adorned with alphabetic structure, rhyme, and alliteration. Its attribution to Tallaght (if not necessarily to Mael Ruain himself) might be strengthened by Mael Ruain's particular devotion to Michael, recorded in the preface to *Félire Oengusso* (ed. & transl. Stokes, pp. 12-13).

[386] The Book of Dimma is associable with Roscrea, which was another *céli Dé* stronghold (Kenney, *The Sources*, p. 633, no. 458). There may be mere accidents of survival involved, but it is perhaps possible that the reforming activities of the *céli Dé* included a particular interest in liturgy.

[387] Byrne, 'The Stowe Missal', p. 44.

6. The Bible

There are two main aspects of the Bible which must be considered here. One is the kind (or kinds) of Bible-text, whether *Uetus Latina* or Vulgate, used in the Irish and other Celtic Churches.[388] The other is the use of the Bible in liturgy and office. The Bible provided material for both reading and singing: lections from the Gospels, the Pauline Epistles and any other parts of the Bible fall into the first category, and the psalms and canticles into the second. Initially, the psalms and canticles provided the main musical (or poetic) element used in the early Western Church, the singing of the psalter being ultimately based on synagogue-practice.

There is much which is now irrecoverable about the Bible as it was used in the British Isles in the first millennium. That the Irish in particular had an outstanding interest in the Old Testament is witnessed both by the legal material and elsewhere,[389] but it has not resulted in the survival of a single codex containing any part of the Old Testament (except the Psalter) from an Irish centre, except for a single folio from a lectionary in an eighth-century Irish hand which contains eighteen verses from a Vulgate text of Genesis.[390] Progress can be made only by studying the Bible-texts quoted by Insular authors, and this has indeed been done for a number of key-figures. The Bible of Patrick was analysed by Ludwig Bieler,[391] and that of Gildas by F. C. Burkitt and Hugh Williams.[392] Both these early British writers show that the Vulgate, which began its slow diffusion across Europe in the fourth century, had not yet superseded the *Uetus Latina* in the British Church. A further piece of evidence for the British Bible is found in the early ninth-century *Liber Commonei*,[393] in Oxford, Bodleian Library, MS. Auct. F.4.32

---

[388] On which see Cordoliani, 'Le texte de la bible', and Ó Cróinín, 'Pride', p. 354. There is some evidence that Vulgate texts began to reach Ireland around the end of the sixth century or the beginning of the seventh. Other aspects of the use made of the Bible in Ireland have been discussed by McNamara, 'A plea', McGurk, 'The Irish pocket gospel book', and in McNamara (ed.), *Biblical Studies*.

[389] Ó Corráin *et al.*, 'The laws', pp. 394-412; see also Kottje, *Studien*, pp. 11-43.

[390] See McCormick, 'Un fragment', and Bischoff & Brown, 'Addenda', pp. 332-3 (no. 1835).

[391] 'Der Bibeltext'.

[392] Burkitt, 'The bible', and Williams, *Gildas*, I.88-99 and 129-32.

[393] Discussed by Hunt, *Saint Dunstan's Classbook*, pp. vii-xii, who described this section as Welsh minuscule of *saec.* ix *in.*.

(S.C. 2176) (also known as 'St Dunstan's Classbook'), fos 19-36.[394] This contains two interesting sets of lections, in parallel Greek and Latin versions, the first of which does not conform, either in the nature of its text or the actual choice of passages, to any Continental liturgy.[395] In particular, the version of Zephaniah quoted by Gildas, and that found in this manuscript, are very close.[396] They are quite distinct from the version found in Sabatier's edition of the *Uetus Latina*[397] and it was therefore suggested by Haddan and Stubbs that there existed a special British revision of the *Uetus Latina*, at least for such lesser books as Chronicles, Job, Proverbs, Ezekiel, and the Minor Prophets.[398] Because traces of these books are relatively rare, it is a plausible suggestion, but hard to substantiate in any detail. An anomalous version of these books could perfectly well have circulated in the British Isles for centuries without being subjected to the kinds of textual comparison and revision which would be applied to the Gospels or the Psalter.

The other set of lections in the *Liber Commonei* is for the Easter-vigil.[399] Again, they are in both Greek and Latin. Schneider pointed out that in some Roman liturgical *ordines* the reading of these lessons and canticles in both languages was prescribed, and that the Welsh manuscript is the only surviving manuscript-witness to this bilingual arrangement.[400] Fischer gave these lections further consideration, and concluded that the *Liber Commonei* Easter-lections contained the lessons and canticles of the Roman Easter-vigil at the time of Gregory the Great's reform (which probably occurred in 592).[401] They thus provide further evidence for the archaism of the biblical material in use in the Welsh liturgy.

---

[394] Hunt, *ibid.*, fos 24r-28v: 'Incipiunt pauca testimonia de prophetarum libris per grecam linguam'.

[395] Baumstark & Botte, *Comparative Liturgy*, pp. 23-4, where he noted a tendency towards suppression of Old Testament lections in all liturgies. The lections of the *Liber Commonei* have been discussed by Lapidge, 'Latin learning', pp. 92-4, who pointed out the 'Irish symptoms' in this collection.

[396] *De Excidio*, II.55 (ed. Winterbottom, p. 114), and Hunt, *Saint Dunstan's Classbook*, fos 26v-27r.

[397] Sabatier, *Bibliorum Sacrorum Versiones Antiquae*, II.973.

[398] *Councils*, I.170-98. The theory was seconded by Sanday *et al.*, *Portions of the Gospels*, pp. ccvi-ccxii. Lapidge, 'Latin learning', has urged caution.

[399] Fos 28v-36r, and 19r/v.

[400] Schneider, *Die altlateinischen biblischen Cantica*, pp. 68-70.

[401] Fischer, 'Die Lesungen'. See also the summary by Hunt, *Saint Dunstan's Classbook*, p. xii.

Gildas used both Vulgate and *Uetus Latina* versions, his non-Vulgate texts being particularly close to the Septuagint.[402] Williams pointed out an instructive contrast in his use of the two: long Old-Testament quotations are often from the Vulgate, when he was presumably working with the book open before him (this is corroborated by Gildas's tendency to produce a batch of quotations from one book and move on to the next); but short quotations made *en passant* are normally *Uetus Latina*.[403] This suggests that the Bible which Gildas had in his memory, and thus the one which he learned in his youth, was *Uetus Latina*, but that the Vulgate was introduced into Britain during his adult life.[404] Burkitt adds:[405]

The quotations of Gildas shew that the Church in Britain about 550 A.D. had already accepted the new version of Jerome for most parts of the Old Testament, but that in Ezekiel, the Minor Prophets, and most of the Sapiential Books including Job, the change had not yet been made and that the 'Old Latin' was still current. Job was still read by Gildas, as also by St Patrick, in the old unrevised text with the additions from Theodotion (which appear in all the Greek MSS and Ambrose) unrepresented.

Further evidence for this British *Uetus Latina* is found in the Breton *uita* of Paul de Leon, VI.17,[406] which quotes Luke X.42 in an extremely anomalous version whose only other occurrence is in the Irish gospel-text of the Book of Mulling.[407] It has 'paucis uero opus est, aut etiam uno; Maria optimam partem elegit', where the Vulgate begins 'porro unum est necessarium; Maria optimam partem elegit'.[408] The version of this verse used in these two Celtic Latin texts is attested in Greek in two manuscripts of the gospels.[409] Curiously, these are two of the most important early Greek manuscripts of the New Testament, *Codex Sinaiticus*[410] and *Codex*

---

[402] Williams, *Gildas*, I.90-7 and 129-32.

[403] Souter, *Pelagius's Expositions*, I.119-20, pointed out that the same pattern of usage can be discerned in the works of St Augustine.

[404] *Ibid.*, I.88.

[405] 'The bible', p. 215.

[406] Written by Wrmonoc in 884: see Lapidge & Sharpe, *A Bibliography*, p. 228 (no. 828).

[407] Williams, *Christianity*, p. 183.

[408] *Uita S. Pauli Leonensis*, VI.17 (ed. Plaine, p. 224).

[409] Ὀλίγων δὲ χρεία εστιν ἤ ἑνός', ed. Wordsworth, *The New Testament* I.211 (only in revised vol. I).

[410] London, British Library, MS. Additional 43725 (*saec.* iv). See Metzger, *The Text*, pp. 42-6, who wrote that its text 'belongs in general to the Alexandrian group, but it also has a definite strain of the Western type of readings'.

Vaticanus.[411] This is consistent with the evidence of Gildas's text of Job, which is based with great fidelity on the original, unrevised version of the Septuagint, and thus extremely archaic in its antecedents.[412] Latin versions of various books of the Bible closely related to the Greek versions in the Septuagint are also found in other early Hiberno-Latin writings, including some of the early hymns[413] and the *Epistolae* of Columbanus.[414] The degree of eccentricity in the Bible-texts used by one author or another naturally varies considerably: the parts of the Old Testament discussed above being by far the most consistently unusual. Adomnán for example used a pure Vulgate Bible,[415] although in the previous century his predecessor Columba had an Old Latin, Gallican version of the Psalter, according to Adomnán's own evidence.[416] On the other hand, the Bible-text of the Irish Augustine, also writing in the seventh century, contained considerable *Uetus Latina* elements.[417]

The possibility of a distinctive Insular text-type has also been raised for the New Testament. Alexander Souter demonstrated that there is a close affinity between the text of the Pauline Epistles in the Book of Armagh and the commentary of Pelagius, in particular a fifteenth-century Italian manuscript of the commentary which was copied from an Insular archetype.[418] If there is indeed a connection between the *Uetus Latina* used by Pelagius and the *Uetus Latina* text in the Book of Armagh, this would seem to imply either that the text found in Pelagius's commentary exerted a controlling influence on subsequent Pauline studies in Ireland, or that the distinctive features of the Insular text-type were established in fourth-century Britain, and remained current in the Celtic Church for the next six centuries. Ludwig Bieler additionally suggested that there were traces of similarity between the bible-

---

[411] Roma, Biblioteca Apostolica Vaticana, MS. Graec. 1209 (*saec.* iv *med.*). See Metzger, *ibid.*, pp. 47-8. Vaticanus is also a representative of the Alexandrian text-type.

[412] Burkitt, 'The bible', and Williams, *Gildas*, I.90 and 129-32.

[413] Burkitt, 'On two early Irish hymns'; *The Irish Liber Hymnorum*, edd. Bernard & Atkinson, II.144.

[414] Smit, *Studies*, pp. 91 and 196-7.

[415] *De Locis Sanctis*, edd. & transl. Meehan [& Bieler], p. 14.

[416] McNamara, 'Psalter text', p. 260. Columba's psalter-text is also discussed by Lawlor, 'The Cathach'.

[417] Esposito,'On the pseudo-Augustinian treatise'.

[418] Souter, 'The character', pp. 263-4, and *Pelagius's Expositions*, I.126, 137-8. See also Frede, *Pelagius*. The Book of Armagh was edited by Gwynn.

text used by Patrick and that of the fifth-century Pelagian writer Fastidius.[419] It is also noteworthy that the eleventh-century Welsh authors Rhigyfarch and Lifris share an almost identical but otherwise unattested version of 2 Thess. III.10, 'qui non laborant, nec manducet' rather than 'si quis non uult operari, nec manducet'. Christopher Brooke has argued that this was a paraphrase, and that there is a verbal connexion between these two authors; but, given the remarkable conservatism of the Welsh Church, it is just possible that they are both independently quoting a non-Vulgate text, even at that very late date.[420]

The psalter was the single most studied book in the early Irish Church, and probably in the other Celtic Churches also, most specifically in the Gallican version.[421] McNamara declared that 'the Irish psalter par excellence was the *Gallicanum*'. It was customary to learn it by heart, as is shown by the Anglo-Saxon Bishop Wilfrid who, on discovering that he had committed the 'wrong' psalter to memory during his early training at Lindisfarne, put himself to the trouble of relearning it in the Roman version,[422] and it may also have been used to teach calligraphy, as is suggested by the Springmount wax-tablets (which may alternatively have been an aide-memoire during the memorising process).[423] In the Rules of Columbanus, psalter-singing is the central part of the celebration of the office. The psalms are divided into threes, of which the first two are sung straight through, and the third antiphonally.[424] At Iona, unison singing seems to have been the practice, for Adomnán recorded how Columba's voice rose above all others.[425] This is

---

[419] Bieler, 'Der Bibeltext', p. 258.

[420] Brooke, *The Church*, p. 72, n. 95, quoting the relevant passages from Rhigyfarch and Lifris.

[421] On devotion to the Psalter in Ireland, see McNamara, 'Psalter text', and 'Tradition', Meyer, *Hibernica Minora*, and Ó Néill, 'The Old Irish Treatise'. See also the entry under *salm* and its compounds and derivatives in *Dictionary of the Irish Language*, gen. ed. Quin, S.42-4, *s.v.*.

[422] Stephanus, *Uita Wilfridi*, §§ 2-3 (ed. & transl. Colgrave, pp. 6-9).

[423] Dublin, National Museum S.A.1914:2; Lowe, *Codices*, S.1684; ed. M.P. Sheehy *apud* McNamara, 'Psalter text', pp. 277-80. See also Brown, 'The oldest Irish manuscripts', p. 312.

[424] Jungmann, *The Early Liturgy*, pp. 204-5, noted that antiphonal psalm-singing seems to have developed in the Syriac Church, superseding the old method with a single cantor, and spread out from there during the fourth century (see also Augustine, *Confessiones*, IX.7,15, ed. Verheijen, pp. 141-2).

[425] *Uita S. Columbae*, I.37 (edd. & transl. Anderson & Anderson, pp. 286-7).

confirmed by Stephanus's *Uita Wilfridi*, in which he claimed that Wilfrid introduced the custom of antiphonal singing into Northumbria (which had learned its customs from Iona), where it had previously been unknown.[426]

The lections used in the British and Irish Churches seem to have been unconventional.[427] The Old-Testament lections referred to above are not found specified in any other liturgy. In general, there was a tendency in both Gallican and Roman liturgies to drop Old-Testament lections while keeping the readings from the Gospels and the Epistles;[428] so this may be another instance of the depth of Irish interest in the Old Testament. Still more peculiar is the Gospel-lection of a mass for the Circumcision in a fragmentary Irish sacramentary, which apparently comes from an apocryphal gospel otherwise unattested.[429] But lectionaries in general have not been well preserved: Klauser listed forty-four manuscripts of the eighth century or earlier which were used as lectionaries.[430] Of these, twenty-five are Scriptural manuscripts with marginal notes, fourteen are carefully-arranged *capitula* with some indication of *incipit* and *explicit*, only three are lectionaries with all the needed material excerpted and arranged, and only two supply the text of the reading along with the mass-prayers.

The canticles seem to have been greatly valued in the early Irish Church, particularly the Old-Testament canticles 'Cantemus Domino' and 'Benedicite' (The Song of the Three Children).[431] These two are singled out for special treatment in the Antiphonary of Bangor. Not only do both appear in this manuscript, but there are also seven collects 'post canticum' and seven 'post benedictionem', suggesting that both were sung at the dawn-office every

426   *Uita Wilfridi*, § 47 (ed. & transl. Colgrave, p. 98-9).

427   Duchesne, *Christian Worship*, pp. 167-9, discussed the lections in use in the Roman Church. On Gallican lections, see Quasten, 'Oriental influences', pp. 64-6.

428   Bishop, *The Mozarabic and Ambrosian Rites*, pp. 21-3; Warren, *The Liturgy*, pp. 98-9.

429   Roma, Biblioteca Apostolica Vaticana, MS. Lat. 3325, ed. Bannister, 'Liturgical fragments', pp. 417-18, and discussion on p. 413. See also McNamara, *The Apocrypha*, pp. 51-2 (no. 45).

430   Klauser, *Das römische Capitulare*, pp. xxx-xxxv. See also Vogel, *Introduction*, pp. 289-320.

431   See Schneider, *Die altlateinischen biblischen Cantica*, pp. 89-98, and Mearns, *The Canticles*.

day of the week.[432] It also contains a series of antiphons on these two canticles. 'Cantemus Domino' and 'Benedicite' are also drawn on by Irish hymn-writers, notably the authors of *Precamur patrem* and the '*Lorica Gildae*'. The other canticles which appear in Irish liturgical contexts are the first Canticle of Moses, and the New Testament canticles of Zacharias and Mary ('Benedictus Deus Israel' and 'Magnificat').[433]

---

[432] These two canticles are specified for Sunday matins in the *Regula ad monachos* of Caesarius of Arles, § 21 (ed. Migne, *Patrologia Latina*, LXVII.1102).

[433] Schneider, *Die altlateinischen biblischen Cantica*, pp. 90-3.

7. Prayers and Collects

Private prayer is, by definition, no part of public worship, and therefore not of my subject. Nonetheless, it is sufficiently related to it to merit a brief mention. Cabrol has noted that,[434] 'À cette époque la prière privée n'est pas isolée…elle reflète la liturgie publique, elle en est tout imbibée; par là le livre appartient au domaine de l'histoire générale'. It highlights some of the features also found in the survivals of the public worship of the Celtic Churches. The first important study of Celtic prayers is that of Edmund Bishop in his 'Liturgical note' appended to Kuypers's edition of the Book of Cerne.[435] Two important facts emerged: first, that the devotional formulae of Hiberno-Latin prayers were directly related to those of the Mozarabic liturgy,[436] and secondly, that Irish prayer influenced English prayer profoundly. Many prayers displaying the features diagnosed as Hiberno-Latin survive in English prayer-books, the Book of Cerne, the Book of Nunnaminster, London, British Library, MS. Royal 2.A.xx, and London, British Library, MS. Harley 7653, all of which overlap in their contents.[437] Even that most eccentrically and egregiously Hiberno-Latin prayer, the so-called 'Lorica Gildae',[438] is not attested in Ireland until the fourteenth century (in Leabhar Breac), but appears in four much earlier English manuscripts.[439] The salient features of Hiberno-Latin prayers are prolixity, a tendency towards various types of litanic structure, and an avoidance of logical development or argument.[440] There is also some liturgical evidence for Irish devotion to Mary in the early

---

[434] 'Le "Book of Cerne"', p. 211.

[435] Kuypers, The Prayer-book, pp. 234-83.

[436] Jungmann, Pastoral Liturgy, pp. 20-1; but see Sims-Williams, 'Thoughts on Ephrem the Syrian', pp. 213-17, for qualifications.

[437] See Kenney, The Sources, pp. 718-22 (nos 575-8), Kuypers, The Prayer-book, pp. xxiv-xxx, and Hughes, 'Some aspects'. A prayer-book from Sankt Emmeram, Regensburg (München, Bayerische Staatsbibliothek, Clm 14248), similar in content, probable date, and Irish influence, has been discussed by Frost, 'A prayer book from St Emmeran', p. 30.

[438] A unique seventh-century Hiberno-Latin prayer based in part on the Song of the Three Children (on which see Mac Eoin, 'Invocation') and in part on Isidore (for which see Herren, 'The authorship').

[439] The Lorica has been discussed by Herren, 'The authorship', and Gougaud, 'Étude', both of whom give details of manuscripts and their provenance.

[440] Curran, The Antiphonary, p. 26.

mediaeval period, particularly a mass for Mary in the Piacenza fragment printed by Bannister, although the alleged early Irish Marian prayer has not stood the test of renewed scrutiny.[441]

The Irish office, or at least the office at Bangor, contained a unique form of prayer, the *oratio communis fratrum*. It is first attested in the *Regula Coenobialis* of Columbanus, and also appears in the Antiphonary. It is a formulary of intercessory prayers, resembling the Roman diaconal litany as far as its structure goes, but transformed in content.[442] Each individual prayer is quite short, but there is obvious scope for revision and addition to fit changing circumstances. The Antiphonary's version gives an antiphon taken from a psalm, followed by a collect, for each petition; Columbanus did not give the antiphons, and his version was only the skeleton of the Antiphonary's, which contains ten additional *preces*. It is quite different from the more widespread 'pro... oramus' formula of intercession, which is found in the Stowe Missal under the title 'deprecatio Sancti Martini pro populo'.[443] It is curious that the *oratio communis* does not offer any intercession 'pro fidelibus defunctorum'. Capelle considered that the Stowe *deprecatio* is based more or less directly on the Greek litany of the *Kyrie*,[444] and is independent of the late fifth century Roman *Deprecatio S. Gelasii* (also based on the Greek litany) which it somewhat resembles.[445]

The Hiberno-Latin collects are interesting. Like almost all collects apart from some prolix Gallican specimens, they are only a few lines or so in

---

[441] 'Some recently discovered fragments', pp. 69-70. The prayer to Mary in the seventh-century 'Liturgie-Fragmente' printed by Dold, p. 283, disappeared when the palimpsest was re-transcribed, and now appears as a much more conventional prayer to Christ in *Das irische Palimsestsakramentar*, edd. Dold & Eizenhöfer.

[442] Curran, *The Antiphonary*, pp. 106-13; and see also Warren, *The Antiphonary*, II.63-6. The diaconal litany was discussed by Callewaert, 'Les étapes', p. 21.

[443] Ní Chatháin, 'The liturgical background', p. 135.

[444] Brightman, *Liturgies*, I.9-12.

[445] Capelle, 'Le *Kyrie*', p. 144. The various Western litanic prayers and their relationships to each other and to Greek originals have been discussed by Callewaert, 'Les étapes', p. 21, and by Cabrol, *The Mass*, p. 74, and 'Litanies'.

length.[446] The collects of the Antiphonary (a manuscript which could almost be rechristened a collectary) cover a wide variety of occasions. There is a set of one for each of the eight hours, a set related to the various parts of the *ad matutinam*, several on the martyrs, and others. There are collects attached to canticles, to psalms, and to hymns. The extent of the Irish affection for collects was such as to draw Continental disapproval, expressed at the Council of Mâcon.[447] One unusual feature of Irish practice was the use of verse collects, attested by the Antiphonary. These resemble hymn stanzas, and consist of four lines of rhymed octosyllables. Some of them are also found in other Irish manuscripts, for example in the Southampton Psalter[448] and the Turin fragment.[449] Verse collects were not used outside Ireland. The sources of the collects in the Antiphonary have been the subject of recent investigation by Curran. His picture confirms that established by Bishop for the prayers of the Book of Cerne: some depend heavily on Mozarabic traditions,[450] but the writers also drew on Gallican formulations, the Old Hymnal, and occasionally on Rome.[451]

---

[446] A collect 'collects' and summarises the prayer for the people. The concept can be seen developing in Cassian, *De Institutis*, II.7, 'is, qui orationem collecturus est...' (ed. Petschenig, p. 23), and in Canon 30 of the Council of Agde (A.D. 506), 'Plebs collecta oratione ad uesperam ab episcopo cum benedictione dimittatur' (ed. Mansi, *Concilia*, VIII.319-42, at col. 329-30), and see also Brou, *The Psalter Collects*.

[447] Discussed above, p. lix

[448] On this unpublished tenth-century Irish psalter, Cambridge, St John's College, MS. C.9 (59), also containing canticles and collects, see James, *A Descriptive Catalogue*, pp. 76-8, and Lapidge & Sharpe, *A Bibliography*, p. 132 (no. 509).

[449] The verse collect, 'Deus altissime rex angelorum' appears in all three of these manuscripts.

[450] Curran, *The Antiphonary*; see particularly pp. 118-24.

[451] *Ibid.*, pp. 150-5.

8. Hymns

Nothing is known about the hymnody of the British, Welsh, or Breton Churches, except for two Breton hymns, probably of late date.[452] That of the Irish Church, on the other hand, is well documented, and outstandingly interesting. Hymnody was a relatively late introduction into liturgy: for a long time, antiphons taken from the psalms were felt to provide all the poetry required in the service of the mass.[453] The initial shift from private devotional poetry to a genre of public worship took place in the monasteries rather than the cathedrals. It was probably influenced to some extent by the development of hymnody in the Syriac Church, of which Ephrem Syrus was the most importand relevant figure. The Syriac liturgy influenced the Greek, which in turn influenced the Latin.[454]

The first dramatic irruption of hymnody into Western public worship was at St Ambrose's church in Milan, where he was besieged together with his followers. According to Augustine (whose mother was there at the time), he began to compose hymns in the metre which has for ever after been associated with his name, in order to rally the spirits of his flock.[455] In the sixth century, Benedict allowed extensive hymnody in the performance of the monastic hours.[456] Every hour had one (sometimes referred to as *hymnus*, and sometimes as *ambrosianum*). Caesarius of Arles made similar provisions.[457] The hymns which were sung in these monasteries were not (with one or two exceptions) the collection which is now associated with Catholic worship, but an earlier set, generally known as the Old Hymnal.[458] Gneuss introduced an

---

[452] Lapidge & Sharpe, *A Bibliography*, p. 270 (nos 983-4).

[453] Mohrmann, *Liturgical Latin*, p. 71. Duchesne, *Christian Worship*, p. 452, n. 1, pointed out that Rome remained conservative on this issue until the twelfth century.

[454] Jungmann, *The Early Liturgy*, pp. 204-5, and Baumstark & Botte, *Comparative Liturgy*, p. 104.

[455] *Confessiones*, IX.7,15 (ed. Verheijen, pp. 141-2). Early Latin hymns are listed in Chevalier, *Repertorium Hymnologicum*, and many are printed by Blume (ed.), 'Hymni antiquissimi', and Walpole, *Early Latin Hymns*.

[456] *Regula S. Benedicti*, §§ 9-18 (ed. de Vogüé, II.510-34).

[457] Gneuss, *Hymnar und Hymnen*, pp. 15-16.

[458] The existence of the Old Hymnal and its contents was worked out by Blume, *Der Cursus*, followed by Walpole, *Early Latin Hymns*, pp. xi-xix.

elaboration of this theory; which postulates three Latin hymnals, Type I (the Old Hymnal, perhaps originating at Milan), Type II, which he calls the Frankish Hymnal, a more or less independent hymnal found in French and German manuscripts of the eighth and ninth centuries, and Type III, the New Hymnal. The Hiberno-Latin hymns are separate from all three groups.[459]

The Old Hymnal circulated extremely widely in the Latin West. However, the Irish took the unusual step of supplementing — or perhaps even replacing — the Old Hymnal with creations of their own. This was not the result of ignorance. Michael Curran has shown that many of the hymns and collects in the seventh-century Antiphonary of Bangor use the hymns of Prudentius, Ambrose, Venantius Fortunatus, and others as source-material.

There are two main collections of the hymns used in early Ireland. The first is the Antiphonary of Bangor,[460] written in Ireland, almost certainly at Bangor, in the late seventh century, which is a liturgical manuscript containing canticles, hymns, and collects.[461] It is supported by the Turin fragment, which contains witnesses to two of its hymns, 'Hymnum dicat' and 'Spiritus diuinae lucis'.[462] The second is the Irish *Liber Hymnorum*, preserved in two manuscripts of the late eleventh century.[463] Although it contains a few collects and prayers along with its hymns, it is basically an antiquarian, not a liturgical, compilation, heavily annotated with glosses, scholia, and anecdotal material. The surviving manuscripts containing Hiberno-Latin hymns show

---

[459] Gneuss, *Hymnar und Hymnen*. See also the valuable summary of his views in 'Latin hymns', pp. 408-12.

[460] Milano, Biblioteca Ambrosiana, MS. C.5.inf., ed. Warren, *The Antiphonary*; Lowe, *Codices*, III.311.

[461] Its purpose was discussed by Warren, *The Antiphonary*, II.ix-xi. See also Bishop, 'A service-book'.

[462] There is also an eleventh-century Irish manuscript-fragment which can probably be grouped with the Antiphonary (or possibly with the contemporary eleventh-century *Liber Hymnorum*), discussed by Bannister, 'Liturgical fragments', pp. 422-7. Its two leaves contain 'Hymnum dicat', 'Spiritus diuinae lucis' (which is otherwise found only in the Antiphonary and the Turin fragment) and 'Te deum'. It does not have the accompanying collects of the two early manuscripts. See Kenney, *The Sources*, p. 716 (no. 573), and Gamber, *Codices*, I.147 (no. 152).

[463] Dublin, Trinity College, MS. 1441 (E.4.2), *saec.* xi; Abbott & Gwynn, *Catalogue*, pp. 391-93 (no. 1441); Killiney, Franciscan House of Studies, MS. A.2, *saec.* xi/xii; Dillon *et al.*, *Catalogue*, pp. 2-5. Both have been discussed in detail by Bieler, 'The Irish Book of Hymns'.

little trace of their intended function, that is, whether they were originally intended for the mass, the office, or private devotion, with the exception of five hymns in the Antiphonary which bear original titles stating their use: 'Sancti, uenite', *Hymnus quando communicant sacerdotes*; 'Ignis creator igneus', *Hymnus quando cereus benedicitur*; 'Mediae noctis tempus est', *Hymnus mediae noctis*; 'Sacratissimi martyres', *Hymnus in natali martyrum, uel sabbato ad matutinam*; 'Spiritus diuinae lucis', *Hymnus ad matutinam dominica*. Columbanus directs the singing of a hymn on Sundays and at Easter only: 'in omnique dominica sollempnitate hymnus diei cantetur dominice et in die inchoante pasche'.[464] This hymn may have formed part of a more elaborate Sunday-office (*ad matutinam*?) or, just possibly, of the celebration of the mass. I know of only one reference to communal singing of a specific hymn, in the *Uita S. Caemgeni*: 'Quadam nocte, ympnum beati Patricii ['Audite omnes'] *cum suis*, dicens...'.[465] A less direct indication is the mention, of an 'ymnorum liber septimaniorum' written by the hand of St Columba, in Adomnán's *Uita*.[466] It would seem that Columba made a larger place for hymn-singing than did Columbanus.[467]

Several of the hymns, such as 'Audite omnes' or 'Audite pantes' (both from the Antiphonary) celebrate some specific Irish saint. The later (eighth-century) hymns 'Martine de deprecor' and 'Cantemus in omni die' celebrate, respectively, St Martin and the Virgin Mary, and therefore find a place in the *cultus* of both these figures who were deeply honoured and venerated in Ireland.[468] Other hymns suggest a possible context by their content. 'Precamur patrem' appears to be a hymn specifically intended for Holy Saturday. Every stanza has some relevance to the paschal mystery, whether directly or typologically.[469]

---

[464] *Regula Coenobialis*, § 9 (edd. & transl. Walker [& Bieler], pp. 158-9).

[465] *Uita S. Caemgeni*, § 9 (ed. Heist, *Vitae*, p. 363).

[466] *Uita S. Columbae*, II.9 (edd. & transl. Anderson & Anderson, pp. 342-3).

[467] See Kenney, *The Sources*, pp. 714-15.

[468] On Martin, see Grosjean, 'Gloria postuma'. There is no equivalent summary of mariolatry in Ireland, but see McNally, *The Bible*, pp. 67-8; and note also that 'Cantemus in omni die' is one of the earliest *Latin* hymns to the Virgin, that the Book of Kells contains the first Western representation of the Madonna and Child, and that the eighth-century poetry of Blathmac (ed. & transl. Carney) gives voice to a fervent personal devotion to Mary.

[469] This has been pointed out by Lapidge, 'Columbanus'.

One hymn in the Antiphonary which raises a particular problem is 'Sancti, uenite'. This is labelled in the manuscript, which is some kind of service-book and should therefore be trusted, *Hymnus quando communicarent sacerdotes*. This unequivocally labels it a eucharistic hymn, and thus as belonging to the mass. This, as indicated above, is unprecedented in the seventh century.[470] A further complication is its relationship to a communion-antiphon also found in the Antiphonary.[471]

It is necessary at this point briefly to discuss the authenticity and character (a related issue) of the Hiberno-Latin hymns. At one end of the spectrum, Blume printed in his 'Hymnodia Hiberno-celtica' practically every hymn which he could find in any manuscript associated with Ireland or with Anglo-Saxon England, confusing the picture completely with a large body of compositions which are almost certainly Anglo-Latin or even Continental. At the other, Coccia pruned away at this material with such savage enthusiasm that he hurled out quite a few important hymns with impeccably Hiberno-Latin forms and antecedents.[472] The Antiphonary, the earliest and purest source of Hiberno-Latin hymns, contains one hymn definitely from the Old Hymnal, 'Mediae noctis tempus est'. It also contains two other metrical hymns, one of which, 'Hymnum dicat', is attributed to St Hilary, but since it is preserved mainly in Insular manuscripts has been argued to be Irish.[473] Unless a reasonably watertight case for the cultivation of Latin metrics in Ireland before the eighth century can be made — rather than the wishful thinking and special pleading which have passed for one — it is best to assume that both 'Hymnum dicat' and 'Ignis creator igneus'[474] are Continental in origin. If so, then they point to the openness of the Irish Church to external influence and its ability to adopt and adapt material of widely divergent original contexts.

---

470 Murphy, 'The oldest eucharistic hymn'.

471 Discussed above, pp. lxiii-lxiv.

472 'La cultura', pp. 274-323.

473 Its texts were discussed by Bannister, 'Liturgical fragments', p. 423. The case for its Irishness has most recently been put by Curran, *The Antiphonary*, pp. 22-34, and see also Culhane, 'The Bangor hymn'. Coccia decisively rejected it ('La cultura', pp. 275-6). Bulst, 'Hymnologica', also discussed it, as did Esposito in 'Notes on Latin learning and literature', pt I, p. 231.

474 Coccia, 'La cultura', pp. 280-2.

This brings us on to the character of the early Hiberno-Latin hymns. The first distinguishing feature is that they are not metrical. They use the Classical forms of the iambic dimeter (the *ambrosianum*) or the trochaic tetrameter catalectic, but re-interpret these forms as *syllabic* metres.[475] Characteristically, they have either eight syllables in a line, or alternate eight- and seven-syllabled lines, and stanzaic form, with an even number of lines. Variations, four plus seven syllables and so on, were also admitted. Accent is regarded only with respect to the end of the line, which is normally proparoxytone in the octosyllables, and alternate paroxytone and proparoxytone in the imitation trochaics.[476] Particularly characteristic of these hymns is the use of rhyme. It is possible, albeit with some tentativeness, to use this as a dating criterion. The hymns which appear to be the earliest, perhaps going back to the sixth century, do not use rhyme, or have only the simplest one-syllable form. By the end of the seventh century, a hymn like 'Munther Benchuir beata' has not only full two-syllable rhyme (for example, 'tonsa'... 'sponsa'), but a true rhyme-scheme, ABCB. In the intervening century, anything was possible, from rhymelessness to full rhyme; so the surviving hymns cannot simply be ranked chronologically on this criterion alone. But the eighth-century hymns 'Cantemus in omni die' and 'In trinitate spes mea' display a profusion of end-rhyme, internal rhyme, and alliteration, which is *not* found in known seventh-century hymns, and which might perhaps be paralleled by the equivalently baroque tendencies of Insular manuscript-decoration.

Obviously, any hymn in the Antiphonary is no later than the end of the seventh century in date.[477] Four of them have been dated even further back, to the sixth century, on various grounds. One is 'Audite omnes', in honour of St Patrick. Its rhymeless octosyllabic structure makes this at least

---

[475] The development of syllabic and accentual metres has been discussed by Norberg in *Introduction* and 'Le vers accentuel'. See also Travis, *Early Celtic Versecraft*, and Murphy, *Early Irish Metrics*, pp. 8-25.

[476] This is using the terminology developed by Norberg, *Introduction*.

[477] Some additional evidence for very early Hiberno-Latin poetry is found fossilised in the prose of Muirchú and Uinniau. See *The Patrician Texts*, edd. Bieler & Kelly, p. 17 (I.10.i), 'origo stirpis regiae / huius pene insolae' (8 + 7pp) and *The Irish Penitentials*, edd. Bieler & Binchy, p. 96 (and note on p. 245), 'ut ab omnibus omnia / deleantur facinora' (8 + 8pp). These fragments are compatible in their characteristics with the chronological scheme outlined above.

possible, although Binchy thought it to fit best in the seventh century, on grounds of content.[478] Three others, 'Sancti, uenite',[479] 'Sacratissimi martyres',[480] and 'Precamur patrem',[481] have often been thought to be particularly ancient; the arguments for all three have been considerably strengthened by finding echoes of these hymns in the genuine works of Columbanus (*ob*. 615).[482]

The *Teagasg Maoil Ruain* and other eighth-century and later documents show Hiberno-Latin hymns being used for private or supplemental devotions, particularly 'Hymnum dicat' (which appears from the surviving records to have been the most consistently popular hymn in Ireland),[483] 'Cantemus in omni die' and 'In trinitate spes mea'.[484] The hymn 'Audite Omnes' seems to have had a special use as a protective charm, attested as early as Muirchú's *Uita S. Patricii*. There are several references to its 'virtue', which rested specifically on its last three stanzas, so that it sufficed to recite these only. This principle may well have been extended to other hymns.[485] There is another testimony to this practice of utilising only the last three stanzas in a hymn to St Brigit in the *Liber Hymnorum*, of which only the first

---

[478] Binchy, 'Patrick and his biographers', pp. 54-5. It has also been analysed by MacNeill, 'The hymn'.

[479] Coccia, 'La cultura', pp. 278-80.

[480] *Ibid.*, p. 283.

[481] *Ibid.*, pp. 276-7.

[482] Curran, *The Antiphonary*, pp. 49 and 211, n. 9 ('Sancti, uenite'); pp. 53 and 57 ('Precamur patrem'); p. 78 ('Sacratissimi martyres'). Lapidge ('Columbanus') would go even further, attempting to show that 'Precamur patrem' was written *by* Columbanus.

[483] For example, it is the only hymn mentioned in the 'Rule of Ailbe', § 24 (ed. & transl. O Neill, 'The Rule', pp. 100-1) which may be as early as the eighth century (Kenney, *The Sources*, p. 315 (no. 123). It is also mentioned in the *Teagasg*, but it is more interesting to see its use attested at a centre which was not linked with either Bangor or Tallaght.

[484] *Teagasg*, § 86 (ed. & transl. Gwynn, 'The Rule', pp. 50-1), § 90 (*ibid.*, pp. 50-3), § 96 (*ibid.*, pp. 56-7). See also 'The monastery of Tallaght', § 8 (edd. & transl. Gwynn & Purton, pp. 130-1), § 28 (*ibid.*, pp. 137-8).

[485] Muirchú, *Uita S. Patricii*, II.4, edd. & transl. Bieler & Kelly, *The Patrician Texts*, pp. 116-17; See also *The Irish Liber Hymnorum*, edd. & transl. Bernard & Atkinson, I.5 and II.6; *The Tripartite Life*, ed. & transl. Stokes, I.116-19 and 246-7; and Colgan, *Trias*, p. 210.

and last three (alphabetic) stanzas have been preserved.[486] Similarly, the fragmentary office found in the Book of Mulling refers to no less than four hymns well known in Ireland, not by their *incipit*, but in each case by the *incipit* of the last three stanzas.[487]

---

[486] *The Irish Liber Hymnorum*, edd. Bernard & Atkinson, I.14-15. Note also that there is a third surviving text of this hymn (in Roma, Biblioteca Apostolica Vaticana, MS. Pal. lat. 482), which is similarly truncated.

[487] Bernard & Atkinson, *ibid.*, I.xxiii, print the fragmentary office from the Book of Mulling. Lawlor, *Chapters*, pp. 145-66, collected the evidence for the 'three-stanza' phenomenon and discussed it in detail.

9. Material Survivals

The liturgical habits of the christian Celts are illuminated by a number of remarkable finds. The value, monetary, spiritual, and sentimental, of the furniture of the mass resulted in a natural tendency to conceal these important objects carefully in times of extreme crisis.[488] As a result, some real treasures have survived, including liturgical vessels from Romano-British, later North British, and Irish sources.

The earliest of these is the Water Newton hoard of early christian silver, which includes a strainer and a two-handled cup which could serve as a chalice.[489] In the fourth century, liturgical vessels were not distinguishable from domestic utensils in shape; so these silver objects need not be Church-furniture, although the context makes this more likely than otherwise.[490] The strainer, like another found in the hoard of loot at Traprain Law (which is dated to the fourth or fifth century),[491] is decorated with an engraved chi-rho monogram.[492] Strainers were adapted from Roman domestic to liturgical use, to filter any impurities from the wine before it reached the chalice. An instrument which appears to be a ladle or strainer of the general form of the Derrynaflan specimen is shown being used to pour wine in the Book of Kells.[493] The Water Newton cup is completely unornamented.

The St Ninian's Isle treasure may also represent Church-property. The case for this was vigorously argued by McRoberts.[494] This hoard does not contain a handled or stemmed cup, but he suggests that the six small bowls are in fact intended as chalices, since *poculum* ('beaker') shapes can be shown to have been used as chalices in the early middle ages side by side with the

---

[488] Ryan, 'The Derrynaflan and other early Irish eucharistic chalices', p. 143.

[489] Painter, *The Water Newton Early Christian Silver*, p. 13 and the photographs on p. 30.

[490] *Ibid.*, p. 22. See also Bishop, 'Observations', p. 166.

[491] Curle, *The Treasure*, p. 5, and Wall, 'Christian evidences', pp. 147-50.

[492] Richardson, 'Derrynavlan', pp. 95-6 (photographs on p. 109), and Curle, *The Treasure*, pp. 75-6.

[493] Pointed out by Richardson, 'Derrynavlan', p. 113, with photograph.

[494] McRoberts, 'The ecclesiastical significance'. But his argument was not accepted by D.M. Wilson (*apud* Small *et al.*, *St. Ninian's Isle*, I.106-7).

calix proper.[495] It was noted above that the Church only gradually developed specific vessels for the eucharist. McRoberts also suggested that the three cones and silver pommel which form part of the hoard are the only surviving remnants of an Insular liturgical *flabellum*. It is beyond doubt that *flabella* formed part of Irish eucharistic equipment; he is able to illustrate many examples, particularly from the Book of Kells.[496] An alleged *flabellum* of Columba is said to have been preserved until 1034, when it was lost at sea.[497]

We are on much more certain ground with the Irish chalices, of which there are three: a silver and a bronze chalice found together at Ardagh and dated to the eighth century, and another silver one recently discovered at Derrynaflan together with a silver paten and a bronze ladle adapted as a strainer.[498] The amazing beauty and equally remarkable technical virtuosity of the Ardagh Chalice are well known, and the Derrynaflan Chalice is not far behind it.[499] They illustrate, as do the high aesthetic standards set by gospel-books like Durrow and Kells, a grandeur and elegance in the presentation of the mass at some few major centres in eighth-century Ireland, which the plain and modest surviving churches would otherwise make hard to imagine.[500]

---

[495] 'The ecclesiastical significance', pp 301-3, and see Leclercq, 'Calice', p. 1632, who illustrates a fifth-century beaker-shaped silver chalice.

[496] 'The ecclesiastical significance', plates xxvii-xxx; Olden, 'On the Culebath'. D.M. Wilson expresses scepticism (*apud* Small *et al.*, *St. Ninian's Isle*, I.118-20). See also Warren, *The Liturgy*, p. 144.

[497] Annals of Ulster, *s.a.* 1034.9 (edd. Mac Airt & Mac Niocaill, p. 472): 'Maicnia H. Uchtan, fer leiginn Cenannsa, do bathad ic tiachtain a hAlbain, 7 culebad Coluim Cille...' ('Maicnia ua hUachtáin, lector of Kells, was drowned coming from *Alba*, and the *culebad* of Columcille...').

[498] On chalices, see Warren, *The Liturgy*, pp. 143-4. The Derrynaflan finds have been dated to the late eighth century by Ryan, 'The Derrynaflan and other early Irish eucharistic chalices', p. 139.

[499] In some ways, the Derrynaflan Chalice is sounder in its construction, on which see Ryan, *The Derrynaflan Hoard*, I.14, but it cannot match the range of goldworking and other decorative techniques on the better-known chalice. Further details on the construction of the Ardagh Chalice itself will become available when the results of the British Museum's conservation and investigation of it are published (forthcoming under the editorship of Etienne Rynne).

[500] Written sources indicate the existence of larger, wooden churches in early Ireland: see Thomas, *Christianity*, pp. 152-4, and Lucas, 'The plundering', pp. 192 and 205-6.

Cogitosus describes the complex architecture and decoration of the seventh-century church of St Brigit at Kildare. Particularly relevant here is his information that the bodies of Brigit and Conlaed rested on either side of the altar 'in monumentis posita, ornatis uario cultu auri et argenti et gemmarum pretiosi lapidis, atque coronis aureis et argenteis desuper pendentibus ac diuersis imaginibus, cum caelaturis uariis et coloribus, requiescunt'.[501] Perhaps the Irish illuminated gospels and ornamented silver vessels belonged in this kind of context. Ryan has shown that the shape of these Irish chalices is closer to Byzantine models than to anything nearer to home, although their techniques of metalworking and decoration are entirely native.[502] This prompts some further speculation on the relationship between the Irish Churches and Eastern christianity, a subject which has been much discussed.[503] Ryan emphasised that the two silver chalices expressed their distance from Byzantine tradition even as they acknowledged its influence, because of their combination of inexpert manufacture and assembly with enormous skill in decorative techniques. He noted, 'it would seem therefore that the craftsmen did not handle imported examples but tried with traditional methods of bowl design, fabrication and decoration to approximate a *reported* pattern'.[504]

Gógan produced the interesting suggestion that the size and shape of the Irish chalices was prompted by that of the very chalice of the Last Supper itself,[505] since the church at Golgotha in the seventh century claimed to preserve this precious relic, and the Gaulish bishop Arculf saw it and described to Adomnán, as:[506]

argenteus calix sextarii Gallici mensuram habens duasque in se ansulas ex utraque parte altrinsecus contenens conpositas.

It may be that reverence for what they believed to be the original led to the Irish making chalices which were two-handled and made of silver, but many other cups and chalices had this form without such an association, including

---

[501] *Uita*, VIII.37 (ed. Bollandists, *Acta Sanctorum*, February, I.129-41, at col. 141A).

[502] Ryan, 'The Derrynaflan and other early Irish eucharistic chalices', pp. 143-5. See also Elbern, 'Eine Gruppe'.

[503] See Raftery, 'Ex oriente...', but also Henry, *Irish Art in the Early Christian Period*, pp. 64-5.

[504] *The Derrynaflan Hoard*, I.15.

[505] *The Ardagh Chalice*, p. 44.

[506] *De Locis Sanctis*, I.7,1 (edd. & transl. Meehan [& Bieler], pp. 50-51).

the Water Newton cup.

Glass chalices were also in use, although none has survived from the British Isles.[507] Gógan noted that two were reported found in the nineteenth century, in contexts which may have been ancient burials, but neither was described or preserved.[508] He also suggested that the combination of a small undecorated bronze chalice and a large ornamented silver one in the Ardagh find may represent normal practice: a humble mass-chalice to remind the priest of the sacrifice,[509] and a magnificent ministerial chalice to remind the congregation of the solemnity of the occasion, since at this time the people communicated in both kinds.[510] This combination is laid down in the tract *Athgabáil* in *Senchus Mór*.[511] St Malachy seems to have felt that magnificence was out of place, for his chalice, seen by Patrick Fleming in 1623, was made of wood.[512]

The Derrynaflan paten is an even more elaborate object than the chalice and, like it, makes use of non-Irish design traditions.[513] Ryan remarked that 'In general terms... it can be argued that the Derrynaflan paten is an insular rendering of a widespread late classical and early christian tradition'.[514] The only other Irish paten known to have survived is a circular dish made of copper and ornamented with a cross in silver, called the 'Mias Tighearnáin'. The basic structure is of four plates of copper riveted together.[515] It is a much

---

[507] See *Uita S. Albei*, § 19 (ed. Heist, *Vitae*, p. 123); *Uita I S. Brendani*, § 32 (ed. Plummer, *Vitae*, I.117).

[508] *The Ardagh Chalice*, pp. 14-15.

[509] As, for instance, St Gall would use only a bronze chalice, following the example of Columbanus, in memory of the bronze nails which fixed the Lord to the Cross (Warren, *The Liturgy*, p. 143).

[510] *Ibid.*, pp. 134-6.

[511] Binchy, *Corpus Iuris*, II.402,9, 'aidme altoire'. For gloss, see *ibid*, II.402,20-21 (London, British Library, MS. Harley 432, fo. 14v), and for commentary, *ibid.*, V.1705,17-18 (Dublin, Trinity College, MS. 1336 [H.3.17], at col. 86). See also Ní Chatháin, 'The liturgical background', p. 138.

[512] Anon., 'Hugh Ward', pp. 63-5. This is actually a rather curious detail, since the *Institutiones* of the Cistercian order called for a chalice of silver and, if possible, silver-gilt (Dugdale, *Monasticon Anglicanum*, V.225).

[513] Described by M. Ryan & R. O'Floinn *apud* Ryan, *The Derrynaflan Hoard*, I.17-30.

[514] *Ibid.*, I.29.

[515] Wilde, 'Description'.

smaller and cruder object than the Derrynaflan paten. Both these patens are round, but square patens are mentioned in Tírechán's notes on the life of St Patrick in the Book of Armagh.[516] He claimed that Bishop Assicus was also a coppersmith, and made various *altaria* ('altar-furniture' rather than 'altars'?) for Patrick's churches, of which three square bronze patens were still extant in Tírechán's time, at the churches of Armagh, Ail Find (Elphin), and Seól (Donagh Patrick).

There is liturgical influence from the *ordo commendationis animae* on some of the iconography of Irish high crosses.[517] In another sense, an aspect of liturgical celebration which is reflected in some physical survivals is the altar itself. A number of these have been identified by Charles Thomas.[518] He suggested that the Irish *leachta*, small flat-topped stone-structures associated with religious sites, and possibly the tombs of martyrs, also served as open-air altars.[519] The design of altars inside the churches is, he pointed out, illustrated by a passage in Cogitosus's *Uita S. Brigidae* which appears to imply that she took her vows as a nun at an altar which was supported on a single wooden pedestal, subsequently kept as a precious relic.[520] This type of pedestal altar is attested at Marseille in the fifth and sixth centuries.[521] The proper material for the construction of an altar was stone: this was the subject of conciliar decree at least as early as the sixth century.[522] But wood was, nonetheless, used, for

---

[516] *The Patrician Texts*, edd. & transl. Bieler & Kelly, p. 140-1 (XXII.1).

[517] Henry, *Irish Art during the Viking Invasions*, pp. 142-4.

[518] *The Early Christian Archaeology*, pp. 167-200. Celtic altars have also been discussed by Warren, *The Liturgy*, pp. 91-2, and see Leclercq,'Autel'.

[519] *The Early Christian Archaeology*, pp. 168-75.

[520] *Uita*, § 1 (ed. Bollandists, p. 136A).

[521] *The Early Christian Archaeology*, pp. 176-7.

[522] *Concilium Epaonense* (Epaon; A.D. 517), § 26, 'altaria nisi lapedea crismatis unctione non sacrentur' (ed. de Clercq, *Concilia*, pp. 20-37, at 30). Cf. Braun, *Der christliche Altar*, I.104. The use of stone altars in Britain is also confirmed by Gildas, *De Excidio*, II.29: 'inter altaria iurando demorantes et hanc eadem ac si lutulenta paulo post saxa despicientes' (ed. Winterbottom, p. 99).

economic and practical reasons.[523] A synod held at Dublin in 1186 sought to regularise Irish practice in this matter:[524]

Ne quis sacerdotum de cetero iuxta consuetudinem huius terrae ueterem super tabulam ligneam missam celebrare praesumat. Et si tantae quantitatis lapis haberi non poterit, qui totam altaris tegat superiorem superfaciem, in medio altaris, ubi consecrandum est corpus Domini lapis quadratus integer et politus arte caementaria firmiter inseratur tantae amplitudinis, ut in eiusdem consecratione quinque cruces spatiosa intercapedine a se distantes contineat et calicis amplissimi pedem ex omni latere excedat.

So St Brigit's altar, although it had a wooden pedestal, could be imagined as having a stone top, or at least a stone surface inlaid into its top. Altars were often, or usually, decorated with linen cloths, as is shown by the Penitential of Cummean.[525] Another customary aspect of the altar is that it included relics within it. This practice was also followed in Ireland, as is witnessed by the *Collectio canonum Hibernensis*, which includes the *dictum* 'Ouius [Mobí of Glasnevin, *ob.* 545?] episcopus dicit… animae uero martyrum sub ara Dei clamant'.[526]

Portable altars must also have been used.[527] A tiny Anglo-Saxon example was found in St Cuthbert's tomb, which is probably roughly similar to contemporary Irish portable altars.[528] A consecrated surface was marked out as such by five crosses, one at each corner and one in the middle.[529] This enables us to identify a stone found at Wick which is only four inches by three-and-a-half inches as a portable altar.[530] There are occasional references to

---

[523] Bede tells us that stone altars were used in the earliest phase of the English Church (*Historia Ecclesiastica*, II.14, edd. & transl. Colgrave & Mynors, pp. 188-9), and the situation in Ireland was probably comparable in terms of material resources. Interestingly, he refers to the use of a portable altar with the phrase 'tabulam altaris uice dedicatam' (V.10, ed. *ibid.*, p. 482), perhaps suggesting that such a slab (because it is wood?) did not qualify as a proper altar.

[524] Quoted by Braun, *Der christliche Altar*, I.87.

[525] *The Irish Penitentials* (edd. & transl. Bieler [& Binchy], pp. 130-1).

[526] *Die irische Kanonensammlung*, ed. Wasserschleben, p. 179 (XLIV.19).

[527] Olden ('On the Culebath', p. 358), suggested that *clár* was a vernacular word for a portable altar. This is not supported by *Dictionary of the Irish Language*, gen. ed. Quin, C.219-21, *s.v.*, which however gives 'writing-tablet' as its sense vi, also a plausible meaning in the verse quoted by Olden.

[528] Radford, 'The portable altar'.

[529] Thomas, *The Early Christian Archaeology*, p. 182.

[530] *Ibid.*, pp. 194-5.

both stone and wooden altars in Irish sources.[531]

It should also be remembered that both wine and oil had to be imported into the British Isles for liturgical use, and so some archaeological traces of this trade may be looked for. Françoise Henry pointed out that large bowls of reddish pottery and small amphorae associated with them on fifth- and sixth-century British and Irish sites may have been associated with this trade rather than purely with the secular trade in luxury-items.[532] The need to import wine and oil remained problematic for centuries. Reenactments of Christ's miracle at Cana are common in Irish sources[533] and probably reflect genuine difficulties with supplies. More prosaically, the *Uita S. Ciarani* specifically mentions 'mercatores cum uino Gallorum'.[534]

The material survivals associated with the Celtic liturgy illustrates some important aspects which would otherwise be less clear. The two great Irish silver chalices bear witness to a splendour and physical dignity in Irish liturgical celebration for which the only other surviving evidence is the illuminated gospel-books. The Romano-British christian silver shows by its shape and decorative motifs the extent to which that community was assimilated into the Roman Empire. And even the humble fragments of amphorae illustrate the supply-problems created by a Church on the furthest Western extremity of the known world.

---

[531] Warren, *The Liturgy*, pp. 91-2.

[532] Henry, *Irish Art in the Early Christian Period*, pp. 46-7.

[533] For example Adomnán's *Uita S. Columbae*, II.1 (edd. & transl. Anderson & Anderson, pp. 324-5).

[534] *Uita S. Ciarani*, § 31 (ed. Plummer, *Vitae*, I.214).

INDEX OF MANUSCRIPTS

MÜNCHEN

Bayerische Staatsbibliothek,
Clm 14248 lxxx
Clm 14429 lxvii

NEW YORK

Pierpoint Morgan Library
M.627 (Drummond Missal) lxx

OXFORD

Bodleian Library,
Auct.F.32 (S.C.2176) (Saint Dunstan's
Classbook) lxxiv-lxxvi
Bodley 579 (S.C. 2675) vii

Corpus Christi College,
282 (Corpus Missal) vii, lxvin, lxx

PADOVA

Biblioteca Capitolare,
D.47 (Sacramentary of Padua) xix

PARIS

Bibliothèque nationale,
latin 12048 (Sacramentary of
Gellone) xix, , livn, lvi
latin 13246 (Bobbio Missal) xvii, lxi, lxv,
lxvi

PIACENZA

Archivio della Basilica di S. Antonio,
C.48 lxvi, lxxx-lxxxi

ROMA

Biblioteca Apostolica Vaticana,
Graec. 1209 (Codex Vaticanus) lxxxvi
Lat. 3325 lxxviii
Pal. lat. 482 lxxxix
Reginensis lat. 257 (Missale
Francorum) xviii
Reginensis lat. 316 xviii, livn

Reginensis lat. 317 (Missale
Gothicum) xvii

SANKT GALLEN

Stiftsbibliothek,
1394 lxiii
1395 lxiii

TORINO

Biblioteca Nazionale,
F.iv.1, fasc. 9 ('Turin fragment') xiin,
xlvi,xlviii, lix, lxxi, lxxviii, lxxx

VERONA

Biblioteca Capitolare,
LXXXV (80) (Sacramentary of
Verona) xviii, lxv

WOLFENBÜTTEL

Herzog-August Bibliothek,
Weissenb. 76 xvii

ZÜRICH

Staatsarchiv,
A.G.19, no. xxxvi xxvi

Zentralbibliothek
Rheinau 30 (Sacramentary of
Rheinau) xix

INDEX

BIBLIOGRAPHY

ABBOTT, T.K.   *Catalogue of the Irish Manuscripts in the Library of Trinity College, Dublin* (Dublin, 1900)

ANDERSON, Alan Orr, & ANDERSON, M.O. (edd. & transl.)   *Adomnan's Life of Columba* (Edinburgh 1961)

ANDERSON, W.B. (ed. & transl.)   *Sidonius: Poems and Letters* (2 vols, Cambridge, Mass. 1936/65)

ANGENENDT, A.   'Missa Specialis. Zugleich ein Beitrag zur Entstehung der Privatmessen', *Frühmittelalterliche Studien* 17 (1983) 153-221

ANGENENDT, A.   'Bonifatius und der *Sacramentum Initiationis*. Zugleich ein Beitrag zur Geschichte der Firmung', *Romische Quartalschrift für christliche Altertumskunde und Kirchengeschichte* 72 (1972) 133-83

ANGLÈS, H.   'Latin chant before St Gregory', in *The New Oxford History of Music, II: Early Medieval Music up to 1300*, ed. A. Hughes (Oxford 1954), pp. 58-91

ANON.   'Irish historical studies in the seventeenth century, 2: Hugh Ward', *Irish Ecclesiastical Record*, 2nd S., 7 (1870/1) 56-77

ANON. (ed.)   *Mélanges offerts à Mlle. Christine Mohrmann* (Utrecht 1963)

ANON. (ed.)   *Report of the Nineteenth Eucharistic Congress, held at Westminster from 9th to 13th September 1908* (London 1909)

BÄUMER, Suitbert   *Histoire du bréviaire* (2 vols, Paris 1905)

BANNISTER, H.M. (ed.)   'Liturgical fragments', *Journal of Theological Studies* 9 (1907/8) 398-427

BANNISTER, H.M. (ed.)   'Some recently discovered fragments of Irish sacramentaries', *Journal of Theological Studies* 5 (1903/4) 49-75

BARLEY, M.W., & HANSON, R.P.C. (edd.)   *Christianity in Britain, 300-700. Papers presented to the Conference on Christianity in Roman and Sub-Roman Britain held at the University of Nottingham 17-20 April 1967* (Leicester 1968)

BARLOW, Claude W. (ed.)   *Martini Episcopi Bracarensis Opera Omnia* (New Haven, Conn. 1950)

BATESON, J.D.   'Further finds of Roman material from Ireland', *Proceedings of the Royal Irish Academy* 76 C (1976) 171-80

BATESON, J.D.   'Roman material from Ireland: a reconsideration', *Proceedings of the Royal Irish Academy* 73 C (1973) 21-97

BATIFFOL, Pierre   *History of the Roman Breviary* (London 1912)

BATIFFOL, P.   'La liturgie du sacre des évêques', *Revue d'histoire ecclésiastique* 23 (1927) 733-63

BATTISCOMBE, C.F. (ed.) *The Relics of Saint Cuthbert. Studies by Various Authors, Collected and Edited with a Historical Introduction* (Oxford 1956)

BAUDOT, Jules *Le bréviaire romain: ses origines, son histoire* (Paris 1907)

BAUMSTARK, Anton, & BOTTE, B. *Comparative Liturgy* (London 1958)

BAUMSTARK, Anton *Nocturna Laus: Typen frühchristlicher Vigilienfeier und ihr Fortleben vor allem im römischen und monastischen Ritus* (Münster in Westfalen 1957)

BERNARD, J.H., & ATKINSON, R. (edd. & transl.) *The Irish Liber Hymnorum* (2 vols, London 1898)

BEST, R.I. 'On the *subscriptiones* in the "Book of Dimma"', *Hermathena*, no. 44 (1926) 84-100

BEST, R.I. (ed.) 'The Canonical Hours', *Ériu* 3 (1907) 116

BEST, Richard Irvine, & LAWLOR, H. J. (edd.) *The Martyrology of Tallaght, from the Book of Leinster and MS. 5100-4 in the Royal Library, Brussels* (London 1931)

BIELER, L. 'Der Bibeltext des heiligen Patrick', *Biblica* 28 (1947) 31-58 and 239-63

BIELER, Ludwig *Libri Epistolarum Sancti Patricii Episcopi* (2 vols, Dublin 1952)

BIELER, L. 'Patrick's Synod: a revision', in *Mélanges offerts à Mlle. Christine Mohrmann*, anon. ed. (Utrecht 1963), pp. 96-102

BIELER, L. 'The hymn of St. Secundinus', *Proceedings of the Royal Irish Academy* 55 C (1952/3) 117-27

BIELER, L. 'The Irish Book of Hymns: a palaeographical study' *Scriptorium* 2 (1948) 117-94

BIELER, Ludwig, & BINCHY, D.A. (edd. & transl.) *The Irish Penitentials* (Dublin 1963)

BIELER, L. 'The mission of Palladius: a comparative study of sources', *Traditio* 6 (1948) 1-32

BIELER, Ludwig, & KELLY, F. (edd. & transl.) *The Patrician Texts in the Book of Armagh* (Dublin 1979)

BINCHY, D.A. (ed.) *Corpus Iuris Hibernici ad Fidem Codicum Manuscriptorum* (6 vols, Dublin 1978)

BINCHY, D.A. (ed.) *Críth Gablach* (Dublin 1941)

BINCHY, D.A. 'Patrick and his biographers, ancient and modern', *Studia Hibernica* 2 (1962) 7-173

BINCHY, D.A. 'St Patrick's "First Synod"', *Studia Hibernica* 8 (1968) 49-59

BINCHY, D.A.   'The passing of the old order', in *Proceedings of the International Congress of Celtic Studies held in Dublin 6-10 July, 1959*, ed. B. Ó Cuív (Dublin 1962), pp. 119-32

BIRCH, Walter de Gray (ed.)   *An Ancient Manuscript of the Eighth or Ninth Century, formerly belonging to St. Mary's Abbey, or Nunnaminster, Winchester* (London 1889)

BISCHOFF, B., & BROWN, V.   'Addenda to *Codices Latini Antiquiores*', *Mediaeval Studies* 47 (1985) 317-66 & 18 plates

BISHOP, Edmund   *Liturgica Historica. Papers on the Liturgy and Religious Life of the Western Church* (Oxford 1918)

BISHOP, E.   'Liturgical note', in *The Prayer-Book of Aedeluald the Bishop, commonly called the Book of Cerne*, ed. A.B. Kuypers (Cambridge 1902), pp. 234-83

BISHOP, E.   'Observations on the liturgy of Narsai', in *The Liturgical Homilies of Narsai*, transl. R.H. Connolly (Cambridge 1909)

BISHOP, W.C.   'A service-book of the seventh century', *Church Quarterly Review* 37 (1894) 337-63

BISHOP, W.C.   *The Mozarabic and Ambrosian Rites: Four Essays in Comparative Liturgiology* (London 1924)

BLUME, Clemens   *Der Cursus s. Benedicti Nursini und die liturgischen Hymnen des 6-9 Jahrhunderts in ihrer Beziehung zu den Sonntags- und Ferialhymnen unseres Breviers. Eine hymnologisch-liturgisch Studie auf Grund handschriften Quellenmateriels* (Leipzig 1908)

BLUME, C. (ed.)   'Hymni antiquissimi, saec. v-xi', *Analecta Hymnica Medii Aevi* 51 (1908) 1-256

BLUME, C. (ed.)   'Hymnodia Hiberno-Celtica', *Analecta Hymnica Medii Aevi* 51 (1908) 257-365

[BOLLANDISTS (ed.)]   'De S. Brigida Virgine Scota Thaumaturga, Kildariae et Duni in Hibernia', in *Acta Sanctorum* (69 vols, Antwerpen 1643–), February, I.99-185

BOWEN, E.G.   *Saints, Seaways and Settlements in the Celtic Lands* (2nd edn, Cardiff 1977)

BRADSHAW, Paul F.   *Daily Prayer in the Early Church: a Study of the Origin and Early Development of the Divine Office* (London 1981)

BRAMBACH, Wilhelm, *et al.*   *Die Handschriften der Badischen Landesbibliothek in Karlsruhe* (10 vols, Karlsruhe 1891– ; rev. imp., Wiesbaden 1970-3)

BRAUN, J.   *Der christliche Altar in seiner geschichtlichen Entwicklung* (2 vols, München 1924)

BRAUNFELS, Wolfgang (ed.)   *Karl der Grosse: Lebenswerk und Nachleben* (5 vols, Düsseldorf 1985-6)

BREWER, J.S., *et al.* (edd.)   *Giraldi Cambrensis Opera* (8 vols, London 1861-91)

BRIGHTMAN, F.E. (ed. & transl.)   *Liturgies, Eastern and Western, 1: Eastern* (Oxford 1896)

BROOKE, Christopher N.L.   *The Church and the Welsh Border in the Central Middle Ages* (Woodbridge 1986)

BROOKS, Nicholas   *The Early History of the Church of Canterbury: Christ Church from 597 to 1066* (Leicester 1984)

BROU, Louis (ed.)   *The Psalter Collects from V-VIth Century Sources (Three Series), edited from the Papers of the late Dom André Wilmart, O.S.B.* (London 1949)

BROWN, T.J.   'The oldest Irish manuscripts and their late Antique background', in *Ireland and Europe: the Early Church*, edd. P. Ní Chatháin & M. Richter (Stuttgart 1984), pp. 311-27

BULST, W.   'Hymnologica partim hibernica', in *Latin Script and Letters A.D. 400-900*, edd. J.J. O'Meara & B. Naumann (Leiden 1976), pp. 83-100

BURKITT, F.C.   'On two early Irish hymns', *Journal of Theological Studies* 3 (1901/2) 95-6

BURKITT, F.C.   'The bible of Gildas', *Revue bénédictine* 46 (1934) 206-15

BUTE, Marquess of [J.P.C. STUART]   'Brendan's fabulous voyage', *Scottish Review* 21 (1893) 371-98

BYRNE, F.J.   '"Senchas": the nature of Gaelic historical tradition', *Historical Studies* [Irish Conference of Historians] 9 (1974) 137-59

BYRNE, F.J.   'The Stowe Missal', *apud* L. de Paor *et al.*, *Great Books of Ireland* (Dublin 1967), pp. 38-50

BYRNE, F.J.   'Tribes and tribalism in early Ireland', *Ériu* 22 (1971) 128-66

CABROL, Fernand, *et al.* (edd.)   *Dictionnaire d'archéologie chrétienne et de liturgie* (15 vols in 30, Paris 1903-53)

CABROL, F.   'Le "Book of Cerne", les liturgies celtiques et gallicanes et la liturgie romaine', *Revue des questions historiques* 76 [N.S., 32] (1904) 210-22

CABROL, F.   'Litanies', in *Dictionnaire d'archéologie chrétienne et de liturgie*, edd. F. Cabrol *et al.* (15 vols in 30, Paris 1903-53), IX.1540-71

CABROL, Fernand   *The Mass of the Western Rites* (London 1934)

CALLEWAERT, C.   'Les étapes de l'histoire du *kyrie*: S. Gélase, S. Benoît, S. Grégoire', *Revue d'histoire ecclésiastique* 38 (1942) 20-45

CAPELLE, B.   'Le *kyrie* de la messe et le pape Gélase', *Revue bénédictine* 46 (1934) 126-44

CARNEY, James (ed. & transl.)   *The Poems of Blathmac son of Cú Brettan, together with the Irish Gospel of Thomas and a Poem on the Virgin Mary* (London 1964)

CARNEY, J. (ed. & transl.)   'Three Old Irish accentual poems', *Ériu* 22 (1971) 23-80

CARVILLE, Geraldine   *The Occupation of Celtic Sites in Medieval Ireland by the Canons Regular of St Augustine and the Cistercians* (Kalamazoo, Mich. 1982)

CHADWICK, Nora K.   *Early Brittany* (Cardiff 1969)

CHADWICK, N.K.   'The colonization of Brittany from Celtic Britain', *Proceedings of the British Academy* 51 (1965) 235-99

CHADWICK, Owen   *John Cassian* (2nd edn, Cambridge 1968)

CHEVALIER, Ulysse   *Repertorium Hymnologicum. Catalogue des chants, hymnes, proses, séquences, tropes en usage dans l'église latine depuis les origines jusqu'à nos jours* (6 vols, Leuven 1892-1921)

CLARKE, H.B., & BRENNAN, M. (edd.)   *Columbanus and Merovingian Monasticism* (Oxford 1981)

COCCIA, E.   'La cultura irlandese precarolina: miracolo o mito?' *Studi Medievali*, 3rd S., 8 (1967) 257-420

COEBERGH, C.   'Le sacramentaire gélasien ancien: une compilation de clercs romanisants du viie siècle', *Archiv für Liturgiewissenschaft* 7 (1961) 45-88

COLGRAVE, Bertram, & MYNORS, R.A.B. (edd. & transl.)   *Bede's Ecclesiastical History of the English People* (Oxford 1969)

COLGRAVE, Bertram (ed. & transl.)   *The Life of Bishop Wilfrid by Eddius Stephanus* (Cambridge 1927)

COLGRAVE, Bertram (ed. & transl.)   *Two Lives of Saint Cuthbert, A Life by an Anonymous Monk of Lindisfarne, and Bede's Prose Life* (Cambridge 1940)

COLGAN, Johannes (ed.) *Triadis Thaumaturgae, seu Divorum Patricii, Columbae et Brigidae, trium veteris et maioris Scotiae, seu Hiberniae sanctorum insulae, communium patronum acta* (Leuven 1647)

CONNOLLY, R.H. (transl.)   *The Liturgical Homilies of Narsai* (Cambridge 1909)

CONSTABLE, Giles   *Medieval Monasticism: a Select Bibliography* (Toronto 1976)

CORDOLIANI, A.   'Le texte de la bible en Irlande du ve au ixe siècle; étude sur les manuscrits', *Revue biblique* 57 (1960) 1-39

CORISH, P.J.   'The early Irish Church and the Western patriarchate', in *Ireland and Europe: the Early Church*, edd. P. Ní Chatháin & M. Richter (Stuttgart 1984), pp. 9-15

CREHAN, J.H.   'The liturgical trade route: East to West', *Studies* [Dublin] 65 (1976) 87-99

CROSS, F.L., & LIVINGSTONE, E.A. (edd.)   *The Oxford Dictionary of the Christian Church* (2nd edn, Oxford 1974)

CULHANE, R.   'The Bangor hymn to Christ the King', *Irish Ecclesiastical Record*, 5th S., 74 (1950) 207-19

CURLE, A.O.   *The Treasure of Traprain* (Glasgow 1923)

CURRAN, M.E.   *The Antiphonary of Bangor* (Blackrock 1984)

DANIEL, H.A.   *Thesaurus Hymnologicus sive Hymnorum Canticorum Sequentiarum circa annum MD. usitatarum collectio amplissima* (5 vols, Halle 1841-56)

DAVIES, Wendy   *Wales in the Early Middle Ages* (Leicester 1982)

DAVIES, W.H.   'The Church in Wales', in *Christianity in Britain, 300-700*, edd. M.W. Barley & R.P.C. Hanson (Leicester 1968), pp. 131-50

DEANESLY, M.   'The Anglo-Saxon Church and the papacy', in *The English Church and the Papacy in the Middle Ages*, ed. C.H. Lawrence (London 1965), pp. 29-62

DEANESLY, Margaret   *The Pre-Conquest Church in England* (2nd edn, London 1963)

DE CLERCQ, Charles (ed.)   *Concilia Galliae, A. 511 - A. 695* (Turnhout 1963)

DE JUBAINVILLE, H. d'A.   'Périodiques', *Revue celtique* 22 (1901) 255-9

DE LABRIOLLE, Pierre (ed. & transl.)   *Les sources de l'histoire du montanisme: textes grecs, latins, syriaques* (Fribourg en Suisse 1913)

DEKKERS, Eligius   *Clavis Patrum Latinorum qua in nouum Corpus Christianorum edendum optimas quasque scriptorum recensiones a Tertulliano ad Bedam commode recludit* (2nd edn, Steenbrugge 1961)

DEKKERS, Eligius, *et al.* (edd.)   *Tertulliani Opera* (2 vols, Turnhout 1954/5)

DE PAOR, Liam, *et al.*   *Great Books of Ireland* (Dublin 1967)

DESHUSSES, Jean (ed.)   *Le sacramentaire grégorien. Ses principales formes d'après les plus anciens manuscrits* (3 vols, Fribourg en Suisse 1971-82)

DE VOGÜÉ, Adalbert, & NEUFVILLE, J. (edd. & transl)   *La Règle de Saint Benoît* (6 vols, Paris 1971-2)

DE VOGÜÉ, Adalbert (ed. & transl.)   *La Règle du Maître* (2 vols, Paris 1964)

DILLON, Myles *et al.*   *Catalogue of Irish Manuscripts in the Franciscan Library, Killiney* (Dublin 1969)

DIX, Gregory   *The Shape of the Liturgy* (London 1945)

DOHERTY, C. 'Exchange and trade in early medieval Ireland', *Journal of the Royal Society of Antiquaries of Ireland* 110 (1980) 67-90

DOLD, Alban (ed.) *Das älteste Liturgiebuch der lateinischen Kirche: ein altgallikanisches Lektionar des 5.-6. Jhs aus dem Wolfenbütteler Palimpsest-Codex Weissenburgensis 76* (Beuron 1936)

DOLD, Alban, & EIZENHÖFER, L. (edd.) *Das irische Palimpsestsakramentar im Clm 14429 der Staatsbibliothek München* (Beuron 1964)

DOLD, A. (ed.) 'Liturgie-Fragmente aus den beiden Palimpsesten Cod. Aug. CXCV und Clm 14429', *Revue bénédictine* 38 (1926) 273-87

DUCHESNE, Louis *Christian Worship, its Origin and Evolution. A Study of the Latin Liturgy up to the Time of Charlemagne* (London 1903, and subsequent editions)

DUDDEN, F. Homes *Gregory the Great, his Place in History and Thought* (2 vols, London 1905)

DÜMMLER, Ernst (ed.) *Epistolae Merowingici et Karolini Aevi* (5 vols, Berlin 1892-1928)

DUGDALE, William (ed.) *Monasticon Anglicanum: a History of the Abbies and Other Monasteries, Hospitals, Frieries, and Cathedral and Collegiate Churches with their Dependencies, in England and Wales, also of all such Scotch, Irish and French monasteries as were in any manner connected with Religious Houses in England... originally published in Latin* (rev. edn by J. Caley *et al.*, 6 vols in 8, London 1819-30)

DUGMORE, C.W. *The Influence of the Synagogue upon the Divine Office* (2nd edn, London 1964)

DUINE, F. *Inventaire liturgique de l'hagiographie bretonne* (Paris 1922)

DUMAS, A. (ed.) *Liber Sacramentorum Gellonensis* (2 vols, Turnhout 1981)

DUMVILLE, D.N. 'Gildas and Maelgwn: problems of dating', in *Gildas: New Approaches*, edd. M. Lapidge & D. Dumville (Woodbridge 1984), pp. 51-9

DUMVILLE, D.N. 'Gildas and Uinniau', in *Gildas: New Approaches*, edd. M. Lapidge & D. Dumville (Woodbridge 1984), pp. 207-14

DUMVILLE, D.N. (ed.) 'Liturgical drama and panegyric responsory from the eighth century? A re-examination of the origin and contents of the ninth-century section of the Book of Cerne', *Journal of Theological Studies*, N.S., 23 (1972) 374-406

DUMVILLE, D.N. 'Some British aspects of the earliest Irish christianity', in *Ireland and Europe: the Early Church*, edd. P. Ní Chatháin & M. Richter (Stuttgart 1984), pp. 16-24

DUMVILLE, D.N.   'The chronology of *De Excidio Britanniae*, Book I', in *Gildas: New Approaches*, edd. M. Lapidge & D. Dumville (Woodbridge 1984), pp. 61-84

EHWALD, Rudolf (ed.)   *Aldhelmi Opera* (Berlin 1913-19)

ELBERN, V.H.   'Eine Gruppe insularer Kelche des frühen Mittelalters', in *Festschrift für Peter Metz*, edd. U. Schlegel & C.Z. von Manteuffel (Berlin 1965), pp. 115-23

ELLARD, Gerald   *Master Alcuin, Liturgist: a Partner of our Piety* (Chicago 1956)

ELLARD, Gerald   *Ordination Anointings in the Western Church before 1000 A.D.* (Cambridge, Mass. 1933)

ESPOSITO, M.   'Notes on Latin learning and literature in mediaeval Ireland, I', *Hermathena*, no. 45 (1930) 225-60

ESPOSITO, M.   'On the pseudo-Augustinian treatise *De Mirabilibus Sacrae Scripturae* written in Ireland in the year 655', *Proceedings of the Royal Irish Academy* 35 C (1918-20) 189-207

EVANS, D. Ellis, *et al.* (edd.)   *Proceedings of the Seventh International Congress of Celtic Studies held at Oxford, from 10th to 15th July, 1983* (Oxford 1986)

FARIS, M.J. (ed.)   *The Bishops' Synod ("The First Synod of St. Patrick"). A Symposium with Text, Translation and Commentary* (Liverpool 1976)

FAWTIER, Robert (ed.)   *La Vie de saint Samson. Essai de critique hagiographique* (Paris 1912)

FÉROTIN, Marius (ed.)   *Le Liber Mozarabicus Sacramentorum et les manuscrits mozarabes* (Paris 1912)

FÉROTIN, Marius (ed.)   *Le Liber Ordinum en usage dans l'église wisigothique et mozarabe d'Espagne du cinquième au onzième siècle* (Paris 1904)

FERRARI, M.   'Spigolature Bobbiesi', *Italia Medioevale e Umanistica* 16 (1973) 1-41

FIREY, A.   'Cross-examining the witness: recent research in Celtic monastic history', *Monastic Studies* 14 (1983) 31-49

FISCHER, Bonifatius, & FIALA, V. (edd.)   *Colligere Fragmenta: Festschrift Alban Dold zum 70. Geburtstag am 7.7.1952* (Beuron 1952)

FISCHER, B.   'Die Lesungen der römische Ostervigil unter Gregor d. Gr.', in *Colligere Fragmenta*, edd. B. Fischer & V. Fiala (Beuron 1952), pp. 144-59

FISHER, J.D.C.   *Christian Initiation: Baptism in the Mediaeval West. A Study in the Disintegration of the Primitive Rite of Initiation* (London 1965)

FLEURIOT, Léon   *Les origines de la Bretagne. L'émigration* (Paris 1980)

FORBES, Alexander Penrose (ed.)   *Lives of S. Ninian and S. Kentigern compiled in the Twelfth Century* (Edinburgh 1874)

FORBES, G.H. (ed.)   *Missale Drummondiense: the Ancient Irish Missal in the Possession of the Baroness Willoughby de Evesby* (Burntisland 1882)

FORTESCUE, Adrian   *The Mass: a Study of the Roman Liturgy* (London 1912)

FREDE, Hermann Josef   *Pelagius, der irische Paulustext, Sedulius Scottus* (Freiburg i.B. 1961)

FREND, W.H.C.   'The christianization of Roman Britain', in *Christianity in Britain, 300-700*, edd. M.W. Barley & R.P.C. Hanson (Leicester 1968), pp. 37-49

FREND, W.H.C.   'Romano-British christianity and the West: comparison and contrast', in *The Early Church in Western Britain and Ireland*, ed. S.M. Pearce (Oxford 1982), pp. 5-16

FROST, M. (ed.)   'A prayer book from St Emmeran, Ratisbon', *Journal of Theological Studies* 30 (1928/9) 32-45

GAMBER, Klaus   *Codices Liturgici Latini Antiquiores* (2nd edn, 2 vols, Fribourg en Suisse 1968)

GAMBER, K.   'Die irischen Messlibelli als Zeugnis für die frühe römische Liturgie', *Römische Quartalschrift für christliche Altertumskunde und Kirchengeschichte* 62 (1967) 214-21

GAMBER, Klaus   *Missa Romensis: Beiträge zur frühen römischen Liturgie und zu den Anfängen des Missale Romanum* (Regensburg 1970)

GAMBER, Klaus, *et al.*   *Sakramentartypen: Versuch einer Gruppierung der Handschriften und Fragmente bis zur Jahrtausendwende* (Beuron 1958)

GAUDEMET, Jean   *L'église dans l'empire romain* (Paris 1955)

GIOT, P.-R.   'Saint Budoc on the Isle of Lavret, Brittany', in *The Early Church in Western Britain and Ireland*, ed. S.M. Pearce (Oxford 1982), pp. 197-210

GNEUSS, Helmut   *Hymnar und Hymnen im englischen Mittelalter: Studien zur Überlieferung, Glossierung und Übersetzung lateinischer Hymnen in England, mit einer Textausgabe der lateinischen-altenglischen Expositio Hymnorum* (Tübingen 1968)

GNEUSS, H.   'Latin hymns in medieval England: future research', in *Chaucer and Middle English Studies in Honour of Rossell Hope Robbins*, ed. B. Rowland (London 1974), pp. 407-24

GÓGAN, L.   *The Ardagh Chalice* (Dublin 1932)

GODEL, W.   'Irisches Beten im frühen Mittelalter', *Zeitschrift für katholische Theologie* 85 (1963) 261-321 *and* 389-439

GODEL, W.   'Irish prayer in the early middle ages', *Milltown Studies* 4

(1979) 60-99 *and* 5 (1980) 72-114

GOUGAUD, L. 'Celtiques (Liturgies)', in *Dictionnaire d'archéologie chrétienne et de liturgie*, edd. F. Cabrol *et al.* (15 vols in 30, Paris 1903-53), II.2969-3032

GOUGAUD, Louis *Christianity in Celtic Lands. A History of the Churches of the Celts, their Origin, their Development, Influence, and Mutual Relations* (London 1932)

GOUGAUD, L. 'Étude sur les loricae celtiques et sur les prières qui s'en rapprochent', *Bulletin d'ancienne littérature et d'archéologie chrétienne* 1 (1911) 265-81 *and* 2 (1912) 33-41, 101-27

GOUGAUD, L. 'Les rites de la consécration et de la fraction dans la liturgie celtique de la messe', in *Report of the Nineteenth Eucharistic Congress*, anon. ed. (London 1909), pp. 348-61

GOUGAUD, L. 'The Celtic liturgies historically considered', *Catholic Historical Review* 16 (1930) 175-82

GREENE, D. 'Some linguistic evidence relating to the British Church', in *Christianity in Britain, 300-700*, edd. M.W. Barley & R.P.C. Hanson (Leicester 1968), pp. 75-86

GRIFFE, E. 'Aux origines de la liturgie gallicane', *Bulletin de littérature ecclésiastique* 52 (1951) 17-43

GROSJEAN, P. (ed.) 'Édition et commentaire du *Catalogus sanctorum Hiberniae secundum diversa tempora* ou *De tribus ordinibus sanctorum Hiberniae*', *Analecta Bollandiana* 73 (1955) 197-213 *and* 289-322

GROSJEAN, P. 'Gloria postuma S. Martini Turonensis apud Scottos et Britannos', *Analecta Bollandiana* 55 (1937) 300-48

GWYNN, Aubrey, & Hadcock, R.N. *Medieval Religious Houses: Ireland With an Appendix to early sites* (London 1970)

GWYNN, A. 'The cult of St. Martin in Ireland', *Irish Ecclesiastical Record*, 5th S., 105 (1966) 353-64

GWYNN, A. 'The Irish missal of Corpus Christi College, Oxford', *Studies in Church History* 1 (1964) 47-68

GWYNN, Aubrey *The Twelfth-century Reform* (Dublin 1968)

GWYNN, E.J., & PURTON, W.J. (edd. & transl.) 'The Monastery of Tallaght', *Proceedings of the Royal Irish Academy* 29 C (1911/12) 115-79

GWYNN, E.[J.] (ed. & transl.) 'The Rule of Tallaght', *Hermathena*, no. 44 (1927), second supplemental volume

GWYNN, John (ed.) *Liber Ardmachanus. The Book of Armagh* (Dublin 1913)

HADDAN, Arthur West, & STUBBS, W. (edd.) *Councils and Ecclesiastical Documents relating to Great Britain and Ireland* (3 vols, Oxford 1869-78)

HALLINGER, Kassius (ed.)   *Initia Consuetudinis Benedictinae* (Siegburg 1963)

HÄNGGI, Anton, & SCHÖNHERR, A. (edd.)   *Sacramentarium Rhenaugiense: Handschrift Rh. 30 der Zentralbibliothek Zürich* (Fribourg en Suisse 1970)

HALLINGER, K. (ed.)   'Ratio de cursus qui fuerunt eius auctores', in *Initia Consuetudinis Benedictinae*, ed. K. Hallinger (Siegburg 1963), pp. 79-91

HALM, Karl (ed.)   *Sulpicii Severi Opera* (Wien 1856)

HAMP, E.P.   'Social gradience in British spoken Latin', *Britannia* 6 (1975) 150-62

HANSON, Richard P.C., & BLANC, C. (edd. & transl.)   *Saint Patrick: Confession et Lettre à Coroticus* (Paris 1978)

HANSON, R.P.C.   'The Church in fifth-century Gaul', *Journal of Ecclesiastical History* 21 (1970) 1-10

HANSSENS, Jean Michel   *Aux origines de la prière liturgique: nature et genèse de l'office des matines* (Roma 1952)

HARRIS, James Rendel   *The Codex Bezae: a Study of the so-called Western Text of the New Testament* (Cambridge 1891)

HEIMING, O.   'Zum monastischen Offizium von Kassianus bis Kolumbanus', *Archiv für Liturgiewissenschaft* 7 (1961) 89-156

HEIST, W.W. (ed.)   *Vitae Sanctorum Hiberniae ex codice olim Salmanticensi nunc Bruxellensi* (Bruxelles 1965)

HENNIG, J.   'Kalendar und Martyrologium als Literaturformen', *Archiv für Liturgiewissenschaft* 7 (1961) 1-44

HENNIG, J.   'Martyrologium and Kalendarium', *Studia Patristica* 5 [= *Texte und Untersuchungen zur Geschichte der altchristlichen Literatur* 80] (1962) 69-82

HENNIG, J.   'Old Ireland and her liturgy', in *Old Ireland*, ed. R. McNally (Dublin 1965), pp. 60-89

HENNIG, J.   'Sacramentaries of the early Irish Church', *Irish Ecclesiastical Record*, 5th S., 96 (1961) 23-8

HENNIG, J.   'Studies in the liturgy of the early Irish Church', *Irish Ecclesiastical Record*, 5th S., 75 (1951) 318-33

HENNIG, J.   'The function of the Martyrology of Tallaght', *Mediaeval Studies* 26 (1964) 315-28

HENRY, Françoise   *Irish Art during the Viking Invasions (800-1020 A.D.)* (London 1967)

HENRY, Françoise   *Irish Art in the Early Christian Period (to 800 A.D.)* (3rd edn, London 1965)

HENRY, Françoise   *Irish Art in the Romanesque Period (1020-1170 A.D.)* (London 1970)

HERBERMANN, Charles G., *et al.* (edd.)   *The Catholic Encyclopedia: an International Work of Reference on the Constitution, Doctrine, Discipline, and History of the Catholic Church* (17 vols, New York 1907-22)

HERREN, M.   'The authorship, date and provenance of the so-called *Lorica Gildae*', *Ériu* 24 (1973) 35-51

HERVAL, René (ed. & transl.)   *Origines chrétiennes: de la IIe Lyonnaise gallo-romaine à la Normandie ducale (ive - xie siècles), avec le texte complet et la traduction intégrale du* De Laude Sanctorum *de Saint Victrice (396)* (Rouen 1966)

HILLGARTH, J.N.   'Ireland and Spain in the seventh century', *Peritia* 3 (1984) 1-16

HILLGARTH, J.N.   'The East, Visigothic Spain and the Irish', *Studia Patristica* 4 [= *Texte und Untersuchungen zur Geschichte der altchristlichen Literatur* 79] (1961) 442-56

HILLGARTH, J.N.   'Visigothic Spain and early christian Ireland', *Proceedings of the Royal Irish Academy* 62 C (1961-3) 167-94

HILLGARTH, Jocelyn [N.]   *Visigothic Spain, Byzantium and the Irish* (London 1981)

HOARE, F.R. (transl.)   *The Western Fathers, being the Lives of SS. Martin of Tours, Ambrose, Augustine of Hippo, Honoratus of Arles, and Germanus of Auxerre...* (London 1954)

HOOD, A.B.E. (ed. & transl.)   *St. Patrick: his Writings and Muirchu's Life* (Chichester 1978)

HOPE, D.M.   *The Leonine Sacramentary. A Reassessment of its Nature and Purpose* (London 1971)

HUGHES, Andrew   *Medieval Manuscripts for Mass and Office: a Guide to their Organization and Terminology* (Toronto 1982)

HUGHES, Anselm (ed.)   *The New Oxford History of Music, II: Early Medieval Music up to 1300* (Oxford 1954)

HUGHES, Kathleen   *Celtic Britain in the Early Middle Ages. Studies in Scottish and Welsh Sources* (Woodbridge 1980)

HUGHES, Kathleen   *Early Christian Ireland: Introduction to the Sources* (London 1972)

HUGHES, K.   'Some aspects of Irish influence on early English private prayer', *Studia Celtica* 5 (1970) 48-61

HUGHES, K.   'The Celtic Church and the papacy', in *The English Church and the Papacy in the Middle Ages*, ed. C.H. Lawrence (London 1965), pp. 1-28

HUGHES, K.   'The Celtic Church: is this a valid concept?', *Cambridge*

Medieval Celtic Studies 1 (1981) 1-20

HUGHES, K., & BANNERMAN, J. 'The Church and the world in early christian Ireland', *Irish Historical Studies* 13 (1962/3) 99-116

HUGHES, Kathleen *The Church in Early Irish Society* (London 1966)

HUNT, R.W. (facs. ed.) *Saint Dunstan's Classbook from Glastonbury. Codex Biblioth. Bodleianae Oxon. Auct. F.4.32* (Amsterdam 1961)

JACKSON, Kenneth *Language and History in Early Britain. a Chronological Survey of the Brittonic Languages, 1st to 12th c. A.D.* (Edinburgh 1953)

JAMES, E. 'Ireland and western Gaul in the Merovingian period', in *Ireland in Early Mediaeval Europe*, edd. D. Whitelock *et al.* (Cambridge 1982), pp. 362-86

JAMES, Montague Rhodes *A Descriptive Catalogue of the Manuscripts in the Library of St. John's College, Cambridge* (Cambridge 1913)

JENNER, H. 'Celtic rite', in *The Catholic Encyclopedia*, edd. C.G. Herbermann *et al.* (17 vols, New York 1907-22), III.493-504

JONES, Cheslyn, *et al.* (edd.) *The Study of Liturgy* (London 1978; rev. imp., 1980)

JUNGMANN, Josef A. *Missarum Sollemnia* (2 vols, Wien 1949)

JUNGMANN. J[osef] A. *Pastoral Liturgy* (London 1962)

JUNGMANN, Josef A. *The Early Liturgy to the Time of Gregory the Great* (Notre Dame, Ind. 1959)

JUNGMANN, Josef A. *The Mass: an Historical, Theological and Pastoral Survey* (Collegeville, Minn. 1976)

JUNGMANN, Josef A. *The Mass of the Roman Rite: its Origins and Development* (2 vols, New York 1951/5)

KENNEY, James F. *The Sources for the Early History of Ireland: Ecclesiastical. An Introduction and Guide* (New York 1929; rev. imp., by L. Bieler, 1966)

KEYNES, Simon, & LAPIDGE, M. (transl.) *Alfred the Great: Asser's Life of King Alfred and Other Contemporary Sources* (Harmondsworth 1983)

KING, Archdale A. *Liturgies of the Past* (London 1959)

KLAUSER, Theodor *A Short History of the Western Liturgy: an Account and Some Reflections* (London 1969; 2nd edn, Oxford 1979)

KLAUSER, Theodor *Das römische Capitulare Evangeliorum: Texte und Untersuchungen zu seiner ältesten Geschichte* (Münster in Westfalen 1935)

KNOWLES, David *Christian Monasticism* (London 1969)

KNOWLES, David *Great Historical Enterprises and Problems in Monastic History* (Edinburgh 1963)

KOTTJE, Raymund *Studien zum Einfluss des alten Testaments auf Recht und Liturgie des frühen Mittelalters* (Bonn 1964)

KRUSCH, Bruno (ed.) *Ionae Vitae Sanctorum Columbani, Vedastis, Iohannis* (Hannover 1905)

KUYPERS, A.B. (ed.) *The Prayer-book of Aedeluald the Bishop, commonly called the Book of Cerne* (Cambridge 1902)

LAMBOT, Cyril (ed.) *Sancti Aurelii Augustini Sermones de Vetere Testamento* (Turnhout 1961)

LAPIDGE, Michael, & SHARPE, R. *A Bibliography of Celtic-Latin Literature 400-1200* (Dublin 1985)

LAPIDGE, Michael, & HERREN, M. (transl.) *Aldhelm: the Prose Works* (Ipswich 1979)

LAPIDGE, M. 'Columbanus and the Antiphonary of Bangor', *Peritia* 4 (1985)

LAPIDGE, Michael, & DUMVILLE, D. (edd.) *Gildas: New Approaches* (Woodbridge 1984)

LAPIDGE, M. 'Latin learning in Dark Age Wales: some prolegomena', in *Proceedings of the Seventh International Congress of Celtic Studies*, edd. D.E. Evans *et al.* (Oxford 1986), pp. 91-107

LAPIDGE, Michael, & GNEUSS, H. (edd.) *Learning and Literature in Anglo-Saxon England. Studies presented to Peter Clemoes on the Occasion of his Sixty-fifth birthday* (Cambridge 1985)

LAPIDGE, M. (ed. & transl.) 'The Welsh-Latin poetry of Sulien's family', *Studia Celtica* 8/9 (1973/4) 68-106

LAPORTE, J. 'Étude d'authenticité des oeuvres attribuées à saint Colomban', *Revue Mabillon* 51 (1961) 35-46

LAWLOR, Hugh Jackson *Chapters on the Book of Mulling* (Edinburgh 1897)

LAWLOR, H.J. (ed.) 'The Cathach of St. Columba', *Proceedings of the Royal Irish Academy* 33 C (1916/17) 241-443

LAWLOR, Hugh Jackson (ed.) *The Rosslyn Missal: an Irish Manuscript in the Advocates' Library, Edinburgh* (London 1899)

LAWRENCE, C.H. (ed.) *The English Church and the Papacy in the Middle Ages* (London 1965)

LECLERCQ, H. 'Autel', in *Dictionnaire d'archéologie chrétienne et de liturgie*, edd. F. Cabrol *et al.* (15 vols in 30, Paris 1903-53), I.3155-87

LECLERCQ, H. 'Calice', in *Dictionnaire d'archéologie chrétienne et de liturgie*, edd. F. Cabrol *et al.* (15 vols in 30, Paris 1903-53), II.1525-1645

LECLERCQ, J., & ROCHAIS, H.M. (edd.) *Sancti Bernardi Opera* (8 vols, Roma 1963)

LESLEY, Alexander (ed.) *Missale Mixtum secundum regulam beati Isidori dictum Mozarabes* (Roma 1755)

LOTH, J. 'Bretons en Irlande', *Revue celtique* 28 (1907) 417

LOTH, J. 'Bretons insulaires en Irlande', *Revue celtique* 18 (1897) 304-9

LOWE, E.A. *Codices Latini Antiquiores. A Palaeographical Guide to Latin Manuscripts prior to the Ninth Century* (11 vols & suppl., Oxford 1934-71)

LOWE, E.A. (ed.) *The Bobbio Missal. A Gallican Mass-Book: MS Paris lat. 13246* (3 vols, London 1920-4)

LUCAS, A.T. 'The plundering and burning of churches in Ireland, 7th to 16th century', in *North Munster Studies*, ed. E. Rynne (Limerick 1967), pp. 172-229

LUFF, S.G.A. 'A survey of primitive monasticism in central Gaul (c. 300 to 700)', *Downside Review* 70 (1951/2) 180-203

LUFF, S.G.A. 'British monasticism and the "Laus Perennis"', *Pax* 43 (1953/4) 146-52

MABILLON, Jean (ed.) *Annales Ordinis S. Benedicti occidentalium monachorum patriarchae*, (6 vols, Paris 1703-39)

MAC AIRT, Seán, & MAC NIOCAILL, G. (edd. & transl.) *The Annals of Ulster (to A.D. 1131)* (2 parts, Dublin 1983–)

MACCARTHY, B. (ed.) 'On the Stowe Missal', *Transactions of the Royal Irish Academy* 27 (Polite Literature and Antiquities Section) (1877-86) 135-268

MCCONE, K. 'Brigit in the seventh century: a saint with three lives?', *Peritia* 1 (1982) 107-45

MCCORMICK, M. (ed.) 'Un fragment inédit de lectionnaire du viiie siècle', *Revue bénédictine* 86 (1976) 75-82

'MAC ECLAISE' (ed. & transl.) 'The Rule of St. Carthage', *Irish Ecclesiastical Record*, 4th S., 27 (1910) 495-517

MAC EOIN, G.S. 'Invocation of the forces of nature in the loricae', *Studia Hibernica* 2 (1962) 212-17

MCGURK, P. 'The Irish pocket gospel book', *Sacris Erudiri* 8 (1956) 249-71

MCKILLOP, S. 'A Romano-British baptismal liturgy?', in *The Early Church in Western Britain and Ireland*, ed. S.M. Pearce (Oxford 1982), pp. 35-48

MCMANUS, D. 'A chronology of the Latin loan-words in early Irish', *Ériu* 34 (1983) 21-72

MCNALLY, Robert [E.] (ed.) *Old Ireland* (Dublin 1965)

MCNALLY, R[obert] E. *The Bible in the Early Middle Ages* (Westminster, Md 1969)

MCNAMARA, M. 'A plea for Hiberno-Latin biblical studies', *Irish Theological Quarterly* 39 (1972) 339-53

MCNAMARA, Martin (ed.) *Biblical Studies: the Medieval Irish Contribution* (Dublin 1976)

MCNAMARA, M. 'Psalter text and psalter study in the early Irish Church (A.D. 600-1200)', *Proceedings of the Royal Irish Academy* 73 C (1973) 201-72

MCNAMARA, Martin *The Apocrypha in the Irish Church* (Dublin 1975)

MCNAMARA, M. 'Tradition and creativity in early Irish psalter study', in *Ireland and Europe: the Early Church*, edd. P. Ní Chatháin & M. Richter (Stuttgart 1984), pp. 338-89

MACNEILL, E. 'The beginnings of Latin culture in Ireland', *Studies* [Dublin] 20 (1931) 39-48 *and* 449-60

MACNEILL, E. 'The hymn of St. Secundinus in honour of St. Patrick', *Irish Historical Studies* 2 (1940/1) 129-53

MACQUEEN, John *St. Nynia. A Study of Literary and Linguistic Evidence* (Edinburgh 1961)

MCROBERTS, D. 'The ecclesiastical significance of the St Ninian's Isle treasure', *Proceedings of the Society of Antiquaries of Scotland* 94 (1960/1) 301-14

MANSI, J. (ed.) *Sacrorum conciliorum nova et amplissima collectio* (31 vols, Firenze 1759-98)

MARKUS, R.A. 'Pelagianism: Britain and the Continent' *Journal of Ecclesiastical History* 37 (1986) 191-204

MARTIMORT, A.-G. (ed.) *The Church at Prayer: Introduction to the Liturgy* (New York 1968)

MAYR-HARTING, Henry *The Coming of Christianity to Anglo-Saxon England* (London 1972)

MEARNS, J. (ed.) *The Canticles of the Christian Church, Eastern and Western, in Early and Medieval Times* (Cambridge 1914)

MEEHAN, Denis, & BIELER, L. (edd. & transl.) *Adamnan's* De Locis Sanctis (Dublin 1958)

METZ, René *La consécration des vierges dans l'église romaine: Étude d'histoire de la liturgie* (Paris 1954)

METZGER, Bruce M. *The Text of the New Testament: its Transmission, Corruption and Restoration* (2nd edn, Oxford 1968)

MEYER, Kuno (ed. & transl.) *Hibernica Minora, being a fragment of an Old-Irish Treatise on the Psalter with Translation, Notes and Glossary and an Appendix containing Extracts hitherto unpublished from MS Rawlinson, B. 512 in the Bodleian Library* (Oxford 1894)

MEYER, W. (ed.) 'Das turiner Bruchstück der ältesten irischen Liturgie', *Nachrichten von der königlich Gesellschaft der Wissenschaften zu Göttingen, phil.-hist. Klasse* (1903) 163-214

MICHELS, Thomas   *Beiträge zur Geschichte der Bischofsweihetages im christlichen Altertum und im Mittelalter* (Münster in Westfalen 1927)

MIGNE, J.-P. (ed.)   *Patrologiæ [graecæ] cursus completus...* (161 vols, Paris 1857-66)

MIGNE, J.-P. (ed.)   *Patrologiæ [latinæ] cursus completus...* (221 vols, Paris 1844-64)

MOHLBERG, Leo Cunibert (ed.)   *Die älteste erreichbare Gestalt des Liber Sacramentorum anni circuli der römischen Kirche (Cod. Padua D. 47)* (Münster in Westfalen 1927)

MOHLBERG, Leo Cunibert (ed.)   *Liber Sacramentorum Romanae Aeclesiae ordinis anni circuli (Cod. Vat. Reg. lat. 316, Paris Bibl. Nat. lat. 7193, 41/56) (Sacramentarium Gelasianum)* (Roma 1960)

MOHLBERG, Leo Cunibert (ed.)   *Missale Francorum (Vat. Reg. lat. 257)* (Roma 1957)

MOHLBERG, Leo Cunibert (ed.)   *Missale Gallicanum Vetus (Cod. Vat. Palat. lat. 491)* (Roma 1953)

MOHLBERG, Leo Cunibert (ed.)   *Missale Gothicum (Vat. Reg. lat. 317)* (Roma 1961)

MOHLBERG, Leo Cunibert, *et al.* (edd.)   *Sacramentarium Veronense (Cod. Bibl. Capit. Veron. LXXXV [80])* (Roma 1956)

MOHRMANN, Christine   *Liturgical Latin: its Origins and Character* (London 1957)

MOONEY, Canice   *The Church in Gaelic Ireland: Thirteenth to Fifteenth Centuries* (Dublin 1969)

MORETON, Bernard   *The Eighth-century Gelasian Sacramentary: a Study in Tradition* (Oxford 1976)

MUNIER, C. (ed.)   *Concilia Africae, A. 345 - A. 525* (Turnhout 1974)

MUNIER, C. (ed.)   *Concilia Galliae, A. 314 - A. 506* (Turnhout 1963)

MURPHY, Gerard   *Early Irish Metrics* (Dublin 1961)

MURPHY, T.A.   'The oldest eucharistic hymn', *Irish Ecclesiastical Record*, 5th S., 46 (1935) 172-6

NASH-WILLIAMS, V.E.   *The Early Christian Monuments of Wales* (Cardiff 1950)

NEALE, J.M., & FORBES, G.H. (edd.)   *The Ancient Liturgies of the Gallican Church; now first collected with an Introductory Dissertation, Notes, and Various Readings, together with Parallel Passages from the Roman, Ambrosian and Mozarabic Rites* (Burntisland 1855-67)

NÍ CHATHÁIN, Próinséas, & RICHTER, M. (edd.)   *Ireland and Europe: the Early Church* (Stuttgart 1984)

NÍ CHATHÁIN, P.   'The liturgical background of the Derrynavlan altar service', *Journal of the Royal Society of Antiquaries of Ireland* 110

(1980) 127-48

NORBERG, Dag   *Introduction à l'étude de la versification latine médiévale* (Stockholm 1958)

NORBERG, D.   'Le vers accentuel en bas-latin', *Mélanges offerts à Mlle. Christine Mohrmann*, anon. ed. (Utrecht 1963), pp. 121-6

O'CARROLL, J.   'Monastic rules in Merovingian Gaul', *Studies* [Dublin] 42 (1953) 407-19

Ó CORRÁIN, D., *et al.*   'The laws of the Irish', *Peritia* 3 (1984) 382-438

Ó CRÓINÍN, D.   'Mo-Sinnu moccu Min and the computus of Bangor', *Peritia* 1 (1982) 281-95

Ó CRÓINÍN, D.   'Pride and prejudice', *Peritia* 1 (1982) 352-62

Ó CRÓINÍN, D.   'The oldest Irish names for the days of the week?', *Ériu* 32 (1981) 95-114

Ó CUÍV, Brian (ed.)   *Proceedings of the International Congress of Celtic Studies held in Dublin 6-10 July, 1959* (Dublin 1962)

Ó FIAICH, T.   'The Church of Armagh under lay control', *Seanchas Ard Mhacha* 5 (1969/70) 75-127

O'MEARA, John J., & NAUMANN, B. (edd.)   *Latin Script and Letters A.D. 400-900. Festschrift presented to Ludwig Bieler on the Occasion of his 70th Birthday* (Leiden 1976)

OLDEN, T.   'On the Culebath', *Proceedings of the Royal Irish Academy* 2 C (1879-88) 355-8

O NEILL, J. (ed.)   'The Rule of Ailbe of Emly', *Ériu* 3 (1903) 92-115

Ó NÉILL, P.   '*Romani* influences on seventh-century Hiberno-Latin literature', in *Ireland and Europe: the Early Church* edd. P. Ní Chatháin & M. Richter (Stuttgart 1984), pp. 280-90

Ó NÉILL, P.   'The Old Irish Treatise on the Psalter', *Ériu* 30 (1979) 148-64

Ó RIAIN, P.   'St. Finnbarr: a study in a cult', *Journal of the Cork Historical and Archaeological Society* 82 (1977) 63-82

Ó RÍORDÁIN, S.P.   'Roman material in Ireland', *Proceedings of the Royal Irish Academy* 51 C (1945-8) 35-82

PAINTER, K.S.   *The Water Newton Early Christian Silver* (London 1977)

PEARCE, Susan M. (ed.)   *The Early Church in Western Britain and Ireland. Studies presented to C.A. Ralegh Radford, arising from a Conference organised in his Honour by the Devon Archaeological Society and Exeter City Museum* (Oxford 1982)

PEPPERDENE, M.W.   'Baptism in the early British and Irish Churches', *Irish Theological Quarterly* 22 (1955) 110-23

PETSCHENIG, M. (ed.)   *Iohannis Cassiani Conlationes XXIIII* (Wien 1886)

PETSCHENIG, M. (ed.)   *Iohannis Cassiani de Institutis Coenobiorum et De Octo Principalium Vitiorum Remediis Libri XII, De Incarnatione Domini contra Nestorium Libri VII* (Wien 1888)

PFAFF, Richard W.   *Medieval Latin Liturgy. A Select Bibliography* (Toronto 1982)

PHILLIMORE, E. (ed.)   'The *Annales Cambriæ* and Old Welsh Genealogies, from *Harleian MS.* 3859', *Y Cymmrodor* 9 (1888) 141-83

PLAINE, F.B. (ed.)   'Vita Antiqua Sancti Samsonis Dolensis episcopi', *Analecta Bollandiana* 6 (1887) 77-150

PLAINE, F.B. (ed.)   'Vita Sancti Pauli Episcopi Leonensis in Brittannia Minori auctore Wormonoco', *Analecta Bollandiana* 1 (1882) 208-58

PLUMMER, C.   'On two collections of Latin Lives of Irish saints in the Bodleian Library, Rawl. B. 485 and Rawl. B. 505', *Zeitschrift für celtische Philologie* 5 (1905/6) 429-81

PLUMMER, C.   'Some new light on the Brendan legend', *Zeitschrift für celtische Philologie* 5 (1905/6) 124-41

PLUMMER, Charles (ed.)   *Venerabilis Baedae Opera Historica* (2 vols, Oxford 1896)

PLUMMER, Charles (ed.)   *Vitae Sanctorum Hiberniae partim hactenus ineditae* (2 vols, Oxford 1910; rev. imp., 1968)

PORTER, H.B.   *The Ordination Prayers of the Ancient Western Churches* (London 1967)

PRINZ, Friedrich   *Frühes Mönchtum im Frankenreich: Kultur und Gesellschaft in Gallien, der Rheinlanden und Bayern am Beispeil der monastischen Entwicklung (4. bis 8. Jahrhundert)* (München 1965)

QUASTEN, J.   'Oriental influences in the Gallican liturgy', *Traditio* 1 (1943) 55-78

QUIGLEY, E.J.   'The Clones Missal', *Irish Ecclesiastical Record*, 5th S., 17 (1921) 381-9, 496-503, 603-9

QUIN, E.G. (gen. ed.)   *Dictionary of the Irish Language, based mainly on Old and Middle Irish Materials* (Dublin 1913-76)

RADFORD, C.A.R.   'The portable altar', in *The Relics of Saint Cuthbert*, ed. C.F. Battiscombe (Oxford 1956), pp. 326-35

RAFTERY, J.   'Ex oriente...', *Journal of the Royal Society of Antiquaries of Ireland* 95 (1965) 193-204

RATCLIFF, E.C. (ed.)   *Expositio Antiquae Liturgiae Gallicanae* (London 1971)

RATTI, A., & MAGISTRETTI, M. (edd.)   *Missale Ambrosianum duplex (proprium de tempore) editt. Puteobenellianae et typicae (1751-1902) cum critico commentario continuo ex manuscriptis schedis aut. M. Ceriani* (Milano 1913)

REEVES, William   *The Culdees of the British Islands, as they appear in History* (Dublin 1864)

REEVES, William (ed.)   *The Life of St. Columba, Founder of Hy; Written by Adamnan, Ninth Abbot of That Monastery. The Text Printed from a Manuscript of the Eighth Century; with the Various Readings of Six Other Manuscripts preserved in Different Parts of Europe. To which are added, Copious Notes and Dissertations, Illustrative of the Early History of the Columbian Institutions in Ireland and Scotland* (Dublin 1857)

REYNOLDS, R.E.   'Virgines subintroductae in Celtic christianity', *Harvard Theological Review* 61 (1968) 547-66

RICHARDSON, H.   'Derrynavlan and other early Church treasures', *Journal of the Royal Society of Antiquaries of Ireland* 110 (1980) 92-115

RICHÉ, P.   'Columbanus, his followers and the Merovingian Church', in *Columbanus and Merovingian Monasticism*, edd. H.B. Clarke & M. Brennan (Oxford 1981), pp. 59-72

ROUSSEAU, P.   'The spiritual authority of the "monk-bishop": Eastern elements in some Western hagiography of the fourth and fifth centuries', *Journal of Theological Studies*, N.S., 22 (1971) 380-419

ROWLAND, Beryl (ed.)   *Chaucer and Middle English Studies in Honour of Rossell Hope Robbins* (London 1974)

RYAN, John   *Irish Monasticism: its Origins and Early Development* (Dublin 1931; 2nd edn, Shannon 1972)

RYAN, J.   'The Church at the end of the sixth century', *Irish Ecclesiastical Record*, 5th S., 75 (1951) 17-29

RYAN, M.   'The Derrynaflan and other early Irish eucharistic chalices: some speculations', in *Ireland and Europe: the Early Church*, edd. P. Ní Chatháin & M. Richter (Stuttgart 1984), pp. 135-48

RYAN, Michael (ed.)   *The Derrynaflan Hoard, 1: a Preliminary Account* (Dublin 1983)

RYNNE, Etienne (ed.)   *North Munster Studies. Essays in Commemoration of Monsignior Michael Moloney* (Limerick 1967)

SABATIER, Petrus (ed.)   *Bibliorum Sacrorum Versiones Antiquae* (3 vols Reims, 1743)

SALMON, Pierre   *L'Office divin au moyen âge: histoire de la formation du brévaire du ixe au xvie siècle* (Paris 1967)

SANDAY, W., et al. (edd.) *Portions of the Gospels according to St. Mark and St. Matthew* (Oxford 1886)

SCHALLER, Dieter, & KÖNSGEN, E.   *Initia Carminum Latinorum Saeculo Undecimo Antiquiorum* (Göttingen 1977)

SCHLEGEL, Ursula, & VON MANTEUFFEL, C.Z. (edd.)   *Festschrift für Peter Metz* (Berlin 1965)

SCHNEIDER, Heinrich   *Die altlateinischen biblischen Cantica* (Beuron 1938)

SELMER, Carl (ed.)   *Navigatio Sancti Brendani Abbatis from Early Latin Manuscripts* (Notre Dame, Ind. 1959)

SHARPE, R.   'Armagh and Rome in the seventh century', in *Ireland and Europe: the Early Church*, edd. P. Ní Chatháin & M. Richter (Stuttgart 1984), pp. 58-72

SHARPE, R.   'Gildas as a Father of the Church', in *Gildas: New Approaches*, edd. M. Lapidge & D. Dumville (Woodbridge 1984), pp. 193-205

SHARPE, R.   'Hiberno-Latin *laicus*, Irish *láech* and the devil's men', *Ériu* 30 (1979) 75-92

SHARPE, R.   'Some problems concerning the organization of the Church in early medieval Ireland', *Peritia* 3 (1984) 230-70

SHARPE, R.   'St Patrick and the see of Armagh', *Cambridge Medieval Celtic Studies* 4 (1982) 33-59

SHARPE, R.   '*Vitae S Brigitae*: the oldest texts', *Peritia* 1 (1982) 81-106

SHEEHY, M.P.   'Concerning the origin of early mediaeval Irish monasticism', *Irish Theological Quarterly* 29 (1962) 136-44

SIMS-WILLIAMS, P.   'Thought, word and deed: an Irish triad', *Ériu* 29 (1978) 78-111

SIMS-WILLIAMS, P.   'Thoughts on Ephrem the Syrian in Anglo-Saxon England', in *Learning and Literature in Anglo-Saxon England*, edd. M. Lapidge & H. Gneuss (Cambridge 1985), pp. 205-26

SLOVER, C.H.   'Early literary channels between Britain and Ireland', *University of Texas Bulletin: Studies in English* 6 (1926) 5-52 *and* 7 (1927) 5-111

SMALL, Alan, *et al.*   *St. Ninian's Isle and its Treasure* (2 vols, London 1973)

SMIT, Johannes Wilhelmus   *Studies in the Language and Style of Columba the Younger (Columbanus)* (Amsterdam 1971)

SMYTH, Alfred P.   *Celtic Leinster. Towards an Historical Geography of Early Irish Civilization A.D. 500-1600* (Blackrock 1982)

SOUTER, Alexander (ed.)   *Pelagius's Expositions of Thirteen Epistles of St. Paul* (3 vols, Cambridge 1922-31)

SOUTER, A.   'The character and history of Pelagius' Commentary on the Epistles of St. Paul', *Proceedings of the British Academy* 7 (1915/16) 261-96

STENZEL, Alois   *Die Taufe. Eine genetische erklärung der Taufliturgie* (Innsbrück 1957)

STOKES, Whitley (ed. & transl.)   *Félire Húi Gormáin: the Martyrology of*

Gorman, edited from a Manuscript in the Royal Library, Brussels (London 1895)

STOKES, Whitley (ed. & transl.) *Félire Óengusso Céli Dé. The Martyrology of Oengus the Culdee, critically edited from Ten Manuscripts* (London 1905)

STOKES, Whitley (ed. & transl.) *The Tripartite Life of Patrick, with Other Documents Relating to that Saint* (2 vols, London 1887)

TANGL, Michael (ed.) *Die Briefe des heiligen Bonifatius und Lullus* (Berlin 1916)

THOMAS, Charles *Christianity in Roman Britain to A.D. 500* (London 1981)

THOMAS, C. 'East and West: Tintagel, Mediterranean imports and the early Insular Church', in *The Early Church in Western Britain and Ireland*, ed. S.M. Pearce (Oxford 1982), pp. 17-34

THOMAS, C. 'Imported Late-Roman Mediterranean pottery in Ireland and western Britain: chronologies and implications', *Proceedings of the Royal Irish Academy* 76 C (1976) 245-54

THOMAS, C. 'Rosnat, Rostat and the early Irish Church', *Ériu* 22 (1971) 100-06

THOMAS, Charles *The Early Christian Archaeology of North Britain* (London 1971)

THOMPSON, E.A. 'Britonia', in *Christianity in Britain, 300-700*, edd. M.W. Barley & R.P.C. Hanson (Leicester 1958), pp. 201-6

THOMPSON, E.A. 'Christianity and the Northern barbarians', *Nottingham Mediaeval Studies* 1 (1957) 3-21

THOMPSON, E.A. *Saint Germanus of Auxerre and the End of Roman Britain* (Woodbridge 1984)

THOMPSON, E.A. 'St. Patrick and Coroticus', *Journal of Theological Studies*, N.S., 31 (1980) 12-27

THOMPSON, E.A. 'The origins of christianity in Scotland', *Scottish Historical Review* 37 (1958) 17-22

THOMPSON, T. *The Offices of Baptism and Confirmation* (Cambridge 1914)

TOYNBEE, J.M.C. 'Pagan motifs and practices in christian art and ritual in Roman Britain', in *Christianity in Britain, 300-700*, edd. M.W. Barley & R.P.C. Hanson (Leicester 1968), pp. 177-92

TRAVIS, James *Early Celtic Versecraft* (Shannon 1973)

VAN DIJK, S.P. 'The urban and papal rites in seventh- and eighth-century Rome', *Sacris Erudiri* 12 (1961) 411-87

VERHEIJEN, Lucas (ed.) *Augustini Confessiones* (Turnhout 1981)

VISMANS, T.A., & BRINKHOFF, L. *Critical Bibliography of Liturgical*

Literature (Nijmegen 1961)

VOGEL, Cyrille   *Introduction aux sources de l'histoire du culte chrétien au moyen âge* (Spoleto 1966)

VOGEL, C.   'La réforme liturgique sous Charlemagne', in *Karl der Grosse: Lebenswerk und Nachleben*, ed. W. Braunfels (5 vols, Düsseldorf 1965-8), II.217-32

WALKER, G.S.M., & BIELER, L. (edd. & transl.)   *Sancti Columbani Opera* (Dublin 1957)

WALL, J.   'Christian evidences in the Roman period', *Archaeologia Aeliana*, 4th S., 43 (1965) 201-26 *and* 44 (1966) 147-64

WALLACE-HADRILL, J.M.   *The Frankish Church* (Oxford 1983)

WALPOLE, A.S. (ed.)   *Early Latin Hymns* (Cambridge 1922)

WARNER, G.F. (ed.)   *The Stowe Missal: MS D.II.3 in the Library of the Royal Irish Academy, Dublin* (2 vols, London 1915)

WARREN, F.E.   'An early Irish liturgical fragment', *Journal of Theological Studies* 4 (1902/3) 610-13

WARREN, F.E. (ed.)   *The Antiphonary of Bangor* (2 vols, London 1893)

WARREN, F.E.   *The Liturgy and Ritual of the Celtic Church* (Oxford 1881)

WARREN, F.E. (ed.)   *The Manuscript Irish Missal belonging to the President and Fellows of Corpus Christi College, Oxford* (London 1879)

WASSERSCHLEBEN, H. (ed.)   *Die irische Kanonensammlung* (2nd edn, Leipzig 1885)

WATT, John   *The Church in Medieval Ireland* (Dublin 1972)

WEBER, R. (ed.)   *Biblia Sacra iuxta Vulgatam Versionem* (2nd edn, 2 vols, Stuttgart 1975)

WEST, R.C.   *Western Liturgies* (London 1928)

WHITAKER, E.C. (transl.)   *Documents of the Baptismal Liturgy* (London 1960)

WHITELOCK, Dorothy, *et al.* (edd.)   *Ireland in Early Mediaeval Europe. Studies in Memory of Kathleen Hughes* (Cambridge 1982)

WILDE, W.R.   'Description of an ancient Irish shrine, called the "Mias Tighearnain"', *Transactions of the Royal Irish Academy* 21 (1848), [Section C:] Antiquities, pp. 16-19

WILLIAMS, Hugh   *Christianity in Early Britain* (Oxford 1912)

WILLIAMS, Hugh (ed. & transl.)   *Gildae De Excidio Britanniae, Fragmenta, Liber de Paenitentia. Accedit et Lorica Gildae* (2 vols, London 1899/1901)

WILMART, A.   'L'âge et l'ordre des Messes de Mone', *Revue bénédictine* 28 (1911) 377-90

WINTERBOTTOM, Michael (ed. & transl.)   *Gildas: The Ruin of Britain and Other Works* (Chichester 1978)

WOOD, I.   'A prelude to Columbanus: the monastic achievement in the Burgundian territories', in *Columbanus and Merovingian Monasticism*, edd. H.B. Clarke & M. Brennan (Oxford 1981), pp. 3-32

WORDSWORTH, Christopher (ed.)   *The New Testament of Our Lord and Saviour Jesus Christ in the Original Greek, With Notes and Introduction* (2nd edn, 2 vols, Oxford 1880-6), with new edn. of Vol I 'with the editor's latest revisions' (Oxford 1886/7)

YOUNG, Karl   *The Drama of the Medieval Church* (2 vols, Oxford 1933)

ZIMMER, H.   'Über direkte Handelsverbindungen Westgalliens mit Irland im Altertum und frühen Mittelalter', *Sitzungsberichte der königlich preussischen Akademie der Wissenschaften* (1909) 363-400, 430-76, 543-613, *and* (1910) 1031-1119

The Liturgy and Ritual of the Celtic Church

F.E. Warren

...factus est qui propter nos homines et propter
nostram salutem descendit de caelo et
incarnatus est de spiritu sancto ex maria virgine
et homo natus est Crucifixus spiritus pro nobis sub
pontio pilato passus et sepultus et resurrexit tertia die secundum scripturas et ascendit
celos et sedit ad dexteram dei patris et iterum
venturus gloria iudicare vivos et mortuos cuius regni non erit finis et spiritum sanctum
et unum statum regni sed patris filii procedentem
patris et filio simul coadorandum et conglorificandum
dum qui loquitur per prophetas et unam sanctam catholicam
catholicam et apostolicam Confiteor unum

THE

LITURGY AND RITUAL

OF THE

CELTIC CHURCH

BY

F. E. WARREN, B.D.

FELLOW OF ST. JOHN'S COLLEGE, OXFORD

Oxford

AT THE CLARENDON PRESS

M DCCC LXXXI

Qualis fuerit apud Britones et Hibernos sacrificandi ritus non plane compertum est. Modum tamen illum a Romano divisum exstitisse intelligitur ex Bernardo in libro de vita Malachiae cc. iii, viii, ubi Malachias barbaras consuetudines Romanis mutasse, et canonicum divinae laudis officium in illas ecclesias invexisse memoratur.

Mabillon, De Lit. Gall. lib. i. cap. ii. § 14.

Hactenus lyturgia Scottica typis vulgata non habetur ; et Britanniae virorum doctorum esset, fragmenta ritus Scottici, circumquaque dispersa, colligere et illustrare.

C. Purton Cooper's (intended) Report on Foedera, Appendix A, p. 94.

CONTENTS.

CHAPTER III.

PREFACE.

THE following pages contain an account of the Liturgy and Ritual of the Celtic Church in these islands, so far as their character can be ascertained from the limited sources of information open to us. They relate to a subject about which, until recently, very little was known. The great continental Liturgiologists of the seventeenth and eighteenth centuries were either silent about it, or dismissed it as offering no data for information and no materials for investigation. Mabillon wrote: 'Qualis fuerit apud Britonos et Hibernos sacrificandi ritus, non plane compertum est. Modum tamen illum a Romano diversum exstitisse intelligitur ex Bernardo in libro de vita Malachiae, capitibus iii et viii, ubi Malachias barbaras consuetudines Romanis mutasse, et canonicum divinae laudis officium in illas ecclesias invexisse memoratur.'—De Liturgia Gallicana, lib. i. c. ii. § 14. Gerbert wrote: 'In dubio est qui et qualis antiquitus ea in orbis plaga fuerit ordo operis Dei.'—Lit. Aleman. i. 76.

In more recent times Dr. Lingard has disclaimed all possibility of any knowledge of the subject: 'Whether the sacrificial service of the Scottish missionaries varied from that of the Romans we have no means of judging.'—Anglo-Saxon Church, edit. 1858, vol. i. p. 271.

Sir W. Palmer in his Origines Liturgicae (i. 176–189) devoted one short chapter to the Liturgy of the Celtic Church, which consisted largely of guesses and of the repetition at secondhand of statements which he was unable to verify, but which, were he to write now, he would either

abandon or modify. Within the last few years extensive
additions have been made to the scanty materials available to
Sir W. Palmer in 1839, in some instances by the discovery,
in other instances by the publication for the first time, of
various ancient Irish and Scottish liturgical fragments; by
the printing of certain important Celtic manuscripts; by
the collection in palæographical and archæological volumes
of the representations in Celtic illuminated MSS.; by the
examination of architectural remains, and of stonework inscriptions and designs.

The sources from which the information contained in the
present volume has been drawn are chiefly the following:

(*a*) Scattered notices in the works of contemporary writers;
viz. fifth century, Fastidius, Patricius, Secundinus; sixth
century, Columba, Fiacc, Gildas; seventh century, Cuminius
Albus, Adamnanus, Columbanus. Bachiarius and Sedulius
are omitted from this list, in consequence of the uncertainty
attaching to their date and nationality. Non-Celtic authors,
e. g. Alcuin, Bede, Bernard of Clairvaux, Jonas, Walafrid
Strabo, &c., have been frequently referred to.

(*b*) Scattered notices in Celtic MSS., viz. Catalogus Sanctorum Hiberniae, Leabhar Breac, Sinodus Hibernensis, Senchus Mor, &c.

(*c*) Fragments of the ancient Celtic Liturgy surviving in
the Stowe (ninth century), Drummond (eleventh century), and
Corpus (twelfth century) Irish Missals; in the Books of Mulling (seventh century), Dimma (seventh century), Deer (ninth
century), Armagh (ninth century); in Irish MSS. on the
Continent, Nos. 1394 and 1395 (ninth century) at St. Gall,
and the Antiphonarium Benchorense (eighth century) at
Milan, and in a few other MSS. enumerated in Chapter iii.

(*d*) Illuminations in Celtic manuscripts, which have lately
become accessible to the untravelled student in the magnifi-

cent volumes of Professor Westwood, Mr. Gilbert, and the late Dr. Todd.

(*e*) Architectural remains of churches, sepulchral inscriptions, sculptured crosses, carved or engraved book-covers, caskets, pastoral staves, bells, chalices, spoons, and other ecclesiastical relics.

In drawing information from such various quarters the author can hardly hope to have escaped all errors of detail, and not to have hazarded some conjectures which will be criticised, and to have drawn some conclusions which will be disputed.

A certain element of incompleteness is still inevitable in the treatment of this subject from the state of a part of the material from which our knowledge is derived. Some important Irish manuscripts, as the Stowe Missal, &c., have never been published ; others, as the Leabhar Breac, &c., have been published in facsimile, without note or comment, and need the editorial explanations of some one who is at once an antiquarian, an ecclesiastical historian, and a palæographer, in order to assign their date and value to the historical, ecclesiastical, and liturgical tracts of which they are composed[1]. There is a vast amount of unsifted and undated, or erroneously dated, material preserved in various collections, especially in the Bollandists' edition of the Acta Sanctorum. Much of it might be useful for illustration in matters of detail, even where it could in no sense be relied upon as historical. But until some discriminating hagiologist shall have undertaken the laborious task of visiting the various European libraries, and critically examining the original MSS. from which such Lives are drawn, and publishing the

---

[1] Since this sentence was written one of the most important of these documents, the Félire of Oengus, has been edited by Mr. Whitley Stokes, with a translation and complete apparatus criticus. Transactions of R. I. A., June, 1880.

result of such investigations, they must be regarded as more likely to mislead than to inform. Occasional reference has been made to a very few of these biographies, viz. those of Cogitosus, Ultan, St. Evin, &c., which have been passed and repassed through the crucible of modern criticism, and the evidential value of which it has therefore been possible approximately to ascertain. The general importance of this hagiologic literature has been discussed by the late Sir Thomas Duffus Hardy, in his Preface to the Rerum Britannicarum medii aevi Scriptores (pp. 18–20), a work which includes a dated catalogue of all the MS. material accessible in Great Britain; and, so far as Ireland and Scotland are concerned, by Mr. Skene (Celtic Scotland, ii. cap. x, and Chronicles of the Picts and Scots, Preface). Its value for liturgical illustration is diminished by the fact that it all belongs to a period subsequent to the conformity of the Celtic Church to the Church of Rome. This appears plainly on the face of such unhistorical passages as the following in Ultan's Life of St. Bridget. The author thus describes her dream and consequent action: 'In urbe Romana juxta corpora Petri et Pauli audivi missas; et nimis desidero ut ad me istius ordo et universa regula feratur a Roma. Tunc misit Brigida viros sapientes et detulerunt inde missas et regulam.'—Cap. 91. The introduction of the Roman Liturgy into the Irish Church is antedated in this passage by many centuries. Its historical value is equal to that of the next chapter, which describes St. Bridget hanging her clothes to dry on a sunbeam.

A part of Chapter ii has previously appeared in the form of an article in the *Church Quarterly Review* (vol. x. p. 50), and a part of Chapter iii in letters to the Editor of the *Academy*.

Latin authorities have been frequently quoted *in extenso*.

Gaelic authorities have merely been referred to. Long passages in the ancient dialects of Ireland, Scotland, and Wales would have added considerably to the bulk of the volume, and would have been unintelligible to the majority of readers.

The retention of an original orthography will explain the occasional occurrence of such forms as 'sinodus,' 'imnus,' 'cremen,' &c., for 'synodus,' 'hymnus,' 'crimen,' &c. The retention of a popular nomenclature will account for such forms as Charlemagne, Iona, &c., instead of Karl the Great, Hi, &c.

It would not be possible to compile such a volume as the present one without being largely beholden to the labours of other writers. The source of information has been generally indicated in foot-notes, but in case of accidental omission the author begs once for all to express his indebtedness to such recently deceased writers as Dr. Todd, Mr. Haddan, and Bishop Forbes, and to such living writers as Professor Stubbs, Mr. Skene, and Dr. Reeves, from whose edition of Adamnan's Life of St. Columba, as from a rich quarry, a knowledge of many facts recorded in this volume has been obtained. It is doubtful whether in the annals of literature so much important information has ever before been so lavishly accumulated and so skilfully arranged within a few hundred pages, or whether any other editorial task has ever been more thoroughly executed.

The author also begs to express his thanks to the Earl of Ashburnham for his kind permission to inspect and copy out the liturgical portion of the MS. volume known as the Stowe Missal, and to Professor Rhŷs, Mr. Whitley Stokes, Professor Westwood, and Mr. Henry Bradshaw for their kindly-afforded assistance in linguistic and palæographical questions respectively.

AUTHORITIES CITED.

[This list is not exhaustive. It only includes certain well-known works, to which frequent reference has been made, in the case of which it seemed desirable to specify once for all the edition made use of; and certain less-known works, to which occasional reference has been made, and to which it seemed desirable to append the date of their composition, and of the earliest MS. authority.]

Adamnani Canones : see Canones.

Adamnani Vita S. Columbae. The Latin text, taken from an early eighth-century MS. at Schaffhausen, was published with copious notes by Dr. Reeves at Dublin, 1857. Adamnan was the ninth presbyter-abbot of Iona, A.D. 679–704. Rolls Series, Descriptive Catalogue, vol. i. pt. i. p. 167.

Antiphonarium Benchorense. A seventh-century MS. originally belonging to the monastery of Bangor, county Down. It is proved from internal evidence to have been written A.D. 680–691, during the life-time of Abbot Cronan. It is now preserved in the Ambrosian Library at Milan. It has been printed in Muratori's Anecdota Bibliothecae Ambrosianae, vol. iv. pp. 121–159 ; Migne, Patrol. Curs. Lat. lxxii. 582 ; Ulster Journal of Archaeology, 1853, pp. 168-179.

Archaeologia : London, from 1770.

Archaeologia Cambrensis : London, from 1846.

Archaeologia Scotica : Edinburgh, from 1792.

B = British Martyrology : London, 1761.

Bedae Historia Ecclesiastica : edited by G. H. Moberly, Oxford, 1869. Rolls Series, Descriptive Catalogue, vol. i. pt. i. p. 433.

Bernardi de Vita Malachiae Liber: fol. Paris, 1586. Rolls Series, Descriptive Catalogue, vol. ii. p. 236.

Betham, Sir W., Irish Antiquarian Researches : Dublin, 1827.

Black Book of Caermarthen: a twelfth-century Welsh MS. (A.D. 1154–1189), published in Skene's (W. F.) Four Ancient Books of Wales, Edinburgh, 1868.

Blight, J. T., Ancient Crosses and other Antiquities in the East of Cornwall : London, 1858.

Book of Armagh : in Trinity College, Dublin, written by Ferdomnach A.D. 807. The evidence for this date, together with a description of the contents of this MS., is given in the Nat. MSS. of Ireland, part i. p. xiv.

Book of Deer : see p. 163.

Book of Dimma : see p. 167.

Book of Hymns : see Liber Hymnorum.

Book of Mulling : see p. 171.

Book of Obits : a fifteenth-century MS. in Trinity College, Dublin, published by Irish Arch. Soc. Dublin, 1844.

Borlase, W. C., The Age of the Saints (Cornish): Truro, 1878.

Bright, W., Early English Church History: Oxford, 1878.

Canones Adamnani: MS. Codex Paris, 3182; saec. xi; printed in Wasser-schleben, Bussordnung. der Abendländ. Kirche, p. 120.

Canones S. Patricii: Irish Canons, (1) Sinodi episcoporum, Patricii Auxilii, Isernini, (2) two single Canons attributed to St. Patrick, (3) Canones secundae S. Patricii sinodi, all erroneously so attributed, and to be referred in their present form to a date A.D. 716–807. Printed in H. and S. vol. ii. pt. ii. p. 328.

Canones Wallici belonging to the period A.D. 550–650; MS. Cod. Paris. S. Germani, 121, saec. viii. Printed in H. and S. i. 127.

Catalogus Sanctorum Hiberniae: traditionally believed to have been composed by Tirechan c. 650, and certainly not later than the middle of the eighth century. Printed by Archbp. Ussher, De Brit. Eccles. Prim. cap. xvii, from two MSS. of which he does not give the date. H. and S. vol. ii. pt. ii. p. 292.

Codex MS. Vetustissimus. A document containing information about the British Liturgy, assigned by Spelman to the ninth century on palaeo-graphical grounds, but proved on internal evidence to have been written in the eighth century. Printed in H. and S. i. 138.

Cogitosi Vita S. Brigidae: printed in Colgan, Trias. Thaum. pp. 518–26. The date of this work is discussed in the Transactions of the Royal Irish Acad. vol. xx. pp. 195–205. The earliest MS. authority for it belongs to the middle of the ninth century. Cogitosus has been identified with the father of Muirchu Macumactheni (ob. A.D. 699); therefore the work must originally have been written c. A.D. 650, unless Mr. Skene is right in his conjecture, that the work has been fathered on Cogitosus, and erroneously assigned to the seventh century (Celtic Scotland, ii. 296); a conjecture supported by internal evidence, see p. 90. Rolls Series, Descriptive Catalogue, i. 106.

Colgan, J., Acta Sanctorum veteris et majoris Scotiae seu Hiberniae: Lovanii, 1645.

Colgan, J., Triadis Thaumaturgae Acta: Lovanii, 1647.

Columbae: Regula, vide Rule; Hymnus, 'Altus Prosator' in Liber Hymnorum, p. 201; Leabhar Breac, 237, col. 1.

Columbani Opera: quoted from Fleming's Collectan. Sacra, printed by him 'ex antiquis monasterii Bobiensis monumentis.'

Cooper, C. Purton: Appendix A, B, C, D, E to intended Report on Foedera, in three vols. printed 1837, published, but not publicly circulated, by the Record Office, 1869.

Corpus Missal = Missale Vetus Hibernicum, q. v.

Culdees: *see* Rule of.

Cuminii De mensura Poenitentiarum, or Poenitentiale. It is doubtful how far this work retains its original Scottish form. Wasserschleben considers that it has so far lost it as to rank it among Frankish rather than Celtic Penitentials. Haddan and Stubbs (Introd. p. xii) incline to consider it the work of a Bishop Cummian at Bobbio, A.D. 711–744. It may how-ever be regarded as founded upon an earlier Celtic work. References are made to Fleming's Collectan. Sacra, p. 197, by whom it was printed from a St. Gall MS., No. 550.

Cuminii Albi (*or* Cummenei, *or* Cumeani), Vita S. Columbae : written by
Cummene Ailbhe, son of Ernan, seventh presbyter-abbot of Iona, A. D.
657–669. The reference, unless otherwise specified, is to Pinkerton's
edit. Rolls Series, Descriptive Catalogue, i. 166.

Cumming, J. G., Runic and other Monumental Remains in the Isle of Man :
London, 1857.

D. = Martyrology of Donegal, q. v.

Descriptive Catalogue of the Materials relating to the History of Great Britain
and Ireland, by T. Duffus Hardy : Rolls Series, London, 1862.

Döllinger, J. von, Geschichte der christlichen Kirche : Landshut, 1833.

Dunraven, Lord, Irish Architectural Antiquities : edited by Margaret Stokes,
London, 1878.

Evin, St., Vita S. Patricii : a ninth, tenth, or eleventh century compilation
(Skene's Celtic Scotland, ii. 442 ; Chron. of Picts and Scots, Pref. xxix),
known as the Tripartite Life of St. Patrick, attributed to his disciple St.
Evin in the sixth century, by whom it was supposed to have been written
partly in Irish and partly in Latin. Translated in Colgan, Trias Thaum.
pp. 117–169, from three Irish MSS. which cannot now be with certainty
identified. Rolls Series, Descriptive Catalogue, i. 65.

F. = Félire of Oengus, q. v.

Fastidii De Vita Christiana Liber unus : addressed by Fastidius, Bishop of
London in the fifth century, to a widow named Fatalis. This book bears
internal marks of genuineness, and is no doubt the work alluded to by
Gennadius of Marseilles writing at the end of the fifth century. 'Fastidius
Britanniarum Episcopus scripsit ad Fatalem (quendam) de Vita Christiana
librum unum, et alium de viduitate servanda, sana et Deo digna doctrina.'
Gennadius (c. 458), De Viris Illustr. in Hieron. Opp. v. 39. Bened. It
has been printed by Migne, Patrol. Curs. Lat. vol. l. p. 385; Galland.
Bib. Vet. Pat. ix. 481.

Félire of Oengus : a metrical account of the festivals of the Church, attributed to Oengus the Culdee in the beginning of the ninth century, but
certainly written after A.D. 982, preserved in the Leabhar Breac, and in six
other MSS. of which an account is given by Mr. Whitley Stokes (pp. 2-6).
It is described in E. O'Curry's Lectures on MS. Materials of Ancient Irish
History (pp. 364–71), and has recently been published by Mr. Whitley
Stokes with translation and glossary in the Transactions of the Royal
Irish Academy, Irish MS. Ser. vol. i. part 1, June, 1880. Arabic
numerals refer to pages in the Leabhar Breac, Roman numerals to pages
in Mr. W. Stokes' edition.

Fiacc, St., Bishop of Slebhte (c. 418–495), Gaelic Hymn of : perhaps composed
as early as the end of the sixth century. The earliest extant MS. copy is
in the Liber Hymnorum, q. v. Printed in H. and S. ii. 2. Mr. Skene
considers this hymn a composition of the ninth century (Celtic Scotland,
ii. 435). Rolls Series, Descriptive Catalogue, i. 62.

Fleming, Patricii, Collectanea Sacra : Louvain, 1667.

Forbes, A. P., Kalendar of Scottish Saints : Edinburgh, 1872.

Gilbert, J. T., Facsimiles of National MSS. of Ireland, in four parts : Ord-
nance Survey Office, Southampton, 1874.

Gildas : British historian (De Excidio Britanniae), sixth century A.D. His
genuine works are, Epistola (c. A.D. 547-550) ; Fragmenta ex Epistola

altera (c. A.D. 565–570); Prefatio de Penitentia (ante A.D. 570), MS. Cod. Paris. 3182, saec. xi. Unless otherwise specified, reference has been made to J. Stevenson's edit., London, 1838. Rolls Series, Descriptive Catalogue, i. 132.

Greith, C. J., Geschichte der altirischen Kirche : Breisgau, 1867.

Haddan, A. W., Remains of: edited by A. P. Forbes, Bishop of Brechin, Oxford, 1876.

H. and S. = Haddan, A. W., and Stubbs, W., Councils and Ecclesiastical Documents of Great Britain and Ireland : Oxford, 1869.

Hardy, T. Duffus : see Descriptive Catalogue.

Hibernensis Sinodus : *see* Wasserschleben.

Howel Dda, Welsh laws of, A.D. 928. Earliest MS. authority twelfth and thirteenth century. Printed in H. and S. i. 211–285.

Hübner, Æmilius, Inscriptiones Britanniae Christianae : Berolini, MDCCCLXXVI.

Jonae Vita S. Columbani. Jonas, a native of Susa in Piedmont, wrote (c. A.D. 624) by order of Attala and Eustace, successors of Columbanus, the former at Bobbio, the latter at Luxeuil. Several MSS. of this Life exist on the continent, none of them probably earlier than a ninth-century copy which was sold in London at M. Liber's sale, March 9, 1858 (Catal. No. 269, p. 63). It is printed in Fleming's Collectanea, ii. 214–243. Rolls Series, Descriptive Catalogue, i. 212.

Irish Archaeological and Celtic Society, Publications of the : Dublin University Press, from 1855. Volumes from 1840–1855 were published by two separate 'Archaeological and 'Celtic' Societies which amalgamated in the latter year.

Keller, F., Bilder und Schriftzüge in den irischen Manuscripten, in Mittheilungen des antiquarischen Gesellschaft in Zurich, vol. vii. p. 61.

Leabhar Breac, or Lebar Brecc : The Speckled Book, otherwise called Leabhar Mor Duna, The Great Book of Dun Doighre ; a large fol. vellum volume in the Royal Irish Academy, Dublin, containing a collection of pieces in Irish and Latin, compiled from ancient sources about the end of the fourteenth century. Published in facsimile from the original MS., Dublin, 1876.

Liber Davidis : MS. Cod. Paris. 3182, saec. xi; printed in H. and S. i. 118.

Liber Hymnorum, or 'Book of Hymns,' a MS. Irish collection of hymns and collects. See page 194. A second MS. copy belongs to S. Isidore's College at Rome.

Liber Kilkenniensis : a fourteenth-century MS. containing lives of Irish Saints; Marsh's Library, Dublin. It is described at length by Dr. Reeves in the Proceedings of the Royal Irish Academy, Second Series, vol. i.

Liber Landavensis: a tenth-century MS. containing lives of Welsh Saints, &c. (see Rees' Preface), written during the episcopate of Bishop Urban, 1107–34; published by L. J. Rees, Llandovery, 1840.

Mart. = Martene, Edm., De Antiquis Ecclesiae Ritibus : Bassani, MDCCLXXXVIII.

Martyrology of Christ Church, Dublin : a fifteenth-century MS. in Trinity College, Dublin, published, together with the Book of Obits, by the Irish Archaeological Society, Dublin, 1844.

Martyrology of Donegal : compiled in the Franciscan Convent of Donegal by Michael O'Clery, and finished on April 19, 1630 ; published by Irish Archaeological and Celtic Society, Dublin, 1863.

Martyrology of Oengus = Félire of Oengus, q. v.

Martyrology of Tallaght. Traditionally said to have been compiled at the end of the ninth century by St. Maelruain and St. Oengus, but certainly as late as the tenth century ; imperfectly edited by M. Kelly, Dublin, 1857, from an early seventeenth-century MS. copy in the Burgundian Library at Brussels.

Missale de Arbuthnott (fifteenth century, Scottish) : edited by A. P. Forbes : Burntisland, 1864.

Missale Drummondense (Irish MS., eleventh century). See p. 269.

Missale Gallicanum : Pitsligo Press edition ; Burntisland, 1855.

Missale Gothicum : Pitsligo Press edition ; Burntisland, 1855.

Missale Mozarabicum : Migne, Patrol. Curs. Lat., vol. lxxxv.

Missale Richenovense (Gallican) : Burntisland, 1855.

Missale Romanum : Mechliniae, 1870.

Missale Rosslynianum : Irish MS., fourteenth century. See p. 269.

Missale Sarisburiense : Burntisland, 1861.

Missale Stowense. See p. 198.

Missale Vesontionense : Pitsligo edition ; Burntisland, 1855, and in Mabillon's Museum Italicum, tom. i. p. 273.   See p. 272.

Missale Vetus Hibernicum (twelfth century) : Pickering, London, 1879.

Montalembert, Comte de, Les moines d'Occident : Paris, 1860–77 ; Authorised translation, Edinburgh, 1861–77.

O'Conor, C., Bibliotheca MS. Stowensis : Buckinghamiae, MD.CCCXVIII. Dr. O'Conor's liturgical remarks and criticisms are often erroneous and misleading (see p. 198), and his palaeographical descriptions must be received with caution.

O'Conor, C., Rerum Hibern. Scriptores Veteres, tom. iv : Buckinghamiae, MDCCCXIV.

O'Neill, H., Sculptured Crosses of ancient Ireland : London, 1857.

Ozanam, A. F., La Civilisation Chrétienne chez les Francs : Paris, 1849.

Patricii Opera : all composed before A.D. 493, i.e. (1) Confessio, in Book of Armagh ; (2) Epistola ad Corotici subditos, in Cotton MS. Nero E. i. (eleventh century) ; (3) Canticum Scotticum, in the Liber Hymnorum ; printed in H. and S. vol. ii. pt. ii. pp. 296–323.

Petrie, G., Christian Inscriptions in the Irish Language : edited by M. Stokes, Dublin, 1870–78.

Petrie, G., The Ecclesiastical Architecture of Ireland anterior to the Anglo-Norman Invasion ; vol. xx. of the Transactions of the Royal Irish Acad.

Pinkerton, J., Vitae Antiq. SS. Scotiae : London, 1789.

Poenitentiale Columbani : printed in Fleming's Collectan. Sac. p. 94, from a sixth-century MS. at Bobbio ; also by Wasserschleben, Bussordnungen, p. 353, who ranks it among Frankish Penitentials, and proves that it has been erroneously attributed to St. Columbanus, p. 12.

Poenitentiale Cuminii : vide Cuminii.

Poenitentiale Gildae : ante A.D. 570.   MS. Cod. Paris. 3182, saec. xi = Prefatio Gildae de penitentia : vide Gildas.

Poenitentiale Vinniani : MS. Cod. Vindob. Theol. 725, 8°. saec. ix, printed in Wasserschleben, Bussordnung. der abendländ. Kirche, p. 108.

Proceedings of Royal Irish Academy : Dublin, from 1836.

Proceedings of the Society of Antiquaries of London : from 1843.

Proceedings of the Society of Antiquaries of Scotland : from 1856.

R. = Missale Romanum, q. v.

Reeves, W., Ecclesiastical Antiquities of Down, Connor, and Dromore : Dublin, 1847.

Reeves, W., Life of Columba : see Adamnan.

Regula : see Rule.

Report on Foedera : see Cooper, C. P.

Rituale Romanum (Rit. Rom.) : Mechliniae, MDCCCLXX.

Rule of St. Columba : from a seventeenth-century MS. in the Burgundian Library at Brussels; itself a transcription by Michael O'Clery, one of the Four Masters, from earlier MS. records. It is probably the compilation of a later Columban monk. Printed in Gaelic, with a translation, by H. and S. ii. pt. i. p. 119.

Rule of St. Columbanus : Regula Sancti Columbani, descripta ex MS. Codice Monasterii Bobiensis, et collata cum aliis exemplaribus MSS. Bib. Oxenhusani in Suevia et SS. Afrae et Uldarici urbis Augustinae. Printed in Fleming's Collectanea, pp. 4, 19.

Rule of the Culdees (Riagail na Celedne o Maelruain cecinit), in the Leabhar Breac, q. v. It is an Irish tract drawn up in its present form in the twelfth or thirteenth century, but regarded by Dr. Reeves to be an amplified and modernised form of the Rule drawn up by St. Maelruain, founder, abbot, and bishop of the Church of Tamlacht (Tallaght), near Dublin, at the close of the eighth century. The pages referred to are those of Dr. Reeves' edition, Dublin, 1864.

S. = Missale Sarisburiense, q. v.

Sacramentarium Gallicanum = Missale Vesontionense, q. v.

Sacramentarium Leonianum, Gelasianum, Gregorianum. All paginal references are to Muratorii Liturgia Romana Vetus : Venetiis, MDCCXLVIII.

Schoell, C. G., De ecclesiasticis Britonum Scotorumque fontibus : Berlin, 1851.

Secundini Hymnus in laudem S. Patricii : Hymn of St. Sechnall, composed before A.D. 448 ; written in the Antiphon. Benchor., q. v. Printed in H. and S. vol. ii. pt. ii. p. 324.

Senchus Mor : a collection of Irish laws drawn up A.D. 438–441, between the sixth and ninth years after St. Patrick's arrival in Ireland, representing the modifications which the ancient Pagan laws underwent on the conversion of Ireland to Christianity ; printed at Dublin, 1865. Four MS. copies exist, the earliest of which was written in the fourteenth century (Pref. vol. i. pp. xxxi–xxxiv), and a few MS. fragments (Pref. vol. iii. p. lxv).

Sinodus Aquilonalis Britanniae : MS. Cod. Paris. 3182, saec. xi ; printed in H. and S. i. 117.

Sinodus Hibernensis : see Wasserschleben.

Sinodus Luci Victoriae, A.D. 569 : MS. Cod. Paris. 3182, saec. xi ; printed in H. and S. i. 116.

Skene, W. F., Celtic Scotland, two vols. : Edinb. 1876.

Stowe Missal, see p. 198.

Stuart, J., Sculptured Stones of Scotland, in vol. xxvi of the publications of the Spalding Club.

T. = Martyrology of Tallaght, q. v.

Todd, J. H., Descriptive Remarks on Illuminations in certain ancient Irish MSS. : London, 1869.

Todd, J. H., Life of St. Patrick : Dublin, 1864.

Transactions of Royal Irish Academy : 4to., Dublin, from 1787.

Transactions of Society of Antiquaries of Scotland : Edinb., from 1792.

Ulster Journal of Archaeology : Belfast, 1853-62.

Ultani Vita S. Brigidae : a tenth-century MS. in the monastery of St. Magnus at Ratisbon, of a work by Ultan Bishop of Ardbraccan (ob. A.D. 656-7); printed in Colgan's Trias. Thaum. pp. 542-5.

Ussher, Archbishop, Brit. Eccles. Antiquitates : Dublin, 1739.

Ussher, Archbishop, Opera Omnia : Dublin, 1847.

V. = Biblia Sacra Vulgatae Editionis : Augustae Taurinorum, 1875.

Walafridus Strabo, Vita S. Galli : quoted from Goldasti, Aleman. Rerum Script. aliquot vetusti, Francof. 1606. There is a ninth-century MS. in the Library at Bern.

Wasserschleben, F. W. H., Die Bussordnungen der abendländischen Kirche : Halle, 1851.

Wasserschleben, F. W. H., Irische Kanonensammlung : Giessen, 1874. A collection of Irish canons of the end of the seventh or beginning of the eighth centuries. The grounds for assigning this date, and the age of various MS. copies collated in different European libraries, are discussed in the Preface. The MSS. vary from the eighth to the eleventh centuries. A tenth-century MS. copy exists in the Bodleian Library (Hatton MSS. No. 42, fol. 1-65), and a ninth or tenth century MS. in C. C. C., Camb., No. 279, both uncollated by Wasserschleben, but mentioned in the Introduction, pp. xvi, xxi.

Wattenbach, Dr., Die Kongregation der schötten Klöster in Deutschland. Translated, with notes, by Dr. Reeves in Ulster Journal of Archaeology, vii. 227, 295.

Westwood, J. O., Lapidarium Walliae : Oxford, 1876-9.

Westwood, J. O., Miniatures and Ornaments of Anglo-Saxon and Irish MSS. : London, 1868.

Westwood, J. O., Palaeographia Sacra Pictoria : London, 1843.

Wilson, D., Archaeology and pre-historic Annals of Scotland : Edinburgh, 1851.

CHAPTER I.

INTRODUCTION.

CHAPTER I.

It would be alien to the purpose with which this volume is written, and impossible within the limits which it is intended to assume, to present to the reader a complete history of the 'Celtic Church;' but it is necessary to define at the outset what is meant by that term, and it will be advantageous to add to this definition a notice of such of its more important features and general characteristics as have an *a priori* bearing on the probable *genus* of its Liturgy and Ritual, which will then be described with as much detail as the nature of the subject-matter and the amount of evidence at our disposal render possible.

§ 1. Extent and Duration of the Celtic Church.—By the term 'Celtic Church' is meant the Church which existed in Great Britain and Ireland (with certain continental offshoots) before the mission of St. Augustine, and to a varying extent after that event, until by absorption or submission the various parts of it were at different dates incorporated with the Church of the Anglo-Saxons[1].

Central England.—The Celtic Church in Central England became extinct at the close of the fifth century, its members being then either exterminated in war, or retiring to the

---

[1] The Scoti and Britones are often mentioned together, as in the letter of the first Anglo-Saxon Bishops preserved by Bede (H. E. lib. ii. c. 4); in the Penitential of Theodore, cap. ix. § 1. See p. 9. n. 2, p. 28. n. 6.

remoter parts of the country for shelter from the attacks of heathen invaders from Jutland, Sleswick, and Holstein. In those more distant quarters the ancient national Church maintained a separate existence and a corporate continuity long after the conversion of the Anglo-Saxons which was begun by the Roman mission under the leadership of St. Augustine.

Wales.—The Britons of North Wales did not conform to the usages of the Anglo-Saxon Church till A.D. 768, those of South Wales not till A.D. 777. The supremacy of the See of Canterbury was not fully established here till the twelfth century.

Southern England.—The British Church in Somerset and Devon, or to speak more exactly the British population dwelling within the territory conquered by the West-Saxons, conformed at the beginning of the eighth century, through the influence of Aldhelm, who became Abbot of Malmesbury A.D. 671, Bishop of Sherborne A.D. 705 [1].

In Cornwall the Bishops of the British Church were not subject to the See of Canterbury before the time of King Athelstan (925-940), the submission of Bishop Kenstec to Archbishop Ceolnoth (833-70) being the only exception. On the conquest of Cornwall by the Saxons the British Bishop Conan submitted to Archbishop Wulfhelm, and was recognised by King Athelstan, who formally nominated him to the Cornish See of Bodmin A.D. 936 [2].

Northumberland.—The Celtic Church, established in Northumberland by King Oswald A.D. 634-5, after having flourished thirty years under the Scottish bishops Aidan, Finan, and Colman, successively, conformed to the Roman practice at the Synod of Whitby A.D. 664; when Colman, who had throughout unsuccessfully opposed the change, 'perceiving that his doctrine was rejected and his sect despised, took with him such as were willing to follow him, and would not comply with the Catholic Easter and coronal tonsure,—for there was much

---

[1] Bede, H. E. v. 18.   [2] H. and S. i. 676.

controversy about that also,—and went back into Scotia, to consult with his people what was to be done in this case[1].'

Strathclyde.—The Britons of Strathclyde conformed A.D. 688, the year after the death of St. Cuthbert, on the occasion of a visit among them of Adamnan, Abbot of Iona, who himself had been persuaded about this time to adopt the new policy. Sedulius, the first British Bishop of Strathclyde who conformed to Roman usage, is mentioned as present at a council held at Rome under Gregory II, A.D. 721 [2].

Scotland.—Adamnan attempted to force the Scottish Church to conform to Roman usage at the close of the seventh century, after his return from his second mission to King Aldfrith in Northumbria A.D. 688, but unsuccessfully. His action is thus recorded by Bede:—

' Adamnan, priest and abbot of the monks who were in the isle of Hii, was sent ambassador by his nation to Aldfrith, King of the Angles, where, having made some stay, he observed the canonical rites of the Church, and was earnestly admonished by many who were more learned than himself, not to presume to live contrary to the universal custom of the Church in relation to either the observance of Easter or any other decrees whatsoever, considering the small number of his followers seated at so distant a corner of the world. In consequence of this he changed his mind, and readily preferred those things which he had seen and heard in the Churches of the Angles to the customs which he and his people had hitherto followed. For he was a good and wise man and remarkably learned in the knowledge of the Scriptures. Accordingly returning home he endeavoured to bring his own people that were in Hii, or that were subject to that monastery, into the way of truth, which he himself had learned and embraced with all his heart, but in this he could not prevail[3].'

---

[1] Bede, H. E. iii. 25.

[2] 'Sedulius, episcopus Britanniae, de genere Scottorum, huic constituto a nobis promulgato subscripsi.' H. and S. ii. 7, with note.

[3] Bede, H. E. v. 15.

After the death of Adamnan, A.D. 704, there were two parties in this controversy, which was eventually settled in favour of the Roman rule by a decree of Nectan, King of the Picts, A.D. 710. 'Not long after which,' says Bede, 'those monks also of the Scottish nation who lived in the isle of Hii, with the other monasteries that were subject to them, were, by the procurement of our Lord, brought to the canonical observance of Easter and the right mode of tonsure. For in the year after the incarnation of our Lord A.D. 716, the father and priest Ecgberct, beloved of God, and worthy to be named with all honour, coming to them from Ireland was very honourably and joyfully received by them . . . and by his pious and frequent exhortations he converted them from the inveterate tradition of their ancestors. He taught them to perform the principal solemnity after the Catholic and Apostolic manner. The monks of Hii by the instruction of Ecgberct adopted the Catholic rites, under Abbot Dunchad (A.D. 710-717), about eighty years after they had sent Bishop Aidan to preach to the nation of the Angles[1].'

But the acceptance of the Paschal rule at Hii in 716 did not settle the practice of that Church finally, for we are informed that the Easter-tide of Ecgberct's death (A.D. 729) was the first Easter celebrated according to the Roman calculation[2]. A schism had taken place at Iona A.D. 704, and rival abbots existed till A.D. 772, when on the death of the Abbot Suibhne the conformity of the whole monastery of Iona to the Roman Church may be considered to have been established[3]. But this remark does not apply to the whole of Scotland. Customs and ritual peculiar to the ancient Church of the country existed long after the

---

[1] Bede, H. E. v. 22.

[2] Ib. 'Cum eo die (i.e. viii. Kal. Maii) Pascha celebraretur, quo nunquam prius in eis locis celebrari solebat.' In 716 the Columban monks were banished from the territories of Nectan, king of the Picts, in consequence of their refusal to comply with a royal edict commanding the adoption of the Roman Paschal cycle and coronal tonsure. Annals of Ulster.

[3] Skene, W. F., Celtic Scotland, ii. 288.

eighth century. When St. Margaret, a Saxon Princess, married King Malcolm III, A.D. 1069, she promoted a religious reformation, which is said to have included the abolition of the following four Scottish customs :—

1. The commencement of Lent on the first Monday in Lent instead of on Ash Wednesday. This is the custom at Milan to the present day. It may perhaps be traced in the Sarum direction to cover up all crosses, &c. on the first Monday in Lent.

2. The non-reception of the Holy Eucharist on Easter Day. It is difficult to understand this statement, because Easter Day in the early Scottish Church was 'the festival of joy[1],' and the Easter Communion was especially singled out for mention[2]. In the early Irish Church it was enjoined on all the faithful by one of the canons attributed to St. Patrick[3]. A King of Leinster is said to have paid a visit to St. Bridget, in order to listen to preaching and celebration on Easter Day[4].

3. Labour on the Lord's Day.

4. Strange customs in the Mass.

St. Margaret's biographer tells us that 'in some places among the Scots there were persons who, contrary to the custom of the whole Church, had been accustomed to celebrate Masses by some barbarous rite, which the Queen, kindled with God's zeal, so laboured to destroy and bring to nothing, that thenceforth there appeared no one in the whole race of the Scots who dared to do such a thing[5].'

---

[1] 'Laetitiae festivitas.' Adamnan, Vit. S. Columbae, iii. 23.

[2] 'Ut in Paschali solemnitate ad altarium accedas, et Eucharistiam sumas. . . . Et post peractam Paschae sollennitatem in qua jussus ad altare accessit.' Ibid. ii. 39.

[3] 'Maxime autem in nocte Paschae, in qua qui non communicat, fidelis non est.' Can. S. Patricii, Secundae Sinodi, xxii.

[4] Leabhar Breac, fol. 64 a.

[5] 'Praeterea in aliquibus locis Scottorum quidam fuerunt, qui contra totius Ecclesiae consuetudinem, nescio quo ritu barbaro, missas celebrare consueverant ; quod regina, zelo Dei accensa, ita destruere atque annihilare studuit, ut deinceps qui tale quid praesumeret, nemo in tota Scottorum gente appareret.' Theoderic, Vit. S. Margaret. cc. 8 sq. ; H. and S. ii. i. 158.

In the absence of any direct statement as to what these
liturgical peculiarities were, we are left to conjecture either
that they were connected with the celebration of Mass in the
vernacular instead of in the Latin language[1], or, with more
probability[2], that up to the eleventh century the Ephesine
and the Roman Liturgies were used contemporaneously in
Scotland, somewhat in the same way that in France a
transition period can be traced through such service books
as the 'Sacramentarium Gallicanum,' in which Ephesine
and Petrine forms present themselves alternately. The
above charges also indicate that the final extinction of the
old Celtic Church in Scotland was partly owing to internal
decay, as well as to the line of policy adopted by Queen
Margaret and Malcolm Canmore, which was the same as
that adopted in the next century by the Anglo-Norman
kings towards Ireland. Neither a national Church nor a
religious movement can be easily extinguished by royal
authority, unless there are other and co-operating influences
at work. St. Margaret was not immediately successful in
her attempts at suppression. Fifty years later, in the reign
of King David, we learn that the Culdees 'in a corner of
their church which was very small used to celebrate their own
office after their own fashion[3].' It is the last spark in the
expiring embers of the controversy and the struggle for supremacy between two elements in the ecclesiastical history
of Scotland; the old national Celtic element represented by

---

[1] This is Mr. Skene's view, who lays stress on the words 'barbaro ritu.'
His words are : 'It is not explained in what this peculiarity existed, but it was
something done after a barbarous manner, so that it is impossible to tell how
it (Mass) was celebrated, and it was entirely suppressed. This is hardly applicable to the mere introduction of some peculiar forms or ceremonies, and
the most probable explanation of these expressions is that in the remote and
mountainous districts the service was performed in the native language and
not in Latin, as was the custom of the universal Church.' Celtic Scotland, ii.
349.

[2] This is Bishop Forbes' view. Missale de Arbuthnot, Preface, lv.

[3] 'Keledei enim in angulo quodam ecclesiae, quae modica nimis erat, suum
officium more suo celebrabant.' Chron. Picts and Scots, p. 190, edited by
W. F. Skene; Edinb. 1867.

the independence of the Scottish episcopate and the retention of the ancient Missal; and the Anglicising element, patronised by the royal authority of Malcolm Canmore and Queen Margaret, subjecting the Scottish episcopate to the supremacy of York, and introducing the Anglicanised (Roman) Missal. It is possible but not certain that this was the Use of Sarum. St. Osmund published that Use in A.D. 1085. St. Margaret died in A.D. 1093. There was therefore time for her to have seen, approved, and initiated the circulation of the Sarum Missal; but considering the slowness of communication in those days, and the time necessarily occupied in the transcription of copies, it is more probable that she introduced the Anglican rite in the form in which it existed before it was arranged by St. Osmund. This probability is increased by the fact that the Sarum Use was not introduced into the Cathedral and See of Glasgow till the time of Bishop Herbert (A.D. 1147-64.)

Ireland.—The Celtic Church in the South of Ireland conformed to Rome on the Paschal controversy, and probably in other respects as well, during the pontificate of Honorius (A.D. 626-638). The letter of that Pope, urging such conformity, has been preserved by Bede[1], and the letter of Cummian, Abbot of Durrow, written A.D. 634 to Segine, fifth Abbot of Iona, announcing the determination of Southern Ireland to conform to Roman usage, is still extant[2]. The Church in Northern Ireland was induced to take a similar step, at the instance of Adamnan, at the Synod of Tara, A.D. 692[3].

But in the case of Ireland, as in Scotland, complete conformity to Roman usage was not secured for many centuries

---

[1] Bede, H. E. ii. 19.

[2] Migne, Bib. Pat. Lat. lxxxvii. p. 969. In this letter Cummian parodies the independent position of the Celtic Church by representing its members as saying, ' Roma errat; Hierosolyma errat; Alexandria errat; Antiochia errat; soli tantum Scoti et Britones rectum sapiunt.'

[3] An account of this synod is given in Reeves' edition of Adamnan's Life of Columba, Appendix to Preface, p. 1.

afterwards. The last vestiges of the old national rite, and of liturgical and ritual independence, were not swept away till the time of St. Malachy, the great Romaniser—the Wilfrid— of the Irish Church. Born A.D. 1075, he became Bishop of Armagh (1134-1148), and in that capacity visited Pope Innocent II, demanded the pallium, which had not hitherto been worn by Irish bishops, and was invested with legatine authority over the Irish Church. His biographer St. Bernard expressly states that 'Roman laws and ecclesiastical customs were introduced by him into his native country[1].' And again, 'He established in all Churches the Apostolical constitutions, and the decrees of the holy fathers, and especially the customs of the holy Roman Church[2].' Gillebert, the papal legate, Bishop of Limerick (1106-1139), implies that there had been more than one Liturgical Use in Ireland previously to that date. He said in the Prologue of a book 'De Usu Ecclesi- astico,' addressed to the whole clergy of Ireland :—

'At the request and also at the command of many of you, most dearly beloved, I have endeavoured to set down in writing the canonical custom of saying the hours, and per- forming the office of the whole ecclesiastical order, not pre- sumptuously, but desiring to serve your most godly command, in order that those diverse and schismatical orders, with which nearly all Ireland has been deluded, may give place to one Catholic and Roman Office[3].'

At a Synod held at Kells A.D. 1152, under the papal legate

---

[1] 'Fiunt de medio barbaricae leges, Romanae introducuntur. Recipiuntur ubique ecclesiasticae consuetudines, contrariae rejiciuntur.' Bernard, Vit. S. Malachiae, cap. 8. § 17.

[2] 'Apostolicas sanctiones, ac decreta sanctorum Patrum, praecipueque con- suetudines sanctae Romanae ecclesiae in cunctis ecclesiis statuebat.' Ibid. cap. 3. § 7.

[3] 'Rogatu necnon et praecepto multorum ex vobis, carissimi, canonicalem consuetudinem in dicendis horis, et peragendo totius ecclesiastici ordinis officio, scribere conatus sum ; non praesumptivo sed vestrae cupiens piissimae servire jussioni ; ut diversi et schismatici illi ordines, quibus Hibernia poene tota delusa est, uni Catholico et Romano cedant officio.' Gilleberti, Lunicensis Episc., De Usu Ecclesiastico. MS. in Camb. Univ. Lib., Ff. i. 27. Art. 16.

Johannes Paparo, further steps were taken to enforce conformity to Roman usage[1].

In the year 1172, at the Synod of Cashel, presided over by Christianus, Bishop of Lismore and papal legate, the Anglican Use, that is to say the Sarum modification of the Roman Missal, was ordered to be introduced into every Church in Ireland, by the following canon:—

'From this time forward let all the divine offices of the Holy Church be performed in all parts of the (Irish) Church, according to the Use of the Church of England[2].'

The above-quoted passages, while implying a previous diversity of liturgical usage and a discrepancy between that of Ireland and that of Rome, unfortunately afford no direct information as to what the nature of the early Celtic Liturgy was. It will be the endeavour of the following pages to throw some light on this at present unsolved and perhaps, to a certain extent, insoluble question.

Continent.—The Celtic Churches on the Continent, founded by the missionary enterprise of the native Church of these islands chiefly during the fifth, sixth, and seventh centuries, included parts of modern France, Belgium, Prussia, Austria, Italy, Switzerland, and Spain. Iceland and the Faroe Islands also were colonised by Celtic missions.

The cessation of Celtic usage in the greater part of this Continental Church is closely connected with the life and efforts of the Anglo-Saxon apostle of Germany, St. Boniface (A.D. 680-755). In Spanish Gallicia Celtic usage as to Easter, &c. was abrogated by the Fourth Council of Toledo, A.D. 633, can. 41. In Brittany British customs prevailed

---

[1] Mansi, Concil. xxi. 768; xxii. 1101; Gams, Series Episc. p. 207.

[2] 'Omnia divina ad instar sacrosanctae ecclesiae, juxta quod Anglicana observat ecclesia, in omnibus partibus ecclesiae [Hibernicae] amodo tractentur,' —with a reason appended which can never have proceeded from genuine Irish sentiment.

'Dignum etenim et justissimum est ut sicut dominum et regem ex Anglia sortita est divinitus Hibernia, sic etiam exinde vivendi formam accipiant meliorem.' Wilkins, Concil. i. 473.

till A.D. 817, when they were abolished under Louis le Dé-
bonnaire, and at the same time the Rule of St. Benedict
was everywhere substituted for that of St. Columbanus[1].

Among the peculiar features and distinguishing characteristics of this wide-spread Celtic Church, the following are
deserving of especial mention :—

§ 2. ITS MONASTIC AND MISSIONARY CHARACTER.—Monasticism was during the best known period of Celtic Church
History a more conspicuous feature and prevailing element
of the Celtic Church than of any other portion of the Western
Church at any other time.   Not only was it *a* feature, as it
is in other Churches East and West, which comprise a regular
and a secular clergy side by side, but the first Church in these
islands seems to have been at one time so far entirely monastic in its character that its hierarchy consisted of regular
clergy almost exclusively, a secular priesthood being, if not
unknown, at most an inconsiderable minority[2].   As it over-
flowed its own territorial limits, and invaded the continent of
Europe, it was rendered for a time doubtful whether the monastic ideal of later Christendom would spring from a Celtic
or an Italian quarter, whether it would be represented in the
Rules of St. Columbanus and St. Columba, or of St. Benedict.   For its exclusively monastic constitution was closely
bound up with its missionary character, and was at once
the cause of its temporary triumph and of its ultimate decay.

Success in missionary enterprise can only be achieved, and
has only been achieved, on any large scale, from the time of
the Apostles downwards, by men who have so far caught the
ascetic spirit as to surrender this world and its ties to the
exclusive and absorbing task of the evangelisation of mankind.   But a Church which attempts to frame almost its

---

[1] H. & S. ii. i. 71, 79, 80.

[2] Bede said of the Celtic Church at Lindisfarne (7th cent.) : ' Omnes presbyteri, diaconi, cantores, lectores, ceterique gradus ecclesiastici monachi monachicam
per omnia cum ipso episcopo, regulam servant.'   Vit. S. Cuth. c. xvi.

whole constitution on a monastic basis, which provides no
outlet for the zeal and earnestness which, while shrinking from
the total self-surrender and separation from the world involved
in the monastic life, will fill the avocations of a secular priesthood, may achieve a brilliant but shortlived success, but aims
at too high an ideal for permanent success. This fact, added
to the intolerable severity of the Columban Rule (p. 17),
seems to be the key to the rise and fall of the Celtic
Church.

There are however passages which prove that a married
priesthood was not unknown in various parts, and at various
periods in the history of the Celtic Church. St. Patrick (fifth
century) says that he was the son of a deacon and the grand-
son of a priest[1]. An early Irish canon alludes to priests'
wives :—

'Quicunque clericus ab hostiario usque ad sacerdotem sine
tunica visus fuerit . . . et uxor ejus si non velato capite am-
bulaverit pariter a laicis contemnentur et ab ecclesia sepa-
rentur[2].'

The words of Gildas (A.D. 547) may imply a married priesthood in Britain in the sixth century, and have been quoted in
that sense by Archbishop Ussher[3]. They form part of the
'increpatio in sacerdotes' with which the 'Epistola i. Gildae'
concludes :—

'[Paulus dicit] "unius uxoris virum." Quid ita apud nos
quoque contemnitur quasi non audiretur et idem dicere et
"virum uxorum." . . . Sed videamus et sequentia. "Domum"
inquit "suam bene regentem, filios habentem subditos, cum
omni castitate." Ergo imperfecta est patrum castitas, si
eidem non et filiorum accumuletur. Sed quid erit ubi nec
pater, nec filius mali genitoris exemplo pravatus, conspicitur
castus? Si quis autem domui suae praeesse nescit, quomodo
Ecclesiae Dei diligentiam adhibebit?'

---

[1] Confessio, c. 1.
[2] Canones Patricii, Aux. Isern. § 6. See Book of Armagh, fol. 18.
[3] Op. iv. p. 294.

Notices of married bishops, priests, and deacons, and of various attempts to enforce clerical celibacy in the tenth century, and of the opposition encountered, prove that a married clergy existed in Wales till the eleventh or twelfth century[1]. There are also allusions to married priests in the Celtic Church in Brittany[2]. These facts have led a modern Roman Catholic author to make the unhistorical assertion that 'l'Eglise Romaine tolera quelque temps chez les Brétons et les Irlandais l'ordination des hommes mariés, comme elle la tolere encore chez les catholiques des rites orientaux[3].' Why did he not add 'comme elle la tolera autrefois chez les catholiques de Rome'? There are allusions to married episcopi, presbyteri, and diaconi in the inscriptions in the Catacombs[4]. But the existence of married priests in the Celtic Church was due to independence of, not to toleration by, the Roman See.

Some idea of the monastic character and extent of the Celtic Church may be gained from a bare enumeration of a few of its more famous houses.

In England (including Northumbria): Lindisfarne, Lastingham, Ripon, Whitby, St. Bees, Malmesbury, Glastonbury, Burgh Castle, Mailros (old Melrose), Coldingham, &c.

In Wales: Hentland-on-the-Wye, Caerworgern, Caerleon, Bangor-Deiniol (or Mawr), Bangor-Garmon, Llandabarnfawr, Llancarvan, Bangor-Iscoed, Clynnog-Fawr, Llan-Iltut, Llanelwy, afterwards St. Asaph, Caergybi, Enlli, Tygwyn-ar Daf, Docwinni.

In Ireland: Durrow, Clonard, Kildare, Clonmacnois,

---

[1] Haddan, A. W., Remains, p. 209; H. and S. i. pp. 155, 285.

[2] Courson, A., Histoire des Peuples Brétons, ii. 163.

[3] Ozanam, La Civilization Chretienne, p. 100; Paris, 1849.

[4] De Rossi, Inscriptiones Christianae, sub ann. 404, 405. Among them there are records of Stephen, son of a priest Melon; Boeckh, Corpus Inscriptt. Graec. vol. iv. fasc. 2. no. 9289; Philip, a son of a priest Alypius; Ibid. no. 9579, &c. Inscriptions to the memory of Roman priests and deacons whose wives were buried with them have been found up to the close of the fourth century; Northcote, J. S., Epitaphs of the Catacombs, p. 117.

Aghaboe, Kells, Bangor, Birr, Tirrdaglas, Glaisnaoidhen, Inismacsaint, Clonfert, Dromore, Moville, &c. One of the successors of St. Patrick, Luan by name, is asserted by St. Bernard to have founded alone a hundred monasteries[1]. The smaller islands round Ireland swarmed with them. Ten monasteries were founded by St. Enda alone on one of the Aran isles off the coast of Galway[2].

In Scotland numerous monasteries were founded by St. Columba and his monks among the Picts and Scots, the names of fifty-three of which, in addition to his own central monastery at Iona, have been preserved, at Soroby, Dunkeld, Inchcolm[3], &c. Many of the Scottish monasteries were placed on islands, which, perhaps on account of their superior safety, had a great fascination for the Celtic monk[4].

In France : Remiremont, Lure, Besançon, Romain-Moutier, Bezieres, Brezille, Cusance, St. Ursanne, Jouarre, Reuil, Rebais, Faremoutier, St. Maur-les-Fosses, Lagny, Moutier-la-Celle, Hautvilliers, Moutier-en-Der, St. Salaberga, Fontenelles, Jumièges, St. Saens, Luxeuil (A.D. 599), Anegray, Fontaines, Peronne, Toul, Amboise, Beaulieu, Strasbourg, in addition to other countless and nameless ' Hospitalia Scotorum,' alluded to in the Capitularies of Charles the Bald, A.D. 846[5].

The above mentioned were Irish foundations. Brittany had been colonised by British Christians at a much earlier date. The single Welsh monastery of Llan-Iltut numbered among its disciples SS. Malo, Samson, Teilo, Magloire, Brieuc, Frugdual, Corentin, Gildas, &c., all of whom are reported to have passed over into Brittany, in consequence of the persecution of the Saxons, and there to have founded

---

[1] Vita S. Malachiae, c. vi.

[2] Skene, W. F., Celtic Scotland, ii. 62. For an extended list see Historians of Scotland, vol. vi. p. xlix ; Edinb. 1874.

[3] Reeves' edit. of Adamnan's Life of St. Columba, p. 289.

[4] Lindisfarne off the coast of Northumbria, St. Michael's Mount in Brittany, and in Cornwall, will at once occur to the reader's mind.

[5] Pertz, Mon. Germ. Hist. Legum, tom. i. 390.

towns, or built monasteries, or established bishoprics, which in many instances still bear their names[1].

In the Netherlands: Namur, Liege, Gueldres, Hautmont, Soignes, &c.

In Germany and Switzerland: Hohenaug, Erfurt, Freyburg, Ettenheimmünster, Schuttern, Nüremberg, Würtzburg, Memmingen, Mentz, Cologne, Regensburg, Constance, St. Gall, Mont St. Victor, Reichenau, Bregenz, Rheinau, Seckingen.

In Italy: Bobbio (A.D. 612), Taranto, Lucca, Faenza, Fiesole.

This list might be largely extended. It does not include many monasteries which, Celtic in their origin, passed subsequently into foreign hands, as was the case with Great St. Martin's at Cologne, where, as elsewhere, when the first fervour of its Celtic inmates dwindled away, their places were filled up by the inhabitants of the country in which the monastery was situated[2]. St. Bernard compared the missionary inundation of foreign countries by the Irish to a flood[3]. A list of 122 monasteries founded by Irishmen in England, Scotland, and on the Continent was collected by Colgan in a lost work, of which the Index has been preserved and is printed in the Proceedings of the Royal Irish Academy, vol. vi. p. 106.

They were of various sizes. Those planted on the barren

---

[1] The travelling tendencies of the members of the British Church are thus attested by Gildas: 'Transnavigare maria terrasque spatiosas transmeare non tam piget [Britannos sacerdotes] quam delectat.' Ep. H. and S. ii. i. 70.

[2] Notice of its Irish origin is preserved in a fragment of an eleventh-century chronicle from a palimpsest vellum leaf printed in Pertz, Monum. Germ. Hist. tom. ii. p. 214. It begins thus:—

'Scoti multo tempore illud incoluerunt, donec a primo fervore tepescentes ex hoc, sicut etiam ex aliis quibusdam monasteriis expulsi sunt, et alii Germani sunt substituti,' &c.

A good deal of detail about the later Celtic monasteries on the Continent will be found in the Chronicle of Marianus Scotus, whose Irish name was Maelbrighte, but who, like most of his countrymen, assumed an equivalent and more pronounceable Latin name. He died in seclusion at Mentz A.D. 1082; Pertz, Monum. Germ. Hist. v. 481.

[3] 'In exteras regiones, quasi inundatione facta, illa se sanctorum examina effuderunt.' Vita S. Mal. c. 6.

islands off the coasts of Great Britain and Ireland must have been small. Others were very large. The Irish monastery of St. Finnian of Clonard, and that of St. Comgall at Bangor, were said to contain three thousand inmates. The Welsh monastery of Bangor-Iscoed contained, according to Bede, two thousand one hundred monks, of whom twelve hundred were slaughtered under the Northumbrian King Æthelfrith[1]. St. Patrick asserted that the number of Irish men and women who embraced the monastic life in his own time was incalculable[2].

The structure of the monasteries was of a simple and inexpensive character. Like the early Celtic churches (ch. iii) they were built at first of earth, and wattles, or wood. It was not till the end of the eighth century that stone buildings began in Scotland and Ireland to be substituted for wooden ones, as a protection against the ravages of the Danes.

The Rule of the Western monks, as laid down in the writings of St. Columbanus, was very severe, far more so than the Rule of St. Benedict. Its principles were absolute and unreserved obedience, constant and severe labour, daily self-denial and fasting; and the least deviation from the Rule was visited with corporal punishment or a severe form of fast, the precise number of blows and of days or hours of fasting being minutely prescribed[3].

---

[1] Bede, H. E. ii. 2.

[2] 'Et filii Scotorum et filiae Regulorum monachi fiebant et virgines Christi quos enumerare nequeo.' Patricii, ad Corot. ep. vi. Further details are given in Reeves' edit. of Adamnan, p. 336.

[3] Ussher, iv. 305; Montalembert, Monks of the West, ii. 447. The Rule itself is printed in Fleming, Collectanea Sacra, p. 4. It is frequently alluded to along with other Irish Rules in the Lives of the Saints, passages from which have been collected by Dr. Reeves in his edit. of Archbishop Colton's Visitation of Derry, p. 109. It was mentioned by Wilfrid in his controversy with St. Colman: 'De patre autem vestro Columba et sequacibus ejus, quorum sanctitatem vos imitari, et *regulam ac praecepta* caelestibus signis confirmata sequi perhibetis, possem respondere.' Bede, H. E. iii. 25.

In describing the success of St. Aidan's mission to Northumberland, Bede speaks of the erection of churches and monasteries where 'imbuebantur prae-

The chief occupation of all the monks, and the only occupation of the more aged, apart from the services of the Church, consisted of reading and writing. It was said of the Irish monastery of Lughmagh under Bishop Mochta, that

> 'Threescore psalm-singing seniors
> Were his household, royal the number,
> Without tillage, reaping, or kiln-drying,
> Without work except reading[1].'

The office of Scribe (Scribhnidh or Scribhneoir) was of such honour and importance in an Irish monastery, that the penalty for shedding his blood was as great as that for killing a bishop or abbot[2]. Sometimes in Scotland, in the seventh to tenth centuries, a scribe was elected to be an abbot or a bishop, and the head of a diocese or monastery thought that it added to the dignity of his position to be able to append the title of 'scriba' to his name. Baithene, the second Abbot of Iona, was an accomplished scribe, and was selected by Columba before his death to finish the Psalter left incomplete by himself[3]. The eighteenth and thirtieth Abbots of Iona, in 797

---

ceptoribus Scottis parvuli Anglorum, una cum majoribus studiis et observatione disciplinae regularis.' Hist. Ec. iii. 3.

The Irish Rule at Bangor in the seventh century is described in the Antiphon. Benchor. p. 156 :—

> 'Benchuir bona regula
> Recta atque divina,
> Stricta, sancta, sedula,' etc.

Ozanam attributes the eventual failure of Columban rule on the Continent to its Eastern severity ; La Civilization Chretienne, p. 140.

[1] Martyrology of Donegal, p. 216; Félire of Oengus, p. cxxxii.

[2] 'Sanguis Episcopi vel excelsi Principis [= Abbot] vel Scribae qui ad terram effunditur, si collirio indiguerit, eum qui effuderit, sapientes crucifigi judicant, vel vii ancillas reddant.' 8th cent. Canon of a Sinodus Hibernensis ; Wasserschleben, Bussordnungen, p. 140. The latter alternative (= vii ancillarum pretium) is St. Patrick's modification of what would be demanded under the older national law of retaliation. See also Sinodus Hibernensis, cap. 29 ; ib. p. 138. Again : 'Patricius dicit omnis qui ausus fuerit ea quae sunt regis vel episcopi vel scribae furari aut aliquod in eos committere, parvi pendens dispicere, vii ancillarum pretium reddat, aut vii annis peniteat cum episcopo vel scriba.' Sin. Hibern. iii. c. 8, ib. p. 141 ; iv. c. 6, ib. p. 142.

[3] Adamnan, Vit. S. Col. i. 23, iii. 23.

and 978, and the Bishop of the Isles of Alba in 961, are also recorded to have been scribes[1].

St. Patrick is said to have first taught his converts letters in a passage which is interpreted as attributing to him the introduction of a written alphabet. If so, it was probably the Irish or Latin-Irish alphabet supplanting the earlier Ogham characters[2]; and the books of Durrow, Kells, Dimma, Mulling, &c. survive to show what apt scholars the Irish were, and to what a marvellous pitch of perfection calligraphy reached within a few centuries after St. Patrick's death[3]. The art of writing was transferred from Ireland to Scotland by St. Columba and his followers. It may have flourished at an earlier date in Southern Pictland at the time of St. Ninian's mission, as doubtless it flourished in the early British Church in England, but invading waves of heathenism had swept that earlier Christian civilisation away, and all traces of its sacred and liturgical writings are irrecoverably lost. But in connection with Iona there are many references to books. St. Columba himself wrote a volume containing hymns for the various services of the week[4]. He possessed a volume containing the Prayers and Ceremonial for the Consecration and Coronation of Kings, which, perhaps on account of its beautiful binding, was called the 'book of glass' and considered to be of celestial origin[5]. His last occupation on earth was the writing of a Psalter, and he was engaged in transcribing the thirty-fourth Psalm for it on the evening before his death[6]. Baithene wrote a Psalter so correctly that a single omission of the vowel 'i' was the only

---

[1] Annals of the Four Masters. For further information see Skene's Celtic Scotland, ii. pp. 423, 444.

[2] Skene's Celtic Scotland, ii. 449.

[3] Facsimiles of National MSS. in Ireland, edited by J. T. Gilbert.

[4] 'Hymnorum Liber Septimaniorum;' Adamnan, Vit. S. Col. ii. 9. The total number of books written by St. Columba was, according to tradition, three hundred; Leabhar Breac, p. 32 b. The same number of books was said to have been written by Dagaeus (ob. 586); Acta SS. Aug. iii. 656.

[5] 'Vitreum ordinationis regum librum;' Adamnan, Vit. S. Col. iii. 5.

[6] Ib. iii. 23.

mistake which St. Columba could find throughout it[1]. There
are many other allusions to books and writing, as in the
case of the awkward monk who dropped the book which
he was reading into a vessel full of water[2], and of the im-
petuous guest who in his anxiety to greet St. Columba
managed to spill that saint's ink-horn[3].

· Sometimes the monks wrote on wax tablets, *ceracula, pu-
gillaria, tabulae,* with a hard pointed instrument, *graphium,* or
stimulus. 'Cum in agro ipse sederet allato angelus Domini
ceraculo eum litterarum docuit elementa[4].'

Adamnan narrates in his work 'De Locis Sanctis' how
Bishop Arnulf 'primo in tabulas describenti fideli et indubit-
abili narratione dictavit quae nunc in membranis brevi textu
scribuntur[5].'

In the Codex Sangallensis, 242, entitled 'De pugillaribus
id est parvis tabulis,' there is a gloss written over v. 3,
Sicut videtur in tabulis Scotorum. The parchment skins
('membranae'), the use of which superseded the 'ceracula,'
were either bound together in the form of a volume[6],
or assumed the shape of a long scroll[7]. The word commonly
in use for writing was *caraxare, charaxare, craxare, cras-
sare, or xraxare.* The Irish monk Arbedoc, who wrote the
MS. Cod. Lat. Paris. 12021, begins by invoking the Divine
blessing thus: 'Mihi xraxanti literas missereatur trinitas.'
Adamnan closes his work 'De Locis Sanctis' by a request that
the reader would offer a prayer 'pro me misello peccatore
eorundem craxatore.' The same Abbot closes his Vita S.
Columbae with this adjuration, 'Obsecro eos quicumque volu-

---

[1] Adamnan, Vit. S. Col. i. 23.

[2] Ib. i. 24.

[3] Ib. i. 25. Many other phrases and allusions to the art of writing have
been collected together by Dr. Reeves in the additional notes to his edit. of
Adamnan's Life of Columba, p. 359.

[4] Vita S. Mochtei, Acta SS. Aug. tom. iii. die xix. 743.

[5] In Prologo Auctoris, Migne, Bib. Pat. Lat. lxxxviii. 781.

[6] Westwood, Facsimiles, Plates x, xxii, xxiii, xxvi.

[7] Ib. Pl. i, xv, xvi.

erint hos describere libellos, immo potius adjuro per Christum judicem saeculorum, ut postquam diligenter descripserint, conferant et emendent cum omni diligentia ad exemplar unde caraxerunt et hanc quoque adjurationem hoc in loco subscribant[1].' Specimens of the early Scottish style of writing survive in an eighth-century MS. Life of Columba by Adamnan, Codex A at Schaffhausen, and in the Book of Deer written by a native scribe of Alba in the ninth century. These two MSS. are specially mentioned because the facsimiles of the originals which accompany the careful editions of the books by Dr. Reeves and Mr. Stuart place samples of early Scottish calligraphy within the reach of every modern reader. Their ornamentation and initial letters, though less elaborate than those of the Book of Kells and other early Irish MSS., confirm the statements so often made in the Lives of the Saints, that the arts of designing, drawing, and illuminating were extensively practised in these early times[2]. Other monks were skilful workers in leather, metal, and wood. St. Patrick himself was said to have been accompanied by workers in bronze and artificers of sacred vessels[3]. It was recorded of St. Dega, an Irish monk and bishop (d. 586), that he spent his nights in transcribing MSS., his days in reading them, and in carving in copper and iron[4]. Among the articles of most frequent construction were costly reliquaries for enshrining the remains of saints, metal cases of embossed

---

[1] Caraxare seems to be a Latinised form of χαράττειν, and to point to the earlier form of writing by engraving letters on wax tablets.

[2] The passages referred to are collected by Professor Westwood in his Palaeographia Sacra, Gospels of Meiel Brith Mac Durnan, p. 7. The epithet 'pictorium' in the passage quoted there from Adamnan, Vit. S. Col. iii. 10, is an erroneous reading for 'pistorium.'

[3] 'Tres fabri aerarii vasorumque sacrorum fabricatores.' Colgan, Trias. Thaum. p. 167 a.

[4] 'Idem Daygeus episcopus abbatibus aliisque Hiberniae sanctis, campanas, cymbala, baculos, cruces, scrinia, capsas, pyxides, calices, discos, altariola, chrysmalia, liborumque coopertoria ; quaedam horum nuda, quaedam vero alia auro atque argento, gemmisque pretiosis circumtecta, pro amore Dei et sanctorum honore, sine ullo terreno pretio, ingeniose ac mirabiliter composuit.' Acta SS. Aug. tom. iii. p. 659 a. Montalembert, Monks of the West, iii. 89.

bronze or silver (cumhdachs) for enclosing copies of the
Gospels or other MSS., and leathern cases (polaires) for
carrying about portable missals and other service books[1].

Education was also carried on by these early monks. Their
monasteries were seminaries for the training of the native
youth[2], and were frequented by adult foreigners, who flocked
to Ireland from all parts of Great Britain, France, and the
Continent generally for purposes of study[3]. Among the distinguished persons who thus visited Irish or Scottish monasteries were Egbert and Chad[4], the French Agilbert, who
succeeded Birinus as second Bishop of Dorchester A.D. 650[5],
Aldfrith, who succeeded his brother Ecgfrith as King of Northumbria A.D. 685[6], Willibrord, the Anglo-Saxon missionary to
Frisia A.D. 690[7], &c.

While the seniors were exclusively engaged in the sedentary
occupations of reading, writing, and teaching, the younger
monks also laboured in the various departments of husbandry,
at least so far as to provide for the wants of their own monasteries. When St. Columba visited the monastery of Clonmacnois the monks at work in the fields flocked together to
receive him[8]. St. Cuthbert and St. Furseus worked with
their own hands[9]. St. Gall went fishing while his monks

---

[1] Further account of these various articles is given in J. O. Westwood's
Facsimiles, &c., pp. 80, 149, 150.

[2] W. Skene, Celtic Scotland, ii. 75.

[3] 'Erant ibidem eo tempore (A.D. 664) multi nobilium simul et mediocrium
de gente Anglorum, qui tempore Finani et Colmani episcoporum, relicta insula
patria, vel divinae lectionis, vel continentioris vitae gratia, illo secesserant.
Et quidam quidem mox se monasticae conversationi fideliter mancipaverunt;
alii magis circumeundo per cellas magistrorum lectioni operam dare gaude-
bant; quos omnes Scotti libentissime suscipientes victum eis quotidianum sine
pretio, libros quoque ad legendum, et magisterium gratuitum praebere cura-
bant.' Bede, H. E. iii. 27.

[4] Bede, H. E. iv. 3.

[5] 'Natione quidem Gallus sed tunc legendarum gratia Scripturarum in
Hibernia non parvo tempore demoratus.' Ib. iii. 7.

[6] Vit. S. Cuthberti auct. anon., quoted in Skene's Celtic Scotland, ii. 422.

[7] 'Et quia in Hibernia scholasticam eruditionem viguisse audivit Hiberniam
secessit,' &c. Alcuin, Vit. Willibrordi, lib. i. cap. 4.

[8] Adamnan, Vit. S. Col. i. 3.

[9] Bede, Vit. S. Cuthberti, cap. 19; H. E. iii. 19.

were, some of them, working in the garden, and others were
dressing the orchard[1].

One short fragment of an ancient Celtic Pontifical survives
in the Public Library, Zurich, in an Irish handwriting of the
tenth century. The first page is quite illegible, having been
made the outside cover of a book. Page 2 contains these
words:—

[De Virgine Investienda.]

'(*a*) Permaneat ad prudentibus qui . . . virginibus vigi-
lantia . . . adferte copuletur . . . per.

(*b*) Oremus, fratres carissimi, misericordiam ut euntum
bonum tribuere dignetur huic puellae N. quae Deo votum
candidam vestem perferre cum integritate coronae in resurrectione vitae aeternae quam facturus est; orantibus nobis,
praestet Deus.

(*c*) Conserva, Domine, istius devotae pudorem castitatis
dilectionem continentiae in factis, in dictis, in cogitationibus;
Per te, Christe Jesu, qui.

(*d*) Accipe, puella, pallium candidum quod perferas ante
tribunal Domini.'

This fragment is interesting as showing that the office for
the reception of a nun into a Celtic monastery included, in
addition to the ceremony of crowning, the formal presentation
of a white dress, which is not part of the 'Ordo de Consecratione Virginum' in the present Roman Pontifical. Nor
are (*a*) (*b*) (*c*) (*d*) found elsewhere, although a formula resembling (*d*) accompanies the presentation of the veil, in a
tenth-century order for the 'Consecratio Sacrae Virginis'
printed in Gerbert, Liturg. Aleman. ii. 96: 'Accipe velum
sacrum, puella, quod praeferas sine macula ante tribunal
Domini nostri Jesu Christi.'

And again in the tenth-century copy of the Pontifical of

---

[1] 'Alii hortum laboraverunt, alii arbores pomiferas excoluerunt, B. vero
Gallus texebat retia,' &c. Wal. Strabo, Vit. S. Galli, cap. 6.

Egbert, Archbishop of York, at the presentation of the 'pallium' in the 'Consecratio Viduae:'—

'*Post haec imponis viduae pallium et dicis.*

'Accipe viduae pallium quod perferas sine macula ante tribunal Domini nostri Jesu Christi[1].'

The monastic was closely connected with the missionary character of the Celtic Church. The list of monasteries given on pp. 14-16 proves how widespread was the area once covered by its evangelistic agency and monastic development; but such development was not the work of one century, nor due to the energy of a single portion of the Celtic Church.

It began by the colonisation of Brittany from the British Church in the fifth century[2].

A British colony was established in Spanish Gallicia in the sixth century, where a Celtic See was occupied by a bishop named Madoc, c. A.D. 570[3].

In the same century the Irish Church began to exhibit its missionary power. The Christianising of the whole of the north and north-west of Scotland and its adjacent islands was due to St. Columba, chief among the missionary Irish. He was Abbot of Iona, and patron saint of Mull, Tiree, Islay, Oronsay, and Lewis. Maccaldus, a native of Down, became Bishop of Man in the fifth century; St. Donnan of Egg; St. Maelrubha of Skye; St. Moluoc of Lismore, and Raasay; St. Brendan of Seil; St. Molaise of Arran; SS. Catan and Blaan of Bute. St. Columba's successors at Iona converted in a similar way the whole of the Anglo-Saxon population north of the Humber. St. Aidan, the Apostle of the Northumbrians (A.D. 634), whose diocese extended from the Humber to the Frith of Forth, was an Irishman

---

[1] Pontif. Ecgb. (Surtees Soc.), p. 114.   [2] See p. 15.

[3] The evidence on these points will be found in H. & S., Councils, vol. i. There was a mission on the part of the British Church to Ireland to restore the faith c. A.D. 550, conducted by SS. David, Gildas, and Cadoc; ib. p. 115.

and a monk of Iona; so were his successors Finan and
Colman, the latter of whom resigned his see after the Synod
of Whitby A.D. 664, and retired to his native country rather
than accept its anti-Scottish decisions [1]. Diuma, the first
bishop of the Mercians, and his successor Ceollach, were
both of them Irishmen, the former certainly and the latter
probably having been brought up at Iona. Other distinguished Irish saints in England were St. Fursa, who
planted Christianity at Burghcastle in Suffolk; Mailduf
(Meildulfus), the founder of Malmesbury; St. Bega, the
foundress of St. Bees in Cumberland; St. Moninna (Mod-
wenna), the patron saint of Burton-on-Trent; St. Ciaran,
or Piran, whose name occurs frequently in the dedications
of Cornish churches [2].

But Irish missionary zeal sought a vent beyond the con-
fines of Great Britain. Early in the sixth century (A.D. 511)
the Irish St. Fridolin appeared at Poitiers, Strasbourg, and
Seckingen near Basle, as the pioneer of future missionary
hosts. Late in the sixth and early in the seventh centuries
St. Columbanus and St. Gall, with their companions, traversed
Gaul, Italy, and Switzerland, founding their chief monas-
teries at Luxeuil, Bobbio, and St. Gall. Soon afterwards St.
Kilian, with his companions the priest Totman and the deacon
Colman, penetrated to Würzburg, where he was martyred
A.D. 687; and the later names of Fiacrius, Chillenus, Furseus,
Ultanus, Foillanus, &c., celebrated at Lagny near Paris, at
Meaux, Peronne, &c., indicate the Irish nationality of many
who laboured successfully in propagating the Christian faith

---

[1] Bede, H. E. iii. 25, 26.
[2] Even for St. Cuthbert an Irish origin has been claimed. Bede introduces
him to the reader of his H. E. without mentioning his birth-place or nationality
(iv. 28), but recognises him as a native of Britain in his poetical life of St.
Cuthbert; Smith's Bede, p. 269. The authority for his Irish origin is a
Libellus de Ortu S. Cuthberti written in the twelfth century, but the earliest
extant copy of which belongs to the fourteenth century. It has been published
by the Surtees Soc. vol. viii. St. Cuthbert's Irish name is said to have been
Mullucc.

in France, Belgium, and other parts of central Europe. Less known Irish missions also carried Christianity to the Faroe Isles c. A.D. 725, and to Iceland A.D. 795[1]. Thus between the fifth and eighth centuries the Celtic Church extended, with intermissions, North and South from Iceland to Spain, East and West from the Atlantic to the Danube, from Westernmost Ireland to the Italian Bobbio A.D. 612, and the German Salzburg A.D. 696.

Even beyond these limits Irishmen were afterwards and occasionally elected bishops, as Cataldus at Taranto and his brother Donatus at Lupiae in the eighth century, and another Donatus at Fiesole a century and a half later.

It will have been noticed that all the great leaders in this Celtic wave of missionary enterprise were of Irish origin, viz. St. Columba, the Apostle of the Picts and Scots; St. Aidan, the Apostle of Northumbria; St. Columbanus, the Apostle of the Burgundians of the Vosges district of Alsace; St. Gall, the Apostle of North-east Switzerland and Alemannia; St. Kilian, the Apostle of Thuringia; and Virgilius, the Apostle of Carinthia.

§ 3. ORTHODOXY OF THE CELTIC CHURCH.—There are no substantial grounds for impugning the orthodoxy of the Celtic Church. On the contrary, there is unimpeachable evidence the other way. But expressions have been sometimes used with reference to it which would lead to a different conclusion. Pope Gregory probably knew very little about the faith of the British Church when he claimed the right of subjecting to the jurisdiction of Augustine 'not only the bishops whom he should ordain, but also all the priests in Britain, that they might learn the rule of believing rightly and living well from his life and teaching[2].'

---

[1] Recorded by Dicuilus (an Irish monk A.D. 825), De Mensura Orbis, pp. 29, 30. His work exists in a tenth-century MS. at Paris (Bibl. Imp. no. 4806), printed by A. C. A. Walckener at Paris, 1807.

[2] Bede, H. E. i. 29.

Certainly Britain, like the rest of Christendom, may have been partially tainted with Arianism in the fourth century, when certain British bishops at Ariminum A.D. 359 were deceived or terrified into signing a semi-Arian creed; and with Pelagianism in the fifth century, which was the cause of the joint visit of Germanus Bishop of Auxerre and Lupus Bishop of Troyes A.D. 429, and of another visit of Germanus with Severus Bishop of Treves, A.D. 447. But the Gallican bishops are recorded to have been eminently successful in their mission, and to have returned across the Channel leaving the Catholic faith firmly established in these islands [1]. The real difficulty here is to understand how the rationalism of Pelagius can have had even a passing attraction for the naturally superstitious and mystic Celt, not how Germanus succeeded in stamping it out. There is nothing in these admitted facts to justify us in inferring from the above-quoted words of St. Gregory that the Celtic Church was destitute of any 'forma recte credendi [2];' or in acquiescing in the language of an Anglo-Saxon Synod (A.D. 705), which took steps for 'the destruction of the malignant and too flourishing heresy of the Britons [3].'

On the other hand, a catena of evidence can be produced to disprove the charge of heresy and in support of the orthodoxy of the first Church of the British Isles. Hilary of Poitiers (A.D 358) congratulates the bishops of the British

---

[1] Authority for this and other statements of a historical character with reference to this period are accumulated in H. and S., vol. i. p. 10. Arianism is referred to by name and Pelagianism by inference in Gildas, Hist. § 12.

[2] 'Tua vero fraternitas . . . omnes Brittaniae sacerdotes habeat . . . subjectos, quatenus ex lingua et vita tuae sanctitatis, et recte credendi et bene vivendi formam percipiant, atque officium suum fide ac moribus exsequentes, ad coelestia, cum Dominus voluerit, regna pertingant.' Bede, H. E. i. 29.

[3] 'Quo maligna quae tunc supra modum pullulabat haeresis Britonum destrueretur.' H. and S. iii. 268. The visit of Victricius Bishop of Rouen, A.D. 396, was for the purpose of settling some British dispute, not, as has been groundlessly surmised, for the purpose of quelling Arianism. The Epistle of Gildas proves the moral depravity of the British priesthood in the sixth century, but is silent as to any charge of heresy.

provinces on 'their having continued uncontaminated and uninjured by any contact with the detestable heresy[1]' (of Arianism). Athanasius (A.D. 363) states that the British Churches had signified by letter to him their adhesion to the Nicene faith[2]. St. Chrysostom (A.D. 386–398) said that 'even the British Isles have felt the power of the word, for there too churches and altars have been erected. There too, as on the shores of the Euxine or in the South, men may be heard discussing points in Scripture, with differing voices but not with differing belief, with varying tongues but not with varying faith[3].' St. Jerome (c. A.D. 400) asserted that 'Britain in common with Rome, Gaul, Africa, Persia, the East, and India, adores one Christ, observes one rule of faith[4].' Venantius Fortunatus (c. A.D. 580) testified to British orthodoxy in the sixth century[5], and Wilfrid in the seventh century. The testimony of the latter, whose hostility to the Celtic Church was notorious, is as honourable to himself, as it is placed beyond all suspicion of inaccuracy or exaggeration. Present at Rome A.D. 680 at a council of a hundred and twenty-five bishops, held in anticipation of the Œcumenical Council of Constantinople in the same year against the Monothelites, Wilfrid asserted that the true Catholic faith was held by the Irish, Scottish, and British, as well as by the Anglo-Saxon Church[6]. It had therefore been no vain boast of Columbanus to Pope Boniface (A.D. 612) that his Church was not schismatical or heretical, but that it held the whole Catholic faith[7].

---

[1] Hilar. Pictav. De Synodis, Prolog. et § 2.

[2] Athanas. Ep. ad Jov. Imp. 2.

[3] Chrys. Quod Christus sit Deus, 12; In Princip. Act. 3. 1.

[4] Hieron. Ep. ad Evangel. c. 1.

[5]   'Currit ad extremas fidei pia fabula gentes
            Ex trans Oceanum terra Britanna fovet.' Ad Justin. Jun. Imp.

[6] 'Pro omni Aquiloni parte Britanniae et Hiberniae, insulisque quae ab Anglorum et Britonum necnon Scotorum et Pictorum gentibus colebantur, veram et catholicam fidem confessus est, et cum subscriptione sua corroboravit.' Eddius, Vit. Wilfrid. c. li.

[7] 'Nihil extra Evangelicam et Apostolicam doctrinam recipientes; nullus

Had it been otherwise, could British bishops have been present certainly at the Council of Arles A.D. 314, perhaps at Nice A.D. 325, probably at Sardica A.D. 347[1]? Could the conferences have taken place at Augustine's Oak A.D. 603, and at Whitby A.D. 664, without at all events far more serious questions having been raised than the form of the tonsure or the calculation of Easter[2]? Would Wini Bishop of Winchester have associated two British bishops with himself in the consecration of St. Chad A.D. 664[3]?

Both direct testimony and indirect inference lead us to conclude with reference to the whole Celtic Church what Montalembert allows with regard to primitive Ireland, that it was 'profoundly and unchangeably Catholic in doctrine, but separated from Rome in various points of discipline and liturgy[4].'

§ 4. INDEPENDENCE OF ROME.—Another noteworthy feature of the Celtic Church was its independence of the Roman Church in its origin, mission, and jurisdiction.

Before the sixth century Roman claims were not opposed, partly because such claims were not yet in existence in the form which they assumed after St. Augustine's mission, partly because, so far as they may have existed potentially, there was an entire unconsciousness of them on the part of the Christian Church in these islands.

The contrary view has notwithstanding been entertained, and rests on the testimony of early and generally trustworthy witnesses on the Roman side, or on later native

---

haereticus, nullus Judaeus, nullus schismaticus fuit, sed fides Catholica sicut a vobis primum, sanctorum scilicet Apostolorum successoribus tradita est, inconcussa tenetur.' Epist. iv. ad Bonifacium; Fleming, Collectan. 139.

[1] H. & S. i. pp. 7–8.

[2] For other minor points of difference raised by Augustine see Bede, H. E. ii. 2.

[3] Bede, H. E. iii. 28. The validity of this consecration was afterwards disputed by Archbishop Theodore, on grounds which are discussed at length in W. Bright's Early Eng. Ch. Hist. pp. 213, 226–7.

[4] Monks of the West, iii. 79.

writers, who however do not profess to be independent or original authorities on this subject.

Bede attributes the conversion of England to the agency of Pope Eleutherus (A. D. 171–190), during the joint reigns of Aurelius and Verus (161–9), in the time of the British prince Lucius[1].

This story is now known to have originated in Rome in the fifth or sixth century, 300 years or more after the date assigned to that event. In the eighth century Bede introduced it into England, where by the ninth century it had grown into the conversion of the whole of Britain, while the full-fledged fiction, connecting it specially with Wales and Glastonbury, and entering into further details, grew up between the ninth and twelfth centuries[2].

Prosper of Aquitaine (A.D. 402–463), who went to Rome on a mission to Pope Cælestine, A. D. 431, and was afterwards secretary to Pope Leo the Great, writing c. 455, asserts with regard to the conversion of Ireland that 'Palladius was consecrated by Pope Cælestine (422–432), and sent to the Scots believing in Christ, as their first bishop[3].' This is the original source of a statement which reappears in substance, though not in this exact form, in many later documents, and with considerable additional detail. It would be difficult to find any other sentence penned by any ecclesiastical historian which has caused so much confusion, or which has been so variously interpreted. In the first place, who were the Scots to whom Prosper refers? We know beyond a doubt that they were the inhabitants of Ireland, but this necessary limitation of the meaning of the term

---

[1] Bede, H. E. i. 4.

[2] This conclusion with further and interesting details will be found in H. and S. i. pp. 25–26. The historical anachronism involved in Bede's account is pointed out by G. H. Moberly, edit. of Bede, p. 14 n. Oxf. 1869.

[3] 'Ad Scotos in Christum credentes ordinatur a Papa Coelestino Palladius, et primus episcopus mittitur.' Prosper, Chron. Consular. ad ann. 429. In another place Prosper says, 'Et ordinato Scotis episcopo, dum Romanam insulam studet servare Catholicam, fecit etiam barbaram Christianam.' Contra Collat. xxi.

before the tenth century has only recently become generally
accepted and understood, and it is probable that the later
legends connecting Palladius with Scotland, as found in the
Aberdeen Breviary, in the Leabhar Breac, and in the Scotichronicon of John of Fordun (14th cent.), have originated in
a misinterpretation of Prosper's language. Secondly, who
was Palladius? Was he, as Prosper intimates rather than
asserts, a Roman, or, as is stated in the Book of Armagh,
an archdeacon of the Church of Rome[1]? or was he, as Dr.
Todd concludes, a Gaul[2], and is to be identified with a certain
Gallican bishop, commemorated under the name of Patricius,
at Clermont, in the Roman martyrology on March 16? or
was he an Irishman? and as the annotations of Tirechan
on the Life of St. Patrick state that 'Palladius was also
called Patrick[3],' has there been some confusion between
St. Palladius and St. Patrick, and can statements which
were meant to apply to the one have become transferred to
the other? Thirdly, what is the force of 'primus'? Is it
to be interpreted chronologically, and accepted as a disproof
of numerous later legends, which allude to the existence of
Christianity and of Christian bishops in Ireland before A. D.
431? or are we to infer that there was previously a presby-
terian form of Christianity in that country? or is 'primus'
to be taken in the sense of precedence, and is it the primacy
of Ireland which was conferred at this early date by a Bishop
of Rome upon Palladius[4]? There is no contemporaneous
evidence for the Roman mission of St. Patrick, for the
earliest authority for which see p. 37.

The first introduction of Christianity into Scotland was
due to the labours of Ninian among the Southern Picts

---

[1] Fol. 2 a.
[2] Todd, J. H., Life of St. Patrick, p. 279.
[3] Book of Armagh, fol. 16 a, quoted in H. & S. ii. pt. ii. p. 290.
[4] We have preferred to enumerate the difficulties of this passage, rather
than to suggest their solution. The question is discussed at much length by
Dr. Todd, Life of St. Patrick, pp. 270-309, and the available evidence is
summarised in H. & S. ii. pt. ii. pp. 290-291.

(c. A. D. 401), who, 'according to Bede,' had been regularly instructed in the faith and the mysteries of the truth at Rome[1] ; and who, according to Ailred[2], had been consecrated a bishop by Pope Siricius.

These statements appear again and again in the later annals and lives of the saints, acquiring a more circumstantial character the further they are removed from the period of which they profess to give an account. Their truth has been generally taken for granted by modern writers[3], until the careful research of Messrs. Haddan and Stubbs has given the death-blow to the story of King Lucius and Pope Eleutherus[4], and it may be suspected, although the difficulty of proving the negative has not been fully overcome, that the stories of the consecration of Palladius by Pope Cælestine and of Ninian by Pope Siricius are equally without foundation. For while Prosper and Bede must be accepted as generally impartial and trustworthy historians, no one can read the works of the former without noticing that his chief object was to magnify the importance of the Papacy[5] ; and,

---

[1] Bede, H. E. iii. 4.

[2] Ailred, Vita S. Niniani, cap. 2. Ailred wrote in the twelfth century.

[3] Mr. Skene, who certainly cannot be suspected of any Roman bias, says, chiefly on the strength of the above authorities, that the early British Church 'regarded the Patriarch of Rome as the Head of the Western Church, and the source of ecclesiastical authority and mission.' Celtic Scotland, ii. p. 6. The reader will find facts on pp. 35-40 which disprove such a statement as far as the later Celtic Church—and therefore inferentially as far as the earlier Celtic Church—is concerned.

[4] Councils, &c. i. 25.

[5] I. p. 17 n. As an instance of Prosper's Roman bias compare his statement that Germanus of Auxerre (and Lupus) were sent by Pope Cælestine to Britain to combat Pelagianism A.D. 429, with the statement of Constantius a presbyter of Lyons (A.D. 473-492) that they were sent by a Gallican synod.

Prosper says, 'Ad actionem Palladii diaconi Papa Caelestinus Germanum Autesiodorensem episcopum vice sua mittit, et deburbatis haereticis Britannos ad Catholicam fidem dirigit.' Chron. [after A.D. 455].

Constantius says, 'Eodem tempore ex Britanniis directa legatio Gallicanis episcopis nunciavit Pelagianam perversitatem in locis suis late populos occupasse, et quamprimum fidei Catholicae debere succurri. Ob quam causam synodus numerosa collecta est; omniumque judicio duo praeclara religionis lumina universorum precibus ambiuntur, Germanus et Lupus, apostolici sacer-

on the other hand, Bede, who was removed by more than a
century from the events recorded in the first Book of his
Ecclesiastical History, was actuated by an intense dislike of
the independent Celtic Church, which has been stigmatised by
a modern Roman Catholic writer in the following words :—

' This (i. e. the feeling and attitude of the British Church)
is called by Bede, in language too like that which Muscovite
writers of our own day employ in respect to the Poles, " a
domestic and immoral hatred : " " Britones maxima ex parte
domestico sibi odio gentem Anglorum et totius Ecclesiae
Catholicae statum Pascha, minus recte moribusque improbis
pugnant." There is no just reason for imputing to the
British Christians a lower rate of morals than those of the
Saxon converts; but our venerable historian, blinded by his
passions and prejudices, goes still further, and yields, as
so many have done after him, to the hateful temptation
of identifying the work of God with a human conquest.
"Tamen et divina sibi et humana prorsus resistente virtute, in neutro cupitum possunt obtinere propositum ; quippe
qui quamvis ex parte sui sint juris, nonnulla tamen ex parte
Anglorum sunt servitio mancipati." (H. E. v. 23.) He says
elsewhere (v. 18) that St. Aldhelm wrote "librum egregium
adversus errorem Britonum, quo vel Pascha non suo tempore
celebrant, vel alia *perplura ecclesiasticae castitati et paci* contraria gerunt." In all Aldhelm's writings that have been
preserved to us there is not the least allusion to the irregular
morals of the Celtic clergy[1].'

So Bede uses such epithets as ' nefanda ' and ' perfida ' of

---

dote qui,' &c. De Vita Germani, i. 19. This is also Bede's account, H. E.
i. 7.

For further evidence of the pro-papal tendency of Prosper, read his Praeteritorum Sedis Apostolicae Episcoporum auctoritates, Praef. cap. vii, viii ;
Liber contra Collatorem, cap. v, xxi, xliii ; Carmen de Ingratis, pt. i. ll. 40,
78, 184.

[1] Montalembert, Monks of the West, v. 25. It has been suggested that
' castitas ' in the above passage may mean ' purity of ecclesiastical discipline '
rather than ' purity of morals.' Bede elsewhere describes Acca, Bishop of
Hexham, as ' in catholicae fidei confessione castissimus ' (H. E. v. 21).

the British nation when he records their defeat by Æthelfrith at the battle of Chester A. D. 613, and the massacre of
the monks of Bangor, in accordance with the prophecy of
St. Augustine[1]. The clue to such language is the fact that
Bede wrote under the influence of two motives, independent
in their origin but conducing to the same result. Firstly,
there was a national hatred of the British Church and nation.
This was no doubt largely due to a feeling of resentment at
the absence of British evangelistic enterprise in Anglo-Saxon
heathendom, of which Bede complains once and again[2].
But we have seen that the British Church was not destitute
of missionary power[3]; and more allowance must be made
in the instance before us than Bede is inclined to make
for the difficulties of the case. It is easier for the conquerors
to preach to the conquered, than *vice versa*[4]. Mission work
must have been very difficult while the state of feeling
between the two nationalities was as embittered as it was
still in the eleventh century, when any Welshman found
armed east of Offa's Dyke was legally punishable by mutila-
tion[5]. A second motive for Bede's violence may have been a
desire to aggrandise Rome at the expense of the rest of Christendom, and to represent her as the mother of all Western
Churches; a desire which began to exhibit itself as early
as the fifth century in the writings of Prosper, and which

---

[1] H. E. ii. 2.

[2] 'Qui, inter alia inenarrabilium scelera, quae historicus eorum Gildus
flebili sermone describit, et hoc addebant, ut nunquam genti Saxonum sive
Anglorum, secum Brittaniam incolenti verbum fidei praedicando committerent.'
H. E. i. 22.

Compare the threat and prophecy with which St. Augustine wound up the
conference with British bishops at 'Augustinæs ac:' 'Quibus vir Domini Augustinus fertur minitans praedixisse, quia si pacem cum fratribus accipere nollent,
bellum ab hostibus forent accepturi; et si nationi Anglorum noluissent viam
vitae praedicare, per horum manus ultionem essent mortis passuri. Quod ita
per omnia, ut praedixerat divino agente judicio patratum est.' Ib. ii. 2. The
state of hostility between the two Churches is further illustrated at p. 42.

[3] p. 15.

[4] Eddius speaks of the 'loca sancta in diversis regionibus, quae Clerus
Britonum, aciem gladii hostilis manu gentis nostrae fugiens, deseruit.' Vit. S.
Wilfr. c. xvii.   [5] Iohannes Sarisbur. Polycraticus, vi. 6.

became intensified instead of diminished in each succeeding
century.

The following facts tend to prove a non-Roman origin
of the Celtic Church.

(*a*) Incidental allusions in ancient documents to the existence of a primitive Christian Church in these islands differing
from the Anglo-Roman or Scoto-Roman Church of later
days.

Giraldus Cambrensis in his description of Ireland (A. D.
1185) narrates how 'in North Munster there is a lake containing two islands; in the greater island there is a church
of the ancient monastic rule ('ecclesia antiquae religionis'), and
in the lesser a chapel wherein a few monks, called Culdees,
devoutly serve God[1].' In South Munster the same traveller
visited the church of St. Michael ('ecclesiam antiquae nimis
et authenticae religionis[2]'). This ancient monastic rule
may have been that not only of SS. Patrick, Columba, &c.,
but also of (1) Mansuetus, first Bishop of Toul in France
(fourth century); (2) Sedulius, the Christian poet (fifth
century); (3) Caelestius, the Pelagian (third and fourth
centuries); (4) Eliphius and Eucharius, martyrs in France
(fourth century). All these were Irishmen, and though much
obscurity hangs over the history and date of (2) and (4),
they may all have been trained under the pre-Roman
'antiqua et authentica religio Hiberniae[3].'

There are also allusions to an 'ecclesia primitiva' in Scotland in the Aberdeen Breviary[4], the strange Masses of which
were finally abolished by Queen Margaret[5].

The independence of the ancient Cornish Church is attested
by a passage in the Leofric Missal, an eleventh-century MS.
in the Bodleian Library, which describes how Eadulf, the

---

[1] Top. Hib. ii. cap. 4, Master of Rolls Ser., v. p. 82.

[2] Ib. ii. 30, p. 118.

[3] For further evidence for the existence of Christianity in Ireland before
St. Patrick, see R. Brash, Eccles. Architecture of Ireland, p. 110; H. and S.
vol. ii. p. 291.   [4] See Index.   [5] p. 7.

first Anglo-Saxon Bishop of Crediton (A.D. 909–34), acquired
three properties in Cornwall that he might more frequently
visit the erroneous and unruly Church in that county [1].

Its divergence from the Roman Church early in the eighth
century had been complained of by Aldhelm Abbot of
Malmesbury A.D. 705 [2].

(*b*) The absence of any allusion to a Roman mission or
jurisdiction in the few surviving genuine writings of Celtic
saints, Gildas [3], Fastidius, Aileran, Patrick, Sechnall, Fiacc,
Columbanus, Columba, Cuminius, Adamnan.

(*c*) The presence in such writings of passages which are
inconsistent with any recognition of Roman mission or
authority. St. Patrick in his Confession and his 'Epistola
ad Corotici subditos' is not only silent as to any commission

---

[1] 'Ut inde singulis annis visitaret gentem Cornubiensem ad exprimendos
eorum errores, nam antea in quantum potuerant veritati resistebant, et non
decretis apostolicis oboediebant.' (MS. no. 579. fol. 2 b.)

[2] 'Auditum namque et diversis rumoribus compertum nobis est, quod
sacerdotes vestri a Catholicae fidei regula, secundum Scripturae preceptum
minime concordent.' Aldhelm, Ep. ad Gerunt. Reg. Damnoniae ; H. & S. i. 672.

[3] An obscure sentence of Gildas quoted by Dr. Lingard (A. S. Church,
i. 335, 345) does not mention and does not seem to refer to Rome. The
following passage occurs in Gildas' description of the British priesthood : 'Praecepta Christi spernentes, et suas libidines votis omnibus implere
curantes, sedem Petri Apostoli immundis pedibus usurpantes, sed merito
cupiditatis in Judae traditoris pestilentem cathedram decidentes.' Epistola, in
H. and S., Councils, i. 74. Bishop Forbes sees in this passage an allusion
to British pilgrimages to Rome (Historians of Scotland, v. p. 263); but
surely the allusion to the two Apostles is purely metaphorical, though British
pilgrimages to Rome, and to Jerusalem also, were probable enough, and
common enough according to the Lives of the Saints : e. g. Ailred, writing a life
of St. Ninian in the twelfth century, attributes these sentiments to him :
'In terra mea quaesivi quem diligit anima mea et non inveni. Surgam et
circuibo mare et aridam . . . Transiensque Britannicum mare, et per Gallicanas
Alpes ingressus Italiam, prospero itinere ad urbem usque pervenit.' Pinkerton, J., Vit. SS. Scot. p. 4. The contemporary evidence of Theodoret, &c.
about British pilgrimages is quoted in H. and S., Councils, &c. i. 13. Gildas
interpreted St. Matt. xvi. 18, 19 as a divine commission given to every priest :
'Vero sacerdoti dicitur, "Tu es Petrus et super hanc petram aedificabo Ecclesiam meam ;" vos quidem assimilamini viro stulto qui aedificavit domum suam
super arenam . . . itemque omni sancto sacerdoti promittitur ; "Et quaecunque
solveris super terram erunt soluta et in coelis, et quaecunque ligaveris," &c.
Sed quomodo vos aliquid solvetis ut sit solutum et in coelis, ob scelera adempti,
et immanium peccatorum funibus compediti,' &c. Epistola, sub finem.

from a Bishop of Rome, but describes himself in general terms
as a bishop in Ireland, deriving his commission directly from
God Himself.   The latter letter opens thus : 'Patricius peccator
indoctus, Hiberione constitutus episcopus, a Deo accepi id quod
sum.'

In other passages he attributes his Irish apostleship to an
inward call, which he regarded as a divine command, and to
a vision of a man (or an angel) in the night beckoning him
over to Ireland [1].   The earliest written records of St. Patrick,
the Hymn attributed to St. Fiacc Bishop of Sletty, near
Carlow, a convert and disciple of St. Patrick—the Hymn
of St. Seehnall (S. Secundinus), another contemporary of
St. Patrick, whose sister's son he is said to have been,—
the ancient Life of St. Patrick, written by Muirchu Mac-
cumachtheni at the dictation of Aedh Bishop of Sletty,
(d. 698), and preserved in the Book of Armagh, all alike are
silent as to any Roman mission of St. Patrick [2].

The language of a later Irish saint—Columbanus—representing the attitude of that portion of the Celtic Church
to Rome at the end of the sixth and the beginning of the

---

[1] The passages are too long to quote. They will be found in English in
Todd's Life of St. Patrick, pp. 377–379.

[2] According to St. Sechnall, St. Patrick :

'Apostolatum a Deo sortibus est.'

This is the more remarkable as St. Peter is mentioned in the previous line
without any allusion to a mission to St. Patrick from his successor in the See
of Rome.   And again :

'Dominus eum elegit ut doceret barbaros,
Quem Deus misit, ut Paulum ad gentes, apostolum.'

St. Fiacc's Hymn mentions the admonition of an angel (stanza 7) ; Liber
Hymnorum, pp. 287–304 ; H. and S. vol. ii. pt. ii. p. 339 n. The earliest Irish
authority for St. Patrick's Roman mission are the annotations of Tirechan in
the Book of Armagh, and the Scholia (ninth century or later) to St. Fiacc's
Hymn.

The unhistorical character of Tirechan's Life of St. Patrick is demonstrated
in Skene's Celtic Scotland, ii. 425. Bede does not mention St. Patrick. The
'Vita S. Patricii' sometimes printed among his works was written by the Irish
Probus, ob. 859. Adamnan makes only one, and that quite an incidental,
allusion to him : 'Nam quidam proselytus Brito, homo sanctus, sancti
Patricii episcopi discipulus, Maucteus nomine,' &c. Vit. S. Colum. Praef. ii.
p. 6.

seventh century, is quite inconsistent with any theory of its
Roman origin, and must sound strange in the ears of a
modern Ultramontane. The position assumed by Columbanus, writing on the Continent to the Pope, substantially
amounted to this: an acknowledgment of the Bishop of
Rome as a true bishop of the Church of Christ, and of the
need of courteous language in addressing the occupant of
so distinguished a See, with, throughout, an implied assertion
of exemption from his jurisdiction, and a claim to be allowed
to criticise freely, and from the independent standpoint of
an equal, the character and conduct of any Roman pontiff.

The language which he used to Boniface IV is not that
of a subordinate, but is couched in terms the freedom of
which may have been resented then, but would certainly be
resented now. He laments over the infamy attaching itself
to the Chair of St. Peter in consequence of disputes at Rome[1].
He exhorts the Pope to be more on the watch[2], and to cleanse
his See from error, because it would be a lamentable thing if
the Catholic faith was not held in the Apostolic See[3]. He
says that many persons entertain doubts as to the purity of the
faith of the Roman bishop[4]. He allows a high post of honour
to the See of Rome, but second to that of Jerusalem, the place
of our Lord's resurrection[5]. He upbraids the Roman Church

---

[1] 'Dolor enim potius me quam elatio compellit vobis indicare, humillima, ut
decet, suggestione, quod nomen Dei per vos contendentes utrinque blasphema-
tur inter gentes; doleo enim, fateor, de infamia cathedrae Sancti Petri.'
iv. Epist. ad Bonif.; Fleming, Collectan. 139. He apparently alludes here to
some dispute among the Italian bishops, for he says afterwards, 'Agnoscite vos
invicem, ut sit gaudium in coelo et in terra pro pace et conjunctione vestra;'
and in another place, 'Unum itaque omnes dicite, et unum sentite, ut utrique
unum sitis toti Christiani,' &c.

[2] 'Vigila, itaque quaeso, Papa, vigila, et iterum dico, vigila, quia forte non
bene vigilavit Vigilius (537–555) quem caput scandali isti clamant qui nobis
culpam injiciunt. Vigila primo pro fide,' &c. Ib. p. 140.

[3] 'Ut mundes cathedram Petri ab omni errore (a later MS. hand has
attempted to substitute 'horrore') si qui est, ut aiunt, intromissus, si non
puritas agnoscatur ab omnibus. Dolendum enim ac deflendum est, si in sede
Apostolica fides Catholica non tenetur.' Ib. p. 141.

[4] 'Rogo vos, quia multi dubitant de fidei vestrae puritate.' Epist. v. ad
Bonifac. § 14.

[5] ·Propter Christi geminos apostolos, vos prope coelestes estis, et Roma

for proudly claiming a greater authority and power in divine
things than was possessed by other Churches merely because
of a certain fact recorded in the Gospels, and denied by no
one, that our Lord entrusted the keys of the kingdom of
heaven to St. Peter, and points out that the prerogative of
the keys stands upon a different basis, and must be wielded
on other grounds[1].

Writers from a Roman standpoint have resorted to curious
devices to escape the necessary inference from such passages.
Dr. von Döllinger collects the courteous expressions contained in the Epistles of Columbanus, and deduces from
them the conclusion that the Celtic saints 'recognised in the
Roman Bishop the Head of the Church, and were in un-
broken communion with him, and through him with the
Church universal!' He sees in St. Columbanus' claim to
Catholicity in a passage previously quoted[2] 'a clear proof of
the Roman mission of St. Patrick[3]!'

Ozanam's explanation of Columbanus' language is still
more amazing. It is due 'to the disordered eloquence of the
seventh century. This period was one of those in which
thought, ceasing to be the mistress of language, betrays itself

---

orbis terrarum caput et ecclesiarum, salva loci Dominicae resurrectionis sin-
gulari praerogativa.' Ep. iv. p. 143.

[1] He warns the Bishop of Rome, 'Ut non perdatis vestram dignitatem per
aliquam perversitatem. Tamdiu enim potestas apud vos erit, quamdiu recta
ratio permanserit; ille enim certus regni coelorum clavicularius est qui dignis per
veram scientiam aperit et indignis claudit. Alioquin si contraria fecerit nec
aperire nec claudere poterit. Cum haec igitur vera sint, et sine ulla contra-
dictione ab omnibus vere sapientibus recepta sint, licet omnibus notum est, et
nemo qui nesciat qualiter salvator noster Sancto Petro regni coelorum contulit
claves, et vos per hoc forte superciliosum nescio quid prae ceteris vobis majoris
auctoritatis ac in divinis rebus potestatis indicatis; noveritis, minorem fore
potestatem vestram apud Dominum si vel cogitatis hoc in cordibus vestris.
Quia unitas fidei in toto orbe unitatem facit potestatis et praerogativae, ita ut
libertas veritati ubique ab omnibus detur, et aditus erroris ab omnibus similiter
abnegetur.' Ep. v. § 10.   [2] p. 28. n. 7.

[3] But Dr. Döllinger wrote thus as far back as 1833; Geschichte der christ-
lichen Kirche, Periode ii. Seite 185. Landshut. Other writers who adduce
Columbanus as a witness in favour of Roman supremacy are Dr. Moran,
Essays on Early Irish Church, p. 99, and Mr. C. F. B. Allnatt, Cathedra
Petri, 2nd edit. pp. 69, 80.

either by an excess or defect of expression, whereby a writer
says less than he means, or more than he means, seldom what
he means to say[1].'

The whole subsequent history of the Celtic Church, both
in these islands and on the continent, exhibits occasional proofs
of its independence of, and hostility to, the claims of Rome.

In A.D. 601 Gregory entirely ignored the existence of the
Celtic bishops, as bishops, in his answer to Augustine's sixth
question whether consecration by a single bishop is valid.
'Yes,' he replied, 'in the English Church, while you are the
only bishop, you can only consecrate in the absence of other
bishops. But when bishops shall come over from Gaul they
will assist you as witnesses at the ordination of a bishop[2].'
In answer to his seventh question Gregory committed all
the bishops of Britain to his supervision and control[3], a
position of subordination which they repudiated, not surely
through any misapprehension of the nature and grounds of
St. Augustine's claims, but because they ignored the theory
of papal supremacy.

In A.D. 604 Augustine was succeeded in the See of Canterbury by one of his companions, Laurentius by name.
'Archbishop Laurence,' Bede tells us, 'not only attended to
the charge of the new Church that was gathered from the
English people, but also regarded with pastoral solicitude
the old natives of Britain, and likewise the people of the
Scots who inhabit the island of Ireland adjacent to Britain.
For observing that the practice and profession of the Scots
in their own country, and also those of the Britons in Britain
itself, were less in accordance with Church order in many
things, particularly because they used not to celebrate the
solemnity of Easter at the proper time . . . he in conjunction
with his fellow-bishops wrote them a letter of exhortation,
beseeching and entreating them to keep the bond of peace and

---

[1] La Civilization Chrétienne, chap. iv. p. 113.
[2] Gregorii Magni Op., Migne; Bib. Pat. Lat. lxxvii. p. 1191.
[3] Bede, H. E. i. 27.

Catholic observance with that Church of Christ which is extended all over the world;' of which letter these were the opening words : 'To our lords and most dear brethren the bishops or abbots throughout all Scotia, Laurentius, Mellitus, bishops, the servants of the servants of God. When the Apostolic See, according to her practice in all the world, directed us to preach to the pagan nations in these western parts, and so it came to pass that we entered into this island which is called Britain, before we were acquainted with it, believing that they walked in the ways of the Universal Church, we felt a very high respect for the Britons as well as the Scots, from our great regard to their sanctity; but when we came to know the Britons we supposed the Scots must be superior to them. However, we have learned from Bishop Daganus coming into this island, and from Abbot Columbanus coming into Gaul, that the Scots differ not at all from the Britons in their habits; for Bishop Daganus, when he came to us, not only would not take food with us, but would not even eat in the same lodging where we were eating[1].'

Daganus was the Celtic bishop of Inverdaoile in Wexford. The Saxon Archbishop's letter cannot have had all the desired effect, for writing 127 years later (A.D. 731) Bede implies that the state of separation and the feelings of enmity between the two Churches remained at least unchanged[2]. In fact they became gradually intensified. The Roman attitude towards the Celtic Church, both British and Irish, in the latter part of the seventh century was one of unmitigated hostility.

Late in A.D. 664 St. Wilfrid went to France for consecration to his Northumbrian See, refusing to be consecrated at home by bishops out of communion with the See of Rome[3]. The

---

[1] Bede, H. E. ii. 4.

[2] 'Sed quantum haec agendo profecerit, adhuc praesentia tempora declarant.' Ib.

[3] 'Sed perstitit ille negare, ne ab episcopis Scotis, vel ab iis quos Scoti ordinaverant consecrationem susciperet, quorum communionem sedes aspernaretur catholica.' Guliel. Malm. de Gestis Pontif. lib. iii; Migne, Bib. Pat. Lat. clxxix, 1555. The speech of Wilfrid on this occasion has been preserved by Eddius, his earliest and most trustworthy biographer : 'Omnibus modis

whole of England, except Kent, East Anglia, Wessex, and Sussex, was at this time in communion with the Scoto-Celtic Church. Of the excepted parts, Sussex was still heathen. Wessex was under a Bishop Wini, in Gallican orders, and in communion with the British bishops. Kent and East Anglia alone remained in complete communion with Rome and Canterbury.

In A.D. 667 Pope Vitalian wrote to Oswy, saying that he would look out for a fit person to fill the Archiepiscopal See of Canterbury, a person who would eradicate the tares from the whole of the island, alluding under this expression to the clergy of the Celtic Church[1].

We learn from the Penitential of Archbishop Theodore (A.D. 668–690) that the validity of its Orders was denied, if not entirely, at least so far as to need a fresh imposition of hands by a Catholic bishop; the consecration of its churches was not recognised; its members were refused communion, without first making a formal submission; and doubts were thrown out even as to the validity of their baptism[2]. And the Arch-

---

nobis necessarium est considerare, quomodo cum electione vestra sine accusatione Catholicorum virorum, ad gradum episcopalem cum dei adjutorio venire valeam ; sunt enim hic in Britannia multi Episcopi, quorum nullum meum est accusare, quamvis veraciter sciam, quod aut quartadecimani sunt ut Britones, ut Scoti, aut ab illis sunt ordinati quos nec Apostolica sedes in communionem recipit, neque eos qui schismaticis consentiunt. Et ideo in multa humilitate a vobis posco, ut me mittatis cum vestro praesidio trans mare ad Galliarum regionem, ubi Catholici Episcopi multi habentur, ut sine controversia Apostolicae sedis, licet indignus, gradum Episcopalem merear accipere.' Vit. S. Wilf. cap. xii. Eddius, like Bede, betrays a strong anti-Celtic bias, speaking of the 'schismatici Britanniae et Hiberniae' (ib. c. v.), and of 'peccatum ordinandi a Quartadecimanis in sedem alterius' (ib. c. xv).

[1] 'Ut ipse et viva voce et per divina oracula omnem inimici zizaniam ex omni vestra insula cum divino nutu eradicét.' Bede, H.E. iii. 29. The meaning of the passage is obvious from the context.

[2] '1. Qui ordinati sunt a Scottorum vel Britonum episcopis, qui in Pascha vel tonsura catholici non sunt, adunati ecclesiae non sunt, sed iterum a catholico episcopo manus impositione confirmentur.

'2. Similiter et aecclesiae quae ab ipsis episcopis ordinantur, aqua exorcizata aspergantur et aliqua collectione confirmentur.

'3. Licentiam quoque non habemus eis poscentibus crismam vel Eucharistiam dare, nisi ante confessi fuerint velle nobiscum esse in unitate ecclesiae. Et qui ex horum similiter gente vel quicunque de baptismo suo dubitaverit, baptizetur.' Poenitentiale Theodori, ii. 9.

bishop gave a practical proof that he meant what he said, by
objecting to the regularity of Chad's consecration as Bishop
of York (A.D. 665-6) because two of his consecrators, assistants
of Wini of Winchester, had been British bishops, probably
summoned from Cornwall for the purpose; and on Chad's
transference to Mercia Theodore 'completed his consecration
afresh in the Catholic manner[1],' A.D. 669.

In A.D. 687 the dying words of St. Cuthbert, himself a
convert to Roman usage, with reference to that Celtic Church
in which he had spent some thirty years of his life, exhibit
much bitterness. 'Keep peace,' he said, 'one with another,
and heavenly charity; and when necessity demands of you
to hold counsel as to your state, take great care that you
be of one mind in your conclusions; and, moreover, maintain
mutual concord with other servants of Christ, and despise
not the household of the faith who come to you seeking
hospitality, but be careful to receive such persons, to entertain
them, and to send them away with friendly kindness; and do
not think you are better than other followers of the same faith
and conversation; but with those that err from the unity of
Catholic peace either by not celebrating Easter at the proper
time, or by living perversely, have no communion[2].'

On the other hand, the members of the British Church
reciprocated by in their turn regarding the Christianity of
the Anglo-Saxons a thing of nought, and refusing to hold
any intercourse with them. In the year A.D. 705, Aldhelm
Abbot of Malmesbury, instructed by a West Saxon Synod,
wrote a letter to Geruntius (Geraint) King of Damnonia
(Devonshire and Cornwall), in which he complained that
'beyond the mouth of the Severn, the priests of Cambria,
proud of the purity of their morals[3], have such a horror of

---

[1] Bede, H. E. iv. 2.

[2] Bede, Vit. S. Cud. xxxvii-xxxix. The date of St. Cuthbert's birth is
unknown, but he entered the monastery of Melrose A.D. 651, conformed to
Roman usage after the Synod of Whitby A.D. 664, and died A.D. 687.

[3] This fact, admitted by Aldhelm, unless his words are sarcastic, contrasts
curiously with the accusations of Gildas, A.D. 547; Epist. in H. and S. i. 74.

communication with us, that they refuse to pray with us in the churches, or to seat themselves at the same table : more than this, what is left from our meals is thrown to dogs and swine, the dishes and bottles we have used have to be rubbed with sand or purified by fire, before they will condescend to touch them. The Britons give us neither· the salutation nor the kiss of peace ; and if one of us went to live in their country, the natives would hold no communication with him till after he had been made to endure a penance of forty days.'

Aldhelm then proceeds to assume that these British Christians, with their bishops, are outside the pale of the Catholic Church, and to assert in language, which has often been heard in more modern times, that it is impossible to be a Catholic and yet not in visible union with the See of St. Peter.

'We entreat you on our knees, in view of our future and common country in heaven, and of the angels our future fellow-countrymen, do not persevere in your arrogant contempt of the decrees of St. Peter and the traditions of the Roman Church, by a proud and tyrannical attachment to the decrees of your ancestors. Whatever may be the perfection of faith and good works, they are unprofitable out of the Catholic Church. . . . To sum up everything in one word, it is vain for any man to take credit to himself for belonging to the Catholic faith, so long as he rejects the doctrine and rule of St. Peter. For the foundation of the Church and the consolidation of the faith, placed first in Christ and secondly in St. Peter, will not waver before the assaults of any tempest. It was on St. Peter that the Truth Himself conferred the privilege of the Church, saying, Thou art Peter, and upon this rock will I build my Church[1].'

In A.D. 816, the Council of Celchyth, under Wulfred Archbishop of Canterbury and Kenulf King of Mercia, passed a

---

[1] H. and S. iii. 268–273.

resolution questioning the ordination of certain Irish clergy
and the efficacy of Sacraments administered by them[1].

The same state of antagonism between the Roman Church
and the Celtic communities existed on the Continent. The
Anglo-Saxon Winfrid, A.D. 680–755, better known as Boniface Archbishop of Mentz, and styled 'The Apostle of
Germany,' regarded the Irish and British missionaries with
whom he came in contact in Germany as little or nothing
else than heretics. He induced Pope Gregory III (A.D. 731–
741) to write a letter exhorting the bishops of Bavaria and
Alemannia to reject the 'teaching and the ritual of the Gentiles,' and 'of those Britons who came there,' as well as of
'other false priests and heretics[2].' He delated two of them,
Virgilius the Apostle of Carinthia, who had been known in
Ireland as Ferghal Abbot of Aghabo, and Sidonius, to Pope
Zachary A.D. 746, for incorrectly administering baptism, and
though the Pope acquitted them on this score, Boniface secured
their condemnation in the following year on a question of
the existence and character of the antipodes. A third Irishman was charged with holding heretical views of baptism,
and a fourth, named Clement, was condemned for heterodoxy
A.D. 742, and afterwards imprisoned by Carloman.

The above facts present to our view a vast Celtic communion existing in Great Britain and Ireland, and sending
its missions among the Teutonic tribes on the Continent,
and to distant islands like Iceland; Catholic in doctrine and
practice, and yet with its claims to Catholicity ignored or
impugned by the Church of Rome; with a long roll of saints,
every name of note on which is either that of one like

---

[1] 'Ut nullus permittatur de genere Scottorum in alicujus diocesi sacram sibi
ministeria usurpare, neque ei consentire liceat ex sacro ordine aliquot attingere,
vel ab eis accipere in baptismo, aut in celebratione missarum, vel etiam
Eucharistiam populo praebere, quia incertum est nobis, unde, en (an) ab aliquo
ordinentur,' &c. Cap. v; H. and S. iii. 581.

[2] 'Gentilitatis ritum, et doctrinam, vel venientium Brittonum, vel falsorum
sacerdotum et haereticorum, aut undecunque sint, renuentes ac prohibentes
adjiciatis,' &c. Greg. III. Epist. ad Episcopos Bajoariae et Alemanniae;
ib. i. p. 203.

St. Columbanus taking a line wholly independent of Rome, or, like Bishop Colman at the Synod of Whitby, directly in collision with her; having its own Liturgy, its own translation of the Bible, its own mode of chanting, its own monastic rule, its own cycle for the calculation of Easter; and presenting both internal and external evidence of a complete autonomy [1].

§ 5. EASTERN ORIGIN.—It is hardly possible to pass over in silence the theory of the Eastern origin of the Celtic Church which was once much in vogue, but which is now generally abandoned as untenable. This theory has, for obvious and polemical reasons, been maintained by all Protestant, and by some Anglican writers, while it has been as uniformly repudiated by writers of the Church of Rome [2]. Neander writes: 'The peculiarity of the British Church is evidence against its origin from Rome, for in many ritual matters it departed from the usage of the Roman Church, and agreed much more nearly with the Church of Asia Minor [3].'

On the other hand, Messrs. Haddan and Stubbs speak of 'the groundlessness of the so often alleged Orientalism of the early British Church,—Oriental in no other sense than that its Christianity originated like all Christianity in Asia, and found its way to Britain through (most probably) Lyons, and not through the then equally Greek Church of Rome, but without imprinting one single trace upon the British Church itself of any one thing in a peculiar sense Greek or

---

[1] The foregoing is for the most part a picture of the early Celtic Church only. The influence of Rome began to predominate in Ireland in the seventh century, and appeals to Rome are recognised in the Book of Armagh. It did not fully establish itself till the twelfth century (see p. 10). All the arguments brought forward by Bishop Greith (Altirischen Kirche, p. 453) to prove the recognition of the papal supremacy by the early Church of Ireland, and the authorities by which he supports them, refer not to the Church of SS. Columba and Columbanus, much less of SS. Patrick and Bridget, but to the Irish Church after conformity to the Roman Church had commenced to set in (for dates see p. 9).

[2] Sir James Dalrymple, Collections, Epist. Dedicat. p. 2 ; Pref. p. xliv ; George Buchanan, Hist. in Rege Aidano ; David Buchanan, Pref. to Knox, Hist. edit. Lond. fol. p. 151 ; Spottiswoode, Vindication of Collections, p. 30 ; Thomas Innes, Civ. and Eccles. Hist. of Scotland, p. 11, Aberdeen 1853.

[3] Gen. Ch. Hist. i. 117.

Oriental [1].' Elsewhere Mr. Haddan speaks of 'the common
but utterly groundless idea of a specially Greek origin of the
British Church [2].'

After such decided expressions of opinion from persons so
qualified to form them, it is yet hoped that it may not be
considered as labour thrown away to accumulate and lay
before the reader the various converging facts which, though
they do not establish a specially Oriental origin of the Celtic
Church, yet go far to save such a theory from the charge
of being 'utterly groundless,' and explain how it grew up.
This theory is of course quite distinct from the ethnological
question as to the origin of Celtic nations, and from the
philological question as to the relation of the Celtic language
to the Indo-Germanic family. Its discussion is complicated
by the fact that the date of the evidence offered is sometimes
difficult to ascertain. Such similarities as that of British
weapons found in barrows, in form and alloy, to those found
in the plains of Phœnicia, and of cromlechs and pillars in
Ireland to stone monuments in Palestine [3], have reference to
an original connection long anterior to the introduction of
Christianity, and are chronologically irrelevant to the subject
in hand. The similarity in these and other points between
Cornwall, Ireland and the East, is almost certainly due to
the fact that in the earliest historical times the great traders
and navigators were the Phœnicians, who brought their
commerce to these shores, and may have influenced the
manners and customs of their inhabitants in their architecture,
arts, and manners. With regard to the carved symbol of the
Greek cross which is frequently found, but not in a majority
of cases, on the ancient sculptured stones of Christian Scotland [4],
while in Cornwall and Brittany the same form of the cross
preponderates [5], and with regard to other supposed signs of

---

[1] Councils and Eccles. Doc. i. p. xix.
[2] Remains, p. 210.   [3] Ulster Journ. Arch. i. 226.
[4] Stuart, J., Sculptured Stones of Scotland, ii. p. lxxxvi.
[5] Blight, J. T., Ancient Crosses of the West of Cornwall, Lond. 1856;
Archaeol. Cambrensis for 1857, p. 370.

an Eastern origin said to be exhibited by the British Christian architectural remains in Cornwall [1], their use may be traced in all early Continental Western art, and is only due to the original connection of all Western Christianity with the East [2].

Architectural Evidence.—Mr. Fergusson makes the following remarks on the general Eastern character of early Christian Irish architecture :—' Ireland possesses what may properly be called a Celtic style of architecture, which is as interesting in itself as any of the minor local styles in any part of the world, and, so far as at present known, is quite peculiar to the island. None of the buildings of this style are large, though the ornaments of many of them are of great beauty and elegance. Their interest lies in their singularly local character and in their age, which probably extends from the fifth or sixth century to the time of the English conquest in 1176. They consist chiefly of churches and round towers [3] ... No Irish church of this period, now remaining, is perhaps even 60 feet in length, and generally they are very much smaller, the most common dimensions being from 20 to 40 feet [4]. Increase of magnificence was sought more by extending the number than by augmenting the size. The favourite number for a complete ecclesiastical establishment was seven, as in Greece, this number being identical with that of the seven Apocalyptic Churches of Asia. Thus, there are seven at Glendalough, seven at Cashel, and the same sacred number is found

---

[1] Journal of Brit. Archaeol. Assoc. vol. xxiii. pp. 221-230.

[2] The Labarum has been found on sepulchral stones, as on the Frampton stone in Dorset, &c., and on an oval tin ornament, fourth century ; Hübner, Æm., Inscript. Britan. p. 12, Nos. 31, 198, 217, 218, 219, 220, 228. For the Greek cross in early Italian art, see J. H. Parker's photographs, No. 442, in Early Irish Art, Kilkenny Archaeol. Soc. 1854, p. 297.

[3] The date of the existing round towers is much later.

[4] Some of the oratories in fact are much smaller. St. Mollagga's oratory, Co. Cork, measures 10 ft. × 7 ft. 2 in. ; St. Declan's at Ardmore, 13 ft. 8 in. × 8 ft. 4 in. ; St. Molua's, Killaloe, 10 ft. 6 in. × 6 ft. 4 in. ; St. Columb's, at Kells, 16 ft. 1 in. × 13 ft. ; St. Kevin's, at Glendalough, 22 ft. 7 in. × 14 ft. 13 in., exclusive of the walls. R. Brash, Eccles. Architect. of Ireland, p. 8. The dimensions of churches are stated ib. p. 121.

at several other places, and generally two or three, at least, are found grouped together.

'No church is known to have existed in Ireland before the Norman Conquest that can be called a basilica, none of them being divided into aisles either by stone or wooden pillars, or possessing an apse, and no circular church has yet been found; nothing in short that would lead us to believe that Ireland obtained her architecture direct from Rome; while everything, on the contrary, tends to confirm the belief of an intimate connection with the farther East, and that her early Christianity and religious forms were derived from Greece by some of the more southerly commercial routes which at that period seem to have abutted on Ireland.

'Both in Greece and Ireland the smallness of the churches is remarkable. They never were, in fact, basilicas for the assembly of large congregations of worshippers, but oratories, where the priest could celebrate the divine mysteries for the benefit of the laity. It is not only at Mount Athos, and other places in Europe, but also in Asia Minor, that we find the method of grouping a large number of small churches together, seven being the favourite number and one often attained[1].'

A little further on Mr. Fergusson alludes to the still older class of antiquities — 'the circular domical dwellings found in the west of the island, constructed of loose stones in horizontal layers, approaching one another till they meet at the apex like the old so-called treasuries of the Greeks, or the domes of the Jains in India[2].' Some words of Tertullian with reference to the Eastern sect of the Marcionites have been somewhat fancifully quoted as fitly describing these early Irish beehive-shaped buildings: 'Habent apes favos, habent et ecclesias Marcionitae,' &c.

Similar Christian architectural remains have been found

---

[1] Fergusson, J., Illustrated Handbook of Architecture, London, 1855, vol. ii. p. 915.   [2] Ib. 925.

in Cornwall (A.D. 250–450), and are described by Mr. Borlase in his ' Age of the Saints [1].'

In his Preface to the Sculptured Stones of Scotland Mr. Stuart quotes Dr. Wise's assertion that there is a striking similarity between the stone monuments of the East and those of Britain [2], and Mr. Chalmers' assertion that there are figures on some of the stones in Scotland identical with those on Gnostic gems [3].

These and such like facts, without amounting to proof, are suggestive of Eastern origin or influence, more probably the latter. On the other hand, the explanation which has already been given [4] of the existence of Greek crosses in Cornwall may be extended to all the other points of architectural similarity between the early Christian remains of Great Britain and Ireland and those of the East [5].

Palaeographical Evidence.—The palaeographical evidence is at first sight strongly in favour of an Eastern connection, though the tendency of recent writers and of fuller investigation has been to modify the extent of the connection, or even to deny it altogether.

The distinctive style of ornamentation adopted or invented by native artists consisted of intricate designs formed—

1. By the use of dots, generally in different coloured inks.

2. By simple lines, straight or curved.

3. By the step-like angulated pattern.

4. By the Chinese-like z pattern.

5. By interlaced ribbons.

6. By interlaced zoomorphic patterns.

7. By various spiral patterns, which are by far the most characteristic of the whole.

8. By the formation of gigantic initial letters, sometimes occupying a whole page, which are filled up with geometrical

---

[1] p. 30. [2] p. iv. [3] p. xiv. [4] p. 48.
[5] Haddan, Remains, p. 238. For an account and explanation of the mixture of Buddhist and Christian symbols on Scottish stones, see Proceedings of Royal Irish Acad. vii. 118.

designs of interlaced work, convoluted serpentine figures, spiral ornaments, grotesque birds, insects, quadrupeds, &c.[1]

What is the origin of this style of Celtic art?

A Roman origin is impossible, because not a single Italian MS. nor a single piece of Italian sculpture can be produced older than the ninth century having a close resemblance to those of this country. The illuminations in the Book of Kells find no exact parallel in Italy. They resemble Assyrian or Egyptian rather than Italian work.

A Scandinavian origin, suggested by the existence of Runic inscriptions on stones found in various places, especially in the Isle of Man, is impossible, because all such stones are several centuries more recent than the oldest Celtic MSS., the writers of which had no intercourse with the inhabitants of Denmark or Norway.

An Eastern origin is suggested by the similarity of much of the Celtic ornamentation to that found in early Syriac, Egyptian, Ethiopic, &c. MSS., by a resemblance in the delineation of birds and animals to Egyptian fresco painting, in the manner of drawing the wings, in the conventional representations of eagles, lions, calves, &c., in the swathed mummy-like figures of Christ[2]. The theory of such an origin is facilitated by the early commercial intercourse which is known to have existed between this country and the East, and by the frequent expeditions recorded to have been made by early Christian pilgrims of the Celtic Church to the Holy Land, and by the immigration of foreign ecclesiastics[3]. On the other hand, it is rendered doubtful by the fact that work resembling Byzantine work, and some features of Oriental ornamentation, are to be found in very early MSS. not only in the East, but also throughout Western Christendom[4].

---

[1] See the monogram of the Book of Kells, Gilbert, J. T., Nat. MSS. of Ireland, i. pl. vii; Westwood, J. O., Facsimiles, &c., p. iv.

[2] Westwood, J. O., Facsimiles, &c., plates xxvi, xxviii.   [3] See p. 56.

[4] 'Professor Westwood said in his Palaeographia Sacra (1845, not paged):

A peculiarity of Greek writing, sometimes adopted by Celtic scribes, as in the Scottish Book of Deer; the Welsh ninth-century Ovid preserved in the Bodleian Library (Auct. F. iv. 32); the Irish Stowe Missal (ff. 18, 20–24); consists in the written letters depending from the line above them, instead of resting on the line beneath.

Another feature suggestive of Oriental influence is the introduction of the serpent as a common form of ornamentation in the elaborate illuminations of interlaced work which adorn the early Irish MSS. It is also prominent among Christian emblems on the rudely carved stone crosses, most of which are earlier than the ninth century, and some of which are coeval with the introduction of Christianity into these islands[1]. This serpentine ornamentation reaches a climax on the case of St. Patrick's Bell (eleventh century), ' one side of which is beautified with stones with ornaments of fine gold representing serpents, curiously and elegantly inter-twined in most intricate folds, and in various knots, like the complicated involutions in the collar of the Order of the Knights of St. Patrick. On one of the ends below the knob and ring by which it is suspended there are eight serpents so singularly infolded and intermingled with one

---

[1] ' The collection of many of these MSS. has also furnished additional though unlooked-for evidence that the ancient Church in these islands was independent of Rome, and that it corresponded, on the contrary, with the Eastern Churches. . . . . These apparently trifling circumstances (ornamental details) seem to me to prove, more forcibly than the most laborious arguments, the connexion between the early Christians in these islands and those of the East, so strongly insisted on by various writers.' It is fair to add that in 1868 the Professor seems so far to have modified his opinion of the Eastern origin of the style of illumination as to speak of it as probable rather than as capable of positive proof; Facsimiles, &c., Introd. p. 5.

[1] For specimens, see Wilson's Archaeology of Scotland, p. 503; Stuart's Sculptured Stones of Scotland, vol. i. plates lxii, lxiv, lxxvii; vol. ii. plate xxv; O'Neil's Sculptured Crosses of Ancient Ireland, plate xxxv; Petrie's Irish Inscriptions, part v. p. xxxvii. For the prominence of the serpent in the ancient worship of Africa, Asia, Egypt, Greece, see Dennis, G., Cities and Cemeteries of Etruria, vol. i. p. 169, note 1. edit. 1878; Fergusson, J., Tree and Serpent Worship, London, 1873, Introd. Essay.

another, that it requires minute attention and singular discrimination to trace each separately and to distinguish it
from its fellows. Their eyes are skilfully formed of blue
glass. Above the cross are four of the same kind, and in
each of the four compartments into which it is divided there
are two golden serpents in relief. Below the knob of suspension, on the opposite end or side, are six other serpents,
with blue eyes, but differently intertwined. On the top is a
strange representation of two of these creatures with two legs[1].'

The serpent continued to make its appearance in the Ritual
of the Anglo-Saxons, according to a traditional use possibly
perpetuated from their Celtic predecessors. On Maundy
Thursday, after Nones, a procession went down to the church
door, bearing with it a staff which ended at the top in the
shape of a serpent. There, fire, struck from a flint, was first
hallowed, and then used for lighting a candle which came
out of the serpent's mouth. From this all other candles were
lighted; and the same ceremonial was repeated on Good Friday
and Easter Eve[2].

The serpent appears in the Mozarabic Liturgy, which contains the following rubric amid the ceremonial of Easter Eve :
' Hic exeat Subdiaconus cum cruce hoc ordine. Ceroferarii
cum cereis pergant coram cruce; et cereus paschalis coram
cereis, et serpens coram cereo,' &c.[3] There is no evidence as to
early Gallican usage on this point, but the serpent-rod was
in use at Rouen as late as the commencement of the eighteenth
century[4], and in England up to the sixteenth century[5].

Another custom common to Ireland and the East, though

---

[1] Reeves, Description of St. Patrick's Bell, Belfast, 1850, p. 6, plates iv, v.

[2] Rayneri, Apostolatus Benedictinorum in Anglia, Appendix, p. 87. 'Dunstani
Concordia praescribens ritus in Coena Domini servandos ait ; Hora congrua
agatur nona, qua cantata .... fratres pergant ad ostium ecclesiae ferentes
hastam cum imagine serpentis ibique .... candela quae in ore serpentis infixa
est accendatur.' Zaccaria, F. A., Onomasticon, ii. 149.

[3] Migne, Pat. Lat. lxxxv. 461, 470.

[4] De Moleon, Voyages Liturgiques, p. 304.

[5] Sarum Processional, edit. 1502, fol. 70. For the serpentine formation of
the pastoral staff of Eastern bishops, see Goar, Euchol. pp. 115, 314.

not exclusively confined to Ireland among Western nations, was that of providing their more precious sacred books with leather satchels called 'polaires,' furnished with straps for slinging round the shoulder, and ornamented in a kind of basso-relievo produced by stamping the leather. Woodcuts of the polaire of the Book of Armagh and of the shrine of St. Maidoc are given in Mr. Petrie's Round Towers, pp. 329, 322; Archæologia, vol. xliii. plate xiv. There are before the writer at this moment the leather satchel of the Irish Missal belonging to C. C. C. Library, Oxford, and the leather satchel of an Æthiopic MS. of about the same date belonging to St. John's College, Oxford. They resemble each other so closely in texture and design that they might be thought to have come from the same workshop.

An independent origin is claimed for the Celtic style of ornamentation by some modern writers; as by Mr. French, who thinks that it is an imitation of the interlaced wickerwork of gigantic animals within which the natives in a pre-Christian period immolated their victims[1]. The anonymous writer of a recent article on this subject gives it as his view that 'English interlacings and Irish spirals are not traditional or taught ornament, but the special fancies of a race;' and again, speaking of the miniatures in the Book of Kells the same writer says that 'they are constructed not without power or beauty, but with the quaintness which marks the work of an isolated Church, which owed Rome nothing, and to which Greece or Syria had taught nothing but the faith[2].'

Liturgical Evidence.—The monastic rule of the Celtic Church has been often ascribed to an Eastern origin[3]. Its canons, so far as they can be judged from the extant remains of the

---

[1] Origin and Meaning of the early Interlaced Ornamentation found on ancient Sculptured Stones of Scotland; 1858, Manchester.

[2] Church Quarterly, vol. v. p. 457. Mr. R. Brash also claims an independent origin for Irish art; Eccles. Architecture of Ireland, p. 29.

[3] e.g. in the Vita S. Guingaloëi in a passage quoted in H. and S. ii. i. 79; Will. of Malmesbury, quoted in O'Conor, Rerum Hibern. Script. vol. ii. p. 166.

Rules of St. Columba, Columbanus, Adamnan, &c., are not identical with any other Eastern or Western code. They are found on comparison rather to resemble the former than the latter in the greater severity of their regulations[1], which probably caused them to give way eventually before the milder Rule of St. Benedict, and in the appearance in the Rule of St. Columbanus of such Eastern words as paximacium, paracaraximus, Archimandrita, Nonnus[2].

The scattered traces of Oriental influence in the remains of the Celtic Litury and Ritual may be summed up as consisting of the following points :—

(*a*) The episcopal benediction immediately preceding the communion of the people, and sometimes bestowed in the Eastern fashion[3].

(*b*) The veiling of women at the reception of the Eucharist[4].

(*c*) The use of unleavened bread[5].

(*d*) The custom of fasting on Wednesdays and Fridays[6] is spoken of by Archbishop Ussher as 'agreeable to the custom of the Grecian rather than of the Roman Church[7].' But there does not seem to be sufficient authority for drawing such a distinction.

(*e*) Several of the points of Celtic Ritual, specified on p. 61 as Gallican, are Oriental in their origin.

Historical Evidence.—Mention may be made, in con-

---

[1] The penalty of beating, which is reserved in the Benedictine Code for a few extreme cases, was assigned in the Penitential of St. Columbanus to the most trivial offences, the number of blows to be inflicted varying from six to two hundred. Montalembert, Monks of the West, ii. 448.

[2] Of these words, Nonnus, though said to be an Egyptian word, appears also in the Reg. S. Bened., and Archimandrita, in a different sense, is used by later Western writers. [3] Ch. ii. § 8. [4] Ch. ii. § 25.

[5] Ch. ii. § 25. Very early Western authority can be found for most of these ritual Orientalisms, in the representations in the Catacombs, or in early Italian mosaics. All that they prove is therefore the Oriental origin of the Celtic Church in common with the rest of Western Christianity.

[6] Ch. ii. § 34.

[7] Op. vol. iv. p. 305. The question is treated at length in Smith, Dict. of Chr. Antiq.; Bingham, Antiq. book xxi. ch. 3. The fast on Wednesday and Friday is ordered in the Eastern Rule of St. Antony, cap. xv; in the Western Rule of St. Caesarius of Arles, c. xxii.

nection with the above facts, of the constant allusions to the East, and especially to Jerusalem, in the legendary lives of the saints; e.g. in the legend connecting Scotland with St. Andrew as its patron saint, and describing the arrival of Regulus, a monkish pilgrim from the city of Constantinople, bringing the bones of the Apostle from the East. The oldest document containing this legend is of the twelfth century, and is printed in the Chronicles of the Picts and Scots[1]. So in the legendary lives of St. Bonifacius[2], St. Servanus[3], and of others enumerated in Haddan and Stubbs' Councils, &c.[4], in the legendary consecration at Jerusalem, in the sixth century, of St. David first Bishop of St. David's, St. Teilo second Bishop of Llandaff, St. Patern Bishop of Llandabarn. Sometimes Eastern pilgrims visited Ireland. Seven Egyptian monks, buried at Disert Ulidh, are invoked in the Félire of Oengus[5].

Celtic saints sometimes referred to Eastern authority in self-defence, in their controversies with Rome. St. Columbanus, soon after the arrival of his mission in Gaul A.D. 590, protected himself from the charge of schism, and defended the Celtic mode of determining the fall of Easter, by referring to the authority of Anatolius Bishop of Laodicea, A.D. 270. He accused the continental Church of innovation; its computation having been altered by Sulpicius Severus A.D. 410, by Victorius of Aquitaine 450, by Dionysius Exiguus 525; and he finally declared to Pope Boniface his readiness to abide by the second canon of the Second Council of Constantinople, 'Let not bishops go out of their dioceses to churches out of their bounds, nor bring confusion on the Churches,' &c.

At the Synod of Whitby, while St. Wilfrid urged the acceptance of the Roman calculation of the fall of Easter on the authority of St. Peter, Bp. Colman defended the Celtic cycle on the authority of St. John. 'Then Colman said, The Easter which I keep I received from my elders who sent

---

[1] p. 138.   [2] Skene, W. F., Celtic Scotland, ii. 229.
[3] Ib. ii. 255.   [4] i. 35; ii. pt. i. 86.   [5] Colgan, Acta SS. Hib. p. 539.

me bishop hither; all our forefathers, men beloved of God, are known to have kept it after the same manner; and that the same may not seem to any contemptible or worthy to be rejected, it is the same which St. John the Evangelist, the disciple beloved of our Lord, with all the Churches over which he presided, is recorded to have observed [1].'

British clergy are recorded to have visited Constantinople during the patriarchate of Methodius (842–847) for the sake of obtaining information about the Paschal cycle [2].

The above facts go far to explain and justify the opinion that there must have been originally some connection between the Celtic and Oriental Churches. But this connection need not have been direct. The most probable hypothesis is that Christianity reached the British isles through Gaul, and that whatever traces of Eastern influence may be found in the earliest Liturgy and Ritual of Great Britain and Ireland are not due to a direct introduction of Christianity from the East, but to the Eastern character and origin of that Church through which Christianity first reached these shores.

§ 6. GALLICAN CONNECTION.—There is strong circumstantial evidence in favour of the immediately Gallican origin of the British Church, and for fixing the date of its foundation between A. D. 176 and 208. In the former year Irenaeus, enumerating the Christian Churches then in existence, made no allusion to any Church in Britain [3]. In the latter year Tertullian wrote a passage which contains the first historical allusion to the existence of Christianity in these islands [4]. The dispersion

---

[1] Bede, H. E. iii. 25. The author does not wish to be considered as endorsing the historical accuracy of Colman's assertions, but merely to call attention to the fact that the Celtic party themselves, however erroneously, claimed an Eastern origin of and sought Eastern authority for their Paschal cycle. Its non-Eastern origin is proved by Messrs. Haddan and Stubbs, Councils, &c. i. 157.

[2] Κληρικοὶ γάρ τινες τῶν εἰς αὐτά που τὰ ἄκρα τῆς οἰκουμένης οἰκούντων ἕνεκα τινῶν ἐκκλησιαστικῶν παραδόσεων, τελείας τε τοῦ πασχαλίου καὶ ἀκριβοῦς καταλήψεως τὴν βασιλίδα πόλιν καταλαβόντες [τῷ ταύτης] τὸν τηνίκαυτα πατριάρχην προσεληλύθασι. Vit. Anon. Chrysost., Op. tom. viii. p. 321. 5; edit. Savile, 1612.

[3] Haer. i. 10.

[4] '. . . . Galliarum diversae nationes, et Britannorum inaccessa Romanis

of the Gallican Church in the fierce persecution which raged
in Gallica Celtica—the district round Lyons and Vienne—
A.D. 177 probably brought Christian refugees across the
Channel, and in accordance with a law of growth often ex-
emplified in the early history of Christianity, the blood of
Gallican martyrs became the seed of the British Church[1].
This early Gallican Church was a colony from Asia Minor.
Pothinus the first Bishop of Lyons had come directly from
that country, bringing with him Irenaeus the disciple of
Polycarp, the disciple of St. John. The names of its bishops
and martyrs were Greek. The writings of its saints and
some of its earliest extant inscriptions are in the same language. The account of its sufferings under Marcus Aurelius
was sent by the Christians of Lyons and Vienne by letter to
their brethren in Asia and Phrygia[2]. Any features of Oriental
ritual in the British Church may be accounted for and traced,
as has been already suggested[3], through this intermediate
Gallican channel.

Other proofs are forthcoming of the intercourse which
existed at a subsequent date between these islands and France.
Passages indicating an intercourse of the British and Gallican
Churches during the first six centuries are found in the writings
of the anonymous author of a tract De Septem Ordinibus
Ecclesiae, Arnobius junior, St. Patrick, and Venantius Fortunatus[4]. During the fourth and fifth centuries there was a
constant emigration of British Christians into Armorica, and
legendary lives exist of many saints who migrated from Wales
or Cornwall into Brittany A.D. 450–600[5]. The presence of

---

loca Christo vero subdita . . . . in quibus omnibus locis Christi nomen qui jam
venit regnat . . . . utpote in quibus omnibus locis populus nominis Christi
inhabitet . . . . Christi autem regnum et nomen ubique porrigitur, ubique
creditur, ab omnibus gentibus supra enumeratis colitur,' &c.   Adv. Jud. vii.

[1] Mr. Pryce would place this mission to Britain before A.D. 177; Ancient
British Church, pp. 60, 61. But in that case we should expect to find some
allusion to it in the writings of Irenaeus.   [2] Eus. Hist. Eccl. lib. v. c. 1.

[3] p. 57.   [4] Quoted at length in H. and S. i. 13.

[5] Enumerated in H. and S. ii. App. B, and in the Journal of the British
Archaeol. Assoc. vol. iv. p. 235.

British bishops at various Gallican Councils is attested by their signatures, as at Tours A.D. 461, at Vannes 465, at Orleans 511, at Paris 555. Mansuetus the first Bishop of Toul was an Irishman [1]; Mansuetus was also the name of the first known Breton bishop; St. Beatus Bishop of Lausanne, and Apostle of Switzerland (fourth century), was likewise Irish. There was also constant commercial intercourse between the two countries. Diodorus Siculus states that tin was exported from Britain to Gaul, and transported through Gaul to the mouths of the Rhone and to Narbonne [2]. Strabo speaks generally of the exchange of commerce between Britain and Gaul [3]. When St. Columbanus was at Nantes, and the authorities there wished to send him back to Ireland, an Irish merchant-ship was found lying in the harbour ready for the purpose [4]. Gallic traders are reported to have visited Clonmacnois in the days of St. Kieran, A.D. 548–9 [5]. Gallic sailors with their ship came to Iona or its immediate neighbourhood in the sixth century [6].

The intimate connection between Wales and Brittany can be traced up to the eleventh century, when Rhys ap Tewdwr, the representative of the royal line of South Wales, took refuge there, returning thence to his throne in 1077 with the unanimous consent of the people [7].

There are traces of the presence or influence of many Gallican bishops in England; St. Martin of Tours [8] (371–97), Hilary of Poictiers [9] (350–67), Victricius of Rouen [10] (c. 407),

---

[1] Martene and Durand, Thes. Nov. iii. 991.

[2] Hist. lib. v. 22, 38.   [3] Books ii, iv.

[4] Jonas, Vit. S. Columbani, c. 22.   [5] Vit. S. Kierani, c. 31.

[6] Vit. S. Columbae, i. 28. These 'Gallici nautae de Galliarum provinciis adventantes' touched at 'Caput Regionis,' probably 'Cantyre.'

[7] Skene, W. F., Four Ancient Books of Wales, i. 20.

[8] Later legends made St. Columba go to Tours, and carry away with him St. Martin's Book of the Gospels, in reward for showing the inhabitants where the saint lay buried. St. Martin was also reported to be the great-uncle of St. Patrick, and the ritual of Tours thus came, it was supposed, to be imported into Ireland; Colgan, Trias Thaum. ; Bede, H. E. i. 26, iii. 4.

[9] There is a Hymnus S. Hilarii in the Liber Hymnorum and in the Antiphon. Benchor. H. and S. i. 9.

[10] Victr. Lib. de Laude Sanctorum ; Gallandus, viii. 228.

Germanus of Auxerre[1] (429 and 447), Lupus of Troyes[2] (429), Severus of Treves[3] (447), Gregory of Tours[4] (573–95), and of Arculfus[5], who was entertained by Adamnan at Iona A.D. 686.

We may also note the dedication of Celtic churches to Gallican saints; as in the case of the very ancient churches at Canterbury and Whithern to St. Martin; the many churches in Cornwall and Wales dedicated to St. Germanus; two churches in Glamorganshire dedicated to St. Lupus[6].

The missions, derived according to some accounts from Gallican sources, of St. Keby into Wales in connection with St. Hilary; of St. Ninian to Scotland, and of St. Patrick into Ireland, in connection with St. Martin.

The employment by the British Church of the Paschal Cycle of Gaul as drawn up by Sulpicius Severus, the disciple of St. Martin, c. 410. The Irish Church followed the still earlier cycle of Anatolius[7].

The use of the Gallican Psalter[8].

---

[1] Bede, H. E. i. 17, 21. See the Cornish Missa S. Germani, ch. iii ; Martyrol. Bedae, Kal. Aug.

[2] Bede, H. E. i. 17; Martyrol. Bedae, iv. Kal. Aug.   [3] Bede, H. E. i. 21.

[4] Greg. Tur. de Mirae S. Martini, iv. 46.

[5] Bede, H. E. v. 15.

[6] Under the name of St. Bleiddian. Rees, R., Welsh Saints, p. 126.

[7] Aldhelm, Ep. ad Geruntium; H. and S. i. 13. See p. 64.

[8] Asserted by Archbishop Ussher on the authority of Sedulius, Works, iv. p. 248. The Roman Psalter is the first revision of the old Latin text made by Jerome c. A.D. 383, at the request of Pope Damasus. It was retained in use in Italy till the pontificate of Pius V (A.D. 1566), who introduced the Gallican Psalter generally, though the Roman Psalter was still allowed to be used in three Italian churches, 'in una Romae Vaticana ecclesia et extra urbem in Mediolanensi, et in ecclesia S. Marci Venetiis.' The Gallican Psalter is the second revision made by Jerome A.D. 387–391. In it he attempted to represent as far as possible, by the help of the Greek versions, the real reading of the Hebrew. It obtained its name from the fact that it was introduced from Rome in the public services of France by St. Gregory of Tours (573–595), and was only accepted south of the Alps at a much later date.

The above account is taken from Smith's Dict. of the Bible, vol. iii. p. 1698. It is the inverse of the account of the two versions given by Bede, so far as Pope Damasus is concerned, who died A.D. 384.

'Sciendum est translationes esse duas apud Latinos in usu atque honore, Romanam, scilicet et Gallicam. Romana est qua utuntur Romani et plerique

The approximation to Gallican usage in certain features of the Liturgy and ritual; e. g. lections [1], proper prefaces [2], position of the benediction [3], the 'deprecatio' for the departed [4], the Hymnus trium puerorum [5], the use of ecclesiastical colours [6], of Eulogiae [7], of bracelets, crowns, &c. [8]

The observance of Rogation Days [9].

The commemoration of S. Eugenia by name in the Canon of the Drummond Missal, as in the Gallican Missale Vesontionense (p. 207), where her name is added in the Commemoratio pro defunctis in the Canon, and where she is commemorated on Dec. 25 instead of S. Anastasia. Her name also appears on Dec. 25 in the Liber S. Trinitatis, a fourteenth-century Irish Martyrology [10]; and also with that of St. Anastasia in the Sacramentary of Leo [11].

Whole passages, in addition to many isolated phrases, from the Gallican Liturgy appear in the Stowe Missal [12], and in the liturgical fragments in the Books of Deer, Dimma, and Mulling [13].

The second and often-quoted question of St. Augustine to Gregory I, together with the papal answer, imply either the identity of the British and Gallican Liturgies, or that St. Augustine found the Gallican Rite in use in Britain; probably in the church of St. Martin at Canterbury, where Liudhard Bishop of Senlis, who had accompanied Queen Bertha from the court of Charibert at Paris, on her mar-

---

Itali, quae de Graeco in Latinum a Symmacho et Aquila sumpta est secundum lxx interpretes Ptolomaei regis. Gallica est qua precipue Galli utuntur. Haec autem praecipue sumpta est rogatu Damasi Papae a beato Hieronymo de Hebraeo ad sententiam.' Praefatio ad Psalmos, tom. viii. col. 423, fol. Basiliae, 1563.

Until a complete collation shall have been made of the Celtic text of the Old Testament it is impossible to verify or refute the inference drawn by Ussher from the doubtful authority of Sedulius. The materials for such a collation are indicated in H. and S., i. pp. 170-198. They seem to prove the existence of a special Celtic revision of the text of the Vetus Latina.

[1] Ch. ii. § 5.   [2] Ib. § 7.   [3] Ib. § 8.   [4] Ib. § 10.
[5] Ib. § 13.   [6] Ib. § 16.   [7] Ib. § 27.   [8] Ib. § 15.
[9] Ib. § 34.   [10] Irish Archaeol. Soc. vi. 191.   [11] viii. Kal. Jan.
[12] Ch. iii. § 14.   [13] Ib. §§ 5, 6, 7.

riage with Ethelbert of Kent, would naturally have been using it.

St. Augustine asked: 'Whereas the faith is one and the same, why are there different customs in different Churches, and why is one form of Mass observed in the holy Roman Church, and another in the Gallican Church?'

To which St. Gregory replied: 'You know, my brother, the custom of the Roman Church, in which you remember you were bred up. But it pleases me that if you have found anything either in the Roman, or the Gallican, or any other Church, which may be more acceptable to Almighty God, you carefully make choice of the same, and sedulously teach the Church of the English, which as yet is new in the faith, whatsoever you can gather from the several Churches. For things are not to be loved for the sake of places, but places for the sake of good things. Choose, therefore, from every Church those things which are pious, religious, and upright, and when you have, as it were, made them up into one body, let the minds of the English people be accustomed thereto [1].'

§ 7. SPANISH CONNECTION.—There are traces of a connection between the Celtic and Spanish Churches in the following facts:—

In A.D. 380 certain Priscillianist bishops were banished from Spain to the Scilly Islands [2].

The existence of a British See of Bretona in Gallicia in N.W. Spain is alluded to in the Council of Lugo (Lucus Augusti), A.D. 569.

The Second Council of Braga, A.D. 572, is subscribed to by Mailoc, a British bishop, suffragan of Martin Archbishop of Braga.

---

[1] Bede, H. E. i. 27. The above facts, while they certainly do not establish the identity of the Gallican and British Liturgies, disprove the assertion of Lingard that this theory is 'without even the semblance of a proof;' Anglo-Saxon Church, i. 385.

[2] Sulpicius Severus, Hist. Sac. ii. 51.

There are traces of the prevalence in Spain of the British mode of calculating Easter c. A.D. 590[1].

The Fourth Council of Toledo, A.D. 633, can. 41, abolished a particular—probably the British—form of tonsure, said to have prevailed in Gallicia, and to have caused an undesirable want of uniformity in Spain. It was subscribed by Metopius, a British bishop.

The signature of an 'Episcopus Britonensis,' sometimes with a Gothic sometimes with a Celtic name, is found appended to the Councils of Toledo VII, A.D. 646; Toledo VIII, A.D. 653; Braga IV, A.D. 675; Toledo XIII, A.D. 683; Toledo XVI, A.D. 693. Traces of the existence of this British See of Britona or Britonia (Sedes Britoniensis) are found in lists as late as A.D. 1156; but the See had become merged in or united with that of Montenedo or Oviedo A.D. 830.

Passages which are found likewise in the Mozarabic Liturgy are incorporated in Celtic liturgical fragments in the Books of Deer, Dimma, Mulling, and in the Stowe Missal[2].

§ 8. POINTS OF DIFFERENCE BETWEEN THE ROMAN AND CELTIC CHURCH.—A consideration of the chief points of difference between the Roman and Celtic Churches will rather incline readers to agree with the old British historian[3], and with St. Augustine of Canterbury[4], that the British were in many respects hostile to Roman customs, than with the more accomplished modern author who says that no traces can be discovered of any permanent divergence between them in doctrine or practice[5].

The chief points of divergence were these:—

1. *The Calculation of Easter.*—There was a difference be-

---

[1] Greg. Tur. v. 17, x. 23.

[2] Ch. iii. §§ 5, 6, 7, 14. Most of the above facts are given more at length in H. and S., ii. pt. i. 99.

[3] 'Britanni toti mundo contrarii, moribus Romanis inimici, non solum in missa, sed in tonsura etiam.' Gildae Epist. ii.

[4] St. Augustine said to the British bishops at the synod of Bangor, ' Quia in multis quidem nostrae consuetudini, immo universalis Ecclesiae contraria geritis.' Bede, H. E. ii. 2.

[5] Skene, W. F., Celtic Scotland, ii. 6.

tween the Roman and Celtic Churches in determining the
date of Easter, which, though intrinsically of an unessential
nature, became the crucial point of controversy in the seventh
century, being prominently insisted on by St. Augustine
at the Bangor conference with the seven British bishops[1].
Some points in connection with it have been already
alluded to[2]. The real state of the controversy and the
important facts to be remembered are these,—that before
the Council of Nice the practice of the British harmonised
with that of the Roman Church, the most ancient Roman
table for Easter agreeing with that of the British Church;
but that owing to its isolation from the rest of Western
Christendom, the Celtic Church had never adopted the
various alterations and improvements which, on astronomical
and not on theological grounds, had been from time to time
accepted by the Continental Church[3].

2. *Baptism.*—One of the conditions of union offered by
St. Augustine to the British bishops was that of their con-
senting to administer baptism according to the custom of
the Roman Church[4]. Bede does not inform his readers in
what the difference between the two baptismal rites consisted, but it probably lay in one or more of the following
points:—

(*a*) *Single immersion.*—The practice of immersion, as
against affusion, is proved by the large size of still surviving fonts, such as the font of sixth-century workmanship
found at St. Brecan's Bed[5], and another of twelfth-century
workmanship at Cashel, in the chapel of Cormac King of
South Munster (1123–38)[6]. Single immersion was the custom
'in tota diocesi Macloviensi' in Brittany up to A.D. 1620[7].

---

[1] Bede, H. E. ii. 2.   [2] p. 56.

[3] The various authorities for this statement are given in H. and S. i. 152,
Appendix D, with a lucid summary of the whole controversy.

[4] Bede, H. E. ii. 2.   A difference is also implied in the thirteenth canon of
the Council of Clovesho, H. and S. iii. 367.

[5] Lord Dunraven, Notes on Irish Architecture, p. 90.

[6] Brash, R., Eccles. Architecture of Ireland, p. 95.

[7] Mart. lib. i. cap. i. art. xv. § 8.

It prevailed in the sixth century in Spain, where Gregory I advised its retention under the peculiar circumstances in which the Spanish Church stood at that time with regard to Arianism[1], and where a British bishopric existed at that date[2]. It is left optional in the three extant ' Ordines Baptismi' of the ancient Gallican Church[3], while a rubric directing trine immersion is contained in the earliest Ordines Romani[4]. Trine immersion, with the alternative of aspersion, is ordered in the earliest extant Irish Baptismal Office, in the composition of which however Roman influence is strongly marked[5].

(*b*) *The omission of unction.*—Lanfranc complained to Tirlagh, chief king of the Irish A.D. 1074, that the Irish baptized their infants without any chrism[6]; and St. Bernard asserted in the twelfth century that they omitted confirmation[7]. This almost incredible accusation of the disuse of confirmation is possibly based on the fact that unction was sometimes omitted in that rite as administered in the Celtic Church. Alcuin sent a present of some oil to a lector named Colcu in Ireland in the eighth century, and requested him to distribute it among the bishops because oil was scarce[8], a fact which suggests that the occasional omission of unction may have been due to the difficulty of obtaining the necessary material. But if St. Bernard's exaggerated accusations were true of the Irish in the twelfth century they do not apply to an earlier date. St. Patrick, writing to the subjects of Coroticus c. A.D. 497, alludes to chrism, along with the sign of the cross and the white chrisom, as all connected with the baptismal rite[9]. The

---

[1] Ep. i. 43. [2] p. 62.

[3] Missale Gothicum, p. 97; Gallicanum, p. 191; Vesontionense, p. 270.

[4] Mart. lib. i. cap. i. art. xviii. ord. iv, v. [5] Stowe Missal, ch. iii. § 14.

[6] Ep. ad Tirdelvac, Op. p. 320, ed. Ben.

[7] 'Usum saluberrimum confessionis, sacramentum confirmationis, contractum conjugiorum (quae omnia aut ignorabant aut negligebant) Malachias de novo instituit.' Bernard in Vita Malachiae, cap. iii.

[8] 'Misi charitati tuae aliquid de oleo quod vix modo in Britannia invenitur, ut dispensares per loca necessaria episcoporum ad utilitatem hominum vel honorem Dei.' Ep. xviii. in Ussher's Works, iv. 467.

[9] 'Postera die qua crismati neophyti in veste candida, dum fides flagrabat in fronte ipsorum.' Ep. ad Corot. subditos, sect. 2. The daughters of King

earliest extant Irish Baptismal Office—in the volume known as the Stowe Missal[1]—enjoins three separate acts of unction:—

(i) At an early point in the service between the interrogations of the candidate : ' Deinde tanges pectus dorsum de oleo et crismate.'

(ii) Shortly before the act of Baptism : ' Incipit oleari oleo et crismate in pectus et item scabulas antequam baptizaretur.'

(iii) Immediately after Baptism : ' Postquam baptizaretur oleatur cresmate in cerebrum in fronte.' The personal formula following, with the vernacular rubric introducing it, is peculiar to the Stowe Missal[2].

Of these three rites, (i) is unrepresented in the present Roman Ordines Baptismi; (ii) is directed to be performed with the oil of the catechumens only; (iii) is performed somewhat differently : ' perungat verticem Electi in modum crucis' (Ordo Bapt. Adult.), 'ungit infantem in summitate capitis,' &c. (Ordo Bapt. Parvulor.)

(c) *The 'Pedilavium,'* or ceremonial washing of the feet after baptism[3].

In connection with the subject it may be mentioned that one of the earliest Anglo-Saxon decrees, under Augustine, provided for the invocation of each Person of the Holy Trinity in Baptism. Pope Zachary writing to Boniface of Mentz A.D. 748 told him that the following canon on Baptism had been passed in England A.D. 597–603 : ' Dinoscitur ut quicunque sine invocatione Trinitatis lotus fuisset, quod sacramentum regenerationis non haberet . . . Hoc quoque observasse in supradicta synodo sacerdotes, ut qui vel unam

---

Leoghaire were clothed in white garments after their baptism by St. Patrick. Book of Armagh, fol. 12 a.   [1] Ch. iii. § 14.

[2] It has been fancifully suggested that certain ancient bronze spoons may have been used for pouring the oil of chrism over the head of the newly baptized person. (Archaeol. Cambr. vol. ii. Fourth Ser. p. 16.) In the anonymous Life of St. Bridget this passage occurs : ' Magus dormiens vidit duos clericos vestibus albis indutos effundere oleum super caput puellae, ordinem baptismi complentes consueto more.' Acta SS. ed. Bolland., Feb., tom. i. p. 119; Leabhar Breac, fol. 62 b.

[3] See note to the passage in the Stowe Ordo Baptismi, ch. iii. § 14.

Personam de Trinitate in baptismo non nominaret, illud bap-
tismum esse non posset, quod pro certo verum est quia qui
Unum ex sancta Trinitate confessus non fuerit perfectus
Christianus esse non potest[1].'

In describing the proceedings of the Synod of Cashel A.D.
1172 Benedict of Peterborough mentions the following curious
facts: ' In illo autem concilio statuerunt, et auctoritate summi
pontificis praeceperunt, pueros in ecclesia baptizari, *In nomine*
Patris, et Filii, et Spiritus Sancti, et hoc a sacerdotibus fieri
praeceperunt. Mos enim prius erat per diversa loca Hiberniae,
quod statim cum puer nasceretur, pater ipsius vel quilibet
alius eum ter mergeret in aqua. Et si divitis filius esset, ter
mergeret in lacte[2].' Archbishop Theodore's doubts of the
validity of British Baptism have been noticed[3]. If there
was any reason for supposing that the abuses in Ireland in
the twelfth century had any counterpart in England in the
seventh century, they would have been justifiable. It is
curious that the formula of Baptism is omitted in the Office
preserved in the Stowe Missal[4].

3. *The Tonsure.*—The Roman tonsure was formed by the
top of the head being shaved close, and a circle or crown of
hair left to grow around it. The Eastern tonsure, styled St.
Paul's, was total. The Celtic tonsure consisted in shaving all
the hair in front of a line drawn over the top of the head
from ear to ear. The Roman party traced their form of
tonsure to St. Peter, and attributed that of their opponents
to Simon Magus. Abbot Ceolfrid discussed the subject at
length in his letter to Nectan King of the Picts A.D. 710[5].

---

[1] Inter Epp. S. Bonifac. lxxxii, edit. Würdtwein, p. 235, quoted in H. and
S. iii. 51. An Irish priest named Sampson was accused by the same pope
of erroneous teaching about Baptism; Ep. xvii. ad Bonifac.; Ussher, iv. 463.

[2] Rolls Ser. 1867, vol. i. p. 28, ed. W. Stubbs. The only allusion to Baptism
in the eight canons of this Council which are extant is in the first, which orders
its administration to take place in the font at church, implying that the laxer
custom of baptizing in private houses was creeping in or had become prevalent.
(Mansi, Concil. tom. xxii. p. 134; Girald. Cambr. Expugn. Hibern. lib. i.
cap. 35; Master of Rolls' Ser. vol. v. p. 282.)

[3] p. 42.   [4] Ch. iii. § 14.   [5] Bede, H. E. v. 21.

Although not brought forward by St. Augustine, this question of the tonsure (together with that of Easter) formed the subject of the most frequent and violent controversy in Britain during the seventh century. There are traces of the same controversy in France, where a Saxon colony at Bayeux had copied the Celtic tonsure from the Bretons before A.D. 590[1]; and in Spain, where a tonsure like the Celtic was condemned by the fourth Council of Toledo[2].

4. *The Ordinal.*

(*a*) *The Consecration of Bishops by a single Bishop.* — In the Life of St. Kentigern it is related that he was consecrated to the episcopate by a single bishop who had been summoned from Ireland for that purpose, according to the custom of the Britons and Scots[3]. A similar fact is recorded in the legendary lives of the Welsh SS. David, Dubricius, Teilo, &c.[4] There is a curious legend of the consecration of St. Columba by Bishop Etchain, who conferred on him priest's instead of bishop's orders by mistake[5]. Was this the flaw which caused Archbishop Theodore to suspect the imperfection of Celtic Orders[6], and think it necessary to confirm the consecration of Chad to the see of York? That consecration had been performed by Wini Bishop of Winchester, assisted by two British bishops, A.D. 665[7], but such assistance may have been regarded as valueless[8]. In Ire-

---

[1] Greg. Tur. Hist. Franc. x. 9.

[2] Conc. Tolet. IV. A.D. 633. can. xli; Mansi, Concil. x. p. 630. Further details are given by Bede, H. E. iv. 1; Gildas, Epist. ii; Aldhelm, Epist. ad Geruntium, in H. and S. iii. 268; Mabillon, Ann. Bened. i. 528; Act. SS. Ord. Ben. saec. ii. pp. 119–20.

[3] 'Rex et clerus regionis Cambrensis (in Glasguo) ... accito de Hibernia uno Episcopo, more Britonum et Scottorum, in Episcopum ipsum consecrari fecerunt.' Vita S. Kentegerni, auctore Jocelino, c. xii.

[4] Acta SS. Mart. i. 44, &c.	[5] Félire of Oengus, at the end of March.

[6] 'Qui ordinati sunt a Scottorum vel Britonum episcopis ... adunati aecclesiae non sunt, sed iterum a catholicŏ episcopo manus impositione confirmentur.' Theodore's Penitential, book ii. sect. ix.	[7] Bede, H. E. iii. 28.

[8] Ib. iv. 2. Theodore's reason is not obvious. Consecration by a single bishop has always been recognised as valid, though irregular. Bingham, Antiq. book ii. cap. xi. sect. 5; Bright, W., Early Eng. Ch. Hist. pp. 227–8.

land the custom of single consecration still obtained in the eleventh century, and was complained of by St. Anselm writing to the Irish king Tirlagh, A.D. 1074, and by Lanfranc writing to King Muriardach, A. D. 1100[1]. It is strange that such a custom should have prevailed in the British Church, as three of its bishops had been present and had subscribed to the canons of the Council of Arles, A.D. 314, which ordered that at least three, and if possible seven, bishops should take part in every episcopal consecration[2].

(*b*) *The Lections of Scripture* used in the British Ordinal differed from those in use in other Western Ordinals. Their variations are exhibited in the following table:—

BRITISH ORDINAL. (From Gildas.)	GALLICAN ORDINAL. (From Lectionarium Luxoviense.)	ROMAN ORDINAL. (From Div. Hieron. Comes Pamelii Liturg. ii. 60.)
At Ordination. 1 Pet. i. 3, 13, 14, 22; ii. 1, 9. Acts i. 15, 16. 'Secunda Lectio Pauli.' 1 Tim. iii. 1 &c. Matt. xvi. 16-18.	*Ordination of Deacons.* Ezek. xliv. 15, 16. 1 Tim. iii. 8-13. Luke ix. 57-62. *Of Priests.* Tit. i. 1-6. Luke xii. 42-44. *Of Bishops.* Mal. i. 6-11. 1 Cor. ix. 7-12. Luke xx. 45-xxi. 4.	*Ordination of Deacons.* 1 Tim. iii. 8. John xii. 24. *Of Priests.* Ecclus. xxxv. 2. Matt. xxiv. 42. *Of Bishops.* Matt. x. 1; xxiv. 42. Mark vi. 6. Luke x. 1. John x. 12; xii. 24. 1 Tim. iii. 1. Tit. i. 7.

St. Gregory, in his celebrated answers to St. Augustine, distinctly recognised the validity of consecration by single bishops in case of necessity, and authorised and commissioned him to consecrate single-handed. 'Truly in the Church of the English, in which as yet you are found the only bishop, you cannot ordain a bishop otherwise than without other bishops.' Bede, H. E. i. 27. Respons. vi.

[1] St. Anselm said, 'Episcopi quoque qui debent esse forma et exemplum aliis canonicae religionis, inordinate, sicut audimus, aut a solis episcopis, aut in locis, ubi non debent, consecrantur.' Ussher, Vet. Epist. Hibern. Sylloge, Ep. xxxv; also in Ep. xxxvi. Lanfranc complained 'Quod episcopi ab uno episcopo consecrantur.' Ib. Ep. xxvii.

[2] 'Ut sine tribus episcopis nullus episcopus ordinetur. De his qui usurpant sibi quod soli debeant episcopos ordinare, placuit ut nullus hoc sibi praesumat nisi assumptis secum septem aliis episcopis: si tamen non potuerit septem infra tres non audeat ordinare.' Mansi, Conc. tom. ii. p. 474. can. xx.

(*c*) *The anointing of the hands* of deacons and priests at ordination. This custom, together with the above use of lections, is vouched for by the contemporaneous authority of Gildas : ' Recurrere tandem aliquando usque ad lectiones illas, quae ad hoc non solum ut recitentur, sed etiam adstipulentur benedictioni, qua initiantur sacerdotum vel ministrorum manus,' &c.[1]

The earliest extant formula for such unction is found in the Pontifical of the Anglo-Saxon Egbert Archbishop of York (732–766), and runs as follows[2] :—

' AD ORDINANDOS PRESBITEROS.

(1) *Consecratio Manus.*

(2) Benedic, Domine, et sanctifica has manus sacerdotis tui Ill. ad consecrandas hostias quae pro delictis atque neglegentiis populi offeruntur, et ad cetera benedicenda quae ad usus populi necessaria sunt ; et praesta, quaesumus, ut quaecunque benedixerint benedicentur, et quaecunque sacrauerint sacrentur, Saluator mundi, qui uiuis et regnas.

(3) *Faciens crucem sanctam de chrismate in manibus eius* (*uel eorum*) *et dicis :*

(4) Consecrentur manus istae, quaesumus, Domine, et sanctificentur ; per istam sanctam unctionem et nostram inuocationem, adque diuinam benedictionem, ut quodquod benedixerint sit benedictum, et quodquod sanctificauerint sit sanctificatum. Per.

(5) *Consecratio capitis oleo.*

(6) Unguatur et consecretur caput tuum coelesti benedic-

---

[1] Gildae Epist. If this interpretation of the passage is correct, Jocelin (twelfth century) must be wrong in stating that unction of the head only formed part of the British rite. ' Mos inolevit in Britannia in consecratione pontificum tam modo capita eorum sacri crismatis infusione perungere, cum invocatione Sancti Spiritus, et benedictione et manus impositione ; quem ritum dicebant disipientes se suscepisse divinae legis institutionem, et Apostolorum traditionem.' Vit. S. Kent. c. xi, ap. Pinkerton, Vit. Antiq. p. 223.

[2] Printed by the Surtees Society, vol. xxvii. p. 24, from a tenth-century MS. in the Imperial Library at Paris.

tione in ordine sacerdotali, in nomine Patris, et Filii, et Spiritus Sancti. Amen.

Pax tibi.

Presp. Et cum Spiritu tuo.'

In the ordination of deacons in the same Pontifical[1] there is the following rubric and collect:—

(7) '*Consecratio manuum Diaconi de oleo sancto et chrisma.*

(8) Consecrentur manus, iste, quaesumus Domine, et sanctificentur per istam unctionem, ut quaecunque benedixerint benedicta sint, et quaecunque sanctificauerint sanctificata sint.'

(1) and (4) are found in the Gregorian Sacramentary[2]; not in the Gelasian; and in three ninth-century Gallican Sacramentaries[3].

The rubric and formula for the unction of the hands in the consecration of priests, in the present Roman Pontifical, are as follows:—

'*Pontifex cum oleo catechumenorum inungit unicuique ambas manus, simul junctas, in modum crucis, producendo cum pollice suo dextero in dictum oleum intincto duas lineas, videlicet, a pollice dexterae manus usque ad indicem sinistrae, et a pollice sinistrae usque ad indicem dexterae, ungendo mox totaliter palmas, dicens, dum quemlibet inungit:*

Consecrare et sanctificare digneris, Domine, manus istas per istam unctionem et nostram benedictionem. *R.* Amen.

Pontifex producit manu dextera signum crucis super manus illius, quem ordinat, et prosequitur:

Ut quaecunque benedixerint benedicantur, et quaecunque consecrauerint consecrentur et sanctificentur in nomine Domini nostri Jesu Christi. Amen[4].'

---

[1] Ib. p. 21.   [2] Muratori, Lit. Rom. Vet. ii. 414, from a tenth-century MS.

[3] Mart. i. viii. xi. ordo iv. vol. ii. p. 41.

[4] There is a passage in a letter from Pope Nicolas I (858–867) to Rodulph Archbishop of Bourges, asserting that the anointing of the hands was not then in use in the Roman Church in the ordination either of priests or deacons: 'Sciscitaris utrum solis presbyteris an et diaconibus debeant cum ordinantur manus chrismatis liquore perungi; quod in sancta hac Romana, cui Deo auctore

The anointing of the hands at the ordination of deacons [(7) and (8)] is not found in any form of the Roman Ordinal, ancient or modern, nor in any Gallican Ordinal[1]. It is found in the Anglo-Saxon Ordinals of St. Dunstan[2], of Egbert[3], of Bec[4]; and is asserted by Martene to have been a peculiarity of the Anglo-Saxon Church[5]. With the passage of Gildas in view[6], it seems a safe inference that it was imported into the Anglo-Saxon Ordinal from the more ancient forms of the British Church.

A similar inference has been drawn with reference to the following points, but with less certainty, as there is no passage of Gildas, or other Celtic author, which can be produced to throw light on the earlier British practice.

(*d*) *The Prayer at the giving of the stole* to deacons at Ordination :—

'In nomine sanctae Trinitatis et unicae divinitatis accipe stolam quam tibi Dominus per humilitatis nostrae famulatum, seu per manus nostras, accipiendam praeparavit; per quam scias sarcinam Domini Dei tui cervicibus tuis impositam, et ad humilitatem atque ministrationem te esse connexum, et per quam te cognoscant fratres tui ministrum Dei esse ordinatum, ut qui in diaconatus ministerio es constitutus, leuitice benedictionis ordine clarescas, et spiritali conuersatione praefulgens gratia sanctificationis eluceas; sed et in Christo Jesu firmus et stabilis perseveres, quatenus hoc quod per hanc stolam significatur in die districti iudicii ante tribunal Domini siue macula representare ualeas; ipso auxiliante cui est honor et gloria in saecula saeculorum. Amen.'

---

deservimus, ecclesia, neutris agitur.' Martene expresses his astonishment at this passage. Certainly Amalarius (ob. 837), writing some years previously, had asserted the custom in the case of the ordination of priests : 'Hunc morem tenent episcopi nostri ; manus presbyterorum ungunt de oleo.' De Div. Off. lib. ii. c. 13. Rodulph and Amalarius were familiar with Gallican, and perhaps also with Anglo-Saxon Ritual.

[1] But (8) is found in the ordering of priests in an early Poitiers Pontifical, Cod. Pictav. saec. vii. in Bibl. Vatican.

[2] Mart. i. viii. xi. ordo iii.   [3] Ib. ordo ii.   [4] Ib. ordo xi.

[5] Ib. i. viii. ix. § 9.   [6] p. 70.

This prayer is found in the Winchester Pontifical[1], and in the English Pontificals of Egbert[2] and St. Dunstan at Paris[3], and in that of Jumièges[4], but not in any other Western ordinals.

(*e*) *Rite of delivering the book of the Gospels to Deacons at Ordination.*

This rite, which is now in general use in the Roman Church, is not found in any of the Ordines Romani in the Western Pontificals prior to A. D. 1000, except in the above-mentioned Pontificals of the Anglo-Saxon Church. The words with which it is there accompanied are these:—

'*Postea tradat ei episcopus sanctum euangelium, dicens:*

Accipe illud uolumen Euangelii. Lege, et intellige, et aliis trade, et tu opere adimple[5].'

It is not mentioned by the early ritualists St. Isidore, Amalarius, or Alcuin. It must therefore have been imported from England into France[6], and through France into the rest of Western Christendom,—and from what other source is the Anglo-Saxon Church likely to have obtained it except from the ancient Celtic Church which preceded it?

(*f*) *Rite of investing priests with a stole at ordination.*

This rite is not mentioned in the Gelasian or Gregorian Sacramentaries, nor in any of the earlier Western Rituals collected by Martene, who conjectures that its absence is due to the fact that the stole had already been given to the deacon at ordination[7]. But the rite does appear in the Office for the Ordination of Priests in the English Pontificals before

---

[1] Harl. MSS. 561. saec. xiv; Maskell, Mon. Rit. iii. 198.

[2] Mart. ii. p. 35.   [3] Ib. p. 39.

[4] Rouen MSS. 362. saec. x; Mart. ii. p. 37.

[5] Ib. p. 39. The present Roman formula is very different: '*Postremo Pontifex accipit et tradit omnibus librum Evangeliorum quem manu dextera tangunt, dicens;* Accipe potestatem legendi Evangelium in Ecclesia Dei tam pro vivis quam pro defunctis. In nomine Domini. Amen.'

[6] '*Cum ergo solemnis fuerit in Anglia evangelii traditio, reperiaturque in omnibus quos inde videremus Libris Ritualibus, ab ea ecclesia hunc ritum initium traxisse facile colligitur.*' Mart. i. viii. ix. § 8.

[7] Mart. i. viii. ix. § 13.

mentioned, whence it probably spread, like the Delivery of the Gospels, into the rest of Western Christendom. The Pontifical of Egbert contains the following directions:—

> '*Presbyter cum ordinatur, circumdentur humeri eius cum stola ab episcopo* [1].

Quando datur stola Presbytero.

Stola(m) iustitiae circumdet Dominus cervicem tuam et ab omni corruptione peccati purificet Dominus mentem tuam [2].'

The same reason exists as in (*c*) for supposing a Celtic origin for this rite.

5. *Peculiar mode of consecrating Churches and Monasteries.*

(*a*) Celtic Churches as a rule, to which those of St. Martin and of the 'Quatuor Coronati [3]' at Canterbury and that of St. Martin at Whithern must be considered exceptions, were not named after departed saints, but after their living founders. On one occasion Archbishop Theodore supplied an Anglo-Roman dedication to the wooden cathedral which had been built some fourteen years previously at Lindisfarne by the Celtic Bishop Finan. Bede narrates how (A.D. 651) 'Aidan, the Bishop, having departed this life, Finan, who was ordained and sent by the Scots, succeeded him in the bishopric, and built a cathedral church in the isle of Lindisfarne; nevertheless after the manner of the Scots, he made it not of stone, but of hewn oak, and covered it with reeds; and the same was afterwards dedicated in honour of St. Peter the Apostle by the most reverend Archbishop Theodore [4].' The dedications of Celtic churches may be divided into two classes, those to native saints before the existence of the Anglo-Saxon

---

[1] The Roman Ordinal has the following : '*Pontifex sedet accepta mitra et reflectit orarium, sine stolam, ab humero sinistro cujuslibet, capiens partem quae retro pendet, et imponens super dexterum humerum, aptat eam ante pectus in modum crucis singulis dicens.*

'*Accipe jugum Domini ; jugum enim ejus suave est et onus ejus leve.*'

[2] Surtees Soc. vol. xxvii. p. 21.   [3] Bede, H. E. i. 26; ii. 7.

[4] Bede, H. E. iii. 25. We are indebted to this Celtic custom of dedicating churches to their living founders or consecrators for the preservation of many saints' names, especially in Cornwall.

Church, those to saints in the Anglo-Saxon or Roman Ca-
lendar imposed at a later date[1]. Sometimes the earlier dedication lingered on in use by the Celtic population, side by
side with the later one, as in the case of 'St. Elider and
St. James,' 'St. Beuno and St. Michael,' 'St. Dogmael and
St. Thomas' &c. in Wales ; 'St. Mawnanus and St. Stephen,'
'St. Manacus and St. Dunstan,' 'St. Meran and St. Thomas
a Becket' in Cornwall.

(*b*) The consecration of a church or monastery was preceded by a long fast. Bishop Cedd of the East Saxons
(653–664) told Æthelwald, King of Deira, that 'it was the
custom of those from whom he had learned a rule of regular
discipline that they should first consecrate with prayer *and
fasting* those places which had been newly obtained for founding a monastery or church.' Accordingly he fasted 'for the
whole forty days of Lent,' and the exercise of fasting and
prayer being completed he built a monastery, which is now
called Lastingham, and established it with religious customs,
according to the practice of Lindisfarne, where he had been
educated[2].

6. *The Liturgy and the Ritual of the Mass.*

The surviving fragments of the Celtic Liturgy have been
put together in ch. iii, and the information which can be
gleaned about its ritual is contained in ch. ii. It will therefore be sufficient to group together here certain passages
which supply historical evidence of the existence of a Liturgy,
other than the Roman, in these islands.

In England and Wales.—The use of a Liturgy here, certainly different from the Roman, and either identical with or
very like the Gallican Liturgy, is an inference from the second
of the questions put by Augustine to Gregory I, and from that

---

[1] Borlase, Age of the Saints, pp. 74–76. Mr. R. Rees has detected a third and
intermediate list of Celtic dedications to St. Michael, ranging from the seventh
to the tenth century. Welsh Saints, p. 65.

[2] Bede, H. E. iii. 23. The detail with which Bede records the above facts
implies that he thought this mode of consecration unusual and deserving of
special mention.

Pope's reply[1]. It is strengthened by the language in which Augustine addressed the British bishops at the Synod of Bangor: 'In many respects you act in a manner contrary to our customs, and indeed to those of the Universal Church; and yet if you will obey me in these three things; to celebrate Easter at the proper time; to perform the office of baptism, in which we are born again to God, according to the custom of the Holy Roman and Apostolic Church; and to join us in preaching the word of God to the English people (Anglorum genti), we will tolerate *all your other customs, though contrary to our own*[2].' The last clause almost certainly includes a difference of Liturgy, which however Augustine had previously received instructions from Gregory not to elevate into a casus belli.

Gildas c. A.D. 570 had asserted a difference between the British and Roman Liturgies in these words: 'The Britons are at variance with the whole world, and are opposed to Roman customs, not only in the Mass, but also in their tonsure[3].'

The Council of Clovesho, A.D. 747, can. xiii, ordered the general adoption of Roman Sacramental usages throughout the English dioceses: 'Tertio decimo definitur decreto: Ut uno eodemque modo Dominicae dispensationis in carne sacrosanctae festivitates, in omnibus ad eas rite competentibus rebus, id est, in Baptismi officio, *in Missarum celebratione*, in cantilenae modo celebrantur, juxta exemplar videlicet quod scriptum de Romana habemus Ecclesia. Itemque ut per gyrum totius anni natalitia sanctorum uno eodemque die, juxta martyrologium ejusdem Romanae Ecclesiae, cum sua sibi convenienti psalmodio seu cantilena venerentur[4].'

This passage proves that in A.D. 747 the Roman Liturgy was only in partial, not in universal use in England. Possibly

---

[1] Bede, H. E. i. 27; Krazer, P. A., De Lit. p. 89, ed. 1787.

[2] Bede, H. E. ii. 2.

[3] 'Britones toti mundo contrarii, moribus Romanis inimici non solum in missa sed in tonsura etiam.' Gildas, Epist. ii; H. and S. i. 112.

[4] H. and S. iii. p. 367.

the Gregorian Canon had been introduced in some places without the whole service having been assimilated to the Roman type, as is concluded, from an examination of the old Gallican Liturgies, to have been the case in France[1].

The Irish Catalogue of the Saints, A.D. 750, asserts that a British Liturgy, different from St. Patrick's, had been introduced into Ireland, in the latter half of the sixth century, by St. David, St. Cadoc, and Gildas[2].

At the close of the eighth century the Scottish Liturgy was said to be still in daily use in the church of York, and Alcuin writing from France (790–800) urged Archbishop Eanbald to abolish it, just as Charles the Great, in 789, had ordered the Roman rite to be substituted everywhere in France for the old Gallican Liturgy[3].

In Ireland.—The following account of the origin of the Scottish (= Irish) Liturgy, and of the British (after A.D. 429) assumed to be the same, tracing it through Germanus and Lupus to St. Mark and distinguishing it from the Gallican, was drawn up by some foreign Scoto-Irish monk probably in the eighth century:—

' *Cursus Romanus*[4].—Beatus Trosimus, Episcopus Arelatensis, et Sanctus Photinus, martir et Episcopus Lugdunensis, discipulus S. Petri, sicut et refert Josephus, et Eusebius Caesariensis Episcopus, cursum Romanum in Galeis tradiderunt.

---

[1] Missale Francorum, p. 692, edit. Muratori ; Mabillon de Lit. Gall. p. 46.

[2] p. 81.

[3] ' (Presbyteri) non despiciant Romanos discere ordines.' Ep. 56. 'Nuncquid non habes Romano more ordinatos libellos sacratorios abundanter ? Habes quoque et veteris consuetudinis sufficienter sacramentaria majora . . . Aliquid voluissem tuam auctoritatem incepisse Romani ordinis in clero tuo, ut exempla a te sumantur, et ecclesiastica officia venerabiliter et laudabiliter vobiscum agantur.' Ep. lxv. Ad Simeonem [= Eanbaldum.]

[4] Transcribed from H. and S. i. 138. The conjectural emendations of Spelman (Concil. i. 167) have been incorporated in the text, so far as is necessary to make it grammatical, and where possible intelligible. The evidence of this confusing document, so far as it is worth anything, asserts the original Irish Liturgy used by St. Patrick to have been neither Roman, nor Gallican, but Alexandrian. In this respect it is an isolated statement, unsupported by any other evidence.

Cursus Gallorum.—Inde postea relatione beati Photini martyris, cum quadraginta et octo martiribus retrusi in ergas-
tulum, relatione ad beatum Clementem IV loci successorem
beati Petri Apostoli deportaverunt, et beatum Irenaeum
Episcopum beatus Clemens ordinavit. Hoc in libro sancti
ipsius Irenaei, Episcopi et martiris, reperies. Edoctus a beato
Polycarpo Smyrnaeorum Episcopo et martyre, qui fuit discipulus Johannis Apostoli, sicut refert Historiographus Josephus, et Irenaeus Episcopus, in suo libro.

Johannes Evangelista primum cursum Gallorum decantavit;
inde postea beatus Polycarpus discipulus Sancti Johannis;
inde postea Irenaeus qui fuit Episcopus Lugdunensis Gallei,
tertius ipse, ipsum cursum decantaverunt in Galleis. Inde
per diversorum prudentium virorum, et modulationibus, series
Scripturarum Novi ac Veteris Testamenti diversorum prudentium virorum paginis, non de propriis sed de sacris Scripturis,
reciproca, antiphonas, et responsus seu sonus, et alleluyas
composuerunt; et per universum mundum peragravit, atque
per universum orbem terrarum Ecclesiae ordo cursus Gallorum diffusus est. Quem beatus Hieronimus presbiter, et
Germanus et Lupus Episcopi, Pelagianam haeresim (non
sicut multi opinantur et Gallicanus quidam clericus Britto
modulatione deditus, quod ipsum edidisset, quod non fecit)
quod beatus Hieronimus presbiter, Germanus et Lupus, Pelagianam haeresim vel Gallianam (quae nomen ipsius titulatur)
ex Britannis et Scotiis provinciis expulerunt.

Cursus Scottorum.—Unde et alium cursum, qui dicitur prae-
senti tempore Scottorum, quae sit opinione, jactatur. Sed
beatus Marcus Evangelista, sicut refert Josephus et Eusebius
in libro quarto, totum Aegyptum vel Italiam taliter praedicaverunt sicut unam Ecclesiam, ut omnis sanctus, vel Gloria in
Excelsis Deo, vel Oratione Dominica, et Amen, universi tam
viri quam foeminae decantarent. Tanta fuit sua praedicatio
unita, et postea Evangelium ex ore Petri Apostoli edidit.

Beatus Hieronimus affirmat, ipsum cursum, qui dicitur prae-
senti tempore Scottorum, beatus Marcus decantavit, et post

ipsum Gregorius Nanzianzenus, quem Hieronimus suum
magistrum esse affirmat. Et beatus Basilius, frater ipsius
sancti Gregorii, Antonius, Paulus, Macarius, vel Johannes et
Malchus, secundum ordinem Patrum decantaverunt.

Inde postea beatissimus Cassianus, qui Linerensi monasterio beatum Honorium habuit comparem. Et post ipsum
beatus Honoratus primus abba, et sanctus Caesarius Episcopus qui fuit in Arelata, et beatus Porcarius abbas, qui in ipso
monasterio fuit, ipsum cursum decantaverunt, qui beatum
Lupum et beatum Germanum monachos in eorum monasterio
habuerunt. Et ipsi sub normam reguli ipsum cursum
ibidem decantaverunt, et postea in Episcopatus cathedra
summi honoris, pro reverentia sanctitatis eorum, sunt adepti.
Et postea in Britannis vel Scotiis praedicaverunt, quae Vita
Germani Episcopi Autisiodorensis, et Vita beati Lupi ad-
firmant. Qui beatum Patricium spiritaliter litteras sacras
docuerunt atque innutrierunt, et ipsum Episcopum pro eorum
praedicatione Archiepiscopum in Scotiis et Britanniis posue-
runt; qui vixit annos CLIII, et ipsum cursum ibidem decantavit.

Et post ipsum beatus Wandilochus senex, et beatus Gomo-
gillus, qui habuerunt in eorum monasterio monachos circiter
tria millia.

Inde beatus Wandilochus in praedicationis ministerium a
beato Gomogillo missus est, et beatus Columbanus, partibus
Galliarum; destinati sunt Luxogilum monasterium, et ibidem
ipsum cursum decantaverunt.

Et inde postea percrebuit forma sanctitatis eorum per universum orbem terrarum, et multa coenobia ex eorum doctrina,
tam virorum quam puellarum, sunt congregata.

Et postea inde sumpsit exordium sub beato Columbano,
quod ante beatus Marcus Evangelista decantavit. Et si nos
non creditis, inquirite in Vita beati Columbani et beati Eus-
tacii abbatis; plenius invenietis, et dicta beati Athleti abbatis
Edbovensis.

Cursus alius Orientalis.—Est alius cursus Orientalis a sancto

Cromacio, et Eliodoro, et beato Paulino, seu Athanasio Episcopo editus, qui in Gallorum consuetudine non habetur ; quem
sanctus Macarius decantavit, hoc est, per duodenas, hoc est,
unaquaeque ora.

Cursus S. Ambrosii.—Est et alius cursus, quem refert beatus
Augustinus Episcopus, quem beatus Ambrosius papa propter
haereticorum ordinem dissimilem composuit, qui in Italia
antea decantabatur.

Cursus S. Benedicti.—Est et alius cursus beati Benedicti,
qui ipsum singulariter pauco discordante a cursu Romano ; in
sua regula repperies scriptum. Sed tamen beatus Gregorius,
urbis Romae pontifex, quasi privilegium monachis, ipsum sua
auctoritate in Vita S. Benedicti in libro Dialogorum affirm-
avit ; ubi dixit, " Non aliter sanctus vir docere poterat, nisi
sicut ipse beatus Benedictus vixit." '

Another document, drawn up about the middle of the
eighth century, is entitled ' Catalogus Sanctorum Hiberniae
secundum diversa tempora.' It is believed to be the work
of Tirechan, the author of the Annotations on the Life of
St. Patrick in the Book of Armagh. It gives the following
information, which is generally accepted as historical :—

' A. D. 440 (?)–534. The first order of Catholic saints was
in the time of Patricius ; and then they were all bishops,
famous and holy, and full of the Holy Ghost ; 350 in number,
founders of churches. They had one head, Christ ; and one
chief, Patricius ; they observed one mass, one celebration, one
tonsure from ear to ear. They celebrated one Easter, on the
fourteenth moon after the vernal equinox ; and what was
excommunicated by one Church, all excommunicated. They
rejected not the services and society of women[1] ; because
founded on the Rock of Christ, they feared not the blast of
temptation. This order of saints continued for four reigns.
All these bishops were sprung from the Romans, and Franks,
and Britons, and Scots.

---

[1] According to another MS., ' They excluded from the churches neither lay-
men nor women.'

'A.D. 534–572. The second order was of Catholic presbyters. For in this order there were few bishops, and many presbyters, in number 300. They had one head, our Lord. They celebrated different masses, and had different rules; one Easter, on the fourteenth moon after the equinox; one tonsure, from ear to ear; they refused the services of women, separating them from the monasteries. This order has hitherto lasted for four reigns. They received a mass from Bishop David, and Gillas and Docus, the Britons.

'A.D. 572–666. The third order of saints was of this sort:—They were holy presbyters and a few bishops; 100 in number; who dwelt in desert places, and lived on herbs and water, and the alms; they shunned private property; they had different rules and masses, and different tonsures, for some had the coronal, and others the hair [behind]; and a different Paschal festival. For some celebrated the Resurrection on the fourteenth moon or on the sixteenth, with hard intentions. These lived during four reigns, and continued to that great mortality[1] [A.D. 666].'

In Scotland. — There are no historical documents extant about the character of the ancient Scottish Liturgy. The existence of such a Liturgy is proved by the character of the solitary fragment in the Book of Deer[2]; by the frequent Liturgical and Ritual allusions in the works of Adamnan and other writers of the Celtic Church in Scotland; by the account of the steps taken by Queen Margaret to get it abolished in the eleventh century[3]. St. Serf is said in the Aberdeen Breviary to have lived ' sub forma et ritu primitivae Ecclesiae[4].' When Palladius arrived in Scotland he is said to have found persons ' habentes fidei doctores et sacramentorum ministros presbiteros et monachos, prima-

---

[1] The original document is printed in H. and S. ii. pt. ii. 292, where it is attributed to an anonymous author, c. A.D. 750. It ncludes the names of many kings, bishops, and presbyters, by the aid of which the date of the periods referred to is ascertained, varying slightly from the dates in the above text, which are taken with the translation from Skene's Celtic Scotland, ii. 12.

[2] Ch. iii. § 5.   [3] p. 7   [4] Brev. Aberd. July i, fol. xv.

tivae ecclesiae solum modo sequentes ritum et consuetudinem[1].' At Culross he found St. Serf ' virum devotum, mansue-
tum, et pium quem, ejus exigentibus meritis, catholicum juxta
Romanae Ecclesiae morem rite ordinavit episcopum, et in
eadem fide divinitus informavit,' &c.[2] Passing on through
Scotland, ' ecclesias consecravit, vestimentis sacerdotalibus
modum imposuit, et ab eisdem horas canonicas dicendas,
prout ecclesia instituebat Romana, sollenniter jussit[3].' The
use of the old Scottish Liturgy at York has been already
alluded to[4].

---

[1] Brev. Aberd. July vi, fol. xxiv. [2] Ib. fol. xxv. Lect. v.

[3] Ib. Lect. vi. It is doubtful whether Palladius ever visited Scotland (Skene, W. F., Celtic Scotland, ii. 27), but documents like the Aberdeen Breviary, even where historically valueless, preserve allusions or indications of otherwise unknown or forgotten circumstances. This is true generally of the ' Acta Sanctorum,' and of some of the Lections in the present Roman Breviary.

[4] p. 77.

CHAPTER II.

CELTIC RITUAL.

CHAPTER II.

It is proposed in this chapter to lay before the reader such information as can be gathered both directly and incidentally about the structure and decoration of Celtic churches, the dress and ornaments of the clergy, and the ritual of the service performed by them. The sources from which such information is forthcoming have been generally summed up in the Preface, and will be more particularly specified in foot-notes.

§ 1. CHURCHES. *Of Earth.* — Celtic churches were occasionally and at a very early date constructed of earth. In Tirechan's Annotations on the Life of St. Patrick it is stated, that 'when Patrick went to the place which is called Foirrgea of the sons of Awley, to divide it among the sons of Awley, he built there a quadrangular church of earth, because wood was not near at hand[1].'

Of Wood.—Where however wood could be obtained it was generally employed, so much so, that the custom of the Irish to use wood for building obtained for it in the middle ages the title of 'mos Scottorum,' 'opus Scoticum,' 'the Scottish style.'

The church of St. Derbhfraich, near Clogher, in Tyrone (fifth century), was a wooden structure[2]. So was that of St. Ciaran of Saighir, in the same century[3].

In the sixth century St. Monenna 'founded a monastery, which was made of smooth planks according to the fashion

---

[1] Book of Armagh, fol. 14 b 2.
[2] Félire of Oengus, April 4, pp. 458, lxxiii.   [3] Colgan, Acta SS. p. 458.

of the Scottish nation, who were not accustomed to erect stone walls or to get them erected[1].' St. Columba's church at Derry was built of timber and wattling[2].

In the seventh century St. Kevin (Coemgen) built his oratory of rods of wood[3]; St. Gobban, a famous builder, constructed a wooden church for St. Mulling[4]. It is told of St. Mochaoi, abbot of Nendrum, that on one occasion he went with sevenscore young men to cut wattles to make his church[5].

In the ninth century the Annals of Ulster record a hurricane which occurred on the festival of St. Martin, and which prostrated a great many trees in the woods, and carried the churches (DIURTHEACHS) from their places[6].

In the twelfth century the custom of building churches of wood was still continued in Ireland, as appears from St. Bernard's notice of a church built by Malachy Archbishop of Armagh[7].

The same custom prevailed in other portions of the Celtic Church. In Scotland St. Ninian's church among the Southern Picts, at the end of the fourth or beginning of the fifth century obtained its name of Candida Casa from the very unusual circumstance that it was built of stone, the use of which material for building purposes was not customary at that date[8].

---

[1] 'Ecclesia in monasterio sanctae Monennae cum supradicta abbatissa construitur tabulis dedolatis, juxta morem Scotticarum gentium, eo quod macerias Scotti non solent facere nec factas habere.' Conchubran's Life of St. Monenna, a twelfth-century compilation, quoted from Cod. Cotton. Cleop. A. 2 by Dr. Reeves in his edition of Adamnan, p. 178. note e.

[2] Leabhar Breac, p. 32 a.   [3] Bolland, Acta SS. June i. p. 316.

[4] ' Quidam famosissimus in omni arte lignorum et lapidum erat in Hibernia nomine Gobbanus, cujus artis fama usque in finem saeculi erit in ea.' Colgan, Acta SS. p. 619.

[5] Martyrology of Donegal, p. 177.   [6] Annals of Ulster, A.D. 891.

[7] 'Porro oratorium intra paucos dies consummatum est de lignis quidem levigatis, sed apte firmiterque contextum, opus Scoticum pulchrum satis.' S. Bernardi, Vita S. Malachiae, c. vi. § 14.

[8] 'Eo quod ibi ecclesiam de lapide, insolito Brittonibus more fecerit.' Bede, H. E. iii. 4.

St. Adamnan implies that the first buildings at Iona,
including the church, were of wood[1].

Early in the eighth century, Nectan king of the Picts
sent into England for builders in stone, after that Benedict
Biscop had introduced there the Roman custom of employing
this more durable material[2].

In the Northumbrian Church, Finan, who had been a monk
at Iona, and who succeeded Aidan as bishop of Lindisfarne
A.D. 651, 'built a church fit for an episcopal see, not of stone,
but altogether of sawn wood covered with reeds after the
Scotic fashion[3].'

In England, the buildings at Glastonbury, as they existed
in the British Church, before the Anglo-Saxon refoundation
of that monastery in the seventh century, were, according to
tradition, of wood[4].

In Wales, when St. Kentigern founded his monastery of
St. Asaph, in the sixth century, he built the church of dressed
wood, 'after the manner of the Britons, since they were not
yet either accustomed or able to build with stone[5].' St.
Gwynllyw, at the close of the same century, is recorded to
have built a cemetery chapel of wood[6].

On the Continent, when the great Celtic missionary St. Columbanus received from the king of the Lombards a site for
his church and monastery at Bobbio A.D. 615, he was said to

---

[1] Adamnan, Vit. S. Columbae, i. 35 ; ii. 41-46.

[2] 'Architectos sibi mitti petiit, qui juxta morem Romanorum ecclesiam de
lapide in gente ipsius facerent.' Bede, Hist. Eccles. v. 21. Biscop had brought
from Gaul ' caementarios qui lapideam sibi ecclesiam juxta Romanorum morem
facerent.' Ib. Vit. SS. Abb. Mon. in Wiramutha, in Migne, Bib. Pat. Lat.
xciv. 715.

[3] 'Fecit ecclesiam episcopali sedi congruam, quam tamen more Scottorum
non de lapide sed de robore secto totam composuit, atque harundine texit.'
Bede, Hist. Eccles. iii. 25.

[4] Dugdale's Monasticon, vol. i. p. 1.

[5] 'More Britonum, quum de lapide nondum construere poterant, nec usum
habebant.' Pinkerton, Vitae SS. Scotiae, Vita Kentegerni, p. 248.

[6] 'Signavit cimiterium, et in medio tabulis et virgis fundavit templum.'
Rees, W. J., Lives of Cambro-British Saints, Vita S. Gundleii, p. 148.

have been supernaturally assisted in procuring the wood necessary for that purpose[1].

Of Stone.—Stone buildings, though not the general rule, were by no means unknown throughout this period. The remains of rude oratories of uncemented stone still survive in Ireland, either like the oratory of Gallerus, of a date antecedent to the mission of St. Patrick, or like that of Crumtherim, coeval with him, or, as in the case of the church of St. Kienan (Cianan, Kenan), built by his disciples[2]. Stone began to be universally adopted in Ireland for building purposes after the first irruption of the Danes, A.D. 794, and the consequent transfer of the monastic establishment of Iona to Kells, A.D. 814.

In Scotland, it has been noticed that St. Ninian's church at Candida Casa, c. A.D. 400, was a stone structure. There are remains of a stone chapel of St. Medan, an Irish virgin and a disciple of St. Ninian, at Kirkmaiden on the Bay of Luce in Wigtonshire, similar to remains found in Cornwall and Brittany. There are also in the same neighbourhood stones, sepulchral slabs, &c., with representations of crosses, animals of interlaced work of Hiberno-British character, like the single stones found in Ireland, and described in detail by Mr. Petrie[3].

The remains of British churches in England and Wales

---

[1] Jonae Vit. S. Columbani, in Mabillon, Acta SS. Ord. Ben. tom. ii ; Vita S. Columbani Abbatis, pp. 28, 40. It must not be inferred that the use of wooden buildings was confined to the Celtic race. Such work in France was known as 'opus Gallicum,' in contradiction to stone-work, 'opus Romanense.' It is described in Italia Monumenta Historiae Patriae, vol. i, Edict. Reg. Langobard. App. xi. p. 245. In Anglo-Saxon times King Edwin (616–633) built a wooden church at Tynemouth ; there was a 'monasteriolum ligneum' in the same town, rebuilt by St. Oswald in stone. The wooden cathedral at Chester-le-Street remained till A.D. 1042. Lelandi Collect. vol. iv. p. 43. The first church of St. Peter at York, A.D. 627, was 'de ligno.' Bede, H. E. ii. 14. There is a wooden church, of the eleventh century, at Greensted in Essex now.

[2] Petrie, G., Round Towers, p. 132 ; Colgan, Trias Thaum. pp. 163, 217. Lime cement has been used in the building ascribed to St. Kienan.

[3] Transactions of Royal Irish Academy, xx. 123; Stuart, J., Sculptured Stones of Scotland, vol. ii. passim.

enumerated and described at length by Messrs. Haddan and
Stubbs exhibit Romano-British stone or brickwork[1].

An examination of these ruins points to the small dimensions of these primitive churches, and this inference is corroborated by early testimony. Sixty feet was the length of the
Great Church of St. Patrick at Teltown in Meath[2]; one hundred
feet that of the first cathedral at Armagh, c. A.D. 445[3]. But
larger churches soon rose. The Annals of Ulster record the
burning of two hundred and sixty persons in a wooden church
A.D. 849. The following is the description of St. Bridget's
church at Kildare, in her life by Cogitosus:—

'The church in which repose the bodies of both, that is,
Bishop Conlaeth, and this Virgin Saint Bridget, on the right
and left of the decorated altar, deposited in ornaments adorned
with various embellishments of gold and silver and gems and
precious stone, with crowns of gold and silver depending from
above. For the number of the faithful of both sexes increasing, the church occupied a spacious area, and was elevated
to a menacing height, and was adorned with painted pictures,
having within three oratories large and separated by partitions of planks under one roof of the greater house, wherein
one partition—decorated and painted with figures, and covered
with linen hangings — extended along the breadth in the
eastern part of the church, from the one to the other party-
wall of the church : which partition has at its extremity two
doors ; and through the one door, placed in the right side,
the chief bishop enters the sanctuary, accompanied by his
regular school, and those who are deputed to the sacred
ministry of offering sacred and dominical sacrifices ; through
the other door, placed in the left part of the above-mentioned
partition, and lying transversely, none enter but the abbess
with her virgins and faithful widows, when going to participate

---

[1] H. and S. i. 37.

[2] Book of Armagh, fol. 10 a, b, quoted in Trans. of Royal Irish Acad. xx. 161.

[3] St. Evin's Life of St. Patrick, ap. Colgan, Trias Thaum. p. 164. Most of
the churches were still smaller ; p. 48. n. 4.

in the banquet of the body and blood of Jesus Christ. But another partition, dividing the pavement of the house into two equal parts, extends from the eastern (western?) side to the transverse partition lying across the breadth. Moreover the church has in it many windows, and one ornamented doorway on the right side, through which the priests and the faithful of the male sex enter the church, and another doorway on the left side, through which the congregation of virgins and faithful women are accustomed to enter. And thus in one very great temple, a multitude of people, in different order and ranks, and sex and situation, separated by partitions, in different order but with one mind worship Almighty God[1].'

The remains of Bishop Conlaeth referred to in this extract were disinterred and enshrined A.D. 799. Cogitosus describes the windows as 'numerous' and the walls as 'covered with mural paintings.' This points to a date at least as late as the eighth century, for Bede assigns the first introduction of glass and painting into England A.D. 676 to Benedict Biscop, and he had to bring glaziers from Gaul[2]; unless Dr. O'Conor[3] is right in seeing in Cogitosus' work only a proof of the early and more advanced state of art in Ireland, or unless Mr. Petrie is right in laying stress on the fact that there is no mention of glass in these windows, which may have been only apertures[4].

The ornamentation of the church need not cause surprise, for there are extant elaborately-worked gold, silver, and bronze utensils and ornaments recently discovered in Ireland, and undoubtedly belonging to a still earlier date. See the description of silver flagons and cups with interlaced and triangular ornamentation found near Coleraine A.D. 1854,

---

[1] Cogitosus, Vita S. Brigidae, ap. Canisii Op. i. 423.

[2] Vit. SS. Abb. Monasterii in Wiramutha, in Migne, Bib. Pat. xciv. 717.

[3] Rerum Hibern. Scriptores, ii. 109.

[4] But Mr. Petrie, on other grounds, assigns this description to the ninth century; Trans. of Royal Irish Acad. xx. pp. 198–206. It is erroneously placed among works of the sixth century in Migne's Patrol. vol. lxxii.

and assigned to a date 400–600 B.C. in the Ulster Journal of Archæology, vol. ii. p. 182.

The surviving architectural remains are a proof of the number of Celtic churches which must at one time have existed. As far as England alone is concerned, there is the direct testimony of the British historian Gildas, who speaks of the multitude of churches destroyed in England during the Diocletian persecution[1] (A.D. 305–313), and again during the invasions of the heathen Saxons in the sixth century[2]. Further details of Irish churches and oratories will be found in Dr. Petrie's Ecclesiastical Architecture of Ireland, p. 186, and of Scottish churches in the Proceedings of the Society of Antiquaries of Scotland, ii. 517.

Certain main features deserve to be further dwelt upon.

Screens. — There appears to have been in early Celtic churches a substantial screen with doors in it, separating the chancel from the nave. This is implied in Cogitosus' description of St. Bridget's church (p. 89), and is stated in a fifteenth-century Gaelic MS. Life of St. Columba preserved in the Advocates' Library at Edinburgh, and translated in Mr. Skene's Celtic Scotland, vol. ii. p. 500.

Altars.—British churches at the beginning of the fourth century had more than one altar. This is inferred from the expressions of Gildas, 'inter altaria' (p. 72), 'inter ipsa sacrosancta altaria' (p. 37). The altar was called 'coelestis sacrificii sedes' (p. 37). It stood at the east end of the church[3]. It was sometimes made of wood, as in the case of the altar in the church of St. Bridget[4]; sometimes of stone. Gildas

---

[1] Specifying their possession of 'altars' and 'towers;' sect. 6.

[2] Sect. 13. Their sites were claimed afterwards by the Anglo-Saxon Church : 'Stans itaque sanctus Wilfridus episcopus ante altare, conversus ad populum, coram regibus enumerans regiones quas ante reges . . . illi dederunt, lucide enunciavit ; necnon et ea loca sancta in diversis regionibus, quae clerus Britonum aciem gladii hostilis manu gentis nostrae fugiens deseruit.' Eddius, Vit. S. Wilfridi, xvii ; H. and S. i. 124.

[3] Ancient Scholiast on Fiacc's Hymn ; Todd's Life of St. Patrick, p. 411 ; unless the church stood N. and S., as was the case at Derry, Saul, and Armagh ; Historians of Scotland, vol. vi. p. 1, Edinb. 1874 ; Leabhar Breac, fol. 26 a.

[4] Canisii Op. i. p. 417. When St. Bridget received the veil at the hands

alludes to the stone altars of British churches[1]. A stone altar is mentioned as having been discovered by St. Patrick in a cave, a possible proof of the existence of Christians in Ireland before the arrival of that saint[2]; and stone altars of the Celtic period have been found on the island of Ardoilan, six miles from the coast of Orney, on the site of the antique monastery of St. Fechin[3]; in the oratory of St. Molaise at Inismurray[4]; at Temple Molaga, with two stone candlesticks close to it[4]; in the oratory of St. Piran at Perranzabuloe in Cornwall[5]; and in that of St. Michael at Penkivel in the same county[6].

Vestry.—There was frequently an outside vestry attached to the church, 'exedra' or 'exedriola[7],' where the sacred vessels were kept, and which served for the other purposes of a sacristy.

Bells.—Each church had its bell, 'clocca' or 'campana,' used for summoning the congregation together for the divine offices[8]. The bells of St. Columba and St. Ninian, the former being possibly the very bell alluded to by St. Adamnan, are still in existence in the collection made by the late Mr. John Bell of Dungannon. Pictures of them, with minute description and measurements, are given in Stuart's Sculptured Stones of Scotland[9], Wilson's Archæology of Scotland[10], Archæologia Scotica[11]. A similar bell was found six hundred years ago in the ruins of Bangor Abbey, of which there is a woodcut in the Ulster Journal of Archæology[12]. There is a handbell in

---

of the British St. Mel (Moel or Mael) Bishop of Ardagh, bowing her head she touched with her hands one of the wooden pillars of the altar, which ever afterwards remained green and sound.

[1] 'Inter altaria jurejurando demorantes, et haec eadem ac si lutulenta paulo post saxa despicientes.' H. and S. i. 49.

[2] St. Evin's Life of St. Patrick, ap. Colgan, Trias Thaum. p. 134; Todd's Life of St. Patrick, p. 222; see Leabhar Breac, fol. 26a.

[3] Transactions of Royal Irish Academy, xx. 421-3.

[4] Dunraven, Lord, Notes on Irish Architecture, pp. 47, 62.

[5] Transactions of Exeter Dioc. Arch. Soc. vol. ii. p. 95.   [6] Ib. vol. iv. p. 91.

[7] Adamnan, Vit. S. Columbae, iii. 19; Id. de Locis Sanctis, i. 8.

[8] 'Cloccam pulsa, cujus sonitu fratres incitati ad ecclesiam ocius currunt.' Vit. S. Columbae, i. 8; iii. 23; Cummian, Vit. S. Columbae, p. 41.

[9] ii. p. liii.   [10] p. 652.   [11] iv. 119.   [12] i. 179.

the hands of a very ancient sculptured figure of an ecclesiastic[1]. A 'campanarius' is mentioned in the list of various persons who formed the household of St. Patrick, who is also said to have given fifty bells to the churches of Connaught[2]. St. Fillan's bell, with its possibly phallic ornamentation, and with an account of the superstitious usages with which till lately it has been connected, is described in the Proceedings of the Society of Antiquaries of Scotland[3]. Small quadrangular hand-bells of great age, very similar in construction to the Irish type of workmanship, have been found in Wales: an account of one dug up on the site of the oratory of St. Cenan, and of another formerly preserved in the church of Llangwynodd, is given in the Archæologia Cambrensis[4]. Various ancient Irish bells still exist, of which the earliest is perhaps that of St. Patrick. A description of it has been published by Dr. Reeves[5].

A short account of the ancient bells of other Celtic saints is given by Professor Westwood[6]. St. Mogue's bell and three others are figured in the Proceedings of the Society of Antiquaries of London[7], where Mr. Franks describes them as presumably 'hand-bells used by the early missionaries and eremitical bishops of the British Church to summon their followers to prayer.' They were kept either in the vestry, or in those round towers both of Scotland and Ireland which were so long a puzzle to antiquaries, but which are believed by some persons to have been belfries, as well perhaps as repositories for relics, books, and other valuables[8].

Strange miracles sometimes attested the sanctity of these

---

[1] Transactions of Royal Irish Academy, xx. 248.

[2] St. Evin's Life of St. Patrick, p. 143.

[3] viii. 265–76.   [4] Fourth Series, ii. 274.

[5] In a folio volume with five plates, 1850.

[6] Facsimiles of the Miniatures, &c., p. 152.   [7] Second Series, iii. 150.

[8] Adamnan, Vita S. Columbae, iii. 15 ; Stuart, Sculptured Stones of Scotland, notice of plate i. p. 1 ; Petrie, Ecclesiastical Architecture of Ireland, p. 120. This theory of the use of the round towers is combated by Mr. Brash in Ulster Journ. Archæol. viii. 280–91. And Miss Stokes, as Editor of Lord Dunraven's Ecclesiastical Antiquities of Ireland, assigns to the earliest of them a date not earlier than the close of the ninth century.

bells, as in the case of the construction of a 'ferrea campana et quadrata suae ecclesiae pernecessaria' by St. Molocus[1], and of the bell which followed St. Ternan day by day all the way from Rome to Scotland[2]. They were also used, as well as pastoral staves, in the administration of oaths[3].

Churchyards.—In close proximity to the British church, then as now, was the churchyard, in the midst of which was planted the emblematic evergreen yew-tree. Many of the trees now standing date from the British period. The yew-tree at Aldworth, Berks, was examined A.D. 1841, and then concluded to be 1377 years old; i.e. it must have been planted c. A.D. 464, shortly after the preaching of St. Germanus against the Pelagian heresy. Crowhurst yew in Surrey is said to be 1450 years, and the yews at Fountains Abbey are of great antiquity[4]. Giraldus Cambrensis noticed the abundance and age of yews in Ireland, especially in churchyards and cemeteries[5].

LITURGY AND RITUAL OF THE CELTIC CHURCH.

We now pass on from the church itself and its surroundings to some account of the service which took place within its walls.

§ 2. TITLES OF THE LITURGY.—The Altar Service itself was entitled Communio[6], Communio altaris[7], Comna[8], Conviaticum[9], Eucharistia[10], Hostia[11], Oblatio[12], Oiffrenn[13],

---

[1] Brev. Aberdon. June 25, fol. vi.   [2] Ib. June 12, fol. cvi.

[3] Kilkenny Archæol. Soc. 1852, p. 51 ; Girald. Cambrens. Top. Hib. iii. 33.

[4] Rock, D., Church of our Fathers, ii. 320 ; Loudon, Arboretum, iv. 2073. The precision with which these calculations have been made is ridiculous, but the author is assured by the Professor of Botany in Oxford that there is nothing abstractly impossible in the existence of certain trees, such as the yew, more than a thousand years old.

[5] 'Maxime vero in coemeteriis antiquis, locisque sacris, sanctorum virorum manibus olim plantatas.' Top. Hib. Dist. iii. c. 10.

[6] Poenitentiale Uinniani, §§ 34, 36 ; Hibernensis, lib. ii. c. 16.

[7] Poenitentiale Uinniani,, § 14.

[8] [= Communion], Senchus Mor, iii. 32, 39 ; Comann, Leabhar Breac, fol. 29 b ; F. cxxxiv, cxciv.   [9] Hibernensis, ii. 16.

[10] Ib. iii. 8 ; Prefat. Gildae de Peniten. ; Book of Dimma.

[11] Hibernensis, ii 21.   [12] Ib. iii. 6 ; Reg. Columbani, cap. iv.

[13] (= Offering, modern Irish Aifrion), Senchus Mor, i. 126 ; ii. 344 ; F. lxxv, cxciv.

Sacorfaicc [1], Sacrificium [2], Sacrificale mysterium [3], Viaticum [4].

The word 'sacrificium' was used equally for that which was offered to God, and for that which was given to and received by the communicant. St. Gall told his scholar Magnoaldus, 'My master Columbanus is accustomed to offer unto the Lord the sacrifice of salvation in brazen vessels [5].' The twelfth canon of the synod of St. Patrick runs thus: 'He who deserveth not to receive the sacrifice in his life, how can it benefit him after his death [6]?' St. Patrick said to the newly-baptized virgin daughters of Laoghaire, 'Ye cannot see the face of Christ except ye taste of death, and except ye receive the sacrifice. And they answered, Give us the sacrifice, that we may behold the Son, our Spouse. And they received the Eucharist of God and they slept in death [7].' The two words 'communion and sacrifice' are frequently used together in one phrase in the Leabhar Breac [8].

To celebrate the Holy Eucharist was expressed by Offerre [9], Sacra offere [10], Offerre sacrificium [11], Christi corpus conficere [12], Eucharistiae celebrare mysteria [13], Sacra Eucharistiae mysteria

---

[1] Book of Deer; Sacarbaic, Leabhar Breac, fol. 29 b; F. ccxxxviii.

[2] Reg. S. Columbani, c. xii; Gildae, Prefat. de Peniten. §§ 6, 7, 8; Hibernensis, xli. 4.

[3] Cuminius, Vit. S. Col. p. 29.   [4] Hibernensis, ii. 16.

[5] 'Preceptor meus beatus Columbanus in vasis aeneis Domino solet sacrificum offerre salutis.' Walafrid Strabo, Vita S. Galli, i. 19.

[6] 'Qui in vita suâ non merebitur sacrificium accipere, quomodo post mortem illi potest adjuvare?' Canons attributed to St. Patrick, xii, H. and S. ii. pt. ii. p. 335.

[7] Book of Armagh, fol. 12 a.

[8] 'Rofaid Patraic aspirut iarsin 7 rogab comaind 7 sacarbaic dolaim tassaig escuip' = 'Thereafter Patrick sent forth his spirit and he received communion and sacrifice from Bishop Tassach's hand.' Leabhar Breac, fol. 29 b; also on fol. 65 a, 66 a. Sacorfaicc is used for the reserved sacrament given to the sick in a rubric in the Book of Deer (ch. iii. § 5); and Sacrificium is used in the same way in a rubric in a tenth century German Rituale printed by Gerbert, Lit. Aleman. ii. 129.

[9] Gildas, Pref. de Penit. xxiv; Hibernensis, lib. xviii. c. 6.

[10] Gildas, ib. xxiii.

[11] Liber Davidis, can. xii; Patricii Confessio, xiv.

[12] Adamnan, Vita S. Columbae, i. 44.   [13] Ib. iii. 12.

conficere [1], Sacra oblationis mysteria ministrare [2], Missarum peragere sollemnia [3], Sacra Eucharistiae consecrare mysteria [4], Missarum sollemnia celebrare [5], Sacram oblationem con secrare [6], Sacrosancta ministeria perficere [7], Frangere panem [8], Sacra celebrare mysteria [9], Sacrosancta mysteria perficere [10], Immolare hostiam [11], Offerre sacrificium [12], Altario jungi [13].

§ 3. MULTIPLICITY OF COLLECTS.—A peculiar feature of the Celtic Liturgy, at least in its Irish form, was a multiplicity of collects. A synod was held at Matiscon (Macon) in Gaul A.D. 623, to consider the charges brought by a certain monk Agrestius against the Rule of St. Columban.

Mabillon gives a full account of the controversy, and mentions, after several trivial objections brought by Agrestius, the following more important one, that the Irish differed from the ritual and rule of other Churches, and celebrated the Holy Eucharist with great variation and multiplication of collects and prayers [14].

Eustasius, the disciple and successor of Columbanus in the monastery of Luxovium (Luxeuil), admitted the charge, but pleaded in defence the general acceptableness of all prayer before God.

It is impossible to decide with certainty to what Agrestius referred in his charge. Benedict XIV interpreted it of the substitution of several collects for the one collect which ordinarily precedes the Epistle in the Roman Missal, and which is thus referred to in one of the opening rubrics in the Gregorian Sacramentary: '*Postmodum dicitur oratio, deinde sequitur Apostolus* [15].' Commenting on this rubric Benedict XIV

---

[1] Adamnan, Vita S. Columbae, i. 40.   [2] Ib.   [3] Ib.   [4] Ib. iii. 17.
[5] Ib.   [6] Ib.   [7] Ib.   [8] Ib. i. 44.   [9] Cuminius, Vita S. Columbae, c. 12.   [10] Ib.   [11] Secundini Hymnus ; Book of Hymns, p. 17.   [12] Patricii Confessio, xiv.

[13] [= to be admitted to communion], Poenitentiale Uinniani, §§ 15, 35.

[14] 'In summa quod a caeterorum ritu ac norma desciscerent, et sacra missarum sollemnia orationum et collectarum multiplici varietate celebrarent.' Annals of the Bened. Order, i. 320.

[15] Migne, Bibl. Pat. Lat. lxxviii. 25 ; on which Menard remarks, 'In hoc sancti Eligii codice ut in Codicibus Rodradi et Ratoldi, atque in Editis, et in

says, 'Una tantum olim in hac Missae parte Collecta seu Oratio dicebatur, ut ostendit Menardus in notis ad Sacramentarium S. Gregorii. Sanctum quondam Columbanum accusavit Agrestinus (Agrestius?) quod contra Ecclesiae morem plures in Missa Orationes recitaret, quem egregie defendit Eustasius,' &c.[1]

But why should not the charge of Agrestius have referred to the existence of other, and to the Roman worshipper unknown collects, which are found in the Gallican and Mozarabic Liturgies, and to which Alex. Lesleus, writing a Latin Preface to his edition of the latter Liturgy, refers thus: 'Tum sacerdos, in utraque Liturgia (i. e. Gallicana et Mozarabica) populum salutat, et ad altare accedens, septem illas solemnes orationes, quibus liturgiae Gallicana, Gotho-Hispana, et Mozarabica praecipue constant, et ab aliis quibuscunque distinguuntur, devote recitabat,' i.e. (i) *Praefatio Missae,* (ii) *alia oratio,* (iii) *post nomina,* (iv) *ad pacem,* (v) *Contestatio aut Immolatio Missae aut Illatio,* (vi) *post mysterium aut post pridie,* (vii) *Dominica oratio* cui brevis oratio praemittitur, *ante orationem Dominicam* Gallis dicta, et subsequitur alia, quae iisdem *post orationem Dominicam* nominatur[2]'?

Dr. O'Conor commenting on this point says, 'This multiplicity of prayers is expressly mentioned by Columbanus himself in his Rule, c. 7[3].' But on reference to that Rule it is found that St. Columbanus is not speaking of the Liturgy at all, but of petitions in the form of versicles inserted in the Day-hours of the Divine Office[4].

Ordine Romano, unica habetur oratio seu collecta in prima parte missae ante Evangelium, raro duae,' &c.　Ib. p. 268. n. 10.

[1] De Sacrosancto Missae Sacrificio, lib. ii. cap. 5. sect. 3; Benedicti XIV, Op. edit. 1777, tom. viii. p. 33.

[2] Migne, Bibl. Pat. Lat. lxxxv. p. 25.

[3] Bibl. MS. Stowensis, vol. i. appendix i. p. 43.

[4] His words are, 'Sed quia orationem canonicarum noscendus est modus, in quo omnes simul orantes horis conveniant statutis, quibusque absolutis unusquisque in cubiculo suo orare debet; per diurnas terni psalmi horas, pro operum interpositione statuti sunt a senioribus nostris cum versiculorum augmento intervenientium, pro peccatis primum nostris, deinde pro omni populo

§ 4. THE LORD'S PRAYER.—The Lord's Prayer formed an essential part of the Celtic as of every other known Liturgy except the Clementine. Heavy penalties were specially enjoined at Iona by the abbot Cuminius in the case of any mistake in its recitation [1].

It was not introduced with the unvarying formula of the Roman Missal in its earliest as well as latest editions, 'Praeceptis salutaribus moniti, et divina institutione formati audemus dicere,' nor was it followed by the Roman embolismus, 'Libera nos, quaesumus, Domine ab omnibus malis,' &c. The varying forms substituted for these in the fragments of the Books of Deer, Dimma, and Mulling, and in the Stowe Missal [2], are one of the strongest proofs of an Ephesine rather than a Petrine origin of the Celtic Liturgy.

The names of local saints were sometimes introduced into the embolismus, as that of St. Patrick in the embolismus in the ancient Irish fragment at St. Gall, MS. No. 1394 [3], and in that of the Stowe Missal [4].

§ 5. LECTIONS.—Lections are mentioned as forming part of the Liturgy. The following is among the directions of the abbot Cuminius : 'Sacrificium non est accipiendum de manu sacerdotis, qui orationes et lectiones secundum ritum implere non potest [5].'

This may imply that in addition to the Epistle and Gospel there was a third lection from the Old Testament—the lectio prophetica—preceding them, as in the Mozarabic and Gallican Liturgies, of which Lesleus says in his Preface, 'In utraque Liturgia tres leguntur Scripturae lectiones una e Veteri, duae e novo Testamento [6].'

Christiano, deinde pro sacerdotibus et reliquis Deo consecratis sacrae plebis gradibus, postremo pro eleemosynas facientibus, postea pro pace regum, novissime pro inimicis.' Migne, Bibl. Pat. Lat. lxxx. p. 212.

[1] 'Si titubaverit sacerdos super orationem Dominicam, quae dicitur periculosa, si una vice quinquaginta plagas secunda centum, tertia superponat.' Cuminii Abbatis, de Mensura Poenitentiarum, c. xiii, ap. Fleming, Collect. Sacra, p. 209.
[2] Ch. iii. §§ 5, 6, 7, 14. [3] Ib. § 9. [4] Ib. § 14.
[5] De Mensura Poenitentiarum, c. xiv, ap. Fleming, Collect. Sacr. p. 210.
[6] Migne, Bibl. Pat. Lat. lxxxv. 25.

The order of the Gallican Service is thus described by Germanus Bishop of Paris : ' Sequebatur lectio ex prophetis et ex apostolo. Nam praeter Evangelii lectionem, duas, unam ex veteri, alteram ex Novo Testamento, lectiones cantabant, quem ritum videre est apud Gregorium Turonensem (Lib. i. de Mirac. S. Martini, cap. 5) ubi haec habet; "Factum est ut illa Dominica, prophetica lectione jam lecta, ante altarium staret, qui lectionem beati Pauli proferret." In sanctorum festivitatibus, sive martyrum, sive confessorum, acta eorum etiam publice legebantur, ut, auditis eorum virtutibus, populi ad similia perpetranda accenderentur. Ita Gregorius Turonensis [1] lectam fuisse S. Polycarpi passionem narrat [2].'

It appears, from a passage in Adamnan's Life of St. Columba, as if an additional lection from the Gospels preceded the Liturgy itself : ' Hi uno eodemque consensu elegerunt ut sanctus Columba coram ipsis in ecclesia sacra Eucharistiae consecraret mysteria. Qui eorum obsecundans jussioni, simul cum eis, die Dominica ex more, post Evangelii lectionem, ecclesiam ingreditur, ibidemque dum missarum sollemnia celebrarentur,' &c. [3]

§ 6. SERMON.—The sermon, when there was one, came next in order after the Gospel, as on the occasion of the Eucharist which followed the elevation of Johannes Diaconus to the rank of bishop, when St. Gall preached the consecration sermon after the Gospel had been read [4].

§ 7. PROPER PREFACES.—The use of a Proper Preface for the Festival of St. Patrick ' sollemnitas dormitationis ejus ' is alluded to in Tirechan's Annotations, but no trace of its wording has survived [5]. In the Book of Armagh it

---

[1] Lib. i. de Glor. Martyrum, cap. 86.
[2] Germani Paris. Expos. Brev. Antiq. Lit. Gall. 6th cent.   [3] Lib. iii. c. 17.
[4] 'Praemissis ergo ex more divinae libationis initiis, post lectionem Evangelii rogavere venerabilem Gallum ut multitudini quae aderat verbi officio sacrae instructionis pabula ministraret.' Walafrid Strabo, Vit. S. Galli, i. 25. The sermon was preached in the vernacular tongue. A list of some extant sermons will be found on p. 157.
[5] Todd, Life of St. Patrick, p. 430.

is ordered that on that Festival 'offertorium ejus proprium immolari.' This probably means that commemoration of St. Patrick should be made in the Liturgy in a Proper Preface, for which the Gallican name was 'Immolatio Missae[1].'

A portion of the Proper Preface for the Feast of the Circumcision survives in a ninth-century MS. fragment of four pages of an ancient Irish Liturgy, No. 1394, in the library of St. Gall[2]. Other Celtic Prefaces have been preserved in the Stowe Missal[3].

§ 8. BENEDICTION.—The benediction was given with the right hand[4] and in the Eastern manner; that is to say, the first, second, and fourth fingers were extended, while the third was closed down upon the extremity of the thumb over the palm of the hand. This may be seen in the representation of our Lord in glory in an Irish ninth-century MS. of the Four Gospels at St. Gall[5]; of St. Matthew surmounted by an angel, both of them extending the right hand in the Eastern attitude of blessing, in the Golden Gospels of Stockholm, of composite sixth-century Celtic and eighth or ninth-century Anglo-Saxon work[6].

There are also traces of the use of the Roman mode of benediction. The thumb, fore and middle fingers are extended, and the third and fourth fingers are bent in the case of a figure sculptured in the attitude of blessing on an Iona cross[7], and on a tenth-century cross at Oransay[8].

With regard to the position in the Liturgy of the episcopal benediction, Dr. Döllinger[9] concludes that it was given after

---

[1] The expression 'immolare hymnum' occurs in the 'Hymnum S. Comgilli' in the Antiphon. Benchor. p. 142.

[2] Ch. iii. § 9.   [3] Ch. iii. § 14.

[4] 'Diormitius tum sanctam sublevat ad benedicendum Sancti monachorum chorum dexteram manum.' Adamnan, Vit. S. Columbae, iii. 23.

[5] Westwood, J. O., Facsimiles of Anglo-Saxon and Irish MSS., plate xxvii.

[6] Ib. plate i. For early and mediaeval Italian representations of this mode of benediction, see J. H. Parker's Photographs, No. 3569.

[7] Stuart, J., Sculptured Stones of Scotland, vol. ii. plate lxii.

[8] Ib. plate lxiii.

[9] Geschichte der christlichen Kirche, vol. i. part ii. p. 183.

the consecration and fraction, and before the immission of the consecrated particle into the chalice. This is an inference from the language in which the celebration of the Eucharist by Bishop Cronan at Iona is described by Adamnan [1].

The episcopal benediction occupied a similar position in the ancient Gallican and Mozarabic Liturgies [2]. The same position was assigned to it in the Liturgy of the Anglo-Saxon Church [3], and was perpetuated in the Sarum Use up to the first vernacular Prayer Book of 1549 [4], as it was also in France at Paris, Arles, Lyons, Rouen, Clermont, Angers, Tours, &c. [5] Dr. Rock argues thus for the Gallican origin of this liturgical peculiarity:—

'That such episcopal blessings formed a part of the old liturgy followed by the Gauls long before Pope St. Gregory and St. Austin's days we learn from the fact that St. Caesarius of Arles [6], who lived almost a whole century before those apostles of our Anglo-Saxon fathers, speaks of this rite as a thing practised everywhere about him. Knowing then as we do from the formal and public visit made to the Church in this island by SS. Germanus and Lupus how the British and

---

[1] Lib. i. cap. 44.

[2] Hammond, C. E., Lit. E. and W. p. xxviii. It can be traced in the old Gallican Liturgies, p. 156, in the Mozarabic Liturgy, p. 563. For the Eastern custom see Syriac Liturgy of St. James, Renaudot, Liturg. Or. Coll. ii. p. 24.

[3] Lingard, Anglo-Saxon Church, i. 295, edit. 1845.

[4] Sarum Missal, p. 622.

[5] De Moleon, Voyages Liturgiques, pp. 59, 76, &c.

[6] 'Ideo qui vult missas ad integrum cum lucro animae suae celebrare, usque-quo oratio dominica dicatur, et benedictio populo detur, humiliato corpore et compuncto corde se debet in ecclesia continere.' (S. Caesarii Arelat. Hom. xii. ed. Binio; Bib. Pat. viii. p. 832, edit. 1677.) 'Unius aut duarum horarum spatium patientiam habeamus, donec in illa spiritali mensâ animarum cibus apponitur, et sacramenta spiritalia consecrantur, Et quia praemissa oratione dominica vobis non ab homine sed per hominem datur, grato et pio animo, humiliato corpore et corde compuncto, rorem divinae benedictionis accipite.' (Ejusdem Hom. viii. ed. Gallandio, Vet. Pat. Bib. xi. 12.) A few years afterwards it was enacted, A. D. 538, in the third council of Orleans: 'De missis nullus laicorum antea discedat quam dominica dicatur oratio, et si episcopus praesens fuerit, ejus benedictio expectetur.' (Concil. Aurelian. III, can. xxix; Mansi, Concil. tom. ix. p. 19.)

Gallic Churches were knit together, not only by the feelings of religious friendship, but by the oneness of true belief, we are warranted in thinking that a ceremonial then in common use throughout a neighbouring country with which this land kept up such an intimate connection in matters of faith, must have been common, too, here; so that our bishops among the Britons, like their brethren beyond the sea in Gaul, used to bestow their episcopal blessing at this part of the holy sacrifice[1].'

§ 9. THE PAX.—The kiss of peace was given after the prayer of consecration, and immediately before the communion of the people, the priest saying these words as he gave the pax: ' Pax et caritas Domini, et communicatio sanctorum omnium sit semper vobiscum.' To which the people replied : ' Et cum spiritu tuo[2].'

The following form is found in the Antiphonarium Benchorense : ' *Ad pacem celebrandam.* Injuste egimus. Redemisti nos Domine Deus veritatis in tuo sancto sanguine, nunc adjuva nos in omnibus Jesu Christe, qui regnas. Pax multa diligentibus ; pax tua Domine, rex coelestis, permaneat semper in visceribus nostris ut non timeamus a timore noctis Qui regnas[3].' Exclusion from communion and from the kiss of peace was the punishment for certain offences in the Welsh Church, A.D. 570[4].

§ 10. PRAYER FOR THE DEAD.—To pray for the dead was a recognised custom in the ancient Celtic, as in every other portion of the primitive Church.

Traces of it are found in the earliest inscriptions on sepulchral or memorial stones. The following words are inscribed in Hiberno-Saxon characters on a stone cross at Gwnnws in

---

[1] Church of our Fathers, vol. iii. pt. 2. p. 40.

[2] St. Gall MS. No. 1394, ch. iii. § 9; Stowe Missal, ib. § 14. This is the Roman, not the Gallican position of the Pax. There is no evidence as to the earlier Celtic usage.

[3] Muratori, Anecdota Bibl. Ambros. iv. 145. The latter of these two forms may be a collect from the night-hours, not a portion of the Liturgy.

[4] Gildae Praefatio de Penitentia, § 1.

Cardiganshire : ' Quicunque explicaverit hoc nomen det bene-
dixionem pro anima Hiroidil filius Carotinn[1].' And on a stone
in the ruins of Caldey Priory, Pembrokeshire, in letters assigned
by Professor Westwood to a date soon after the departure
of the Romans from these islands in the fifth century : ' Et
singno crucis in illam fingsi ; rogo omnibus ammulantibus ibi
[ut] exorent pro anima Catuoconi[2].'

Ancient inscriptions on gravestones at Iona in Scotland,
and Lismore, &c. in Ireland, contain requests for prayers for
the departed, facsimiles of which may be seen in the Ulster
Journal of Archaeology[3], Lord Dunraven's Notes on Irish Architecture[4], Æmilius Hübner's Inscriptiones Britanniae Christianae[5]. Others in vernacular Irish, centuries vi–x, are given
in Petrie's (G.) Christian Inscriptions in the Irish Language[6].
In one instance a bilingual inscription (Irish and Latin) has
been found on a stone at Inismurray : ' Ordo Moredach hu
chomochain hic dormit[7].'

The writers of manuscripts in old days would end their
volumes by requesting the prayers of their hereafter readers.
On the fly-leaf of the book of Durrow, or Gospel of St. Columba, a sixth-century MS. in the Library of Trinity College,
Dublin, there is this entry : ' Rogo beatitudinem tuam, sancte
presbyter Patrice, ut quicunque hunc libellum manu tenuerit
meminerit Columbae scriptoris, qui hoc scripsi ipsemet evangelium per xii dierum spatium, gratia Domini nostri.' A
little below in a contemporary hand : ' Ora pro me frater mi ;
Dominus tecum sit[8].'

The colophon at the end of the Book of MacRegol (end
of eighth or beginning of ninth century) is : ' Quicunque

---

[1] Archaeologia Cambrensis, Fourth Series, vol. v. p. 245.
[2] Ib. vol. i. p. 139 ; Westwood, J. O., Lapidarium Walliae, pt. iii. p. 107.
[3] Vol. i. pp. 85-6.   [4] pp. 48, 58, 88, 89.
[5] pp. 33, 75, &c.   [6] Parts i-vi.
[7] Ib. Very similar prayers abound in the sepulchral inscriptions in the
Catacombs. See Boeckh, Corpus Inscriptionum, vol. iv. Facs. ii. Nos. 9644,
9650, et passim.
[8] Westwood, J. O., Facsimiles, &c., p. 23.

legeret et intelligeret istam narrationem orat pro Mac Reguil scriptori[1].'

Adamnan ends his tract De Locis Sanctis (seventh century) with these words: 'Obsecro itaque eos quicunque breves legerint libellos ut pro eodem sancto sacerdote Arculfo divinam precentur clementiam, qui haec de sanctis experimenta locis eorum frequentator libentissime nobis dictavit. Quae et ego quamlibet inter laboriosas et prope insustentabiles tota die undique conglobatas ecclesiasticas sollicitudines constitutus, sibi quamvis sermone describens declaravi. Horum ergo lectorem admone experimentorum, ut pro me misello peccatore, eorundem craxatore, Christum judicem saeculorum exorare non neglegat[2].'

The colophon at the end of Adamnan's Vita S. Col. (Codex A, an early eighth-century MS.) is:—

'Quicunque hos virtutum libellos Columbae legerit pro me Dorbbeneo Dominum deprecetur, ut vitam post mortem aeternam possideam[3].'

That at the end of St. John's Gospel (seventh century) in the Stowe Missal runs thus: 'Deo gratias. Amen. Finit. Amen. Rogo quicunque hunc librum legeris ut memineris mei peccatoris scriptoris. i.————————[4] peregrinus. Amen. Sanus sit qui scripsit et cui scriptum est. Amen.'

It was part of the constant duty of the Irish Culdees in the eighth century to offer intercessions, in the shape of litanies, on behalf of the living and the dead[5]. The old Irish civil law recognised the fact that tithes, first-fruits, and alms were due from the people to the Church, the Church in return being bound to provide for the people, offering or communion, baptism, and preaching, and burial and requiem or hymn of souls[6]. The old Irish ecclesiastical law enumerated benefit to the souls of the departed among the three chief objects for which the Eucharistic offering was made[7]. In one of the

---

[1] O'Conor, Rer. Hibern. SS. Lib. Nuncupat. i. 230.

[2] Mabillon, Acta SS. Ord. Bened. saec. iii. pt. ii. p. 472, Venet. 1734.

[3] Reeves' edit. p. 242.   [4] = Sonid if read forward, Dinos if read backward.

[5] Rule of the Culdees, p. 95, &c.   [6] Senchus Mor, ii. 344; iii. 33, 39.

[7] 'Nunc ecclesia multis modis offert Domino; primo, pro se ipsa; secundo,

canons of the Synod of St. Patrick the question is asked how
the Sacrifice could be expected to benefit a person after his
death, who had not received it during his lifetime[1]. The
monks at Iona were enjoined to display 'fervour in singing
the office for the dead as if every dead person was a particular
friend of theirs[2].' The Eucharist was celebrated on the
day of the funeral, and on the third or seventh day afterwards[3]. When St. Gall was informed of the death of St.
Columbanus he forthwith gave orders for preparations to be
made to enable him to offer the sacrifice of salvation for the
repose of the departed saint[4]. A like kind office was performed on behalf of St. Gall by a surviving episcopal friend[5].

The commemoration of the departed, being one aspect and
object of the Eucharist, naturally occupied a recognised
position in the Liturgy.

Diptychs containing the names of the deceased were brought
by the deacon to the celebrant, and their contents were
announced by him during the offertory, after the first oblation
of the unconsecrated elements and before the Canon. A
special penance was assigned to the deacon who forgot
this part of his duty[6]. This recitation of names was followed

---

pro commemoratione Jesu Christi qui dicit; hoc facite in meam memoriam;
tertio, pro animabus defunctorum.' Sinodus Hibernensis, lib. ii. cap. 9.

[1] 'Qui enim in vita sua sacrificum non merebitur accipere, quomodo post
mortem illi poterit adjuvare.' Syn. S. Patricii, cap. xii.

[2] Regula S. Columbae, sect. 13.

[3] Cuminius de Mens. Poenitent. cap. xiv.

[4] 'Post hujus vigilias noctis cognovi per visionem Dominum et patrem meum
Columbanum de hujus vitae angustiis hodie ad Paradisi gaudia commigrasse.
Pro ejus itaque requie sacrificium salutis debet immolari, et signo pulsato
oratorium ingressi prostraverunt se in orationem, et coeperunt missas agere, et
precibus insistere, pro commemoratione B. Columbani.' Walafrid Strabo, Vita
B. Galli, i. cap. xxvi. St. Columba acted in the same way when he heard of
the death of Columbanus of Leinster; Adamnan, Vita S. Col. iii. 12.

[5] 'Intraverunt ergo ecclesias et episcopus pro carissimo salutares hostias
immolavit amico.' Wal. Strabo, Vita B. Galli, i. cap. xxx.

[6] 'Diaconus obliviscens oblationem adferre donec auferatur linteamen,
quando recitantur nomina pausantium, similiter poeniteat.' Cuminius, De
Mens. Penitent. c. xiii. For the use of the word 'pausantium' see Stowe
Missal, ch. iii. § 14, where the Irish form of collect in use after the reading of
the diptychs is preserved.

by an anthem in an authorised form of words called the
'deprecatio.' It contained an enumeration of the names of
those departed saints for whose repose the prayers of the
congregation were requested, and of those by whose intercessions such prayers would be assisted. We know that this
collect at Iona ended with the name of St. Martin, and that
on one occasion St. Columba, celebrating on the day following
his reception of the news of the death of Bishop Columbanus,
suddenly turned to the cantors, and bade them add that
bishop's name to the deprecatio. The words of Adamnan
in narrating this incident are these: 'Sed forte dum inter
talia cum modulatione officia, illa consueta decanteretur
deprecatio in qua sancti Martini commemoratur nomen, subito
sanctus ad cantores ejusdem onomatis ad locum pervenientes,
Hodie, ait, pro sancto Columbano episcopo decantare debetis.
Tunc omnes qui inerant fratres intellexere quod Columbanus,
episcopus Lagenensis (=Leinster), carus Columbae amicus,
ad Dominum emigraverit [1].'

This passage affords a presumption in favour of the identity
of the Celtic and Gallican Liturgies. In the latter Liturgy,
the priest after presenting the oblations on the altar, and praying
for the illapse of the Holy Ghost, recited from the diptychs
the names of saints both quick and dead, in whose memory
and for whom the offering was made. The liturgical
formula in use for this purpose in the Church of Arles in
the time of St. Aurelian (545–553) has been preserved, and
in spite of its length is here subjoined in full, as being
probably identical with the form of words which constituted
the deprecatio in the Celtic Liturgy in use at Iona. The words
suggesting such identity are printed in italics. 'Simulque
precantes oramus etiam, Domine, pro animabus famulorum
tuorum Patrum atque institutorum quondam nostrorum,
Aureliani, Petri, Florentini, Redempti, Constantini, Himiteri,
Hilarini, Januarini, Reparati, Childeberti, Ultrogothae, vel om-

---

[1] Adamnan, Vit. S. Columbae, iii. 12.

nium fratrum nostrorum, quos de hoc loco ad te vocare dignatus es.   Cunctorumque etiam hujus loci memores fidelium, pariterque parentum nostrorum atque servientium hujus loci, et pro animabus omnium fidelium famulorum tuorum, vel famularum, ac peregrinorum in pace ecclesiae defunctorum, ut eis tu, Domine Deus noster, peccatorum tribuas veniam et requiem largiaris aeternam ;   meritis et intercessionibus sanctorum tuorum, Mariae genitricis Domini nostri Jesu Christi, Joannis Baptistae et praecursoris Domini nostri Jesu Christi, Stephani, Petri, Pauli, Joannis, Jacobi, Andreae, Philippi, Thomae, Bartholomaei, Matthaei, Jacobi, Simonis, Judae, Matthiae, Genesii, Symphoriani, Baudilii, Victoris, Hilarii, episcopi et confessoris, *Martini episcopi et confessoris*, Caesarii episcopi, haec propitius praestare et exaudire digneris, qui vivis et regnas in unitate Spiritus sancti Deus in saecula saeculorum.   Amen [1].'

The first group of names in this 'deprecatio [2]' (this title being suggested by the word 'precantes') consists of fathers and founders of the Church of Arles; the second group consists of fifteen saints of Holy Scripture, followed by certain leading Gallican saints, the last of whom is Caesarius Bishop of Arles, died A.D. 542.   His name, which appears here on account of a local relation, would probably have been omitted at Iona, and so the name of St. Martin, who was held in special veneration in these islands, would be the last on the list, until on the occasion referred to by Adamnan St. Columba ordered the name of Columbanus to be added to it [3].   Two specimens of the 'deprecatio' or 'Collectio post nomina' of the ancient Irish Liturgy have survived in the Stowe Missal [4].

This position of the commemoration of the living and the

---

[1] Mabillon, de Liturg. Gallic. lib. i. cap. v. sect. 12 ;   Migne, Bib. Pat. Lat. lxviii. 395.

[2] For another liturgical use of the word 'deprecatio,' see Stowe Missal, ch. iii. § 14.

[3] Transcribed nearly verbatim from Dr. Reeves' note in his edit. of Adamnan, p. 211.   For an example of a Deprecatio pro vivis, see Stowe Missal, ch. iii. § 14.   [4] Ch. iii. § 14.

dead survives in the Anglican Liturgy, while in the Roman it occupies a different place, being within and a portion of the Canon itself.

There are no instances recorded of the modern practice of praying to departed saints, although there was a strong and devout belief in the efficacy of their prayers for those left on earth. St. Columba's power of prevailing with God by intercession was recognised as continuing to be exercised after his death [1]. Several instances of it are recorded by Adamnan [2], among them the exemption of the Picts and Scots from a pestilence which devastated the rest of Great Britain and Ireland. Adamnan's belief is expressed in these words: 'Now to what other person can this favour granted them by God be attributed unless to St. Columba, whose monasteries lie within the territories of both these people, and have been regarded by both with the greatest respect up to the present time? But what I am now to say cannot I think be heard without a sigh, that there are very many stupid people in both countries, who in their ignorance that they owe their exemption from the plague to the prayers of the saint, ungratefully and wickedly abuse the patience and the goodness of God [3].' In a very early collect for St. Patrick's Day preserved in the Corpus Missal [4] God is directly besought to receive St Patrick's intercessions on behalf of His people.

§ 11. Prayer of Consecration.—The original Celtic formula of consecration does not survive, but there are allusions to it which imply that, like the rest of the service, it was pronounced

---

[1] Adamnan, Vit. S. Col. i. 1. [2] Ib. ii. 44, 45, 46.

[3] 'Cui alii itaque haec tribuitur gratia a Deo collata, nisi sancto Columbae cujus monasteria, intra utrorumque populorum terminos fundata, ab utrisque ad praesens tempus valde sunt honorificata. Sed hoc quod nunc dicturi sumus, ut arbitramur non sine gemitu audiendum est, quia sunt plerique in utrisque populis valde stolidi, qui se sanctorum orationibus a morbis defensos nescientes, ingrati Dei patientia male abutuntur.' Ib. ii. 46. It is easy to understand how this belief produced in the course of time the habit of invocation of saints, as found in the later Litanies in the Stowe Missal (ch. iii. § 14), St. Gall MS. 1395 (ib. § 10), and in the later lives of the saints passim.

[4] Ch. iii. § 15. Similar forms of Collect abound in the Leon. and Gelas. Sacramentaries.

in an audible voice[1]. The breaking of the bread formed so integral a portion of its ritual that 'frangere panem' is used as an equivalent term for 'missarum sollemnia celebrare[2].' The use of the words of institution and consecration is sometimes indicated in Celtic MSS., as in surviving Gallican fragments, by the opening words, 'Qui pridie[3].' In both cases the Prayer of Consecration seems to have been brief, the introductory clauses up to this point varying with each festival.

If this inference is admitted, we are able to reconstruct the Canon of the Celtic Church, as used on saints' days, in the following form :—

'Vere sanctus, vere benedictus, vere mirabilis in sanctis suis, Deus noster Jesus Christus ipse dabit virtutem, et fortitudinem plebi suae; benedictus Deus, quem benedicimus in Apostolis, et in omnibus sanctis suis, qui placuerunt ei ab initio saeculi, per eundem Dominum nostrum Jesum Christum,

Qui pridie quam pateretur, in sanctis manibus suis accepit panem, respexit in coelum ad te, sancte Pater, omnipotens aeterne Deus, gratias agens, benedixit, fregit, fractumque apostolis suis et discipulis suis tradidit dicens ;

Accipite et edite ex hoc omnes ; hoc est enim corpus meum, quod pro multis confringetur.

Similiter etiam calicem postquam coenatum est, pridie quam pateretur, accepit, respexit in caelum ad te, sancte Pater, omnipotens aeterne Deus, gratias agens, benedixit, apostolis suis et discipulis suis tradidit dicens ;

Accipite et bibite ex hoc omnes ; hic est enim sanguis meus[4].'

---

[1] 'Quendam *audiens* presbyterum sacra eucharistiae mysteria conficientem.' Adamnan, Vit. S. Columbae, i. 40.

[2] Ib. i. 44. A reference to this passage will show the untenability of Dr. Reeves' suggestion that the expression 'frange panem' may be an allusion to the distribution of the consecrated bread to the communicants, and not to the fraction in the act of consecration. [3] Stowe Missal, ch. iii. § 14.

[4] The first part of this Prayer of Consecration is taken from the Stowe

The absence of the full text of the Consecration Prayer as used in the earliest Liturgies of the Churches of Britain and Gaul has been sometimes accounted for by a theory, supported rather by conjecture than by evidence, that it was supplanted by the Roman Canon before the 'disciplina arcani' had been altogether abandoned, so that though the rest of the service was written, the Canon was recited by the priest from memory, only its opening words 'Qui pridie' being sometimes indicated in writing.

The presence of the Roman Canon in the Stowe Missal[1] proves that it was introduced into at least partial use in Ireland late in the eighth century, the numerous passages interpolated into it being probably survivals of the earlier and now lost Celtic rite.

§ 12. Communion Anthems.—In the ancient Irish Church a hymn was sung after the prayer of consecration, during the communion of the clergy and before that of the people. In the Preface to the Leabhar Breac, a composition assigned to the seventh or eighth century, there is a legend which speaks of a choir of angels being heard in the church of St. Sechnall chanting the hymn 'Sancti Venite,' &c., which hymn, the writer adds, has been sung in the Irish Church while the people were communicating[2]. No trace of such a hymn has been hitherto found in any mediaeval Breviaries or Antiphonaries, but it is preserved in the Antiphonarium Benchorense, where it is entitled *Hymnum quando communicarent sacerdotes*[3].

During the communion of the people anthems were sung, slightly varying forms of which have been preserved in the St. Gall MS. No. 1394[4], the Antiphonary of Bangor[5], and the Stowe Missal[6].

They occupied a position corresponding to that of the

Missal, ch. iii. § 14. Compare the Collectio post Sanctus for Christmas Eve in the Missale Gothicum, p. 33. The second part is taken from the Gallican work known under the title of Ambros. de Sacramentis, lib. iv. cap. v.

[1] Ch. iii. § 14. [2] Liber Hymnorum, p. 44. [3] Ch. iii. § 12.
[4] Ib. § 9. [5] Ib. § 12. [6] Ib. § 14.

anthem called 'Transitorium' in the Ambrosian, the 'Tre-
canum' in the Gallican, the anthem 'Gustate et videte' &c.
in the Mozarabic, and the 'Communio' in the Roman rite.

§ 13. THE BENEDICITE.—The 'Song of the Three Children'
appears in various forms and occupies a prominent position
in the Antiphonary of Bangor[1], from which fact we infer
that this canticle with its antiphons formed a constituent
part of the Celtic, as it did of the Gallican[2] and Mozarabic
Liturgies[3], where it was sung before the Gospel (Gall.), or
before the Epistle (Moz.), on all Sundays and saints' days.

We pass on from the service itself to some account of its
ritual accessories.

§ 14. POSITION OF THE PRIEST.—The position of the celebrant
was before the altar ('ante altare'), that is to say, facing the
altar and with his back to the congregation. This we infer
from the expression 'de vertice' in Cuminius' description
of the four brothers watching St. Columba celebrate at Iona,
and seeing a strange light streaming down upon his head[4].
Gildas speaking of the degenerate character of the British

---

[1] Chap. iii. § 12.

[2] 'Lectionibus pronuntiatis chorus hymnum trium puerorum decantabat, et
quidem ut reor per modum responsorii, quem sane hymnum a Gregorio
Turonensi (Hist. Franc. lib. viii. cap. 3) psalmum responsorium dici conjicio.'
Germani Parisiens. Expos. brevis Antiq. Lit. Gall. sect. vii.

[3] One of the liturgical irregularities which had grown up in Spain in the
sixth century was a tendency to omit this canticle. 'Hymnum quoque trium
puerorum in quo universa coeli terraeque creatura Dominum collaudat, et quem
Ecclesia catholica per totum orbem diffusa celebrat, quidam sacerdotes in
missa Dominicorum dierum et in solemnitatibus martyrum canere negligunt;
proinde hoc sanctum consilium instituit ut per omnes ecclesias Hispaniae vel
Galliae in omnium missarum sollemnitate idem in pulpito decantetur; communionem amissuri, qui et antiquam hujus hymni consuetudinem nostramque
definitionem excesserint.'

The fourteenth canon of the Fourth Council of Toledo, A.D. 633, was in
these words:—'Diebus Dominicis atque in martyrum sollemnitatibus ante
epistolam cantatur canticum trium puerorum.'

[4] 'Sed illi post Evangelii recitationem viderunt quendam igneum globum et
valde luminosum de vertice sancti Columbae ante altare stantis et sacram
oblationem consecrantis tamdiu ardere, et ad instar alicujus columnae sursum
ascendere donec eadem perficerentur sacrosancta mysteria.' Cuminius, Vit. S.
Col. cap. xii.

priesthood describes them as 'seldom sacrificing and never with clean hearts standing at the altar[1].'

Extended hands.—Gildas also makes mention of extended hands as part of the ritual of the Mass, speaking of British priests as 'extending their hands over the holy sacrifice[2];' an expression which may find a counterpart in the rubric which in the Sarum Missal immediately follows the consecration of the chalice, 'Deinde sacerdos elevet brachia sua in modum crucis;' in the 'extensis manibus' of the Roman rite; and in various rubrical directions in the Anglican and Eastern Liturgies[3]. It is also the ordinary attitude of prayer in early Italian art[4].

§ 15. VESTMENTS.—Special vestments were in use at the altar. It is recorded among the instances of the generosity of St. Bridget that 'she gave away to the poor the transmarine and foreign vestments of Bishop Condlaedh, of glorious light, which he was accustomed to use when offering the holy mysteries at the altars, on the festivals of our Lord and the vigils of the Apostles[5].' Adamnan relates how on one occasion the vestments and books of St. Columba were placed on the altar[6].

Among the episcopal or sacerdotal vestments and ornaments alluded to in these passages as being in use in these early times we have proof of the existence of the following:—

The Chasuble.—This vestment in its primitive full circular shape[7], with embroidered orphreys, is represented on figures

---

[1] 'Raro sacrificantes, et nunquam puro corde inter altaria stantes.' Gildae Epist. § 66. Compare a similar phrase, 'Et quum altari adsistitur semper ad Patrem dirigatur oratio,' Con. Carth. III, can. xxiv. A.D. 397.

[2] 'Manus sacrosanctis Christi sacrificiis extensuri.' Epist. § 67.

[3] Hammond, C. E., edit. pp. 211, 242.

[4] Parker, J. H., Photographs, Nos. 479, 1710, 1806, &c.

[5] 'Vestimenta transmarina et peregrina Episcopi Conlaith, decorati luminis, quibus in solempnitatibus Domini et vigiliis Apostolorum, sacra in altaribus offerens mysteria utebatur, pauperibus largita est.' Cogitosus, Vita S. Brigid. cap. 29.

[6] 'Beati viri vestimenta et libros, inito consilio, super altare, cum psalmis et jejunatione, et ejus nominis invocatione posuimus.' Lib. ii. cap. 45.

[7] 'Cum scriptorum plerique casulam a casa dictam scribunt, quod totum

in the reliquary of St. Maedoc[1] (eighth-century, Irish), on
Evangelists depicted in the Book of Deer[2] (ninth-century,
Scottish), and on figures of priests sculptured on the very
ancient Kirriermuir stones in Scotland. Two of these priests
hold books, the third has no book, but a Δ-shaped ornament
on the lower front part of his dress just above the feet[3].
Several of these figures will be seen to have in front of them
a rectangular ornament which may be taken for a book borne
in the hand, but which is possibly the rationale.

Rationale.—The rationale is an ancient but little known
ornament of the Celtic bishops, which according to Dr. Rock
is never found in Anglo-Saxon times, but which re-appeared
among the episcopal ornaments in Anglo-Norman days, and
dropped entirely out of use in the fourteenth century. It was
fashioned in all shapes, at one time round, at another a trefoil
or a quatrefoil, but more generally an oblong square. It was
made of gold or silver, studded with precious stones, and it
was worn in imitation of the rational of the Aaronic priesthood, from which it took its name[4]. Another example of it

---

hominem ut casa tegat, respexerunt ad veterem casularum formam, quae
totum revera sacerdotem a collo ad pedes ambibat, atque adeo brachia ipsa et
manus tegebat, ita ut si iis ad sacra facienda, aut ad alios usus vellent uti,
necesse haberent casulam ad utrumque latus erigere, aut fibula cohibere.'
Du Cange, sub voc.

[1] Archaeologia, xliii. 140.

[2] Westwood, J. O., Facsimiles, &c., plate li.

[3] Stuart, J., Sculptured Stones of Scotland, vol. i. plate xliii. Alcuin asserts
that the pallium has taken the place of the rationale in the case of archbishops;
Lib. de Div. Offic. p. 64 A, edit. Hittorp.

[4] The following Oratio ad induendum rationale occurs in the ' Missa Illyrici:'
'Da nobis Domine veritatem tuam firmiter retinere, et doctrinam veritatis
plebi tuae digne aperire.' Mart. i. p. 177. Du Cange says of the rationale,
'Vestis episcoporum novae legis vel ornamentum, sed cujusmodi fuerit hactenus
incertum manet.' Garland, a thirteenth-century writer, is more explicit :
'Hoc est ornamentum episcopale et dicitur alio modo logion quod debet reponi
in pectore episcopi ad modum laminae aureae in quo cernuntur duodecim
lapides, et in illis xii. nomina prophetarum, et scripta erant in illa lamina
aurea ita duo nomina, "justicia et judicium."' Caius Coll. MS. 385 ; quoted
by Dr. Rock, Church of our Fathers, i. 369. See Honorius Augustod. Gemma
Animae in Migne's Bibl. Pat. Lat. clxxii. p. 608 ; Gerbertus, Vet. Liturg.
Aleman. i. 261 ; Bock, Fr., Geschichte der Liturgischen Gewänder des Mittel-

may be seen on a figure of St. Gall in the Golden Psalter[1].
It corresponds to the Greek *Peristethion*, an oblong plate of
jewelled gold or silver worn over the chasuble by patriarchs
and metropolitans in the Eastern Church.

Alb.—The figures above referred to on the shrine of St.
Maedoc are vested in albs with embroidered borders (apparels)
under their chasubles[2]. So also are those on the Soiscel
Molaise[3].

Maniple.—The maniple appears to have been worn not on
the wrist, but over, and depending from the forefinger of the
left hand, as on the figure of St. Jerome in the Golden Psalter
at St. Gall[4]. The same mode of wearing it prevailed in the
Anglo-Saxon Church, as may be seen by the vested figure
worked on St. Cuthbert's stole at Durham, and proved by
the inscription on it to have been embroidered by Queen
Elfleda, wife of King Edward the Elder, 905–906; and at
Rome up to the eleventh century, as in the fresco of St.
Clement[5].

Ring.—There was a ring in the tomb of Ebregesilus
Bishop of Meaux, a monk of the Columban school, when it
was opened in the seventh century[6]. There is still earlier
evidence of the use of the episcopal ring in Gaul, which is
a presumption in favour of its use among contemporaneous
British bishops. Clovis I, writing to the Gallican bishops
A.D. 510, promised to pay every attention to their letters
provided that they sealed them with the seals of their pastoral
rings[7]. Avitus, Bishop of Vienne, writing to Apollinaris

---

alters, vol. i. p. 375. Taf. vi, where it is part of the dress of a thirteenth-century
Italian bishop.

[1] Unless this is a book which is so often represented in the hands of saints,
held where the rationale would appear, if worn. Westwood, J. O., Unpublished
Facsimiles.

[2] Archaeologia, xliii. plate xviii.   [3] Ib. plate xx.

[4] Westwood, J. O., Unpublished Facsimiles. See Rahn, J. F., description of
this Psalter, Taf. vii ; St. Gallen, 1878.

[5] Marriott, W. B., Vestiarium Christianum, plate xliii.

[6] Mabillon, Annal. Bened. i. 456.

[7] Nouveau Traité de Diplom. iv. 318.

Bishop of Valence, requested that his monogram might be
engraved on his ring[1].

Pectoral Cross.—The pectoral cross of St. Aidan, a monk
of Iona and first Bishop of Lindisfarne (635–652), was preserved among the relics at Durham in the fourteenth century[2].
There is evidence in the writings of St. Gregory of Tours
that pectoral crosses were worn by Gallican bishops in the
sixth century[3].

Pastoral Staff.—There is varied evidence for the early use
of the pastoral staff as an ornament and emblem of authority
borne by bishops. Its Celtic name was cambutta, cambota,
or more rarely cambo[4]. St. Patrick's staff is alluded to in
a seventh-century Irish prophecy, preserved by the Scholiast
on Fiacc's Hymn[5], and later authority asserts that it was
made of gold, and adorned with precious stones[6]. His
disciples St. Dagaeus and St. Asic were traditionally famous
for their skill in gilding and bejewelling pastoral staffs and
other ecclesiastical ornaments[7]. St. Columba is said to have
made many crosses, book-satchels (polaires), and pastoral
staffs[8]. When he and St. Kentigern met they exchanged
staffs, and St. Kentigern's staff, as given to him by St.
Columba, covered with gold and jewels, was still preserved

---

[1] Epist. 78.

[2] Raine, J., St. Cuthbert, p. 9. The ring and the pectoral cross were also
worn by bishops in the Anglo-Saxon Church. Id. pp. 216–17.

[3] 'Hujus beatae Virginis reliquias . . . super me in aurea cruce positas exhi-
bebam. Tunc extractam a pectore crucem elevo,' etc. De Gloria Martyrum,
lib. i. cap. 11. St. Gregory of Tours evidently wore a gold pectoral cross within
the folds of his garment on his breast, which also served as a reliquary.

[4] Walafrid Strabo, Vit. S. Galli, i. 26; Fleming, Collectan. p. 243. In
Durandus (Rat. vi. 24) the word has become modified into sambuca. Accord-
ing to Du Cange it is an Armoric word. It is used in a rubric in the Gregorian
Sacramentary; Migne, Bibl. Pat. Lat. lxxviii. p. 153.

[5] Todd, J. H., St. Patrick, p. 411.

[6] 'Porro Nigellus videns sibi imminere fugam tulit secum insignia quaedam
aedis illius, textum scilicet Evangeliorum, qui fuit beati Patricii, baculumque
auro tectum, gemmis pretiosissimis adornatum,' &c. S. Bernardi de Vita
Malachiae, c. 8.

[7] Acta SS. in Vita Dagaei.

[8] Ancient Irish Life of St. Columba in the Leabhar Breac, translated in
Skene's Celtic Scotland, vol. ii. App. p. 488.

at Ripon in the beginning of the fifteenth century [1]. In the tenth century it was held in great veneration, and was carried as a standard in going to battle under the name of 'Cathbhuaidh [2]' (= Battle Victory).

In its original shape the episcopal staff was short, rounded at the top, truncated at the bottom, and made of wood. A specimen may be seen in the hands of one of the figures engraved on the ancient Irish shrine of St. Maedoc of Ferns [3]; and in the hand of an ecclesiastic, vested in an embroidered chasuble, engraved on the Soiscel Molaise, a small box of tenth-century work at the latest, which once contained a now lost copy of the Gospels written in the sixth century by St. Molaise of Devenish. It is fair to add that it rather resembles an aspersory than a pastoral staff [4], in which case it might be appealed to as evidence for the early use of holy water, and the small circular vessel, like a pome, held by another figure, might be a holy-water stoup [5], but the smallness of the vessel and the largeness of the staff seem fatal to this explanation. It is not unlike the baton of a ruler of a choir. St. Padarn, who arrived in Wales from Armorica A.D. 576 and became first bishop of Llandabarn, had a choral cap and staff presented to him by the people in recognition of his musical talent [6]. But on the whole it may be with most probability inferred that it is an early form of a Celtic bishop's pastoral staff, which in the ninth or tenth century began to assume its more modern and now usual form. Other

---

[1] 'Ac nunc cambo, quem beatus Kentigernus a beato Columba receperat in ecclesia Sancti Wilfridi de Ripoun, aureis crustulis inclusus, ac margaritarum diversitate circumstellatus cum magna reverentia adhuc servatur.' Fordun, Scotichronicon, iii. 30.

[2] Irish Annals, quoted in Reeves' edit. of Adamnan's Life of Columba, p. 333. Compare the anxiety of the detected thief to swear to his innocence over the staff of St. Serf; Brev. Aberdon., July 2, lect. viii. fol. 16 a.

[3] St. Maedoc was born A.D. 555, but the shrine is at least a century later. Archaeologia, xliii. 140. [4] Archaeologia, xliii. plate 20.

[5] Ib. plate 18. There is a reference to the miraculous power (not the liturgical use) of holy water, blessed by St. Columba, in Adamnan, Vit. S. Col. ii. 4, 5, 6, 17; and by St. Bridget, in her Life by Ultan, cap. 45.

[6] Liber Landavensis, ch. iii. sect. 1.

specimens of the primitive cambutta, in its transition size
and shape, may be seen in the hands of St. Matthew
and St. Luke, as depicted in the MS. Gospels of Meiel
Brith Mac Durnan, c. A.D. 850 [1], and in the case of a figure
carved on the cumhdach, or metal-work cover, of the Stowe
Missal [2]. The Bachal-more of St. Moloch, in the possession
of the Duke of Argyll, and figured in the Origines Parochiales
(ii. 163), is a black-thorn bludgeon, with traces of a metal
covering, measuring only 2 feet 10 inches in length. Several
of the bronze cambuttas preserved in the museum of the Irish
Academy are little longer.

Bracelets.—It has been suggested that bracelets or cuffs
formed part of the sacerdotal costume of a British priest.
In the absence of documentary or other reliable evidence
this is merely an inference from the custom of the early
Gallican priesthood to wear metal bracelets or cuffs of silk
or other handsome texture [3].

'If,' says Dr. Rock, 'the ritual observances of our Britons
were like those of their nearest neighbour, Gaul,—and there
is every reason for thinking so,—then do we, far off as we
are from their times, catch a glimpse of another among the
sacred appurtenances of a priest in the British era of our Church
history; and beholding him vested for the holy sacrifice of

---

[1] Westwood, J. O., Facsimiles, &c. plate xxii; Stuart, Sculptured Stones of
Scotland, vol. ii. p. lxxviii.

[2] Westwood, J. O., Facsimiles, &c. plate li. fig. 9. Further descriptions and
details are given in Stuart, Sculptured Stones of Scotland, ii. p. lv ; O'Neil, H.,
Fine Arts and Civilization of Ireland, 1863, plates 7, 10 ; figures of Kilklispeen
and Monasterboice Crosses, Ulster Journal of Archaeology, ix. 51 ; in an account
of the Shrine of St. Manchan in Kilkenny Archaeol. Soc. 1874, p. 147; Proceedings
of the Soc. of Antiq. of Scotland, vol. ii. pp. 14, 125. An account of Welsh Relics,
including the staff of St. Cyric, the bell of St. David, &c., is given in the
Welsh itinerary of Giraldus Cambrensis, edit. Lond. 1806, pp. 6, 7, 13, 14.

[3] The evidence for the Gallican custom in the middle of the sixth century
is explicit : ' Manualia vero, id est manicas induere sacerdotibus mos est instar
armillarum, quas regum vel sacerdotum brachia constringebantur. Ideo ex
quolibet pretioso vellere, non metalli duritia extant, vel ut omnes communiter
sacerdotes, etiam minoris dignitatis in saeculo facilius inveniant.' Germani
Paris. Expos. Brev. Antiq. Lit. Gall. A somewhat similar ornament —τὰ
ἐπιμανίκια—is worn by the Greek clergy. Marriott, W. B., Vest. Christ. p. 169.

the Mass, we shall perceive that along with the fine full
chasuble he wore a kind of apparel on the sleeves of his alb.
Cuffs of this sort are still found in use among the Greeks, who
call them ἐπιμανικία[1],' &c.

Bracelets have frequently been found in ancient tumuli,
and in other places and positions. A gold bracelet found
in a loch in Galloway, and consisting of two very artificially
intertwining circles, has been assigned to a late Celtic period[2].
Celtic circular ornaments of gold have been found in Peebles-
shire[3]; bracelets, armlets, earrings, bead and jet ornaments
have been discovered in British burial-places[4], and in Ireland[5].
But there is nothing in the shape of proof, it is mere conjecture to assign to these bracelets, as has been sometimes
done, any ecclesiastical connection. Such a connection, in
any case, would more probably be with Druidism than with
Christianity. The Druid priests of Great Britain may have
resembled those of Gaul, who, Strabo informs us, wore golden
bracelets, and coloured vesture variegated with gold[6]. But
the tendency of recent investigation has been to assign to
all such relics a distant prehistoric date, perhaps as far back
as the neolithic period of mankind[7].

Comb.—The ritual use of the comb, now long since obsolete,
but as it was employed in Anglo-Saxon times before High
Mass[8], was probably derived from the Celtic Church. The

---

[1] Church of our Fathers, i. 438.
[2] Stuart, J., Sculptured Stones of Scotland, ii. p. ix.
[3] Archaeol. Scot. iv. 217.
[4] Archaeol. Cambrensis, xiv. 220.   [5] Ulster Journal of Archaeol. ix. 28, &c.
[6] Χρυσοφοροῦσί τε γὰρ περὶ μὲν τοῖς τραχήλοις στρεπτὰ ἔχοντες, περὶ δὲ τοῖς
βραχίοσι καὶ τοῖς καρποῖς ψέλια, καὶ τὰς ἐσθῆτας βαπτὰς φοροῦσι καὶ χρυσοπά-
στους ἐν ἀξιώματι. Strabo, Geog. lib. iv. marginal p. 197, edit. Amsterdam.
1707. Diodorus Siculus mentions bracelets and brooches among the personal
ornaments of the Celts; lib. v. p. 351, edit. 1745.
[7] Greenwell and Rolleston, British Barrows. In an article in the Edinburgh
Review for April, 1878, it is concluded that most of these ornaments belong
either to the iron age, or to the third and last, the Maeringian, period of the
bronze age.
[8] The Anglo-Saxon ritual was as follows:—If a bishop pontificated, the
deacon and sub-deacon combed his hair as soon as his sandals had been put on
his feet, while seated on his episcopal chair within the chancel; if a priest

comb of St. Kentigern was one of the relics kept in Glasgow Cathedral[1]. That of St. Cuthbert was buried with him[2]. Representations of a comb, sometimes accompanied with scissors, are frequently found in the early sculptured stones of Scotland, where its appearance has been variously interpreted as a trace of the Eastern custom of designating the sex of a person by a single-toothed or double-toothed comb or as a sign of his trade, or dignity, or as having some ecclesiastical significance. These and other theories are discussed at length and with much ingenuity by Mr. Stuart[3]. The Christian character of the device is just possible, but is incapable of proof, and is more nearly disproved by the probable date of the stones themselves. The profession of a Christian priest is usually indicated by other symbols, such as a book in the hand, a chalice and paten, or a consecrated host as in the Nigg stone[4].

Crowns.—The Celtic bishops wore crowns instead of mitres. St. Sampson, a Welshman, generally but incorrectly described as Archbishop of York, and subsequently of Dol in Brittany[5], c. A.D. 557, is said to have dreamed that he saw 'three eminent bishops adorned with golden crowns standing before him[6].'

---

celebrated, the same office of the comb was performed for him seated in the sedilia. More curious was the ritual at Viviers in France, A.D. 1360, where the ceremony of combing was performed several times during Mass : 'Sacra celebraturus sedet dum in choro Kyrie, Gloria, et Credo decantantur ; unde quoties assurgebat, ipsi capillos pectebat diaconus, amoto ejus capello seu almucio, licet id officii jam in secretario antequam ad altare procederet, sollicite ei praestitisset.' Du Cange, in verbo Sedes Majestatis.

[1] Regist. Glasg. vol. ii. p. 330, Edinb. 1843.

[2] Reginald de Adm. S. Cuthberti Virtut. p. 89.

[3] Stuart, J., Sculptured Stones of Scotland, vol. ii. p. 5, &c. The comb as found on sepulchral tablets in the Roman Catacombs is a mark of the wool-combing trade of the deceased. Withrow, W. H., The Catacombs of Rome, p. 231.

[4] Ib. vol. i. plate xxviii ; vol. ii. plate lvii.

[5] For the facts in the life of St. Sampson and of other Celtic saints, see H. and S. i. Appendix C. p. 142.

[6] 'Sanctus Samson admirabilem vidit visum. Quadam nocte circumseptari se a delicatis ac densissimis candidatorum turbis cernit, et tres episcopos egregios diadematibus aureis in capite ornatos, atque holosericis ac pulcherrimis amictos vestibus in faciem sibi adsistere,' &c. Vita S. Samsonis ab

There is a representation of an Irish bishop thus crowned on a sculptured bas-relief of great antiquity, part of a ruined chapel in the valley of Glendalough[1]. The use of this crown in a modified form[2] continued in Anglo-Saxon times until the tenth century, when representations of the mitre, properly so called, begin to be found; which originally resembled a flat cap, and did not assume its present cloven and horned shape till after the Conquest[3].

Sometimes crowns were suspended over shrines, as in the case of the early Irish church of St. Bridget described by Cogitosus[4], where there was a richly decorated altar with gold and silver crowns hanging over it. This was an Eastern custom. According to Du Cange, the custom of hanging crowns over the altar in the church of St. Sophia dated from the time of Constantine the Great[5]. It was also a Gallican custom. Crowns were suspended over the tomb of St. Martin at Tours[6], a tomb to which the early Irish made frequent pilgrimages[7].

Discs or Brooches.—Two figures carved on an old stone at Invergowrie[8] have on their necks ornaments which

---

auctore anonymo subaequali apud Mabillon, Acta Sanct. tom. i. p. 176. sect. 43. The crown or mitre of an Eastern priest is alluded to in the rubrics of the Armenian Liturgy; Hammond, C. E., Lit. E. and W. p. 168.

[1] Woodcut in Transactions of Royal Irish Academy, vol. xx. pp. 248, 265.

[2] There is a figure of an ecclesiastic wearing a circlet of gold set with precious stones in the Benedictional of St. Æthelwold; edited by J. Gage, London, 1832, plate xxx. Can this crown represent the petalum of St. John the Divine, ὃς ἐγενήθη ἱερεὸς τὸ πέταλον πεφορεκὼς (Eus. H. E. v. 24)? Bock, Fr., Geschichte der Liturgischen Gewänder, vol. i. p. 387.

[3] See the flat mitres on the bishops in the twelfth-century set of chessmen, made of the tusk of the walrus, and found in the isle of Lewis; Archaeol. xxiv. plate xlvii.   [4] p. 89.

[5] Du Cange, Constantinopolis Christiana, l. iii. 43 ; Histor. Byzantina, part ii. p. 37.

[6] S. Greg. Tur. de Mirac. S. Mart. lib. i. cap. 2.

[7] O'Conor, Bib. MS. Stow. vol. i. appendix i. p. 23. There are traces of the same custom in Italy. Leo III, 719–816, gave a crown to the monastery of St. Pancras, near the Lateran (Mis. Lateran. p. xxvi). See Smith's Dictionary of Christian Antiq. for an account of the three crowns preserved in the treasury of the cathedral of Monza.

[8] Stuart, J., Sculptured Stones of Scotland, vol. i. plate lxxxvii.

look like discs of metal, fastened to the dress by laces passed
through small holes perforated in the discs.   They are possibly
insignia of either lay rank or sacred dignity, or else large
brooches which are often represented as fastening up the
dress at the shoulder in the case of ecclesiastics on the early
Irish crosses[1].   The Brehon laws assign the brooch as one
of the distinctive emblems of royalty; 'brooches of gold having
crystal inserted in them with the sons of the King of Erin,
and of the king of a province, and brooches of silver with the
sons of a king of a territory,' &c.[2]   The following account
gives a quasi-supernatural sanction for the brooch becoming
part of a saint's dress: 'Then Diarmoyt, the son of Cearbuyll
King of Ireland, who ruled in the city of Themoria in the
country of Midhi, saw in a dream two angels take the royal
necklace from off his neck and give it to a man unknown
to himself.   On the next day St. Brendan came to that king.
And when he beheld him, he said to his friends, "This is
the man to whom I saw my necklace given."   Then the wise
men said to the king, "Hitherto the rule of Ireland has
been in the hands of kings; hereafter thy kingdom will be
divided among Ireland's saints[3]."'

We may take the fact that the brooch, which was originally part of the regal insignia, became a part also of ecclesiastical dress, as a sign of the great honour which was paid in
early times to the saints in Ireland[4].

---

[1] O'Neill, Irish Crosses, plates xiv, xxii, xxiv.

[2] Senchus Mor, vol. ii. p. 147.

[3] 'Tunc Diarmoyt, filius Cearbuyll rex Hyberniae (A.D. 544-64), qui regnabat
in urbe Themoria in regione Midhi sompnium uidit, id est, duos angelos torquem regiam de collo eius tollentes et dantes homini sibi ignoto.   Crastino iam
die peruenit sanctus Brendanus ad regem illum.   Cumque uidesset eum rex,
dixit amicis suis : hic est uir ille cui uidi torquem meam dari.   Tunc sapientes
dixerunt regi : Regnum Hyberniae usque nunc erat regibus, amodo diuidetur
inter sanctos Hyberniae regnum tuum.'   Vita S. Brendani, cap. xxiv, Liber
Kilkenniensis.

A serpentine bird-headed silver brooch resembling in its design some of the
initial letters in early Irish MSS. is figured in the Proceedings of the Kilkenny
Archaeol. Soc. vol. for 1872, p. 74.

[4] Westwood, J. O., Facsimiles, &c., p. 30, plate x, etc.

Sandals.—Sandals are represented on the feet of St. Matthew and St. John in the Book of Kells, and in the case of
many other figures in early Celtic MSS. They were worn
at Iona, and were called 'calceus,' or 'calceamentum,' or
'fico,' all words frequently employed in the Lives of
Celtic saints[1]. Curiously-shaped slippers are to be seen on
the feet of four ecclesiastics on a sculptured stone at St.
Vigean's, to whom the Roman tonsure on their heads compels
the assignation of a date subsequent to A.D. 710[2].

Caracalla.—The ordinary outer dress of a British priest
was a long hair cassock called a 'caracalla.' This was worn
by the priest Amphibalus[3], and assumed by St. Alban in
exchange for his own clothes in order to facilitate the escape
of the former[4]. The ordinary outer cloak of a monk at Iona
was called 'amphibalus[5]' or 'cuculla[6],' worn over a white
under-dress, 'tunica candida' or 'pallium[7].'

§ 16. USE OF COLOURS.—It has been asserted that the
assigning of special colours to certain seasons for sacerdotal
vestments or altar coverings does not belong to the first
eight centuries of Christianity[8]. This is true as far as any

---

[1] Adamnan, Vit. S. Colum. ii. 13 ; iii. 12 ; Du Cange, sub voc.

[2] Stuart, J., Sculptured Stones of Scotland, vol. i. plate lxx ; vol. ii. p. 8.

[3] For the possible origin of the name Amphibalus, which is not mentioned
by Bede, see G. H. Moberly, edit. of Bede's H. E. p. 18. n. 7.

[4] 'Qui cum ad tugurium martyris pervenissent mox se sanctus Albanus pro
hospite ac magistro suo, ipsius habitu, id est caracalla qua vestiebatur indutus,
militibus exhibuit, atque ad judicem vinctus perductus est.' Bede, H. E. i. 7.
But the caracalla was not an exclusively sacerdotal dress. Du Cange, Faccio-
lati, sub voc.

[5] Adamnan, Vit. S. Col. i. 3 ; ii. 6. Also in Britain : 'sub sancti abbatis
amphibalo ;' Gildae Ep., H. and S. i. 49. 'Amphibalus' was also, at least in
Gaul, the Latin for a chasuble. Germani Paris. Epist. ii. in Martene et
Durand. Thesaur. Anecd. tom. v. col. 99. Sulpicius Severus represents St.
Martin as celebrating the Eucharist in an 'amphibalum ;' Dial. ii. § 1. p.
545, Lugdun. Batav. 1647.

[6] Adamnan, Vit. S. Col. ii. 24.   [7] Ib. ii. 44.

[8] Hefele, Beiträge zur Archaeologie, ii. 158. There is no allusion to any
systematic sequence of colours in the earlier Ordines Romani, or in the writings
of the earlier ritualists. The first reference to the regular Roman sequence of
four colours is found in the works of Innocent III (1198-1216), De Myst.
Missae, lib. i. cap. lxv, black being there substituted for violet.

elaborate cycle of colours is concerned, such as is prescribed
in mediaeval Missals and Rituals, but allusion to the ecclesiastical use in the Celtic Church of at least two colours has
been preserved to us.

Purple.—Gildas refers to the custom of covering the altars
in British churches with purple palls[1]. The three choirs of
saints which appeared to St. Brendan were clad 'in vestibus
candidissimis jacinctinis purpureis' (Navigatio S. Brendani,
eleventh century MS. Nat. Lib. Paris, No. 3784). St.
Cuthbert was buried in a purple dalmatic A.D. 687, but
this fact illustrates early Anglo-Saxon rather than Celtic
usage[2]. In the legend of St. Mulling, as preserved in the
Book of Leinster, an Irish MS. of the earlier half of the
twelfth century, Christ is represented as appearing to that
saint, in a vision vouchsafed to him in church, in a purple
garment[3]. Purple is very largely introduced into the earliest
extant specimens of Celtic illumination, as in the Book of
Kells, and into the later Irish MSS. at St. Gall[4]. A passage
in Bede's works alluding to the ease with which a red or
purple dye could be obtained from shells on the Irish coasts,
at once explains and renders probable the preponderating
ecclesiastical use of this colour[5]. We have evidence of the
use of purple altar-cloths—pallae—in the early Gallican
Church. St. Germanus of Paris, c. A.D. 550, explains the
use of this colour by referring to the mention of purple in

---

[1] 'Sub sancti abbatis amphibalo latera regiorum tenerrima puerorum inter ipsa,
ut dixi, sacrosancta altaria, nefando ense hastaque pro dentibus laceravit, ita ut
sacrificii coelestis sedem purpurea ac si coagulati cruoris pallia attingerent.'
Gildae Epist. p. 37.

[2] 'Christianorum more pontificum post haec tunica et dalmatica indutus est,
quarum utrarumque genus ex pretioso purpurae colore et textili varietate satis
venustum et permirabile est.' Reg. Dunelm. p. 87, Surtees Soc. 1835, and
Bolland, Acta SS. Mart. xx. tom. iii. p. 140.

[3] Reeves, W., British Culdees, p. 77. F. civ.

[4] Facsimiles of National MSS. of Ireland, plate viii, &c.

[5] 'Sunt et cochleae satis superque abandantes quibus tinctura coccinei coloris
conficitur, cujus ruber pulcherrimus nullo unquam solis ardore, nulla valet
pluviarum injuria pallescere. Sed quo vetustior est, solet esse venustior;'
quoted in Ulster Journal of Archaeology, viii. 221, and in Keller's Bilder
und Schriftzüge, p. 70.

the Levitical account of the tabernacle[1]. St. Gregory of Tours, in the same century, mentions the defence of the Abbess of St. Radegund against the charge of cutting up one of these purple altar-coverings for a dress for her niece[2]. And the use of these purple altar-palls was perpetuated, like other British and Gallican customs, in the Anglo-Saxon Church[3].

White.—The second colour, of the ecclesiastical use of which there is distinct mention, is white. It was the festal colour at Iona. Adamnan describes how white vestments were worn by St. Columba and his attendants on the occasion of the celebration in memory of Columbanus, as if it was a holy day[4].

The same saint when dying before the altar at Iona was clothed in a white dress[5]. White is the only colour referred to in the early Irish Canons, which order that the deacon at the time of oblation should be clad in a white vestment[6]; whereas in a mediaeval Irish tract on the origin and meaning of colours in the mass-vestments, as many as seven colours are named, yellow, blue, white, green, red, black, purple[7]. In this employment of white the custom

---

[1] 'Siricum (vid. Du Cange) autem ornatur aut auro vel gemmis quia Dominus Moysae in tabernaculo fieri velamina jussit ex auro jacintho et purpura coccoque bis tincto et bysso retorta.' Germani Paris. Expos. Brev. Antiq. Lit. Gall.

[2] 'De reliquo vero quantum opportunum fuit ad ornatum altaris pallam condigne condiderit, et de illa inscissura quae pallae superfuit, purpuram nepti suae in tunica posuerit.' Gregorii Tur. Hist. lib. x. c. 16.

[3] 'Altaria purpura et serico induta' are mentioned in Vita S. Wilfridi, c. xxi, ap. Mabillon, Acta Sanct. tom. v. A purple altar-cloth is depicted in the Benedictional of St. Æthelwold; Archaeologia, vol. xxiv. p. 116. Five purple altar-coverings were among the gifts of Bishop Leofric to Exeter Cathedral; Codex Dip. Anglo-Sax. iv. 275, &c.

[4] 'Et his dictis fratres obsequuntur, et juxta Sancti jussionem, eadem ociantur die, praeparatisque sacris ad ecclesiam ministeriis, quasi die solenni albati cum sancto pergunt.' Adamnan, Vit. S. Columbae, c. 12.

[5] 'Candida tunica qua in hora exitus indutus erat.' Cuminii Vit. S. Columbae, c. 26.

[6] 'Diaconus tempore oblationis alba utatur veste.' Hibernensis, lib. iii. cap. 6.

[7] Buide, gorm, gel, uāie, dond, dg, dub, corcair. Leabhar Breac, fol. 108 a. For information about the mediaeval use of colours, the reader is referred to C. C. Rolfe, The Ancient Use of Liturgical Colours, Oxford, 1879.

of the Celtic agreed with that of the early Gallican Church. In the fifth and sixth centuries white was recognised there as the festal, and especially as the Paschal colour. St. Remigius Bishop of Rheims, in his will A.D. 499, bequeathed to his successor his white Easter vestment[1]. Similar allusions are found in the case of St. Caesarius of Arles[2], and of St. Gregory of Tours[3]. St. Germanus of Paris c. 550 mentions the appearance of angels clad in white at the sepulchre as the symbolical reason for the selection of white as the liturgical colour at Eastertide[4].

The predominant employment of white and red in the Sarum Use may be a survival of the early British preference for those colours.

Is it only a coincidence that the Rule of St. Columba recognised but two classes of martyrdom, 'red martyrdom' (= death), 'white martyrdom[5]' (= self-mortification)?

§ 17. CHORAL SERVICE.—The services of the Celtic Church, both at the altar and in the choir, were choral. Gildas, referring to Britain, speaks of 'ecclesiastical melodies,' and the musical voices of the young sweetly singing the praises of God[6]. The word 'decantare' is used of the introduction of the Liturgy into Ireland in the fifth century[7], and of its performance at Iona in the sixth century[8]. Adamnan states

---

[1] 'Futuro episcopo successori meo amphibalum album paschalem relinquo.' Migne, Bibl. Pat. Lat. lxv. 971.

[2] 'Casulamque quam processoriam habebat albamque Paschalem ei dedit.' Greg. Tur. Op. p. 1187, note 1.

[3] 'Diacono quidam casulam tribuit . . . cappa cujus ita dilatata erat atque consuta, ut solet in illis candidis fieri quae per paschalia festa sacerdotum humeris imponuntur.' Greg. Tur. Op. 1188.

[4] 'Albis autem vestibus in Pascha induetur secundum quod angelus ad monumentum albis vestibus cerneretur.' Germani Paris. Expos. Brev. Antiq. Lit. Gall.

[5] H. and S. ii. pt. i. 120. The fragment of an Irish sermon in the Codex Cameracensis adds a third, or 'green' martyrdom. The original Gaelic with a Latin translation is given in Zeuss. Grammat. Celtic. p. 1007.

[6] 'Ecclesiasticae melodiae'—'Dei laudes canora Christi tyrorum voce suaviter modulante.' Epist. p. 44.

[7] Cotton MS. c. 800, de Officiorum Ecclesiasticorum Origine.

[8] Adamnan, Vit. S. Columbae, iii. 12.

that the voice of St. Columba was so powerful that when he
was chaunting he could be heard sometimes half a mile,
sometimes even a mile off,—a statement not necessarily involving either miracle or exaggeration,—in the still air of an
autumn day on one of the western islands of Scotland[1].   In
Ireland music was an art early cultivated, and intimately
connected with divine worship.   Harpers are represented on
the most ancient sculptured stones of Ireland, and pipers are
introduced as decorations of initial letters in sacred manuscripts of the eighth and ninth centuries[2].   In the Félire of
Oengus a good man is compared to 'an altar whereon wine
is shed, round which is sung a multitude of melodies[3].'   Irish
Annals speak of the destruction of church organs A.D. 814[4].
There is nothing improbable in such an entry, as organs are
known to have been in general use in Western Europe before
that date[5].   The more interesting question is, What was the
style and character of the music in the Celtic Church?   To
this enquiry, unfortunately, no answer can be given beyond
the negative one, that it was not the Roman chaunt in its

---

[1] 'Sed et hoc silere non debemus quod ab expertis quibusdam de voce beati
psalmodiae viri indubitanter traditum est.   Quae scilicet vox venerabilis viri
in ecclesia cum fratribus decantantis aliquando per quatuor stadia hoc est D.
passos, aliquando vero per octo, hoc est M. passus incomparabili elevata modo
audiebatur.' Adamnan. Vit. S. Colum. i. 37.   The distance has grown to 1500
paces in an old Gaelic poem preserved in the Leabhar Breac, fol. 31 b.

[2] Zurich. Antiq. Gesellschaft, vii. 65.   [3] p. cvi. June 17.

[4] 'Direptio organorum ecclesiae Clooncrene.'   Annales Ultonienses, ann.
DCCCXIV.

[5] There are drawings of two organs in the Utrecht Psalter (sixth or ninth
century) in the illustrations to Pss. cl, cli.   There is a still earlier representation
of an organ on one of the catacomb stones in the monastery of San Paolo
fuori le Mura at Rome.   St. Augustine says that organs with bellows were used
in his day; Comment in Ps. lxi.   These organs must have been curious and
cumbrous structures if they resembled that which Ælfeah Bishop of Winchester
(934–51) caused to be constructed in his monastery, which required seventy
men to blow it.

'Bisseni supra sociantur in ordine folles,
   Inferiusque jacent quattuor atque decem.
Flatibus alternis spiracula maxima reddunt,
   Quos agitant validi septuaginta viri.'

Wolstanus in Prologo ad Vitam Metricam S. Swithuni,
Leland. Collect. i. 152.

Gregorian, nor probably in any other form. Bede asserts
that the Roman style of singing was first introduced into
England generally by Benedict Biscop, Abbot of Wearmouth,
A.D. 678, and into the monasteries founded by Scottish missionaries in the North of England by St. Wilfrid, who died
c. A.D. 709[1].

Dr. O'Conor discusses the question with much ingenuity
and research in his ' Rerum Hibernicarum Scriptores[2].' He
endorses to a certain extent the conclusion of Mabillon, that
the choral service of the British Church which was not
' juxta morem Romanum' was therefore ' juxta morem Ori-
entalem.' The Eastern course having been introduced into
the monasteries of Lerins and Marseilles (as described by
Cassian[3]), and having been learned there or elsewhere in
Gaul by Germanus and Lupus (and Patrick), was by them
introduced into Great Britain and Ireland in the fifth century, and was transferred thence to Scotland by Irish missionaries in the sixth century[4]. The subject is hardly sufficiently
relevant to the Liturgy to be discussed here at further
length.

§ 18. INCENSE.—We have been unable to discover any
passage referring to the use of incense in the Celtic Church[5].
Thuribles or incense-cups have often been found in British
burial-places, as at Lancaster Moor[6], at Brixworth[7], &c. The
perforation of these cups near the upper rim implies that they
were to be swung, and the occurrence of ornamentation on the
under surface, which is not found in cinerary and other urns,

---

[1] Hist. Eccl. iv. 18.   [2] Vol. iv. pp. 153–160.
[3] Lib. ii. Instit. an. 420.
[4] The words of Mabillon are: 'Alterum (ecclesiasticum cursum) voco Alexan-
drinum auctore Marco Evangelista, qui cursus in monasteriis Lerinensi et
Massiliensi Cassiani receptus sit ; atque inde per sanctos Germanum Autisio-
dorensem et Lupum Tricassinum antistites in Scotiam, et per Caesarium in
Arelatensem ecclesiam inductus ; quem demum Columbanus in Luxovium ad-
miserit.' De Cursu Gallicano, p. 381.
[5] A single allusion to it in Aileran's Interpretat. Moralis (Migne, Bibl. Pat.
Lat. lxxx. 338) is plainly metaphorical.
[6] Brit. Archaeol. Journal, xxi. 161.   [7] Ib. xix. 21.

proves that they were intended to be suspended above the level of the eye. The symbol of the cross has been found on some of these cups, as on those discovered at Bryn Seiont, Carnarvonshire, and at other places[1]. The date of such relics is undetermined. The mark of the cross used generally to be referred to as an evidence of their connection with Christianity, and was often relied upon by antiquarians as a proof of a post-Christian date, as in the case of bronze spoons found at Llanfair in Wales, and of inscribed stones, &c. elsewhere[2]. But it has been found as an emblem on vases, ornaments and relics, both in the British islands and in continental pile-wrought villages, and lacustrine dwellings and cemeteries, many centuries anterior to the Christian era[3]; and the most recent and experienced archaeologists are decided in their view that these incense urns have no connection with Christianity[4]. The psalm 'Dirigatur,' &c. which accompanies the act of censing in the modern Roman Missal is indicated for use in the Stowe Missal, but there are no rubrical directions there for the use of incense[5]. It may be added that no trace exists of the use of incense in the early Gallican Church. It is not mentioned in any rubric of the surviving Missals, nor is there any allusion to it in the somewhat full 'Expositio Missae' of Germanus Parisiensis (sixth century.)

§ 19. JOINT CONSECRATION.—A very singular custom existed at Iona of two or more priests being ordinarily united in the Eucharistic prayer and act of consecration; to consecrate singly being the prerogative of bishops, or of individual priests specially selected and empowered to consecrate on account of their sanctity or eminence.

Adamnan records how 'on one occasion a stranger from the

---

[1] Archaeol. Cambrensis, Third Series, vol. xiv. p. 25, figs. 18, 19; p. 260, figs. 23, 24.

[2] Ib. Third Series, vol. viii. p. 219; vol. for 1856, p. 49.

[3] Gabriel de Montillet, La signe de la Croix avant le Christianisme, Paris, 1866.

[4] Greenwell and Rolleston, British Barrows, p. 76, &c.

[5] Ch. iii. § 14. Fol. 18 a in the later handwriting.

province of Munster, who concealed through humility the fact that he was a bishop, was invited, on the next Sunday, by Columba to join with him in consecrating the body of Christ, that as two priests they might break the bread of the Lord together. Columba, on going to the altar, discovered his rank, and addressed him thus: "Christ bless thee, brother; consecrate alone as a bishop; now we know that thou art of episcopal rank. Why hast thou endeavoured to disguise thyself so long, and to prevent our giving thee the honour due to thee [1]?"'

On another occasion four illustrious visitors from Ireland paid a special mark of respect to St. Columba by requesting him to offer the Eucharist in their presence [2].

This custom of joint celebrants in the case of priests, and of a single celebrant in the case of a bishop, is peculiar to the Celtic rite, no similar practice existing in any other country or at any other time. There was something exactly opposed to it in the once general but now nearly obsolete rule of the Western Church, that when a bishop cele-brated the priests present should unite with him in the words and acts of consecration [3]. This direction still sur-vives in the Roman service for the 'Ordering of Presbyters,' when the newly-ordained priests join with the bishop in repeating the words of the Canon [4]. The same custom

---

[1] 'Alio in tempore, quidam de Muminensium provincia proselytus ad sanctum venit, qui se, in quantum potuit, occultabat humiliter ut nullus sciret quod esset episcopus; sed tamen Sanctum hoc non potuit latere. Nam alia die Dominica a Sancto jussus Christi corpus ex more conficere, Sanctum advocat, ut simul quasi duo presbyteri Dominicum panem frangerent. Sanctus proinde ad altarium accedens, repente intuitus faciem ejus, sic eum compellat, Benedicat te Christus, frater, hunc solus, episcopali ritu, frange panem; nunc scimus quod sis episcopus. Quare hucusque te occultare conatus es, ut tibi a nobis debita non redderetur veneratio?' Adamnan, Vita S. Columbae, i. 44.

[2] 'Hi uno eodemque consensu elegerunt ut sanctus Columba coram ipsis in ecclesia sacra Eucharistiae consecraret mysteria.' Ib. iii. 17.

[3] 'Ut in confectione immolationis Christi adsint presbyteri et simul cum pontifice verbis et manu conficiant.' Martene, de Antiq. Eccles. Rit. i. 3. 8; Conf. Amalarius, lib. i. cap. 12.

[4] The rubric in the Pontifical (De Ordinatione Presbyteri) directs the celebrating bishop to speak 'aliquantulum alte, ita ut ordinati sacerdotes

existed at Chartres, on Maundy Thursday, as late as the fifteenth century[1].

§ 20. OBLATIONS AND OFFERTORY.—The oblations of bread and wine for the Eucharistic service, and offerings of money, ornaments or other precious gifts, were made, in accordance with the general custom of the Gallican and Mozarabic Liturgies, just before the recitation from the diptychs of the names of departed saints[2]. St. Augustine seems to have found this custom in existence in England, for one of his first questions to St. Gregory was as to the proportion in which such alms and offerings were to be distributed[3].

Early Irish canons, attributed to St. Patrick, lay down that the offerings of the wicked and the excommunicate are not to be accepted[4]. St. Patrick mentions in his Confession how the devoted and warm-hearted Irish women among his disciples made offerings at his altar of ornaments and personal presents, and how he offended them by always returning them afterwards, lest the unbelieving should have appearance of ground for scandal against him[5]. When St. Columba was making 'the offering of Christ's Body and Blood' in the presence of Comgall and Cainnech, at their special request, 'then it was

---

possint secum omnia dicere, et presertim verba consecrationis, quae dici debent eodem momento per ordinatos quo dicuntur per pontificem.'

[2] 'Le Jeudi-saint six Archidiacres Prêtres celebrent la grand' Messe conjointement avec l'Eveque ... l'Eveque est au milieu de l'Autel ; il a trois Prêtres a sa droite, et trois a sa gauche, sur la meme ligne. Ils chantent tous sept unanimement, et pratiquent ensemble toutes les cérémonies de la Messe.' De Moleon, Voyages Liturgiques, p. 231.

[3] See p. 105. n. 6.

[4] 'Prima interrogatio beati Augustini episcopi Cantuariorum ecclesiae. De episcopis, qualiter cum suis clericis conversentur, vel de his quae fidelium oblationibus accedunt altaris ; quantae debent fieri portiones, et qualiter episcopus agere in ecclesia debeat.' Bede, H. E. i. 27, Interrogatio i.

[5] 'Contentus tegmento et alimento tuo cetera dona iniquorum reproba.' S. Patric. Synodus, c. 2. 'Quicunque Christianus excommunicatus fuerit, nec ejus eleemosyna recipiatur.' Synodus Episcoporum Patricii, &c. xii.

[6] The passage is corrupt, but the meaning is obvious. 'Nam etsi imperitus sum in omnibus, tamen conatus sum quispiam servare me etiam et fratribus Christianis, et virginibus Christi, et mulieribus religiosis, quae mihi ultronea munuscula donabant, et super altare reddebant, ex ornamentis suis, et iterum reddebam illis,' &c. Patricii Confessio, c. xxi.

that Cainnech beheld a pillar of fire over Colombcille's head while at the offertory[1].

In the Mozarabic and Gallican Liturgies an anthem or hymn was sung during the offertory called 'Sacrificium' or 'Sonum[2].' Such may be this short anthem in the Antiphonary of Bangor, which resembles an offertory sentence of the Anglican Liturgy rather than the offertorium of the Roman Missal.

'*Pro eleemosynariis.*—Dispersit, dedit pauperibus, iustitia ejus manet in saeculum saeculi, cornu ejus exaltabitur in gloriâ.

Eleemosynas facientibus in hoc mundo retribue, Domine, in regno tuo sancto.'

An account is preserved in the Leabhar Breac of the ritual accompanying the oblation of the elements which is probably a genuine survival of the ancient Celtic Liturgy. First three drops of water were placed in the chalice, the priest saying, 'Peto [or Quaeso] te, pater, deprecor te, filii, obsecro te, spiritus sancte;' then three drops of wine, with the accompanying formula, 'Mittet pater, indulgeat filius, misseretur spiritus sanctus[3];' or, 'Remittet pater, indulget filius, misseretur spiritus sanctus[4].'

§ 21. Unleavened Bread.—Dr. Döllinger enumerates the use of unleavened bread in the Eucharist among the peculiarities of the British Church, and as one of the points on which it differed from the rest of Western Christendom: 'Dass der Gebrauch der Azyma eine Eigenthumlichkeit der Briten gewesen sey, schliesse ich aus einer Stelle der capitula selecta canonum Hibern bei D'Achery, Spicileg. i. 505 : Gildas ait : Britones toto mundo contrarii, moribus Romanis inimici non solum in missa, sed etiam in tonsura cum Judaeis umbrae futurorum servientes. Gerade so drückt sich Nicetas contra

---

[1] Leabhar Breac, p. 32 b. The word used here is idpairt, to which no technical meaning is affixed. The usual word for the Eucharistic offering itself was oiffrenn = 'the mass.'

[2] Leslei, Praefatio in Liturg. Moz. sect. 76; Germani Paris. Expos. Brev. Ant. Lit. Gall., De Sono. [3] Fol. 251 a. [4] Stowe Mis. fol. 64 b.

Latinos, Bibl. PP. Max. xviii. 405. aus; Qui azymorum adhuc participant, sub umbra legis sunt, et Hebraeorum mensam comedunt[1].'

This ingenious inference is supported, as far as the later continental Celtic Church is concerned, by a statement of Walafrid Strabo that it was the custom of St. Gall to use unleavened bread[2]. The design at the foot of the monogram of the Book of Kells may be taken to prove that circular wafer bread, stamped with a ×, was in use in Ireland in the sixth century. The consecrated wafer bread is there drawn between animals which seem to hesitate to destroy or devour it[3]. The host in a circular form, with a chalice or portable altar underneath it, is represented between two kneeling figures on the Nigg stone in Ross-shire[4]. In mediaeval Celtic literature there are plentiful allusions to wafer bread.

'I asked the secular priests,
To their bishops and their judges,
What is the best thing of the soul?
The Paternoster, and consecrated wafers, and a holy
Creed[5].'

Dr. Döllinger is not quite right in inferring that in their use of unleavened bread the British Church differed from the rest of Western Christendom,—' wahrend man sich damals in der Römischen Kirche und im übrigen Occident noch des gesäuerten Brodes bediente,'—and Bingham is quite wrong in asserting that it is 'a matter beyond all dispute that the Church for a thousand years used no other but common or

---

[1] Geschichte der christlichen Kirche, p. 217, Landshut, 1833.

[2] 'Dum de hujusmodi colloquium rebus haberent, superveniens Ioannes Diaconus secundum consuetudinem obtulit ei panes azymos et lagunculam vini.' Wal. Strabo, Vita S. Galli, i. 17.

[3] Dr. Todd suggests that these animals are beavers with their young; Illumination of Ancient Irish MSS. plate i; Descriptive remarks, p. 10. An uncrossed wafer is depicted on another page of the same MS. See S. Ferguson's Cromlech of Howth, App. p. 21. For a similar representation of the wafer in a thirteenth-century Italian fresco, see J. H. Parker's Photographs, No. 1123.

[4] Stuart, J., Sculptured Stones of Scotland, vol. i. plate xxviii.

[5] Black Book of Caermarthen, xxvii. plate ii. (twelfth century).

leavened bread in the Eucharist[1].' Unleavened bread was
not only used in the early Celtic Church, but also in the
African Church in St. Cyprian's time[2], in the Spanish Church
in the ninth century[3], in the Anglo-Saxon Church under
Archbishop Theodore[4], and in Alcuin's time[5].

§ 22. MIXED CHALICE.—The universal custom of the primitive Church to mix water with the wine for consecration in the
Eucharistic cup[6] obtained in the Celtic Church also. This
may be inferred from Adamnan's account of St. Columba in
his youth, in Ireland (Scotia), acting on one occasion as
deacon and fetching water for the celebration of the Eucharist[7].

On one occasion, when St. Finden of Movilla was celebrating,
water only, and not wine, had been provided. St. Columba,
who was present, removed the difficulty by turning the water
into wine[8].

The cross engraved on bronze spoons found at Llanfair
in Wales has been held to be a proof of their connection
with Christian usage[9]; and it has been suggested that they
were Eucharistic spoons used for the administration of the
consecrated wine. This is merely conjecture, faintly supported
by the fact that a bronze chalice was used by St. Columbanus
in the sixth century, and that another bronze chalice of eighth-
century Irish workmanship is still preserved in the convent
of Kremsmünster on the Rhine. But if these bronze spoons
had any liturgical use at all, they were more probably

---

[1] Antiq. xv. ii. 5.   [2] Ep. 63. 3.

[3] Martene, de Antiq. Eccles. Rit. i. iii. vii. 26.

[4] Thorpe, B., Anc. Laws, fol. ed. 1840, p. 304.

[5] Alcuini Ep. lxxv, Ad Fratres, Lugdun. t. i. p. 107.

[6] Martene, de Eccles. Antiq. Rit. iii. vii. 30.

[7] 'Ad fontem sumpto pergit urceo, ut ad sacrae Eucharistiae ministeria
aquam, quasi diaconus, fontanam hauriret.' Vita S. Columbae, ii. 1. Or
was this water required for the 'lavabo,' the symbolical washing of the
priest's hands, a practice asserted by St. Augustine of Hippo to have prevailed
universally in the primitive Church? 'Nam utique et altare portarent, et vasa
ejus, et aquam in manus funderent sacerdoti sicut videmus per omnes ecclesias.'
Quaest. V. et N. Test. 101.   [8] Leabhar Breac, f. 31 b.

[9] Archaeol. Cambrens. Third Series, vol. viii. p. 219. For the question of the
date to be assigned to the use of a cross, see p. 128.

employed for conveying a little water into the chalice of wine before consecration, in accordance with a custom which prevailed almost universally in the early Church [1]. Such might have been the use of the small bronze spoon found under St. Martin's Cross at Iona, and now in the possession of the Duke of Argyll [2], and of a diminutive gold spoon found in the river Bann, and figured in the Ulster Journal of Archaeology [3]. An account of ancient bronze spoons found at Weston is given in the Proceedings of the Society of Antiquaries for Scotland [4]. Notwithstanding the sacred character which has been conjecturally assigned to their ornamentation, it is probable that all these spoons were put to ordinary culinary, rather than to any ecclesiastical use.

§ 23. COMMUNION IN BOTH KINDS.—We might infer the fact of communion in both kinds from such words as these of Columbanus: 'If thou art thirsty, drink the Fount of life; if thou art hungry, eat the Bread of life. Blessed are they who hunger for this Bread, and thirst for this Fount, for ever eating and drinking, they still desire to eat and drink [5].' They form a metaphor the full force of which would have been lost in a Church where communion in one kind only was the rule. But more direct proof is obtainable. In the Rule of Columbanus a special penalty is assigned to any who injure the chalice with their teeth [6]. In St. Sechnall's Hymn in praise of St. Patrick that saint is described as one 'who draws heavenly wine in heavenly cups, and gives drink to the people of God from a spiritual chalice [7].' The

---

[1] Bona, Rer. Lit. lib. ii. c. ix. § iii; Leabhar Breac, f. 251 a.

[2] A woodcut representation is given in Ulster Journal of Archaeol. i. 80.

[3] Vol. i. p. 81.   [4] Vol. viii. p. 363. plate viii.

[5] 'Si sitis, bibe fontem vitae; si esuris ede panem vitae. Beati qui esuriunt hunc panem, et sitiunt hunc fontem; semper enim edentes et bibentes, adhuc edere et bibere desiderant.' S. Columbani, Instructio xiv. de fonte vivo Christo Jesu adeundo et potando.

[6] 'Similiter qui pertuderit dentibus calicem salutaris, sex percussionibus.' S. Columbani, Regula Coenobialis, cap. iv.

[7] 'Qui celeste aurit vinum in vasis celestibus,
Propinansque Dei plebem spirituali poculo.'
Liber Hymnorum, p. 19.

Communion Hymn of the early Irish Church [1] is full of allusions to the reception of the chalice. So are the formulae of Administration and of the Communio preserved at the close of the Antiphonary of Bangor [2].

In the later lives of the saints such expressions as these abound : ' After the girl had received the Body of Christ and His blood she died without anxiety ; ' and ' The old man pointed out to them the land of which they were in search, i.e. the Land of Promise, and having received the Body of Christ and His blood he went to heaven [3].' Reference has been already made to the possible connection of certain ancient spoons with the administration of the Eucharist [4]. In the church at Kildare there was ' a special door through which St. Bridget and her virgins passed, that they might enjoy the banquet of the Body and Blood of Jesus Christ [5].' The act of communion was called ' going to the chalice ' in the Rule of the Irish Culdees [6]. St. Cuthbert, who cannot be supposed in his later days to have deserted on such a point as this the Celtic traditions of his youth [7], was entreated by an officer of the court of Egfrid King of Northumberland to send a priest to visit his wife before her death, and to administer to her ' the Sacrament of the Body and Blood of Christ [8] ; '

---

[1] Chap. iii. § 12.

[2] Chap. iii. § 12. Some of these passages appear also in the Books of Deer (ib. § 5), Dimma (ib. § 6), and Mulling (ib. § 7); St. Gall. MS. 1394 (ib. § 9); the Stowe Canon (ib. § 14) ; to which notes are appended indicating the source of all, and the Mozarabic connection of some, of the antiphons.

[3] Irish Life of St. Brendan, quoted in Todd's Life of St. Patrick, p. 460, n. Although the separate mention of the Body and Blood of Christ indicates the double administration, the absence of such two-fold mention does not necessarily disprove it. In Jonas' Life of St. Columbanus, that saint is described as giving the viaticum to another person named Columbanus in these words, 'Corpus Christi abeunti de hoc vita viaticum praebet.' Fleming, Collectan. p. 228.   [4] p. 133.

[5] ' Per alterum ostium abbatissa cum suis puellis et viduis fidelibus tantum intrant, ut convivio corporis et sanguinis fruantur Jesu Christi.' Cogitosus, Vita S. Brigidae ; Canisii Op. i. 423.

[6] Reeves' edit. p. 86.

[7] Communion in both kinds was also the practice of the Anglo-Saxon Church.

[8] 'Mittas presbyterum qui illam, priusquam moriatur, visitet, eique Dominici corporis et sanguinis sacramenta ministret.' Bede, de Vit. Cuthbert. pros. cap. 15.

and himself, immediately before his own death, received the Blessed Sacrament in both kinds from the hands of Herefrid Abbot of Lindisfarne[1].

The cup was administered by the deacon. There are extant certain canonical regulations of the Welsh Church c. A.D. 589, where among the penances attached to greater crimes are a refusal of permission to a priest to celebrate or to a deacon to hold the chalice[2]. The chalice from which St. Bridget was communicated was administered by 'unus de pueris Episcopi[3].'

§ 24. COMMUNION OF INFANTS.—There are traces of the once universal custom of administering the Eucharist to children after baptism in the Stowe Missal, where a formula of communion and several collects of thanksgiving after eucharistic reception are placed at the close of a Baptismal Office, the language of which implies that it was intended to be used in the case of infants as well as of adults[4]. In a later Irish Ordo Baptismi (twefth century) it is directed that the newly-baptized infant shall be confirmed if a bishop be present[5]. There may also be some significance in the appointment of St. Matt. xix. 14 (Sinite parvulos, &c.) as an Antiphon ad Communionem in the Stowe Missal[6] and in the St. Gall MS. 1394[7].

§ 25. WOMEN TO BE VEILED AT THE RECEPTION OF THE SACRAMENT, AND NOT TO APPROACH THE ALTAR.—Among the regula-

---

[1] 'Exitum suum Dominici corporis et sanguinis communione munivit.' Ib. cap. 39. The following language of Jonas is still more explicit : 'Quaedam ex illis cum jam corpus Domini accepisset ac sanguinem libasset.' Vita Burgundofarae, § vi, ap. Mab. Acta SS. ii. 443. It could hardly, like previous quotations, be used, with theological exactness, of communion in one kind.

[2] 'Hinc autem presbitero offerre sacrificium, vel diacono tenere calicem non licet; aut in sublimiorem gradum ascendere.' Twelfth-century MS. Paris. No. 3182, H. and S. i. 119. 'Diaconus, praesente presbytero, eucharistiam populo si necessitas cogat, eroget.' Syn. Hibernens. lib. iii. c. 8.

[3] Ultani, Vita S. Brig. cap. 94. The story is told rather differently in the Leabhar Breac, fol. 65 b.   [4] Ch. iii. § 14.

[5] 'Hic vestitur infans, et si episcopus fuerit statim confirmare eum chrismate oportet.' Corpus Missal, p. 203. Similar directions are found in the Service Books of the Anglo-Saxon Church.

[6] Ch. iii. § 14.   [7] Ib. § 9.

tions laid down in the Penitential of Cuminius is one that
' women shall receive the Holy Communion under a dark veil;'
and St. Basil is referred to as an authority for this undoubtedly
Eastern custom[1]. There was a similar order for women to approach the altar with their heads veiled in the Apostolic Constitutions, in a passage relied upon by Bunsen[2] as a proof of
their Eastern origin : Καὶ γυναῖκες κατακεκλυμμέναι τὴν κεφαλὴν,
ὡς ἁρμόζει, γυναικῶν τάξει προσερχέσθωσαν[3].

This was also a custom of the early Gallican Church, where
a head-covering (dominicale) was ordered to be worn by women
at the time of communion, by the 42nd canon of the Council
of Auxerre[4].

In later times we hear of a church in North Munster into
which no woman, or any animal of the feminine gender, ever
entered but it immediately died[5]. There was another church
where Irish women were prohibited from going near the altar,
or taking the chalice in their hands: 'Nulla femina ad altare
Domini accedat, nec calicem Domini tanget[6].' The latter
part of this direction proves it to be of considerable antiquity.
It occurs in a ' Sermo sinodalis parrotianis prespeteris,' but
must surely apply only to some particular monastic altars.
Yet injunctions of a similar character were not confined to
Ireland. The Gallican Constitutions of Theodulf Bishop of
Orleans (A.D. 802–11) ordered ' ut feminae ad altare non

---

[1] 'Mulieres possunt sub nigro velamine accipere sacrificium ; Basilius hoc
judicavit.' Cuminii de Mensura Poenitentiarum, cap. xiv. The same direction
occurs in the Penitential of Theodore, vii. 3.

[2] Reliquiae Liturgicae, iii. 248.

[3] Book ii. ch. 57.

[4] 'Ut unaquaeque mulier quando communicat dominicale suum habeat, quod
si qua non habuerit, usque ad alium diem Dominicum non communicet.' Conc.
Autissiodor. can. 42. There was formerly some uncertainty about the interpretation of the word ' dominicale;' Gavant, Thes. Rit. i. 269; Scudamore, W.
E., Notit. Euchar. edit. 1876, p. 723. n. 5. Women are represented as veiled in
early and mediaeval Italian sacred art; J. H. Parker's Photographs, Nos.
479, 1710.

[5] Giraldus Cambrensis, Top. Hib. ii. c. 4. A.D. 1185; Master of the Rolls'
Ser. vol. v. p. 80. No woman might enter the church or mill of St. Fechin at
Fore; ib. ii. 52. p. 134.   [6] Leabhar Breac, f. 248. col. 1.

accedant[1].' Women were not allowed to enter the chancel
of Durham Cathedral within a line of blue marble which ran
across the nave[2]. In a collection of tenth-century Anglo-
Saxon laws the Gallican rule of Theodulf was incorporated
and expanded thus: 'Eac we beodað þæt þæm tidum þe
mæsse-preost mæssan singe þæt nan wif ne ʒenealæce þam
weofode, ac standen on hyra stedum, and þe mæsse preost þær
æt hiom onfó þære ofrunge þe hiʒ Gode ofrian wyllath[3].'

§ 26. RESERVATION.—The consecrated elements were reserved
for the use of the sick or absent, to whom they were afterwards conveyed. A person going to procure Communion for
the sick was exempt from liability to arrest and from the law
of distress[4]. Special warnings were directed against the loss
of the reserved Sacrament from a boat or a bridge or while on
horseback[5]. It was carried in a vessel called a ' chrismal,' or
in a satchel suspended from the neck[6]; and various penalties
were assigned by St. Columbanus for dropping it accidentally,
or for leaving it behind through negligence[7]. It is not
always clear whether these directions contemplate the Eucharist being conveyed to the sick, or worn as an amulet
about the person, but in the absence of proof of the existence
of the latter custom we may conclude that they are connected with administration to the sick[8]. The reserved Eu-

---

[1] Pertz, Leges, i. 107, 171.

[2] Irish Life of St. Cuthbert, Surtees Soc. Biog. Misc. pp. 63–87.

[3] Anglice, 'We also command that when the priest sings mass, no women
draw near the altar, but stand in their places, and let the mass priest there
receive from them the offerings which they are ready to make to God.' A
great deal of information as to the mediaeval custom on this head is collected
by Canon Simmons (Lay Folks' Mass Book, pp. 233–236), from which it
appears that such injunctions had reference generally to the approach to the
altar for offering alms (or for vesting the altar, B. Thorpe, Ancient Laws,
folio edit. 1840, pp. 303, 375), not for the purpose of communicating.

[4] Senchus Mor, i. 267.

[5] Cuminii de Mensura Poenitentiarum, cap. xiii.

[6] 'Perula, quam, more patriae, presbyter itinerans sub indumento a collo
suspensam deferebat.' Girald. Cambrens. Top. Hib. dist. ii. c. 19.

[7] Regula Coen. xv. For the number of blows inflicted on these occasions,
see Migne, Pat. Lat. Curs. lxxx. 218.

[8] Both customs existed in Anglo-Saxon days. Rock, D., Church of our
Fathers, i. 134.

charist was at a very early date placed on a person's breast
when he was buried, as in the case of St. Cuthbert, whose
body was found 'oblatis super sanctum corpus positis[1].'
May we infer from the use of the plural number here that
the reservation took place in both kinds, just as Dr. Rock
infers from the employment of the singular number in another case that in Anglo-Saxon days the reservation was of
one kind only[2]? The decolorisation of the reserved Sacrament
alluded to as a test of its corruption in the Regula St. Columbani, cap. xv, possibly points to the twofold but conjoint
reservation of both elements[3]. The Eastern custom of simultaneous administration of both reserved elements is implied
in the cases of sick or death-bed Communion previously
referred to[4], and in the Celtic remains of services for the
Communion of the Sick in the Books of Deer, Dimma,
Mulling, and Stowe[5].

§ 27. EULOGIAE.—It was a primitive Eastern custom to bless
a loaf of bread at the conclusion of the Liturgy, which was
then cut up into small pieces with a knife specially consecrated for that purpose, and distributed to the congregation,
who came forward and received it at the priest's hands; there
is ample evidence for the existence of such a custom universally prevailing in the primitive and mediaeval Church,
where it was variously known by the names of Eulogiae,
Panis Benedictus, and Pain Béni[6].

There are proofs of its use in the Celtic Church. Adamnan
states that at St. Kenneth's monastery at Aghaboe in Ireland
there was a table in the refectory on which the Eulogiae were
cut up for distribution. The passage is curious, as showing
that in Ireland in the sixth century it was customary to par-
take of the Eulogiae, not in connexion with the Eucharist in

---

[1] Raine, J., St. Cuthbert, p. 34; Lingard, Anglo-Saxon Church, ii. p. 44,
edit. 1858.

[2] 'Oblationis particula,' Bede, H. E. iv. 14; Rock, Church of our Fathers,
i. 133.   [3] Fleming, Collectanea Sacra, 24.

[4] p. 135.   [5] Chap. iii. §§ 5, 6, 7, 14.

[6] For authorities, see Rock, Church of our Fathers, i. 133.

the oratory, but at the afternoon meal in the refectory[1]. The same practice existed at Iona in Scotland[2], and, as has been inferred from a passage in the old hymn attributed to St. Columba, under the same conditions of time and place as at Aghaboe[3]. At Lindisfarne, in St. Cuthbert's time, it was distributed at the third hour, after Mass[4].

In the continental monasteries of St. Columbanus it was distributed on Sundays and holy days after Mass. It is recorded of the saintly and humble Ermenfried, who presided over the Columban monastery of Cusance (625–670), that he always kissed the hands of the poorest persons before distribution[5]. Its unworthy reception was forbidden by special enactment[6].

§ 28. FREQUENCY OF CELEBRATION.—There does not appear to have been a daily Eucharist in the Celtic Church, but only on Sundays, saints' days, and days specially appointed by the head of the monastery.

By the old law of distress in Ireland a stay of two days was granted in the case of church furniture, and the requisites of the Mass, though it be not celebrated every day[7].

On Sundays.—When four distinguished Irish saints visited St. Columba at Iona and requested that he would celebrate

---

[1] 'Et cum forte post nonam coepisset horam in refectorio eulogiam frangere, ocius deserit mensulam,' &c.   Vit. S. Columbae, ii. 12.

[2] 'Die crastina, his quae necessaria sunt citius praeparatis, Silnanus accepto de manu Sancti pane benedicto, in pace enagavit.'   Ib. ii. 4.

[3] Skene, Celtic Scotland, ii. 99 ; Liber Hymnorum, part ii. 220.

[4] 'Facto jam signo diei horae tertiae et oratione consummata mensam statim apposuit, quia enim panis casu aliquo non erat in diversorio, tantum micas pro benedicto pane congregatas super mensam constituit.' S. Cuthberti Vita Anon., quoted by Rock, Church of our Fathers, i. 138. 'Repente unus eorum intulit, quia secum haberet panem quem sibi nuper vir Domini Cuthbertus benedictionis gratia dedisset.'   Bede, Vit. S. Cuthberti, c. ix.

[5] 'Dicebant etiam de beato viro, quod, humilitatis causa, cum Dominicis vel festivis sanctorum diebus post expletionem Missarum, ut mos est ecclesiasticus eulogias populis daret, si vidisset aliquem operatorem aut pauperrimum crepatis manibus, non ante eulogias dabat quam benignissimus Pater conversa vice manus ipsas oscularetur ; et tunc demum eulogias dabat.' Egilbertus, Vita S. Ermenfredi, ap. Bolland. t. vii. Sept. p. 120.

[6] 'Eulogias immundus accipiens xii. percussionibus.'   Reg. Columb. c. iv.

[7] Senchus Mor, vol. i. p. 126.

in their presence he complied with their request, as usual on Sunday[1]. The same saint is described as celebrating on the last Sunday (June 2, 597) before his death, which took place on the Saturday following[2]. Cuminius in his Penitential defends and explains these Sunday celebrations by a reference to the custom of the Greeks[3]. In the eighth century in Ireland there was a seven years' probation for admission into the society of the Culdees. In the first year the novice was not allowed to communicate at all, only to be present at the sacrifice. In the second year his communions began, and gradually increased in number, till they mounted to communion every Sunday in the seventh year[4].

On Saints' Days.—We read of St. Columba at Iona giving special orders for the celebration of the Eucharist in commemoration of St. Brendan[5] and of Columbanus, and it is noted that the latter order was carried out in detail, as if it had been a regular and recognised holy-day[6]. Passengers on their way to Iona pray that they may reach the island in time to celebrate the Eucharist on the day dedicated to St. Columba and St. Baithene, on whose joint festival (June 9) the wished-for Eucharist is offered[7]. In Ireland, in the sixth century, we read of celebration on a holy-day in the church of St. Finnian at Movilla, county Down[8]. In St. Bridget's

---

[1] 'Die dominica ex more.' Adamnan, Vit. S. Columbae, iii. 17 ; Cuminius, Vita, &c. cap. 12.

[2] Adamnan, Vit. S. Col. iii. 23. On this occasion his face was illumined with a glow of light which he described as caused by his vision of an angel who had been sent 'to demand a deposit dear to God,' and whose appearance was vouchsafed to Columba 'dum missarum sollemnia, ex more, Dominica celebrarentur die.'

[3] 'Graeci omni Dominica communicant, clerici et laici ; et qui in tribus Dominicis non communicaverint, excommunicentur sicut canones habent.' Cuminius, De Mensura Poenitentiarum, cap. xiv.

[4] Rule of the Culdees, p. 87.

[5] ' Vir venerandus mane primo suum advocat saepe memoratum ministratorem Diormitium nomine, eique praecipit, inquiens, Sacra celeriter Eucharistiae ministeria praeparentur. Hodie enim natalis beati Brendani dies ' (= dies obitus). Adamnan, Vit. S. Col. iii. 11.

[6] 'Quasi die solenni.' Ib. iii. 12. See the whole chapter.

[7] ' Ut in tua celebremus ecclesia tui natalis missarum sollemnia.' Ib. ii. 45.

[8] 'Quadam solenni die.' Ib. ii. 1.

church at Kildare, early in the sixth century, there was a
celebration on Sundays and on the vigils of the feasts of
Apostles[1]. In the mother church of every Irish monastery
in the eighth century there was an offering upon every altar
on Sundays and solemnities[2].

St. Gall ordered a special celebration in commemoration of
St. Columbanus on receiving intelligence of his death[3], and
no doubt from that day forward the festival of St. Columbanus
was added to the Kalendar of St. Gall.

§ 29. HOURS OF CELEBRATION.—Mass was always celebrated
at an early, generally at a very early, hour of the day. The Mass
of St. Columbanus was celebrated by St. Columba at Iona
'in the morning[4],' by St. Gall in Switzerland 'at daybreak[5].'
That of St. Brendan at Iona was 'in the very early morning[6].'
The solemn Mass of St. Baithene was sung at the later hour
of noon[7]. An early hour was ordered in the continental
Irish monasteries under a heavy penalty[8].

In all these passages, as usually in the language of the
seventh century, the word 'Missa' means the Liturgy proper,
and such phrases as 'Missarum sollennia' and 'sacra Eucharistiae ministeria' are used as synonymous expressions, but
the word Missa is also used occasionally to denote any sacred
office. The last service at which St. Columba was present
is called the 'vespertinalis Dominicae noctis Missa[9].' This
service was evidently not an evening communion, but 'Vigiliae
nocturnae' or 'nocturns.' The word 'Missale' or 'Missal'
was also used to denote not only the text of the Mass itself,

---

[1] 'In solemnitatibus Domini et vigiliis Apostolorum.' Cogitosus, Vit. S. Brig.
cap. 29. [2] Rule of Culdees, p. 94.

[3] Walafrid Strabo, Vit. S. Galli, tom. i. part ii. c. 27.

[4] 'Mane.' Adamnan, Vit. S. Columbae, iii. 12.

[5] 'Primo diluculo.' Walafrid Strabo, Vita S. Galli, cap. xxvi.

[6] 'Mane primo.' Adamnan, Vita S. Columbae, iii. 11.   [7] Ib. ii. 45.

[8] 'Obliviscens oblationem facere usque dum itur ad officium centum percussionibus.' Reg. Columban. cap. iv.

[9] Adamnan, Vit. S. Col. iii. 23. So in the Regula Caesarii Arel. cap. xxi,
the word 'Missa' is used as equivalent to 'Lectio.' Migne, Bibl. Pat. Lat.
lxvii. p. 1162.

but also other Office Books. The book which in the Irish
life of St. Columba is called the Book of the Gospels, but
which is no longer extant, is called by Colgan in his Latin
translation ' Missarum Liber.'

§ 30. DUPLICATING.—Priests were allowed at Iona, in the
seventh century, to celebrate twice, and by implication, as
a general rule, not more than twice on the same day[1].

§ 31. PATEN AND CHALICE.—The paten (called ' discus' or
patena[2], ' patinus[3]') and chalice (called ' Calix Domini[4],'
'vas[5],' ' laguncula[6],' 'coilech[7],' 'cailech[8]') were probably
originally made of glass. A stone altar with four glass
chalices upon it is mentioned by later writers as having been
discovered by St. Patrick in a cave, and as evidence of the
existence of Christianity in Ireland before the arrival of that
saint[9]. The cups and patens brought by that saint on his
arrival from beyond the sea were possibly of the same
material[10], for there is testimony as to the early use of glass
chalices in Gaul[11]. Bronze chalices were used at a little
later period, in the Irish continental monasteries. St. Gall
refused to use silver vessels for the altar, saying that St.
Columbanus was accustomed to offer the sacrifice in vessels
of bronze, in memory of the fact that his Saviour was fastened
to the cross with brazen nails[12].

A golden chalice, a relic of Iona, perhaps coeval with St.
Columba himself, once existed, but has in recent times been

---

[1] Cuminii De Mensura Poenitentiarum, cap. xiv.

[2] St. Evin, Vita S. Patricii, ii. 54.   [3] Book of Armagh, fol. 8, 11.

[4] Adamnan, De Locis Sanctis, i. 8.   [5] Wal. Strabo, Vit. S. Galli, i. 17.

[6] Ib. i. 19.   [7] = chalice. Leabhar Breac, fol. 31 b.   [8] F. cvi.

[9] St. Evin, Vita S. Patricii, ii. 35. The story is copied in other and still
later biographies. Glass as well as wooden chalices were forbidden by later
Irish authority: 'Nullus presumat missam cantare in ligneo vel in vitreo
calice.' Leabhar Breac, p. 248. col. i.

[10] Scholiast on St. Fiacc's Hymn, seventh century. The original Irish, with
a translation, is given in Dr. Todd's Life of St. Patrick, p. 411.

[11] St. Hilary of Arles possessed ' patenae et calices vitrei.' Honorati, Vita S.
Hilarii, ap. Bolland. Acta SS. ad v. Maii, tom. ii. p. 28.

[12] ' Praeceptor meus B. Columbanus in vasis aeneis Domino solet sacrificium
offerre salutis.' Walafrid Strabo, Vit. S. Galli, i. 19.

unfortunately lost[1]. A similar fate has attended the relics of St. Kieran (sixth century). When his grave was opened A.D. 1791 his relics comprised beads strung on brass wire, a crozier, a hollow brass ball which opened, resembling the ball (possibly a pome) in the hands of one of the figures on the Breac Moedog (Archaeol. xliii. pl. 18), and a paten and chalice[2].

§ 32. FAN.—The only evidence for the use of this well-known Eastern accessory of liturgical worship is derived from illuminations in ancient books. There is a ' flabellum ' or fan represented in the right hand of St. Matthew in a Hiberno-Saxon MS. of the Gospels (eighth century) at Treves[3], also in the hands of the angels in the monogram of the Book of Kells (sixth century, Irish), where they seem to be constructed of thin plates of metal surrounded by little bells like those used by the Maronites[4].

Plentiful evidence of the early use of the flabellum in Western Christendom is adduced by Gerbert[5], and especially as to Gaul in Smith's Dictionary of Christian Antiquities[6]. In a thirteenth-century illumination in a French MS., a facsimile of which is given in Bastard's Peintures et Ornements[7], a priest vested in an ample chasuble is represented in the act of consecration at Mass. Behind him stands the deacon in a dalmatic, waving a flabellum composed of peacocks' feathers.

Knife.—A knife is depicted in the left hand of St. Matthew in the Treves Gospels[8], and in the right hand of the right-hand figure in the monogram of the Garland of Howth[9]. It

---

[1] The circumstances attending its loss are recorded in Wilson's Archaeology of Scotland, pp. 668-9.

[2] There are early and frequent allusions to golden chalices in Gaul ; Greg. Tur. De Glor. Confess. clxiii ; Hist. Franc. lib. iii. cap. 10 ; lib. vii. cap. 24. For information as to other countries, see Scudamore, Notit. Eucharist., second edit. p. 558. [3] Westwood, J. O., Facsimiles, &c., plate xx.

[4] Ib. plate liii. No. 7 ; Todd, J. H., Descriptive Remarks, &c.

[5] Liturg. Aleman. i. 228. [6] Sub voc. Flabellum. [7] Tom. iii.

[8] Westwood, J. O., Facsimiles, &c., plate xx.

[9] Todd, J. H., Descriptive Remarks, &c., plate iii.

is impossible without further evidence to decide for what purpose this knife was employed, although its character as a sacred symbol is evident. It may have been used as the holy spear (λόγχη) is used in the Eastern Church, for the ceremonial piercing of the Amnos and severing the host into portions during the Liturgy[1], or as the knife specially set apart in the Anglo-Saxon Church for the purpose of cutting up the Eulogiae[2].

§ 33. SIGN OF THE CROSS. Frequent mention is made of the use of the sign of the cross for various purposes by the Scottish monks at Iona and by Irish monks under St. Columbanus. It was the sign ordinarily attending the sacerdotal act of benediction. We may infer therefore that it was employed in every Celtic act of consecration, although there is no direct evidence extant to that effect. There are directions for its use once over the chalice in St. Gall MS. 1394[3]; once in the Rite of Unction in the Book of Dimma[3], and in the Stowe Missal[4]; once in the Ordo Baptismi, and five times in the Gelasian Canon in the latter volume[4]. Instances of its use at Iona have been collected by Dr. Reeves in his edition of Adamnan[5]. It was made over the pail before milking[6], over tools before using them[7], over a spoon[8], over a lantern[9]. It was considered effectual to banish evil spirits[10], to restrain a river monster[11], to stop a wild boar[12], to unlock a door[13], to endow a pebble with healing virtue[14], or bread[15], or water[16], or salt[17]. It deprived a spear[18] or a dagger[19] of its power of hurting, etc. etc. In the first eight of these instances the sign of the cross is mentioned, in the latter seven it is implied in the word 'benedixit.' It was made 'extensa,' *or* 'elevata manus,' *or* 'manus protensione.' There are numerous allusions to its use in all the later lives of the saints.

---

[1] There is slight evidence in favour of the use of a knife in the early Gallican Liturgy in the account of the vision recorded by Germanus Paris. in the Expos. Missae, Mart. i. p. 168. col. 2.   [2] Rock, D., Church of our Fathers, i. 36.
[3] Ch. iii. §§ 6, 9.   [4] Ib. § 14.   [5] p. 351.   [6] Ib. ii. 16.
[7] Ib. ii. 29.   [8] Reg. Columban. cap. i.   [9] Ib. cap. ii.
[10] Adamnan, ii. 17.   [11] Ib. ii. 27.   [12] Ib. ii. 26.   [13] Ib. ii. 35.
[14] Ib. ii. 33.   [15] Ib. ii. 4.   [16] Ib. ii. 5.   [17] Ib. ii. 6.
[18] Ib. ii. 25.   [19] Ib. ii 29.

§ 34. FASTING.—There is no direct evidence of the practice of fasting reception of the Communion, but we may infer it from the early hour at which the Eucharist was celebrated [1], and from the prominent position assigned to fasting generally in the regulations of the Celtic Church.

Wednesday and Friday were observed as fast-days at Iona, but a dispensation was granted by the abbot in the case of the reception of strangers [2], &c.; also at Lindisfarne, where the Celtic custom of fasting till three o'clock (except in Easter-tide) had been introduced by St. Aidan from Iona [3]. The Rule of St. Columbanus prescribed the same custom for the Irish continental monasteries [4]. In the Rule of the Irish Culdees (eighth century) skimmed milk was allowed on St. Patrick's Day even if it fell on a Wednesday or Friday [5]. The non-eating of flesh on Wednesdays and Fridays was one of the customary laws by which the soul-friend (anmcara) bound the Irish people [6].

Lent (dies quadragesimales) was observed at Iona as a season of preparation for Easter [7]. The severity of the Lenten Rule may be gathered from the statement of Bishop Cedd that the strict rule which he observed had been learned by him in the Columban monastery in which he had been brought up [8].

The three Rogation Days, before the Feast of the Ascen-

---

[1] p. 142.   [2] Adamnan, Vit. S. Col. i. 26.

[3] 'Per totum annum, excepta remissione quinquagesimae paschalis, quarta et sexta sabbati jejunium ad nonam usque horam protelare.' Bede, H. E. iii. 5.

[4] 'Si quis ante horam nonam quarta sextaque feria manducat, nisi infirmus, duos dies in pane et aqua.' Cap. xiii. p. 23.

[5] p. 84. In the Black Book of Caermarthen (Welsh, twelfth century) this charge is brought against an irreligious person : 'Thou respectedst not Friday, of thy great humility,' &c.; v. 30.

[6] Senchus Mor, iii. 15.   [7] Adamnan, Vit. S. Col. ii. 39.

[8] 'Diebus cunctis, excepta Dominica, jejunium ad vesperam usque *juxta morem* protelans, ne tunc quidem nisi panis permodicum, et unum ovum gallinaceum cum parvo lacte aqua mixto percipiebat. Dicebat enim *hanc esse consuetudinem eorum, a quibus normam disciplinae regularis didicerat.*' Bede, H. E. iii. 23 The rule of St. Benedict was the same as to the hours of food both on Wednesdays and Fridays and in Lent, and it appears to have been still more strict as to quality (cc. 39, 41, 49).

sion, were observed, with fasting up to the ninth hour, and
their observation was perpetuated in the Anglo-Saxon Church
by the 16th canon of the Council of Clovesho (A.D. 747),
which expressly refers to their observation not as a custom derived from Rome, but as a traditional custom of the country :
'Sexto decimo condixerunt capitulo : Ut Laetaniae, id est
rogationes, a clero omnique populo his diebus cum magna
reverentia agantur, id est, die septimo kalendarum Maiarum,
juxta ritum Romanae Ecclesiae, quae et Letania major apud
eam vocatur. Et item quoque, *secundum morem priorum nostrorum,* tres dies ante Ascensionem Domini in caelos cum
jejunio usque ad horam nonam et Missarum celebratione
venerantur[1],' &c.

The wording of this canon is noteworthy. The observance
of the Rogation Days was a Gallican custom, unknown at
that date in the Roman Church, into which it was first introduced by Leo III (795–816) ; and their recognition in the
British Church, and their perpetuation from that source in
the Anglo-Saxon Church, if we may see an allusion to that
Church in the words 'priores nostri,' is a link in the proof
of the early connection between the British and Gallican
Churches.

The connection of a special fast with the Celtic rite of the
consecration of churches has been already pointed out[2].

§ 35. CONFESSION.—There is plentiful evidence of the practice of confession in the Celtic Church, but there is no trace
of its connection with or of its use as a preparation for the
celebration or reception of the Eucharist. Gildas uses the
general expressions 'poenitentiae medicamen' and 'ut peccata
sua delerentur humilitate confessionis[3].' The ordinary Irish
title for a confessor was 'anmcara' or 'soul's friend,' and
every person seems to have attached some priest to himself in
that capacity.

---

[1] H. and S. iii. 368.   [2] p. 75.

[3] Epist., H. and S. i. 78, 80.

St. Donnan of Eig requested St. Columba to act as his anmcara. 'This Donnan went to Columcille to make him his soul's friend; upon which Columcille said to him, "I shall not be soul's friend to a company of red martyrdom; for thou shalt come to red martyrdom, and thy people with thee." And it was so fulfilled[1].' St. Columba is said to have been 'anmcara' to Aidan King of Dalriada A.D. 574[2].

Adamnan acted as anmcara to Finnsnechta, who became monarch of Ireland A.D. 675[3]. Minute regulations about confession are laid down in the Irish Rule of the Culdees (pp. 88–90). In some of the later entries in the Annals of Ulster the office of chief confessor is named[4]. There are various regulations on the subject of penance and confession in the Welsh laws of Howel[5]. In the Black Book of Caermarthen an irreligious Welshman is taunted with the question, 'What gavest thou of thy wealth before private confession[6]?'

Three points are worthy of note with regard to the practice of confession in the Celtic Church.

(*a*) It was public rather than private.

We read how a certain Irishman (de Scotia), named Feachnaus, touched with remorse for some crime committed by him, came to Iona, and falling at St. Columba's feet, lamenting bitterly, 'confessed his sins before all that were there present.' Whereupon St. Columba, weeping together with him, absolved him in these words: 'Rise up, my son, and be comforted; thy sins which thou hast committed are forgiven, because, as it is written, a contrite and a humble heart God doth not despise[7].'

---

[1] Félire of Oengus, p. 86. line 3; also p. cxxix and passim.

[2] MS. H. 2. 16. Trin. Coll., Dublin, p. 858, quoted in Reeves' Adamnan, p. lxxvi.   [3] MS. quoted in Reeves' Adamnan, p. xliii.

[4] As in the case of Oengus O'Donnellan, primh anmcara, wrongly translated by O'Conor 'primus anachoreta' of the Columban monks; anno MCIX.

[5] H. and S. i. pp. 211–283.   [6] v. 21.

[7] 'Feachnaus, cum fletu et lamento, ante pedes ejus [sc. Columbae] ingeniculans flexis genibus amarissime ingemuit, et *coram omnibus qui ibidem inerant*

On another occasion, when St. Columba was visiting the little monastery of Trevet, co. Meath, a priest who had been chosen by the brethren to celebrate the Eucharist on account of his supposed superior sanctity, was conscience-stricken by some words uttered by St. Columba, and 'was compelled to confess his sin in the presence of them all[1].'

An old Irish canon speaks of confession of sins in the presence of priest and people[2].

(*b*) It was optional rather than compulsory.

In early Irish law there is frequent mention of the anmcara, and of confession to him being profitable (not necessary), and of his power to impose penances, such as a pilgrimage after a murder[3].

The direction on the subject in the Penitential of Cuminius ran in these words: 'Confessio autem Deo soli ut agatur, si necesse est, licebit[4].' It was perhaps owing to its optional character that the practice of confession seems to have dropped into disuse in the later Irish Church. Alcuin writing to certain brethren in Ireland (eighth century) urged the practice of confession very strongly on men and women, secular and religious, young and old[5]. In another letter he complained

---

peccantias confitetur suas. Sanctus tum, cum eo pariter illacrymatus, ad eum ait, Surge fili, et consolare; dimissa sunt tua quae commisisti peccamina; quia sicut scriptum est, Cor contritum et humiliatum Deus non spernit.' Adamnan Vit. S. Col. i. 30.

[1] 'Presbyter ille " de quo haec dicebantur verba *coram omnibus* peccantiam compulsus est suam confiteri."' Ib. i. 40.

[2] 'Post confessionem peccatorum coram sacerdote et plebe.' Sin. Hibern. ii. c. 4. [3] Senchus Mor, iii. 39, 73.

[4] The same direction appears in the Anglo-Saxon Penitential of Theodore (668-690): 'Confessio autem Deo soli agatur licebit si necesse est. Et hoc *necessarium* in quibusdam codicibus non est;' cap. xii. sect. 7. The meaning of these directions depends upon the interpretation which is placed upon the conditional clause. Is the necessity alluded to 'objective' as maintained by Roman writers, such as would be caused by a stroke of paralysis, or by the impossibility of access to a priest? or is it 'subjective,' of the existence of which each person is judge according to his own spiritual needs? Lingard, A. S. Church, i. 304.

[5] Alcuini Epist. ccxxv. ad fratres qui in Hibernia insula per diversa loca Deo deservire videntur.

that 'it is reported that none of the laity are willing to make their confession to the priests, whom we believe together with the holy Apostles to have received the power of binding and loosing from God in Christ[1].'

St. Bernard asserted that the custom of going to confession had died out in Ireland in the twelfth century, and that its restoration was one among the reforms of St. Malachi[2].

(c) It was not the custom to pronounce absolution until after the penance assigned had been fulfilled.

An early Irish canon assigned a year of penitence as the punishment for certain crimes. When the year was accomplished the penitent might come with witnesses and receive absolution from the priest[3]. Bede records how an Irish youth named Adamnanus made confession to a priest, and on hearing the penance imposed complained of it, not on account of its severity, but because he wished more quickly to receive absolution. The penance had been imposed for an indefinite time, and absolution was deferred until the priest should see him again. No second interview ever took place, in consequence of the sudden death of the priest in his native country (Ireland), whither a sudden emergency had caused him to return, and Adamnanus continued to comply with the conditions of the penance for the rest of his natural life[4].

This regulation, although it led to a practical inconvenience in the case of Adamnanus, is more in accordance with the discipline of the primitive Church than the modern

---

[1] 'Dicitur vero neminem ex laicis suam velle confessionem sacerdotibus dare, quos a Deo Christo cum sanctis Apostolis ligandi solvendique potestatem accepisse credimus.' Epist. cxli. ad fratres in provincia Scotorum [al. Gothorum].

[2] 'Usum saluberrimum confessionis, sacramentum confirmationis, contractum conjugiorum (quae omnia aut ignorabant aut negligebant) Malachias de novo instituit.' S. Bernard in Vita Malachiae, cap. iii. ad finem; see also cap. viii. § 17.

[3] 'Christianus qui occiderit, aut fornicationem fecerit, aut more gentilium ad aruspicem juraverit, per singula cremina annum poenitentiae agat; impleto cum testibus veniat anno poenitentiae, et postea resolvetur a sacerdote.' Sinodus Patricii, Auxilii, Isernini, cap. xiv.

[4] This story is told at some length in Bede, H. E. iv. 25.

practice of making the absolution precede the performance of the penance[1].

The following portion of an Irish Penitential survives among the MSS. at St. Gall[2] :—

'Capitula quaedam ad emendationem vitae.

INCIPIT ORDO AD POENITENTIAM DANDAM.

Credis in Patrem et Filium et Spiritum Sanctum? *R.* Credo.

Credis quod istae tres personae, quo modo diximus, Pater et Filius et Spiritus Sanctus, tres sunt, et unus Deus est? *R.* Credo.

Credis quod in ista ipsa carne in qua nunc es habes resurgere in die iudicii et recipere siue [bonum] siue malum quod egisti? [*R.* Credo.]

Uis dimittere illis quicunque in te peccauerint, Domino dicente, Si non remiseritis hominibus peccata eis, nec Pater uester coelestis dimittet uobis peccata uestra? (*R.* Dimitto.)

Et require diligenter si sit incestuosus[3] *; si non uult ipsa*

---

[1] Bingham, Antiq. book xix. c. 2.   For the present Roman rule and practice, see Schouppe, F. X., Elementa Theol. Dog. vol. ii. tract xiv. c. ii.

[2] F. F. iii. 15.

[3] The presence of this question as a typical question to be put to an Irish penitent corroborates the dark picture drawn by St. Bernard of the morals of the Irish; p. 150. n. 2. Statements about the prevalence of incest in Ireland in the eleventh century are also made by Lanfranc Archbishop of Canterbury, in letters addressed to Gothric King of Dublin (Ep. xxvi ; Ussher's Works, iv. 490), to Terdelvacus King of Ireland (Ep. xxvii ; ib. 493); by Anselm, in letters to Muriardachus King of Ireland (Ep. xxxv ; ib. p. 521 : Ep. xxxvi ; ib. p. 523); by Giraldus Cambrensis, writing A.D. 1185 ; Topograph. Hibern. distinct. iii. cap. 19.   The first canon of the Synod of Cashel, A.D. 1172, is directed against the same irregularity (Mansi, Concil. vol. xxii. p. 134).   But the early Irish ecclesiastical law of marriage was strict ; Canones S. Patricii, ii Synod. xxv–xxviii. Compare the decision of Columba in a matrimonial dispute in the island of Rechrea, off the coast of Antrim ; Adamnan, Vit. S. Col. ii. 41.   It is also noteworthy that the same question is directed to be put to the penitent in a tenth-century German Office published by Gerbert (vol. ii. p. 25, ex Cod. MS. Bibl. Caes. Vindob. Theol. No. 685), and in an almost identical French Ordo Penitentiae printed in Martene, de Antiq. Eccl. Rit. lib. i. cap. vi. art. vii. ordo vi, ex MS. Gellonensi, saec. ix aut x, in diocesi Lodevensi.   Possibly therefore the question was a necessity of the times rather than indicative of any special

incesta dimittere, non potes ei dare poenitentiam; et si uult ipsa incesta dimittere, fac eum confiteri omnia peccata sua, et ad ultimum dicere,

Multa sunt peccata mea in factis, in uerbis, in cogitationibus.

Tunc da illi poenitentiam, et dic istas orationes super eum,

Oremus.

Preueniat hunc famulum tuum *ill.* Domine misericordia tua, et omnes iniquitates eius celeri indulgentia deleat. Per[1].

Oremus.

Exaudi, Domine, preces nostras, et confitentium tibi parce peccatis, et quos conscientiae reatus accusat, indulgentia tuae pietatis absoluat[2].

Et caeteras si tempus habueris sic in sacramentario continentur. Si tibi non uacat istae sufficiant.

Et si homo ingeniosus est, da ei consilium ut ueniat tempore statuto ad te aut ad alium sacerdotem in Coena Domini, et reconciliaretur sic in Sacramentario continetur. Quicquid manens in corpore consecutus non fuerit (hoc est reconciliatio) exutus carne consequi non poterit. Si uero minus intelligens fuerit, quod ipse non intelligit, in uno statu reconciliare potes eum, ita dicendo,

Oremus.

Presta, quesumus, Domine, dignum poenitentiae fructum huic famulo, ut Ecclesiae tuae sanctae, a cuius integritate deuiarat peccando, admissorum ueniam consequendo reddatur innocuus[3]. Per.

Si infirmus est homo, statim reconciliare eum debes.

---

degradation in the morality of Ireland. It should also be remembered that marriages with persons occupying positions of spiritual affinity as well as with near kindred fell under the designation of incest. (Hook, W. F., Archbishops of Canterbury, i. 372. § 7.) The charge of 'incest' was frequently brought against the Anglo-Saxons in the ninth century. (Lingard, A. S. Church, ii. 220.)

[1] Sacr. Gelas. p. 504; Greg. p. 209; Sarum Missal, p. 132.   [2] Ib.

[3] This collect occurs in the Ordo Excommunicandi, &c. in the Pontif. Rom.

CHAPTER III.

Together with certain Missae and Collects, which, though not portions of the original Celtic Liturgy, were used in the later
Celtic Church, or are associated with the names of Celtic Saints,
or refer to incidents in their lives, or have relics of the ancient
Liturgy interwoven in their structure or contents.

§ 1. No traces of a vernacular Liturgy. — § 2. Cornish Fragment. Missa S.
Germani. — § 3. Welsh Fragments. Missa de S. David. — § 4. Missa
de S. Teilao. § 5. Scottish Fragment. Book of Deer. — § 6. Irish
Fragments. Book of Dimma. — § 7. Book of Mulling. — § 8. Book of
Armagh. — § 9. St. Gall. MS. No. 1394. — § 10. St. Gall. MS. No. 1395.
— § 11. Basle MS. A. vii. 3. — § 12. Antiphonary of Bangor. — § 13.
Book of Hymns. — § 14. Stowe Missal. — § 15. Drummond, Corpus, and
Rosslyn Missals. — § 16. Paris MS. 2333 A. Colbert. — § 17. Missale
Vesontionense.

Throughout the documents printed in this chapter the original orthography
and accentuation have been retained. The punctuation has been modernised
and capital letters have been introduced after full stops. Words or letters
within square brackets [ ] are not in the MS. text. Those within round
brackets ( ) have been added by a later hand. Rubrics have been printed
in italics, Titles in small capitals. Contractions and abbreviations have been
expanded.

§§ 2, 3, 4b, 5, 6, 7, 8, 13, 14, 15, 16 have been printed from the original MSS ;
§§ 9, 10 from facsimiles of the original MSS.; §§ 4 a, 11, 12 from collations
with the original MSS., kindly supplied by P. B. Davies-Cooke, Esq., Dr. L.
Sieber, and the Very Rev. W. Reeves, D.D.

CHAPTER III.

§ 1. No traces of a Vernacular Liturgy.

THERE is no trace of a vernacular Liturgy having been in use in any portion of the Celtic Church; but in the absence of any liturgical remains of an earlier date than the seventh century, only negative evidence can be produced on this point. The undoubtedly Celtic liturgical fragments of a later date which have survived are in the Latin language, relieved by an occasional vernacular rubric, as in the case of the St. Gall MSS., the Stowe Missal, and the Books of Deer, Dimma, and Mulling[1]. But there is not only an absence of direct proof, but also of any indirect evidence which points to a vernacular Liturgy having once existed, if we except a possible interpretation of the 'ritus barbarus,' abolished in Scotland by Queen Margaret[2].

As far as the earliest British Church is concerned many facts suggest a partially Latin origin. The most important British bishoprics belonged to the capitals of Roman provinces— York, London, and possibly Caerleon. The earliest Christian martyrs in Britain bore Roman, or at least not Celtic names— Albanus, Julius, Aaron. The earliest antiquarian remains of British Christianity are connected with Roman stations, as at Canterbury, Dover, Lyminge, Richborough, &c. Ptolemy, writing in the earlier part of the second century (c. A.D. 120), enumerates under their Latin titles fifty-six cities then

---

[1] §§ 5, 6, 7, 9, 10, 14.
[2] Theoderic. Vita S. Margaret. c. 8, quoted on p. 7. n. 5.

existing in Britain[1]; Marcianus in the third century reckons fifty-nine[2]. Other names of towns have been collected from the pages of Asser, Nennius, Henry of Huntingdon, and the Saxon Chronicle[3]. The walls by which some of these places are still surrounded, the ruins of theatres, villas, baths, and other public and private buildings, the vases, coins, inscriptions discovered from time to time, prove that they once contained a flourishing Roman population. Possibly, therefore, the earliest Christian Church in these islands consisted of converts to Christianity among its Roman invaders and of such natives as were brought into immediate connection with them[4]. Gradually, as the Roman power dwindled away, the Church spread over the population of these islands; but in quite early days Latin, and not any form of Gaelic, may have been, if not the vernacular language, at least a language understood by all the members of the Christian Church in Britain. Tacitus informs us that the Roman language was adopted by the leading inhabitants of Britain under the 'policy' of Agricola[5]. Most of the writings of the British, Scottish, and Irish authors of the first six centuries[6], all the extant Psalters and Books of the Gospels, and the few liturgical fragments which have been preserved, are written in the Latin language by scribes who not only understood what they wrote, but were so far masters of the language in which they were writing as to have compiled a special British and Irish revision of the old Latin text of the Bible for use in their own Church[7]. The ecclesiastical use of the ancient

---

[1] Geogr. lib. ii. cap. 2.   [2] Heracleot. Περίπλους, edit. M.DC. p. 92.

[3] Their Celtic names, and where possible the Roman equivalents, are given by Thomas Gale (Hist. Brit. Script. p. 135) and W. Gunn (Edit. of Nennius, p. 97).

[4] The remains of Celtic churches, crosses, &c. in Cornwall are to be referred to this period.   [5] Tacitus, Vit. Agric. c. 21.   [6] p. 36.

[7] Including the Domnach-Airgid MS., written in the fifth century and believed to have belonged to St. Patrick, now in the Royal Irish Academy at Dublin; an ancient version of the Gospels, fifth to seventh century, in Trinity College, Dublin; the Psalter styled Cathach, and the volume of the Gospels known as the Book of Durrow (Vulg.), both written by St. Columba in the sixth century.

Celtic tongue, if this theory is correct, commenced when the
Church began to include among its members and to receive
into its priesthood persons who were ignorant of Latin; but
even then it was confined to the rubrics, and to sermons or
addresses. A large fragment of a sermon on self-denial and
compassion in the old Irish language from the Codex Camara-
censis (eighth century) is printed in Zeuss, Grammatica Celtica[1]. Vernacular sermons are in existence for the Feast of
All Saints[2], on the Beatitudes[3], Judgment and Resurrection[4].

The above is virtually Mr. Haddan's theory of the Latin
character of the earliest Church in Britain. A counter
theory of its non-Latin and purely Celtic character has
been more recently advanced by Mr. Brewer, and supported by the following considerations :—(1) Christianity was
not as yet (second and part of third centuries) tolerated by
Roman law, and those who under Roman law had just been

Facsimiles of some of their pages are given in The National MSS. of Ireland,
part i. plates i–vi; Dublin, 1874. The evidence for a special Scoto-Britannic
version is collected in H. and S. i. 170-198.

Bede says that, through the study of the sacred Scriptures, Latin had become
'a common language for the Angles, Britons, Picts, and Irish;' Hist. Eccl. lib.
i. cap. 1. There are traces of the use of Greek. Greek words are introduced
into the Hymnus Sancti Comgilli, and in the Antiphon. Benchor. (ch. iii. § 11).
Occasional Graecisms occur in Adamnan's Life of Columba, and in the writings
of other early Irish saints. Examples of Hiberno-Greek characters are given
in Keller's Bilder, &c., plates xii, xiii. In the Book of Armagh Greek characters occur frequently, e. g. in the Gospel of St. Matthew, where the Latin
text of the Lord's Prayer is written in Greek letters. The same is also found in
Codex A, an eighth-century Irish MS. Vita S. Columbae, by Adamnan, of which
a facsimile is given in Reeve's edit. plate 3. The colophon at the end of the
Second Book is likewise in Greek. Ib. Preface, p. xiv; see pp. 158, 354. There
is a story extant of St. Brendan finding a Missal written in Greek characters
in the Welsh monastery of St. Gildas : 'Et habebat Sanctus Gylldas missalem
librum scriptum Graecis litteris, et possitus est ille liber super altare. Et
custos templi ex iussione sancti Gilldae dixit sancto Brendano; uir Dei, praecipit tibi sanctus senex noster ut offeras corpus Christi; ecce altare hic et librum
Graecis litteris scriptum et canta in eo sicut abbas noster. Aperiensque
sanctus Brendanus librum ait : Demonstra michi Domine ihesu istas litteras
ignotas sicut aperuisti ostia clausa ante nos. Profecto possibilia sunt omnia
credenti. Ilico iam litteras grecas sciuit sanctus Brendanus sicuti Latinas quas
didicit ab infancia.' Vita S. Brendani, cap. xv, in the Liber Kilkenniensis.

[1] p. 1004.   [2] Leabhar Breac, fol. 187 a.
[3] In Bodl. MS. Laud 610, twelfth century.
[4] In the Leabhar na h-Uidre, eleventh century.

trampled upon would hardly seek Romans for the materials
of a Church. (2) Tertullian's words imply that Christians
were numerous where the Roman arms had not reached:
'Britannorum inaccessa Romanis loca Christo vero subdita[1].'
(3) The founders of the British Church had come from Celtic
districts of Gaul; in many instances they themselves probably
were Celts, or mixed Celts, and therefore mostly attracted to
the Celtic blood of Britain. (4) The subsequent history, which
must have sprung from these beginnings, is the history of
a Celtic Church, the Roman architecture of existing remains
proving no more than that when Britons built churches they
built as those great builders the Romans taught them[2].

It may be concluded that both elements, the Latin and the
Celtic, coexisted in the British Church of the third and
fourth centuries, but exactly how far this composite character
affected its Liturgy there is no documentary evidence, and it
is a chimera to expect that there ever will be such evidence
forthcoming to show.

The Roman Canon of the Mass seems certainly, but not
universally, to have been introduced into the Irish portion of
the Celtic Church in the course of the ninth century. This
is proved by its presence in the earliest extant Irish Missal,
where it is largely intermingled with fragments of an earlier
pre-Roman Use[3]. There are signs of local friendly intercourse
beginning to grow up between the Irish and Anglo-Saxon
Churches about this time, and of the spread of Anglo-Saxon
influence in the former Church. Among such signs are the
introduction of the names of the second, third, and fourth
archbishops of Canterbury among the Irish saints commemorated in the Canon of the Mass[4], although the appeal
of one of them (Laurence) to the Irish bishops to conform
to Roman usage in the seventh century had been ineffec-
tual[5]. We may also notice the reference to Roman authority
in early Irish canons (late seventh and eighth centuries),

---

[1] H. & S. i. 3. [2] Quarterly Review, No. 294. p. 519.

[3] Stowe Missal, § 14. See § 8. [4] p. 239. [5] p. 40.

where such expressions abound as 'Synodus Romana' or
'Romani dicunt,' 'Regula Canonica dicit Romana,' 'Dispu-
tatio Romana,' 'Institutio Romana.' Extracts from Greek,
African, and even native early Irish conciliar decrees are
sometimes erroneously quoted under the above headings.
But the earliest extant MS. copies of these canons vary
between the ninth and eleventh centuries, when the desire
of assimilation to Rome, the habit of referring to Roman
authority, and the spread of Roman influence had become
strong and more wide-spread.

§ 2. CORNISH FRAGMENT—MISSA S. GERMANI.

The following fragment of an ancient Cornish Liturgy
was written in the ninth century on fol. 1 of a MS. in the
Bodleian Library, No. 572. It was composed after the
Cornish Church had fallen under Anglo-Saxon influence,
and has no claim to be considered as a genuine Celtic Missa
either in form or substance.

MISSA PROPRIA GERMANI EPISCOPI.

Fol. 1. Deus[1], qui famulantibus tibi mentis et corporis sub-
sidia misericorditer largiris, presta quesumus ut hi qui pro
amore supernę patriae ardenter cęlestia premia per fidem
et spem caritatemque adipisci cupiunt, intercedente beato
archimandrita[2] confessore tuo germano[3], ab omnibus iniqui-
tatibus liberentur per dominum.

et item alia.

Propitiare, domine deus, omni populo christiano ex diversis
partibus linguarum conuenienti in unum, ut hi qui locum

---

[1] The first thirteen words of this collect occur in Sacram. Gregor. p. 230.

[2] Archimandrita is often used, as in the text, for 'Prelate' in mediaeval
non-Liturgical writings; Alcuin, Ep. 72, &c. (see Du Cange, Gloss.) There is
a Vita de S. Theodoro Archimandrita, Surius, tom. ii. p. 727.

[3] A Gallican Missa S. Germani records in its Proper Preface how 'hic tuus
devotissimus Germanus episcopus Tartarum eorum [= Auturicorum] vestigiis
subsecutus, per totas Gallias, inectalia [= in Italia] Roma, in Brettania annis
triginta corpore adflictus Janius [= jejuniis] jugiter in tuo nomine praedicavit,
haereses abstulit, adduxit populum ad plenam et integram fidem,' &c. Missale
Gallicanum, p. 153.

preclarum atque notum ubique lannaledensem[1] ubi reliquię
germani episcopi conduntur, quanto ardensius tanto cicius
uisitare cupiunt ab omnibus infirmitatibus anime et corporis
fideliter liberentur. Per.

SECRETA.

Concede nobis, omnipotens et misericors deus, ut haec n[obis
sit] salutifera oblatio, et intercedente beato germano con-
fessorae tuo atque episcopo, a nostris reatibus liberet, et
a cunctis tueatur aduersitatibus. Per dominum[2].

[PRAEFATIO.]

U[ere] D[ignum] eterne deus. Et te laudare mirabilem dominum in sanctis tuis, quos ante constitutionem mundi in aeternam tibi gloriam preparasti, ut per eos huic mundo ueritatis tuę
lumen ostenderes, de quorum collegio iste germanus episcopus,
a sancto gregorio romane urbis apostolico ad nos missus[3],
lucerna et columna cornubiae et preco ueritatis efulsit, qui
in lannaledensis aeclesiae tuae prato sicut rosae et lilia floruit,
et tenebras infidelitatis quae obcecabant corda et sensus nostros
detersit. Propterea suppliciter atque lacrimabiliter deprecamur totis uiribus claementiam tuam, ut licet meritis non ex-
sigentibus misereri tamen nostri semper digneris, quia priscis
temporibus legimus te irasci magis quam misereri, propter
uesaniam dementiamque imp[ii] et crudelis regis guortherni[4].

---

[1] The date and character of this fragment are indicated by this preservation
of the old British but otherwise unknown name of Llanaledh for St. Germans.
There was a monasterium Lanaletense [= of Alet] in Brittany, to which the
Pontificale Gemmeticense (tenth century) once belonged; Archaeologia, xxv. 247.

[2] Compare the Secret 'Concede nobis,' &c. in Sacr. Gelas. pp. 692, 714;
Gregor. p. 172.

[3] The ecclesiastical influence of the neighbouring Saxons so far prevailed when
this Missa was composed as to induce its compilers by a violent anachronism
to attribute the mission of St. Germanus to Gregory the Great.

[4] Note this mention of Vortigern and his enormities. The contest between
him and St. Germanus is thus described by a ninth-century historian : 'Et
super haec omnia mala adjiciens, Guorthigernus accessit filiam suam propriam
in uxorem sibi quae peperit ei filium, Hoc autem cum compertum esset a S.
Germano, venit corripere regem cum omni clero Britonum. Et dum conventa
esset magna synodus clericorum ac laicorum in uno consilio, ipse rex praemonuit
filiam suam, ut exiret ad conventum, et ut daret filium suum in sinu Germani,
diceretque quod ipse erat pater ejus. Ac ipsa fecit sicut edocta erat. S. Germanus eum benigne accepit; et dicere coepit : Pater tibi ero; nec te permittam,

Idcirco petemus, obsecramus, deprecamur in his ultimis diebus indulgentiam pietatis tuę, ut per te ueniam peccatorum
nostrorum mereamur accipere, et post finem huius seculi, te
interpellante, cum deo et sanctis eius immaculati conregnare
possimus. Et ideo

POSTCOMMUNIO.

Sumptis, domine, sacramentis in honore sancti confessoris
tui germani episcopi, cuius uenerandam hodię celebramus
festiuitatem, nos claementer exaudi tuam misericordiam obsecrantes; ut ab hac[1] * * *

§ 3. WELSH FRAGMENTS. MISSA DE S. DAVID.

These so-called Welsh fragments have no real claim to be
called Celtic. The oldest, the ' Missa de S. David,' is based
upon the Lectiones taken from Ricemarch's Life, and can
hardly have been compiled before the Welsh Church had
become Normanised or Anglicised.

The following Missa is written by the original scribe in
MS. Cott. Vesp. A. xiv, a MS. of the latter part of the
twelfth century, after the conclusion of the Life of St. David
by Ricemarch. Fol. 69 b.

MISSA DE EODEM.

[ORATIO.]

Deus, qui beatum confessorem tuum Dauid atque pontificem,
angelo nuntiante, Patricio prophetante, triginta annos antequam nasceretur predixisti; quesumus, ut cuius memoriam
recolimus, eius intercessione ad eterna gaudia perueniamus,
per secula seculorum[2]. Per.

---

nisi mihi novacula cum fornice pectineque detur, et ad patrem tuum carnalem
tibi dare liceat. Mox ut audivit puer, obedivit verbo senioris sancti, et ad
avum suum patremque suum carnalem Guorthigernum perrexit, et dixit illi:
Pater meus es tu, caput meum tonde, et comam capitis mei pecte. Ille autem
siluit, et puero respondere noluit ; sed surrexit iratusque est vehementer, et ut
a facie S. Germani fugeret quaerebat : et maledictus est, et damnatus a B.
Germano et omni consilio Britonum.' Nennius, Hist. Britonum, cap. xxxix.

[1] The fragment breaks off here abruptly at the end of the last line on the
verso of fol. 1.

[2] This collect is written with slight verbal variations in Add. MSS. 5810,

SECRETA.

Hostias laudis et preces deuotionis, quas tibi in honore beati confessoris tui Dauid atque pontificis, omnipotens deus, deferimus, placatus intende ; et quod nostrum non optinet meritum, tua clementia et illius pro nobis frequens intercessio efficiat. Per.

POSTCOMMUNIO.

Repleti, domine, participatione sacramenti, quesumus, ut sancti Dauid confessoris tui atque pontificis meritis, cuius gloriosam celebramus festiuitatem, ineffabilis misericordie tue patro(ci)nia sentiamus. Per.

§ 4 a. WELSH FRAGMENTS. ORATIO DE S. THELYAO.

This collect is written in a fourteenth-century hand on the fly-leaf at the end of the Liber Landavensis, now in the possession of P. B. Davies-Cooke, Esq. of Owston in Yorkshire.

Omnipotens sempiterne deus, qui de beato corpore sancti thelyai confessoris tui atque pontificis tria corpora consecrasti, et per illud miraculum pacem et concordiam inter inimicos reformasti ; concede propitius per eius suffragia pietatis tue ueniam consequamur, per dominum nostrum. amen [1].

§ 4 b. WELSH FRAGMENTS. MISSA DE S. TEILAO.

This Missa is written in a fifteenth-century hand upon a vacant space at the end of a MS. Sarum Missal in the Cambridge University Library, MS. Add. 451, which belonged formerly to the Hungerford family, who owned property on the marches of Wales.

[MISSA] DE SANCTO TEILAO.

Omnipotens sempiterne deus, virtutum omnium fons et origo, qui per beatum theilaum gloriosissimum confessorem tuum atque pontificem ingentis vipere seuisiam in mare demersisti ; da, quesumus, vt antiqui hostis nequicia superata, diuini amoris igne succensi, pie peticionis consequamur effectum.

---

fol. 198 a, Brit. Mus., and is printed in the Camden Soc. 1880, New Ser. xxvi. p. 36. It is the collect of the Sarum Breviary, March 1.

[1] The miracles of St. Teilo commemorated in this collect and in the following collect and Postcommunion will be found in the Liber Landav. pp. 104, 110.

SECRETA.

Beati theliai confessoris tui atque pontificis supplicacione, munus oblatum, domine, quesumus fiat nobis imperpetuum salutare, per christum dominum.

POSTCOMMUNIO.

Quesumus, omnipotens deus, vt meritis reparati sanctissimi confessoris tui atque pontificis theilai, pro quo tue gentis belligere munitiua tria funera mirifice prodidisti, triplici seueritate hostium superata, mereamur indiuidue trinitatis percipere uisionem, per dominum.

§ 5. SCOTTISH FRAGMENT. BOOK OF DEER.

Dr. Lingard writing in 1844 asserted that we had no means of judging whether the sacrificial service of the Scottish missionaries varied from that of the Roman Church[1]. But since that date a single liturgical fragment has been discovered, belonging to the Celtic period of the Scottish Church, which, though brief, exhibits sufficiently distinctive marks to enable us to answer the question which Dr. Lingard considered insoluble. It is a portion of the Service for the Communion of the Sick written before the year 1130 on a vacant space in the Book of Deer (ff. 28 b, 29 a), an early Evangeliarium in the Cambridge University Library[2]. This MS. was published by the Spalding Club, 1869, under the editorship of Dr. J. Stuart. A good account of it is given in the preface to that work. There is a close coincidence between many expressions in the short Eucharistic Office which it contains and those of the Mozarabic and Gallican Missals, and there is a marked deviation from certain invariable features of the Roman Liturgy. Therefore this fragment, short as it is, affords evidence that the Scoto-Pictish Liturgy of the Columban Church in Scotland belonged to the 'Ephesine' and not to the 'Petrine' family of Liturgies. The reasons for this conclusion are given in detail in the following notes.

---

[1] Anglo-Saxon Church, vol. i. 271. [2] Ii. 6. 32.

BOOK OF DEER.

ITEM ORATIO ANTE DOMINICAM ORATIONEM.

Crętor naturarum omnium[1] deus et parens uniuersarum in celo et interra originum, hás trementis populi tui relegiosas preces exillo inaccessibileis lucis trono tuo[2] suscipe, et inter-hiruphín et zaraphin indefessas circumstantium laudes exaudi spei nonambigue precationes[3].

Pater noster quies· *usque in finem.*

Libera nós, domine, a malo, domine christe ihesu, custodi nos semper inomni opere bona, fons et auctor omnium bonorum deus euacua nos uitiis, et reple nos uirtutibus bonis. per te christe ihesu[4].
Hisund dubar sacorfaicc dau[5].

Corpus cum sangine domini nostri ihesu christi sanitas sit tibi in uitam perpetua et salutem[6].

---

[1] This phrase occurs in the Mozarabic service for the Nativity of St. John the Baptist, of whom it is said, ' Qui nobis naturarum omnium creatorem necdum natus ostendit.' Mis. Moz. 332 c.

[2] Compare the petition, ' Respice nos de excelso throno gloriae tuae.' Mis. Moz. 312 c.

[3] The Roman Liturgy, in all its forms, has a fixed introduction, ' Praeceptis salutaribus moniti,' &c., and conclusion, ' Libera nos, quaesumus, ab omnibus malis,' &c. ; which never vary. The very fact of there being even a fixed introduction is enough to show a connection in remote times with what is called the Ephesine family. In the Ephesine family, on the other hand, the introduction and embolismus vary with every service. The fact alone would be sufficient to establish a generic difference between the Petrine Liturgy and the Celtic Services preserved here in the Scottish Book of Deer, and in the Irish Books of Dimma, p. 169, Mulling, p. 172, Stowe Missal, § 14, St. Gall MS. 1394, p. 177.

[4] This embolismus resembles in its wording very closely the forms preserved in the Gallican Liturgies : ' Libera nos a malo, omnipotens Deus, et custodi in bono. Evacua nos vitiis et reple virtutibus,' pp. 33, 144 ; ' Libera nos, omnipotens Deus, a malis, et constitue nos in bonis ; evacua nos a vitiis et reple virtutibus tuis,' p. 147 ; ' Libera nos a malo, evacua nos vitiis et reple nos virtutibus,' p. 19. The last passage is taken from the Mis. Richenovense, the most pure and ancient specimen yet discovered of the Ephesine Liturgy, without any trace of its having been interpolated with Roman collects.

[5] Anglice, ' Here give the sacrifice to him.' Mark the use of ' sacrificium' for ' sacramentum.' There is a similar use of it in the Leofric Mis. fol. 324 a ; in a rubric in a ninth-century Pontifical of Prudentius of Troyes, ' *Hinc detur sacrificium infirmo ita dicendo,* Corpus et sanguis,' &c. Mart. i. p. 304 ; see Ch. ii. § 2.

[6] Book of Dimma, p. 170; Book of Mulling, p. 173; Antiphon. Benchor. p. 192;

Reffecti christi corpore et sanguine tibi semper dicamus domine. alleluia, alleluia[1].

Quia satiauit animam inanem, et animam essurientem satiauit bonis[2]. alleluia, alleluia.

Et sacrificent sacrificium laudis et *usque* exultatione[3]. alleluia, alleluia.

Calicem salutaris accipiam, et nomen domini inuocabo[4]. alleluia, alleluia.

Reffecti christi corpore. alleluia, alleluia[1].

Laudate dominum omnes gentes[5]. alleluia, alleluia.

Gloria.

Reffecti christi[1]. alleluia, alleluia.

et nunc. Et semper.

Reffecti[1].

Sacrificate sacrificium iustitiae et sperate indomino[6].

Deus[7], tibi gratias agimus per quem, misteria sancta celebrauimus et ate sanctitatis dona deposcimus, miserere nobis, domine, saluator mundi. Qui regnas insecula seculorum, amen.

Finit.

Stowe Missal, p. 224. Both consecrated elements seem to have been administered at once. For evidence as to the prevalence of this custom of intinction in the West between the seventh and twelfth centuries, see Scudamore, W. E., Notit. Eucharist. second edit. p. 705. Compare the formula of joint administration in the Syriac Lit. of St. James, and in the Armenian Lit. (Hammond, C. E., Lit. E. and W. pp. 81, 165).

[1] This formula of thanksgiving, coupled with a thanksgiving collect, as in the Book of Dimma, p. 171, Book of Mulling, p. 173, Stowe Missal, p. 224, Antiphon. Benchor. p. 192, is a mark of Ephesine origin : ' Refecti Christi corpore et sanguine te laudamus, Domine, Alleluia, alleluia, alleluia.' Mis. Moz. 452 A. The Gloria Patri forms part of the Mozar. Ant. ad Accedentes, pp. 343, 377.   [2] Ps. cvi. 9 ; Stowe Missal, p. 224.

[3] Ps. cvi. 22 ; Book of Mulling, p. 173.

[4] Ps. cxv. 13 ; Book of Dimma, p. 170 ; Book of Mulling, p. 173 ; Stowe Missal, p. 225.

[5] Ps. cxvi ; Book of Dimma, p. 171 ; Book of Mulling, p. 173 ; Stowe Missal, p. 225.

[6] Ps. iv. 16 ; Book of Dimma, p. 171 ; Book of Mulling, p. 173 ; Stowe Missal, p. 225.

[7] This collect, occurring also in the Books of Dimma (p. 171), Mulling (p. 173), and Stowe Missal (p. 225), appears twice in a nearly similar form in the Missale Gothicum : ' Deus, gratias tibi agimus per quem mysteria sancta celebramus ; a te quoque sanctitatis et misericordiae dona deposcimus. Per.' pp. 144, 150. It is not found in any of the Roman Sacramentaries.

The same MS. contains at the close of the volume, and in the handwriting of the original scribe, the Apostles' Creed, which runs as follows :—

FOL. 85. a. Credo indeum patrem omni potentem, creatorem c̨eli et terre. Et inhesum christum filium eius, unicum dominum nostrum, qui conceptus est de spiritu sancto, natus ex maria uirgine, passus sub pontio pylato, crucifixus etsepultus. Discendit ad inferna. Tertia die resurrexit amortuis, ascendit in celum, sedit addexteram dei patris omni potentis, inde uenturus est iudicare uiuos et mortuos. Credo et inspiritum sanctum, sanctamque aeclisiam catholicam, sanctorum communionem, remissionem peccatorum, carnis resurrectionis, uitam eternam. amen [1].

Immediately below this Creed the scribe has written a rhyming couplet in his own language.

No other MS. liturgical remains known to exist in Scotland are connected with the Scoto-Celtic Church.

(1) The Arbuthnott Missal [Liber Ecclesiae beati Terrenani de Arbuthnott] is a Sarum Missal with certain Scottish additions and modifications, written in 1491 by an ecclesiastic named Sybbald, Vicar of Arbuthnot. It was printed at the Pitsligo Press, 1864, under the editorship of the late Bishop of Brechin (A. P. Forbes), and his brother the Rev. G. H. Forbes.

(2) The Celtic Kalendar printed by Bishop Forbes (Kalendar of Scottish Saints, pp. 79–92) is a late and unimportant document. The Antiquae Litaniae published in the same work (Appendix to Preface, No. iii. pp. lvi–lxv; H. & S. ii. i. 278) belong in their present form to the sixteenth century, though they may contain portions of a genuine earlier Culdee document.

(3) The Drummond and Rosslyn Missals will be referred to hereafter in connection with the Irish Church [2].

---

[1] Other early forms of the Creed are given in Antiphon. Benchor. p. 189 ; Stowe Missal, p. 231.

[2] § 15.

§ 6. Irish Fragments. Book of Dimma.

The following 'Missa de Infirmis' is written between the
Gospels of St. Luke and St. John on ff. 52–54 of the 'Book
of Dimma,' a Book of the Gospels, preserved in the Library
of Trinity College, Dublin[1]. The writer having been identified with one Dimma, who lived in the middle of the
seventh century, the MS. has on that account been attributed
to that date.

The remarks in the Notes appended to the 'Missa de
Infirmis' in the Scottish 'Book of Deer[2],' proving its
Ephesine character, apply equally to the Missae which have
survived in the ancient Irish Books of Dimma and Mulling,
and in the Stowe Missal. Additional indications of the same
connection are noted below.

Extract from the Book of Dimma.

Oremus, fratres[3], dominum deum nostrum pro fratre nostro
.n. quem duri adpresens malum langoris adulcerat, ut eum
domini pietas caelestibus dignetur curare medicínís; qui dedit
animam det etsalutem, perdominum nostrum.

Deum[4] uiuum omnipotentem, cui omnia opera restaurare
[et] confirmare facillimum est, fratres carissimi[3], profratre
nostro infirmo supliciter oremus, quo creatura manum sentiat
creatoris aut inreparando aut inrecipiendo; inhomine suo pius
pater opus suum recreare dignetur, perdominum nostrum.

Domine[5], sancte pater, uniuersitatis auctor[6], omnipotens
aeternae deus, cui cuncta uiuunt, qui uiuificas mortuos et uocas

---

[1] A. 4. 23.   [2] p. 164.

[3] These addresses to the people, or 'biddings,' called 'Prefaces' in the Gallican Liturgies, are a distinct mark of Ephesine origin. The Roman Liturgy,
which consists almost exclusively of collects addressed to God, nevertheless
retains still in the Good Friday service a remnant of the Ephesine character,
which was no doubt eschewed by the Italian, as much as it was cultivated
by the Gallican branches of the Church. See Stowe Missal, p. 221 (note 2),
where these two addresses occur again verbatim, together with some of the
following collects and lections. This address also occurs in a tenth-century
German Ritual, Gerbert, Lit. Al. ii. 33.

[4] Stowe Missal, p. 221.   [5] Ib.   [6] p. 271, n. 1.

ea quae non sunt, tanquam ea quae sunt, tuum solitum opus, qui es artifex, pie exerce in hoc plasmate [1] tuo, perdominum.

Deum [2] in cuius manu tam alitus uiuentis quam uita morientis, fratres dilectissimi [3], deprecemur, ut corporis huius infirmitatem sanet et animae salutem prestet; ut quod per meritum non meretur, misericordiae gratia consequatur, orantibus nobis, perdominum.

Deus [4], qui non uís mortem peccatoris, sed ut conuertatur et uiuat [5], huic adte excorde conuerso peccata dimite, et perennis uitae tribu[e] gratiam, perdominum.

Deus [6], qui facturam tuam pio semper do[mi]nares afectu, inclina aurem tuam suplicantibus nobis tibi; ad famulum tuum .n. aduersitate ualitudinis corporis laborantem placitus respice; uisita eum insalutare tuo, et caelestis gratiae ad medicamentum, per dominum.

LECTIO APOSTOLI AD CORINTHEOS.

Sí in hac uita tantum in christo sperantes sumus misserabiliores sumus omnibus hominibus. Nunc hautem christus resurrexit a mortuis, primitiae dormientium : quoniam quidem per hominem mors, et per hominem resurectio mortuorum ; et sicut in adam omnes moriuntur, ita [7] in christo omnes uiuificabuntur [8].

---

[1] The word 'plasma' is not found in the Roman, but is frequently used in the Mozarabic and Gallican Liturgies ; as in the exorcismus in the Ordo Baptismi in Sacram. Gall., Mab. edit. p. 324 ; Mis. Mozar. p. 314 ; also in a collect in Anglo-Saxon Missal of Leofric (Surtees Soc. lxi. p. 348). It also occurs in this same collect in the Stowe Missal, p. 220. It is interesting to find it in the hymn assigned for the first Vespers, 'In natali unius Apostoli,' in the Sarum Breviary, 'Salva, Redemptor, plasma tuum nobile' (line 5), of which Daniel says, 'Videtur carmen Galliae et Angliae fuisse proprium.' Thes. Hymnol. i. 273.   [2] Stowe Missal, p. 221.

[3] See p. 167, note 3.   [4] Stowe Missal, p. 222, q.v.

[5] 'Rex gloriae qui non vis mortem peccatoris, sed ut convertatur et vivat,' Miss. Goth. p. 93.

[6] Stowe Missal, p. 222 ; Corpus Mis. p. 207 ; Gerbert, Lit. Aleman. ii. 29, 37. This collect occurs almost verbatim in an old Ritual of St. Benedict of Fleury, given in Martene de Rit. Antiq. iii. p. 377, and very nearly in its present form in the Breviarium Gothicum, Migne's edit. p. 974. Sac. Gelas. p. 735, Gregor. p. 211.   [7] V. + et.

[8] I Cor. xv. 19-22. For this lection the Stowe Missal (p. 222) substitutes Matt. xxiv. 29-31.

In illo die accesserunt ad eum saducei qui dicunt non esse resurrectionem, et interrogauerunt eum. Respondens hautem ihesus ait illis; erratis nescientes scripturas neque uirtutem dei. In resurrectione enim neque nubent neque nubentur, sed erunt sicut angueli[1] in caelo. De resurrectione hautem mortuorum non legistis quod dictum est a deo, dicente uobis; Ego sum deus abraam[2], deus isac, [3] deus iacob? non [4] deus mortuorum sed uiuentium[5]. Audientes turbae admirabantur[6] in doctrinam[7] eius[8].

Diuino magisterio edocti, et diuina institutione formati, audemus dicire[9].

Credo in deum patrem omnipotentem;

Credo et in ihesum christum filium ejus;

Credo et in spiritum sanctum;

Credo uitam post mortem;

Credo me resurgere.

Ungo te deoleo sanctificato in nomine trinitatis, ut salueris in saecula saeculorum[10].

Concede nobis famulis tuis ut orantes cum fiducia dicire mereamur[11] Pater noster.

Infirmus canit si potest; si non, persona eius canit sacerdos.

Agnosce, domine, uerba quae precipisti; ignosce presumpsioni quam imperasti; ignorantia est nobis, non agno-

---

[1] V. + Dei.   [2] V. Abraham + et.   [3] V. + et.   [4] V. + est.
[5] V. + et.   [6] V. mirabantur.   [7] V. doctrina.
[8] Matt. xxii. 23-33.   This passage also forms one of the lections in the Stowe Missal, p. 222.

[9] 'Divino magisterio edocti et divina institutione formati audemus dicere. Pater.' Miss. Gall. p. 74. Nowhere, except here, has this or any similar Preface been found to introduce the Creed. Compare Stowe Missal, p. 242. n. 150. The Credos are written continuously in the original MS.

[10] Book of Mulling, p. 172 ; Stowe Missal, p. 223.

[11] Stowe Missal, p. 223. This is an old Gallican preface to the Pater Noster. 'Concede, Domine, famulis tuis ; ut orantes cum fiducia dicamus, sicut.' Mis. Gall. p. 144. Very similar forms of preface will be found in Mis. Gall. pp. 46, 60, 66; Mis. Moz. § 18. line 12 ; § 66, ad finem; § 74. line 65 ; § 243, 3 ; § 249, 31 ; § 333, 63 ; § 447, 42 ; § 263, 18 ; § 281, 37 ; § 330, 6 ; § 464, 75. It occurs verbatim together with the following embolismus (Libera, &c.) in a Constantinopolitan Pontifical ; Mart. ordo xxi. vol. i. p. 333.

scere meritum; contumacie non seruare preceptum, quo iubemur dicere[1] Pater noster.

Libera nos, domine, ab omni malo, et custodia nos semper in omni bono, christe ihesu, auctor omnium bonorum, qui regnas in saecula[2].

Páx et caritás domini nostri ihesu christi sit semper nobiscum[3].

Hic pax datur ei, et dicis[4].

Pax et commonicatio sanctorum tuorum, christe ihesu, sit semper nobiscum[3].

Respondit, Amén.

Dás ei euchari[s]tiam dicens,

Corpus et sanguis domini nostri ihesu christi filii dei uiui conseruat animam tuam in uitam perpetuam[5].

Post adsumptum ait,

Agimus deo patri omnipotenti gratias quod terr[en]ae nos originis atque naturae, sacramenti sui dono in celestem uiuificauerit demotationem[6].

Item oratio.

Ostende[7] nobis, domine, missericordiam.

Conuerte[8] nos deus salutum nostrarum, et firmare presta salutem nostrorum; qui regnas in saecula saeculorum.

Alleluia.　Calicem salutaris *usque* inuocabo[9].

---

[1] 'Agnosce, Domine, verba quae praecepisti; ignosce praesumptioni quam imperâsti; ignorantia est nobis non agnoscere meritum; contumacia non servare praeceptum, quo jubemur dicere, Pater noster.' Mis. Gall. pp. 150, 153.

[2] Book of Deer, p. 164. n. 4.

[3] For similar forms of words to be used at the bestowal of the Pax, see Stowe Missal, pp. 224, 242; St. Gall. MS. 1394, p. 177.

[4] This is the Roman position of the Pax, which is placed before the Canon in the Ephesine Liturgy; but as the Canon would not be repeated at all in the case of communicating a person from the reserved gifts, no argument can be based upon this circumstance; but the same position is assigned to the Pax in the St. Gall. MS. No. 1394 (p. 177), and in the Stowe Missal (p. 242), neither of which is a private Office 'ad communicandum infirmum.'

[5] Book of Deer, p. 164. n. 6.　　　[6] Ib. p. 165; Stowe Missal, p. 243.

[7] Ps. lxxxiv. 8; Stowe Missal, pp. 220, 232.

[8] Adapted from Ps. lxxxiv. 5; Stowe Missal, p. 224.

Ps. cxv. 13; Book of Deer, p. 165; Book of Mulling, p. 173; Stowe Missal, p. 225.

Alleluia.   Fortitudo mea *usque* in salutem[1].

Alleluia.   Refecti christi corpore et sanguine, tibi semper dicamus[2].

Alleluia.   Laudate dominum omnes gentes[3] *usque in finem.*

Alleluia.   Sacrificate sacrificium iustitiae *usque* in domino[4].

Tunc signas et dicis[5],

Pax tecum.   Benedicat tibi dominus, et custodiat té, conseruat uultum tuum ad té, ut det tibi pacem[6].

Respondit.

Deus, tibi gratias agimus per quem ministeria sancta celebramus, et ate dona sanctitatis deposcimus, qui regnas in saecula[7].

§ 7. IRISH FRAGMENTS.   BOOK OF MULLING.

The following ' Missa de Infirmis' is written in a ninth-century hand at the end of St. Matthew's Gospel in the Book of Mulling, containing the entry 'nomen scriptoris Mulling,' and therefore ascribed to Mulling Bishop of Ferns, who died A.D. 697.   It is now in the Library of Trinity College, Dublin.

Oratio communis pro infirmo incipit.

Oremus, fratres carissimi[8], pro spiritu cari nostri .n. qui secundum carnem egritudinem patitur, ut dominus ei reuelationem dolorum presentet, uitam concedat, tutellam salutis remunerationem bonorum operum impertiat, per dominum.

Prefatio[9] *communis incipit.*

Oremus, fratres carissimi[8], pro fratre nostro .n. qui in-

---

[1] Ps. cxvii. 14 ; Stowe Missal, p. 225.   [2] See p. 165. n. 1.

[3] Ps. cxvi ; Book of Deer, p. 165 ; Book of Mulling, p. 173 ; Stowe Missal, p. 225.

[4] Ps. iv. 16 ; Book of Deer, p. 165 ; Book of Mulling, p. 173 ; Stowe Missal, p. 225.

[5] The sign of the cross is also directed to be made at the conclusion of the Office for Unction in the Stowe Missal, p. 225.

[6] This blessing is given in an amplified form in Stowe Missal, p. 225 ; Book of Mulling, p. 172.   [7] Book of Deer, p. 165. n. 7.

[8] Book of Dimma, p. 167. note 3.

[9] This use of the word ' Praefatio' for a short exhortation to the people is peculiar to and common in the old Gallican Liturgies.

commodo carnis et egretudine uexatur, ut domini pietas per angelum medicinę celestis uisitare et corroborare dignetur, per dominum. . . . .

[pate]r omnipotens, et conserua famulum tuum hunc .n. quem [sancti]ficasti et redemisti pre[tio] magno sancti sanguinis tui, in secula seculorum.

BENEDICTIO SUPER AQUAM.

Oremus et postulemus de domini missericordia, ut celesti spiritu hunc fontem benedicere et sanctificare dignetur, per dominum.

BENEDICTIO HOMINIS.

Benedicat[1] tibi dominus et custodiat te; illuminet[2] dominus faciem suam super[3] te[4] et misseriatur tui, conuertatque[5] dominus uultum suum adte, et det tibi pacem et[3] sanitatem[3]. Misserere n. d. a.

Tum unges eum oleo.

Unguo[6] te deoleo sanctificationis in nomine dei patris, et filii, et spiritus sancti, ut saluus eris in nomine sanctę trinitatis.

Simul canit.

Credo in deum patrem.

Tum dicitur ei ut dimittat omnia.

COLLECTIO ORATIONIS DOMINICAE.

Creator naturarum omnium[7], deus, et pariens uniuersarum in celo et interra originum has trinitatis populi tui relegiosas preces ex illo inaccessę lucis throno tuo suscipe, et inter hiruphin et saraph[in i]n-deffessas circu[m] st[an]tium laudes exaudi spei non ambi[gue] precationes.

P[ater] noster.

Collectio nunc sequitur.

Libera nos a malo, domine christe ihesu, et custodies nos in

---

[1] Num. vi. 24–26; Book of Dimma, p. 171.   [2] V. ostendet.
[3] V. *om.*   [4] V. tibi.   [5] V. *om.* que.
[6] Book of Dimma, p. 169.   [7] Book of Deer, p. 164.

omni opere bono, auctor omnium bonorum, manens et regnans in saecula saeculorum[1], amen.

Tum reficitur corpore et sanguine[2].

Corpus cum sanguine domini nostri ihesu christi sanitas sit tibi in uitam ęternam.

Oratio post sumptam euchari[s]tiam.

Custodi intra nos, domine, glorię tuę munus, ut aduersus omnia presentis saeculi mala euchari[s]tiae quam percipimus uiribus muniamur[3], per dominum.

Alleluia.

Et sacrificent sacrificium laudis *usque* annuntiant opera eius in exultatione[4], alleluia.

Calicem salutaris accipiam et nomen domini inuocabo[5].

Reffecti christi corpore et sanguine, tibi semper, domine, dicamus, alleluia[6].

Laudate dominum omnes[7].

Glo[ria patri].

Sacrificate sacrificium iustitię et sperate in domino[8].

Deus[9], tibi gratias agimus, per quem misteria sancta cele-brauimus, et ate sanctitatis dona deposcimus, per dominum nostrum ihesum christum filium tuum, cui gloria in saecula saeculorum.

§ 8. Irish Fragments. Book of Armagh.

The following extracts are from the Book of Armagh, a New Testament with Latin and Irish additions, written in A.D. 807 by Ferdomnach, a scribe of that city, now in the Library of Trinity College, Dublin.

---

[1] Book of Deer, p. 164.   [2] Ib.

[3] 'Custodi intra nos, Domine, gloriae tuae munus, ut contra omnia praesentis saeculi macula eucharistiae viribus quam accepimus muniamur.' Mis. Goth. p. 146.

[4] Ps. cvi. 22 ; Book of Deer, p. 165.

[5] Ps. cxv. 13; Book of Deer, p. 165; Book of Dimma, p. 170; Stowe Missal, p. 225.

[6] Book of Deer, p. 165.

[7] Ps. cxvi; Book of Deer, p. 165; Book of Dimma, p. 171 ; Stowe Missal, p. 225.

[8] Ps. iv. 16; Book of Deer, p. 165 ; Book of Dimma, p. 171; Stowe Missal, p. 225.

[9] Book of Deer, p. 165; Book of Dimma, p. 171.

Hanc igitur oblationem seruitutis nostrae sed et cunctae
familiae tuae quesumus domine ut placatus accipias
+ diesque nostros in tua pace disponas atque ab aeterna
dampnatione nos eripi et in electorum tuorum iubeas
grege numerari, per christum dominum nostrum.

Lib. Armacan. fol. 19 a.

These lines, containing a portion of the Roman Canon,
with the words 'diesque nostros,' &c. said to have been
inserted by St. Gregory, are interesting as proving that the
Roman Canon in its Gregorian form was known in Armagh
early in the ninth century.

The following collect is written at the end of St. Matthew's
Gospel. Though intended for private rather than liturgical
use, it may be added here for the sake of comparison with the
Anglican Collect for St. Matthew's Day :—

Deus, inmensae clementiae atque ineffabilis pietatis, sub-
missa uoce rogare presumo, ut quomodo ex puplicano matteum
preclarum apostolum fecisti, ita per missericordiam tuam
arcessere me digneris adperfectam in hoc saeculo uiam,
atque anguelicis hierusalem caelestis choris collocare, ut perpetuo solio infinitae laetitiae ymnidicis archanguelorum
laudibus conlaudare te merear, per unigenitum filium tuum,
qui tecum uiuit in unitate spiritus sancti, per omnia saecula
saeculorum. Amen.

Lib. Armacan. fol. 52 b.

§ 9. Irish Fragments. St. Gall MS. 1394.

At St. Gall there is the following fragment of an Irish
Sacramentary, supposed to be written in the ninth century,
and now forming one of a collection of fragments marked
MS. 1394. A facsimile of the original was sent from St.
Gall to Mr. C. Purton Cooper, and was printed by him [1] :—

---

[1] Appendix A to (intended) Report on Rymer's Foedera, p. 95. There is
mention made of a 'Missalis' among the 'Libri Scottice scripti' in a ninth-

petimus omnipotens deus nost[er . .]¹

placatus accipere p[er Dominum]

Deus qui unigenito tuo not[am (=vam)] creaturam nos tibi
esse fecisti respice in [opera misericordiae]
tuae et ab omnibus nós mac$\d{}$lis vetustatis emunda]
ut per auxilium gratiae tuae [in illius invenianur]
forma in qua tecum [est nostra substantia. per]²

IN tuis tibi domine gratias . . .

primordis quibus sub . . .

hodie fructus offerimu[s] . . .

Uere dignum et iustum es[t. Qui ut nos a servitute]
gravi legis eximeret le[galis circumcisionis]
natur purgationis in qua [et observationis antiquae]
probatur existeret, et hum[anam in se naturam vetus-]
tate expoliens ut inuocanti [praeteriti sacramentorum con]
sumator misteri idemque be [=le-gislator et custos precipie]
ns et obediens diues in su[o pauper in nostro par tur-]
torum aut dûs pullûs co[lumbarum sacrificio vix]
subffecit coeli terraeq[ue possessori grandaevi Sy-]
meonis inualidis gastati [=gestatur manibus a quo mundi]
rector et domini predicator [=dn̄s predicatur accedit etiam
testificantis ora-]

---

century catalogue of MSS. in the monastery of St. Gall. This Missal has been
lost, but it is possible that this fragment is a portion of it (Keller, F., Bilder und
Schriftzüge, p. 61). In Haenel's Catalogus Librorum MSS. Monasterii B.V. M.
Rhenoviensis (p. 734) there is this entry : 'Missale antiquissimum Saec. viii.
Hoc Missale ab aliquo Scoto scriptum S. Fintanus noster, ex Scotia oriundus,
forsan vel ipsemet scripsit, vel scriptum secum in monasterium nostrum
Rhenoviense attulit' (Pertz, Archiv der Gesellschaft für ältere deutsche
Geschichtkunde, vii. 182). No trace of this Missal can be found, and the
notice is now believed to be due to some mistake on the part of the compiler of
the Catalogue (Keller, ut supr., p. 94). Professor Westwood has searched for
such a volume in vain at Rheinau, Zurich, Carlsruhe, &c.

¹ Letters and words in brackets have been supplied conjecturally. The
original rubrics are written continuously with, and in the same handwriting as,
the rest of the text. Contracted and abbreviated words have been written at
length. *Al, all, alle* are the various abbreviations used for alleluia here and
in other Irish fragments.

² This collect occurs in Gerbert, Liturg. Aleman. i. 14, for the Festival of the
Circumcision, Kl. Jan. in octava Domini. Sacram. Gelas. p. 500.

culum uiduae quoniam dicebat [=decebat ut ab utroque
 adnunciaretur sexu utriusque salvator]
et ideo cum angelis [et arch]an[gelis][1] . . .

Participes a diabulici(o) co[nvivio jubes abstinere]
aeterne deus qui tuae mens[ae].[2]
da quaesumus plebi tuae ut gu[stu mortiferae pro]
sanitatis abiecto puris [mentibus ad epulas]
aeternae salutis accedant [per.][3]

ut salutare tuum no[va coelorum luce]
[Concede nobis] omnipotens deus et misericors[2]
mirabili quod ad salutem [mundi hodierna]
uirtute processit nostris sem[per innovandis]
cordibus innovatur. per dominum[4].

 [Coelesti lumine quaesumus Domine]
 semper et ubique nos p[raeveni ut mysterium]
[cuju]s nos participes esse uo[luisti et puro cernamus]
 intuitu et digno particip [=percipiamus effectu per]
 dominum nostrum[5]

. . . enus ad [altare] . . . me per christum dominum
[nostrum . . . nen . . . sce] nos stella christi ante
dominum
deum de . . . editum deum nostrum . . . ut
[a]perti[s thesauris . . . laetus suscipe . . . in illa]
[munera mistica . . . dispensat[6]] . . .

P . . . [mun]demus[7] conscientias nost[r]as ab omni labe
uitiorum ut nihil sit in [nobis subdolum vel] superbum,
 sed in

---

 [1] Gerbert, Liturg. Aleman. i. 14; Mis. Ambros. in Pamel. Liturg. i. 312.

 [2] This line and the previous line ought to be transposed.

 [3] Sacr. Leon. p. 301; Gelas. p. 501. The references in this collect are to
the 'Missa de prohibendo ab Idolis' formerly appointed for Jan. I.

 [4] Sacr. Gregor. pp. 11, 17. Read 'festivitate' for 'virtute,' 'oriatur' for
'innovatur.'

 [5] This collect occurs in the Benedictio Thymiamatis in Sabbato Sancto,
Sarum Missal, p. 336. Sacr. Gelas. p. 503; Gregor. p. 78.

 [6] Report on Foedera, App. A, plate xxviii.   [7] Ib. plate xxix.

humilitatis studium et c[a]ritatis pen[sum et] sanguinem
dominici corporis fraternitas uincta copuletur . . . dicere :—
 Diuino magisterio edocti et diuina institutione
formati audiemus dicere[1], Pater nost[er]
Lib[era] nos, domine, ab omni malo praeterito prae-
[senti] et futuro, et intercedentibus pro nobis
be[atis a]postolis tuis petro et paulo et patricio
[episcopo] da propitius pacem tuam in diebus nostris [ut op]e missericordiae tuae adiuti et a peccatis s[empe]r simus liberi et ab omni perturbatione
securi . . . per dominum[2].

[*Sacerdos*] *tenens sancta in manibus signat calicem cruce,*
 et hic pax datur[3] *et dicit sacerdos.*

P[a]x et caritas domini et commonicatio sanctorum omni[u]m sit semper uobiscum[4].

 populus respondit . .

Et cu[m spiritu] tuo
 et mittit sacerdos sancta in calicem, et dat sibi populus p[a]cem,
 [*atque commo*]*nicant, et iuxta commonionem canitur . .*

Pacem meam do uobis, [meam pa]cem relinquo uobis[5]. alleluia.
Dominus reget me[6]

Qui manducat corp[us meum et bi]bit meum sanguinem.
 alleluia.

ipse in me manet et ego in illo[7]. alleluia.

[Hic est] panis uiuus qui de coelo discendit[8]. alleluia.

Qui manducat [ex eo uiuet in et]ernum[9]. alleluia.

---

[1] Book of Deer, p. 164; Stowe Missal, p. 242.

[2] This embolismus after, as well as the introduction to, the Pater Noster show
strong traces of Latin influence. They approximate to without being identical
with the Roman form. The same wording occurs in the Stowe Missal, p. 242.
Compare Book of Deer, p. 164. n. 4.

[3] For this position of the Pax see Book of Dimma, p. 170. n. 3.

[4] Book of Dimma, p. 170.

[5] St. John xiv. 27. The whole of this anthem [pacem—meus alleluia]
occurs in an extended form in the Stowe Missal, q. v. p. 242. Many of its
expressions imply (perhaps simultaneous) communion in both kinds.

[6] Ps. xxii. 1. Stowe Missal, p. 242.

[7] St. John vi. 57. Stowe Missal, p. 242.

[8] St. John vi. 59. Stowe Missal, p. 243; Antiphon. Benchor. p. 192.

[9] St. John vi. 15. Stowe Missal, p. 243.

Ad te, Domine, leuaui[1].

Uenite, comedite panem me[um et bibite ui]num quem
misc[ui] uobis[2].

Iudica me, domine, quoniam ego[3].

Comedite amici[4].

rngeiorn[5].

Et nolite eos prohibere, alleluia, talium enim est regnum
coelorum[6]. alleluia.

Et uiolenti rapiunt illud[7]. alleluia.

Penitentiam agite, alleluia, adprop[inq]uauit enim regnum
coelorum[8]. alleluia.

Hoc sacrum corpus domini et saluator[is] sanguinem, alleluia, sumite uobis in uitam

perennem[9]. alleluia.

In labis meis meditabor [hymnum]. alleluia. Cum docueris
me ego iustitias respondebo[10]. alleluia.

Uenite bene[di]cti patris mei, possedete regnum, alleluia,
quod uobis paratum est

ab origine [m]undi[11]. alleluia.

Ubi ego fuero illic erit et minister m[eus[12]]. alleluia.

In natale domini[13].

Nos oportet celebrare, alleluia, magni regis in natale, alleluia.

Christum mundi salu[ator]em, alleluia.

sacrosancto sanguine, alleluia.

In aepiphania.

Babtiz[atus est dominus] ap[er]ti sunt coeli, alleluia. et
uidit spiritum descendentem super se, alleluia[14].

---

[1] Ps. xxiv. 1. Stowe Missal, p. 243.   [2] Prov. ix. 5. Ib.
[3] Ps. vii. 9. Ib.   [4] Cant. v. 1. Ib.
[5] These eight letters are rudely written as if by a scribe testing his pen. A
facsimile of this page is contained in Appendix A to (intended) Report on
Rymer's Foedera, plate xxx.   [6] Matt. xix. 14. Stowe Missal, p. 243.
[7] Matt. xi. 12. Ib.   [8] Matt. iii. 2. Ib.
[9] Stowe Missal, p. 243 ; Antiphon. Benchor. p. 192.
[10] Ps. cxviii. 171. Stowe Missal, p. 243 ; Antiphon. Benchor. p. 192.
[11] Matt. xxv. 34. Stowe Missal. p. 243.   [12] Ioan. xii. 26. Ib. p. 243.
[13] For the festivals for which there is special commemoration in the Stowe
Missal, see p. 235.   [14] Compare Matt. iii. 16.

IN DIE PASCHE.

Saeculi saluator dominus hodie resurrexit, et in dextera dei
pat[ris] uirtute consedit, alleluia.

IN PENTI[COSTE].

Effundam de spiritu meo, alleluia, super omnem [car]nem,
alleluia, et quidam in seruos meos et in ancellas [m]eas[1], alleluia.

POST[COMMUNIO].

Quos caelesti, domine, dono satiasti praesta ut a nostris
mundemur occultis et ab hostium liberemur insidis, per
dominum nostrum ihesum °.

Gratias tibi agimus, domine, sancte pater, omnipo[t]ens
aeterne deus, qui nos corporis et sanguinis christi filii tui
commo[ni]one satiasti, tuamque misericordiam humiliter
postulamur, ut hóc tuum domine sacramentum non sit nob[is]
reatus ad poenam sed intercessio salutaris ad [uen]iam sit[3]...

§ 10.—IRISH FRAGMENTS.   ST. GALL MS. 1395.

The following Litany occurs in MS. 1395 at St. Gall. It
is on a single leaf in an Irish handwriting of the eighth or
ninth century. A facsimile of the original MS. is given in
the (intended) Report on Rymer's Foedera[4].

Peccauimus, domine, peccauimus par*.

Parce peccatis nostrís et salua nos. qui gubernasti nóe
super undas dilui exaudi nos, et ionam de abiso uerbo
reuocasti libera nos. Qui petro mergenti manum porrex(is)ti
auxiliare, christe, filíi dei, fecisti mirabilia, domine, cum patribus nostris, et nostrís propitiare temporibus, emitte manum

---

[1] Compare Acts ii. 17, 18.

[2] This post-com. which is not part of the Canon in the Roman and Sarum
Missals, occurs in the Stowe Canon (p. 243), and in the Sarum Domin. vi. post
Trin. (p. 478) and the Missa contra paganos (p. 824*), in both of which places
a different post-com. is provided in the Roman Missal. Sacr. Gel. p. 687; Greg.
p. 167.

[3] The fragment breaks off here abruptly at the bottom of fol. ii. verso. The
rest of the collect may be supplied from the Stowe Missal, p. 243.

[4] Appendix A, plates xxiii, xxiv.

tuam de alto, libera nos, christe audi nos, christe audi nos, christe audi nos[1].

> Sancta maria, ora pro [nobis]
> sancte petre, ora pro [nobis]
> sancte paule, ora pro [nobis]
> sancte andria, ora pro [nobis]
> sancte iacobe, ora pro [nobis]
> sancte iohannis, ora pro [nobis]
> sancte pilippe, ora pro [nobis]
> sancte bartholomei, o[ra] pro [nobis]
> sancte thomas, ora pro [nobis]
> sancte mathái, ora pro [nobis]
> sancte simón, ora [pro nobis]
> sancte iacobe, ora [pro nobis]
> sancte thathe, [ora pro nobis]
> sancte madiane[2], [ora pro nobis]
> sancte marce, [ora pro nobis]
> sancte lucas, [ora pro nobis]
> sancte stefane, [ora pro nobis].

The following fragment of an 'Officium Defunctorum' is written on a single leaf of a small Irish Missal of the eighth or ninth century, formerly the property of the monastery of St. Gall[3], but now lost. It is bound up in MS. 1395. A facsimile page is given in the (intended) Report on Rymer's Foedera[4].

Te decet, domine, [hymnus] deus in sion, et reddetur uotum in hirusalem, exaudi orationem meam, ad te omnis caro ueniet[5].

[6] In[7] illis diebus dixit ihesus addiscipulos suos; lazarus amicus noster infirmabatur et manifeste mortuus est[7]; et gaudeo

---

[1] This anthem occurs at the commencement of the Stowe Canon, p. 226. It seems to be a peculiarity of the Celtic Liturgy, taking the place of the Kyrie in the Roman rite.

[2] Madianus occupies this position in the lists of saints in the Stowe Missal, pp. 226, 240. It is the Hiberno-Latin form of Matthias; p. 262. n. 91.

[3] p. 175. [4] Appendix A, plate xxxi. [5] Ps. lxv. 2, 3.

[6] St. John xi. 14–44. The whole passage is printed in H. and S. vol. i. p. 197, with much additional and valuable information as to the affinities of the text in this and other fragments of the Holy Scriptures as used in the Celtic Church.

[7]–[7] An adaptation of vv. 11 and 14. Variations from V. are marked in the following notes.

propter uos, ut credatis, quoniam non eram ibi, sed eamus ad
eum. Dixit autem¹ thomas, qui dicitur didimus, ²cum
discipulis suis², eamus et nos³ moriamur cum illo⁴. Uenit⁵
ihesus et inuenit eum ⁶iam quartum diem⁶ in monumento
habentem. Erat autem bethania iuxta hirusolimam quassi
stadiis quindecim. Multi autem a⁷ iudaeis uenerunt⁸ . . .
[ob]uiam ⁹uenit ei⁹. Maria autem domi sedebat. Dixit
ergo martha ad ihesum, domine, si fuises¹⁰, ¹¹non fuiset
mortuus frater meus¹¹. Sed¹² nunc scio quoniam¹³ quae-
cumque petieris¹⁴ a domino¹⁵ dabit tibi dominus¹⁶. Ait¹⁷
ei¹⁸ ihesus; resurget frater tuus. Dicit ei martha, scio quia
resurget in resurrectione in novissimo die. Dixit¹⁹ ihesus,
ego sum resurrectio et uita; qui credit in me, etsi²⁰ mortuus
fuerit, uiuet; et²¹ qui uiuit et credit in me non morietur²².
Credis hoc? Dixit²³ ei²⁴, utique, domine, ego credidi
quoniam²⁵ tu es christus, filius dei²⁶, qui hunc²⁷ [in²⁷]
mundum uenisti. Et cum hec dixisset, abiit et uocauit
mariam sororem suam si[lentio] dicens, magister uenit²⁸ et
uocat te. At²⁹ illa . . . iudaei autem³⁰ qui erant cum ea³¹
et consolabantur eam ut³² uid[erunt] mariam quod³³ fes-
tinanter³⁴ surrexisset³⁵ et exisset³⁶, subsequuti³⁷ sunt³⁸ dicentes, quoniam³⁹ uadit ad mon[umen]tum ut ploret ibi.
Maria au[tem⁴⁰ cum] uenisset ubi erat ihesus, et⁴¹ uid[isset⁴²
eum] procedit⁴³ ad pedes eius⁴⁴, domine [si fuis]ses⁴⁵, ⁴⁶frater
meus non fuis[set mor]tuus⁴⁶. Ihesus autem⁴⁷ cum⁴⁸
uidisset⁴⁹ flentem, et iudeos qui uene[rant cum] ea flentes⁵⁰,

---

¹ ergo.   ²⁻² ad condiscipulos.   ³ + ut.   ⁴ eo.
⁵ + itaque.   ⁶⁻⁶ quatuor dies jam.   ⁷ ex.   ⁸ venerant.
⁹⁻⁹ occurrit illi.   ¹⁰ + hic.   ¹¹⁻¹¹ frater meus non fuisset mortuus.
¹² + et.   ¹³ quia.   ¹⁴ poposceris.   ¹⁵ Deo.
¹⁶ Deus.   ¹⁷ dicit.   ¹⁸ illi.   ¹⁹ + ei.
²⁰ etiamsi.   ²¹ + omnis.   ²² + in aeternum.   ²³ ait.
²⁴ illi.   ²⁵ quia.   ²⁶ + vivi.   ²⁷⁻²⁷ *transpose.*
²⁸ adest.   ²⁹ *om.*   ³⁰ ergo.   ³¹ + in domo.
³² cum.   ³³ quia.   ³⁴ cito.   ³⁵ surrexit.
³⁶ exiit.   ³⁷ secuti.   ³⁸ + eam.   ³⁹ quia.
⁴⁰ ergo.   ⁴¹ *om.*   ⁴² videns.   ⁴³ cecidit.
⁴⁴ + et dicit ei.   ⁴⁵ + hic.   ⁴⁶⁻⁴⁶ non esset mortuus frater meus.
⁴⁷ ergo.   ⁴⁸ ut.   ⁴⁹ vidit.   ⁵⁰ plorantes.

[1] turbatus est [1] sp[iritu et] commotus [2] dixit, Ubi posu-
isti[s eum]? Dicunt [3], domine, ueni et uide. Et [lacri]-
matus est ihesus. Dixerunt autem [4] [iudei] Ecce quomodo
amabat illu[m] [5] ... [6] nunt quidam ex eis [6] non po[te-
rat]......[toll]ite lapidem. Dixit [7] ei martha [8], domine iam
pudet [9], [10] qua[triduu]m enim habet [10]. Ait [11] ihesus, Nonne
[dixi tibi] quoniam [12] sic ne di [12] ... uidebitis [13] gloriam dei?
Sustulerunt [14] ergo la[pidem]. Ihesus autem [15] eleuauit oculos
sussum et [15] dixit, pater gra[tias ag]o tibi quoniam audisti
me. [Ego aut]em sciebam quoniam [16] semper [me aud]is, sed
propter turbam [17] que [18] [circum]stat dixi, ut credant quoni[a]m [19]
me misisti. Et [20] cum [21] hec [21] di[xisset,] exclamauit [22] uoce
magna [23], [Lazar]e, prodi [24] foras. Et confestim [25] [prodiit]
qui [26] mortuus erat [27], ligatis [28] pedibus [29] [et ma]nibus [30]
fasceis [31] et facies eius [32] ...

A fragment of an office ' De Visitatione Infirmorum,' of the
same date as the preceding fragment of an Officium Defunctorum, is now bound up in the same volume with it,
No. 1395. A facsimile of it is given in the (intended) Report
on Rymer's Foedera [33].

... iustitiae demonstra ei, et aperi ei portas iustitiae et
repelle ab ea principes tenebrarum. Agnosce, domine, de-
positum fidele quod tuum est. Suscipe, domine, creaturam
tuam non exdís alienis creatam, sed a te deo solo uero et uiuo ;
quia non est deus alius praeter te, domine, et non est saecundum
opera tua. Laetifica, domine, animam serui(ae) tui(ae) .n.

[1—1] infremuit.   [2] turbavit seipsum et.   [3] + ei.

[4] ergo.   [5] eum.   [6—6] quidam autem ex ipsis dixerunt.

[7] dicit.   [8] + soror ejus qui mortuus fuerat.   [9] fetet.

[10—10] quatriduanus est enim.   [11] dicit ei.   [12—12] si credideris.

[13] videbis.   [14] tulerunt.   [15—15] elevatis sursum oculis.

[16] quia.   [17] populum.   [18] qui.   [19] quia tu.

[20] om.   [21] transpose.   [22] om.   [23] + clamavit.

[24] veni.   [25] statim.   [26] + fuerat.   [27] om.

[28] ligatus.   [29] pedes.   [30] manus.   [31] institis.

[32] illius. In twenty-nine of the above various readings the Text agrees with
the unpublished MS. copy of the Vetus Itala preserved in Trinity College,
Dublin, A. 4. 15.   [33] Appendix A, plates xxv-xxvii.

Clarifica, domine, animam, serui(ae) tui(ae) .n. reuertentem
ad te. Ne memineris pristinae iniquitatis et ebrietatis quam
suscitauit feruor mali desiderii. Licet enim peccauit, patrem
tamen et filium et spiritum sanctum non negauit, sed credidit
et zelum Dei habuit, et deum fecisse omnia adorauit. Suscipe, domine, animam serui tui(ae) .n. reuertentem ad te ;
indue e(a)m uestem caelestem et laua eam in fontem uitae
aeternae, ut inter sapientes sapiat, et inter gaudentes gaudeat,
et inter martres possedeat, et inter profetas proficiat, et inter
apostolos se custodiat, et inter angelos et archangelos claritatem
dei inueniat, et inter rutulos lapides paradisi gaudium possedeat,
et notitiam misterior [1] . . .

Three forms of benediction of water, or of salt and water,
written on a single page, in a different and smaller handwriting than the foregoing collect, of about the same date,
are bound up in the same volume, No. 1395. A facsimile
of this page is given in the (intended) Report on Rymer's
Foedera [2]. The headings are written continuously with the
text, but in a still smaller handwriting.

BENEDICTIO AQUAE ET SALIS AD SPERGENDUM IN DOM[IBUS].

Domine, sancte pater omnipotens, instaurator et conditor
omnium el[emen]torum, qui per christum ihesum fi[lium tuum
in] hanc creaturam spiritum creantem iussisti, té deprecamur,
domine, ut hanc creaturam salis et aquae [benedicere et
sanctificare digneris], ut ubicumque asparsa fuerint, omnis
spiritus inmundus ab eo loco confusus et increpatus effugiat,
ne[c] ulterius in eo loco habeat potestatem commorandi. Item
presta, domine, per hanc creatam asparsionis sanitatem mentis,
integritatem corporis, tutellam salutis, securitatem spei, cor-

---

[1] The fragment breaks off abruptly at this point. The same prayer occurs
in the Sacram. Gelas. p. 747, in a ninth-century French (Fleury) Ritual, printed
by Martene (lib. iii. cap. 13, vol. ii. p. 381), and in a twelfth-century Salzburg
Pontifical (ib. p. 387), where it opens thus, ' Omnipotens sempiterne Deus qui
humano corpori animam,' &c.

[2] Appendix A, plate xxii.

roborationem fidei, híc et in aeterna saecula saeculorum.
Amen [1].

ITEM BENEDICTIO AQUAE SPARGENDUM IN DOMO.

Deus, qui ad salutem humani generis maxima queque
sacramenta in aquarum substantia condidisti, adesto inuocationibus nostris, et elemento huic omnimodis purificationibus
preparato uirtutem tue benedíctionis infundes, ut creature
mysteriiss túis seruens ad abigendos demones morbosque
pellendos diuinę gratię tue sumat effectus, ut quidquid in
locis in domibus fidelium hęc unda resparserit, careat in-
munditia, liberet a noxia, non illic resedeat spiritus pestilens,
non aura corumpens, abscedant omnes insidię latentes inimici,
et si quid est quod incolmitati habitantium inuidet aut quieti,
aspersione huius aquae effugiet, ut salubritas per inuocationem
tui nominis expetita ab omni sit inpugnatione defensa, per
dominum nostrum ihesum christum filium tuum, qui uenturus
est iudicare uiuos et mortuos et seculum [2].

ITEM ALIA.

Exorcizo te, creatura aquae, in nomine dei patris omni-
potentis, et in nomine ihesu christi filii eius, et spiritus sancti,
omnis uirtus aduersárii, omnis incursus diabuli, et omne
fantasma, omnes inimici potestates eridicare et effugare ab
hac creatura aquę. Unde exorcizo te, creatura, per deum
uerum, per deum uiuum, per deum sanctum, et per dominum
nostrum ihesum christum, ut efficiaris aqua sancta, aqua benedicta, ut ubicunque effusa fueris uel sparsa, siuę in domo
siue in agro, effuges omnem fantasiam, omnem inimici potestatem, et spiritus sanctus habitet in domo hac, per dominum
nostrum ihesum christum filium tuum, qui uenturus est iu-
decare uiuos et mortuos et sęculum per ignem [3].

---

[1] This Benediction occurs, with some variation of text, in the Sacramentarium
Gallicanum, Mab. edit. p. 387.

[2] Sacramen. Gelas. p. 738 ; Greg. p. 264; Rit. Rom. p. 288 ; Sacram.
Gallican. Mab. edit. p. 387 ; Stowe Missal, pp. 207, 211.

[3] Stowe Missal, p. 213 ; Gerbert, Lit. Aleman. vol. ii. p. 10; Sacram. Gelas.
P. 739.

§ 11.—Irish Fragments. Basle MS. A. vii. 3.

Among the MSS. in the Library at Basle, there is a ninth-century Greek Psalter with an interlinear Latin version, No. A. vii. 3[1]. The first three leaves are occupied by some liturgical fragments, in a later Irish handwriting, consisting of two Hymns, (a) in honour of St. Mary the Virgin, (b) of St. Bridget[2]; two prayers addressed (a) to St. Mary, (b) to all Angels and Saints, and the following prayer for use before the altar:—

De conscientiae reatu ante altare.

(Fol. 2 b) Domine, deus omnipotens, ego humiliter te adoro. Tu es rex regum, et dominus dominantium. Tu es arbiter omnis saeculi. Tu es redemptor animarum. Tu es liberator credentium. Tu es spes laborantium. Tu es paraclitus dolentium. Tu es uia errantium. Tu es magister gentium. Tu es creator omnium. Tu es amator omnis boni. Tu es princeps omnium uirtutum. Tu es amator uirginum. Tu es fons sapientium. Tu es fides credentium. Tu es lux lucis. Tu es fons sanctitatis. Tu es gloria dei patris in excelso. Tu sedes ad dextram dei patris, in alto throno regnans in saecula. Ego te peto ut des mihi remissionem omnium peccatorum meorum, deus meus, ihesu christe. Tu es qui neminem uis perire, sed omnes uis saluos fieri, et ad agnitionem ueritatis uenire. Tu es qui ore tuo sancto et casto dixisti, In quacunque die conuersus fuerit peccator, uita uiuet et non morietur. Ego reuertor ad te, et in toto corde meo clamabo at te, domine deus meus. Delictum meum cognitum tibi facio, et iniustitiam meam non abscondo. Tibi humiliter confiteor, domine deus meus, quia peccaui in cęlum et in terram coram te, et coram angelis tuis sanctis, et coram facie omnium sanctorum, tam per negligentiam mandatorum tuorum, et q[uam] malefactorum meorum. Ego corde, ego

---

[1] Haenel, F., Catal. Libr. MSS. p. 590; Keller, F., Bilder und Schriftzüge, p. 86.
[2] Mone, F., Lateinische Hymnen, Nos. 572, 858.

ore, ego opere, et omnibus uitiis coinquinatus sum. Peccaui
per superbiam et inuidiam. Peccaui per detractionem et
auaritiam. Peccaui per superbiam et malitiam. Peccaui per
fornicationem et gulam. Peccaui per falsum testimonium et
per odium hominum. Peccaui per furtum et rapinam.
Peccaui per blasfemiam et carnis desiderium. Peccaui per
ebrietatem, et per otiosas fabulas. Peccaui in dictis, in factis,
in cogitationibus. Peccaui per contentiones et rixas. Peccaui
per iuramentum et iracundiam. Peccaui per terrenam et
transitoriam lętitiam. Peccaui per mentis meę suauitatem.
Peccaui per dolorem et murmurationem. Peccaui in oculis [1]
et in auribus meis. Peccaui in lingua et in gutture. Peccaui
in pectore et in collo. (f. 3 a) Peccaui in manibus et pedibus.
Peccaui in medullis et in renibus. Peccaui in anima et in
toto corpore meo. Si iniquitates obseruem, domine, domine
quis sustinebit. Quanta in me ipsa fuerunt peccata mea, si
multiplicaueris judicium tuum, quomodo sustineam, si nunc
erit uindicta tua. Ideo confiteor tibi, domine, deus meus, qui
solus sine peccato es. Et obsecro te, ihesu christe, deus miseri-
cordiarum, per passionem et per effusionem sanguinis tui,
atque per signum ligni salutiferi crucis tuę, ut concedas mihi
remissionem omnium peccatorum meorum, non secundúm
meum meritum, sed secundúm magnam misericordiam tuam.
Iudica me secundúm iudicium indulgentię tuę. Ego homo
te adiuro, omnipotens deüs, ut non reddas mihi peccatorum
poenam meorum, sed suscita timorem et amorem tuum per-
seuerantem in me, ac ueram penitentiam peccatorum meorum,
et fletum praeteritorum propter nomen propter nomen sanctum tuum; et da mihi memoriam mandatorum tuorum, ut
faciam. Adiuua me, domine deus meus, secundum multitudinem miserationum tuarum dele iniquitatem meam usque
semper; et ne auertas faciem tuam ab oratione mea; et ne
proicias me á facie tua. Ne discesseris, et ne derelinquas me,

---

[1] Another and more exhaustive enumeration of the parts of the body is contained in the Lorica of Gildas, Leabhar Breac, fol. 241; and in a collect in
the Stowe Ordo Baptismi, p. 207.

sed confirma me in tua uoluntate, et doce me facere uoluntatem tuam, et quae debeam loqui a [ut] tacere. Defende me, domine, ab omnibus inimicis meis, inuisilibibus et uisibilibus. Defende me, domine deus meus, contra iacula diaboli, et contra angelum tartari, de quo dixisti, uenit princeps mundi huius et in me non habet quicquam. Quapropter extingue mea peccata, et carnalia desideria in me. Redemptor animarum, ne me derelinquas unum miserum indignumque famulum tuum N. sed ut per te ambulem, et ad te perueniam, et in te requiescam, domine, deus meus, quia sive te nil possumus, qui uiuis et regnas cum deo patre, deus in unitate spiritus sancti, per omnia saecula saeculorum. Amen [1].

§ 12.—Irish Fragments. Antiphonary of Bangor.

This relic of the ancient Church of Ireland [2] contains chiefly hymns and other portions of the day and night Hours, but it includes the following passages, the liturgical use and connection of which are evident or probable.

i. Ymnum quando commonicarent sacerdotes.

> Sancti venite [3], christi cor-
> pus sumite; sanctum
> bibentes quo re-
> dempti sanguine.

---

[1] This long prayer, though not found *verbatim* elsewhere, resembles in substance the private devotions for the priest frequently introduced into early Missals under the title of 'Apologia Sacerdotis' or 'Confessio Peccatoris.' Other examples, resembling the text in the enumeration of the parts of the human body by which sin has been committed, or in the multiplication of clauses commencing with the word 'Peccaui,' will be found in a 'Praeparatio ad Missam,' published by Gerbertus ex Cod. S. Blasian. saec. x (Lit. Aleman. i. 351); in the 'Missa Flacii Illyrici,' published by Martene (ordo iv. pp. 176-9); and in a tenth-century Tours Sacramentary (ordo vii. ib. p. 193).

[2] For its date, see List of Authorities. It has been printed nearly in extenso, and not very correctly, by Muratori in the fourth volume of his Anecdota Bibliothecae Ambrosianae, to the pages of which reference is made in the following foot-notes. The extracts have been grouped according to their subject-matter.

[3] Page 132. This hymn is printed in Daniel, H. A., Thes. Hymnol. i. 193. It is familiar to English readers from its translation in Hymns Ancient and Modern. The original arrangement of the quatrains has been retained here.

Salvati christi corpore
et sanguine, a quo
refecti laudes di-
camus deo.

Hoc sacro mento corporis et sanguinis omnes ex-
uti ab inferni
faucibus.

Dator salutis, christus
filius dei, mundum
saluauit per cru-
cem et sanguinem.

Pro uniuersis im mo-
latus dominus ipse sa-
cerdos existit
et hostia.

Lege praeceptum immolari hostias qua ad-
umbran-
tur diuina misteria.

Lucis indultor et
saluator omnium
praeclaram Sanctis
largitus est gratiam.

Accedunt omnes pu-
ra mente creduli,
sumant aeternam
salutis custodiam.

Sanctorum custos, rector
quoque dominus, uitae perennis largitur cre-
dentibus.

Caelestem panem dat
esurientibus,

de fonte
uiuo praebet sitientibus.

Λλϝα et ω,
ipse christus dominus
uenit,
uenturus iudicare homines.

ii. Ad pacem celebrandam.   See ch. ii. § 9.

iii. Incipit Symmulum.

CREDO in deum patrem omnipotentem inuisib[i]lem, omnium creaturarum uisibilium et inuisibilium conditorem.

Credo et in ihesum Christum, filium eius unicum dominum nostrum, deum omnipotentem, conceptum de spiritu sancto, natum de maria virgine, Passum sub pontio Pylato, qui crucifixus et sepultus descendit ad inferos, tertia die resurrexit a mortuis, ascendit in caelis, seditque ad dexteram dei patris omnipotentis, exinde uenturus iudicare uiuos ac mortuos.

Credo et in spiritum sanctum, deum omnipotentem, unam habentem substantiam cum patre et filio. sanctam esse aecclesiam catholicam, ab remisa peccatorum, sanctorum commonionem, carnis resurrectionem. credo uitam post mortem, et uitam aeternam in gloria Christi.

Haec omnia credo in Deum.   Amen[1].

Oratio diurna.   Pater noster, &c.

---

[1] Page 145. This Creed differs in its wording from all other forms which are known to exist. Its liturgical position immediately before the Lord's Prayer is that of the Mozarabic rite, regulated by can. ii. of the Third Council of Toledo, A.D. 589 : 'Sancta constituit synodus ut per omnes ecclesias Hispaniae vel Gallaeciae [= Gallia Narbonensis] secundum formam orientalium ecclesiarum, hoc est cl. episcoporum symbolum fidei recitetur, ut priusquam dominica dicatur oratio, voce clara a populo decantetur ; quo et fides vera manifestum testimonium habeat, et ad Christi corpus et sanguinem praelibandum pectora populorum fide purificata accedant.' Mansi, Concil. tom. ix. p. 993. Other early forms of the Creed are preserved in the Book of Deer, p. 166, and in the Stowe Missal, p. 231.

iv. Benedictio Puerorum[1].

Benedicite omnia opera domini, dominum; ymnum dicite, et superexaltate eum in saecula, &c.

Collectio post benedictionem puerorum.

Exaudi praeces nostras, omnipotens deus, et praesta ut sicut indecantato Imno beata puerorum instituta sectamur, Ita pro tuo munere peccatorum laqueys absoluti aeterni ignis non ambiamur incendiis, saluator mundi, qui cum patre uiuis[2].

Super benedictionem trium puerorum.

Sancte Domine, et gloriosae mirabilium uertutum effector, qui tribus pueris inter supplicia constitutis quartus adsistis, cui factum facilium est ignium temperare naturam, et uim quodammodo exusstantium coercere flammarum, ut inter incendia frigida ymnum tibi canentes cum magna uictoria exultarent, eandem nunc, domine, ad liberandos ac protegendos nos dona uirtutem, saluator mundi[3].

Post benedictionem trium puerorum.

Deus, qui pueris fide feruentibus fornacis flammam frigidam facis, et tribus inuictis, morte diuicta, quartus adsistes, praecamur nobis aestibus carnis talem uirtutem praestes adustis per te, Ihesu Christe[4].

Post Benedi[ci]te.

Deus, qui tres pueros de fornace eripuisti, sic nos eripias de supplicis inferni, qui regnas in saecula[5].

---

[1] Page 131. See ch. ii. § 13. For the use of the Benedicite in both the Gallican and Mozarabic Liturgies between the Lections, see Mis. Mozar. pp. 25, 523; Germani Expos. Brev. Lit. Gall., sub tit. De Hymno; Mabillon, Mus. It. i. 283,

[2] Page 150.

[3] Page 151.

[4] Page 152. Compare the collect 'Deus qui tribus pueris mitigasti,' which occurs in the present Roman Missal in the Gratiarum actio post Missam, and after the Canticle from Daniel on the four Ember Saturdays.

[5] Page 153.

Post ymnum trium puerorum.

Te enim, omnipotens deus, benedicimus iure, qui tres pueros liberasti ab igne nos quoque de supplicio mortis aeterne propter misericordiam tuam eripe, qui regnas[1].

Post Benedicite.

Ut tres pueros in flamma saluasti discensu in fornacem caelestis nuntii, sic nos per angelum magni consilii liberare digneris ab igne inferni, qui regnas[2].

Super benedictionem trium puerorum.

Tres ebrei uenerabiles numero, sacramento muniti, aetate teneri, sed fidei soliditate robusti, amore diuinae relegionis regis adorare imaginem contempserunt, utpute qui ipsum contempserant regem, qui ira sufflatus solito septies amplius caminum iusit incendi, ac pice et stuppa armatum citari in cendium aestuantibus globis. Erubescit quoque ipsum alienis ignibus coelum. Illo praecipitantur insontes, ibidemque te, propter quem praecipitantur inueniunt, Christe. Taliter nos ex tyranni intellectualis furore, et ab ingenito igni digneris liberare, saluator mundi, qui cum aeterno patre uiuis[3].

Incipiunt antefani super cantemus ei benedicite.

Tres pueri in camino missi sunt, et non timuerunt flammam ignis, dixerunt laudem domino nostro.

Tres pueri te orabant de medio ignis, ad te clamabant ex una uoce, ymnum dicebant.

Fornacis flammas pueri contempserunt, Christo iugiter immolauerunt, uiam iniquam diriliquerunt[4].

v. Ad commonicare[5].

Corpus domini accipimus, et sanguine eius potati sumus, ab omni malo non timebimus, quia dominus nobiscum est.

---

[1] Page 153. [2] Page 154. [3] Page 155. [4] Page 157.
[5] Page 158. These seven Communion formulae are written consecutively.

Item alia.

In labiis meis meditabor ymnum, alleluia; Cum docueris me ego iustitias respondebo, alleluia[1].

Item alia.

Gustate et uidete, alleluia, quam suauis est dominus, alleluia[2].

Item alia.

Hoc sacrum corpus domini, et saluatoris sanguinem sumite uobis in uitam perennem[3]. alleluia.

Item alia.

Quam dulcia faucibus meis eloquia tua, Domine[4].

Item alia.

Hic est panis uiuus qui de caelo descendit, alleluia. Qui manducat ex eo uiuet in aeternum, alleluia[5].

Item alia.

Refecti christi corpore et sanguine tibi semper, Domine, dicamus, alleluia[6].

vi. Collectio post Euangelium.

Exsultantes gaudio pro reddita nobis huius diei luce omnipotenti deo laudes gratiasque referamus, ipsius misericordiam obsecrantes, ut diem dominicae resurrectionis nobis sollempniter celebrantibus, pacem et tranquillitates, laetitiam praestare dignetur, ut a uigilia matutina usque ad noctem

---

[1] Ps. cxviii. 171. St. Gall. MS. 1394, p. 178; Stowe Missal, p. 243.

[2] Ps. xxxiii. 9. Stowe Missal, p. 243. See p. 267, n. 178.

[3] St. Gall. MS. 1394, p. 178; Stowe Missal, p. 243. The formula in the Drummond Missal (eleventh century) seems also to imply simultaneous communion in both kinds: 'Corpus et sanguis Domini nostri Jesu Christi maneat ad salutem et proficiat ad remedium in vitam eternam.'

[4] Ps. cxviii. 103.

[5] St. John vi. 59. St. Gall. MS. 1394, p. 177; Stowe Missal, p. 243.

[6] Book of Deer, p. 165; Book of Dimma, p. 171; Book of Mulling, p. 173; Stowe Missal, p. 225.

clementiae suae fauore protecti exultantes laetitia perpetua
gaudeamus, per dominum nostrum ihesum christum [1].

Post euangelium.

Dominicam nostrae resurrectionis initium uenerantes trini-
tati deo nostro debitas laudes, et grates unito refferamus
affectu obsecrantes misericordiam eius ut nobis domini et
saluatoris nostri beatae resurrectionis participium tam in
spiritu quam etiam in corpore concedat, qui cum patre
uiuit [2].

Post euangelium.

Resurgentem in hoc diluculo dominum dipraecamur ut et
nos in uitam aeternam resurgamus per omnia saecula saeculorum [3].

Post euangelium.

Canticis spiritalibus dilectati imnos, christe, consonantes
canimus tibi, quibus tua maiestas possit placari, oblata laudis
hostia spiritali, qui tecum uiuit [4].

Item post euangelium.

Deluculo lucis auctore resurgente exultemus in domino,
deuicta morte, quo peccata possimus semper obire, uitaeque
ambulemus in nouitate, qui tecum uiuit [5].

Ad uesperum et ad matutinam.

Gloria in excelsis deo, et in terra pax hominibus bonae
uoluntatis. Laudamus te, benedicimus te, adoramus te, glorificamus te, magnificamus te, gratias agimus tibi propter
magnam misericordiam tuam, domine rex caelestis, deus pater
omnipotens, domine filii unigenite iesu christe, sancte spiritus

---

[1] Page 150. No collect is found in any other than Irish Liturgies thus
entitled or placed. An example of its position and use survives in the Stowe
Missal, p. 231; Book of Hymns, p. 196. The present short and invariable
prayer used at the conclusion of the Gospel in the Roman rite, 'Per evangelica
dicta deleantur nostra delicta,' may be the petrified survival of once varying
collects.

[2] Page 152.   [3] Ib. 153.   [4] Ib. 153.   [5] Ib. 154.

dei, et omnes dicimus, amen, domine, filii dei patris, agne dei qui tollis peccatum mundi, miserere nobis, suscipe orationem nostram qui sedes ad dexteram dei patris, misserere nobis, quoniam tu solus sanctus, tu solus dominus, tu solus gloriosus cum spiritu sancto in gloria dei patris. amen [1].

§ 13. IRISH FRAGMENTS. BOOK OF HYMNS.

The MS. known as the 'Liber Hymnorum,' or Book of Hymns, now in the Library of Trinity College, Dublin (E. 4. 2), is a collection of Hymns, Canticles, and Collects once used in the Irish Church. It has been assigned to the ninth or tenth century, but its heavy even angular writing and the mediaeval character of some of its contents point to a date two or three centuries later. About one-half of it (fol. 1 a– 15 a) has been published by the Irish Archæological and Celtic Society, under the careful and competent editorship of Dr. J. H. Todd (vol. xvii). It is to be regretted that the work has never been completed. Among the devotions on the unpublished pages (ff. 20 b–34 b) are a lengthy 'Lamentatio Ambrosii episcopi Mediolaniae' (f. 20 a), to the recitation of which special virtue was attached, and a collection of 'ccclxii orationes quas beatus papa gregorius sparsim de toto psalterio, deo gubernante et adiuuante congregauit. Si deuota mente cantentur, uicem, ut fertur, omnium psalmorum, et sacrificii, et fidelis animarum commendationis continent.' But, although indulgenced with a sacrificial efficacy, neither these nor any of the devotions in the volume have a necessary eucharistic connection. It must therefore suffice here to exhibit a few sample forms of collects &c. which, at the most, are not necessarily non-eucharistic in their association.

Prayer of St. Mugint, tutor of St. Finnian, in the earlier part of the sixth century :—

---

[1] Page 159. Other early Irish versions of this hymn occur in the Book of Hymns, p. 196, where see note, and in the Stowe Missal, p. 227.

Fol. 4 a. 'Parce, Domine, parce populo tuo quem redemisti, Christe, sanguine tuo, et non in eternum irasceris
nobis[1].'

Fol. 4 b. 'Deprecamur te, domine, in omni misericordia tua
ut auferatur furor tuus et ira tua a ciuitate ista et de domu
sancta tua. Quoniam Peccauimus, Peccauimus tibi, domine, et
tu iratus es nobis, et non est qui effugiat manum tuam. Sed
supplicemus ut ueniat super nos misericordia tua, domine, qui
in ninuen pepercisti inuocantes dominum. Exclamemus ut
respicias populum tuum conculcatum et dolentem, et protegas
templum sanctum tuum ne ab impiis contaminetur, et mise-
rearis nimis afflictę ciuitati tuę. Exclamamus omnes ad
dominum dicentes.

'Peccauimus tibi, Domine, peccauimus, patientiam habe in
nobis, et erue nos a malis que quotidie crescunt super nos.
Dimitte, domine, peccato populi tui secundum multitudinem
misericordię tuę.

'Propitius fuisti patribus nostris, propitius esto nobis, et
implebitur gloria tua in uniuersa tua[2]. Recordare, domine,
dic angelo tuo percutienti populum tuum, Sufficit[3], contene
manum tuam, et cesset interfectio que grassatur in populo ut
non perdas animam uiuentem.

'Exurge, domine, adiuua nos et redime nos propter n[omen]
t[uum].'

To which is appended in a different handwriting :—

'Parce domine peccantibus, ignosce penitentibus, misere
nobis te rogantibus, saluator omnium christe, respice in nos
ihesu et miserere. Amen[4].'

---

[1] Corpus Mis. p. 211; Gerbert, Liturg. Aleman. ii. p. 34; Mart. i. pp.
321-323 ; Sarum Breviary, edit. 1879, p. 249.

[2] For 'terra.'   [3] 2 Sam. xvi. 24.

[4] These collects were evidently written for the use of some city or monastery
(civitas) in the time of an epidemic or of a hostile invasion. Their language is
inconsistent with the curious Irish legend of their origin as given in the
Vernacular Preface, f. 4 a, translated in Lib. Hym. p. 97. Compare the wording
of the collect in the Stowe Missal commencing 'Ante oculos tuos,' p. 230.

Collect written at the end of the Hymnus S. Colmani Mic
Ui Cluasaigh:—

Fol. 6 a. 'Orent pro nobis sancti illi in celis, quorum
memoriam facimus in terris, ut deleantur delicta nostra per
inuocationem sancti nominis tui, ihesu, et miserere qui regnas
in secula seculorum.'

Prayers written at the end of the Hymnus S. Hilarii in
laudem Christi:—

Fol. 8 a. 'Te decet ymnus, deus, in sion, et tibi reddetur
uotum in hierusalem [1].

'Canticis spiritualibus dilectati, ymnos, christe, consonantes
canimus tibi quibus tua, domine, maiestas possit placari
oblata deo laudis hostia spiritali, per te, christe ihesu, saluator [2].

'Unitas in trinitate te deprecor, domine, ut me semper
trahas totum tibi uotum uouere.'

Collects written after a copy of the Epistle of Christ to
Abgarus King of Edessa:—

Fol. 15 a. 'Domine, domine, defende nos a malis, et custodi
nos in bonis, ut simus filii tui, hic et in futuro: saluator
omnium, christe, respice in nos, ihesu, et miserere nobis.

'Euangelium domini nostri ihesu christi, liberet nos, protegat nos, custodiat nos, defendat nos, ab omni malo, ab
omni periculo, ab omni langore, ab omni dolore, ab omni
plaga, ab omni inuidia, ab omnibus insidiis diabuli et malo-
rum hominum hic et in futuro. amen [3].'

GLORIA IN EXCELSIS.

Fol. 9 a. 'Gloria in excelsis. Angeli dei cecinerunt primum
uersum huius ymni in nocte dominicae natiuitatis.

'Ic tur gabdur morro do ronsat .i. mile o hierusalem sair

---

[1] Ps. lxv. 2, 3. St. Gall MS. 1395, p. 180.
[2] Antiphonary of Bangor, p. 193.
[3] Ib. n. 1.

do faillsigud morro connid macc de in ti ro genair ann do ronsat he.   In ainisir octauin augusti do ronad.

'Ambrosius hautem fecit hunc ymnum a secundo uersu usque ad finem ymni[1].'

'Gloria in excelsis deo et in terra pax hominibus bonę uoluntatis.

'Laudamus te, benedicimus te, adoramus te, glorificamus te, magnificamus te.

'Gratias agimus tibi propter magnam miserecordiam tuam, domine, rex celestis, deus pater omnipotens.

'Domine, fili unigenite, ihesu christe, sancte spiritus dei, et omnes dicimus, amen.

'Domine, fili dei patris, agne dei, qui tollis peccata mundi, miserere nobis.

'Suscipe orationem nostram, qui sedes ad dexteram patris, miserere nobis, domine.

'Quoniam tu solus sanctus, tu solus dominus, tu solus gloriosus, cum spiritu sancto, in gloria dei patris. amen[2].'

---

[1] This Preface is translated, with notes, in the Liber Hymnorum, part ii. p. 177.   It occurs also in F. p. clvii, with a translation by Mr. Whitley Stokes.

[2] This Irish version of the Gloria in Excelsis, adapted from the Greek version (Bunsen, Analecta Ante-Nicaena, iii. 86), occurs again, in its liturgical position, in the Stowe Missal, p. 227. It is here followed by six antiphons from the Psalms, which indicate that it was used in the night Offices of the early Irish Church. The rubric preceding it in the Antiphon. Benchor. directs its use 'at vespers and matins;' p. 193.

§ 14. IRISH FRAGMENTS.

THE STOWE MISSAL.

Little is known about the history of the MS. which bears this name, and which is the earliest surviving Missal of the Irish Church [1].

The inscriptions on its cumhdach, a metal-work cover of eleventh-century workmanship, indicate that it originally belonged to some church in Munster, that church being possibly the monastery founded by St. Ruadhan at Lothra in the barony of Lower Ormond and County of Tipperary, where he died as its first abbot and patron [2] A.D. 584. The monastic character of the service book is also evidenced by the insertion of the words 'et abbate nostro' in the clause of the canon 'Te igitur' &c. (p. 234) and by the long lists of monastic Irish saints enumerated on pp. 238, 240. Pos-

---

[1] Transactions of the Royal Irish Academy, vol. xxiii. ad finem. See also O'Conor's Rerum Hibernicarum Scriptores, vol. ii. ad finem, and Bibliotheca MS. Stowensis, vol. i. App. Dr. O'Conor's description is full of inaccuracies. The absence of any allusion to the mixed chalice is accounted for because that ceremony is only of human institution (p. 46). Natalis Calicis is translated 'Lent' (p. 47). The antiquity of the Creed is deduced from the absence of the article of 'The descent into hell' (p. 45), as if that clause had ever formed part of the Nicene Creed. The contraction 'scōrum' for sanctorum is lengthened into 'Scotorum' (p. 48). The musical notes, of which he gives a long description (p. 43), are the creation of his own imagination, and do not exist in the original MS.

[2] Hardly anything is known about St. Ruadhan. He is included in the list of Saints on p. 238, but the name is written without any change in the size of letters, or exceptional ornamentation. His life is published by the Bollandists (Acta SS. Ap. 15, p. 382), from a twelfth-century MS., a long tissue of such ludicrous and improbable miracles that the compilers confess in their Preface to having suppressed part of it, for fear of exciting ridicule. His abbey at Lothra was destroyed by the Danes A.D. 843 (Annal. IV. Magistr. sub anno), when this volume, if written before that date, must have been saved.

sibly the presence of two collects, headed 'Oratio in sollemnitatibus Petri et Christi' (p. 227) and 'Oratio prima Petri'
(p. 228), may point to the monastery having been dedicated
to St. Peter.   At an early date, probably in the twelfth
century, it left Ireland, perhaps transferred to the Continent
by some of those Irishmen who carried donations from
Tordelbach O'Brian, king of Munster, to the monastery of
Ratisbon A.D. 1130.   It was discovered abroad in the
eighteenth century by John Grace, Esq., of Nenagh in Ireland,
an officer in the German service, who died without leaving
any memorandum respecting the monastery or library where
it was found.   From his hands it passed into those of the
Duke of Buckingham, where it remained until the sale of
the Stowe Library (1849), when it was bought by the Earl
of Ashburnham, in whose library at Ashburnham Place it is
now preserved.

The present contents of the volume are arranged as follows:—

Fol. 1 a–12 b. St. John's Gospel, written at a very early
date by a scribe who at its conclusion appends his name in
Ogham characters.

Fol. 13 a–37 a. Ordinary and Canon of the Mass, with the
colophon 'moel caich scripsit.'

Fol. 37 a–40 b. Misa apostolorum, et martirum, et sanctorum, et sanctarum uirginum.

Fol. 40 b–43 b. Misa pro penitentibus uiuis.

Fol. 43 b–45 a. Misa pro mortuis pluribus.

Fol. 45 b–64 a. Ordo babtismi.

Fol. 64 b–66 b. An old-Irish treatise on the Eucharist,
followed by three old-Irish charms.

The Sacramental portion of the volume, with which alone
we are here concerned, is in various handwritings, the oldest of
which cannot, on liturgical grounds, be assigned to an earlier
period than the ninth century, though several of the features
enumerated on pp. 201–203, taken singly, seem to point to a
still earlier, and others to a still later date.

Palæographical evidence does not appear to be inconsistent

with such a conclusion so far as it has been possible to compare the text of the Stowe Missal with such Irish or Hiberno-Latin MSS. as have been found accessible either in the original, or in the facsimiles presented in the pages of the National MSS. of Ireland, and the publications of the Palæographical Society.

The following facts make it impossible to accept Dr. Todd's hasty assignation of the earlier portion of the Missal to the sixth century [1], and in part suggest a date not earlier than the ninth century:—

(*a*) The use and position of the Nicene Creed; p. 236. n. 35.

(*b*) The presence of the Agnus Dei; p. 266. n. 156.

(*c*) The structural completeness of the Ordinarium Missae.

(*d*) The presence of the words 'diesque nostros in tua pace disponas, atque ab aeterna damnatione nos eripias, et in electorum tuorum jubeas grege numerari' (p. 236), which are known to have been added to the Canon by Gregory the Great (590–604) [2], and which prove that we have not here a pure Gelasian text (p. 232).

(*e*) The date of several of the saints who are commemorated in the list commencing on f. 31 a, including Laurence, Mellitus, and Justus, Archbishops of Canterbury, the latter of whom died in A. D. 627; p. 263. n. 113. The list of saints on fol. 29 is written in the later hand on an interpolated leaf, and need not here be taken into account.

The following parts of the Missal are written in the older and larger handwriting, of which a sample is presented in the frontispiece:—f. 13 a, from the first Peccavimus; f. 13 b; f. 14 a, from 'Rogo . . ad finem;' f. 14 b, 'ascendat . . rex caelestis;' f. 15 a, except the collect 'Deus qui diligentibus,' &c.; f. 15 b, except the collect 'Deus qui nos,' &c.; ff. 16 a, b, 17 a; f. 17 b, to 'aceptos per dominum;' f. 19 a, b; f. 20 a, to 'emunda

---

[1] Transactions of R. I. A., Appendix, p. 16. Dr. Todd saw the volume under disadvantageous limitations of time and action.

[2] Bede, H. E., lib. ii. cap. 1.

per dominum;' f. 25 b, from 'Et memoriam;' f. 26 a, b;
f. 27 a, except from 'in mei memoriam;' f. 27 b, from 'unde
et memores;' f. 28 ab; ff. 31 ab, 32 ab, 33 a; f. 33 b, to
'peccatorum nostrorum;' ff. 36 b–45 a; ff. 46 a–64 a.

Of the above, f. 28 ab, ff. 31 a–33 b, ff. 57 a–64 a are written
in a darker ink and a more cursive and flourishing handwriting than the rest, which seems to denote a change of
scribe but not any material change of date. A similar change
of style is noticeable in other Celtic MSS., as in the Book
of Kells (Palæogr. Soc. Publications, Plate 88, last line),
the Codex S. Dunstani (Bodl. Lib. Auct. F. iv. 32, f. 46 b),
and the diamond-shaped centre on f. 103 a in the Book of
Armagh, and especially in the 'Argumentum pilagii in aepi-
stulam ad Romanos' on f. 107 b of that MS.

The excepted pages and portions of pages in the above
list[1] are written in a smaller and later minuscule hand (that of
Moel Caich, f. 36 a), depending from single ruled lines, the
older text having been in some places erased to make way for
it. The headings of Missæ and Collects, all the Irish and
Latin Rubrics, are in various and later handwritings, except
the Rubrics in the Ordo Baptismi, which are coaeval with
the text.

The collects 'Deus qui nos,' &c. on f. 15 b, and 'Quaesumus
Domine' on f. 18 b, have been added at a still later period.

In spite of these variations of handwriting there seems
little reason to doubt that the whole Ordo Missæ, as it now
stands, was in use in some Church in Ireland in the tenth,
and the older portion of it perhaps in the ninth century.

Though written in Ireland and by Irish scribes, it contains
petitions 'pro piissimis imperatoribus et omni Romano
exercitu' (p. 229), 'pro imperio Romano' (p. 235), and the

---

[1] Viz., f. 14 a, Profeta—caelis per dominum; 14 b, deus pater—amen; 15 a,
Deus qui diligentibus—per dominum; 15 b, Deus qui nos – nostrum; 17 b,
from Ante oculos; 18 ab; 20 a, from Hostias; 20 b; 21 ab; 22 ab; 23 ab;
24 a b; 25 a; 25 b, to discendit; 27 a, from in mei memoriam; 27 b, to de
caelis; 29 ab; 30 ab; 33 b, from fiat; 34 ab; 35 ab; 36 a; 45 b.

heading 'Orationes et Preces Ecclesiae Romanae' (p. 228). The canon is headed, 'Canon dominicus papae Gilasi' (p. 234). Internal evidence of the truthfulness of this description is borne out by an examination of the text, and by the presence of such distinctly Gelasian peculiarities as the omission of the words 'Deum de Deo' from the Creed, and of the clauses 'Dominus vobiscum,' 'Et cum spiritu tuo' before the Sursum corda. The interest of the MS. partly lies in its containing one of the earliest known copies of the Gelasian text, partly in its being interspersed with fragments of an ancient Celtic Liturgy which have either not been preserved elsewhere, or have been only recently discovered in the pages of other early Irish MSS. printed in this chapter.

Among its many liturgical peculiarities and indications of an early date, the following seem to deserve special and separate mention :—

1. The Litany at the commencement of the Ordo Missæ (p. 226).

2. The unique position of another ancient Missal Litany, entitled 'Deprecatio Sancti Martini,' between the Epistle and the Gospel (p. 229).

3. The presence of vernacular rubrics (pp. 210, 216, 230, 232, 233, 234, 241).

4. The long lists of early saints, chiefly Irish, inserted in the text of the canon.

5. The absence of any special 'Proprium Sanctorum,' and the simple provision of a single Missa Commnis Sanctorum (p. 244) for all commemorations of saints, which, together with a single Mass for Penitents (p. 246) and another for the Dead (p. 247), make up the smallest known volume which ever passed under the title of a Missal.

6. The absence of the 'Filioque' from the Nicene Creed (p. 232. See frontispiece).

7. The fixed use of an unchanging Epistle and Gospel (pp. 228, 231).

8. The interpolation of various forms of private devotion

for the priest in the shape of an Apologia or Confessio Sacerdotis (pp. 226, 227, 230, 239).

9. The enumeration of only three orders, Bishops, Priests, and Deacons, all notice of the minor orders being omitted (pp. 229, 233, 235).

10. The general paucity of rubrics, together with the absence of any allusion to the mixed chalice or to the use of incense, &c.

11. The absence from the text of the canon of the tenth-century additional clause, 'pro quibus tibi offerimus vel' (p. 234).

12. The paucity of crosses, only five being marked for use as against thirty-one in the present Roman Canon, and none occurring at the words of institution.

13. The presence of early and rare liturgical terms, e. g. senior, augmentum, stella, kalendae, natalis calicis, quinquagensima, sacrificium spirituale, anathleticus gradus, liber vitae.

14. Singular usages, e. g. the position of the fraction of the Host before the Pater Noster (p. 244), the crossing of the child's hand and the washing of the feet in Baptism (pp. 217–8).

15. The petition that the founder of the church and all the people may be converted from idolatry (p. 236).

There is a general resemblance in this Irish Mass to the ninth- or tenth-century Ordo Missae which was first published by M. Flacius Illyricus A.D. 1557 under the title of 'Missa Latina quae olim ante Romanam in usu fuit,' and which was afterwards printed by Martene[1]. Certain prayers and phrases (p. 249, notes 3, 7, 28, 46) are common to both, but there the resemblance ends. The text, especially in the 'Gloria in Excelsis' and the 'Nicene Creed,' is very dissimilar, and there is no ground for supposing that there

---

[1] Lib. i. c. 4. art. 12. ordo 4, i. p. 176, where the name is misprinted as Flaccus.

can be any original connection, or anything more than an accidental resemblance, between the two.

The Stowe Missal affords no certain proof, but throws some light on the question as to what was the earliest form of Liturgy in use in the Hiberno-Celtic Church. It proves that the Roman Canon was introduced into at least partial use in Ireland as early as the ninth century, while it retains certain portions of an earlier and a different Liturgy interwoven with it. The admixture of passages from the Ambrosian, Gallican, and Mozarabic rites with the Roman Canon is suggestive of a period when the diversity had not ceased to exist which is alluded to in Tirechan's sketch of the ancient Irish Church, when Irish saints ' diversas regulas et missas habebant, et diversam tonsuram[1].'

The following ' Ordo Baptismi,' where it agrees with the Roman rite, follows the text of the Gelasian Sacramentary, but it does not altogether resemble the Gelasian or any other extant Ordo Baptismi, and is remarkable partly for its great length, partly for the differences which it exhibits both in text and ritual from every other known rite. It is important and interesting as presenting a hitherto unpublished MS. text of the earliest surviving Baptismal Office known to have been used in any part of the Church of these islands.

It consists of four clearly marked divisions :—

I. Ordo ad Catechumenum faciendum.

II. Consecratio Fontis.

III. Ordo Baptismi.

IV. Ordo Communionis nuper Baptizatorum.

I. The ordinary rites in use at the admission of catechumens, and which were repeated at the seven ' scrutinia catechumenorum' held during Lent, with however great local variety of usage[2], were :—

---

[1] Quoted in full on p. 81.   [2] Mart. lib. i. cap. i. art. vi. i.

1. The sign of the cross upon the forehead.
2. The imposition of hands with prayer.
3. Exorcism.
4. Insufflation (Exsufflatio).
5. Touching the nose and ears with saliva.
6. Unction of the breast and shoulders.

Of these rites, 3, 4, and 6 are found in the Stowe Rite, while there is no mention of 1, 2, and 5 [1].

In addition to these points, there is here the blessing of salt, and its imposition in the mouth of the catechumen, (as in the Gelasian Sacramentary [2], and in the present Roman Ordines Baptismi, though with a different arrangement of words, p. 210), and a twofold application of the threefold questions of renunciation, separated by the threefold questions as to the candidate's faith (p. 209), an arrangement which does not appear to be found elsewhere.

II. The Benedictio or Consecratio Fontis opens with verses drawn from Psalms xli, xxviii, whereas the present Roman tract and verses sung during the procession to the font are drawn from the former Psalm only (xli. 1, 2, 3). Then follows the lengthy Roman form of consecration substantially as found in the Gelasian Sacramentary, and as laid down for use in the present Roman Missal on Easter Eve. An older and shorter Benedictio aquae, consisting of two collects drawn, one from a Petrine, the other from an Ephesine source, are curiously placed, as if by way of appendix, at the conclusion of the Baptismal Office (Benedic Domine, &c. fol. 58 b, Exorcizo te spiritus immunde, &c. fol. 59 a).

III. The rite of baptism, differing both in language and ritual from any extant Ordo Baptismi, and especially remarkable for the presence of the 'Pedilavium' and the ceremonial crossing of the right hand of the candidate, and for the omission of the verbal formula of Baptism and of the presentation of the lighted taper (pp. 216, 217).

---

[1] See Introd. p. 65.			[2] Lib. i. ordo xxxi. p. 534.

IV. The Communion of the newly-baptized in both kinds conjointly, with thanksgiving collect and antiphons (p. 218).

Then follow various short offices :—

1. Ad Visitandum Infirmum (p. 220).
2. De Sacramento Extremae Unctionis (p. 223).
3. Ad Communicandum Infirmum (Ib.)

It is hardly consistent with technical accuracy to print this ' Ordo Baptismi' under the heading of ' Reliquiae Liturgicae,' but a Eucharistic character is given to it by its retention of the custom, now obsolete in Western Christendom, of the immediate communion of the newly-baptized, and by there being appended to it offices for the Visitation, Unction, and Communion of the Sick, bearing a close resemblance, both verbal and substantial, to the similar Celtic offices surviving in the Books of Deer, Dimma, and Mulling.

INCIPIT ORDO BAPTISMI.

Fol. 45 b. Deus, qui adam de limo terrae fecisti, et ille in paradiso peccauit, et illum peccatum mortis non reputasti, sed per per sanguinem unigeniti tui recuperare digneris et in sanctam hirusalem glorientem reducis. Ergo, maledicte, recognosce sententiam tuam, et da honorem domino et recede ab hoc famulo dei quia hunc (hanc) deus et dominus noster ad suam sanctam gratiam atque missericordiam babtismi uocare dignatus est, per hoc signum crucis quod tu, diabule, nunquam adetis designare, per dominum nostrum.

Fol. 46 a.　　　Ordo babtismi.

Domine[1], sancte pater, omnipotens aeterne deus, expelle diabulum et gentilitatem[2] ab homine isto, de capite, de cappillis, de uertice, de cerebro, de fronte, de oculis, de auribus, de naribus, de ore, de lingua, de sublingua, de gutore, de faucibus, de collo, de pectore, de corde, de corpore toto, intus, de foris, de manibus, de pedibus, de omnibus memris, de copaginibus memrorum eius, et de cogitationibus, de uerbis, de operibus, et omnibus conuersationibus híc et futuro per te, ihesu christe, qui reg[nas].

Fol. 46 b. Deus[3], qui ad salutem humani generis maxima queque sacramenta in aquarum substantia condidisti, adesto propitius inuocationibus nostris, et alimento huic multimodi purificationis tuae benedictiones infunde, ut creatum misterii

---

[1] This collect is found among the 'Orationes contra Daemoniacum' in a tenth-century codex in the library at Vienna, published by Gerbertus, Mon. Vet. Lit. Aleman. ii. p. 132. A still more exhaustive enumeration of the parts of the body is found in other collects of this date; Ib. pp. 131, 136; Leofric Missal, fol. 312 a.

[2] This and similar expressions still found in the Roman Baptismal Offices point to a date when the candidate for Baptism was generally a convert from heathenism.

[3] Sacram. Gelas. p. 738; Gregor. p. 264; Rit. Rom. p. 288, Ordo ad faciendam aquam benedictam, with variations. This collect is repeated in extenso on p. 211, and in St. Gall. MS. No. 1395, p. 184.

seruiens ad abieciendos demones morbosque expellendos diuinae gratiae tuae sumat effectus, ut qui quid locu[m] in
domibus fidelium hec un[d]a resperserit, careat immunditia,
liberetur a noxia, non illic residiat spiritus pestilens, non aura
corrumpens, abscedant omnes insidiae latentis inimici, et si
Fol. 47 a.   quid est quod incolomitate habitantium inuidit aut
quieti, aspersione aquae huius effugiat, ut salubritas per inuocationem nominis expetita ab omni sit impugnatione deffensa,
per dominum nostrum.

Consecratio salis incipit.

Deus, qui ad salutem hominis medicinam per hunc salubrem
salem, presta ut de errore gentilitatis anima illius conuertatur,
et eripiatur, et trinum deum confiteatur, et diabulum repellat
per abrenuntiationem, signumque crucis domini nostri ihesu
christi, qui regnat cum patre et spiritu sancto in in saecula
saeculorum.

Item alia oratio[1].

Exorcizo té creatura salis, in nomine dei patris omnipo-
tentis, et in caritate domini nostri ihesu christi, et in uirtute
Fol. 47 b.   spiritus sancti.   Exorcizo te per deum uiuum, per
deum uerum, qui te ad tutellam generis humani procreauit,
et populo uenienti ad credulitatem per suos seruos conse-
creaisti precipit.   Proinde rog(a)mus té, domine deus noster,
ut hec creatura salis IN nomine trinitatis efficiatur salutare
sacramentum ad effugandum inimicum, quod tu domine sanc-
tificando sanctificis, benedicendo benedices, ut fiat omnibus
accipientibus perfecta medicina permanens in uisceribus eorum,
in nomine domini nostri ihesu christi, qui uenturus est iudicare
uiuos et mortuos et saeculum per ignem[2].

---

[1] Rit. Rom. p. 24. Where this 'Benedictio salis' differs from that provided
in the present R. Ordo Baptismi parvulorum, it follows the readings of the
form given in the Gelasian Sacramentary, lib. i. No. xxxi. p. 534.

[2] Here follows in the Gelas. Sacram. the rubrical direction, substantially
preserved in the present Rit. Rom., '*Et post hanc orationem pones sal in ore
infantis et dices. Accipe illi* sal sapientiae propitiatus in vitam aeternam.'

Fol. 48 a. *De abrenuntiatione*[1].

Abrenuntias satanae ?   *Res.* Abrenuntio.
Et omnibus operibus eius ?   *Res.* Abrenuntio.
Et omnibus pompis eius ?   *Res.* Abrenuntio.

De confessione incipit.

Credis in deum patrem omnipotentem ?   *Respon.* Credo.
Credis et in ihesum christum ?   *Respon.* Credo.
Credis et in spiritum sanctum ?   *Respon.* Credo.

Exsufflas et tanges eum. Deinde tanges pectus dorsum de oleo et crismate, dicens[2].

Ungo té de oleo sanctificato, in nomine patris, et filii, et spiritus sancti.

Abrenuntias satanae ?   *Res.* Abrenuntio.
Et omnibus operibus eius ?   *Res.* Abrenuntio.
Et omnibus pompis eius ?   *Res.* Abrenuntio.

Fol. 48 b. Rogamus té, domine sancte pater, omnipotens aeterne deus, misserre famulo tuo .N. quem uocare ad rudimenta fidei dignatús es ; caecitatem cordis omnem ab eo expellens disrumpe omnes laqueos satanae quibus fuerat colligatus; aperii ei ianuam ueritatis tuae, + ut signo sapientiae tuae indutus omnibus cupiditatem fetoribus careat, atque suaui odore preceptorum tuorum laetus tibi in aeclesia deseruiat, et proficiat de die in diem, ut idoneus efficiatur promisae gratiae tuae, in nomine patris, et filii, et spiritus sancti, in saecula saeculorum.

Fol. 49 a. Medellam[3] tuam deprecor, domine sancte pater

---

[1] These three questions occur in the Gelas. Sacram. in the Redditio Symboli (Catechumenorum) in Sabb. Sancto (Ordo xlii. p. 563), but they are not repeated twice as here, and the three questions ' Credis' &c. are postponed till immediately before the act of baptism (Ib., Ordo xliv. p. 570). The renunciation in every Roman Office from the Gelas. Sacram. onwards is triple as here ; in the Milanese rite it was double, and in the Gallican single.

[2] In the Gelas. Sacram. the rubric runs thus : ' Postea vero tangis ei pectus et inter scapulas de oleo exorcizato' (Ordo xlii. p. 563). See Introd. p. 66.

[3] This collect, with very considerable variations, appears in the Baptismal Office in an ancient Limoges Ritual, published by Martene, de Ant. Ec. Rit. lib. i. c. i. art. xviii. ordo 18, and in a tenth-century German Ordo (Cod. Theol.

omnipotens aeterne deus, qui subuenis in periculis, qui temperas flagillas, té, domine, supplices exoramus ut uisitatione tua sancta erigas famulum tuum .N. de hac ualitudine temtationem. Sicut in iob terminum pone, ne inimicus de anima ista sine redemtione babtismatis incipiat triumpare. Defer, domine, exitum mortis et spatium uitae distende. Reuela quem perducas ad babtismi sacramentum, nec redemptione tuae inferas damnum. Tolle occasionem diabulo triumphandi, **Fol. 49 b.** et reserua quem triumphis compares esse christi, ut sanus tibi in aeclesia tua gratia babtismatis renascatur, facturus cuncta quae petimus, per dominum.

Nec te lateat, satanas imminere tibi poenas, immine tibi gehinam, diem iudici, diem suplícii sempiterni, diem qui uenturus est uelud clibanus ignis ardens, in quo tibi adque angelis tuis sempiternus praeparatus est interitus ; et ideo pro tua nequitia, dampnate atque damnande, da honorem deo **Fol. 50 a.** uiuo, da honorem ihesu christo, da honorem spiritu sancto paracleto, in cuius uirtute precipio tibi, quicumque es immundus spiritus, ut exeas et recedas ab his famulis dei, et eos deo suo reddas, quos dominus deus noster ihesus christus ad suam gratiam et benedictionem uocare dignatus est, ut fiat eius templum aquam regenerationis in remisionem omnium peccatorum, in nomine nostri domini ihesu christi, qui iudicaturus est iudicare uiuos et mortuos et saeculum per ignem [1].

Isund doberar insalann imbelu indlelacti [2].

Effeta, quod est apertio, effeta est hostia in honorem suauitatis, in nomine dei patris, et filii, et spiritus sancti [3].

---

685 ; Bibl. Caes. Vind.) published by Gerbert, Liturg. Aleman. vol. ii. p. 10. col. 1. In the Sacramentarium Augiense (Ib. Cod. Colbertin. No. 1927 ; Mart. i. p. 71), and in the Sacram. Gregor. p. 263, it is entitled, as its contents indicate it to be, Oratio ad baptizandum infirmum.

[1] R. Ordo Bapt. Adult., with verbal variations.

[2] Anglice, ' Here salt is put into the mouth of the child.'

[3] In the present Roman Offices for Baptism, both of infants and adults, this formula, which is placed in the later and more strictly baptismal portion of the service, runs thus : ' Eppheta, *quod est*, Adaperire in odorem suavitatis. Tu autem effugare, diabole, appropinquabit enim judicium Dei.' It is used, not as here at the imposition of salt, but while the priest is touching the ears and

Domine[1] sancte, pater omnipotens, aeternae deus, qui es, et
Fol. 50 b. qui eras, et qui uenturus es, et permanens usque in
finem, cuius origo nescitur, nec finis comprehendi potest; te,
domine, supplicis inuocamus super hunc famulum tuum .N.
quem liberasti de errore gentilium et conuersatione turpissima;
dignare exaudire eum qui tibi ceruices suas humiliat, perueniat
ad babtismatis fontem, ut ut renouatus ex aqua et spiritu
sancto, expoliatus ueterem hominem, induatur nouum qui
sécundum té creatus est, accipiat uestem incorruptam et
immaculatam tibi qui domino nostro seruire mereatur, in
Fol. 51 a. nomine domini nostri ihesu christi, qui uenturus est
iudicare uiuos et mortuos et saeculum per ignem.

Deus[2], qui ad salutem humani generis maxima in aquarum
substantia quecumque sacramenta in aquarum substantia
condidisti, adesto propitius inuocationibus nostris, et elimento
huic multimodo purificationis tuae effunde benedictionis, ut
creatura misterii seruiens et abiecendos demones morbosque
expellendos diuinae gratiae tuae sumat effectus, ut quicquid
loqui[3] in domibus fidelium hec unda resparserit, cariat immunditia, liberetur a noxia; non illic resideat spiritus pestilens,
Fol. 51 b. non aura corrumpens, abscedant omnes insidiae
latentes inimici; et si quid est quod incolimitate habitantium
inuidit aut queti, asparsione aque huius effugiat, ut salubritas
per inuocationem tui nominis expetita ab omni sit impugnatione deffensa. per.

Exaudi[4] nos, domine deus, pater omnipotens, aeternae deus,

---

nose of the candidate with saliva; in the Gelas. Sacram. at the Catechismus
Infantium in Sabbato Sancto (Ordo xlii. p. 563). The curious but intelligible
reading of the text occurs in the Sacram. Gallican. (Mab. edit. p. 324): 'Effeta,
effecta est hostia in odorem suauitatis.'

[1] Rit. Rom. Ordo Bapt. Adult., with variations.

[2] Rit. Rom. Ordo ad faciendam aquam benedictam; with variations. This
collect has been previously given *in extenso* on p. 207, q. v. for further references.

[3] c and qu are sometimes interchanged by early Irish scribes. See Corpus
Missal., Introd. p. 34. So 'scaloribus' is read infra, p. 215; 'corum' p. 241.

[4] This collect occurs in the 'Benedictio domorum facienda cum aspersione
aquae benedictae' in the Rit. Rom. p. 300; Sacram. Gregor. p. 227; Gelas.
p. 759; in the 'Benedictio Salis et Aquae' in the Sarum Brev. [Cambridge

et mitire dignare angelum tuum sanctum de caelís, qui custodiat, subeat, protegat, uisitat, et defendat omnes inhabitantes in hoc habitaculo famuli tui illuc.

Huc usque catacominus. Incipit oleari oleo et crismate in pectus et item scabulas antequam babtizaretur[1]. *Deinde letania* cir[ca] *fontem canitur. Deinde benedictio fontis. Dcinde ii. psalmi;* Sitiuit anima mea[2] *usque* uiuum.

Quemadmodum uox domini super aquas multas[3].

Adferte[4].

Exorcizo[5] té, creatura aquae, per dominum uiuum, per dominum sanctum qui te in principio uerbo separauit ab

FOL. 52 a. arida, cuius spiritus super té ferebatur, qui té de paradiso emanere et in .iiii. fluminibus totam terram rigari precipit, qui té de petra produxit, [6]ut populum quem ex egypto liberauerat siti fatigatum rigaret, qui te amarissimam per lignum indulcauit[6].

Exorcyzo[7] té et per ihesum christum filium eius[8], qui té in c(h)annan galiliae signo ammirabile sua potentia conuertit in uinum, qui pedibus superambulauit, et ab ionne in iordane in te babtizatus est, qui te una cum sanguine de latero suo produxit, et discipulís súis precipit dicens ; ite, docete, docete omnes gentes, babtitzantes eas in nomine patris, et filii, et spiritus sancti.

FOL. 52 b. Tibi[9] igitur precipio omnis spiritus immunde, + omne fantasma, omne mendacium, eradicare, effugare ab hac creatura aquae ut discensurus in ea sit ei fons aquae sallientis

---

reprint, 1879, p. 354], and in the Office of Extreme Unction in the Rit. Rom. p. 130.

  [1] For the Unctions prescribed in this Office, see Introd. p. 66.

  [2] Ps. xli. 2.   [3] Ps. xxviii. 3.

  [4] Ps. xxviii. 1. The R. Tract and vv. are from Ps. xli. 1, 2, 3.

  [5] R. Benedico, from the Benedictio Fontis in Sabbato Sancto in Mis. Rom. p. 199; Sacram. Gel. p. 568 ; see Corpus Missal, fol. 201 a, with considerable variations. This and the following paragraph are transposed from their present R. position, where they come after 'consequantur' (on p. 214.)

  [6–6] R. om.   [7] R. Benedico.   [8] R. + unicum.

  [9] This and the following paragraph are strangely placed here. The R. Benedictio Fontis proceeds with the clause 'Haec nobis praecepta,' &c., as on p. 215.

in uitam aeternam.　Efficae ergo, aqua sancta [a]qua benedicta, ad regenerandos filios deo patri omnipotenti, in nomine domini nostri ihesu christi, qui uenturus est in spiritu sancto iudicare seculum per ignem.

Exorcizo té, creatura aquae, in nomine dei patris omni- potentis, et in nomine domini nostri ihesu christi filii eius, et spiritus sancti, omnis uirtus aduersarii, omnis incursus dia- Fol. 53 a.　buli, omne fantasma eradicare et effugare ab hac creatura aquae, ut sit fons sallientes in uitam aeternam, ut cum babtizatus fuerit fiat templum dei uiui in remisionem peccatorum, per dominum nostrum ihesum christum, qui uenturus est iudicare saeculum per ignem[1].

Omnipotens sempiternae deus[2], adesto magnae pietatis tuae misterís ; adesto sacramentís, et ad creandos[3] nouos populos Fol. 53 b.　quos tibi fons babtismatis parturit ; spiritum adop- tionis emitte ut quod humilitatis nostrae gerendum est ministerio tuae uirtutes compleatur effectu.　per.

Deus[4], qui inuisibili potentia sacramentorum tuorum mira- biliter operaris effectu, et licet nos tantís misterís adsequandi sumus indigni, tú tamen gratiae tuae dona non deferens, etiam ad nostras preces aures tuae pietatis inclina, per dominum nostrum deum.

Deus[5], cuius spiritus, super aquas inter ipsa mundi pri- mordia fereabatur, ut etiam tunc uirtutem sanctificationis aquarum natura conciperet.

Deus[6], qui innocentes mundi cremina per [a]quas abluens Fol. 54 a.　regenerationis speciem in ipsa diluii effussione sig-

---

[1] This form of ' Exorcismus aquae' occurs in a tenth-century German Ordo Baptismi, printed by Gerbert, Lit. Aleman. vol. ii. p. 10 ; and in part in St. Gall MS. No. 1395, p. 184.　There is a collect resembling this one, but not identical with it, although opening with the same words, in the Ordo ad faci- endam aquam benedictam. Rit. Rom. p. 287.

[2] Mis. Rom. p. 191, Benedictio fontis in Sabbato Sancto, with verbal variations ; Corpus Missal, p. 199 ; Sacram. Gelas. p. 568 ; Gregor. p. 63.

From this point down to the unction immediately following the act of baptism the readings of the Gelasian Sacramentary are closely followed.

[3] So Gel. ; recreandos Rit. Rom.　　　[4] Ib. Part of the Proper Preface.

[5] Ib.　　　　　　　　　　　　　　　　[6] Ib.

nasti, ut unius eiusdemque elementi ministerio, et finis esset
uitís et origo uirtutibus, respice in faciem aeclesiae tuae, et
multiplica in ea generationes tuas, qui gratiae affluentes im-
petu laetificas ciuitatem tuam, fontemque babtismatis aperis
toto orbe terrarum gentibus innouandís, ut tuae maiestatis
imperio sumat unigeniti tui gratiam de spiritu sancto, qui
hanc aquam regenerandís hominibus preparatam arcana sui
luminis[1] ammixtione fecundet, ut, sanctificatione concepta,
ab immaculato diuini fontes utero in nouam renouatam crea-
Fol. 54 b.　turam progenies coelestis emergat ; et quos aut
sexus in corpore, aut aetas discernit in tempore, omnes in una
pariat gratiam atque infantiam. Procul ergo hinc, iubente
té, domine, omnis spiritus immundus abscedat. Procul tota
nequitia diabuliticae fraudis absistat. Nihil hic loci habeat
contrariae uirtutis ammixtio, non insidiando circumuolet, non
latendo subripiat, non inficiendo corrumpat. Sit hec sancta
et innocens creatura libera ab omni impugnationis incursu, et
totius nequitiae purgata discessu. Sit fons uiuus, regenerans
Fol. 55 a.　aqua, unda purificans, ut omnes hoc lauacro salu-
tifero diluendi, operante in éis spiritu sancto, perfectae purificationis indulgentiam consequantur. per[2].

Unde benedico[3] té, creaturae aquae, per deum uiuum, per
deum sanctum, qui te in principio uerbo separauit ab arida[4] et
in quatuor fluminibus totam terram rigari precipit, qui té in
deserto amaram suauitate indita fecit esse potabilem, et siti-
Fol. 55 b.　enti populo de petra produxit. Benedico te et
per ihesum christum filium eius unicum, dominum nostrum ;
qui te in channan galileae signo ammirabili sua potentia
conuertit in uinum ; [5]qui pedibus super té ambulauit, et ab

---

[1] R. numinis.

[2] For the rubrics inserted here in the later Irish rite, see Corpus Missal,
p. 200.

[3] Ib. This and the following paragraph have already occurred once on
p. 212, ' exorcizo ' being there substituted for ' benedico.'

[4] So Gel.; R. + cujus spiritus super te ferebatur qui te de paradisi fonte
manare fecit.

[5]—[5] qui—sancti. A zigzag mark on the margin calls attention to the fact that
this passage has already occurred in the form of ' Exorcismus aquae ' on p. 212.

iohanne in oirdane in té babtizatus est ; qui té una cum
sanguine de latera suo produxit, et discipulís suís iusit ut
credentes baptizare(n)t in te, dicens, ite docete omnes gentes,
baptizantes eos in nomine patris, et fili, et spiritus sancti[5].

Haec nobis precepta seruantibus tú, deus omnipotens,
clemens adesto, tú benignus aspira, tú has simplices aquas
tuo ore benedicito, ut per te naturalem emundationem quam
Fol. 56 a. lauandís possunt adhibere corporibus sint etiam
purificandís mentibus efficaces, discendat in hanc plenitudinem
fontis uirtus spiritus tui[1], et totam huius aquae substantiam
regenerandi fecundet effectu. Hic omnium pecatorum maculae
deleantur. Híc natura ad imaginem tuam condita, ad honorem sui reformata principii, cunctís uetustatis scaloribus[2]
emundetur, ut omnis homo hoc sacramentum regenerationis
ingressus in uerae innocentiae nouam infantiam renascatur,
per dominum nostrum ihesum christum[3].

Fol. 56 b. *Deinde, benedictio completa, mittit sacerdos crisma
in modum crucis in fontem, et quique uoluerit[4] implet uasculum
aqua benedictionis ad domos consecrandas, et populus pressens
aspargitur aqua benedicta. Iterum roga a diacono si credat in
patrem, et filium, et spiritum sanctum.*

Credis in deum patrem omnipotentem[5] ? *R.* Credo.

Credis et in ihesum christum filium eius unicum dominum
nostrum natum et passum ? *R.* Credo.

---

[1] So Gel.; R. + sancti, totamque.

[2] p. 211. n. 2.   [3] R. + qui venturus est, &c.

[4] There is a similar direction to the members of the congregation generally
in the Corpus Missal, p. 202. The present R. rubric confines the right of
taking away the consecrated water to 'unus ex ministris ecclesiae.' There
too a triple use of oil is prescribed instead of the single application ordered
here, viz. i. of the oil of the catechumens ; ii. of the chrism ; iii. of both oils
combined. The Benediction of the font being now complete, the Baptismal
Office proper is resumed. The Gelasian rubric runs thus, ' *Inde benedicto
fonte baptizas unumquemque in ordine suo sub his interrogationibus,*' p. 570).
In the later Roman Ordines Bapt. these three questions as to belief are
immediately preceded by three questions as to the renunciation of Satan and
his works. It is remarkable that while they are omitted here in accordance
with Gelasian precedent, they should have occurred twice close together in the
earlier portion of the service ; p. 209.

[5] So Gel. ; R + creatorem coeli et terrae.

Credis et in spiritum sanctum, aeclesiam catholicam[1], remisionem peccatorum, carnis resurrectionem[2]? *Res.* Credo.

[3]*Discendit*[4] *in fontem et tingitur ter uel aspargitur.* [5]*Post-quam babtizaretur oleatur cresmate in cerebrum in fronte*[5],[3] *et dat uestem candidam diacunus super capute in frontae, et dicit pres-piter*[6];

Deus omnipotens, pater domini nostri ihesu christi, qui té regenerauit ex aqua et spiritu sancto, quique tibi dedit re-misionem omnium peccatorum, ipse té lineat crismate salutis in christo.

Fol. 57 a.   *isund dognither intongath*[7].

Ungo[8] té de oleo et de crismate salutis et sanctificationis, in nomine dei patris, et filii, et spiritus, nunc et per omnia in saecula saeculorum.

Operare[9], creatura olei, operare in nomine dei patris omni-potentis, et filii, et spiritus sancti, ut non lateat híc spiritus

---

[1] Gel. sanctam.

[2] So Gel.; R. + et vitam aeternam. The text follows the Gelas. Sacram. in omitting the additional question now found in the Ordines Rom.:—'Vis baptizari. R. Volo.'

[3]—[3] Gel. Sacram., Deinde per singulas vices mergis eum tertio in aqua. Postea, cum ascenderit a fonte infans signatur a Presbytero in cerebro de chrismate his verbis. (See Introd. p. 65.) The actual baptismal formula is omitted here as in the Gelas. Sacram. (Ordo xliv. p. 570; Gregor. Sacram. p. 65); in the description of baptism given in the Gallican work known under the title of St. Ambrose *De Sacram.* lib. ii. cap. 7; and in a ninth-century Sacramentary (Cod. Colbert, No. 1348) printed by Martene, Ordo v. vol. i. p. 66. The omission is strange. Perhaps, as in the case of the Eucharistic words of consecration, so often omitted, as on p. 246, it was presumed that the priest would know them by heart.

[4] It is to be noticed that the direction to go down into the font implies that immersion was the general rule.

[5]—[5] Rit. Rom., 'Deinde intingit pollicem in sacro chrismate et ungit infantem in summitate capitis dicens.'   [6] Rit. Rom. p. 30.

[7] Anglice, ' Here the unction is made.'

[8] The only other place where a formula of unction occurs with the verb in the first person is in the Missal. Goth., ' *Dum chrisma eum tangis dicis,* Perungo te chrisma sanctitatis.' (Mab. ed. p. 248.)

[9] This address to the oil occurs in the Ordo Baptismi in the Sacramentarium Gallicanum (Mart. i. p. 65; Mab. Lit. Gal. p. 324), but in connection with the rite of Unction before the act of Baptism; in an ancient but undated Ordo Vis. Infirm. in a Beauvais Pontif., Mart. i. p. 332; in the Codex Vat. of the Greg. Sacram. editedby Rocca, Antv. 1615, p. 224.

immundus nec in membris, nec in medullis, compaginibus membrorum, sed operetur in té uirtus christi filii dei uiui altisimi, et spiritus sancti, per omnia saecula saeculorum. Amen.

Et dat uestem candidam diaconus super caput eius in frontae, et dum uestimento candido tegitur dicit prespiter [1];

Accipe uestem candidam, sanctam, et immaculatam, quam
Fol. 57 b.   perferas ante tribunal domini nostri ihesu christi.

Res. Accipio et perferam [2].

Et dicit prespiter,

Aperiatur manus pueri [3].

Dicens,

Signum crucis christi + accipe in manum tuam dexteram, et conseruet te in uitam aeternam.   *R.* Amen.

Tunc lauantur pedes eius, accepto linteo accepto [4].

---

[1] Rit. Rom. p. 30. The presentation of the white dress is followed in the R. Ordo Bapt. Parv. by the presentation of a lighted taper, of which there is here no trace. Although not mentioned in the Gelas. and Gregor. Sacram., the latter ceremony is found in all mediaeval office books except those of Mayence.

[2] This response does not seem to occur elsewhere.

[3] This ceremony is not found in the R. Ordo Bapt. nor in any of the Baptismal Offices printed by Martene, nor is any allusion made to it by him or by other writers on Baptism. But a similar rite is found in an eleventh century Jumieges Ritual, where it occurs at a much earlier point in the service, after the sign of the cross has been made on the infant's forehead: '*Tunc presbyter faciens crucem cum pollice intra palmam dextram infantis dicat.* Trado signaculum Domini nostri Jesu Christi in manu tua dextera, ut te signes et te de adversa parte repellas, et in fide catholica permaneas, et habeas vitam aeternam, et vivas cum Domino semper in saecula saeculorum. Amen.' (Mart. Ordo xiii. vol. i. p. 73.)

[4] This ceremonial washing of the feet, or 'pedilavium,' is not found in any Roman Office, but is common to the early Gallican 'Ordines Baptismi,' and was still in use in France in the eighth century, as we gather from a work, which usually passes under the name of St. Ambrose, and is bound up with his writings, but is now ascertained to be a Gallican production of about A.D. 800, 'Ascendisti de fonte ? Quid secutum est ? Audisti lectionem. Succinctus summus sacerdos pedes tibi lavit . . . Non ignoramus quod Ecclesia Romana hanc consuetudinem non habeat.' (Ambros. *De Sacram.* lib. iii. cap. 1, and Gallican Liturgies, ed. by G. H. Forbes, pp. 97, 189, 267.) Its presence in this ancient Irish Missal possibly supplies the clue to the meaning of one of the conditions of union offered, but without success, by St. Augustine to the British bishops, the precise interpretation of which has been hitherto left to

Alleluia.   Lucerna pedibus mieis uerbum tuum, domine[1].

Alleluia.   Adiuua me, domine, et saluus ero[2].

Alleluia.   Uisita nos, domine, in salutare tuo[3].

Alleluia.   Tu mandasti mandata tua custodire nimis [4].

Mandasti missericordiam tuam, opus manuum tuarum ne despicias[5].

Si[6] ego laui pedes uestras dominus et magister uester, et uos debetis alterutrius pedes lauare ; exemplum enim dedi uobís ut quemadmodum feci uobis et uos faciteis[7] aliis.

Dominus[8] et saluator noster ihesus christus, pridie quam pateretur, accepto linteo splendido, sancto, et immaculato[9], precinctís lumbís suís, misit aquam in piluem, lauit pedes discipulorum suorum.   Hoc et tu facias exemplum domini nostri ihesu christi hospitibus et peregrinis tuis.

Fol. 58 a.   Corpus[10] et sanguinis domini nostri ihesu christi sit tibi in uitam aeternam.   Amen.

---

conjecture :—'Ut ministerium baptizandi, quo Deo renascimur, juxta morem sanctae Romanae et Apostolicae Ecclesiae compleatis.' (Bede, H. E. ii. 2 ; H. and S. i. 153.) This passage has by some been supposed to refer to confirmation.   Dr. Lingard states, without giving any authority, that the Britons did not confirm after baptism. (A. S. Church, i. 295.) This rite of pedilavium obtained also at one time in Spain, but was abolished by Can. 48 of the Council of Eliberis, A.D. 305. (Mansi, Concil. tom. ii. p. 14).

[1] Ps. cxviii. 105.   [2] Ib. 117.   [3] Ps. cv. 4. p. 225.

[4] Ps. cxviii. 4.   [5] Ps. cxxxvii. 8.

[6] Ioan. xiii. 14, 15.   A sentence resembling this is ordered to be repeated at the Pedilavium in the three extant Gallican Ordines Bapt. Mis. Goth., Mab. ed. p. 249 ; Mis. Gallican., Mab. ed. p. 364 ; Sacram. Gallican., Mab. ed. p. 325. The formula in the latter runs thus : 'Ego tibi lavo pedes, sicut Dominus noster,' &c. ; n. 8.

[7] For faciatis.

[8] Compare the following formula in the Sacram. Gallican. (Mab. ed. p. 325) : 'Dominus noster Jesus Christus de linteo, quo erat praecinctus tersit pedes discipulorum suorum, et ego facio tibi, tu facies peregrinis, hospitibus et pauperibus.'

[9] Compare the three epithets applied to the chrisom, *supra*, 'Accipe vestem,'&c.

[10] [Communion of the newly-baptized.]   The immediate approach to the altar of the newly-baptized, still clad in their white dress, 'familia candidata,' is described at length in the Gallican work usually printed as S. Ambros. de Sacram. lib. iii. 2. § 15 ; iv. 2 ; v. 3. § 14.   The confirmation or communion (generally both) of such persons is ordered in every mediaeval Ritual till the fourteenth century.   The rubric in the Gelasian Ordo Bapt. (Murat. ed. p. 571) simply prescribes, 'Deinde ab episcopo datur eis Spiritus septiformis.'   In the

Refecti[1] spiritalibus escís, cibo coelesti, corpore et sanguine domini recreati, deo domino nostro ihesu christo debitas laudes et gratias referamus, orantes indefessam eius missericordiam, ut diuini muneris sacramentum ad incrementum fidei et profectum aeternae salutis habeamus. per.

Oremus, fratres carisimi[2], pro fratre nostro N. qui gratiam domini consecutus est, ut babtismi quod accipit immaculatum atque integrum perferat ante tribunal domini nostri ihesu christi, qui.

Fol. 58 b. Deus[3], tibi gratias agimus per quem misteria sancta celebrauimus, et a té sanctitatis do[num] deposcimus, per dominum.

Alleluia. Memento nostri, domine, in beneplacito populi tui, uísita nós in salutari tuo[4].

Alleluia. Ó domine, saluum fac[5].

Ó domine, bene prosperare[6].

---

ninth-century Gelasian Codices (Colbert. 1348, Reg. 3866) there is this order:—
'Postea si fuerit oblata, agenda est missa, et communicat. Sin autem, dabis, eis tantum sacramenta Corporis et Sanguinis Christi dicens, Corpus Domini nostri Jesu Christi sit tibi in vitam aeternam;' followed by two short collects of thanksgiving for baptism. (Mart. i. p. 66.)

For this purpose altars were usually erected in baptisteries, a custom which can be traced back to the time of Pope Hilary (461–7). (Mart. vol. i. pp. 5, 55.)

In a tenth-century Parisian Codex this rubric occurs : ' Et vestitur infans vestimentis suis. Si vero episcopus adest statim confirmari eum oportet chrismate et postea communicare ; Et si episcopus deest, communicetur a presbytero dicente ita,' &c. (Mart. Ordo x. vol. i. p. 70.) Book of Deer, p. 164. n. 5 ; Book of Dimma, p. 170 ; Book of Mulling, p. 173.

[1] For the Ephesine character of this and the following thanksgivings, see Book of Deer, p. 165. n. 1. Compare the post-reception collects in the Book of Dimma, p. 171 ; Book of Mulling, p. 173.

[2] p. 167. n. 3. There are one or two post-baptismal collects of thanksgiving resembling this one in their tenor in all the Gallican Offices. Compare the following from the Sacram. Gallican. (Mab. edit. p. 325) : ' Laudes et gratias Domino referamus, fratres dilectissimi, quod augere dignatus est ecclesiae suae congregationem per caros nostros qui modo baptizati sunt. Petamus ergo de Domini misericordia ut baptismum sanctum quod acceperunt, inlibatum, inviolatum, et immaculatum perferant ante tribunal Christi.'

[3] Book of Deer, p. 165. n. 7; Book of Dimma, p. 171 ; Book of Mulling, p. 173.

[4] Ps. cv. 4. The latter half of this verse is repeated in the Ordo ad Com. Infirm. p. 225.

[5] Ps. cxvii. 25.   [6] Ib.

Alleluia. Ostende nobís, domine, *usque* nobís[1].

Salua nos, ihesu, qui potes saluarae, qui dedit animam det et[2] salutem, per dominum.

Benedíc[3], domine, hanc creaturam aquae, ut sit remedium
Fol. 59 a. generi humano salutare, presta, per inuocationem nominis tui, per hanc creaturam aquae, corporis sanitatem, et animae tutellam, rerum defensionem. per.

Exorcizo[4] té, spiritus immunde, per deum patrem omni-potentem, qui fecit caelum et terram, mare, et omnia quae in eis sunt, ut omnis uitus aduersarii, omnis exercitus diabuli, omnis incursus, omne fantasma inimici eradicetur et effugetur ab hác creatura aquae, ut sit sancta et salutifera, et ignis ardens aduersus insidias inimici, per inuocationem nominis domini nostri ihesu christi, qui iudicaturus est saeculum per ignem in spiritu sancto. Amen.

[ORDO AD VISITANDUM INFIRMUM.]

Oremus[5], fratres, dominum deum nostrum pro fratre
Fol. 59 b. nostro ad pressens malum langoris adulcerat, ut

---

[1] Ps. lxxxiv. 8.   Book of Dimma, p. 170 ; Stowe Mis. p. 232.

[2] p. 221, line 2.

[3] Sacr. Gregor. p. 229.   This and the following Exorcism are apparently misplaced here.   They seem to be appended as forms once in use, but now rendered useless by the insertion of the larger Roman 'Benedictio Fontis' (p. 212) in its proper place.

[4] This is a Gallican and Milanese Exorcism.   It occurs in the Ordo Baptismi in the Sacramentarium Gallicanum (Mab. edit. p. 324), and in an Ambrosian Ritual quoted by Martene (Ordo, xxi. vol. i. p. 80).   In both cases it is an 'Exorcismus hominis,' not 'aquae.'   We append the Gallican text : 'Exorcidio te, spiritus immunde, per Deum Patrem omnipotentem, qui fecit coelum et terram, mare et omnia quae in eis sunt, ut omnis virtus adversarii, omnes exercitus diaboli, omnes incursus, omne fantasma eradicetur ac fugetur ab hoc plasmate, ut fiat templum Dei sanctum in nomine Dei Patris omnipo-tentis, et Jesu Christi Filii ejus, qui judicaturus est saeculum per ignem in spiritu sancto in saecula saeculorum.'   Its introductory rubric in the Milanese rite is this : ' *Exsufflat in faciem ejus in similitudinem crucis dum dicit.*'   Com-pare the forms of 'Exorcismi' at the benediction of each of three oils on Maundy Thursday in the Roman Pontifical.   That employed in the ' Benedictio chris-matis' most closely resembles the text.

[5] Here commences an Office for the 'Visitatio Infirmi.'   It corresponds very closely with that preserved in the Book of Dimma, p. 167, to which the reader is referred for notes, and of which this forms the opening address.   Gerbert, Lit. Al. ii. 33.

eum domini pietas coelestibus dignetur curare medicinis, qui
dedit animam det et salutem. per.

Deum [1] uiuum omnipotentem sua omnia opera restaurare,
confirmare facillimum est, fratres carissimi [2], pro fratre nostro
infirmo .N. supliciter oremus, quo creatura manuum sentiat
creatoris, ut aut in reparando aut in recipiendo in nomine suo
pius pater opus suum recreare dignetur. per dominum nostrum
ihesum christum.

Domine [3], sancte pater, uniuersitatis auctor, omnipotens
aeterne deus, cui cuncta uiuunt, qui uiuificas mortuos, et uocas
Fol. 60 a.   ea quae non sunt tanquam sunt, qui quod est tuum
solitum opus, qui es magnus artifex pie exercere in hoc tuo
plasmate [4], per christum.

Deus [5], in cuius manu tam alitus uiuentes quam uita
morientis, fratres delectissimi, deprecemur ut corporis huius
infirmitatem sanet, et animae salutem prestet, ut quod per
merita non meretur, missericordiae gratiae consequatur orantibus nobis prestet, per dominum nostrum ihesum christum.

Domine [6], sancte pater, omnipotens aeterne deus, qui es
uia, et veritas, et uita, exaudi et conserua famulum tuum
Fol. 60 b.   hunc N. quem uiuificasti et redemisti pretio magno
sancti sanguinis filii tui, qui regnas.

---

[1] Book of Dimma, p. 167.

[2] For the Ephesine character of these addresses to 'fratres carissimi' or
'fratres dilectissimi,' see p. 167. n. 3.   In the Mozarabic Lit. the 'Missa,' the
'Ad orationem dominicam,' the 'Alia oratio post missam,' the 'Post pridie'
are frequently so addressed (pp. 257, 830, 879, &c.)   In the Gallican Lit. the
'Praefatio,' the 'Collectio post nomina,' the 'Ante Orationem Dominicam,' the
'Post communio' assume the same form (Mis. Goth. pp. 37, 40, 46, 51).   See
Books of Dimma and Mulling; Corpus Missal, fol. 100 a.

[3] Book of Dimma, p. 167.   This collect also occurs in an eleventh-century
Narbonne Pontif., Mart. i. p. 318; in a twelfth-century Salzburg Pontif.,
Ib. i. p. 325.   The phrase 'uniuersitatis auctor' occurs again in a Postcom.
on p. 271.

[4] For the use of this word 'plasma,' see p. 167. n. 7.

[5] Book of Dimma, p. 168.

[6] This collect occurs among the Prayers for the Sick in a tenth-century MS.
published by Gerbert, Liturg. Aleman. ii. 30.   Also in an Ordo Extremae
Unctionis, Ib. p. 33; in a twelfth-century Salzburg Pontif., published by
Mart., Ordo xv. vol. i. p. 324.

Deus[1], qui non uís mortem[2] sed ut conuertatur peccatoris[2] et uiuat, huic ad té ex corde conuerso peccata dimite, et perennis uitae tribue gratiam, per dominum.

Deus[3], qui facturam tuam pio semper donaris affectu, inclína aurem tuam suplicantibus nobís tibi ad famulum tuum .N. aduersitate uelitudinem corporis laborantem placidus respice, uissíta eum in salutari tuo et coelestis gratiae concede medicamentum. per.

Fol. 61 a.   In[4] illo tempore accesserunt saducei ad eum dicentes non esse resurrectionem, et interrogauerunt eum. Respondens ihesus illís ait ; erratis nescientes scripturas neque uirtutem dei ; in resurrectione enim neque nubent neque nubentur, sed erunt sicut angeli dei in caelo.   De resurrectione autem mortuorum non legistis quomodo dictum est a domino dicente uobís, Ego sum deus abracham, deus issac, deus iacob ; non est ergo deus mortuorum, sed deus uiuentium. Et audientes turbae mirabantur doctrina eius.

In[5] illis diebus dixit ihesus ; Statim hautem post Fol. 61 b.   tribulationem dierum illorum sol obscurabitur, et luna non dabit lumen suum, et stellae cadent de caelo, et uirtutes caelorum commobebuntur, et tunc apparebit signum filii hominis in caelo, et tunc plangent sé omnes tribús terrae,

---

[1] Book of Dimma, p. 168 ; Gerbert, Liturg. Aleman. ii. 30 ; also in a twelfth-century Salzburg Pontif., Mart., Ordo xv. vol. i. p. 324 ; in a Latin Ordo in use in Syria in the twelfth century ; Mart., Ordo xxiii. vol. i. p. 335.

[2] There has been an accidental transposition of words here.

[3] Book of Dimma, p. 168 ; Gelas. Sacram., Murat. edit. p. 735 ; Greg. p. 211 ; Corpus Missal, p. 207. Also in a tenth-century German Ordo (Cod. Th. v. 683) published by Gerbert, Lit. Aleman. ii. 29.   Again in an eleventh-century Cod. Rhenaug., Ib. p. 37 ; in Codex Colbertin. No. 2585 (a French Ritual), copied by Mart. i. p. 311 ; in a twelfth-century Salzburg Pontif., Mart. i. p. 323, Ordo xv ; in a twelfth-century Remiremont Missal, Ib. Ordo xvii. p. 328 ; a ninth-century Fleury Codex, Ordo i, Ib. vol. ii. p. 377 ; a fourteenth-century Rouen Ritual, Ordo xii, Ib. p. 400.

[4] Matt. xxii. 23–33.   This forms the second of the two lections in the Book of Dimma, p. 168, the readings in which differ in some particulars from those presented here.

[5] Matt. xxiv. 29–31. For this lection the Book of Dimma (p. 168) substitutes 1 Cor. xv. 19–22. None of these lections occur among those provided in the Ordo de Visitatione Infirm. in the Rit. Rom.

et uidebunt filium homines uenientem in nubibus caeli, cum
uirtute multa et maistate, et mittet angelos suos cum tuba
et uoce magna, et congregabunt electos suos a quatuor uéntis,
a summis caelorum usque ad terminos eorum.

[ORDO MINISTRANDI SACRAMENTUM EXTREMAE
UNCTIONIS] [1].

Fol. 62 a. Ungo té de oleo sanctificato, ut salueris in nomine
patris, et filii, et spiritus sancti, in saecula [2].

Concede, domine, nobís famulís túis ut orantibus cum
fiducia dicere meriamur [3] :

Pater noster.

Libera nos, domine, ab omni malo, et custodi nós in omnibo [4],
ihesu christe, aucto[r] omnium bonorum, qui regnas in saecula
saeculorum.

[ORDO AD COMMUNICANDUM INFIRMUM] [5].

Oramus té, domine, pro fratré nostro .N. cui infirmitate
sua officium commonionis, ut si qua eum saecularis macula
inuassit, aut uitium mondialem ficit, dono tuae pietatis indulgeas et extergas. per.

---

[1] The earliest extant Ordines Extremae Unctionis are found in certain ix–x
cent. MSS. of the Gregor Sacram., Tilianus, Remensis, S. Eligii, Ratoldi, &c. They
are elaborate in their structure, and bear no resemblance to the simple rite in
the Stowe Missal. A later and more expanded Irish Office, including the
Unction of the various parts of the body, is given in the Corpus Missal, p. 208.

[2] This very nearly resembles the formula of Unction in the Book of Dimma,
p. 169 ; Book of Mulling, p. 172.

[3] This Preface and the following Enbolismus to the Pater Noster occur in the
Book of Dimma, p. 169. Compare the Book of Deer, p. 164. n. 3 ; Book of
Mulling, p. 172.   [4] For omni bono.

[5] It appears from the order in which these services are arranged that Communion is intended to follow the rite of Unction, as in the case of the tenth-
century German Offices published by Gerbert, Lit. Aleman. ii. 33, and in
accordance with the almost universal custom of the Western Church (Mart. i.
p. 297). The whole 'Ordo' differs almost entirely from any extant Roman
Office of Communion of the Sick. Its points of resemblance to other Celtic
Offices are pointed out in the following notes.

Fol. 62 b.　Domine [1], sancte pater, te fideliter deprecemur ut accipiendi fratri nostro [2] sacrosanctam hanc æucharistiam corporis et sanguinis [2] domini nostri ihesu christi, tam carnis quam animae sit salus. per dominum.

Exaudi nós, domine ihesu christe, deus noster, pro fratre nostro infirmo, té rogantes ut tua sancta euchoristia sit ei tutella per dominum.

Páx et caritás domini nostri ihesu christi et commonicatio sanctorum tuorum sit semper uobiscum [3]. ℟. Amen.

Corpus et sanguis domini nostri ihesu christi filii dei uiui altisimi. *rl* [4].

Fol. 63 a.　Accepto salutari diuini corporis cibo lalutari nostro, ihesu christo gratias agimus [5], quod sui corporis et sanguinis sacramento nos á morte liberauit, et tam corporis quam animae homano generi remedium donare dignatus est, qui regnat.

Agimus deo patri omnipotenti gratias, quod terrenae nos originis atque naturae sacramenti sui dono in coelestem uiuificauerit denotationem, per dominum [6].

Conuerte nós, deus salutum nostrarum, et infirmorum praesta salutem nostrorum [7].

Fol. 63 b.　Quia satiauit animam inanem, et animam essurientem satiauit [8].

---

[1] This collect occurs with various readings in Rit. Rom. p. 123, and in the Corpus Missal, p. 209.

[2]—[2] R. sacrosanctum corpus.

[3] Compare the formula in the Book of Dimma, p. 170, where see note 3 as to this position of the Pax; Stowe Missal, p. 242. The Pax and Communion are curiously blended together in one clause in the tenth-century German Office, printed by Gerbert, Lit. Aleman. ii. 33: 'Pax et communicatio corporis et sanguinis Domini nostri Ihesu Christi conservet animam tuam in vitam eternam.'

[4] For the remainder of this formula of administration, see Book of Deer, p. 164. n. 6; Book of Dimma, p. 170; and Book of Mulling, p. 173.

[5] This resembles in principle, but differs verbally from, the collects of thanksgiving in the Books of Deer (p. 165. n. 1), Dimma (p. 170), and Mulling (p. 173), and the Praefatio post Eucharistiam in the Gallican Missa in Symboli Traditione (Mart. i. p. 35).

[6] Book of Dimma, p. 170.　　[7] Ps. lxxxiv. 5. Book of Dimma, p. 170.

[8] Ps. cvi. 9. Book of Deer, p. 165.

bis.   Alleluia.   Alleluia.

Uissita nos, deus, in salutari tuo [1].   Alleluia.

Fortitudo mea, *usque* salutem [2].   Alleluia.

Calicem salutaris accipiam *usque* inuocabo [3].   Alleluia.

Refecti christi corpore et sanguine tibi semper, domine, dicamus [4].   Alleluia.

Laudate dominum omnes gentes [5], *usque in finem.*

Sacrificate sacrificium iustitiae, et sperate in domino [6].

Fol. 64 a.   Deus, tibi gratias agimus per quem misteria sancta celebrauimus, et ad té sanctitatís dona deposcimus, qui regnas in saecula saeculorum [7].

Benedicat tibi dominus et custodiat te, ostendatque dominus faciam suam tibi, et misseriatur tui, conuertat dominus uultum suum ad té, et det tibi pacem [8].

      et respondit.   Amen.

Tunc signans eum dicito [9],

Signaculo crucis christi signaris.

Páx tecum in uitam eternam.

     et respondit.   Amen.

     Finit ordo commonis.

---

[1] Ps. cv. 4. This verse is also used in the Communion of the newly-baptized, p. 218.

[2] Ps. cxvii. 14. Book of Dimma, p. 170; Stowe Mis. p. 229.

[3] Ps. cxv. 13. Book of Deer, p. 165; Book of Dimma, p. 170; Book of Mulling, p. 173.

[4] Book of Deer, p. 165; Book of Dimma, p. 171; Book of Mulling, p. 173; Antiphon. Benchor. p. 192.

[5] Ps. cxvi. Book of Deer, p. 165; Book of Dimma, p. 171; Book of Mulling, p. 173.

[6] Ps. iv. 16. Book of Deer, p. 165; Book of Dimma, p. 171; Book of Mulling, p. 173.

[7] Book of Deer, p. 165; Book of Dimma, p. 170; Book of Mulling, p. 173; Mis. Goth. pp. 144, 150.

[8] This Benediction occurs in an abbreviated form in the Book of Dimma, p. 171, and in its present form with various readings in the Book of Mulling, p. 172. Similar but not identical Benedictions occur near the end or at the conclusion of most mediaeval offices for the Visitation of the Sick.

[9] Compare the rubric in Book of Dimma, p. 171.

[ORDINARIUM MISSÆ.]

Fol. 13 a.

LETANIA[1] APOSTOLORUM AC MARTIRUM SANCTORUM ET UIRGINUM INCIPIT (2).

Deus in adiutorium nostrum intende (2).

Peccauimus (3), domine, peccauimus, parce peccatis nostris, et salua nos, qui gubernasti noe super undas dilui exaudi nós, et ionam di abiso uerbo reuocasti libera nos, qui petro, mergenti manum porrexisti auxiliare nobis, christe.

Fol. 13 b. Fili dei, ficisti mirabilia domini cum patribus nostris, et nostris propitiare temporibus. Emite manum tuum de alto.

Libera nos christe

Audi nos christe	cyrie elezion
sancta maria	sancte tathei
sancte petri	sancte madiani (4)
sancte pauli	sancte marce
sancte anrias	sancte lucae
sancte iacobi	omnes sancti orate pro nobis.
sancte bartholomei	propitius esto, parcae nobis,
sancte tomae	domine; propitius esto, libera nos,
sancte mathei	domine;
sancte iacobe	ab omni malo libera nos, domine,
	per crucem tuam (5) libera nos, domine.

Fol. 14 a. ORATIO AUGUSTINI (6).

Profeta omnes iustitae nostrae sicut pannus menstruate. Indigni sumus, domine christe, ut simus uiuentes, sed tú, deus,

---

[1] In consequence of their necessary length the notes referred to by numbers between parentheses have been postponed to p. 249.

non uis mortem peccatoris; dá nobís ueniam in carne con-
stitutís, ut per penitentiae labores uita aeterna perfruamur in
caelis, per dominum.

Rogo (7) té, deus zabaoth altissime, pater sancte, uti me
tonica caritatis digneris accingere, et meos lumbos ba(l)theo (8)
tui amoris ambire, ac renes cordis mei tuae caritatis igne
urire, ut pro peccatís méis possim intercedere, et adstantes
populi peccatorum ueniam promeriri, ac pacificas singulorum
hostias immolare, me quoque tibi audaciter accidentem non
sinas perire (8), sed dignare lauare, ornare, et leniter suscipere,
(8) per dominum nostrum.

Fol. 14 b. *Hec oratio in omni misa cantatur.*

Ascendat oratio nostra usque ad tronum claritatis tuae,
domine, et ne uacua reuertatur ad nos postulatio nostra, per.

In sollemnitatibus petri et christi (9).

Deus, qui beato petro apostolo tuo, conlatis clauibus regni
caelestis, animas ligandi autque soluendi (10) pontificium tradidisti, suscipe propitius preces nostras, et intercessione eius,
quesumus, domine, auxilium, ut a peccatorum nostrorum
neximus liberemur, per dominum (11).

Imnus angelicus (12).

Gloria in excelsis deo, et in terra pax hominibus bonae
uoluntatis. Laudamus té, benedicimus té, adoramus té, glorificamus té, [1]magnificamus te[1], gratias agimus tibi pro[2] magnam misericordiam[3] tuam, domine[4], rex caelestis[5], deus pater
omnipotens, domine filii dei[6] unigeniti ihesu christe, [7]sancte
spiritus dei, et omnes dicimus amen, domine, filii dei patris,
agne dei, qui tollis peccatum mundi, misserere nobís, suscipe
orationes nostras[7], qui sedis ad dexteram dei[6] patris, misserere

---

[1-1] om.   [2] propter.   [3] gloriam.   [4] + Deus.
[5] After this word the writing is continued in a later hand on a slip inserted
between fol. 14 b and fol. 15 a.   [6] om.
[7-7] Domine Deus, Agnus Dei, Filius Patris, Qui tollis peccata mundi
miserere nobis, Qui tollis peccata mundi suscipe deprecationem nostram.

nobis ; quoniam tú solus sanctus, tú solus dominus, [1]tú solus dominus[1], tú solus [2]gloriosus cum spiritu sancto[2] in gloria dei patris. amen.

Fol. 15 a. *Hec oratio pro uice dicitur qui culpa in coti-dianís diebus . . .*

Deus qui diligentibus té bona inuisibilia preparasti, effunde cordibus nóstrís tui amoris affectum, ut té in omnibus et super omnia diligentes promisiones tuas que omne desiderium superant consequamur, per dominum(13).

Órationés et precés misericordiae aeclesiae romane (14).

Hec oratio prima petri.

Deus,(15) qui culpa offenderis, penitentia placaris,(15) ad-flictorum gemitus respice, et mala que iustae inrogas miseri-corditer auerte, per.

Híc augmentum(16).

Lectio pauli apostoli ad corintheos incipit(17).

Fratres[3], quotiescumque[4] manducabítis panem hunc, [5]et Fol. 15 b. bibetis calicem istum[5], mortem domini adnuncia-bitis donec ueniat. Itaque quicumque manducauerit panem[6], uel biberit calicem domini indigne, reus erit corporis et sanguinis domini. Probet hautem séipsum homo, et sic de pane illo edat et de calige bibat. Qui enim manducan[7] et bibit[8] non discernens[9] corpus domini. Propterea[10] inter uos multi infirmi et egri[11], et dormiunt multi. Quodsí nosmetipsos iudicaremus[12], non utique iudicaremur. Dum

---

[1-1] om.   [2-2] altissimus Jesu Christe.
[Differences from the Vulgate (Textus receptus) are noticed below, except in the case of merely orthographical discrepancies.]
[3] V. om.   [4] V. + enim.   [5-5] V. et calicem bibetis.
[6] V. + hunc.   [7] V. manducat. A later hand has written t over this word.
[8] V. + indigne judicium sibi manducat et bibit—words which a later hand has also written over the line.   [9] V. dijudicans.   [10] V. Ideo.
[11] V. imbecilles.   [12] V. dijudicaremus.

hautem[1] iudicamur[2], a domino corripimur, ut non cum hoc mundo damnemur.

Deus, (18) qui nós regendo conseruás, parcendo iustificás, a temporali tribulatione nós eripe, et gaudia nobís eterna largire, per dominum nostrum. rl.

Omnipotens sempiterne deus, qui populum tuum unigeniti Fol. 16 a. tui sanguine redimisti, solue opera diabuli, rumpe uincula peccati, ut qui ad eternam uitam in confessione tui nominis sunt adepti nihil debeant mortis auctori. per.

Querite dominum et confirmamini, querite faciem eius semper (18 a).

Confitemini, et inuocate nomen eius, *usque*, querentium do-minum—querite (18 b).

(19) Grata sint tibi, domine, munera quibus (19) misteria celebratur nostrae libertatis et uitae, per. alleluia.

Fortitudo mea et laudatio (20) *usque in* salutem.

Sacrificiis presentibus, domine, quesumus, intende placatus, ut deuotionis nostrae proficiat ad salutem (21).

Fol. 16 b. DEPRECATIO (22) SANCTI MARTINI PRO
POPULO INCIPIT.

Amen. Deo gratias.

(a) Dicamus (23) omnes, domine, exaudi et missere, domine, misserre.

(β) Ex toto corde et ex tota mente quí respices super terram et facis eam tremere. oramus.

(γ) Pro altissima pace et trancillitate temporum nostrorum, pro sancta aeclesia catholicaque a finibus usque ad terminos orbis terrae. oramus.

(δ) Pro pastore .n. episcopo et omnibus episcopis, et praes-peteris, et diaconis, et omni clero (24). oramus.

(ε) Pro hoc loco, et inhabitantibus in eo, pro pissimis im-peratoribus (25), et omni romano exercitu (25). oramus.

(ζ) Pro omnibus qui in sublimitate constituti sunt, pro uirginibus, uidúis, et orfánis. oramus.

---

[1] V. *om.*   [2] V. + autem.

Fol. 17 a. (η) Pro perigrinantibus, et iter agentibus, ac nauigantibus, et poenitentibus, et catacominis. oramus.

(θ) Pro his qui in sancta aeclesia fructus misserecordiae largiuntur, domine deus uirtutum, exaudi preces nostras. oramus.

(ι) Sanctorum apostolorum ac martirum memores símus, ut, orantibus éis pro nobís, ueniam meriamur. oramus.

(κ) Christianum et pacificum nobís finem concedi a domino deprecemur. Presta, domine, presta.

(λ) Et diuinum in nobís permanere uinculum caritatis sanctum dominum deprecemur. Presta.

(μ) Conseruare sanctitatem et catholicae fidei puritatem dominum deprecemur. Presta. Dicamus.

Fol. 17 b. Sacrificium tibi domine celebrandum placatus intende, quod et nos a uitíis nostrae condicionis emundet, et tuo nomine retdat aceptos, per dominum (26).

Ante oculos tuos, domine, reus conscientiae testes adsisto ; rogare pro alís non audio quod impetrare non meriar ; tú enim scís, domine, omnia que aguntur in nobís ; erubescimus confiteri id quod per nós non timemus admitti ; uerbís tibi tantum obsequimur, corde mentimur, et quod uelle nós dicimus **Fol. 18 a.**′ nostrís actibus adprobamus. Parce, domine confitentibus, ignosce peccantibus, misserere té rogantibus (27) sed quia in sacramentís tuís meus sensus infirmus est, presta, domine, ut qui ex nobís duro corde uerba non recipis per te nobís ueniam largiaris, per dominum (28).

Lethdírech sund (29).

Dirigatur domine *usque* uespertinum (30).

Ter canitur. Híc eleuatur lintiamen de calice (31).

Ueni, domine, sanctificator omnipotens, et benedic hóc sacrificium praeparatum tibi (32).

Ter canitur.

Fol. 18 b.

INCIPIT LECTIO EUANGILII SECUNDUM
IOHANNEM (33).

[1]Dominus nóster ihesus christus dixit[1]; ego sum panis
uiuus qui di coelo discendi. Sí quis manducauerit ex eo[2]
uiuet in aeternum, et panis quem ego dabo ei caro mea est
pro huius[3] mundi uita. Litigabant ergo iudaei ad inuicem,
dicentes, quomodo potest hic nobís dare[4] carnem suam man-
ducare[4]? dixit ergo eís ihesus; amen, amen, dico uobís, nisi
manducaueritis carnem filii hominis sicut[5] panem[5], et bibe-
ritis[6] sanguinem huius[7], non habebitis (34).

ORATIO GREGORIANA SUPER EUANGELIUM (34a).

Quesumus, domine, omnipotens deus, ut uota nóstra tibi
immulata clementer respicias, atque ad defentionem nóstram
dextram tuae maestatis extendás, per dominum nóstrum
. . . . rl :

Fol. 19 a. bitis uitam in uobís. Qui manducat meam carnem, et bibet meum sanguinem habet uitam aeternam, et
ego resuscitabo eum in nouissimo diae. Caro enim mea uere
est cibus, et sanguis meus uerus est potus; qui manducat
meam carnem, et bibit meum sanguinem ipse in me manet,
et ego in illo.

Credo (35) in unum deum patrem omnipotentem, factorem
caeli et terrae, uissiuilium omnium et uisiuilium[8], et in unum
dominum nostrum[9] ihesum christum, filium dei unigenitum[10],

---

Variations from the Textus Receptus of the Vulgate.
[1-1] V. om.   [2] V. hoc.   [3] V. om.   [4-4] V. carnem
suam dare ad manducandum.   [5] V. om.   [6] V. + eius.   [7] V. om.
Variations from the Textus Receptus of the Creed.
This Creed agrees with the form given in the Ordo ad Catechum. faciendum
in the Gelas. Sacram. in the following readings, 2, 4, 5, 14, 15-15, 17, 18 (Muratori, Lit. Rom. i. 540). Other early forms of the Creed are found in the Book
of Deer, p. 166, and the Antiphon. Benchor. 189.
[8] + omnium. The writer evidently intended this for visibilium et invisi-
bilium.
[9] R. om.   [10] + et.

¹natum ex patre¹ ante omnia saecula², lumen de lumine, deum
uerum de deo uero, natum³ non factum, consubstantialem patri,
Fol. 19 b.   per quem omnia facta sunt, qui propter nós homines
et propter nostram salutem discendit de caelo⁴, et incarnatus est
de spiritu sancto et⁵ maria uirgine, et homo natus⁶ est, crugi-
fixus hautem⁷ pro nobís sub pontio pilato, passus et sepultus⁸;
et resurrexit tertia die secundum scripturas, et ascendit in
caelos⁹, et sedit a[d] dextram dei¹⁰ patris, et iterum uenturus¹¹
cum gloria iudicare uiuos et mortuos, cuius regni non erit
finis. Et¹² spiritum sanctum, dominum¹³ et uiuificatorem¹⁴,
¹⁵ex patre procedentem, cum patre et filio coadorandum et con-
glorificandum¹⁵, qui loqutus est per profetas, et unam sanctam
aeclesiam¹⁶ catholicam et apostolicam; confeteor unum bab-
Fol. 20 a.   tismum in remisionem pecatorum; spero¹⁷ resur-
rextionem mortuorum, et uitam futuri¹⁸ saeculi. Amen.

landírech sund (36).

Ostende nobís, domine, misericorer salutare tuum dabis (37).

ter canitur (38).

Oblata, domine, munera sanctifica, nosque a peccatorum
nostro[rum] maculis emunda, per dominum (39).

Hostias, quesumus, domine, nostrae deuotionis benignus ad-
sume, et per sacrificia gloriosa subditorum tibi corda purifica,
per dominum (39a).

Hás oblationes (40) et sincera libamina immolamus tibi,
Fol. 20 b.   domine, ihesu christe, qui passus es pro nóbis, et

---

¹⁻¹ ex patre natum.

² + Deum de Deo. This clause was inserted at the Council of Nice (A.D. 325),
omitted at Constantinople. It is usually found in Western forms of the Creed,
with the exception of the Creed of the Gelasian Sacramentary.

³ genitum.   ⁴ coelis.   ⁵ ex.   ⁶ factus; Gel. humanatum.
⁷ etiam (in later handwriting).   ⁸ + est.   ⁹ coelum.   ¹⁰ om.
¹¹ + est.   ¹² + in.   ¹³ et.   ¹⁴ vivificantem.

¹⁵⁻¹⁵ qui ex patre filioque procedit, qui cum patre et filio simul adoratur et
conglorificatur. A later interlinear hand has written, 'qui . . . filioque procedit . . simul' over the line, inserting a small 'qui' after procedentem, and a
small 'tur' over the fourth syllable of co-adorandum, and over the fifth
syllable of conglorificandum. The Gelasian Creed has 'ex (or et) Patre procedentem qui cum Patre et Filio simul adoratum et conglorificatum.'

¹⁶ Postpone to after apostolicam.   ¹⁷ et expecto.   ¹⁸ venturi.

resurrexisti tertia die a mortuís, pro animamus carorum nostrorum .n. et cararum nostrarum quorum nomina recitamus,
et quorumcumque non recitamus sed a té recitantur in libro
uitae (41) aeternae, propter missericordiam tuam eripe, qui
regnás in secula seculorum. Amen.

Secunda pars augmenti. híc super oblata (42ª).

Grata sit tibi hec oblatio plebis tuae quam tibi offerimus in
Fol. 21 a. honorem domini nóstri ihesu christi, et in commemorationem beatorum apostolorum tuorum, ac martirum
tuorum, et confessorum, quorum híc reliquias (42ᵇ) spicialiter
recolimus .n. et eorum quorum festiuitas hodie celebratur,
et pro animamus omnium episcoporum nostrorum, et sacerdotum nóstrorum, et diaconorum nóstrorum, et carorum nóstrorum (43) et cararum nóstrarum, et puerorum nostrórum,
et puellarum nostrarum, et paenitentium nóstrorum, cunctis
proficiant ad salutem, per dominum.

Sursum corda (44). Habemus ad dominum.

Gratias agamus domino deo nóstro.

Dignum et iustum est.

Fol. 21 b. Uere (45) dignum et iustum est aequm et salutare
est, nos tibi híc semper et ubique gratias agere, domine
sancte, omnipotens aeterne deus, per christum dominum nostrum, qui cum unigenito tuo et spiritu sancto deus es unus et
inmortalis, deus incorruptibilis et inmotabilis, deus inuisibilis
et fidelis, deus mirabilis et laudabilis, deus honorabilis et fortis,
deus altisimus et magnificus, deus uiuus et uerus, deus sapiens
et potens, deus sanctus et spiciosus, deus magnus et bonus,
deus terribilis et pacificus, deus pulcher et rectus, deus purus
Fol. 22 a. et benignus, deus beatus et iustus, deus pius et
sanctus, non unius singulariter personae sed unius trinitatis (46) substantiae, té credimus, té benedicimus, té adoramus, et laudamus nomen tuum in eternum et in saeculum
seculi, per quem salus mundi, per quem uita hominum, per
quem resurrectio mortuorum.

*isund totét dignum intórmaig ind maid per quem bes inna-
diudidi thall* (47).

Per quem maestatem tuam laudant angeli, adorant domi-
nationes, tr[e]ment potestates, caeli caelorumque uirtutes ac
Fol. 22 b. beata saraphim socia exsultatione concelebrant, cum
quibus et nóstras uoces uti admitti iubeas deprecamur, supplici
confessione dicentes ; Sanctus.

*isund totét dignum intórmig ind máid sanctus bess inna-
diudidi thall* (48).

Sanctus, sanctus, dominus deus sabaóth ; pleni sunt caeli et
uniuérsa terra gloria tua. Ossanna in excelsís, benedictus qui
uenit in nomine domini. Ossanna in excelsis, benedictus qui
uenit de celís ut conuersaretur in terrís, homo factus est ut
dilicta carnis deleret, hostia factus est ut per passionem suam
uitam aeternam credentibus daret, per dominum (49).

Fol. 23 a.   CANON DOMINICUS PAPAE GILASI.

Té igitur, clementisime pater, per ihesum christum filium
tuum dominum nostrum supplices té[1] rogamus, et petimus,
uti accepta habeas et benedicás haec dona, haec munera, haec
sancta sacrificia inlibata, inprimís, que tibi offerimus pro tua
sancta aeclesia catholica, quam pacificare, custodire, et[1] unare[2],
et regere digneris toto orbe terrarum, una cum beatissimo[1]
Fol. 23 b. famulo tuo .n. papa nóstro[3], episcopo [4]sedis apostolicae, et omnibus ortodoxís atque apostolice fidei cultoribus,
et abbate nostro .n. episcopo[4] (50).

Híc recitantur nomina uiuorum (51).

Memento etiam, domine, famulorum tuorum[5] .n.[5] famularumque tuarum, et omnium circum adstantium, quorum tibi
fides cognita est et nota deuotio (52), qui tibi offerunt hoc
sacrificium laudis pro se suisque omnibus, pro redemptione
animarum suarum, [6]pro stratu seniorum (61) suorum, et ministrorum omnium puritate, pro intigritate uirginum, et con-
tinentia uiduarum, pro aeris temperie, et fructum fecunditate

---

Variations from the text of the Gelasian Canon of the Codex Vaticanus, as
printed by Muratori (Lit. Rom. Vet. tom. i. p. 695), are here appended.

[1] om.   [2] adunare.   [3] + et antistite nostro ill.   [4–4] om.
[5–5] om.   [6–6] om.

Fol. 24 a. terrarum, pro pacis redetu et fine discriminum, pro incolimitate regum, et pace populorum, ac reditu captiuorum, pro uotís adstantium, pro memoria martirum, pro remisione pecatorum nóstrorum, et actuum emendatione eorum, ac requie defunctorum, et prosperitate iteneris nostri, pro domino papa episcopo, et omnibus episcopís, et prespeterís, et omni aeclesi- astico ordine, pro imperio romano (25), et omnibus regibus christianís, pro fratribus et sororibus nostrís, pro fratribus

Fol. 24 b. in uia directís (53), pro fratribus quos de caliginosís mundi huius tenebrís dominus arcisire dignatus est, uti eos in aeterna summae lucis quietae pietás diuina suscipiat, pro fratribus qui uarís dolorum generibus adfliguntur, uti eos diuina pietás curare dignetur⁶, pro spé salutís et incolimi- tatis suae, tibi reddunt uota sua eterno deo uiuo et uero commonicantes,

In natale domini (54).

¹ Et diem sacratisimam celebrantes in quo incontaminata uirginitas huic mundo edidit saluatorem :

kl. (54)

Fol. 25 a. Et diem sacratisimam celebrantes circumcisionis domini nóstri ihesu christi :

stellae (54).

Et diem sacratisimam celebrantes natalis calicis (54) domini nostri ihesu christi :

pasca.

Et noctem uel diem sacratisimam ressurrectionis domini nóstri ihesu christi :

in clausula pasca (54).

Et diem sacratisimam celebrantes clausulae pascae domini nóstri ihesu christi :

ascensio (54).

Fol. 25 b. Et diem sacratisimam celebrantes ascensionis domini nóstri ihesu christi ad caelum :

pentacostén (54).

Et diem sacratisimam celebrantes quinquagensimae (54)

---

¹ ¹ om

domini nostri ihesu christi, in qua spiritus sanctus super
apostolos discendit[1].

Et memoriam uenerantes, inprimís gloriosae semper uirginis
mariae, genetricis (55) dei et domini nostri ihesu christi, (56)
sed et beatorum apostolorum ac martirum tuorum, petri, pauli,
Fol. 26 a. anriae, iacobi, iohannis, thomae, iacobi, pilippi, bar-
tholomei, mathei, simonis et thathei, lini, ancliti[2], clementis,
xisti, córnili, cipriani, laurenti, crisogini, iohannis et pauli,
cosme, et damiani, et omnium sanctorum tuorum, quorum
meritis precibusque concedas ut in omnibus protectionis tuae
muniamur auxilio. per[3].

Hanc igitur oblationem seruitutis nostrae, sed et cunctae
familiae tuae, [4]quam tibi offerimus in honorem domini nostri
ihesu christi, et in commemorationem beatorum martirum
tuorum, in hac aeclesiae quam famulus tuus ad honorem
nominis gloriae tuae aedificauit[4], (56), quesumus, domine, ut
Fol. 26 b. placatus suscipias[5], [6]eumque, adque omnem populum ab idulorum cultura eripias, et ad té deum uerum patrem
omnipotentem conuertas[6] (57), diesque (58) nostros in tua
pace disponas, atque ab aeterna damnatione nos eripias[7], et
in electorum tuorum iubeas grege numerari (58), per[8] dominum nostrum.

Quam oblationem té[9], deus, in omnibus, quesumus, benedictam, + ascriptam, ratam, rationabilem, acceptabilemque
facere dignareque[10] nobís corpus et sanguis fiat dilectissimi
fili tui domini[11] nostri ihesu christi.

Qui pridie quam pateretur, accipit panem in sanctas ac
Fol. 27 a. uenerabiles manus suas, eleuatis oculis suís[12] ad[13]
caelum ad té deum patrem suum omnipotentem, tibi gratias
egit[14], benedixit, fregit, dedit[15] discipulís suís, diciens, accipite et manducate ex hoc omnes. Hoc est enim corpus meum.
Simili modo posteaquam cenatum[16], accipit[17] et hunc pre-

---

[2] Cleti.   [3] + Christum Dominum nostrum.   [4–4] om.   [5] accipias.
[6–6] om.   [7] eripi.   [8] + Christum.   [9] tu.   [10] digneris ut.
[11] + dei.   [12] om.   [13] in.   [14] agens.   [15] + que.   [16] + est.
[17] accipiens.

clarum calicem in sanctas ac uenerabiles manus suas, item tibi
gratias agiens, benedixit, dedit discipulís suís, dicens, accipite
et bibite ex hoc[1] omnes. Hic est enim calix sancti[2] sanguinis
mei, noui et aeterni testamenti, misterium fidei, qui pro uobis
et pro multis effundetur in remisionem peccatorum. Haec
quotienscunque feceretis, in mei memoriam faciatis[3], [4]passi-
onem (59) meam predicabitis, resurrectionem meam adnuntia-
Fol. 27 b. bitis, aduentum meum sperabitis, donec iterum
ueniam ad uós de caelís[4] (59).

Unde et memores sumus, domine, nos tui serui, sed et plebs
tua sancta, christi filii tui domini[5] nostri tam beatae passionis,
nec non et ab inferis resurrectionis, sed et in caelos gloriosae
ascensionis, offerimus preclarae maiestati tuae de tuís donís
ac datís, hostiam puram, hostiam sanctam, hostiam immaculatam, panem sanctum uitae aeternae, et calicem salutis per-
petuae.

Supra quae propitio ac sereno uultu aspicire[6] dignare[7],
et accepta habere, sicuti accepta habere dignatús es munera
Fol. 28 a. pueri tui iusti abel, et sacrificium patriarchae
nostri abrache, et quod tibi obtilit summus sacerdos tuus
melchisedech, sanctum sacrificium, immaculatam hostiam.

Supplices té rogamus, et [2]petimus,[2] omnipotens deus, iube[8]
perferri m[9] per manus sancti[2] angeli tui in [10]sublimi altari
tuo[10], in conspectu diuinae maistatis tuae, ut quotquot ex
[11]hoc altari sanctificationis[11] sacrosanctum filii tui corpus et
sanguinem sumserimus, omni benedictione[12] et gratia re-
plemur[13].

Fol. 28 b. [14]Memento etiam, domine, et eorum nomina qui
nos praecesserunt cum signo fidei, et dormiunt in somno pacis,
cum omnibus in toto mundo offerentibus sacrificium spiritale (60) deo patri, et filio, et spiritui sancto sanctis ac uenera-
bibus sacerdotibus offert senior noster .n. praespiter, pro sé,

---

[1] eo.   [2] om.   [3] facietis.   [4–4] om.   [5] + Dei.   [6] respicere.
[7] digneris.   [8] + haec.   [9] Erroneous commencement of manus.
[10–10] sublime altare tuum.   [11–11] hac altaris participatione.
[12] + coelesti.   [13] + per Christum Dominum nostrum.   [14–14] om.

et pro súis, et pro totius aeclesie cetu catholicae; et pro commemorando anathletico gradu (60a) uenerabilium patriarcharum, profetarum, apostolorum, et martirum, et omnium quoque sanctorum, ut pro nobís dominum deum nostrum exorare dignentur (61).

Fol. 29 a.

     sancte stefane, ora pro nobís (62).

     sancte martini, ora pro nobís.

     sancte hironime, ora pro nobís.

     sancte augustine, ora pro nobís.

     sancte grigorii, ora pro nobís.

     sancte hilari, ora pro nobís.

     sancte patricii (63), ora pro nobís.

     sancte ailbei (64), ora pro nobís.

     sancte finnio (65), ora pro nobís.

     sancte finnio (66), ora pro nobís.

     sancte ciarani (67), ora pro nobís.

     sancte ciarani (68), ora pro nobís.

     sancte brendini (69), ora pro nobís.

     sancte columba (70), ora pro nobís.

     sancte columba (71), ora pro nobís.

Fol. 29 b.

     sancte comgilli (72), ora pro nobís.

     sancte cainnichi (73), ora pro nobís.

     sancte findbarri (74), ora pro nobís.

     sancte nessani (75), ora pro nobís.

     sancte factni (76), ora pro nobís.

     sancte lugidi (77), ora pro nobís.

     sancte lacteni (78), ora pro nobís.

     sancte ruadani (79), ora pro nobís.

     sancte carthegi (80), ora pro nobís.

     sancte coemgeni (81), ora pro nobís.

     sancte mochonne (82), ora pro nobís.

     sancte brigta (83), ora pro nobís.

     sancte ita (84), ora pro nobís.

     sancte scetha (85), ora pro nobís.

sancte sinecha (86), ora pro nobís.

sancte samdine (87), ora pro nobís.

Fol. 30 a.   omnes sancti, orate pro nobís.

Propitius esto.   Parce nobís domine.   Propitius esto.

Libera nós, domine, ab omni malo.

Libera nós, domine, per crucem tuam.

Libera nós, domine, peccatores.

Té rogamus audi nós.

Filii dei, té rogamus audi nós.

Ut pacem donés té rogamus.

Audi nós, agne dei.

Qui tollis peccata mundi, misserere nobís.

Christe, audii nós.   Christe, audi nós.   Christe, audi nós.

ORATIO AMBROSI (88).

Ante conspectum diuinae maestatis tuae, deus, adsisto, qui inuocare nomen sanctum tuum presumo, misserere mihi, do-
Fol. 30 b.   mine, homini peccatori luto feccis inmunde inherenti, ignosce indigno sacerdoti per cuius manus haec oblatio uidetur offerri ; parce, domine, pulluto peccatori labe pre ceterís capitalium (creminum) et non intres in iudicio cum seruo tuo, quia non iustificabitur in conspectu tuo omnis uiuens, scilicet uitís ac uoluntatibus carnis grauati sumus, recordare, domine, quod caro sumus, et non est alius tibi comparandus ; in tuo conspectu etiam caeli non sunt mundi, quanto magis nos homines terreni, quorum ut dixit (89) :—

Fol. 31 a.

ablis (90)	dauid	nauum	iohannis
zeth	heliae	ambacuc	baptiste
enóc	helessiae	sophoniae	et uirginis
noe	essaiae	agiae	mariae
melch	heremiae	sachariae	petri
sedech	ezechelis	malachiae	pauli
abrache	danielis	tobiae	andriae
isac	hestre	ananiae	iacobi

iacob	osse	azariae	iohannis
ioseph	iohel	misahelis	pilipi
iob	amos	macha-	bartha
mosi	abdiae	beorum	lomae
essu	ionae	item in-	tomae
samuelis	michiae	fantum	mathei

Fol. 31 b.

iacobi	et ceterorum	isernini (97)	cuáni (111)
simonis	patrum	cerbáni (98)	declach (112)
tathei	heremi	erci (99)	laurenti (113)
madiani (91)	sciti (92)	catheri (100)	melléti (114)
madiani (91)	item	ibori (101)	iusti (115)
marci	episcoporum	ailbi (102)	aedo (116)
lucae	martini	conlai (103)	dagani (117)
stefani	grigori	maic (104)	tigernich (118)
cornili	maximi	nissae (105)	muchti (119)
cipriani	felicis	moinenn (106)	ciannani (120)
et ceterorum	patrici (93)	senani (107)	buiti (121)
martirum	patrici (94)	finbarri (108)	eogeni (122)
pauli	secundini (95)	ni (109)	declani (123)
antoni	auxili (96)	colmani (110)	carthain (124)

Fol. 32 a.

maile (125)	columbe (136)	et omnium
ruen (126)	colmani (137)	pausantium, (140)
item et	comgelli (138)	qui nós in domi-
sacerdotum	coemgeni (139)	nica pace preces-
uinniani (127)		erunt, abad-
ciarani (128)		am usque in ho-
oengusso (129)		diernum diem,
endi (130)		quorum deus non
gilde (131)		nominauit (140a)
brendini (132)		et nouit,
brendini (133)		ipsis, et omnibus in
cainnichi (134)		christo quiescentibus,
columbe (135)		locum refrigerii,

Fol. 32 b.   lucis et pacis, ut indulgeas deprecamur.

Nobís quoque peccatoribus fanulís tuis de multitudine
misserationum tuarum sperantibus partem aliquam, et so-
cietatem donare dignare[1], cum tuís sanctis apostolís et
martiribus, cum [2] petro, paulo, patricio[2], iohanne, stefano,
mathia, barnaba, ignatio, alaxandro, marcellino, petro[3],
perpetua, agna, cicilia, felicitate, anatassia, agatha, lucia[3],
et cum omnibus sanctis tuís; intra corum[4] nós consortia,
Fol. 33 a.   non estimatir meritis, sed ueniam, quesumus, largitor
admitte.   per[5].

Per quem haec omnia, domine, semper bona creas, +
sanctificas, + uiuificas, + benedicis, + et prestas nobís, per
ipsum, et cum ipso, et in ipso, est tibi deo patri omnipotenti
in unitate spiritus sancti, omnis honor et gloria per omnia
saecula saeculorum[6].

*Ter canitur. isund conogabar indablu tuaír forsincailech
fobdidithir leth nabairgine is in cailuch* (141).

Fiat domine misericordia tua super nos quemadmodum
sperabimus in te (142).

isund conbongar in bairgen (143).

Cognouerunt dominum. alleluia. in fractione panis (144).
alleluia.

Fol. 33 b.   Panis quem frangimus corpus est domini nostri
ihesu christi (145). alleluia.

Calix quem benedicimus. (alleluia.) sanguis est domini nostri
ihesu christi. (alleluia.) in remisionem peccatorum nostrorum
(145). (alleluia.)

Fiat domine misericordia tua super nós. alleluia. quemadmodum sperauimus in té. alleluia (146).

Cognouerunt dominum (147). alleluia.

Credimus (148), domine, credimus in hác confractione (149) corporis et effussione sanguinis nós esse redemptos, et confidimus,

---

[1] digneris.   [2-2] om.   [3-3] after Petro + Felicitate, Perpetua, Agatha,
Lucia, Agnem, Caecilia, Anastassia.   [4] quorum.   [5] + Christum Dominum nostrum.   [6] Amen.   The variations from the Gelas. Text in the
remainder of the Stowe Canon are too numerous for foot-notes.

sacramenti huius adsumptione munitos, ut quod spé interim hic tenemus mansuri in celestibus uerís fructibus perfruamur, Fol. 34 a. per dominum :

Diuino magisterio edocti, et diuina institutione formati, audimus dicere (150).

~~~ Pater noster, . . rl.

Libera (151) nós, domine, ab omni malo preterito, presenti, et futuro, et intercedentibus pro nobís beatís apostolís tuís petro et paulo, patricio, dá propitius pacem tuam in diebus nóstrís, ut ope missericordiae tuae adiuti et a peccato simus semper liberi, et ab omni perturbatione securi, per dominum.

Páx (152) et caritas domini nostri ihesu christi, et commoni- Fol. 34 b. catio sanctorum omnium, sit sempèr nobíscum.

Et cum spiritu tuo (153).

Pacem mandasti, pacem dedisti, pacem dirilinquisti. Pacem tuam, domine, dá nobís de celo, et pacificum hunc diem et ceteros dies uitae nóstrae in tua pace disponás (154), per dominum.

Commixtio corporis et sanguinis domini nostri ihesu christi sit nobís salús in uitam perpetuam (155). amen.

Ecce agnus dei (156).

Ecce. qui tollis peccata mundi.

Pacem meam do uobís (157). alleluia.

Fol. 35 a. Pacem relinquo uobís (157). alleluia.

Pax (158) multa diligentibus legem tuam, domine. alleluia : et non est in illís scandalum (159). alleluia.

Regem caeli cum pace (160). alleluia.

Plenum odorem uitae (161). alleluia.

Nouum carmen cantate (162). alleluia.

Omnes sancti uenite (163). alleluia.

Uenite, comedite panem meum. alleluia. et bibite uinum quod miscui uobis (164). alleluia.

Dominus reget me (165).

Qui manducat corpus meum et bibit meum sanguinem (166). alleluia.

Ipse in me manet ego in illo (167). alleluia.

Domini est terra (168).

Fol. 35 b.   Hic est panis uiuus qui de celo discendit (169). alleluia.

Qui manducat ex eo uiuet in eternum (170). alleluia.

Ad té, domine, leuaui animam meam (171).

Panem caeli dedit eís dominus. alleluia. panem angelorum manducauit homo (172). alleluia.

Iudica mé, domine (173).

Comedite amici mei. alleluia. et inebriamini carissimi (174). alleluia.

Hoc sacrum corpus domini saluatoris sanguinem; alleluia. sumite uobís in uitam eternam (175). alleluia.

In labís meís meditabor ymnum, alleluia. cum docueris mé et ego iustias respondebo (176). alleluia.

Fol. 36 a.   Benedicam dominum in omni tempore. alleluia. semper laús eius in ore meo (177). alleluia.

Gustate et uidete. alleluia. quam suauis est dominus (178). alleluia.

Ubi ego fuero. alleluia. ibi erit et minister meus (179). alleluia.

Sinite paruulos uenire ad mé, alleluia. et nolite eos pro- hibere. alleluia. talium est enim regnum caelorum (180). alleluia.

Penitentiam agite. alleluia. adpropinquauit enim regnum celorum (181). alleluia.

Regnum celorum uim patitur, alleluia. et uiolenti rapiunt illud (182). alleluia.

Uenite, benedicti patris mei, possidete regnum. alleluia. quod uobís paratum est ab origine mundi (183). alleluia.

Gloria. Uenite. Sicut erat. Uenite (183 a).

móel caích (184) *scripsit.*

Fol. 36 b.   Presta ut quos celesti, domine, dono satiasti, et a nostris enundemur occultis, et ab ostium liberemur insidis (185).

Gratias tibi agimus, domine, sancte pater, omnipotens aeterne deus, qui nos corporis et sanguinis christi filii tui commonione

satiasti, tuamque missericordiam humiliter postulamus, ut hoc
tuum, domine, sacramentum non sit nobís reatus ad penam,
sed intercessio salutaris ad ueniam, sit ablutio scelerum, sit
fortitudo fragilium, sit contra mundi periculo firmamentum,
hec nos commonio purget a cremine, et caelestis gaudi tribuat
esse participes (186). per.

misa acta est (187).

in pace :—(188).

Fol. 37 a. Mísa apostolorum et martirum et sanc- torum et sanctarum uirginum (189).

Deum patrem, deum filium, deum spiritum sanctum, unum
et solum dominum dominantium, et regem regnantium, et
gloriam futurorum per preuelegia clara patriarcharum, et
gloriosa presagia profetarum, per sancta merita apostolorum,
per marteria martirum, per fidem confessorum, per sanctitatem
Fol. 37 b. uirginum, per teoricam uitam anchoritarum (190), per
silentium spiritale munachorum, per episcoporum ac abbatum
catholicorum principatum, innixís ac continuis orationibus
fideliter opsecremus spicialiter hoc per sancta sufragia sanctorum, uel sanctarum uirginum, quorum hodie sollemnítas á
nobis celebratur, ut hec oblatio plebís tuae, quam sanctae
trinitate in honorem eorum .n. offerimus, acceptabilis fiat
deo, cunctis proficiat ad salutem. per.

Domine, deus noster, ihesu christe, splendor paternae
Fol. 38 a. gloriae, et dies claritatis aeternae, gratias tibi
agimus, quoniam accendere dignatus és .xii. apostolos tuos
igne sancti spiritus tui, quique .xii. horas diei lumine solis
inlustratas quibus dixisti, uos estis lux mundi, et iterum,
nonne .xii. horae diei súnt, si quis ergo ambulauerit in lumine
diei hic non offendit, orire nobís, domine, deus noster, ihesu
christe, sol iustitiae, in cuius pennís est sanitas timentibus
té, ut ambulemus in luce dum lucem habemus, ut simus filii
lucis, qui inluminasti apostolos, quique luminaria huic mundo
Fol. 38 b. et alios sanctos, quique tuos uel eorum uicarios
gratia spiritu sancti ac doctrina preditos, discute a nobís

tenebras ignorantiae, et iustitiae tuae per horum patrocinia .n.
quorum festiuitas hodie colitur, ut in te, et per té, semper
manemus. per.

Deus qui nos sanctorum tuorum beatisimorum spirituum,
angelorum, archangelorumque, principum et potestatum,
dominationum, uirtutum, ciruphín et saraphin, patriarcharum,
profetarum, apostolorum, martirum, confessorumque, et
uirginum, anchoritarum, coenouium, omniumque sanctorum
conciuium supernorum et intercessionibus gloriosís circumdas
Fol. 39 a. et protegis, presta, quesumus, eorum et emitatione
proficere, et interpellatione tueri, et, intercedentibus sanctis,
a cunctís nós defende periculis. per.

Domine, deus omnipotens, qui sanctos tuos cum mensura
probas, et sine mensura glorificas, cuius precepta finem habent,
et premia terminum non habent, exaudi preces nostras per
marteria et merita illorum, et tribue eorum patrocinia
adiuuent nos ad fidei profectum, ad bonorum operum fructum,
ad prosperitatis bonum, ad salubritatis commodum, ad religionis
Fol. 39 b. cultum, ad diuini timoris augmentum. Orent
pro nobís sancti martires, et pro defunctís nostris, et pro
pecoribus, et pro omnibus terrae nostrae fructibus, et pro
omnibus in hoc loco commorantibus, et omnipotentem deum
creaturarum caelestium et terrestrium innumerabilis multi-
tudinis sanctorum tuorum et angelorum chori incessabili uoce
proclamant dicentes ;

Sanctus, Sanctus, Sanctus.

Dignum et iustum, aequm et iustum et gloriosum est,
nos tibi semper gratias agere, omnibus diebus uitae
Fol. 40 a. nostrae, domine deus omnipotens, sed in hac
die gratias et habundantius debemus gratulari cum gaudio
spiritus sancti solemnitatem apostolorum .n. siue sanctorum
uel sanctarum .n. presta ergo nobís, omnipotens deus, fidem,
spem, et caritatem, et catholicum finem ac pacificum, per
merita ac commemoratione sanctorum tuorum .n. in quorum
honorem hec oblatio hodie offertur, ut cunctís proficiat ad
salutem, per dominum nostrum ihesum christum, cui omnes

angeli et archangeli, profete et apostoli, martires et confessores,
Fol. 40 b. uirgines et omnes sancti, immo perpetuo et in-
defessís laudibus, cum quatuor animalibus, uenti quatuor
senioribus concindunt dicentes.

S[anctus].

Uere (191) sanctus, uere benedictus, uere mirabilis in sanctis
suis, deus noster ihesus christus ipse dabit uirtutem et
fortitudine plebis suae; benedictus deus quem benedicimus
in apostolis, et in omnibus sanctis suís, qui placuerunt ei
ab initio sae[culi], per eundem dominum nostrum ihesum
christum.

Qui pridie (192).

Sumpsimus, domine, sanctorum tuorum sollemnia celebrantes
caelestia sacramenta; presta, quesumus, ut quod temporaliter
gerimus aeternis gaudiis consequamur. per (192 a).

INCIPIT MISA PRO PENITENTIBUS UIUÍS.

Fol. 41 a.   PRO PENITENTIBUS UIUIS.

Exultatio diuina, paterna pietas, inmensa maestas, te supplices trementes depraecamur pro famulís tuís, ut des eís
mentem puram, caritatem perfectam, in actibus sinceritatem,
in corde puritatem, in opere uirtutem, in moribus disciplinam,
et que iustiae tuae timore intigra mentes uel deuotione pro ipsis
.n. tibi offerimus pietatis tuae obtinentia agnoscant. per.

Indulge, domine, penetentibus nobís famulís tuís poscentibus
secura mente tibi, domine, deo nostro uictimam pro ipsís
Fol. 41 b.   .n. offerri ualeamus, et pie dictís suís ueniam
obteniant, sanitatis, per té, pater sancte, munere consequti,
ad salutem gratiae aeternae possint cum tuo adiutorio
peruenire.

Iteramus, omnipotens deus, deprecationem (193) nostram ante
conspectum maiestatis tuae, quam spicialiter pro famulis tuís
.n. in honore sanctorum, mariae, petiri, pauli, iohannis, et
omnium sanctorum tuorum, oblationem pro peccatís eorum
offerimus, uota perficias, petitiones eorum ascendat ad aures

Fol. 42 a.　clementiae tuae, discendat super eos pia benedictio.
ut sub umbra alarum tuarum in omnibus protegantur, et
orationes nostrae, té propitiante, pro ipsís non refutentur a
conspectu pietatis tuae, sed in omnibus auxiliare atque de-
fendere digneris. per.

U[ere] d[ignum] per dominum nostrum ihesum christum,
filium tuum, cuius potentia deprecanda est (194), missericordia
adoranda, piatas amplectare. Quis enim aliís putare poterit
omnis potentiae tuae miracula? nec aures hominis audire, nec
in cór hominis ascendere, nec estimatio hominum poterit
Fol. 42 b.　inuenire quanta praeparas sanctis electis tuis (195);
sed in quantum possimus misseri terrenique de incontinentia
sed de tua missericordia ueniam misserationis et refugium pos-
tulantes, atque in commemoratione sanctorum, per quorum
suffragia sperantes ueniam, ut famulis tuis .n. remisionem
tribuas peccatorum, opera eorum perficias, uota condones; dona
eís denique séruis tuís, intercedentibus sanctis, remedium animarum suarum quod postulamus, ut uota desideriorum eorum
Fol. 43 a.´ perfeciat, presta, omnipotens, suplicantibus nobís
indulgentiam, postulantibus ueniam, poscentibus uota pingesce,
protege eís nomen dei iacob, iube eis auxilium de sancto
et de sion tueri .n. memor esto, missericors deus, sacrificium
eorum, et holochaustum eorum ante conspectum sanctorum
apinge fiat; tribue eís desideria sancta eorum, et omne
consilium eorum confirmá in bonum, ut inletentur coram té
corda desiderium eorum. per christum.

Deus (196) qui confitentium tibi corda purificas, et accus-
santes sé conscientius et omnium iniquitate absoluis, dá
Fol. 43 b.　indulgentiam reís, et medicinam tribue uulneratis,
ut, percepta remissionem omnem peccatorum, in sacramentis
tuis sincera deinceps deditione permanent, et nullam redemptionis aeternae susteniant tetrimentum. per dominum
nostrum.

Misa pro mortuís pluribus.

Praesta, quesumus, omnipotens et missericors deus, ut

animas famulorum tuorum .n. indulgentiam peccatorum et gaudia perpetua lucis inueniant.

Dá nobís misseridordiam tuam, quesumus, domine, ut animas famulorum tuorum .n. ab omnibus uitiís expiatae, cum tua protectione securae diem futurae resurrectionis expecta(n)t. per christum.

Intende, domine, munera que altaribus tuís pro sanctorum tuorum .n. commemoratione deferimus, et pro nostris offentionibus imbulamus (197).

U[ere] d[ignum] cuius promisionis plenus aeternorum bonorum in ipso expectamus manifestandus, in quo scimus eas absconditas domino nostro ihesu christo, qui uera est uita credentium, resurrectio famulorum tuorum .n. illorum pro quibus hoc sacrificium offerimus, obsæcrantes ut regenerationis fontae purgatos, et a temptationibus exceptos, beatorum numero digneris inserere, et quos adoptionis participes iubeas hereditatis tuae esse consortes. per.

Oremus, fratres carisimi (198), pro carís nostrís .n.(199) qui iam in dominice pace praecesserunt, quos finis debitus et ordo transmigrationis conclusit, ut deus omnipotens, pater domini nostri ihesu christi, iubeat carnem animamque et spiritum eorum suscipi in locum lucis, in partem refregéri, in sinibus abrache, et isác, et iácob, dimittat quoque si quicquid incongrue per ignorantiam, atque subripiente inimico, peccauerunt, et spiritu oris sui eos refrigerare dignetur. per.(200)

NOTES.

1. This title, together with the following Versicle, 'Letania—intende,' is written on the top margin of fol. 13 a. Compare the wording of the title on p. 244.

2. This is the second Versicle at Matins, and the Introit for Dom. xii. Pentec. (S. R.).

3. The same Litany occurs in the St. Gall fragment, MS. No. 1395, p. 179, and seems to be peculiarly Irish. A short Litany of this kind used always to precede Mass, intervening between it and the preceding office of Terce or Sext. Its use in the Cluniac constitutions was thus prescribed: 'Majorem missam in privatis diebus solet iterum letania praevenire, quae tamen non est multum prolixa, tribus tantum Sanctis de singulis ordinibus nominandis.' Udalricus, Antiq. Consuet. Cluniacens. lib. i. c. 6.

The opening rubric of the Mass edited by Mat. Flac. Illyricus (Mart. i. p. 176) runs thus: '*In primis quomodo sacerdos Apologetica celebrare debeat, antequam ad missarum celebrationem accedat. Mox antequam sacerdotalibus induatur vestibus, si locus acciderit, vel tempus permiserit, flexis genibus coram altare cantet vii. Psalmos poenitentiales cum litania, qua finita dicat* "Pater Noster," Credo in Deum Patrem omnipotentem. *Post has preces.*' Among these preces the following bear resemblance, partly verbal, partly substantial, to the opening devotions of the Stowe Missal:—

'Peccavimus cum patribus nostris, injuste egimus, iniquitatem fecimus Domine.'

'Adjuva nos, Deus salutaris noster, et propter gloriam nominis tui, Domine, libera nos, et propitius esto peccatis nostris propter nomen tuum.'

'Extende, Domine, brachium tuum; et libera animas nostras ne pereamus.'

'Domine exaudi orationem meam.'

The triple Kyrie eleison is the sole surviving relic in the present Roman Ordinary of the Mass of an older Litany; De Vert, Cérémonies de l'Eglise, i. 67.

4. St. Madianus occupies the same position in the list of saints within the Canon (p. 240), and in the Litany in the St. Gall fragment, No. 1395, p. 180. See note 91.

5. The preparatory absolution in a Tours Missal, A.D. 1533, is given: '. . . per auxilium et signum sanctae crucis . . . et per intercessionem . . . et omnium Sanctorum et Sanctarum' (Mart. i. p. 130).

6. The words which follow are the usual conclusion of the prayer of St. Ambrose; see p. 239. n. (89). Possibly the scribe intended to insert the 'Prayer of St. Augustine' given at the commencement of the Sarum Ordinary of the Mass under this title (p. 566), and printed at the commencement of the Roman Missal under the title of Oratio Sancti Ambrosii Episcopi (p. lxii). The Roman rubric directs it to be said '*Pro opportunitate sacerdotis ante celebrationem et communionem.*' The rubric in a Sarum Missal given by a Lord Prior of Worcester to the church of Bromsgrove, A.D. 1511, runs thus: '*Oratio Sancti Augustini dicenda a sacerdote in Missa dum canitur* Officium *et* Kyrie

et Gloria in Excelsis *et* Credo in unum ; *vel tota dicitur ante missam quod melius est.'*

7. This prayer occurs in a ninth-century Troyes Pontifical, at vesting, 'ad tunicam' (Mart. ordo vi. p. 191) ; in a ninth-century Tours Missal among the apologiae after vesting (ib. ordo vii. p. 193) ; in a Rheims Pontifical, undated (ib. ordo ix. p. 195) ; in a tenth-century Corbie Sacramentary, 'ad baltheum' (ib. ordo xi. p. 203) ; in the Missa 'Flacii Illyrici postquam sacerdos infulatus fuerit' (ib. ordo iv. p. 177) ; in the Codex Chisii in the Preparatio sacerdotis ad Missam, after vesting (ib. ordo xii. p. 205) ; in the Ambrosian rite, as the 'Oratio secreta antequam sacerdos accedat altare' (Pamel. Liturg. i. 293). The presence and position of this and similar prayers for the personal use of the priest are in themselves a proof of the antiquity of any Missal.

8. A later hand had added 'l' over 'batheo ;' 'neque permittas' over 'perire ;' 'praesta' before 'per dominum ;' and seems to suggest the abbreviation of the collect by the omission of the words from 'ut—pacificas.'

9. The scribe must have been an ardent devotee of St. Peter to write down Petri et Christi instead of Christi et Petri ; or is Christi a clerical error for Pauli ?

10. Compare the language of the Absolution in the Reconciliatio poenitentiam on Maundy Thursday: 'Absolvimus vos vice beati Petri, apostolorum principis cui collata est a Domino potestas ligandi atque solvendi,'&c. Sar. Mis. p. 300 ; Corpus Mis. p. 210. The words 'Deus—tradidisti' are the opening words of the collect 'in Com. S. Petri Ap.' on June 30 in the Rom. Mis. p. 438, Sar. Mis. p. 790. In a Syrian collect of Absolution quoted by Mart., ordo xxiii. vol. i. p. 335, the words 'ceterisque discipulis suis' have been significantly added after 'beato Petri ;' also in a fourteenth-century Rouen Rit., ordo xii. Mart. vol. ii. p. 402.

11. This is the Roman collect, with verbal variations, in Cathedra S. Petri, Jan. 18, 25, Feb. 22, and the memorial collect of St. Peter on June 30. Its earliest occurrence is in the Gelas. Sacram. lib. ii. ordo xxx. It also occurs in the Missale Vesontionense under the heading of 'Missa Romensis Cottidiana,' p. 206.

12. The 'Gloria in Excelsis' was introduced into the Roman Liturgy by Pope Symmachus, 498–514 (Wal. Strabo, De Rebus Eccles. c. 22). Several variations from the received Western text will be observed here. Compare the text in the Ant. Bench. p. 193 ; Book of Hymns, p. 197. It forms no part of the Eastern nor of the ancient Gallican Liturgy, judging from the omission of any reference to it in Germanus's Expos. Brev. Antiq. Lit. Gallican. (Mart. i. p. 167). It is noteworthy however that in the Sacramentarium Gallicanum it occurs as in the Anglican Liturgy, in the position of a thanksgiving after the Communion (Mabillon, Mus. It. i. p. 281).

13. This collect is assigned to Dom. v. Pentec. (R.), Dom. vi. post Trin. (S.), Gelas. Sacr. iii. coll. i ; Greg. Sacr. Hebd. vi. post Pentec.

14. There are frequent allusions in later Missals to the 'Romanus Ordo' or 'Ecclesia Romana' (York Missal, i. pp. 168, 169), as differing from the local or national use ; or to the latter as differing from the former (Sarum Missal, pp. 6, 15). In the case of the York Missal such expressions have been taken to date from the time of Charlemagne, when the Ordo Romanus was introduced into France by royal authority, and probably into York by Alcuin or his pupil Archbishop Eanbald II. In the present text a contrast seems to be implied between the devotions of the foreign Church of Rome and those of the ancient national Church of Ireland.

15-15. Deus—placaris.   These are the opening words in the Greg. Sacr. for the Feria v. in Quinquagesima, but the rest of the collect is different.   The present collect occurs nearly in this position in the Sacramentarium Gallicanum (Mabillon, Mus. It. i. p. 279).

16. This is a rare word of sacrificial signification used by Arnobius, Adv. Gentes, lib. vii. c. 24, and defined by Varro as 'quod ex immolata hostia dejectum in jecore in porriciendo augendi causa;' De Lingua Lat. lib. v. § 112. p. 44, edit. 1833.   I have not met with its use elsewhere as a term of Christian ritual.   It may refer to some unwritten addition made at this point of the service, or can it refer merely to the concluding unwritten words of the collect 'Jesum Christum,' &c.?   Compare the rubric on p. 233.   The word 'augmentum' occurs in cap. 7 of the Regula S. Columbani quoted on p. 97.

17. 1 Cor. xi. 26–32.   This is a portion of the Epistle assigned to Coena Domini in the Roman and Sarum Missals (1 Cor. xi. 20–32), in the Sacram. Gallican. (1 Cor. xi. 20–26).   The presence here of single fixed lessons is remarkable, and an evidence of great antiquity.   The only other case where the same Epistle and Gospel are conjectured to have been always used is that of the Liturgy of the Church of Malabar; Le Brun, Explication de la Messe, tom. vi. p. 487.   The suitableness of the passages of Scripture selected here for constant use, both of them bearing on the institution of the Eucharist, is obvious.

18. This collect is written on the lower margin of fol. 15 b, in the later hand.

18 a. Ps. civ. 4.   18 b. 1 Par. xvi. 8–10.

19. These are the opening words (Grata—quibus) of a Secret in the Corpus Missal, p. 190, and in the Gelasian Sacram. p. 682.

20. Ps. cxvii. 14.   V. Laus, Bk. of Dimma, p. 170, Stowe Missal, p. 225.

21. This only differs slightly from the Roman Secret for Dom. iv. Adv.: 'Sacrificiis praesentibus quaesumus, Domine, placatus intende : ut et devotioni nostrae proficiant et saluti.'   Sacr. Leon. p. 482 ; Gelas. p. 682 ; Greg. pp. 29, 43, 105, 108, 124, 138.

22. It is curious to find this word lingering as the title of mediaeval devotions of the same character.   The York Bidding Prayers, A.D. 1405, commence thus : 'Deprecemur Deum Patrem Omnipotentem pro pace et stabilitate sanctae matris Ecclesiae' (Early Eng. Text Soc. vol. 71. p. 64).   Another form of Bidding Prayers (A.D. 1440–50) is headed 'Deprecacio pro pace Ecclesiae et regni in diebus dominicis' (ib. p. 68).   For another use of the word 'deprecatio,' see p. 106.   The association of these prayers with the name of St. Martin, Bishop of Tours (371–401), indicates that, though of Eastern origin, they reached Ireland through a Gallican channel.

That such a Litany existed in the ancient Gallican rite is proved by the allusions of various writers.   Caesarius of Arles speaks of the 'Oratio (quae) Diacono clamante indicitur' (Serm. cclxxxvi. in App. ad Opp. S. Aug., Migne, Bib. Pat. Lat. xxxix. 2285).   Germanus Parisiensis devotes a paragraph to its description under the name of 'Prex,' and indicates its position after the homily and before the expulsion of the catechumens (Mart. i. p. 167).   No traces of the wording of this 'Prex' exist in any extant Gallican Missal, except that the Mozarabic Litany for Passion Sunday occurs in the Sacramentarium Gallicanum for Easter Eve (Mus. Ital. i. 317 ; Mis. Moz. p. 372) ; and the expression 'Collectio post precem,' which is the title of a prayer in the Missale Gothicum on Christmas Day and Easter Day, possibly refers to a preceding Litany, although Mabillon gives a different interpretation of it (Lit. Gallic. p. 190).

It is noteworthy that the character of these intercessions corresponds to those enumerated, in a somewhat different order, in a passage in the Regula S. Columbani : ' Cum versiculorum augmento intervenientium pro peccatis primum nostris, deinde pro omni populo Christiano, deinde pro sacerdotibus, et reliquis Deo consecratis sacrae plebis gradibus, postremo pro eleemosynas facientibus, postea pro pace regum, novissime pro inimicis, ne illis Deus statuat in peccatum quod persequuntur nos, et detrahunt nobis, quia nesciunt quod faciunt.'

23. Similar passages are found in the Rogation Litany printed from a tenth-century Pontifical of the diocese of Münster in Westphalia (Mart. lib. iv. c. 27. p. 185). Compare the 'Orationes Sollemnes' after the Gospel on Good Friday and the Litany before Mass on Easter Eve in the present Roman Missal; the petitions after the Ingressa on four Sundays in Lent in the Milanese rite; after the Psallendo and before the Epistle on the first five Sundays in Lent in the Mozarabic rite; in the Liturgies of St. Chrysostom and St. Basil before the Introit; in the Liturgies of Armenia and Malabar before the first lection. The present position between the Epistle and the Gospel appears to be unique. There is also a strong resemblance to the ' Bidding Prayers,' or Preces Dominicales, which immediately preceded the sermon in the mediæval English Church, and were said in the Procession before Mass in cathedral and collegiate churches, but after the Gospel and Offertory in parish churches. Compare the tenth-century form in use at York, printed in Early English Text Society, vol. 71. p. 62, with Mr. Simmons' exhaustive note, ib. p. 315. Similar prayers in the vernacular were drawn up for the use of lay people during the recitation of the Canon by the officiating priest ; ib. pp. 32–36, Text B. They are a survival from an Eastern source. A near approach to this whole passage, both in form and substance, is to be found in the following Missal Litany, transcribed by Wicelius from an ancient MS. in the Library of Fulda, and printed by Bona, Rer. Litur. lib. ii. cap. iv. § 3 :—

' In Codice Fuldensi Litania Missalis.

(α) Dicamus omnes ex toto corde totaque mente : Domine miserere.

(β) Qui respicis terram et facis eam tremere. Oramus te, Domine, exaudi et miserere.

(γ) Pro altissima pace et tranquillitate temporum nostrorum. Oramus, &c.

Pro sancta ecclesia catholica, quae est a finibus usque ad terminos orbis terrarum. Oramus, &c.

(δ) Pro patre nostro episcopo, pro omnibus episcopis, ac presbyteris, et diaconis, omnique clero. Oramus, &c.

(ε) Pro hoc loco et habitantibus in eo. Oramus, &c.

Pro piissimo imperatore et toto Romano exercitu. Oramus, &c.

Pro omnibus qui in sublimitate constituti sunt, pro virginibus, viduis, et orphanis. Oramus, &c.

(ζ) Pro poenitentibus et catechumenis. Oramus, &c.

(θ) Pro his qui in sancta ecclesia fructus misericordiae largiuntur. Domine Deus virtutum exaudi preces nostras. Oramus, &c.

(ι) Sanctorum apostolorum ac martyrum memores sumus, ut, orantibus eis pro nobis, veniam mereamur. Oramus, &c.

(κ) Christianum ac pacificum nobis finem concedi a Domino comprecemur. Praesta, Domine, praesta.

(λ) Et divinum in nobis permanere vinculum charitatis, Dominum comprecemur. Praesta, Domine, praesta.

(μ) Conservare sanctitatem ac puritatem catholicae fidei sanctum Deum comprecemur.   Praesta, Domine, praesta.

Dicamus omnes, Domine exaudi et miserere.'

We subjoin another form of Missal Litany, Gallican in its wording and character, written in a ninth-century hand on fol. 13 a, b of the Leofric Missal. It is not part of the Leofric Sacramentary, properly so called, but occurs on one of the miscellaneous leaves which have been bound up together at the commencement of the MS. volume which bears that name :—

'Oremus, fratres karissimi, domini misericordiam pro fratribus ac sororibus nostris ab oriente usque ad occidentem, ut et illi orent pro nobis unusquisque in diversis locis per christum dominum nostrum.

'Oremus etiam pro unitate aecclesiarum, pro infirmis, pro debilibus, pro captiuis, pro poenitentibus, pro laborantibus, pro nauigantibus, pro iter agentibus, pro elemosinas facientibus, pro defunctorum spiritibus, et pro his qui non communicant, ut det illis dominus dignam agere poenitentiam, per christum dominum nostrum.

'Oremus etiam domini misericordiam pro spiritibus carorum nostrorum pausantium .ill. ut eis dominus placidum refrigerium tribuere dignetur, et in locum quietis ac refrigerii sanctorum suorum intercessione eos transferat, per ihesum christum dominum nostrum.

'Offerimus tibi, domine ihesu christe, hanc orationem ab ortu solis usque ad occidentem, a dextera usque ad sinistram, in honorem et gloriam diuinitatis christi et humanitatis, in honorem et gloriam omnium graduum coelestium, michahelem, gabrihelem archangelum ; in honorem et gloriam patriarcharum, prophetarum, apostolorum, ac martyrum ; pro omnibus uirginibus, fidelibus poenitentibus, pro omnibus matrimoniis, pro bonis non ualde, pro malis non ualde, pro omnibus merentibus orationem et deprecationem [note 22] nostram, per eundem.'

We may also compare the Deacon's Litany or Bidding Prayer (διακονίκα, εἰρηνικὰ, δεήσεις, μεγαλὴ συναπτή) in the Liturgy of St. Chrysostom, extracts from which are here appended in Goar's Latin translation (Eucholog. pp. 64–65) :—

(α) 'In pace Dominum precemur.   Domine miserere.

(γ) Pro pace totius mundi [altissima = ὑπὲρ τῆς ἄνωθεν εἰρήνης] stabilitate sanctarum Dei ecclesiarum, et pro omnium concordia, Dominum precemur.

(δ) Pro Archiepiscopo nostro N.   Venerandis presbyteris, in Christo Diaconis, universo clero Dominum precemur.

(ε) Pro hac sancta domo, et iis qui cum fide, religione, et Dei timore ipsam ingrediuntur, Dominum precemur.

Pro piissimis et a Deo custoditis regibus nostris, toto palatio et exercitu ipsorum Dominum precemur.

Pro sancta hac mansione, omni urbe, et regione, et cum fide habitantibus in ipsis Dominum precemur.

(η) Pro nauigantibus, iter agentibus, aegrotis, laborantibus, captivis, et salute ipsorum, Dominum precemur.

(γ) There is a corresponding prayer in the Clementine Liturgy : Ὑπὲρ τῆς ἁγίας καθολικῆς καὶ ἀποστολικῆς ἐκκλησίας τῆς ἀπὸ περάτων ἕως περάτων δεηθῶμεν.

(ε) Ὑπὲρ τῆς ἐνθάδε ἁγίας παροικίας δεηθῶμεν.

(ζ) Ὑπὲρ . . . παρθένων, χηρῶντε, καὶ ὀρφανῶν δεηθῶμεν.

(θ) Ὑπὲρ τῶν καρποφορούντων ἐν τῇ ἁγίᾳ ἐκκλησίᾳ καὶ ποιούντων τοῖς πένησι τὰς ἐλεημοσύνας δεηθῶμεν.

(κ, λ, μ) Ὑπὲρ ἀλλήλων δεηθῶμεν, ὅπως ὁ Κύριος τηρήσῃ ἡμᾶς καὶ φυλάξῃ τῇ αὐτοῦ χάριτι εἰς τέλος. Hammond, C. E., Lit. E. and W. p. 8.

The presence of these devotions in the Stowe Missal goes to support Goar's assertion that similar petitions were found in Western Liturgies before the ninth century (Euchol. p. 123. n. 62). We append the following specimen from the Ambrosian Missal, which also bears a close resemblance to the Stowe text (Pamel. Liturgicon, i. 328) :—

'*Dom. Quadrag. dicta De Samaitana.*

Finita ingressa, preces per Diaconum pronunciatae, respondente choro (after each petition) :—

(α) Domine miserere.

(β)* Divinae pacis et indulgentiae munere supplicantes ex toto corde et ex tota mente precamur te.

(γ) Pro ecclesia tua sancta catholica, quae hic et per universum orbem diffusa est precamur te.

(δ) Pro papa nostro .N. et pontifice nostro .N. et omni clero eorum, omnibusque sacerdotibus ac ministris precamur te.

(ε) Pro famulo tuo .N. imperatore, et famula tua .N. imperatrice, et omni exercitu eorum, precamur te.

Pro famulo tuo .N. rege, et duce nostro, et omni exercitu ejus, precamur te.

Pro pace ecclesiarum, vocatione gentium, et quiete populorum, precamur te.

Pro civitate hac et conversatione ejus, omnibusque habitantibus in ea, precamur te.

Pro aeris temperie, ac fructuum, et foecunditate terrarum, precamur te.

(ζ) Pro virginibus, viduis, orphanis, captivis, ac poenitentibus, precamur te.

Pro navigantibus, iter agentibus, in carceribus, in vinculis, in metallis, in exiliis constitutis, precamur te.

Pro his qui diversis infirmitatibus detinentur, quique spiritibus vexantur immundis, precamur te.

(θ) Pro his qui in sancta tua ecclesia fructus misericordiae largiuntur, precamur te.

(α) Exaudi nos, Deus, in omni oratione atque deprecatione nostra, precamur te.'

24. Notice the absence of any mention of the Pope or of the minor orders.

25. These words, 'piissimi imperatores,' are a direct translation of the εὐσεβέστατοι βασιλεῖς of the Liturgy of St. Chrysostom. They seem to suggest one of those various periods in the fourth century between the death of Constantine, A.D. 337, and the division of the Empire into East and West, A.D. 395, when several persons were associated on the imperial throne. It is as fruitless to enquire what possible meaning the Latin words can have borne in Ireland, as it was for Goar to ask to whom the Greek words referred, when he heard them used at Constantinople in the beginning of the seventeenth century (Euchol. p. 46. n. 2) ; or as it would be to ask who is meant in the petition, 'Oremus et pro christianissimo imperatore nostro,' which occurs in the present Roman Missal on Good Friday. The phrase has been imported verbatim from the continent into the Irish Liturgy, without consideration that it thereby became unmeaning. It is noteworthy that the above-quoted Fulda Litany reads 'piissimo imperatore' in the singular, and that in the much later Corpus Irish Missal the 'rex' and 'exercitus Hiberniensium' are prayed for instead of the Roman emperor and army. See Introd. to Corpus Missal, p. 47.

Curious instances of a similar confusion may be found in foreign liturgical codices. In the Gregorian Sacramentary (Codex Ratoldi) the King of the Franks is elected to the 'regnum totius Albionis' (Migne, Pat. Lat. lxxviii. 257). The following passage occurs in the office for the Coronation of a King (Benedictio Regis) in a ninth-century Rheims Pontifical (Col. Agrip. Bib. Eccles. Metrop. no. 141 ; Hartzeim, Catalogus MSS. p. 111), in another Pontifical of the same date in the monastery 'Sancti Germani a Pratis' (Migne, Bib. Pat. Lat. lxxviii. 572), and in the service used at the coronation of Charles V of France (Cott. Tib. B. viii; Maskell, W., Mon. Rit. iii. 14):—

'Ut regale solium, videlicet Saxonum, Merciorum, Nordan-Humbrorumque sceptra non deserat, sed ad pristinae fidei pacisque concordiam eorum animos, te opitulante, reformet, ut utrorumque horum populorum debita sibi subjectione fultus, cum digno amore per longum vitae spatium paternae apicem gloriae tua miseratione unatim stabilire et gubernare mereatur.'

The real explanation of the above passages is this. When Charles the Great abolished the national Liturgy in France, there was a sudden and great demand for new liturgical codices. Under Alcuin's directions, Anglo-Saxon Office Books were imported into France for the purpose of being copied, and French scribes wrote them out, word for word, forgetting the geographical and dynastic differences of the two countries.

Menard's remarks on the above extracts illustrate the danger of basing historical conclusions on liturgical expressions: 'Quae quidem verba satis manifestant aliquem Francorum regem id temporis in Anglorum regem unctum fuisse ; quod tamen est difficile scitu, cum nihil tale in historicis antiquis, cum Francorum, tum Anglorum, repereris, per quos huic difficultati lucem afferre quis possit.' Migne, Bib. Pat. Lat. lxxviii. 571, note 1090.

26. S. secret for Domin. prox. ante Adv. ; Sacr. Leon. p. 364; Gelas. p. 681.

27. Compare collect in Book of Hymns, p. 195.

28. This prayer is found in a similar position in the Mass published by M. Flacius Illyricus, its rubric directing 'inter lectionem et evangelium, id est tempore Gradualis, Alleluia, ac Sequentiae, episcopus dicat has orationes ;' Martene, De Ant. Eccles. Rit. I. iv. art. xi. ordo 4. p. 182: also in a French Missal, c. A.D. 800 ; ib. ordo v. p. 187 ; in a ninth-century Troyes Pontifical after the Gospel; ib. ordo vi. p. 191 ; ib. viii. p. 194; ib. xiii. p. 207 ; ib. xvi. p. 215 : after vesting ; ib. xv. p. 210. Similar prayers under the title of 'Apologia' or Confessio Sacerdotis' are found in the Missale Gothicum, No. xxxvii ; Mis. Moz., Leslie, tom. i. p. 224. Fifteen such forms exist in the Gregor. Sacram. as edited by Menard, pp. 228, 526, n. 78 b. A trace of it may exist in the solitary 'Oremus,' not followed by any prayer, in the present Roman Missal before the Offertory.

29. Anglice, 'A half uncovering here.' Some light is thrown on the meaning of this rubric, together with the corresponding Irish rubric on p. 232, by the following extract from a tract on the Eucharist preserved in the Leabhar Breac:—

'The two uncoverings, including the half of the chalice of the Offertory and of the Oblation, and what is chaunted with them, both in the Gospel and Alleoir (= Alleluia ?), figure the written law in which Christ was manifestly foretold but was not seen until his birth. The elevation of the chalice of the Offertory and the paten, after the full uncovering at which is sung the verse "Immola Deo sacrificium laudis."' Fol. 251. col. 1. Compare Stowe Mis. f. 64 b.

30. Ps. cxl. 2. It occurs as the Grad. and Vers., Fer. iii. post Invocavit ; Dom. xix. post Trin. ; Sabb. iv. Temp. Sept. (S. R.) It is also used in the Roman Ordinarium Missae, at the point where the priest incenses the altar.

31. This seems to have been the ancient Gallican position of the Preparation of the Chalice. It survived in the mediaeval French Uses of Amiens, Soissons, Chalons-sur-Saone, and in the English Use of Sarum (Mis. p. 587). The mixture of water with wine took place here also at Salisbury (ib.), and in other places (Mart. iv. 57); but there are no traces of such a rite here.

32. This prayer is said, with slight variation of reading, after the presentation of the elements in the present Roman rite. It is ordered in this form in the VI. Ordo Rom. § 10. Micrologus asserts that it was introduced into the Roman from the Gallican Use : ' Dicit sacerdos hanc orationem juxta Gallicanum Ordinem' (De Eccles. Observ. c. xi). In a ninth-century Rheims Missal it is said 'dum elevatur Sanctum a sacerdote' (Mart. i. p. 197).

33. St. John vi. 51–57. Various portions of this passage of St. John's Gospel occur among the Gospels in the ' Missae Defunctorum,' and in Festo Corporis Christi (R. S.).

34. Here follows a mutilated leaf two-thirds of which have been cut away. On the recto are written the words from Oratio Gregoriana—rl. The verso is blank.

34 a. Other collects 'post Evang.' are provided in the Antiphon. Benchor. p. 193; Book of Hymns, p. 196. This collect occurs twice in Sacr. Greg. pp. 34, 39.

35. This Creed was first introduced into the Liturgy of Constantinople by the Patriarch Timotheus, A.D. 511; into the Church of Spain and France (Gallia Narbonensis) by the second canon of the third Council of Toledo, A.D. 589; into the Roman Liturgy, probably in the reign of Henry II, A.D. 1002–1024, but possibly in that of Charlemagne (ninth century). There are no traces of its present liturgical use in the Gelasian and Gregorian Sacramentaries, or in the earliest Ordo Romanus. Mart. i. p. 138. Its position here may be accepted as prohibitive of the assignation of an earlier date than the ninth century to the Stowe Missal.

36. Anglice, 'A full uncovering here.' See note 29.

37. Ps. lxxxiv. 8. Book of Dimma, p. 170; Stowe Mis. p. 220.

38. This rubric has been added by a later hand.

39. R. S. Sec. in Nativ. Dmi. ad iii. Missam; Sacr. Gregor. pp. 10, 159. The wording of these collects seems to imply the joint presentation of both paten and chalice, in accordance with the later custom of Hereford (Mis. p. 117), Sarum (Mis. p. 593), and the following French churches—Moysac (Mart. i. p. 194), St. Thierry by Rheims (ib. p. 197), Soissons (ib. p. 220), Fécamp (ib. p. 229), Lehon (ib. p. 238), Le Bec (ib. p. 242). On the other hand, the Roman and York Missals (i. p. 171) direct that the elements shall be offered separately and consecutively, providing a separate collect of oblation for each.

It seems hardly fair to infer with Dr. O'Conor (Stowe Catalog. i. App. p. 47), from the absence here of any allusion to wine and water, that the mixed chalice was omitted 'as merely of human institution.'

39 a. Sacr. Leon. p. 352.

40. The allusion to the diptychs in this and the following collect, and the position of these intercessions for the departed before the Canon, is distinctly Ephesine, and has never been found in any Petrine Liturgy. They are specimens of the ' Collectio post nomina' of the Gallican and the ' Oratio post nomina' of the Mozarabic rite. A similar allusion to diptychs is contained in a passage in the Rede Boke of Darbye (an Anglo-Saxon MS. c. 1061, C. C. C. C. 422); but it has been shifted from its Gallican position before the Preface to

its Roman position within the Canon, where it forms part of the present Commemoratio pro vivis : 'Memento, Domine, famulorum famularumque tuarum, omnis congregationis beatae Dei genitricis semperque virginis Mariae, omniumque propinquorum nostrorum, et quorum eleemosynas suscepimus, seu quorum nomina super sanctum altare tuum scripta habentur,' &c. This reading occurs nearly verbatim and in the same position in a tenth-century Sacramentary belonging to the monastery of Corbie, and quoted by Martene, vol. i. p. 146 ; and a similar allusion to diptychs placed on the altar is found in the marginal reading of an early Cologne Codex of the Gregorian Canon, printed by Pamelius (Liturgicon, vol. ii. p. 180).

There are references to both the 'reliquiae' and 'nomina sanctorum' in one of the many 'Secrets' supplied in the Missa Flacii Illyrici, introduced with this rubric :—

'Istae orationes cum oblationes offeruntur ad altare dicendae sunt, et haec est prima quotidiana et generalis.

'Suscipe, sancta Trinitas, hanc oblationem, quam tibi offero in memoriam incarnationis, nativitatis, passionis, resurrectionis, ascensionis Domini nostri Jesu Christi, et in honorem sanctorum tuorum qui tibi placuerunt ab initio mundi, et eorum quorum hodie festivitas celebratur, et quorum hic nomina et reliquiae habentur, ut proficiat ad honorem,' &c. The collect of oblation now in the Roman Liturgy, p. 213, was introduced into it from a foreign source in the twelfth century (Le Brun, Explic. de la Messe, i. 354 ; Microl. § xi).

The above collect and similar phrases occur in the eighth-century Gallican Missal published by Martene, ordo v. p. 189, which consists of the Roman Canon as introduced into Gaul under Charlemagne, interspersed with relics of the national but superseded Liturgy, and in a ninth-century Troye Pontifical (ib. ordo vi. p. 192), of Reims (ix. p. 196 ; x. p. 197 ; xv. p. 213 ; xvi. p. 215 ; xvii. p. 216 ; xxvii. p. 230). The Ordo Missae Flacii Illyrici (Mart. i. p. 185) contains a reference, under the title 'liber vitae,' to the diptychs with the names of the departed inscribed on them, in the later passage within the Canon, entitled in the present Roman Missal Commemoratio pro defunctis, but there

'Item pro salute vivorum et mortuorum.

'Memento etiam . . . . et animabus famulorum famularumque tuarum, videlicet omnium orthodoxorum, quorum commemorationem agimus, et quorum corpora hic et ubique requiescunt, vel quorum nomina hic in libro vitae scripta esse videntur, indulgentiam et remissionem omnium tribuas peccatorum, et in consortio electorum tuorum habere digneris.

'Hic recites nomina quorum velis.

'Istis et omnibus fide catholica quiescentibus locum pacis, refrigerii et quietis indulgeas deprecamur.'

The expression 'the Book of Life' for the 'Diptychs' was perhaps derived from the East. Renaudot quotes a Nestorian writer as saying with reference to two Metropolitans, 'eorum nomina libro vitae inscripta non fuisse, eo quod contra leges ecclesiasticas dignitatem usurpaverant' (Liturg. Or. Coll. 1234).

41. There are frequent references to the Book of Life in the Gallican Orationes post nomina. 'Litteris mereantur conscribi coelestibus;' Miss. Goth. ordo iii: 'in aeterno vitae libro conscribi;' Sacram. Gall., Mab. ed. p. 359: 'in coelesti pagina conscribi praecipias;' Miss. Goth. xxii: 'coelesti chirographo in libro vitae jubeas ascribi;' ib. xxiii, xxiv: 'in libro vitae censeas deputari;' ib. lv: 'in coelesti pagina jubeas intimari;' ib. lviii: 'in coelestibus paginis conscribantur;' ib. lxv: 'aeternalibus indita paginis;' ib. xl: 'nomina jubeas scribi in aeternitate;' ib.

iv: 'nomina faciat in beatitudinem aeterni gaudii recenseri;' ib. liii: 'nomina aeternitatis titulo jubeas praesignari;' ib. xxvi: 'nomina figere in scriptione sempiterna digneris;' ib. xxv: 'in aeterno vitae libro nomina conscribe;' Sacram. Gall., Mab. edit. p. 359: 'in libro vitae jubeas paginam intimare;' ib. 384. also in some Gallican prayers, surviving in an unpublished tenth-century French Greg. Sacr. (Bodl. Auct. D. i. 20, fol. 40 b). Similar phrases occur occasionally in the Mozarabic Liturgy (pp. 226, 286, 346, 415, 483, &c.), always including a reference both to the living and the dead. There is only one instance of such a phrase in the Roman books, and there the reference is to the living only (Sacram. Leon., Murat. edit. p. 318). For further information as to Celtic usage on this point, see p. 105. There is reference to a 'beatae predestinationis liber,' in which are written 'nomina fidelium eorum quos in oratione commendatos suscepimus,' in a ninth-century French Codex (Mart. ordo x. p. 201). This collect reappears in the Anglo-Saxon Leofric Missal, fol. 237 b.

42 a. See p. 227, n. (16).

42 b. Oct. 1 was the Feast of the Holy Relics; F. cciv.

43. These tender expressions are peculiarly characteristic of the Gallican Liturgies. See Missale Richenovens. missa ii; Mis. Goth. ordo iii, xviii, xxxiii, xxxvii, liii, lviii; also Milanese fragment quoted in Peyron, Cic. Frag. Orat. p. 226.

44. The absence of the formulae of mutual salutation, 'Dominus vobiscum, Et cum spiritu tuo,' is worthy of notice. It formed part of the Gregorian, but not of the Gelasian Canon.

45. This Preface does not occur elsewhere, but there was a great wealth and beauty of Prefaces in early Western Liturgies. A variety of festivals is recognised in the paragraph 'Communicantes,' &c. within the Canon, p. 235, and other Prefaces occur on pp. 245-7-8.

46. Some of the expressions in this Preface, 'sanctus, fortis, immortalis,' occur in the Reproaches on Good Friday. Others, 'non unius singulariter personae sed unius trinitatis substantiae,' occur in the Roman Preface for the Feast of Trinity.

47. Anglice, 'Here the "Dignum" receives the addition if "per quem" follows in the text.' The Irish words run continuously together in the original text, both here and in the next rubric.

48. Anglice, 'Here the "Dignum" receives the addition if "sanctus" follows in the text.' 'The addition' referred to in both these Irish rubrics seems to be the 'Proper Preface' appointed for the festival.

49. This resembles the Mozarabic Post-Sanctus for Christmas Day (Migne Edit. p. 189), and that in the Missale Gothicum in Vigil. Natal. Domini. It is a survival of the varying Ephesine Canon, where it immediately precedes the 'Qui pridie.'

50. These words, sedis—episcopo, are omitted in the Gelasian and many Sacramentaries earlier than the tenth century, and do not form part of the text of the Canon as given by Micrologus, cap. 25. They are found, except the last four words, in the Codex Othobonianus, but not in the Codex Vaticanus of the Gregor. Sacram. Martene supplies two other instances of Missals (de Prez and Monte Casino) containing here a petition 'pro abbate nostro' (i. p. 145).

51. There is no rubric here in the later Irish Missals. The recitation of names is not ordered in any of the varying forms of this short rubric in the Roman Canon, or in the English Uses of Sarum, Hereford, and York; but in some mediaeval Gallican forms of the Canon this 'Memento' includes a petition

for those 'quorum nomina super sanctum altare tuum scripta habentur' (in a Reims Pontifical, Mart. ordo ix. p. 197). See note 40.

52. Note the absence of the tenth-century additional clause 'pro quibus tibi offerimus vel.' Comp. Corpus Missal, p. 3, where the omission still survives in a twelfth-century text.

53. Cap. lxvii. of the Rule of St. Benedict is entitled 'De fratribus in viam directis.' Comp. the language in a Contestatio Paschalis in the Sacram. Gallicanum, 'dum justos per viam rectam gradientes coelestem ducit ad patriam' (Mabillon, Mus. Ital. i. 332).

54. The festivals here commemorated are—

(1) 'Natale Domini' = Christmas Day.

(2) 'Kl.' (= Kalendis Januariis), Feast of the Circumcision.

(3) 'Stella' = Feast of the Epiphany.

(4) 'Natalis Calicis' = Maundy Thursday. So in the Kalendar of Polemius Silvius for March 24, 403; Migne, Bib. Pat. Lat. xiii. 678. Both Dr. O'Conor and Dr. Todd unaccountably refer this phrase to 'Ash Wednesday.' Neither interpretation suits the preceding heading 'Stellae.'

(5) 'Pasca' = Easter Day.

(6) 'Clausula Pasca' = Low Sunday, or Clausum Paschae. Mis. Goth. No. xliv. p. 108.

(7) 'Ascensio' = Holy Thursday.

(8) 'Dies Quinquagensimae,' or 'Pentacosten' = Whitsun Day.

The occasions on which a variation occurs in the clause 'Communicantes,' &c. in the present Roman Canon are Christmas, Epiphany, Maundy Thursday, Eastertide, Holy Thursday, Whitsuntide. We have independent testimony that some such variation formed part of the original Gelasian text in a letter written by Pope Vigilius to Profuturus Bishop of Braga in Spain, A.D. 538, in which he said: 'Ordinem quoque precum in celebritate missarum nullo nos tempore, nulla festivitate, significamus habere divisum, sed semper eodem tenore oblata Deo munera consecrare. Quoties vero Paschalis, aut Ascensionis Domini, vel Pentecostes, et Epiphaniae, Sanctorumque Dei fuerit agenda festivitas singula, capitula diebus apta subjungimus, quibus commemorationem sanctae solemnitatis, aut eorum faciamus quorum natalitia celebramus, caetera vero ordine consueto persequimur.' Migne, Bib. Pat. Lat. lxix. p. 18.

55-55. The presence here of these seven words is not inconsistent with Mr. Simmons' suggestion that they may have been introduced into the Canon by Eugenius I, 655-8. The Gelasian title of this Canon must not be pressed to confirm his other supposition that they may have formed part of the Canon before the time of St. Gregory. (Early Eng. Text Soc. vol. 71. p. 356.)

56. An allusion to a special Church is contained in the Deacon's Litany or Bidding Prayer in the Liturgy of Constantinople : ὑπὲρ τοῦ ἁγίου οἴκου τούτου, καὶ τῶν μετὰ πίστεως, εὐλαβείας, καὶ φόβου Θεοῦ εἰσιόντων ἐν αὐτῷ τοῦ Κυρίου δεηθῶμεν. (Hammond, C. E., edit. p. 91.) Another instance is found in the earliest extant form of those bidding prayers which, derived from the East through the ancient Gallican Church, form one of the distinguishing character-istics of the Anglican Liturgy : 'Wutan we gebiddan for ealles thæs folces gebed þe þas halgan stowe mid ælmesan seceth,' &c. = Let us pray for all those people's prayer who seek this holy place with alms, &c. (From a York MS. saec. x, printed by Early Eng. Text Soc. vol. 71. p. 62.)

57. This passage suggests the possibility of the Stowe Canon being part of a Missa Dedicationis. A special 'Hanc igitur' is very common in the Gelasian,

rare in the Gregorian Sacramentary, and only occurs thrice in the present Roman Missal. There is a 'Hanc igitur' similar in intent but with little verbal identity in an 'Ordo ad dedicandam basilicam,' ex MS. Missal. Gellonens. (eighth century), published by Martene, tom. ii. p. 246. The present passage refers to a particular church, the founder or builder of which was still living; and the prayer that he and all the people may be converted from idolatry may imply that the founder was himself a pagan, and proves that when the words were written paganism was not extinct in Ireland. This is important as bearing upon the date of the Stowe Missal. It affords an instance of literal compliance with can. 19 of the Council of Emerita, A.D. 666 : 'Salubri deliberatione censemus, ut pro singulis quibusque ecclesiis, in quibus presbyter jussus fuerit per sui episcopi ordinationem praeesse, pro singulis diebus Dominicis sacrificium Deo procuret offerre, et eorum nomina a quibus eas ecclesias constat esse constructas, vel qui aliquid his sanctis ecclesiis videntur aut visi sunt contulisse si viventes in corpore sunt ante altare recitentur tempore missae ; quod si ab hac discesserunt vel discesserint luce, nomina eorum cum defunctis fidelibus recitentur suo ordine.' (Labbe, tom. vi. col. 507.)

58-58. These words (diesque—numerari) are said by Bede (Hist. Ec. lib. ii. cap. i) to have been added to the Canon by Gregory the Great, but they are found in the Codex Vaticanus of the Gelasian Canon published by Muratori (p. 696).

59-59. This passage (passionem—coelis) occurs at the close of the 'Qui pridie' in the Ambrosian Liturgy. (Pamel. Liturg. i. p. 302.) A similar passage occurs in the Greek Liturgies of St. James, St. Basil, St. Chrysostom, St. Mark, in the Coptic St. Cyril and St. Basil, and in the Æthiopic. (Hammond, C. E., Lit. pp. 70, 111, 112, 187, 211, 220, 258; compare also the closing words of the Prayer of Consecration in the Mozarabic Liturgy, p. 117.)

60. This expression (sacrificium spirituale) occurs in the Post-com. for St. Patrick's Day in the Drummond, Corpus, and Rosslyn Irish Missals, p. 271. It is uncommon in Western liturgical phraseology, although 'spiritualis' as an epithet of 'cibus' or 'poculum' is frequently met with. Compare the following passage in the Mozarabic Preface for ii. Domin. post Oct. Epiphan. : 'Nam licet verum corpus edatur, et sanguis manifestissimus hauriatur, nullus tamen horror incutitur, cum salus animarum in spirituali cibo et poculo ministratur ;' p. 249. The equivalent ἡ πνευματικὴ θυσία is used by St. Cyril of Jerusalem, Catech. Myst. v. § vi, ed. A.D. 1631, p. 241.

60 a. The expression 'Electus dei anthleta' occurs in Lib. Hymn. f. 31 b. For the superfluous 'n' see Corpus Missal, p. 35.

61. There is a passage similar to this in the Commemoratio pro vivis in the Mozarabic Liturgy, § 225 : 'Offerunt Deo Domino oblationem sacerdotes nostri, Papa Romensis et reliqui pro se et pro omni clero ac plebibus ecclesiae sibimet consignatis, vel pro universa fraternitate. Item offerunt universi presbyteri, diaconi, clerici, ac populi circumstantes, in honorem sanctorum pro se et suis.' Compare also the following Collectio post nomina for Easter Eve in the Missale Gothicum ; 'Oremus pro his qui offerunt munera Domino Deo nostro sacrosancta spiritalia, pro se, et pro caris suis, et pro spiritibus carorum suorum, in commemoratione sanctorum martyrum ; ut Dominus Deus noster preces illorum clementer exaudire dignetur. Per Resurgentem.' Mis. Goth. p. 98.

The order of intercessions as arranged in St. Columbanus' Rule has been already referred to, p. 251, n. 22. The word 'senior' has occurred on fol. 23 b. It also occurs in the Regula Columbani, c. 7 ; Poenitentiale, c. 28 ; in the Missale

Gallicanum, p. 159 ; Tertullian, Apolog. 39. It is explained by Alcuin, Lib. de Div. Off. p. 61, edit. Hittorp. In the Irish Rule of St. Columba the head of a community is entitled 'senóra.' (H. and S. ii. p. 119.) In the Missa Flacii Illyrici there is a collect commencing 'Suscipe Sancta Trinitas hanc oblationem quam (offero tibi) pro seniore nostro, et cuncta congregatione sancti Petri,' &c. (Mart. i. p. 184.) The presence of this passage here is one of various slight indications that this Ordo Missae, which was written c. A.D. 900, and for which such various origins have been claimed (ib. p. 176), may have been of Irish origin. The word 'seniores' occurs repeatedly in consecutive clauses in a charter of confederation of German monasteries in an eleventh-twelfth century Cod. Vindobonensis printed by Gerbert, ii. 140. The Latin 'senior' and Celtic 'senóra' became 'aldor' or 'aldermann' in Anglo-Saxon times. In the ecclesiastical laws of Wihtred King of Kent, promulgated at Bersted in 696, it was enacted, 'Mynstres aldor hine cænne in preostes canne' = Let the senior of a minster clear himself with a priest's clearance (No. xvii. H. and S. iii. 236). In the Ormulum (thirteenth century, line 6304) the word 'alderrmann' occurs in the same sense; for several other instances of this use of the word in the same work, see R. M. White's edit., Oxford, 1852, vol. ii. p. 442.

62. Many of the names of saints in the following lists are in the genitive case —a common occurrence in ancient martyrologies—the word festum being understood. The writer appears to have copied out the names forgetting always to change the genitive into a vocative case. The frequent repetitions are caused by the existence of more than one saint bearing the same name. I can detect no paleographical evidence for the statement endorsed by Mr. Scudamore (Notit. Euch. p. 425, second edit.) that the 'ora pro nobis' has been added throughout by the later hand of a scribe who was ignorant of the real purport of the list, but the whole of fol. 29 a b is written in a later handwriting on an interpolated leaf. Fol. 30 a b is also an addition to the original text, which passed on at once to the long list of departed saints commencing on fol. 31 a. For similar Litanies to the Saints, see Gerbert, Lit. Al. ii. 34. Brit. Mus. Add. MSS. 28, 188.

63. March 17. Apostle of Ireland, ob. 493.

64. Sept. 12. First Bp. of Emly, patron of Munster, ob. 534. [B. F. p. ccxii.]

65. March 2. Bp. of Cluain-Iraird, now Clonard, ob. 549. [B. Book of Obits, p. lxxxvi.]

66. March 16. Abb., ob. 615. [B. F. p. cclxii = Finan.]

67. March 5. Of Saighir, = Cornish Piran, older than St. Patrick. [B. F. p. ccxxxii.]

68. Sept. 9. Kieran, *or* Queranus, first Abb. of Clonmacnoise, ob. 549. [B. D.]

69. May 16. The elder Abb. of Clonfert, ob. 576. [B. D.] There are ten saints bearing this name in D. = Brenann of Cluain-ferta, F. p. ccxxvi.

70. Dec. 13. Abb. of Tyrdaglas, one of the twelve apostles of Ireland. [B. D. F. p. ccxxxvii.] The names of the twelve Irish apostles are given in F. p. cxviii.

71. June 9. Abb. of Iona, ob. 597. Two other Columbs are commemorated in F., June 7, Sept. 6.

72. May 10. Comgallus, Abb. and Conf. of Bangor in the sixth century. [Book of Obits, p. lxi; F. p. ccxxxvii.] There are seven saints of this name commemorated in D.

73. Oct. 11. Cannicha, *or* Canice, Abb. and Conf., founder of Achad-bho, now Aghaboe, ob. 598. [B. D.] = Caindech, F. p. ccxxviii.

74. Sept 25. Barrus, Bp. of Cork. [B. D.] Or July 4, Findbarr of Magh Bile, F. p. cclxii.

75. Dec. 6. Nessan, *or* Neassan, Bp. [B. D. F. p. ccxlix.]

76. Jan. 19. Factnae, Bp. of Nuachonghbail. [D. F. p. cclix.]

77. Aug. 4. Luan, *or* Molua, *or* Lugeus, *or* Lugidus, Abb. of Cluain-ferta-molua, ob. 622. [B. D.] Or Abb. of Lismore in the Hebrides; [Book of Obits, p. lxv.]

78. March 18. Lactenus, *or* Lactinus, Abb. of Achadh-Ur, and Bp., ob. 622. [B. D. Colgan, Acta SS. p. 655.]

79. April 15. Abb. of Lothra, ob. 584. [B. D. F. p. cccix.]

80. March 5. Carthach, Abb. and Bp., succeeded St. Kieran the elder. [B. D. F. p. ccxxx.]

81. June 3. Coemgen, *or* Kevin, Abb. of Gleann-da loch = Glendalough, ob. 615. [B. D. Book of Obits, p. xlvii,; F. p. ccxxxvi.]

82. March 8. There are eleven saints of this name commemorated in D. The person represented by this name may be S. Mochonna, ob. 704; F. ccxciii.

83. Feb. 1. Virgin, Abbess of Kildare, ob. 523. [B. D. F. p. ccxxvii.]

84. Jan. 15. Ite, *or* Ythe, *or* Mida, Virgin of Cluain-creadhail and Abbess, ob. 569. [B. D. F. p. cclxxix.]

85. Jan. 1. *Or* Sceath, Virgin, of Feart-Scethe. [D. T.] Perhaps she may be identified with Scite or Scithe, commemorated on May 13 in the Lib. S. Trinitatis [Book of Obits, pp. lxi, 115], or with Sciath, Sept. 6; F. cccxi.

86. Nov. 9. Sincha, *or* Sinech, of Cluain-Leith-teangadh, Virgin. There are three other saints of this name commemorated in D. [Book of Obits, p. lxxix; F. cccxv.]

87. Dec. 19. Perhaps Samhthann, Virgin, of Cluain-Bronaigh, ob. 734. [D.] Samthann, Samdann, F. p. cccxi.

88. This prayer of St. Ambrose is found in a ' Libellus sacrarum precum' written at Fleury c. A.D. 900, and printed by Martene (De Ant. Eccl. Rit. lib. iv. c. 34, tom. iii. p. 245). Its liturgical use is found in many a French Missal written c. A.D. 800–900. (Ib. lib. i. cap. iv. art. xii. ordd. v, vi, vii, ix, xiii, xiv, xv, xvi.) There are many variations in the text. Its usual position is at a much earlier point in the service, either among the ' Orationes ante Missam,' or immediately before the ' Secreta.'

89. For these unintelligible words (quorum ut dixit) most forms of the prayer substitute ' immundi sicut pannus menstruatae. Indigni sumus, Jesu Christe ut simus viventes sed tu qui non vis mortem peccatoris da nobis veniam in carne constitutis, ut per poenitentiae labores vita aeterna perfruamur in coelis, per te, Jesu Christe, qui,' &c.

90. = Abel. These ' Nomina justorum ac prophetarum' occur at the commencement of a long Litany in an eleventh-century Psalter at Florence (Bibl. Laur. Plut. xvii. cod. iii. fol. 144 a), where Seth, Melchisedech, Joseph, Job, Joshua, Tobit, the tres pueri, and the Machabeorum infantes are omitted, and Aaron, Elijah, and Elisha are added. Patriarchs and prophets are also commemorated in the Félire of Oengus, in the Kalendar of the Drummond Missal, and in the Book of Obits of Christ Church, Dublin. See S. Hieron. Martyrologium, Migne, Pat. Lat. Curs. xi. 437. In the York Bidding prayer, tenth century, people are invited to pray for the souls of all that have believed in Christ, ' fram Adames dæge to þisum dæge.' Early Eng. Text. Soc. vol. 71. p. 62. The same wide range is included in the language of early Eastern Liturgies, as in the Oratio generalis of the Syro-Jacobite Ordo : ' Memoriam

agimus . . . eorum etiam qui nobiscum adstant et orant, cum omnibus qui a saeculo tibi placuerunt ab Adamo ad hanc usque diem.' Renaudot, Liturg. Orient. Coll. ii. 16.

91. Dots placed over the lower Madiani imply that the word has been repeated by error. Matthias and Barnabas usually occupy the place here assigned to Madianus [D. Jan. 24]. Forbes, A. P., Kalendar of Scot. Ch. p. 382. But this name occupies the same anomalous position elsewhere; pp. 180, 226. Madianus is the mediaeval Hiberno-Latin form of Matthias, who is commemorated under the name of Madian in the Félire of Oengus; Leabhar Breac, fol. 82 b; in a list of the Apostles, ib. p. 91; Hymnus Cuminei, Lib. Hymn. p. 77; on the last page of the Appendix to the Glamis copy of the Aberdeen Breviary, printed in facsimile by D. Laing at the end of his Pref. to the Brev. Aberdon.

92. Did the scribe mean to write 'tarum'?

93. March 17. Apostle of Ireland, ob. 493.

94. Aug. 24. Abb. and Bp., nephew of the former, Or is one of these two Patricks to be identified with Palladius?

95. Nov. 27. *Or* Sechnall, British by birth, coadjutor of St. Patrick, ob. 448. [Book of Obits, p. lxxxv. F. p. cccxii.]

96. Sept. 16. British by birth, coadjutor of St. Patrick, ob. 454. [Book of Obits, p. lxxvii.]

97. Dec. 2. British by birth, coadjutor of St. Patrick.

98. A disciple of St. Kieran, ob. 499. [Colgan, Acta SS. 473.]

99. April 16. First Bp. of Slane, ob. 514. [B.] Nov. 2, F. clxii.

100. Not identified. The name Cathar occurs in F. lxiv, lxxii.

101. April 23. Iobhar, Bp., coadjutor of St. Patrick, ob. 500. [B. D. F. p. cclxxiv.]

102. See note 64.

103. Feb. 2, or May 3. Conlaedh, Bp. of Kildare, ob. 519.

104. Aug. 1. Is this Mica of Ermudhe? [D.]

105. Is this Mac Nisse, founder and first bishop of the See of Connor, ob. 513? [Book of Obits, p. lxxii]; or one of the five Nessans commemorated in D?

106. March 1. Maoinenn, Bp. of Clonfert, disciple of St. Brendan, ob. A.D. 572. [Four Masters, D.]

107. March 1 and 8. Senan, Bp. of Inis-Cathaigh, ob. 544. [F. cccxiii.]

108. See note 74.

109. A portion of this word is erased in the MS.

110. Is this Colman, Bp. of Glendalough, ob. Dec. 13, 659? There are ninety-seven persons of this name commemorated in D. 17, in F. p. ccxxxvi.

111. April 2. *Alias* Mochua, Abb. [B.] Twelve persons named Cuanus are commemorated in Colgan's Acta SS. St. Cuana of Kill-chuana, *alias* Killskanny, Co. Clare, ob. 650.

112. Nov. 17. Is this Dulech, *or* Duileach, *or* Doulough, Bp. and Conf.? [D. Book of Obits, pp. xlvi, lxxx.]

113, 114, 115. Second, third, and fourth Archbps. of Canterbury. The presence of these names proves the existence of intercourse between the Anglo-Saxon and Irish Churches. The absence of St. Augustine's name is remarkable, but may be accounted for by the feeling of hostility which existed between him and the Celtic clergy. Laurence is known to have written a letter to the Irish bishops, urging them in vain to come to terms of union with the Anglo-Saxon Church. Bede H. E. ii. 4. St. Augustine is commemorated in F., May 24.

116. Nov. 10. Aedh, Bp. of Ciltair, ob. 588. There are twenty-six saints of this name commemorated in D. See F. p. ccxi.

117. Sept. 13. Bp. of Inver-Daoile ; see also March 12. [D. F. p. ccxliv.]

118. April 4 or 5. Bp. of Clogher, founder of Clones (Cluaineois), ob. 548. [B. D. F. p. cccxxiii.]

119. Aug. 22. Mochteus, first Bp. of Louth, ob. 535 = Mochta. D. *Or* Aug. 19, *or* March 24, as in Colgan's Acta SS.

120. Nov. 24. Bp. of Daimhliag, ob. 488. [D.] The other saints of this name are found under Feb. 25, Nov. 29, Nov. 24. F. p. ccxxxii.

121. Dec. 7. Buite, *or* Boetius, *or* Beo, now St. Baoithin, Bp., ob. 520. The festival of his elevation is on Dec. 11. [D. Book of Obits, p. xlix. F. p. ccxxxviii.]

122. Aug. 23. Eoghan, *or* Eugesius, Bp. of Ard-sratha (Ardstraw, Tyrone), ob. 570 or 618. There are nine other saints of this name commemorated. [D. F. p. cclvi.]

123. July 24. Declan, Decclan, *or* Deglan, Bp. of Ard-mor, fifth century. [B. D. F. p. ccxlv.]

124. March 5. Is this Carthach, Bp. and Abb. of Druim-fertain ? [B. D. F.] Two other saints of this name are commemorated on March 26, May 14. A Carthagius is named in Colgan's Acta SS. p. 473.

125. Feb. 6. Perhaps = Mel, Bp. of Ard-achadh, nephew and disciple of St. Patrick, ob. 487. [B. D.]

126. Sept. 25. Ruine. [T.]

127. Dec. 1. Uinnian, *or* Finnian, *or* Finnen, Bp. and Conf., of Maghbile, ob. 578. [Lib. Hymn p. 100.]

128. See note 67.

129. Nov. 17. Of Cill-mor. Six saints of this name (Oenghus) are commemorated in D. F. ccci.

130. March 21. Enda, Abb. of Isle of Aran. [B. D.] See Dec. 31, F. cclvi.

131. Nov. 4. Gildas the elder, ob. 512 ; the younger, ob. 570. Jan. 29. [B.]

132. See note 69.

133. Nov. 29 or 30, the younger. Abbot of Birra, ob. 577. [B. D.]

134. See note 73.

135. See note 70.

136. See note 71.

137. There are 230 Irish saints bearing this name. [B. D.]

138. See note 72.

139. See note 81.

140. This word occurs in the Collectio post nomina in Mis. Goth. ordd. xvii, xl. In ordo xxxiii. there is an Oratio pro spiritibus pausantium ; so in the Sacram. Gallican., Mab. edit. p. 321 ; in the Commemoratio pro defunctis in the Mozarabic Liturgy, §§ 226, 252, pp. 114, 168, 603, 730 ; in the Poenitentiale of Cuminius, p. 23. n. 1. Adamnan speaks of St. Columba's grave as 'locus in quo ipsius sancta pausant ossa' (lib. iii. cap. 23). 'Pausantes' for 'mortui,' 'pausatorium' for 'sepulchrum,' are words of rare use in late Latin ; vid. Du Cange, sub voc. 'Pausare' is the word generally employed in the Annals of Ulster (saec. xiv-xv. Rawl. MSS. B. 489, fol. 9 b, &c.) in recording the deaths of bishops and abbots, whereas 'quievit, mortuus est,' &c. are used in the case of kings and other lay persons. Pausare is used in the same sense in early mortuary inscriptions in the Roman Catacombs (De Rossi, Inscriptiones Christianae, sub an. 353), and in early Christian inscriptions in Gaul

(Le Blant's edit. nos. 230, 511, 534). It occurs also in a collect in the Coemiterii Benedictio in the Roman Pontifical, 'Deus sancte, Pater O,' &c. Ἀνάπαυσις and ἀναπαύσασθαι are words in frequent use in the Eastern Liturgies of St. Clement, St. James, St. Basil, St. Chrysostom (Hammond's, C. E., edit. pp. 20, 36, 38, 115, 118, &c.). Compare the Oratio post Diptycha in the Coptic Lit. (Anaphora of St. Cyril, Hammond's edit. p. 210) on behalf of 'omnium quorum nomina recitamus et quorum non recitamus, quos unusquisque nostrum in mente habet, et eorum quorum memoria non occurrit nobis qui dormierunt et quieverunt in fide Christi,' &c. The whole of the paragraph 'Memento etiam Domine famulorum' in the Roman Canon is preceded in some ancient MSS. by the title 'Super Diptycha.' In a tenth-century Tours Sacramentary that title is followed by the rubric, '*Si fuerint nomina defunctorum recitentur. Dicat sacerdos :* Memento etiam, &c. . . . in somno pacis. *Deinde postquam recitati fuerint, dicat sacerdos :* Ipsis et omnibus,' etc. It is not easy to assign the exact date at which the custom fell into desuetude. Martene (i. p. 150) quotes at length the diptychs as read at Amiens early in the twelfth century, but the custom had become generally obsolete a century or two before that date. The diptychs in this Irish Missal, consisting of forty-seven names from Abel to Coemgeni, are of unusual length. One would at least equally have expected to find them connected with the two collects preceding the Sursum Corda (q. v. p. 233).

140 a. Compare the following ancient and anonymous inscription in the church of St. Allyre in Gaul : 'Hic requiescunt corpora sanctorum quorum nomina Deus scit.' Le Blant, Inscript. Chrét. de la Gaule, No. 563, where further instances of the early use of the phrase are supplied in the notes.

141. Anglice, 'Here the oblation is lifted over the chalice, and half of the bread is dipped into the chalice.'

142. Ps. xxxii. 22. See below, n. 146.

143. Anglice, 'Here the bread (lit. cake or wafer) is broken.' The fraction of the Host in the present Roman rite takes place during the Embolismus after the Pater Noster.

144. Luc. xxiv. 35. See below, n. 147.

145. Adapted from 1 Cor. x. 16.

146. Ps. xxxii. 22. See above, n. 142.

147. Luc. xxiv. 35. See above, n. 144.

148. Similar confessions of faith are found in various Eastern Liturgies ; the Syriac Lit. of St. James, Hammond's edit. p. 77 ; the Ethiopic Lit., ib. p. 261. They are also found in the Mozarabic Liturgy, pp. 116, 118, 1009.

149. Confractio. The word confringo is found in the Gallican and Ambrosian words of Institution, and we may infer from this passage that it was employed in the ancient Celtic Prayer of Consecration. Compare the Gallican Post Secreta for Christmas Day : 'Credimus, Domine, adventum tuum, recolimus passionem tuum. Corpus tuum in peccatorum nostrorum remissionem confractum. Sanguis sanctus tuus in pretium nostrae redemptionis effusus est, qui cum Patre,' etc. (Missale Gothicum, Mab. edit. p. 192).

150. 'Praeceptis salutaribus moniti' Miss. Rom. This difference from the unvarying Roman formula of introduction to the Pater Noster is noteworthy. See St. Gall MS. No. 1394, p. 177 ; Book of Dimma, p. 169.

151. 'Libera nos, quaesumus, Domine ab omnibus malis praeteritis, praesentibus, et futuris, et intercedente pro nobis beata et gloriosa semper Virgine Dei Genitrice Maria, cum beatis Apostolis tuis Petro, et Paulo, atque Andrea'

Miss. Rom. The name of Patrick is substituted for Andrew in the text, in accordance with the very early custom of the priest inserting here at his option the names of patron or local saints. St. Andrew is also omitted in a ninth-century Gallican Missal quoted by Martene (i. p. 152). St. Ambrose is added in a Milanese Missal, A.D. 1560; Dionysius, Eletherius and Rusticus, in a eighth and ninth century Gallican Missal (Mart. i. ordo v. p. 190; see ordo ix. p. 197).

152. The Roman formula is 'Pax Domini sit semper vobiscum.' This is the Roman position of the Pax. In the Gallican and Mozarabic Liturgies it preceded the Sursum corda. The wording of the text resembles somewhat the Mozarabic formula, 'Gratia Dei Patris omnipotentis, pax ac dilectio Domini nostri Jesu Christi, et communicatio Spiritus Sancti sit semper cum omnibus nobis' (p. 115). It occurs again with a verbal alteration on p. 224; Book of Dimma, p. 170.

153. Here follow in the Gelas. Canon. twelve Postcommuniones and fifteen Benedictiones super populum. Muratori edit. p. 698.

154. Similar words accompany the bestowal of the Pax in the Mozarabic Liturgy, § 226, p. 115.

155. The Commixture here precedes the Agnus Dei, according to the Roman Use, differing from that of Sarum, Hereford and York, and from mediaeval French Liturgies. Mart. i. ordo v. p. 190; vi. p. 192; vii. p. 193; viii. p. 194.

156. The Agnus Dei was appointed to be sung here by Sergius, i. 687–701. It was always sung once or thrice. Here apparently it is to be used twice (so John of Avranches, de Eccles. Offic. c. xlviii). There was some variation in the wording of the third clause, which does not however appear to have been elsewhere entirely omitted (Gerbert, Disquis. iv. vol. i. p. 381). The Agnus Dei is omitted altogether from other editions of the Gelas. Sacram.; Muratori, Lit. Rom. i. 698; Scudamore, W. E., Notit. Euchar. 2nd edit. p. 679.

157. Ioan. xiv. 27. St. Gall MS. 1394, p. 177.

158. For the whole of this passage compare the Irish fragment of St. Gall MS. No. 1394, p. 177; the extracts from the Antiphonarium Benchorense (p. 192), and from the Books of Deer (p. 165), Dimma (p. 170), and Mulling (p. 173). This is very nearly the anthem sung in the Mozarabic Liturgy by the choir at the Kiss of Peace, § 226, p. 546. I have not found any passage resembling it in any printed or MS. edition of the Gelasian or Gregorian Sacramentaries.

159. Ps. cxviii. 165.

160. Not identified.

161. Not identified.

162. Perhaps Ps. xcv. 1.

163. Perhaps the communion hymn in the Antiphon. Benchor. p. 187.

164. Prov. ix. 5. St. Gall MS. 1394, p. 178.

165. Ps. xxii. 1. St. Gall MS. 1394, p. 177.

166. Ioan. vi. 57.

167. V. *om.* ipse. Ib. St. Gall MS. 1394, p. 177. This is the Mozarabic 'Ant. ad Accedentes' for the Friday after the first Sunday in Lent, p. 316.

168. Ps. xxiii. 1.

169. Ioan. vi. 59. V. *om.* vivus. St. Gall MS. 1394, p. 177; Antiphon. Benchor. p. 192. This passage occurs as part of the Communio in the Ethiopic Liturgy, Hammond's edit. p. 262. It is also part of the Mozarabic Ad Accedendum for the third Sunday in Lent, p. 343.

170. Ib. For ʻex eoʼ V. reads ʻhunc panem.ʼ Ib. comp. the ʻAd Accedentesʼ for the fifth Sunday in Lent; Mis. Mozar. p. 377.

171. Ps. xxiv. 1.   St. Gall MS. 1394, p. 178.

172. Ps. lxxvii. 24, 25.

173. Ps. vii. 9.   St. Gall MS. 1394, p. 178.

174. Cant. v. 1.   St. Gall MS. 1394, p. 178.

175. This formula of administration is found in the St. Gall. MS. No. 1394, p. 178; Antiphon. Benchor. p. 192.   It appears, like the formula in the Book of Deer, &c. (p. 164), to involve Communion in both kinds at once.

176. Ps. cxviii. 171.   V. ʻEructabunt labia mea hymnum, cum docueris me iustificationes tuas.ʼ   St. Gall MS. 1394, p. 178; Antiphon. Benchor. p. 192.

177. Ps. xxxiii. 2.   Mozar. Lit. § 232. p. 565.

178. Ps. xxxiii. 9; Antiphon. Benchor. p. 192.   This is sung during the fraction in the Greek Lit. of St. James (Hammond, C. E., edit. p. 51).   The whole of this psalm was ordered to be sung during the Communion of the people, in the Apostolic Constitutions (lib. viii. c. 13, al. 20).   St. Cyril speaks of this verse being sung in his time (348–86) at Jerusalem : Μετὰ ταῦτα ἀκού-ετε τοῦ ψάλλοντος μετὰ μέλους θείου προτρεπομένου ὑμᾶς εἰς τὴν κοινωνίαν τῶν ἁγίων μυστηρίων καὶ λέγοντος, Γεύσασθε καὶ ἴδετε ὅτι χρηστὸς ὁ Κύριος, κ. τ. λ.   St. Ambrose alludes to it as sung at Milan in the same century : ʻUnde et ecclesia videns tantam gratiam hortatur filios suos GUSTATE ET VI-DETE QUONIAM SUAVIS EST DOMINUS,ʼ &c.   It is the ordinary Antiphona ad accedentes in the Mozarabic Liturgy, except from the first Sunday in Lent to the vigil of Pentecost (Hammond, C. E., edit. p. 349).   It does not form part now, though it did form part of the Roman Liturgy in St. Jeromeʼs days, who said, ʻQuotidie coelesti pane saturati dicimus, Gustate et videte quam suavis est Dominusʼ (Comment. in Es. ii. c. v. 20; Migne, Bib. Pat. Lat. xxiv. 88).

179. Ioan. xii. 26.   V. ʻUbi sum ego, illic et minister meus erit.ʼ   St. Gall MS. 1394, p. 178.

180. Mat. xix. 14.   V. ʻSinite parvulos et nolite eos prohibere ad me venire,ʼ &c.   The employment of this verse as a Communion anthem points to the custom of infant communion.   There is a rubric in the twelfth-century Irish Ordo Baptismi in the Corpus Missal, ordering the confirmation of infants, which was probably a prelude to their communion (fol. 203 a); St. Gall MS. 1394, p. 178, commencing with ʻNolite.ʼ

181. Mat. iii. 2.   St. Gall MS. 1394, p. 178.

182. Mat. xi. 12.   St. Gall MS. 1394, p. 178.

183. Mat. xxv. 34.   V. ʻpossidete paratum vobis regnum a constitutione mundi.ʼ   St. Gall MS. 1394, p. 178.   This is the Mozarabic ʻSacrificiumʼ in festo SS. Servandi et Germani, p. 884.

183 a. See p. 165, n. 1.

184. This is an early Irish name belonging to a period when Pagan names were still retained, but the bearer of it has not yet been identified.   Used as a prefix, Maol, Mael, or Moel, means the servant or devotee of the person whose name follows, as Maol Colaim, Maol Seacnaill; so here Moel Caich.   It is the old Irish word for ʻtonsus.ʼ

185. St. Gall MS. No. 1394, p. 179, where see note 2.

186. This prayer is the ʻConsummatio Missaeʼ in the Sacramentarium Gallicanum, p. 209.   It occurs in the ninth-century Irish fragment at St. Gall, No. 1394 (p. 179).   The first part, ʻGratias ueniam,ʼ occurs in the Leon. Sacr., mense Jul. No. xxiv, the remainder in mense Sept. No. iii, with verbal

variations. Comp. the thanksgiving collect in the Sarum Canon, 'Gratias tibi ago,' &c., p. 626. For the generally Ephesine character of these forms of thanksgiving, see Book of Deer, p. 165, n. 7.

187. This is the Mozarabic formula for conclusion 'in feriali officio.'

188. The omission of any allusion to the ablutions and to the final Gospel 'In principio' is common to all Missals written before the twelfth-thirteenth century. The earliest date of any allusion to those customs in the Church of these islands is given in the Early Eng. Text Soc. vol. 71. pp. 301, 383.

189. This Missa bears a general resemblance in its length of collects, possession of a Proper Preface, width of application, exhaustive enumeration of orders of saints, to a Missa generalis printed by Martene from a ninth-century codex belonging to a monastery at Rheims (De Eccles. Antiq. Rit. i. p. 197). Compare the title on p. 226.

190. Compare the language in the Faeth Fiada, the ancient Irish Hymn of St. Patrick : 'I bind to myself to-day the power of the love of seraphim, in the obedience of angels, in the hope of Resurrection unto rewards, in prayers of patriarchs, in predictions of prophets, in the precepts of apostles, in the faith of confessors, in the purity of holy virgins, in works of just men. (Kilkenny Archaeol Soc. 1868, p. 295 ; Todd, J. H., Life of St. Patrick, p. 427.)

191. In these words we have at least one form of the opening words of the Prayer of Consecration in the Celtic Church. As in the case of the Gallican Liturgy the opening words of the Canon down to 'Qui pridie' varied with each festival. The Gallican Canon for Christmas Eve opened with the words of the Canon in this Irish Missa, 'Vere sanctus, vere benedictus,' &c. Daniel, Cod. Lit. i. p. 83 ; Mabillon, Lit. Gall. p. 188. See p. 109.

192. The words of consecration in full are not found in any extant Gallican Missal, but their presence is sometimes indicated as here by the opening words 'Qui pridie.' So in an eighth-century Gallican fragment found by the Rev. H. B. Swete, A.D. 1867, attached to one of the covers of MS. 153 in Gonville and Caius College, Cambridge. Miss. Richenov. ii. p. 4; Miss. Goth. No. lxxv. p. 142. See Post Sanctus in Miss. Moz. pp. 181, 198, &c. The remainder may be supplied in the case of the Gallican Liturgy, and therefore by implication in the case of the Celtic Liturgy, from S. Ambros. de Sacram. lib. iv. cap. 5. See pp. 109–10.

192a. Sac. Leon. p. 305 ; Gregor. pp. 100, 182.

193. We have here an example of the 'Deprecatio' of the Celtic Liturgy, in its proper position before the Preface, offered here pro vivis instead of pro defunctis. See p. 106.

194. See note 193. The same word (deprecari) occurs in Prefaces peculiar to the Drummond Missal. 'Et tuam immensam dementiam humiliter deprecari, ut mentibus nostris in beati apostoli,' &c. (fol. 65 b). 'Deprecantes majestatem tuam ut venturam beati ,N. confessoris tui festivitatem,' &c. (fol. 83 a).

195. 1 Cor. ii. 9. These words occur in the Great Oblation in the Greek Liturgy of St. James, and in the Preface of that of St. Mark.

196. This collect occurs at the conclusion of an office for the Unction and Communion of the sick in a French thirteenth-century codex in the Library of St. Victor de Paris ; Mart. vol. i. ordo xxii. p. 335 ; Sac. Gelas. p. 553.

197. A similar framework of a collect occurs in Sac. Leon. p. 461.

198. See p. 167. n. 3.

199. See note 43.

200. The rest of fol. 45 a is blank.

§ 15.—Irish Fragments. Later Irish Missals.

Three Irish MS. Missals are extant of considerably later date than the Stowe Missal; viz. the Drummond Missal (eleventh century), the property of Lady Willoughby d'Eresby, found at Drummond Castle in Perthshire A.D. 1787; the Corpus Missal (twelfth century), in the Library of Corpus Christi College, Oxford, published by Messrs. Pickering, London, 1879 (several coloured photozincograph facsimiles of pages in this Missal are exhibited in the Second Part of the National Manuscripts of Ireland, Dublin, 1878); the Rosslyn Missal (thirteenth or fourteenth century), which once belonged to the Sinclairs of Rosslyn, and is now in the Advocates' Library at Edinburgh.

All these Missals are mainly Roman or Sarum in their structure and contents, and throw no light on the liturgical use of the early Celtic Church, except in the exhibition of various modifications of ritual, the retention of certain Irish and other names of saints[1], and the use of certain collects, postcommons, &c. which are not found in other Missals, and the allusions in which are evidently drawn from some purely local source. It would be impossible here to present all these variations in a tabular form[2]. Attention has been drawn to a few of the more important of them, in illustration of points touched upon in the foregoing pages. As a sample of such collects, &c. we append the Missae for the festivals of St. Bridget and St. Patrick as contained in the Corpus and Rosslyn Missals, calling attention to the evident antiquity of the language. The Roman Missal contains no proper

---

[1] e.g. In the Canon of the Drummond Missal the names of 'Eugenia' and 'Brigita' follow Anastasia. The name of S. Eugenia also appears twice in the Sacramentarium Gallicanum, following that of Lucia within the Canon (Mab. Mus. It. i. 281), and occurring in the 'Collectio ad Pacem' for Christmas Eve (Ib. p. 289). This service book of the Ephesine family was discovered in the Irish monastery of Bobbio, and thus we may have a slight indication of an original Gallican influence on the Irish Liturgy. See p. 61.

[2] The collects, &c. of the Drummond Missal are indexed at the end of G. H. Forbes' edit. of the Sarum Missal.

Missa for St. Bridget, only a special collect for St. Patrick.
The Sarum Missal contains proper Missae both for St. Bridget
and St. Patrick, but in neither Missal do any of the following
collects occur.   There is nothing, however, technically Celtic
about them.   They are either native compositions on the
Roman model, or consist of Gelasian or Gregorian frames
with the names of Celtic saints patchworked into them.

Missa Sancte Brigide Uirginis.   Kal. Feb. [1]
Oratio.

Celorum atque terrarum conditor et gubernator, omnipotens
deus, precanti populo succurre tua pietate, et presta ut qui
in honore sancte brigide presentem dei huius gerimus sollennitatem per ipsius suffragia perhenni misericordia tua potiamur.
per.

Secreta.

Eclesię tuę quesumus domine preces et hostias beate brig ide
commendet oratio, ut qui pro illius meritis maiestatem tuam
indefessa[m] atque exorabilem humiliter imploramus.   Cuius
precibus adiuti misericordiam tuam sentiamus. per.

Postcommunio.

Adiuuent nos, quesumus, domine, hec misteria sancta que
sumpsimus, et beate uirginis tuae brigitae intercessio ueneranda,
per dominum nostrum.

Missa Sancti Patricii Episcopi.   xvi. Kal. Ap. [2]
Oratio.

Deus, qui sanctum patricium scotorum apostolum tua pro-
uidentia elegisti, ut hibernenses gentes in tenebris et in errore
gentilitatis errantes ad uerum dei lumen scientie reduceret,
et per lauacrum regenerationis filios excelsi dei efficeret, tribue
nobis, quesumus, eius piis intercessionibus ut ad ea que recta
quantocius festinemus [3]. per.

---

[1] Corpus Missal, fol. 130 a ; Rosslyn Missal, fol. 80 a.
[2] Corpus Missal, fol. 135 a ; Rosslyn Missal, fol. 87 b.
[3] Indications of an early date of composition are furnished (1) by the equiva-

SECRETA.

Hostias tibi quas in honore sancti patricii offerimus deuotus accipias, ut nos a timore iudicii liberemur. per.

POSTCOMMUNIO.

Omnipotentem deum uniuersitatis auctorem [1] suppliciter exoramus, ut qui spirituale sacrificium in honorem sancti patricii offerimus fiat nobis remedium sempiternum. per.

§ 16.—IRISH FRAGMENTS. PARIS MS. 2333 A. COLBERT.

The following Missa is written at the close of a life of St. Brendan in a fourteenth-century MS. 2333 A. Colbert. Nat. Libr. Paris. Fol. 147 b. Printed Catalogue, iv. 504.

[MISSA IN FESTO SANCTI BRENDANI.]
ORATIO.

Deus, qui hodiernam diem sacratissimam nobis, beati brendani confessoris tui atque abbatis solempnitate tribuisti, adesto piis ecclesie tue precibus, ut cuius gloriatur meritis muniatur suffragiis. per.

SECRETA.

Sacris altaribus, domine, hostias superpositas beatus brendanus abbas in salutem nobis peruenire deposca[t] dominum nostrum.

---

lent use of the words 'Scoti' and 'Hibernenses,' which ceased to be convertible terms in the tenth century; (2) the reference to the previous heathenism of Ireland; (3) the oblique mode of the Invocation of Saints which marks the above collects; (4) the description of the Eucharistic offering as 'spirituale sacrificium,' Stowe Missal, p. 237; (5) the allusion in the secreta to the ancient tradition found both in the Gaelic hymn of St. Fiacc and the Latin hymn of St. Sechnall, that on the day of judgment the men of Erin will stand round St. Patrick before the judgment-seat of God (Lib. Hymn., part ii. p. 297; part i. p. 22. n. 92). The memoirs of St. Patrick in the Book of Armagh speak of his 'conductio omnium sanctorum Hiberniae in die judicii' (fol. 15, 16). An old Gaelic Life of St. Patrick preserved in the Leabhar Breac asserts that 'though great is St. Patrick's honour still among men, it will be still greater at the meeting of Doom, where he will be like every chief apostle, passing judgment on the men of Ireland unto whom he preached' (fol. 29 b). It was one of the three requests granted to St. Patrick before his death 'ut Hybernenses omnes in die judicii a te judicentur' (Vit. S. Patric. ii. p. 333, inter Bedae Op., Basil. 1563).   [1] p. 167. n. 6.

Postcommunio.

Protegat nos, domine, cum tui perceptione sacramenti beatus brendanus abbas pro nobis intercedendo, ut conuersacionis eius experiamur insignia, et intercessionis eius experiamur suffragia. per.

§ 17.—Missale Vesontionense.

This Sacramentary, which is described by Dr. O'Conor at some length as 'Missale Hibernicum Bobiense[1],' and by Dr. Lanigan as 'Cursus Scotorum[2],' is a Gallican, not an Irish Missal, and has been printed as such by Mabillon under the title of 'Sacramentarium Gallicanum[3],' by Muratori[4], and by G. H. Forbes, with a complete apparatus criticus, under the title of Missale Vesontionense[5] (=of Besançon). It is a seventh-century MS. found by Mabillon in the monastery of Bobbio, and believed to have been carried thither by St. Columbanus from Luxeuil. It is now in the National Library at Paris, No. 13246.

As frequent and confusing allusions have been made to this supposed Irish Missal in the pages of various writers, in recent times[6], it may be useful to summarise the reasons against an Irish and in favour of its Gallican origin.

(a) The non-Irish character of its handwriting. This can be proved by an inspection of the facsimiles presented by Mabillon[7] and O'Conor[8].

---

[1] Rerum Hibern. Script. i. cxxx–cxliii.

[2] Eccles. Hist. of Ireland, iv. 371; Dublin, 1829.

[3] Mus. It. i. 273–392.   [4] Lit. Rom. Vet. ii. 766.

[5] Gallican Liturgies, p. 205. See also Dr. Todd's remarks in Transactions of R. I. A. vol. xxiii. p. 26, ad finem.

[6] e.g. Ozanam, Civilization Chretienne, A.D. 1849, p. 100; Bishop Greith, Altirischen Kirche, A.D. 1867, p. 437; Dr. Moran, Essay on Early Irish Church, Dublin, 1864, pp. 276–296; Allnatt, C. F. B., Cathedra Petri, Lond. 1879, p. 47; Malone, S., Ch. Hist. of Ireland, Dublin, 1880, vol. i. ch. 10. These writers appear to have been misled in the first instance by Dr. O'Conor, of whose competence to argue on a liturgical or palaeographical point some specimens have been given, p. 198. n. 1.

[7] Mus. It. i. 276.   [8] Rer. Hibern. Script. i. p. xxxi.

(*b*) The absence throughout of the names of any Irish saints.

(*c*) The presence of the names of various Gallican saints ; e.g. of St. Hilary and St. Martin in the clause ' Communicantes,' &c. within the Canon[1]. There are proper Missae for St. Martin of Tours, ' In depositione Sancti Martini Episcopi[2]; ' and for St. Sigismund, King of the Burgundians, ' Missa Sancti Sigismundi Regis[3].' Sigismund was defeated and murdered by Chlodomir A.D. 523. The commemoration of this king suggested the title of ' Missale Vesontionense ' for this Sacramentary.

(*d*) The use throughout of Gallican terms ; e.g. Collectio post nomina, Collectio ad pacem, Contestatio, Benedictio turris[4].

(*e*) Certain well-known Gallican features of arrangement ; e.g. the Rogation Days are marked for observance before Ascension Day by the provision of Legenda and a Missa in Letaniis. The ' Missa in Adsumptione Sanctae Mariae ' is assigned to Jan. 18 (instead of Aug. 15), immediately preceded by the ' Missa in Cathedra Sancti Petri[5].'

Further forms of devotion not of a technically liturgical character, and in their present shape only very remotely connected with the Celtic Church, survive in a tenth-century Breton Litany, first published by Mabillon[6] from a Rheims MS., and printed in H. and S., Councils, ii. i. 81 ; and in the sixteenth-century Scottish Litany (Antiquae Litaniae) referred to on p. 166.

---

[1] Mabillon, Mus. Ital. i. p. 207.   [2] Ib. p. 303.

[3] Ib. p. 297.   [4] Ib. p. 362.

[5] It is fair to add that the same arrangement occurs in the Félire of Oengus, Leabhar Breac, p. 80. In the same ' Félire ' St. John and St. James are simultaneously commemorated on Dec. 27 (ib. p. 102), a curious association which is also found in the Sacramentarium Gallicanum, p. 226, and the Missale Gothicum, p. 41. These and such like coincidences, instead of proving the Irish origin of the Missale Vesontionense, prove how far certain early Irish ecclesiastical documents were affected by Gallican influence.

[6] Analect. tom. ii. p. 669, edit. 1676.

INDEX

Of Collects and other Liturgical Formulae.

An asterisk (*) prefixed to a Collect, &c. indicates that it occurs in Roman Office-Books, but with frequent and important variations of text.

æ. = aeternus.	b. = beatus.	D. = Deus.	Dns. = Dominus.
I. = Jesus.	n. = noster.	o. = omnipotens.	p. = pater.
q. = quaesumus.	s. = sanctus.	Xtus. = Christus	

Deus, qui pueris fide ferventibus fornacis, 190.

Deus, qui s. Patricium Scotorum apostolum, 270.

Deus, qui tres pueros de fornace eripuisti, 190.

*Deus qui unigenito tuo notam creaturam, 175.

Deus, tibi gratias agimus per quem, 165, 171, 173, 219, 225.

Dicamus omnes, Dne., exaudi et, 228.

Diluculo lucis auctore resurgente exultemus, 193.

*Dirigatur, Dne, [oratio mea], 230.

Dispersit dedit pauperibus, iustitia eius, 131.

Diuino magisterio edocti et diuina, 169, 177, 242.

Domine D. n. I. Xte. splendor paternae, 244.

Domine, D. o. ego humiliter te, 185.

Domine D. o. qui s. tuos cum mensura, 245.

Domine, Dne., defende nos a malis et, 196.

Domine sancte p. o. ae. D. expelle diabulum, 207.

*Domine s. p. o. ae. D. qui es et qui eras, 211.

Domine s. p. o. ae. D. qui es uia et ueritas, 221.

Domine s. p. o. instaurator et conditor, 183.

*Domine s. p. te fideliter deprecemur, ut, 224.

Domine, s. p., uniuersitatis auctor, 167, 221.

Domini est terra, 243.

Dominicam nostrae resurrectionis initium, 193.

Dominus et saluator noster I. Xtus., pridie, 218.

Dominus n. I. Xtus. dixit. Ego, 231.

Dominus reget me, 117, 242.

Ecce agnus Dei, 242.

Ecce qui tollis peccata mundi, 242.

Eclesie tue q. Dne. preces et hostias, 270.

Effeta, quod est apertio, effeta est hostia, 210.

Effundam de spiritu meo super omnem, 179.

Eleemosynas facientibus in hoc mundo, 131.

Et sacrificent sacrificium laudis et, 165, 173.

Euangelium Dni. n. I. Xti. liberet nos, 196.

*Exaudi, Dne., preces nostras et confitentium, 152.

*Exaudi nos Dne. D. p. o. ae. d. et mittere, 211.

Exaudi nos, Dne. I. Xte. d. n. pro fratre, 224.

Exaudi preces nostras, o. D. et presta ut sicut, 190.

*Exorcizo te, creatura aquae, in nomine D., 184, 213.

*Exorcizo te, creatura aquae, per Dnm. uiuum, 212.

*Exorcizo te, creatura salis, in nomine, 208.

Exorcizo te, spiritus immunde per D. patrem, 220.

INDEX

OF PASSAGES OF SCRIPTURE.

GENERAL INDEX.

A.

Aaron, p. 156.
Aberdeen Breviary, 35, 81, 82, 116.
Abgarus, 196.
Ablutions, 268.
Adamnan, xiii, 5, 6, 9, 20, 36, 60, 148.
Adamnanus, 150.
Aedh, St., 37, 240.
Aengus = Oengus.
Aghaboe, 15, 139, 45.
Agilbert, 22.
Agnus Dei, 242, 266.
Agrestius, 96.
Aidan, bishop, 17, 24, 26, 115, 146.
Aidan, king, 148.
Ailbe, St., 238, 240.
Aileran, 36, 127.
Ailred, 32, 36.
Alb, 114.
Alban, St., 122, 156.
Aldermann, 261.
Aldfrith, 5, 22.
Aldhelm, St., 4, 33, 36, 43.
Altars, 91 ; of wood, 91 ; of stone, 92 ;
  in baptisteries, 219.
Amboise, 15.
Ambrosian Liturgy, see Milanese.
Ambrosii oratio, 239, 249, 262.
Amphibalus, 122.
Anathleticus gradus, 203, 238.
Anegray, 15.
Anmcara, 146, 147, 149.
Anthems sung during Communion, 110,
  187, 191, 242.
Anthleta, 260.
Antiphonary of Bangor, xiii, 131, 187.
Apologia Sacerdotis, forms of, 185, 226,
  227, 230, 239, 250.
Aran, 15.
Arbedoc, 20.
Arbuthnott Missal, 166.
Archimandrita, 55, 159.
Architecture, Celtic, 48, 85.
Arculfus, 60.
Ardbraccan, xix.
Ardoilan, 92.
Ariminum, Council of, 27.
Arles, Council of, 29.

Armagh, 10 ; Book of, xiii, 37, 173.
Arnulf, bishop, 20.
Arran, 24.
Asaph, St., 14.
Ascensio, 235.
Asic, St., 115.
Assumption of B.V.M., 273.
Athanasius, St., 28.
Athelstan, king, 4.
Attala, xvi.
Augmentum, 203, 228, 233, 251, 252.
Augustine, St., of Canterbury, 26, 34,
  40, 61, 62, 63, 64, 263.
Augustine's Oak, 29.
Augustini Oratio, 226, 249.
Auxilius, St., 240.

B.

Bachalmore, the, 117.
Baithene, St., 18, 19, 141, 142.
Bangor, 15, 17.
Bangor, Antiphonary of, see Anti-
  phonary.
Bangor, Rule of, 18.
Bangor-Deiniol, 14.
Bangor-Garmon, 14.
Bangor-Iscoed, 14, 17.
Baoithin, St., 264.
Baptism, Celtic Ritual of, 64, 204 ;
  Office of, 207 ; unction at, 66 ; by a
  parent, 67 ; in milk, 67 ; validity of,
  doubted by Archbishop Theodore, 42.
Baresy, 15.
Barrus, St., 262.
Basle, Irish fragments at, 185.
Beatus, bishop, 59.
Beaulieu, 15.
Bede, anti-Celtic bias of, 33 ; pro-papal
  bias of, 34.
Bega, St., 25.
Bells, 92.
Benedicite, the, 111, 190.
Benedict XIV, 96.
Benedict Biscop, 87, 90.
Benedict, St., Rule of, 12, 17, 146.
Benedictio aquae, 184, 207, 211, 214.
Benedictio aquae et salis, 183.
Benedictio Fontis, 205, 212.

ERRATA.

Page 158, note 4, *for* 239 *read* 240
Page 168, note 1, line 5, *for* 220 *read* 221
Page 199, lines 28, 29, *omit* old-